HIGHER
EDUCATION

"Doubt is the enemy of success."

Jim "The Bird" Bridwell

(1944~2018)

HIGHER EDUCATION

A BIG WALL MANUAL

Andy Kirkpatrick

ANDREW
KIRKPATRICK

Higher Education
A Big Wall Manual

First Edition

WARNING

Climbing is dangerous Enthusiasm is no substitute for knowledge and experience

This manual is designed to give climbers the skills necessary to stay safe, but rock climbing and mountaineering is inherently dangerous, and so this manual is written for experienced rock climbers and mountaineers only. No one should undertake climbing without the proper training or equipment, and must take personal responsibility for learning the proper techniques and employing good judgment. I strongly recommend that every climber seek instruction by a qualified professional if they are unsure of any aspect of this manual.

By using the information contained within this manual you acknowledge that the information therein may be out of date or inaccurate and you agree that the author cannot be held liable for any damage that may be caused by use of this manual.

This book is designed to provide helpful information on the subjects covered, including climbing, abseiling and hauling. It is particularly designed for people who are actively participating in, or would like to train for, rock climbing and mountaineering.

All of the information contained in this book, including text, graphics, images, exercises, techniques and references to third party material are for information and educational purposes only. The author and publisher of this book shall have no liability or responsibility to any reader or third party arising out of any injury or damage incurred as a result of the use of the information provided in this book.

COVER PHOTO The Author alone on the Sea of Dreams.

MIX
Paper from
responsible sources
FSC FSC® C084699
www.fsc.org

Printed in the UK
ISBN
978-1-9997005-9-1
978-1-9997005-8-4 (ebook)

Editor: Vanessa Kirkpatrick
Photo Editor: Andy Kirkpatrick
Illustrations: Andy Kirkpatrick
Design and Production: Andy Kirkpatrick

PUBLISHED AND DISTRIBUTED BY
Andrew Kirkpatrick Limited
Ireland

HOUSE KEEPING

Structure

The complexity of big walling and the fact we cannot go from A to B to C means this is a book that probably needs to be read twice at first, and will then be dipped into many times thereafter. I'm guessing there will be parts of this book that will not make sense when you read them (in fact I'm sure of it), but will make sense a few chapters later, when you read something else. Very often the confusion and frustration that you experience when trying to grasp this, and your own search for understanding, is what leads to you really 'getting it', more so than anything I can write.

Naming Conventions

Throughout this book I've tried to simplify and make things clearer by avoiding slang terms, such as 'jumar', 'wall hauler' or 'GriGri', as this can often lead to confusion when instructing or learning, for example "use a hauler" can be misconstrued as using your hands, a micro ascender, a pulley, a micro traxion, a pro traxion or some other brand of pulley. Instead I've abbreviated a few pieces of big wall equipment, so instead of 'GriGri' I've used the term **ABBD** (Assisted Braking Belay Device) as there are many such devices on the market (although the Petzl 'GriGri' is probably the best). I've used **PCP** (Progress Capture Pulley) to replace the term 'wall hauler', a term that comes from the first commercial big wall pulley, and **PCD** (Progress Capture Device) for micro ascenders such as the Petzl Tibloc. I've also been a little bold in swapping out the term "daisy" for "lanyard", as again the variety of ways of connecting yourself to the wall is vast, and such restrictive slang can be a hindrance to learning.

CONTENTS

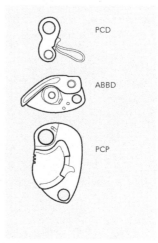

PCD

ABBD

PCP

Feedback And Updates

If you have any feedback or questions regarding this book, perhaps where more clarity is needed (like a diagram), then please contact me at andy@psychovertical.com.

FOREWORD

Big wall climbing requires grit. The kind of grit that requires problem solving skills and creativity to overcome obstacles and unforeseen snags, often those in the literal sense. What comes clear from reading Andy's entertaining advice and recollections based on his vertical experiences, is that Andy's got grit. Not only grit, but has a knack for sharing the workings of his particular type of grit, sprinkled with a bit of good old British humour, and a healthy splash of improvisation.

Back in 1984, I wrote a mini-treatise on big wall climbing by compiling what I had learned during my previous six years obsession with big walls, and the result was the "The Big Wall Tech Manual". It was a 52-page give-away booklet shipped to anyone whacky enough to be still interested in big walls and who ordered specialised equipment from my fledgling big wall gear company, A5 Adventures. When I first set up my company, after living in the dirt of Yosemite for the previous three years, no one believed at the time that a big wall specialist company would be viable, as big walls were thought of as a dying art. Writing about these fading tools and techniques was considered an even bigger fool's errand—free climbing was making leaps and bounds in standards thanks to new climbing shoe rubber coupled with an explosion of mechanical protection options, and the focus was on the clean ascent of the vertical—the hammered pitons that big walls required were considered archaic and the realm of the outlaw.

Before the Big Wall Tech Manual, there was very little specific information on the tools and techniques of big walls—perhaps a few titbits in the Chouinard catalogues, but the only real source of information for a beginner was Royal Robbin's "Advanced Rockcraft", published in 1970. But later in the 1970's, the Silver Age of big wall climbing had come and gone, with legends like Charlie Porter, Jim Bridwell, Chuck Kroger, Jimmy Dunn, and the prolific duo of Hugh Burton and Steve Sutton having scored most of the classic lines on the big walls of Yosemite, and by 1978, when I started visiting the big wall mecca, most of these heroes had already fled the valley for bigger and better things, their collective knowledge never documented and only sparsely recorded in every dreamer's well-thumbed picture book, "Yosemite Climber".

So for my generation of big wall climbers of the 80's (perhaps best called the "Bronze Age" of Yosemite big walls), we had very little to go by. The outdated Advanced Rockcraft was of little use, so when I did my first big wall climb in 1978, the Northwest face of Half Dome, we learned the craft of living and moving on a wall the hard way mostly through trial and error, while others were not so lucky—as soon as we got to the base of that great monolith, a climber already on the first pitch cratered 50 feet from his first attempted aid placement and was helicoptered out in a stretcher as we began our own journey upwards.

A few years later I properly began my big wall obsession and spent summers living in the dirt of Yosemite, where there was still a small group of big wall aficionados who

John Middendorf on the summit of Great Trango Tower 1992 © Xaver Bongard were elite yet frankly, not always very inclusive (one of them actually told me to "fuck off" as I approached him with newbie questions after I'd heard he had climbed one of the harder nailing routes on El Cap). As I sought partners for my first true nailing big wall, there was no interest among these hard-men in climbing with a neophyte, so I set off to solo the Prow. During those three days by myself, the engineer in me realised that a systems approach to the vertical could create an efficiency that could possibly lessen the torment and fear and wasted energy so typical of climbing a big wall for me at the time. Experimentation to make things easier was balanced by a conservative approach based on fear, and slowly but surely I figured a few things out.

I learned to invent and improvise. Not always did it go well—one time, having recently "invented" a new solo system involving a Figure-of-Eight descender and a Prusik knot, I set off to solo Zodiac. After a piton blew on what should have been a short fall right off the first belay, 80 feet up, my solo system (despite having been successfully tested once in a Camp 4 tree) completely failed, and during the ensuing head-first screamer—first pondering the mechanics of the top heavy gear rack causing my involuntary head down rotation—I realised that nothing was going to stop me from hitting the ground—so confident I was in my invention that I failed to incorporate any sort of backup into the system. In the time-slowed seconds of the fall, as the ropes were floating dreamily around me, I grabbed a loop of rope, wrapped it around my chest, and suddenly, normal time returned as I slammed hard to a stop in mid-air 20 feet above the ground, the ropes digging deep into my skin under my arms, creating deep bloody channels that resulted in extreme pain as I jumared back up to the belay to untangle myself so I could rappel back down to safety. During the several hours of thirsty immobilised agony at the base, coveting the swimmers I could see in the Merced far below, I realised that to become a big wall climber, one would need to become a better innovator of techniques to survive.

Specialised big wall gear was also very limited in those days. Chouinard made pitons and hooks, but very little else specific to climbing the big stones—his excellent forged Yosemite hammer was out of production. Ed Leeper made a few tools, and Bill Forrest sold a few odds and ends, including his eponymous and notorious vertebrae-crushing hammock designed for bivouacs and respite from one's harness, but actual sleep was a monumental task in the Forrest hammock, and it would transform into a cold bathtub in even the lightest storm. So we improvised. We knotted aiders, duct-taped and speedy stitched loops onto cotton duffel bags to function as haulbags, constantly repaired our soft tennis shoes, and tried a number of belay seat ideas to offer respite from thin waist harnesses that still required tying webbing tape knots to secure. Daisy chains were unknown (instead, Robbin's recommended a ligament destroying deep aider knee lock to rest on steep aid), gear slings were simply unpadded neck-gouging webbing, and the smallest cam was Jardine's one inch #1 rigid stemmed Friend, with only 3 sizes in all. No one wore helmets, though I can't recall anyone ever banging their head, not even Yabo who once took a huge whipper on an attempt of the Shield, accelerating downward to certain death on Heart Ledge, but was saved when his rope miraculously caught on a flake stopping his fall. Luck, in other words, was an essential attribute in those days.

For water bottles, we used rinsed out old Clorox bottles, notwithstanding the everlasting heavy chlorine taste, these were very weak and prone to cracking, and it was not uncommon to see growing wet patches appear on the side of the haulbag after even the most careful lower out, as we saw on my first time up the Nose, and had to endure two days in horrible Yosemite summer heat with no water.

Eventually I moved to live on the rescue site all year around, and climbed with a great cohort of like minded big wall sufferers, such as Walt Shipley, John Barbella, Rich Albushcat, Dave Shultz, Scott Cosgrove, Mike Corbett, Werner Braun, Alex Lowe, Russ Walling, Hidetaka Suzuki, Derik Hersey, and Steve Quinlan. Slowly but surely over the years, we developed new techniques, like how to follow a pendulum, three-rope systems, the use of tag lines, and a better method for free hanging jumaring (a very short lead jumar attachment and both legs in aiders in the bottom jumar). Evolving from the whack and dangle technique on difficult nailing pitches, we learned to systematically test pieces to ensure the safest and most controlled method of upward progress on tricky aid. Body hauling was still a new invention, and we still often leg hauled as recommended in the Robbin's bible, but eventually began full rope free-hanging body hauling, making even the most brutal loads seem manageable.

We learned how to climb more efficiently, to free climb whenever possible, and developed new tools. Eventually my business A5 Adventures produced new tools such as better portaledges, relatively indestructible haulbags, and tools that revolutionised hard aid, like the A5 BirdBeak. Sharing information on all these tools and techniques, and inventing new tools and systems over the years has been a joy, to watch how the sport has blossomed and how all these tools and techniques laid down the necessary groundwork of the current new revolution of free climbing on the big walls, the ultimate expression of purity on the vertical.

And there are endless looming challenges and whole new realms to explore in the wild corners of the Earth. Throughout my climbing career, I was primarily inspired by Chouinard's 1963 prophecy: "Yosemite Valley will, in the near future, be the training ground for a new generation of super alpinists who will venture forth to the high mountains of the world to do the most aesthetic and difficult walls on the face of the earth." Remote alpine big walls are a realm where grit is preferenced over all else. Absorbing and practicing the current wisdom as you will find in this book, persevering over all the clusterfuckery that will likely happen as you gain experience (and forgiving yourself by remembering the adage, "Judgement comes from experience, but experience comes from bad judgement"), and learning to improvise and develop self-reliant solutions to any problem, the magic that can often only be sensed for fleeting moments will be there to be shared as Andy has done in this book.

John Middendorf
Hobart Tasmania

PREFACE

"Fools learn from experience.
I prefer to learn from the experience of others."

Otto Von Bismarck

People often ask me when I learnt to climb, first tied into a rope and began my long journey up. I tell them that although I can remember learning to swim and ride a bike I don't remember becoming a climber, something so long ago it's as forgotten as my first steps. Ask me instead about when I became a big wall climber and I can pinpoint that very moment.

Before I get to that I should note that I grew up in the least big wall place in Britain, the port city of Hull, a fact that might actually explain how I ended up as I did, that lack of a thing – in this case mountains and walls and faces – making them holy, desired, and pined for. Luckily for me the architects of the age gave me a head start by furnishing me with the perfect training ground - a council estate of fabricated tower blocks, meaning for most of my childhood I lived in the sky, a fine place to banish any silly fear of heights. Further still the builders of these flats had done a shoddy job, throwing up already poorly designed buildings – like pound store knock off Lego - creating slum conditions; cold, draughty, damp and a grimness matching 1970's Britain. During this period I learnt a lot of skills that would set me in good stead for later life.

My parents were divorced, my dad a mountaineering instructor in the air force. On one visit he brought with him a slide projector and a box of slides, and after setting it up in my grandma Kirkpatrick's living room, we switched off the lights and saw a world very different to the one we lived in, the magical world of Yosemite. I can remember the pictures still, my dad climbing up steep golden corners in nothing but a pair of shorts, the rock above him endless. He told a story of sleeping on a ledge – imagine that - and how in the night there had been an earthquake, the whole mountain moving beneath them. It was forty years later that I learned he'd climbed the South West face of Half Dome, quite a thing for a Brit back then, but such details were unimportant in my seven year old mind. I just wanted to climb big walls.

The author hanging out on the Lafaille route (A4), Petit Dru © Ian Parnell

After that night when I looked up at the crumbling pebble dashed tower blocks I didn't see them for what they were, storage for the poor, but as miniature big walls. When I looked at the ripping seams between ten ton sections of prefab I didn't see shoddy workmanship, but possibilities, cracks, the way up and out. When I went to bed with my clothes on, or got dressed next to the crappy central heating, or listened to the single glazed windows rattle in a storm, I was not living the reality of some small squalor, but living on that ledge.

The first big wall, well a big wall for me, was the Humber Bridge, opened on my tenth birthday, the longest single span bridge in the world. Bridges require far more care and duty than housing for the poor, and so here was something far from pebbledash. At two kilometres long, with two, one hundred and fifty five metre high towers, this structure blew my mind. Standing with my nose pressed against one of the towers I could hardly grasp how high it was, understanding for the first time how something could scrape the sky, and that up there was where I had to go.

I guess everything that came was training for what was to come, both life and climbing, beginning on ten metre high gritstone crags and slowly working up. Working in climbing shops was a boon as it gave me access to lots of gear to play with, as well as climbers and also cavers who could share their knowledge. The first aid climbs were done on a top rope on rainy days, shunting up and learning the art of going from one piece to another. This was a steep learning curve, not without incident, teaching me that a half rope stretches a lot when you fall onto it when shunting, and that careless jumaring can snap a sheath with alarming ease. Nevertheless I developed my skills in nuts and cams, and rope soloing, finding that although one twenty metre pitch could take all day to aid, that day felt more like a true adventure into oneself than pushing my free grade.

The first big wall climber I met during this time was Andy Scott, a crazy haired madman from the Lake District. He worked in the same shop as me, but was everything I wasn't; cool, strong, like someone in a rock band. But he wasn't all show, and had just made an ascent of Jim Bridwell's El Cap classic Pacific Ocean Wall. The route involved climbing far removed from anything I had tried - heading, hooking, RURPs, pendulums. Andy said that they only climbed it due to being 'heavily sedated'. I probably bugged Andy endlessly with questions, about what kind of edges you could hook, how to high step, how to place heads, you name it. Luckily John Middendorf and John Long's book 'Big Walls' came out around the same time, which helped to fill in some gaps – although not all.

It's hard to grasp just how hard it was to learn big wall techniques back then, before the Internet, with information in books often out of date, and climbers you could ask few and far between. The only way to learn was by working it out yourself, such as when word came back about the new technique of 'short fixing'. Very often when you did meet climbers who had done hard aid climbs, such as Paul Pritchard, Noel Crane, or Adam Wainwright, their grasp of the nitty gritty was as poor as your own, simply going by sketchy gut instinct most of the time.

I remember talking to Adam Wainwright (the UK climber who'd climbed the hardest walls I knew) about climbing Aurora, which was graded A5 at the time. He described how he'd been so scared climbing a copper heading pitch that he 'd had to sit on a head for twenty minutes psyching himself up for each placement to come. I think what I learnt from Adam was that often the most important skill to develop is the ability to switch off your brain.

My big wall prep finally came to an end when I met Paul Tattersall, a climbing drifter, who started part time at the shop I worked at, before heading off on a trip to Greenland. He'd climbed the Nose in a day, as well as Lurking Fear and the Salathe, and was keen to go back and do some 'proper' walls. We got on well, more as people than as climbers, and so we went out to Yosemite together.

To say we were keen is an understatement, and the day after we arrived we set off up the Shield, which for me was a typical giant leap over a traditional apprenticeship on easier walls. My training on damp quarry walls turned out to be poor prep for El Cap, meaning I found every pitch an education. A1 nutting felt like A4 to begin with, that fear of falling always on my heels. My problem was I had never understood bounce testing, and so just crept up from placement to placement, which grew more terrifying as the climb went on. Slowly things like hauling and jumaring began to become second nature, along with living on the wall, yet leading still remained a process of sketchiness.

It was on the crux of the route that I came unstuck, on the triple cracks, trying – stupidly – to climb it sans pegs. I was back cleaning most pieces, especially our valuable Alien cams, meaning there was big air below me. Top stepping I clipped a sturdy looking fixed cable, ignoring the thinner one beside it and stepped up, the ground maybe eight hundred metres below me, then reached down and back cleaned, fully committing to the piece. Then I felt it, as much in my heart as through my feet - the swage was pulling apart, I was going to fall and there was nothing I could do to stop it. BANG. I was off, the next piece at least twenty feet below me. The first thing that happened was I flipped upside down due to the weight of the rack. Then I opened my eyes and saw Paul below in the portaledge, eyes closed, asleep on duty. Instead of fear I only heard one thought going through my head: "I'm falling off a big wall!"

When the rope came tight, sending Paul flying up into the ledge, I was level with him, both of us asking if the other was OK. We were, but this was a turning point for both of us, realising that big walls are risky places, full of danger, and that just crossing your fingers wasn't enough, that sooner or later your luck runs out. From that moment on we took bounce testing seriously.

That trip ended with an ascent of Pacific Ocean Wall in a very rapid five days, showing we'd learned a lot during our stay in Yosemite, that we were now big wall climbers.

My big wall studies continued, with Iron Hawk and Lost In America coming next, each a grade higher than each other in my mind, a fall from the crux of LIA when a large expanding flake broke off, close to being terminal. The following day I ended up – due to my own incompetence - having to jumar up on a rope only secured by a single cam hook, which crossed a threshold for me. The following year I soloed Aurora, my hardest route to date and first solo, followed by a one day ascent of Tangerine Trip in winter conditions (which took three days!), then Zenyatta Mondatta, and finally an eleven day solo of the Reticent Wall, one of the hardest walls at the time.

If big walling had been my school, college and university, I guess the Reticent was my final exam, the pass nothing more than a still beating heart.

I drifted away from big walls for a while, well apart from repeating the Lafaille route on the West face of the Dru, trying to become an alpinist, a frustrating and dangerous game, but using my big wall skills on walls in Norway, Alaska, Patagonia and Antarctica. It was only when I'd come to the end of my tether with alpinism that I found myself back in Yosemite, climbing El Cap a further twenty four times, with stand outs being solo ascents of The Sea Of Dreams and South Seas.

Each time I climbed El Cap I always felt I was learning new things, new things and old things I'd forgotten or swapped out for other ways of doing things. Each wall was like a test of skill, stamina, and mental control, and through writing about my adventures, and passing on some of what I'd learnt, I realised that there remained so much people did not quite understand, so many questions that needed filling in. I thought back to my own early days, all the mistakes I made, all those humble questions asked in car parks and at picnic benches. Yes, part of learning is learning to find your own answers, but another part is teaching, no one a master until they teach others.

And so this is how this book came about, far from being a way to generate money, but rather an attempt to get as much information down for other climbers to read and learn. Yes this might be cheating, rob climbers of that buzz of working it out, but I think what will happen is it will free those climbers to focus on other things, new things we have not thought about, that and keep them alive through the dangerous days of groping in the dark for the way on.

I have tried to make this book as complete as can be, and the mining of my thoughts has taken nearly two years, the reason being I climbed five more walls during its writing, each wall making me question if I had been true to the realities of such things. This is a book for novice big wall climbers, but is also only for experienced climbers, so there is much that will be missing for anyone looking for a dot-to-dot of how to climb. I have also tried to keep the book true to my own philosophy of climbing and life, to keep it as simple and as un-showy as possible, to stick with what is practicable and works, rather than pseudo techniques and thought experiments beloved by the forum. If I've not used it, then it's probably not in this book.

Lastly this book, be you novice or expert, is not the end point of knowledge, of skills and understanding, but the starting point, a map if you like, to lead you up to where your mind scrapes the sky.

Andy Kirkpatrick
Bray, Ireland

INITIATION

WHY ARE YOU READING THIS BOOK?

So you want to be a big wall climber, or if not a big wall climber, then proficient at the big wall game, aiding, climbing ropes, hauling, spending nights on the vertical. Maybe you want to just aid walls, or maybe you want to free them, but have the sense to know that leading - even free - is just a small part of getting to the top. Maybe you're an alpinist, and have noticed that the great alpinists of the past, the ones who climbed the really hard walls - like the Poles and Slovenians - were big wall climbers first, that this old fashioned game of whack and dangle, is a vital skill to understand. And so you've found yourself here, wanting to learn. I hope I can help.

WHERE TO BEGIN

Big wall climbing is an advanced sub set of climbing, and so it's vital that you've served a long and deep apprenticeship there. This is a game, unlike free climbing, that does not take prisoners, and I've known a few young climbers who came unstuck due to not really having served their time.

The idea of nailing all the skills, and I mean really nailing them, using ascenders, hauling and aiding, training hard until you can do it in your sleep (lowering bags, docking, following pendulums, everything) is the key to getting up the wall, not just because you need these skills, but because to realise you don't have them when you're on the wall, will kill your psych stone dead.

I always try and think of it as just being professional and taking it seriously, which you should, as a wall is a high risk environment, and not the place to learn. This view has been reinforced over the years by the terrible teams I've seen who seem incapable of hauling even a shopping bag up a boulder, let alone a mile high wall, and who invariably hold everyone else up and then bail.

DO I HAVE WHAT IT TAKES?

Well you're reading this book, which is a start, but perhaps you're a little delusional, or only have romantic notions? Well first off, big wall climbing is fucking grim, fucking grim and hard - like the hardest job you've ever had. It is not like rock climbing, which is fun, fun, fun, but rather just work, work, work, with the fun being when the work stops (and then it gets dark).

I think climbers who have some background in mountaineering often make the best big wall climbers, as they're under no illusions of the reality of big objectives, well mountaineers or those who do manual labour for a living.

Grade wise, if you learn to aid safely, I'd say you need to be a solid HVS or 5.9 leader, happy on all rock types, can get up and down multi pitch routes, and have a solid grasp of rope work (people who can't even put their harnesses on right need not apply).

Physically you do not have to be mega strong, but you need a good base fitness and stamina, so you can do long days

The upside down world, Mescalito

without falling to bits. The wall does make you strong, but you need to meet it halfway. In my life as a wall climber I've climbed with men and women, straight and gay, black and white, able and disabled, even with gingers, and the one thing they all shared was an old fashioned thing called fortitude. If you've got that, the rest can come.

TRAINING

You need to set aside a good period of time to create a solid foundation for what is to come, first learning the basics, then applying them in a safe environment, then trying them on easy objectives. Here are the foundation skills you need to develop:

- **Progression**: You need to learn how to aid up a series of placements, what those placements are being less important here than the movement itself (so a line of bolts in a gym would be fine for this type of training). This should cover understanding how to use aiders, fifi and lanyards, and aiding with one, two and three aiders, plus top stepping.

- **Rope Climbing**: You need to be able to safely climb a rope with a minimum of effort, ropes that are free hanging, vertical and on slabs. You need to be able to clean steep pitches, pass gear and lower out, plus down jumar and pass knots.

- **Belays**: You need to know how to set up a belay that is non standard, i.e., Not a free climbing belay.

- **Hauling**: You should know how to haul both light bags and heavy, and lower out and dock the bags. You should have a solid grasp of 1:1 and 3:1 systems, plus space hauling.

- **Descent**: You should know how to abseil with heavy loads, and pass knots, plus use your lanyards.

WHERE TO LEARN

You need to be someone who enjoys learning new skills and does not see it as a hindrance to just going climbing. The more time you put into it the safer and more effective you'll be. Here is how I'd break down training.

Indoors

I've taught hundreds of climbers how to climb big walls on climbing walls with routes less than five bolts long, teaching the nuance of moving up aiders, cleaning tricky pitches as well as hauling, docking and lowering bags. Doing so indoors removes the problem of putting in and taking out protection, which saves a lot of time, and enables you to just focus on the actions and systems. Here are some ideas on how to train each skill.

- **Aiding**: Start off with the two aider method on a vertical wall, learning the rhythm of moving from one aider to another. Try out differing foot positions and play a game with a piece of chalk to see how high you can leave a mark. Avoid using any holds for your hands when practising aiding, but do practice going from aid to free and free to aid. Now move to a steeper wall and do it again until you can do it without sweating your ass off (focus on resting on your fifi, not hanging off your arms). Now practice the one aider method, then the three, playing around using a fifi hook or a karabiner. Can you get into your second step and stand comfortably?

- **Rope Climbing**: Begin with a free hanging rope and the Texas system of

Chimney, wide cracks and aid on Ulvetanna

ascending. Focus on moving between rests, rather than move, hang off your arms. When ascending the rope, it can be set up like a top rope, lowering the climber down when they're finished ascending (if practising like this, just make sure the belayer uses an ABBD and the rope is long enough to do this, and always tie a large figure of eight in the end). If they're not going to be lowered, they can practice setting up an abseil from the top. Add some knots to the rope and practice passing gear (the knots), focusing on backing yourself up. Once at the top, rap the rope and pass the knots while descending. Now switch to a vertical wall, cleaning a pitch (bolts). Once you have this nailed add in an ABBD when cleaning, and zigzag the rope between two lines of bolts. As each climber is lowered off they should rig up the rope for the next, making it as hard as possible. One way to do this is to make a spider's web with the rope, running it both up and down from clips. At all phases don't forget backup knots. Now switch to steeper climbs, with roofs being perfect. Throw in cleaning a pendulum and a traverse.

- **Hauling**: Fill a haul bag with bottles of water, climbing holds or weight bags (cordon off the area you're using to avoid anyone getting whipped off the wall by falling bags). Practice setting up an anchor using two bolts at the top of the wall, then practice 1:1 and 3:1 hauling, plus a 2:1 Chongo haul if you have one. When the bag arrives at the belay practice docking it to the masterpoint, and taking the PCP off, then reverse the process and lower the bag back down again using a Monster Munter.

- **Putting It All Together**: Set up a hanging belay at the bottom of the longest steepest wall in the gym, making sure everyone's feet are off the ground and the bag is hanging. Now have one person lead and then haul while the second cleans. Then swap and repeat.

AN IRON LAW

They say when you're having a baby to never stand when you can sit, never sit when you can lie down. You should view aid climbing in the same way, in that you should never find it hard, and if you do, it means you're doing it wrong. If your arms are tired when aiding you're not resting on your fifi hook, or when ascending a rope it means your lanyards aren't set right or you're standing in the wrong step of your aider. The same goes for hauling, if you're busting a gut then switch up to 2:1 or 3:1, or space hauling. Almost everything physical should be a movement sandwich, movement placed between two slices of rest. Move, sit back, move, sit back.

Outside

Now you've nailed the foundation skills it's time to apply them to actual rock. If you're dreaming of big granite walls then you should be training on granite crags, or sandstone quarries. The worst place to train is on limestone, as it just doesn't lend itself to easy aid and you could end up damaging routes. On this subject avoid using hooks or hammered pegs on any route where you could damage it.

- **Aiding**: The aim now is to learn how to test gear, and understand what will work, then how to move between poor gear. On some routes this could be micro wires, hand placed pegs (beaks or angles), cam hooks (on granite), giving you a feel for leading. If you're doing this on wet weather days then you can always do this on a solo top rope (self lining) to save your partner from spending hours sat while you figure it out.

- **Rope Climbing**: Now you can try cleaning for real.

- **Hauling**: This tends to be tricky to do outdoors on a normal crag, so I would just focus on nailing this indoors as much as possible.

- **Bivvying**: If you can I'd try and practice bivvying out on a crag somewhere, especially if you're going to use a portaledge, as putting up a ledge, on the wall of a dark quarry, is a good eye opener to just how hard it can be.

FIRST WALLS

So you've put in the time to get your skills ready for the real deal, your first wall, but what and where should that be? I've met many climbers who go looking for walls to build up their experience before going to Yosemite, walls in Switzerland and Italy, Norway and Spain, but I always say they've got it the wrong way round. You go to Yosemite to learn to climbs walls, then move on to those other places (or Patagonia or Alaska or Gangotri). In the valley you have perfect weather, perfect rock, a huge amount of beta and info, bolted belays and easy approaches. Yes if you live outside of the US you might spend a few more hundred pounds getting there, but if you convert this to metres climbed I don't think you can get any better value, something you'll appreciate after a week of rain in the Val di Mello.

Which Walls?

If you've done your homework, trained well, and have a solid working team, then I don't see why you can't just jump on any wall up to A2+, which is what I did, climbing the Shield as my first wall. Smaller walls, such as Leaning Tower, can be great places to iron out the subjective reality from the objective, being safe but very steep. Here you'll really have your skills tested, spend a night out, discover many things aren't as bad as you thought, while others you'd not thought about are worse (climbing a single rope over a roof ten pitches up is something new for most climbers). The trick is to bolster your psych, to find your feet and nerve without stumbling.

OVERCOMING INEPTITUDE

One of my favourite books is 'Beyond No Mean Soldier' by Peter McAleese, the story of a British soldier who starts out in the British army, gets into the SAS, then goes on to Rhodesia, then South Africa, and finally becomes a mercenary. What I like about this book is how McAleese talks about training men to go into combat, how through constant drilling, and more drilling, they are able to overcome huge odds. In one chapter he trains ten men to kill Pablo Escobar, building up his drills and rehearsals for eleven weeks, building a scale model of Escobar's ranch. Each man knows what the other is doing, knows each step of the plan. The sides of the main house are given colours so there is no confusion with left and right. When the team finally step onto the helicopter on the morning of the attack no one is in any doubt they are ready and can overcome the odds against them (you'll have to read the book to find out what happens next).

The idea of treating a wall like combat is actually spot on, as wall climbing is not free and easy like free climbing, but a highly complex mix of tasks, requiring skill, fitness and strategy. Many climbers look down their noses at aid climbers, with their aiders and haul bags, feeling themselves superior, until they try and climb a wall. It's like a swimmer thinking themselves fitter and stronger than a transatlantic sailor - yes they are, but not in the middle of the Atlantic ocean. I've seen this problem on the wall countless times, especially on hard free walls like El Nino, where a climber cruises a hard pitch, but then takes several hours to haul a bag.

BABY STEPS

Another way to build both your skill set and psych is to take baby steps, learning the skills, then applying them to an easy wall. Once these learned skills are used in anger they become modified, less abstract, more solid and reliable, especially the basic movements such as easy aiding, jumaring and hauling.

Now you take this foundation and work out what more you need to learn for your next project. Perhaps it needs a lower out, a pendulum, some beaks or hooking.

You train again, you drill it in, and then you execute the climb. Again you cement these skills, the hooking easier in reality, the pendulums not as big, other things you didn't drill for actually dealt with based on what you knew already.

At this point, two walls in, and several days of intensive training, you feel you have a good base to try something harder. Added to this, you're not only strong in skills and the quiet confidence this brings, but also your team psych is good, you trust each other because you are learning together.

AFTER ACTION

In these early days try and keep notes, either after each climb, or on the climb, noting what you've learnt and what you need to learn. Talk to each other as you climb about little bits of learning you're discovering, pros and cons of different systems, and basically play around (it's better to go a little slower and learn by what you're doing, than just stumble up your early walls). Once down take an hour to go through what went right and what went wrong, and nail what can be done differently when you go back on the wall again. I still do this even though I've done fifty walls as I'm always learning new things the whole time, as well as re-learning things I've forgot.

FINAL EXAM

There is no real final exam in wall climbing as every wall is a test in itself, but your first proper big wall is different, as it will test all your skills to the full, and be totally demanding physically and mentally. This will be your baptism of fire, and once you get to the summit you'll be wired for all the walls to come.

Steve Bate being careful about what he pulls on, on Zodiac

HEAD GAMES

"An integral part of belief is to doubt"

Malcolm Muggeridge

Climbing a big wall is not easy physically, yet such hurdles as a weak body can be overcome with training, hitting the gym and the climbing wall, beasting yourself on harder and harder training climbs, until your body is as hard as rock. But what about a weak mind?

I have spent many summers in Yosemite, seen the defeated, those who do not climb the wall, or who bail, fail because they are not mentally prepared or able. Yes they have the kit, yes they have the skill, but what they forget to bring with them is the will to succeed. And so I thought it best to start this book with the head, as without it you're going nowhere.

OVERCOMING THE IMPOSSIBLE

The biggest hurdle for many climbers is the sheer scale of what they are attempting, to stand at the base of a thousand metre wall and believe they can make it to the top. This is understandable, in fact, it's why you're standing there, the nature of the game the search for near impossibility, so make sure you embrace that fact. If you can't, then walk away.

The first move on such an undertaking is never physical, but mental, and so if you've made it to the first move, travelled across the world with all your gear, forfeit blood and treasure for this ambitious dream, then you have it in you to make it come true.

If you feel overawed then consider this: think about a skyscraper like the Empire State building, how although a marvel of engineering, over a thousand feet high, it is nothing but one hundred and two floors set one on top of another. Think how each floor, massive in itself, is nothing but a complex arrangement of rooms made from steel and granite blocks, that each block is made up of interlocking feldspar, quartz and mica. Now think about a successful climb, how it is built up from pitches scaled, how each pitch is made up of successful placements, cams, nuts, beaks, hooks, how each placement is made from solving nothing more than one single little puzzle. If you are willing to make that first move, to solve that puzzle of engineering, but also fear, ambition, anxiety, hope and joy, you can solve them all.

FEAR AND ANXIETY

There is a lot of fear in big wall climbing, as well as doubt, uncertainty and anxiety. It is very much a game of psych and so it's good to understand this and be able to identify these feelings, and know they are natural, healthy and important. Otherwise they will affect your ability to climb. Here are some thoughts on the fear and anxiety.

Feel The Fear: A climber who does not feel fear is a dangerous climber, and that

Cian O' Leary knowing his place during a Winter ascent of the Nose.

Head Games / 25

feeling should be noted when it peaks. At the same time don't confuse nerves with raw fear, or simple anxiety. Learn to identify when these feelings are irrational and can be overridden, such as a hook move above a 10 mm bolt, and rational, a hook move on a fragile flake over ten metres of heads.

Fake It To Make It: When in a team, try and talk through how you feel and rationalise it, but don't dwell or focus on it too much. Yes you are scared when you're leading, but so is everyone, it's your lead and the reason you're here is that you want to be tested, the fear part of the game (maybe 'The' game). Faking it to make it isn't really the point, but you need to develop some backbone, some stiff upper lip, to literally lead by example. Yes you feel scared, but by controlling it you do not let it control you.

Fear Of Falling: This is a big one, and one that can only partly be overcome by becoming used to falling off sport climbs (an aid fall is very different). The problem with big wall falls versus free climbing is that with free climbing you feel in control and lack fear until you have good reason to think you're going to fall, whereas when aid climbing you can feel fearful for a whole pitch, and only lose that fear when you fall. Solid testing and understanding gear is the best way to overcome irrational fear, as well as ignoring ideas about clean climbing on routes that cannot go clean for you (which means placing beaks, and maybe the odd sawn off peg). When you feel this fear very close, you can often feel yourself falling, feel that lurch in your bones, the sound of your gear, the rush of the wind. Yes all such aid climbing falls tend to be short (although some are not!), and over

before you know you're falling, but they should not be something you want to get used to. The aim is not to fall, and so this fear of falling needs to be sidestepped by solid leading skills, and when that does not work, the bull headed ability to push through the fear.

Support: How those around you support you on a hard lead can make a big difference. It is often best to let the leader focus on the leading and avoid giving suggestions or imagining that you are them. If you do this too much then you are imagining leading as they lead, and so feel the fear too, which means you never get a rest from it, this rest being vital on a hard wall. Try instead to be positive, attentive and maybe even respectful, by which I mean when they say "Watch me" that you actually do. Remember that one pillar of the leader's psych and confidence is their belayer. I've had a few experiences of being dropped by belayers on a wall, and I can tell you it does no good for your head.

Fear Cramping: On hard solo climbs I've sometimes pushed myself so far into fear that my body reacts in a physical way, the slightest little scare — like a bird flying past — creating an actual physical pain in my body, like a cramp. This is the result of taking all the fear on, too much too soon, rather than sharing it with fellow climbers or building up your tolerance of such fear more gradually.

Identifying And Categorising Fear

I've stolen the following from my book 'Me, Myself & I' as it's my best effort on this subject:

Mild Fear: Although the most common emotion for a soloist, this is not really fear at all. It usually manifests itself as a background hum of fear, static, people describing themselves as 'worried' or 'scared' about what is to come; the start of the climb, the pitch you must lead tomorrow, committing to a skinny rope running over a sharp edge.

The greatest threat from this fear is that it's a petri dish for negative thought and failure. Within this hum of fear you begin to magnify both the danger and magnitude of the task at hand, the fear feeding on itself until you either bail before you've begun, or you find the power to overcome it. First off, like I said, this is not fear, this is anxiety and is normal. It is your primitive brain trying to prepare itself for fight, flight or freeze. Like an animal you are about to enter a situation in which there is a chance you may be killed or injured, after all you don't feel like this when you walk around IKEA. It is important to recognise this anxiety and deal with it point by point until you are able to dim it enough for it to be irrelevant.

Here are some examples:

Thought: What if I make a mistake and kill myself?

Answer: *I've been training and practicing for over a year, I've climbed harder single pitches at home, as well as in the rain, storm and darkness.*

Thought: I know I've done lots of training, but this would be a real climb on a big wall!

Answer: *Think about it rationally, it's just a bunch of single pitch routes one on top of the other. If I can climb one safely, then I can climb them all.*

Thought: But what if I get to the crux ten pitches up and I can't do it?

Answer: *I believe I can do it, and have all the skills and tools needed to climb that pitch. Maybe it's just one move, who knows, but I know I can do it.*

Thought: It's easy to say that now, but what about when you're up there looking at a huge fall onto a ledge?

Answer: *I will place solid gear and test everything. I will equalise runners as I go to make mini running belays. I have offset cams, beaks, and countless other stuff they didn't have when these routes were first done.*

Thought: But what if you can't?

Answer: *I accept that I may fail, and will back off if I think it's not justifiable. Even if I fail I know it is better to try, and fail in the doing of it, not in the thinking of it.*

Real Fear: Perhaps it's only when you've experienced real, heart pounding fear, that you know mild fear for what it is - not fear at all. Real fear is unpleasant (it's best not to get into the habit of enjoying it) but is part of the game and needs to be viewed as a sharpener for the senses.

Sharp Fear: This is 'piano falling out of a window and just missing you' fear, striking fast and hard, the nature of the close call determining how long the after shock lasts for. What triggers this response in a person varies, depending on their past experiences, as what may have you shitting your pants as a beginner (such as a krab shifting as you hang on it), won't even raise an eyebrow a few routes on. Also, the more experienced you become, the faster you tend to deal with a red-lining heart, as you can rationalise what scared you. This is not to say you should totally ignore sharp fear, but in my experience it tends to come after the danger has passed. If it hasn't (an example being a flake moving when you start climbing on it), then it's paramount that you remain in control in order to escape the situation - be that by fight or flight.

Rolling Fear: This is the most difficult fear to deal with, and is a slowly increasing sense of alarm/danger/deep anxiety that can climb into you for minutes, hours or even days. If you're in this constantly scared state you will not be able to act or think clearly, and worse still you'll just have a really crap time! The first wall I did was very much like this for me, as I didn't have enough experience to feel comfortable, and so just blindly pushed on (getting to each belay my only sanctuary). On a wall, all alone, you could perhaps feel this sense of fear and dread even more, but in fact I think as you have to face these things alone when soloing, you do a better job of it. The idea of 'just switching off' doesn't work that well, but you can use positive thinking and language to detune this fear. Instead of viewing the wall as something malign and dangerous, out to kill you, think of it as a crafty opponent, each piece you place a victory in a chess match. Use positive language, such as saying 'train stopper' each time you get some good gear. Try and focus on the fun, the adventure, the 'place', how you're doing something beyond 'hardcore', the fact that you are thriving and enjoying every minute. Try and have a smile on your face.

FIRST WALL PSYCH

So you've set your sights on climbing your first wall, perhaps it's the Nose, an obvious choice for many good climbers: lots of beta, lots of traffic (must be easy), close to the road. You buy your tickets and spend a day or two down at the crag jumaring and hauling. It's not easy, but you're E5 wads, you'll free most of it, maybe even do something harder like Zodiac or the Shield.

You arrive and see El Cap for the first time. It's big, like bigger than anything you've ever seen. It's also hot. You hang around in camp 4, sorting gear, going cragging, looking for water bottles. Everyone else seems to want to climb the Nose or has bailed from the Nose. A few people, 'Nose In A Day' people, tell you it's a path, and you believe them (they don't tell you they've climbed it ten times), while the bailers, who tell you how much harder it all was - leading, hauling, jugging - are ignored.

After more than a week you go up, you have psyched up and spent the previous day packing, but find you're there at the back of a long queue, some loser faffing around on the first pitch. You bail.

You come back the next day, this time at 5am. Now the route ahead is clear up to Sickle Ledge, the other teams ahead of you having bailed as well. You set off, but straight away the climbing feels super hard. The rock feels slick and polished, and you find French free does not work like it says in the books. You break out your aiders but still find you can't get any gear to fit. Your feet start to hurt in your tight rock boots, and your arms too as you hold onto the gear. You run out of the right size cams after an hour, and after two your partner is shouting up "how's it going?", shorthand for "fucking hurry up". You get to a free section at last, something you should be able to walk up, but it feels impossible. There are no holds and no gear. "I think something must have broken off" you shout down, and look for a sky hook move on the slab. You've never used a hook before, but brought one for a joke. You don't know what to hook, and so snatch a finger-nail flake and after ten minutes build up the courage to step up. The flake rips and you take a whipper. You try and free climb again, on what feels like impossible smears, and then, you reach the belay, and looking down, you see a long line of climbers waiting for you to stop faffing around, all grumbling at your lack of skill. You bail.

Such a story is common, and I could go on and on, the same stories I've seen countless times: strong climbers who could not haul or aid or jumar, who felt they were 'going too slow', or who were just beaten by the time they dragged themselves onto Sickle Ledge.

MOMENTS OF DOUBT

There will come a time on any wall where things go wrong, and it's how you deal with these things that can make or break a team. First off, you must expect bad luck, misfortune and chaos to visit you at some point. After all the complexity of what you are doing just invites it in. But when these things visit — a storm, a damaged rope, a dangerous pitch — you must be able to bend, to flow around them, to sidestep and rationalise, not see them as reasons to fail. In some ways these moments of doubt and their overcoming, are what big wall climbing is about, like tangled ropes and stuck or dropped gear. If you butt heads with problems, take each one personally (telling yourself that they mean you're crap) then they'll wear you down. Instead just deal with them one after another, and take them on the chin.

WHY PEOPLE BAIL

Someone once asked me how not to fail on the Nose, and I replied "Climb, and when things get hard, don't come down". The next time we met he told me they'd failed. "Why?" I asked. "Things got hard and we came down", he said sheepishly. Not bailing from a wall is the best way to climb a wall, so here are some typical excuses for bailing, and ideas on how to overcome them.

Going Too Slow

A common one on many walls, but especially on popular routes, where you get bogged down in other climbers epics and ineptitude.

Fix: *There are many ways to deal with this and here's a few:*

- **Define fast: Are you really saying that you'll run out of water, food or time?** Well, water consumption always decreases as you climb higher, and the bags get lighter as well, meaning your speed increases. Keep climbing.

- **Are you saying you're crap?** Well give it thirty more pitches and you might get the hang of it, get into a groove. Keep climbing.

- **Are you scared?** Again, give it time and just being on the wall might slowly feel more like home. Keep climbing.

- **Did you underestimate the climb or overestimate your skill to climb it?** What do you know of the climbing above you? A good example of this is the Nose, who's hardest pitches come at the start below Sickle ledge. If you've taken all day to climb four "easy" pitches your psych may be in tatters, choruses of 'we're too slow' echoing throughout the team, not realising the climbing above becomes easy, often highway cracks that can be aided in less than an hour. Keep climbing.

- **Are you being held up?** Most slow parties will bail, often that slowness the last gasp of their dreams, especially if you're on their tails. Being held up for a few hours should be down as a possibility on a popular route like the Nose or any route from 'Fifty Classic Climbs Of North America' for example, and you should have planned for this. Most slow teams, will let you pass if you offer to fix a rope for them, but the bottom line is, make being held up a day part of your strategy to get to the top. Keep climbing.

Sickness

Very often one of the team will become ill; flu, the shits, feeling sick.

Fix: There's generally nothing wrong, and what they feel is just the malady of the wall - like sea sickness, the heat, the hard work. Make sure everyone is drinking and eating, and if that does not work, then just stop for the day. If they don't recover by morning, then go down.

Bottling It

It's less common for a team member to want to let people down once they start up the wall (before they start is a different matter), but it does happen. One problem with two person teams is that the belayer's psych can drift when sat for ages belaying, while at the other end the leader's soars. A high tide might raise all ships, but not on a wall, where the magnitude of the undertaking requires everyone rise to the challenge.

Fix: Climbing in a three person team can help reduce this problem, as the two at the belay can keep each others morale up, plus each member only needs to lead a third of the route. If they're simply not able to face leading (common after a long belay session), then offer to lead all day and see how they feel the next morning (a good wall climber should feel able to lead anything).

Bad Weather

Another common one, and caused both by actual bad weather (rain and snow), presumed and un-forecast bad weather (clouds or distant thunder), or the fear that either may arrive soon (maybe you have no way to check tomorrow's weather).

Fix: First off, most teams on a wall are equipped to climb Trango Towers in winter, with four season sleeping bags, bivvy bags, ledges and flysheets that can withstand Patagonian tempests. As a big wall climber, you must be prepared for such storms, as well as being prepared to climb through them (meaning setting up camp and waiting for the storm to pass). If the weather looks like it's turning, then stop, set up for a storm and fix a few pitches if it hasn't turned by the time you've done this, but don't bail. This might be controversial, but I tend to not even look at weather forecasts, and just plan for bad weather (when it's going to rain in a few days the walls become empty, which has its advantages). This might be high risk, but sitting out a storm, and experiencing what it's like, gives you confidence when an unexpected storm you're not prepared for hits another time. The exception to this rule are climbers who are speed climbing and have little or no protection, and these climbers should only ever set off with zero chance of bad weather, same for climbers without portaledges and flysheets.

Heavy Bags

Another common one, and really just as bullshit as the rest. You will often find people sat below the Nose, having bailed off Dolt Tower giving this excuse.

> **Fix**: Having hauled 50+ days of food and water (4 person team on 10 day ascent) this is just an excuse for being clueless and out of your depth, and failing is a good thing. Any team on a wall less than a week long should be able to haul their bags with relative ease, meaning knowing how to space haul or do a 3:1 or 2:1 early on, then a 1:1 higher up.

Stuck Bags

Another one you see from the clueless, hauling bags up slabs and corners with total confidence they'll come quietly.

> **Fix**: Again, good training will teach a team that on less than overhanging terrain someone needs to mind the bags.

We Were Crap

This is one that's often unsaid, or could be worded as "it was harder than we expected", and is a reason that can encompass many of the ones already discussed.

> **Fix**: Well obviously don't be crap, take it seriously, have some humility. If you do get on the wall and find

yourself wanting, do you have what it takes to work it out quite quickly, to learn from your mistakes, the school of hard knocks (and do it without killing yourself or anyone else)?. I've seen this a few times on the wall, teams who look on the surface to be clueless, doing it all wrong, but somehow overcoming their own crapness with every pitch climbed. For such teams what they have is conscious incompetence - they know how shit they are, but can become unconsciously competent bit by bit, pitch by pitch. The dangerous team is the one that's unconsciously incompetent, it does not understand why everything is going wrong instead of right, each error not a reason to learn, but another coin in the death meter!

Reality Sucks

I've met many climbers who were just totally unprepared for being on a big wall, the heat, the faff, the slowness of everything. The problem is rock climbing is fun, yes scary at times, but fun. Big wall climbing is category 2 fun. It is slow, sometimes scary, but often not what people thought they'd signed up for.

> **Fix**: If you can stick to it, it will get faster and more fun, and you'll soon find yourself in wild places doing very technical and absorbing climbing, but to get there takes the kind of fortitude many rock climbers lack.

Ego

It's very hard to be a very good rock climber who is struggling on an easy route. If you're climbing E7 at home, but are getting passed out by a HVS leader on the Nose, it can be just too humiliating. People whose egos tell them they

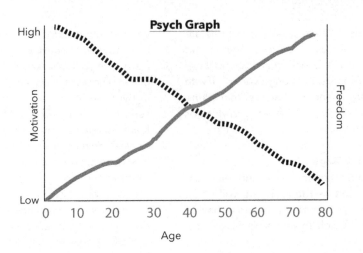

Psych Graph

(Graph: y-axis left labelled "Motivation" from Low to High; y-axis right labelled "Freedom"; x-axis labelled "Age" with values 0, 10, 20, 30, 40, 50, 60, 70, 80. One dotted line descends from High to Low, one grey line ascends from Low to High.)

don't need to practice, that they'll figure it out, are actually both arrogant and naive, something that will bite them in the ass from day one on a wall. I have seen the same thing many times, a climber flailing around trying to climb a rope, or pass a piece of gear, shouting and swearing at everyone and everything but themselves. When such people force everyone to bail, because "big wall climbing is shit", they're only half right.

Fix: *Climb with people who have some humility.*

FAILURE LOOKING FOR AN EXCUSE

I've talked about this already and it is very common. With the team's psych precariously balanced between up and down, any excuse that can be found, such as 'we don't have enough water' or 'I feel ill' will have the whole team rapping the wall.

In reality though, the above fixes may not help. This is because very often, the reason given for bailing is not the real reason at all, but an excuse, the team simply trying to find a way out that allows them to save face, and not divulge the real reason they failed.

SHADOW

I'll finish this chapter with a quote from Richard Bandler and John Grinder's book 'Frogs Into Princes' and leave it up to you to interpret as you will:

"At any moment that you find yourself hesitating or if at any moment you find yourself putting off until tomorrow something that you could do today, then all you need to do is glance over your left shoulder and there will be a fleeting shadow. That shadow represents your death, and at any moment it might step forward, place its hand on your shoulder and take you. So that the act that you are presently engaged in might be your very last act and therefore fully representative of you as your last act on this planet. When you hesitate, you are acting as though you are immortal."

Selfie by Neil Chelton on A4 crux of the Russian route, Eiger North Face

PLACEMENTS

The world of protection has expanded dramatically since Long and Middendorf's book 'Big Walls' in 1994. Back then you had twin stem BD Camalots, flexible and rigid Friends, Wired Bliss and Metolius cams. The biggest commercial cam was a black Camalot 4, while the smallest and most common cam was a Wild Country 0.5. Nuts had some variety, but the only real micros were RPs and HB offsets, and the A5 Birdbeak had only just come on the market. Perhaps due to the book itself, and the explosion of big walling that came from so much knowledge being shared all at once, it seemed that overnight there was a revolution in big wall gear.

The biggest development was the Alien cam from Colorado Custom Hardware, which was a quantum leap in terms of its ability to hold in the smallest placements, the red, yellow and green Aliens being as important on a hard wall as your rope.

Nuts improved, with better offsets coming along, such as the DMM Peanut and many more varieties of micros. The A5 Birdbeak was joined by the Black Diamond Pecker, its primary benefit the introduction of a medium and large size, which all but put to bed all other pitons. The Leeper Cam Hook was rediscovered by big wall climbers, and BD introduced the Talon and Grappling hook, which helped to open hard aid. Cams also got bigger, with the Camalot 5 and Wild Country 5 and 6 helping to tame the wide stuff.

With each revolution in passive gear from one company there was a response from someone else, all of it trickling down into free climbing (I think aid climbers led the way in passive pro, not free climbers).

Today we have new benchmark pro, such as the Moses Tomahawk, the Totem

basic (standard and offset) and classic Totem, Superlight Camalots, plus many lightweight nuts such as the Wild Country Superlight Offset. And who knows what will come next?

In this chapter I will cover aid placements, clean gear, pitons, hooks, rivets and bolts.

NUTS

MICRO NUTS

Until the introduction of the true micro wire (and not just small nuts on rope) thin cracks could only be tackled with knifeblades or RURPs. The small nuts available were limited by thick cables or worse still, cord that was so thin it was only as effective as a shoelace (in fact some were threaded with shoe lace!). The answer to this gap in protection was first filled by an East German boilermaker living in Australia called Roland Pauligk, who created a set of micro nuts that have never been equalled, although they have been copied many times. Silver soldering cables into the smallest brass nuts you could imagine (size 0 is 3 mm thick),

Tomahawk deadhead placement on South Seas.

Roland produced six nuts that became known as RPs and opened up hard routes throughout the world. These brass nuts, which I think of as true micros, have been joined by alloy micros, such as the classic Black Diamond Stopper #1 to #3 and micro Wallnuts and Rocks (00 to 3/4), which differ from the brass micros in that they are drilled for wire, which makes them cheaper and easier to produce at the cost of strength (a 1.5 mm wire passing around such a small radius creates problems, meaning they are viewed as body weight protection only).

tion) (1-5, with the smallest size being 4 mm), with the Black Diamond Micro stoppers (1-6) having a little more side flare (a little like a plain Jane nut versus a more complex DMM Wallnut). The reason why such small pieces can achieve relatively high strengths is that a wire does not need to be threaded through the nut itself, but instead is soldered.

- **Offset**: The HB Offset set the standard in this style of nut and the design works really well in more complex placements. DMM brass Offsets (0 -

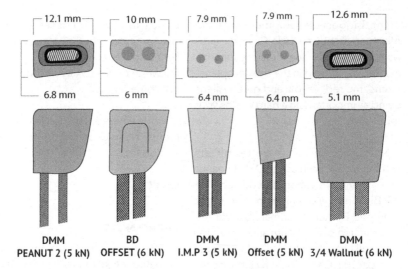

| DMM PEANUT 2 (5 kN) | BD OFFSET (6 kN) | DMM I.M.P 3 (5 kN) | DMM Offset (5 kN) | DMM 3/4 Wallnut (6 kN) |

Micro Shapes

Micro nuts come in three distinct styles:

- **Boxy**: This is the classic RP shape, a gentle taper with hard edges, and only a slight variation in faces (unlike a normal nut). This is great for exploiting very shallow placements, as the load is focused onto a smaller area, which is also important when you need to exploit very subtle constrictions. The best version on the market is the DMM I.M.P (Immaculate Marginal Protec-

6) and Peanuts (1 – 5), Black Diamond Offset Micro Stoppers (1 – 6), and Metolius Astro nuts (1-10), are the stand out models, with the softer alloy DMM Peanut often going where brass offsets won't. One area where offsets excel is in the bottom of piton scars, and they are vital when aiding on sandstone (three full sets of micro offsets is the minimum for harder routes).

- **Micro Stoppers**: These are just the smallest cabled alloy nuts, cheaper to make than the soldered brass version, but not as strong. The smallest version, like the Wallnut 00, is as narrow as the I.M.P 1 (4 mm), but much wider (9.7 vs 5.6 mm) and half as strong (2 kN vs 4 kN). The advantages of an alloy micro wire is that it has a larger contact surface area (although it can't be placed sideways like a brass micro), which can be helpful in very soft rock (the alloy used on micros tends to be harder than on full sized nuts).

So What's Best? The answer is very simple; all styles are best, depending on the placement, meaning you need a good mix of nut types, and both brass and alloy. Beyond the cost, micro nuts weigh so little, meaning four full sets to cover any placement (DMM Offsets, I.M.P, Micro Wallnuts and Peanuts for example) would fit well on one krab and weigh nothing.

What To Carry: I would recommend for standard trade routes to carry one set of brass boxy nuts and one set of brass offsets, probably DMM. These can all live on a little dedicated 'trick wires' krab. If this is too much of an outlay then a set of Peanuts and a set of micro alloys will also work. On harder walls I'd expand this out to four sets, focusing on the mid to large sizes (the size 1 micros rarely get used, but 3 to 6 do). Having a mix of BD and DMM nuts give you more tools in your micro crack tool box.

Micro Placements: Unlike most micros used when free climbing, on a big wall you will be fully weighting these nuts, so you should note their strength before doing any full on bounce testing as they will either break or deform (some will only hold 200 kg, which can easily be generated in a hard bounce test).

Cleaning: Due to being weighted it's easier to end up with fixed pieces when aid climbing and a great deal of care needs to be taken in cleaning your micros. Always employ a nut tool and make sure its tip is sharp so you can direct the force into the nut's cleaning sweet spot. Do not yank out micros as you clean as you will bend or kink the wire, and bent micros are less strong than straight micros.

REGULAR NUTS (STOPPERS)

These are your standard bread and butter aluminium nuts, the most common being Wild Country Rocks, DMM Wallnuts and Black Diamond Stoppers.

I find that on most routes on granite, where I have bolt belays and a good supply of cams, I can get away with just one or one and a half sets of these nuts, and double that on sandstone or limestone. If I have to make my own belays I will always stick to two sets, but make sure I also have other specialised nuts to call on (offsets, super lights).

You tend to find that the smaller nuts get called on more than the larger, as nuts are slower to both place and clean than cams. This does not mean that you need to carry more smaller nuts as the larger micro nuts also cover this size range.

It's worth noting that nut brands have a sizing system that means you will have two nuts that will cover the same size. For example, a Wallnut 6 placed face on covers 22.6 mm while an 8 placed sideways (traditionally) covers 22.3 mm.

OFFSET NUTS

These larger alloy offsets are vital on many routes and give the leader another tool at their disposal. On some routes you might need more than one set. One of my favourite nuts is the Wild Country offset Superlight, which is light and compact, and perfect for aiding, the weight important as it's just less to carry while leading.

PLACING NUTS

Everyone should know how to place a nut, but on an aid climb you may often be forced to place one far beyond where it would be placed while leading when free climbing, and sometimes blindly. Nuts, being soft alloy, have a high degree of 'grip', and will deform when bounce testing, often creating some semi custom nut.

Nuts can also be hammered into place, creating a 'stopper head', but this should be your last resort, with small taps being used to seat the nut rather than trying to paste it into the crack.

One of the biggest advantages of nuts is the lower outward force they apply when compared to cams, meaning they are safer to use in expanding or loose placements.

CLEANING NUTS

The fact you're weighting your nuts, sometimes very aggressively, means they can easily become stuck. A stuck wire will become fixed, the wire will rust, then break, eventually leaving behind an unsightly chunk of battered alloy on the route. For this reason you should always carry a lightweight hammer (even just a light one from a DIY store) to aid in cleaning your nuts, otherwise you'll end up having to leave them, which can also result in you running low on gear as you climb.

I tend to follow a policy of also cleaning any fixed gear left by others that I feel can be cleaned without damaging the route, as fixed gear spoils a route. Yes, it's nice to come to a fixed piece when you're leading, but it reduces the grade and robs you of your own little win.

I've climbed the Nose many times and have always come away with at least a full set of nuts each time (often DMM offsets). Is that ethical? Well I cleaned the Glowering Spot on the Nose of every single fixed wire in 2017, turning it from a via ferrata back into a cool pitch (one of the few technical aid pitches on the Nose, with small nuts above an ankle breaking ledge).

When I climbed it a few weeks later, for the second time that season, I was passed by Brad Gobright and Jim Reynolds, who were gunning for the new speed record. I knew on their last attempt the whole pitch had been fixed, crucial when every second counts, so I felt a little guilty as Jim set off up the pitch, using his aiders where before he could have just monkeyed up on the fixed gear. But Jim did it, and they broke the record, climbing the Nose in 2 hours, 19 minutes and 44 secs.

FIXED NUTS

The issue of fixed nuts is worth considering further as you will come across them, sometimes virtually creating a ladder (such as on the Great Roof pitch on the Nose). First of all you should never just blindly jump on a fixed nut. Several times I've clipped into a nut only to have it just fall out of the crack (slings are the same), which means someone simply dropped a nut and it fell into the crack below, a time bomb for some luckless (or careless) climber. Such booby-trapped pieces are dangerous when you're leap-

New Dawn rack

frogging for a long way, as they might hold you for a second, long enough to clean the piece below, but no more than that. If the nut is good, then check out the state of the cable. Is it rusty or frayed? I've had several fixed wires break when they were rusty and had damaged wires break while being bounce tested. You can try to just creep up on such gear with your fingers crossed, but it's often better to empty the nut instead, by either threading a sling around it, using a cinch hanger on the cable (if frayed), or hooking a beak over the top of the nut.

WHAT IS A TYPICAL NUT RACK?

STANDARD RACK
Brass Micros: DMM I.M.P 2, 3, 4, 5
Brass Micros: DMM Offset 2, 3, 4, 5, 6
Alloy Micros: DMM Peanuts 1, 2, 3, 4, 5
Alloy Micros: DMM 00, 0, 0.5, 0.75
Standard: DMM Wallnuts: Full set
Standard: BD Stopper: 3, 5, 7, 9, 11
DMM Offsets: 2x7, 2x8, 2x9, 10, 11

SPEED CLIMBING RACK
Brass Micros: DMM I.M.P: 2, 4, 6
Brass Micros: DMM offset: 2, 4, 6
Standard Nuts: Wallnut: 1, 3, 5, 7
DMM Offset: 7, 9, 11

Sandstone / Limestone Rack: Same as a typical nut rack but doubles in standard nuts and perhaps doubles or triples in all micro nuts for harder aid (Desert Shield for example).

Hard Aid: On very bleak aid I might dump all my larger nuts and just take my micros, while on sandstone or limestone I would add in two full sets of nuts from 1 to 10. Nuts that are not being used can always be left at the belay.

RACKING NUTS
I tend to carry my skeleton rack of standard nuts on a single oval karabiner, then my micros on two other ovals, standard on one (including 3/4 to 00 nuts), offsets on the other (including DMM Peanuts). These are kept at the back of my racking loops, as they are used very little unless I'm climbing on sandstone.

HEXENTRICS
The late great Walt Shipley would never climb a wall without a set of Black Diamond Hexes, and although old school they have many pros and few cons. Being large a hex can replace a cam in a belay or as a runner, which can be important when new routing or when cams are limited. They also work in icy cracks, loose or expanding rock, can be hammered into place, and stack very well with pitons. Hexes on cord or slings can also be used in non traditional loading positions, cammed like a tricam or twisted and locked into place (they can even be placed lengthways, in holes, and cammed into position). For granite walls I'd probably skip carrying hexes, but on big scrappy big walls, on sandstone or limestone, they have their place. Of the few models on the market, my favourite is the DMM Torque, due to its improved ability to cam.

TRICAMS
Often overlooked, the cheap and lightweight tricam can be invaluable on some climbs, especially on limestone or for funky sandstone weirdness. The smaller micro sizes are also worth having for very tricky placements as their width is much smaller than any cam, they can be used as nuts also, and like nuts I find they seem to exert a lower outward force than a cam in expanding rock. Also due to their broad

Tricam on Mount Dickey

camming range, they will not rip like a nut when the rock flexes under load.

Rack: On a granite wall I will often carry a 0.125 (2 kN / 10 - 16 mm) and 0.25 (5 kN / 13.5 - 22 mm), racked along with my nuts (so they are there when I need them), and perhaps up to 1.5 if I know there will be a lot of peg scars (the Shield for example). On sandstone I'd carry up to size 4, and a double set up to size 5 on limestone.

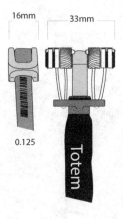

Tricam Placement: When placing a tricam in a vertical crack try to find a depression for the 'spike' and always visually check you're achieving a good strong 'tripod' between the spike and the two 'rails'. Ideally the sling should pass between the two 'rails', but good placements can be achieved even if placed sideways, with the tape running sideways and twisted over just one 'rail'. In horizontal placements it's best to have the spike on the bottom, with the sling running over the top of the nut, as this tends to help keep its position better. Once placed give it a big tug to set it and then extend it to reduce the likelihood of it being unset.

Cleaning: To clean a tricam you'll need a nut tool and this should be used either to push the bottom 'rail' side back, or pull the 'spike' side forward to return it to its unset position. If it has been fallen on then you may need two hands, using a krab to hammer the nut tool.

SLIDER NUTS

This style of opposing nut – although niche - was once far more common, designed to exploit micro cracks that were too small or narrow for cams, with the smallest size Trango BallNutz 1 covering 3.75 - 6.4 mm (a black Alien has a range of 8 - 14 mm). How effective they were in this role is debatable, as often they were used by free climbers on routes where falling off was not really an option.

My own experience of sliders for direct aid was never great, so I have doubts how many of those climbers would have lived if they'd fallen on that single slider. Luckily, since the introduction of smaller and smaller camming units, like the black CCH Alien and other 000 units, the slider nut has all but disappeared, with only the Camp Ballnut and Trango Ballnutz remaining. In practice I've always found sliders very tricky to use, with the very hard steel body of the Camp Ball-nut often stopping it from getting that initial and important 'stick' in very smooth cracks (one reason Aliens work so well is their soft alloy), which is vital in order to get a solid placement (the old Metolius slider worked much better as it had a softer alloy body). A second problem was that if you got a slider to stick then it would often be very hard to clean, meaning you'd often find fixed broken sliders.

This leads to the question; is there still a place for the slider nut? I think the answer needs to be broken down into two halves:

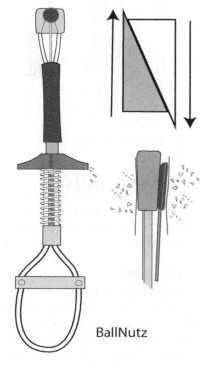

BallNutz

Progression: For aid climbing the slider nut's role tended to be as a replacement for a piton when trying to climb a route clean, or in very narrow placements where a higher strength piece might be achieved with a slider compared to a tied off piece (tip of #7 Lost Arrow or stacked RURPS etc). These days the slider nut has been killed off by the adoption of the cam hook, which works excellently well in classic slider 'letterbox' slots, especially inverted placements. The one place where the slider still has a place is on very soft rock, such as sandstone, where a cam hook can break away the edge of a crack.

Protection: It's rare to leave a cam hook behind as protection, meaning if you come across a small slot in the middle of a section of bleak aid you might be missing a solid piece if you just cam hook through it. Stacked micro pitons might work, but again they might be marginal, and so a slider nut might offer you the best option possible.

Placement: The amount of play between the two sides of the nut is minimal, growing smaller and smaller as you go down in size, meaning any expansion in the rock, or a less than tight fit, will see the opposing force lost and the stack will collapse. For this reason I always try and find a very tight placement, so you have as much room for compression and expansion in the rock as possible. Although a slider will work in a parallel slot, you should try to view it as neither a cam or a nut, but a mix of both, looking to exploit even the slightest constriction to aid it's holding power. If using the upside down nut you can match it with RP style micros or even offsets.

Rack: Perhaps it's worth carrying a set of the smallest, size 1 and 2 sliders, for the 0.1% of placements where a cam hook won't go, but I tend to fall back onto piton stacks or improvised sliders instead. Nevertheless the concept is one that should be understood, as although I don't use slider nuts myself anymore, I do use the concept occasionally, both via improvised methods and my own custom slider set up.

Improvised Slider: Every now and then you'll come across some funky slot that won't take a micro cam, but will take a cam hook, but you want some protection as well. One option is to create your own slider nut by placing two opposed (one inverted) micro nuts. The best nuts for this are micro alloy sub #1 nuts (such as DMM Wallnut 00 or 0), although you can also stack a nut with an inverted RURP or beak (the crucial point is that you need two opposing tapers). When stacking pro always make sure both pieces are somehow connected so they aren't lost if they fail. To do this simply slide one nut over the other larks footing their cables together (as you would when extending a wire with another wire).

Upside Down Nut: This piece of DIY gear goes into your bag of big wall tricks for hard aid, and can be used both as a blocking piece with nuts or with micro pitons (beaks). It works the same way as the improvised method but due to it lacking a full length cable makes it easier to use in very tight spots where a cable would get in the way. To make one of these take a micro nut (BD stopper 1 or DMM Wallnut 00) and cut off the cable, then rewire it with a loop of 1.5 mm cable and swage it in order to create an upside down nut. The nut itself is not load bearing, but only there to act as a way to secure it to the primary nut.

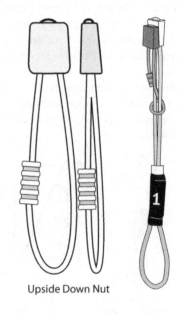

Upside Down Nut

CAMMING UNITS

Walls are primarily climbed on cams, from cams the size of a pencil to cams as big as your head.

MICRO CAMS

The deflation in big wall difficulty has come about primarily due to the introduction of more sophisticated camming units, with the first great leap coming in 1977 with the Wild Country rigid Friend. This was followed by many competing designs, but perhaps the first 'aid cam' was Steve Bryne's flexible stemmed Wired Bliss TCU (three cam unit), allowing narrower placements to be exploited (when you compare an old Wild Country

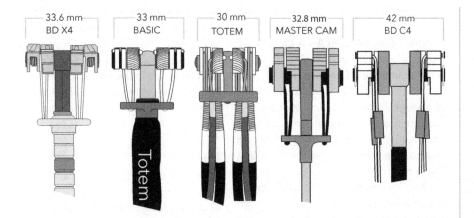

| 33.6 mm | 33 mm | 30 mm | 32.8 mm | 42 mm |
| BD X4 | BASIC | TOTEM | MASTER CAM | BD C4 |

0.5 Flexible Friend with a green Alien it's amazing we ever climbed anything).

The CCH Alien, invented by Dave Waggoner, was the biggest game changer, with it's super soft cams (6061-T6) and greedier camming angle (16 degrees), flexible stem, and narrow head, allowing it to go where no other cam could. On a hard route you could never have enough green, yellow or red Aliens, with at least four of each being the minimum for hard aid, with the blue, and later black, sizes further banishing pitons from even hard walls.

The next step was the offset cam, which was a game changer. Again it was CCH who took the offset idea and produced the amazing offset Alien, opening up many clean placements from the hammer.

Unfortunately CCH was more of a garage enterprise and so suffered some manufacturing faults that damaged their reputation, and so when Dave Waggoner passed away the company was sold to Fixe.

The new Fixe CCH Alien Revolutions are very good (avoid first generation models that have plastic trigger components), being lighter, stronger and narrower. The Totem cam also appeared on the market at the same time, another leap, like some mutant Alien cam injected with Hulk DNA.

The Totem featured the same camming angle as the Alien which meant it would go where other cams could not (there is an associated loss in general holding power, but I've never had one fail).

Totem then began producing its own version of the Alien in the form of the Totem Basic, both as straight cams and as offsets. Parallel to this, Black Diamond and Metolius pushed the free cam designs with the Camalot family and Master cams, which covered standard camming units very well (many other brands of cams are available but I find Camalots work the best in terms of general use, but most of all due to their ability not to end up fixed). Black Diamond also produced the C3 (discontinued), and later the C4 and C4 offset. I personally feel the C4 and Master cams are more focused towards free climbing, having more traditional, hard, alloy cams.

What Makes A Cam An Aiding Cam?

An aid cam starts around 8 mm and ends around the off-finger range (30 mm) - in other words black Alien to red Alien - as above this standard cams take over. An aid cam has to be as narrow as possible and feature a flexible stem, so it can be placed safely without the stem becoming bent or damaged or causing the cam to shift. It's worth noting the strength of the smallest units (5 kN), which although good for falls does signify that such units are more fragile. Another factor is that the softer cams on the Alien style units deform more, with ten or so walls and constant bounce testing mushrooming out the cams. It's best not to imagine something so small as a black Alien can be twisted, bent, bounced and fallen on and just stay the same, and I've broken (bent head stems or axles) a handful of such tiny cams. How long do they last? I'd say, at a rough guess, about twenty walls.

OFFSET CAMS

These feature two sizes of cam and are crucial for moderate to hard aid, with two sets (or more), being pretty much vital. The Totem Basic Offset and Alien Revolution Offset are the only ones I'd use. Although offset, these should not be viewed as simply for trick placements, but as standard cams as well. When climbing I tend to see these as being cams I can sacrifice (leave in as protection when leading instead of back cleaning) more easily than my standard micros, and even in what might look like a parallel crack you will often find a flare. On standard aid pitches I tend to carry one full set of offsets on a single karabiner, treating them like nuts, with a second set ready to be sent up from the belay.

Offset Specific Placements: Offsets work like a standard cam, but in the most technical flared placements you need to really think about exploiting parallel opposing surfaces, making sure the cam will be loaded in the correct orientation. In some placements you can get away with only three cams in play, but each has to be spot on.

TCU

Three cam units had a place in the past, but narrower four cam units have all but replaced them. The one exception was the BD C3 (discontinued), which was an excellent cam and useful in sizes 0 to 000. These worked very well when matched with four cam units, often going in places where they will not. I carry one set of these with their draws cut off, racking them like nuts on a single karabiner.

STANDARD CAMS

I would class standard cams as your normal free climbing cams, solid, robust and high strength. These can overlap your aid cams (wider finger sized cams such as a 0.5 Camalot for example), as most cracks will take this style of cam the same as it will take an aid cam, and often you will place your standard cams as pro, and keep your aid cams for progression. There are tons of cams on the market, but personally I prefer Black Diamond Camalots due to the fact these cams cannot invert leading to fixed cams or broken cables. They are also very hard to get stuck, something that I can't say about other models. The newer Camalot Ultralights are a game changer in terms of weight, especially for alpine walls, but their cost and lower life span means you really need to want them (buying the bigger cams as Ultralights, such as the 2, 3, and 4 is a good option).

STAND OUT MICRO AID CAMS

There are many cams on the market but I would focus on these for pure aid:

TOTEM	TOTEM BASIC
0.50 **Black** (6 kN / 11.7 - 18.9 mm) 0.65 **Blue** (8 kN / 13.8 - 22.5 mm) 0.80 **Yellow** (9 kN / 17 - 27.7 mm) 1 **Purple** (10 kN / 20.9 - 34.2 mm) *The best aid cam in my opinion.*	0.50 **Blue** (5 kN / 11.2 - 17.4 mm) 0.65 **Green** (7 kN / 13.6 - 21.4.4 mm) 0.75 **Yellow** (9 kN / 16.6 - 26.1 mm) 0.95 **Red** (11 kN / 19.9 - 31.6 mm) *The Basics fit in between the standard Totem cams and are narrower, meaning they are ideal as a third set of cams, or as stand alone cams.*

FIXE ALIEN REVOLUTION	BLACK DIAMOND X4
1/3 **Black** (5 kN / 8 - 14 mm) 3/8 **Blue** (6 kN / 10 - 17 mm) 1/2 **Green** (7 kN / 13 - 22 mm) 3/4 **Yellow** (10 kN / 15 - 25 mm) 7/8 **Grey** (10 kN / 17 -30 mm) 1 **Red** (10 kN / 20 - 33 mm) *A slightly different size than the Basics, plus lighter and narrower.*	0.1 (5 kN / 8.4 - 13.8 mm) 0.2 (6 kN / 9.9 - 16.5 mm) 0.3 (8 kN / 12.4 - 21.2 mm) 0.4 (9 kN / 15.5 - 26.6 mm) 0.5 (9 kN / 19.8 - 33.7 mm) 0.75 (9 kN / 24 - 41.2 mm) *More focused towards free climbing, with the harder cams and less flexible stem making them less effective for the toughest placements.*

METOLIUS ULTRA-LIGHT MASTER CAM	BLACK DIAMOND C4
00 (5 kN / 8.5 - 12 mm) 0 (5 kN / 10 - 15 mm) 1 (8 kN / 12.5 - 18 mm) 2 (10 kN / 15.5 - 22.5 mm) 4 (10 kN / 23.5 - 33.5 mm) *Same as the X4.*	0.3 (8 kn / 13.8 - 23.4 mm) 0.4 (10 kN / 15.5 - 26.7 mm) 0.5 (12 kN / 19.6 - 33.5 mm) 0.75 (14 kN / 23.9 - 41.2 mm) 1 (14 kN / 30.2 - 52.1 mm) *The classic and standard wall cam.*

OMEGA LINK CAMS

This is an esoteric cam that needs to be singled out as it can be very handy, especially for free climbing. Although heavy and expensive, the Link cam design allows you to have one unit that covers the range of around four cams, with the yellow size 2 (25.4 - 64 mm) being the stand out. For routes like the Nose you can just clip one of these into each daisy and just jug some of the cracks. Due to the design, this style of cam can also create quite extreme offsets. The downside is that these cams require a good level of skill to avoid getting them fixed. The last time I climbed the Nose I found three stuck in the Stove Leg cracks alone, and have come across many others on other walls.

RACK

The number of cams you carry comes down to the difficulty of the route and how cool you are with running it out. On a route like the Nose you can get away with two full sets of cams, but this means you'll be back cleaning almost everything, using nuts or fixed gear as protection. For this reason most climbers will carry three sets of cams as a minimum, switching back to doubles for Camalot 3 and above (unless the wall features a lot of wide cracks). As things get harder you tend to want to increase your small and micro cams (0.5 Camalot and down), and I tend to carry the following rack on most walls:

- 2x Alien Revolution Black
- 2x Alien (Totem Basic) Blue, Green, Yellow, Red
- 2x Totem Black, Blue, Yellow, Purple, Red
- 2x Alien Revolution Black/Blue
- 2x Offset Alien (Totem Basic) Blue/Green, Green/Yellow, Yellow/Red
- 2x Black Diamond C4 0.5 to 6

ADVANCED CAM PLACEMENTS

If you're about to head up onto a big wall you should already know how to use a cam, but there are a few little add-ons that can help on a wall, and the harder the wall the greater the demands on your cam placement skills.

Granular Thinking: Ninety percent of placements, even on A4 routes, will be straightforward, able to be exploited by even standard free climbing cams.

Another nine percent will require more specialised cams, narrower, more flexible, or just more trustworthy. This nine percent require far more skill then your normal free climber has, and a fuller understanding of how the cam interacts with the rock.

And then there is the one percent of placements that I would call granular placements, where moving the cam 1 mm either way will see it rip out. Here you require a master's understanding of the cam's cohesion to the rock, how a rough area the size of your fingernail in a flair will help snag a cam that keeps popping, how a radical flare where nothing fits actually contains two parallel bumps that can take a cam on two lobes.

Such granular placements not only require skill, but also care, as any shifting can cause them to fail, meaning you need to know how for instance a BD C3 can shift if loaded on its rigid side (a C3 is flexible in two directions, rigid in two), the difference between the body weight and the train stopper placement.

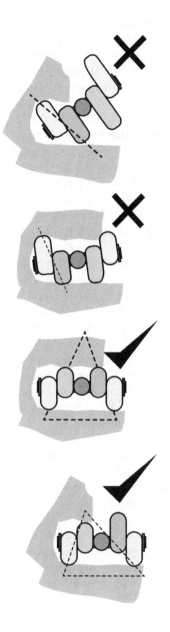

become shallower, and will not accept the full width of the cam, you need to start paying attention.

If the narrowness and shallow depth of the crack mean that 25% of the cam will not fit, or even 50%, this can look to an untrained eye like a cam is unplaceable, or can result in a cam being placed in a dangerously weak orientation, when in fact a full strength placement can be achieved, even if it looks like the cam is hanging out of the crack.

The most important thing to remember is that a cam has two orientations, a wide and a narrow one, and if a cam is unstable and weak one way, it may be solid if you flip it over (this is most noticeable in a Tricam or TCU).

Imagine a cam working like a triangle, with the force coming from the outside cam lobes being the base, and the two central lobes the point. Very often a shallow crack in a corner will have a broad face on one side and a shallow one on the other, so by placing the cam with the wide cam lobes on the broadest face and the central lobes touching the shallow side, you can achieve a full strength placement. If the crack is very shallow you may find that one of the central lobes is not touching at all, don't be alarmed, it may not be 100% but the strength of 3 cam lobes should still be effective, the cam is working like a TCU.

Shallow Cams: One of the most crucial skills in big wall cam placements is getting the correct orientation of your cam lobes, so that all four, or maybe three, or two, achieve the highest degree of holding power. In straight deep cracks you don't have to worry, but as cracks

As you can imagine, the narrower the cam (Aliens, Basic, Totems, C3 and C4), the greater the possibility of all lobes engaging the rock, and of being able to provide effective protection in the shallowest of cracks.

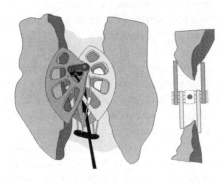

Overlapping: You will occasionally come across cracks that are very jagged and have no parallel sides, meaning the placement requires a non standard approach. This can be achieved by having the cam held by the interior edges of the cam lobes, more of a gripping action than a straight cam. This works especially well on some wide cracks.

Nut Cams: Cams that feature cam stops or have double axles can be used as a nut in some placements, although their stability tends to be very poor. Another variation of this, is to use the cam sideways like a nut, which will give you a narrower placement (body weight only). On this point you can sometimes end up having a cam, or a part of a cam, acting as a nut unbeknownst to you, say when the trigger terminus on a Basic or Alien is jammed in a crack, rather than the cam itself as you intended. Here the vital thing, as with all aid climbing, is being observant.

Opposing Forces: You will sometimes come across very loose, shifting or fractured rock or cracks, where the only placements you have move, like broken crockery. If the looseness is blocked by other sections of more solid rock, such

as when the whole looseness is within a wider crack, you can just use the loose rock as you would opposing or stacked gear, with the force of the cam being transferred and securing everything in place.

Two Lobe Placements: Although theoretically most cams should be able to be loaded on two cam lobes, it is only the twin stemmed Totem that allows you do this with a modicum of self soilage. To do this simply clip the correct side of the stem and test carefully.

Back Cleaning: Aiding is gear intensive; with one piece going in roughly per metre meaning you will quickly find yourself out of gear if the climbing is uniform, say a forty metre size two Camalot crack. The only way to avoid running out of gear is to reuse crucial pieces, leapfrogging them up the crack. To do this safely requires some skill and confidence, as often you'll be hanging from a single piece of protection.

Back cleaning requires a great deal of practice and if you get it wrong you could end up finding yourself at the bottom of the last pitch!

The trick is to never remove the last piece, meaning you always have a backup in case the piece you're currently on blows (it shouldn't because you've tested it). This means once you're on the new piece, before you crank up the aider you should reach down and remove the piece below the one you were on (the second piece below the top one, or the third piece).

As you progress you should leave bomber pieces in for protection every now and then as you would if you were

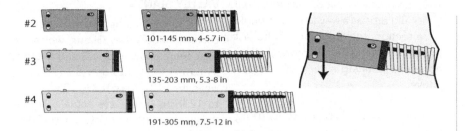

#2 101-145 mm, 4-5.7 in

#3 135-203 mm, 5.3-8 in

#4 191-305 mm, 7.5-12 in

free climbing, and these are usually wires, as cams are generally the most useful pieces to have on your harness for progression as they are quick to place and quick to remove.

If you find yourself running short of gear and the end is still not in sight then consider building a belay with two equalised pieces then lowering down to clean all the gear below.

MONSTER GEAR

Dealing with very wide cracks can be a feature of many walls, the Bismarck on Mescalito on El Cap being a great example. Some pitches can be thrutched and free climbed by those adept at offwidthing, or climbed on tipped out cams (Such as the big off width on Zodiac), but others have to be aided. If you're climbing a new route you should always have a plan on how to deal with something wide and nasty, rather than just rivet up it (when I climbed in Antarctica the two most used cams were probably the Camalot 5 and 6!). You have a number of options at your disposal:

BIG STANDARD CAMS

For me this covers Camalot 4 to 6, and these seem to cover most wide sections on standard walls. Due to their weight and bulk you will only carry these if they are called for on the topo.

The best way to employ these cams is either to aid off them one after the other, or attach your lanyards to them and try and squirm yourself up. When aiding I find it's best to have the top cam for your body, and the bottom for your feet, pushing up one at a time (rather than leapfrogging). Always be very aware of the danger of cams being tipped out and ripping, and make sure you have enough cam expansion in the unit to remain secure.

TUBE CHOCKS

These can be homemade from sections of aluminium scaffolding or old Chouinard Tube Chocks, but most often come in the form of the Big Bro, an expanding tube chock designed by the late Craig Luebben. The Big Bro is cheapish (cheaper than a custom cam), light and compact (important on a first ascent where you may not need them), and covers a fair range. Although there are four sizes of Big Bro (the gold five has been discontinued), you only need sizes above Camalot 6, meaning the #3 (235 g / range: 135 - 203 mm / 5.3 - 8 inch) and #4 (338 g / 191 - 305 mm / 7.5 - 12 inch). The main problem with a Big Bro compared to a cam is that it cannot be pushed up or leapfrogged up a crack, and so works best as protection or for one off moves. Some climbers, faced with some fearsome wideness have resorted to leapfrogging between bolts/rivets and big bros, but this is a very long and messy way to climb. I have tended to use Big Bros as a way to span a single wide section, top stepping on the last piece and getting the Big Bro high, then hopefully reaching a narrower section above.

Tube Chock Placement: Getting a Big Bro to lock in place requires two parallel and slightly opposing sections of crack, with one side placed in position then the tube opened. A strong placement can also be created by exploiting a concave spot, small edges, or crystals or bumps that fit within the tube. Once you have a secure fit tighten down the collar as much as you can. As an aside it is possible to step on the tube chock as long as it's straight down, but only press on the higher end up the tube (wrapping the top in finger tape makes it less slippery). I would also recommend sticking a line of tape alone the very bottom of the Big Bro, so when you're below it you can tell when it's correctly orientated. In extremes I have also hammered the Big Bro to fit, but being aluminium this is for emergencies only.

WOODEN BLOCKS
Another option is to use a standard large cam (5 or 6) and stack it with a block of wood. This block can just be a simple block of sawn wood (with a hole drilled for a keeper cord), or a block with a slightly concave face with the other side having a sheet of sticky rubber screwed and glued onto it. This kind of placement is really just for aid, but can be very secure. If you find yourself faced with a wide section then you can make use of the wood in your belay seat as an emergency stacking option.

VALLEY GIANTS
The largest cams you can get are custom made Valley Giants, which are best seen as being size 7 and 8 cams. #9 covers 145 to 229 mm (5.7 to 9 inch), while the #12 covers 188 to 305 mm (7.4 to 12 inch). These are actually lighter than you would think (880 g and 990 g), and are designed to be pushed above you as you climb, rather than aided on(I doubt anyone could afford two sets of Valley Giants).

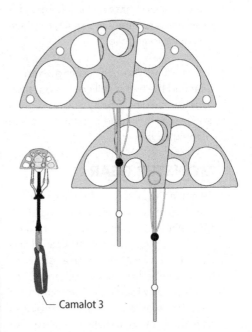

Camalot 3

WIDE CRACKS WITHOUT WIDE GEAR
If you come across a wide section and have nothing that fits you might be able to place a cam deeper inside where the crack narrows. When doing this you can get some height by leveraging your body up, so the cam is being pulled straight out. Look out for edges that can be hooked, or foot holds that can be used to get past the hard section.

Big crack climbing on Holstinnd, Antarctica

CAM CARE

On hard, intensive walls, where cams are being placed and removed hundreds of times, as well as being twisted, bent, and abused, trigger wires will break. Such problems when they appear on the ground are annoying, something to fix when you've got time, but on a wall, the loss of a single unit can mean the loss of a climb. Scale that up to a long trip far from home, and you could have a problem that unless remedied could ruin a trip of a lifetime. Here are some ideas on how to stop your wires breaking, and how to deal with them when they do.

#1 LOOK AFTER YOUR CAMS!

This is a big one, as the trigger wires that come with camming units should last the lifetime of the cam, and I have cams that are worn to a nub and yet still have the cables they came with.

How wires get broken is often due to poor transportation, all your rack just dumped into your pack after a climb, or onto the floor. Cables and wires have a tendency to get hung up, snagged and tangled on everything else, and yanking your rack apart just wrecks them. Any kink added to a stiff wire is a future break. Instead, you should get into the habit of bunching your cams together and in line, and ideally store them in a stuff sack when not being used.

Large cams such as size 4, 5 and 6 need more care, and I would try and use a stick to keep the lobes retracted when not being used, as they tend to snag on everything.

It's important also to keep your cams clean and lubricated. Dirty cams resist the trigger and so require more pressure on the trigger. Keep them clean and free from dirt and salt by washing them every now and then with hot water and soap, scrubbing them clean with a toothbrush. Lubricate the cams with a graphite lubricant that will not attract dirt (bike shop), or with good old WD40, which does attract dirt, but has seen climbers proud for several decades.

Don't set off with dodgy wires. If your Camalot 3's trigger is hanging by a thread, with just a single strand of wire the only thing between working and not working, then sort it out before you leave the ground!

WALL REPAIRS

Being able to fix your cams on the fly is vital on any big wall, doubly so if you're on an expedition, and by carrying a few specialist items in your tool kit, you can quickly make running repairs.

Trigger Kits: Most brands sell trigger kits that can be used to replace damaged units, and it's always best to go with what the manufacturer recommends. The downside of this approach is that you never have such kits when you need them, and the moment the ones you've ordered arrive you'll find a broken cam you missed. Having a lot of cams, I tend to just repair them all myself at home.

Cam Repair Kit: A basic cam repair kit can vary from nothing but a roll of dental floss to a kit comprising of multiple thicknesses of wire, swages, and a multi tool, the emergency repair versus a repair that lasts for years.

Tools: Very few climbers will have the correct tools to hand for a professional job, namely wire cutters and a swaging tool, and instead, you will need to improvise. The best tool for this is a multi tool, and you will need this to cut away old cables, pull cables out, then cut the new wire and crimp your swages. Cutting multi strand wires cleanly can be difficult without professional clippers, leaving stray wires that affect insertion or make it impossible, and for this reason, I'm a fan of single strand wire, monofilament or fluorocarbon as it can be cut easily. One method that can work for multi filament wire is to use the tip of a blade or sharp piton and hammer it, creating a guillotine.

Cables: The diameter of the wire used on camming units varies, but as a rule of thumb the standard hole drilled into cam lobes on small to medium cams tends to be around 1.3 mm, so avoid anything more than 1.3 mm (clean out holes with the stiff broken cable to make insertion of new cable easier). Holes on micro cams such as the blue alien or C3 are smaller still, around 0.8 mm, working best with 0.75 mm cable, while the smallest units require 0.5 mm wire.

The factory built cables are designed for decades of hard use and the trigger is designed to look and feel like a cam trigger. Your on the run repairs do not need to be up to the same standard. I expect most companies could switch to a monofilament or fluorocarbon cable which would be cheaper and easier to replace, but don't, because climbers are resistant to change (just look at the resistance to the excellent Metolius Master Cam's kevlar trigger cables). Again, you don't face the same commercial worries and can make use of whatever you want. When making repairs it's good to have a good selection of materials to choose

from, and a few mini z-lock bags containing a metre of rolled up wire weighs nothing.

Swages: Swages are soft alloy or copper sleeves into which you insert two wires and then crimp together. If crimping with a multi tool use the wire cutter to carefully crease the sleeve without actually cutting into it. If you don't have a multi tool, then use a hammer/rock to hit a blunt edged piton to compress the sleeve. Alloy swages are easier to crimp than copper. Make sure you match the correct swage to the correct cable. Industrial wire or fishing tackle sites are the best places to buy swages, as well as swaging tools.

Replacing Broken Cables

The following can be used to repair your cams.

- **Monel Seizing Wire**: This is 0.8 mm marine wire that comes in a 10 metre spool and having a few metres in your repair kit always pays dividends. The wire is very stiff but flexible enough for the job and does not seem to weaken after being bent at right angles.

- **#2 1.2 mm Brass Picture Frame Wire**: This is fantastic emergency repair wire, being thin enough for the smallest cams, stiff but easily twisted or bent. This wire works best on micro cams and does not require any other components or swages. I've also used this to repair broken triggers.

- **Paper Clips**: Always worth having in your repair kit, these make good stiff wire replacement for medium to large cams, ranging in diameter between 0.7 mm and 1 mm, and can be used alone or swaged into a cable.

- **1.2 mm Monofilament Strimmer Line**: This is one of my favourites as it's the easiest to use on the fly, and needs no special tools to be used on medium to large cams (Camalot 4s and 5s, which tend to suffer trigger damage often). Cut the line at an angle to make it easier to insert and melt the ends so they ball up and act as stoppers.

- **0.48 mm Steel Guitar String**: This works very much like picture frame wire, being very stiff and high strength, but also available in diameters below 0.5 mm. I find this is the best way to repair tiny camming units such as black Aliens.

- **3/64 (1.19 mm) 7x19 Aircraft Grade Stainless Wire**: This is the best wire for standard cams, with 7x19 construction far more effective than 7x7 as it's much more flexible and high strength. Make sure your swages match the wire.

- **0.75 mm 7x19 Stainless Wire**: Very thin but still strong, this is ideal for micro cams.

- **Dental Floss:** Much higher strength than you'd imagine, and suitable for temporary cam repair.

- **Fishing Line:** Heavy duty fishing line is easy to tie and cheap, and can be used for fishing too! Heavy duty deep sea fishing line with high breaking strains is surprisingly strong, with fluorocarbon line being even stronger than monofilament line. This can also double up for other repairs, even sewing.

- **Whipping Twine**: Designed for yachting ropes, this high strength waxed cotton is an excellent all round cord for repair kits, suitable for heavy duty sewing too.

HOOKS

I can still remember my first A4 death lead, the first time I knew, without a doubt, that failure was not an option.

Such thoughts often run through your head, looking down at a long string of copper heads for example, but experience tells you that often such joke pro does actually stop you dying, or that ripping all the gear to the belay is no biggie when you're falling into space.

But no, on this lead I was in no doubt that to fuck up here, to be slapdash or too hasty, would see me either dead or pretty badly smashed up. So where was I? Well, I was on the crux of Lost In America, an A4+ route put up by Randy Leavitt and Greg Child, the pitch a horizontal traverse elusively on small hooks set on flat edges. The only protection on the traverse was two fixed cruddy #2 heads, with a fall onto the belay being a huge killer swing into a big corner beneath the haul bags.

The idea of skyhooking is one of those terrifying things you read about as a novice, buy the gear, and know you'll have to do it someday, but don't look forward to that day. When you've never used a skyhook the very idea is the stuff of nightmares, and then when that day comes you find it very much lives up to top billing in the theatre of fear.

My first ever hook move, beyond messing around at crags, my feet an inch above the deck, was on the Shield headwall. So far we'd made it up my first ever big wall without the use of hooks, but there I was, out of options, the only thing to link where I was to where I wanted to go, a small edge. Out came the Black Diamond Cliffhanger hook I'd bought long before, and clipping this into my aider, I leant way left and hooked it onto the edge. Transferring over to the hook, committing to it, was beyond terrifying. I could feel the metal flexing under my weight, felt as if it was just going to flex out and break. I stepped over and back several times, until finally I committed my weight fully to it, and tried to move over without slipping off the hook in fright. I doubt I'd ever been so afraid. I somehow found the strength to step up my aiders for some far off piece of gear - I forget what - and was just so happy to be off the hook.

And so it was funny to look back six walls later, to be out on that A4+ lead, the only gear on my harness a set of hooks and rivet hangers, feeling comfortable, even relaxed on hooks a tenth of the size of that cliffhanger, going from hook to hook to hook. What had changed in all that time to give me this skill? I guess the walls I'd climbed had taught me that hooks, like automatic weapons, were safe if used correctly. The trick was understanding how they worked, what they could and could not do, and then taking your time, moving like an artist, not a bullfighter.

Since then I've done many hundreds of hook moves, and beyond the odd one – or ten – that were terrifying, due to the fact they broke the rules of what constituted a safe move, such as micro edges that could chip off, all have been fun.

UNDERSTANDING HOOKS
What your novice brain does not know is that most hooks are bomber, solid sinker flakes or flat edges with some dimple eroded by the passage of hooks or enhanced by a drill or chisel. There tend to be very few matchstick edges or sloping rounded horror holds.

On all trade routes, even the hard classics, where you put a hook will be visible. As the climbing becomes more difficult, it often becomes a game of just knowing where to look, trying to read the rock like the first ascensionists had to, sometimes unfortunately leading to 'not the move', where under duress you hook something terrible imagining 'that's all there is'.

In actual fact, in almost all cases, on anything but the hardest first ascents and repeats there tends to be something good - although my definition of 'good' might not be the same as someone else's.

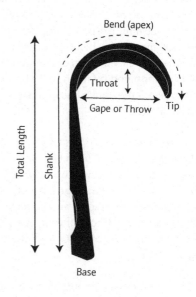

Practise: As with most gear in this book, it's important to play with the tools you have, pick up hooks and look at their differing shapes and sizes, find out where one works better than another. As with everything else, it's a game of forces, how they are applied and how other forces, such as leverage, can make or break a hook placement.

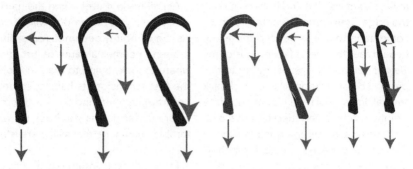

A hook will always attempt to align its tip to its base.

The most important features of the hook are its point, and its 'throw', the distance from the spine or shank of the hook to its point, this distance varying from 5 to 50 mm. The point engages with the rock and can be blunt or sharp, the steepness or shallowness of the point's angle determined by the hook's throat. Lastly, there's the hook's base, where the load is applied.

When loaded, the point of the hook will always try and move in line with the base, this being the reason why skyhooks don't work well on flat edges. An effective skyhook is a complex and balanced design, with the throw, throat, length of the shank, base and point all working together.

On micro edges a hook needs a small throw and throat so forces are minimised, the hook held in place by both the stickiness/friction and the bite of a sharp point, exploiting depressions on a granular level. Medium to large hooks most often simply wrap over flakes, rails, bumps and into holes, cracks and depressions, making use of larger throws and throats. Flat, smooth edges are the most problematical, and you can test this by hooking the edge of a laminated work surface,

such as a kitchen table. With nothing to grab or check the point's desire to get in line with the base, the hook will almost always pop. Such real work placements, including sloping edges, require some mall depression, and this is most often created by previous hooks, or by a drilled or chipped hole. The idea of chipping perhaps sounds outrageous, but most often something the size of a match head is all that's required.

Placement: On most hook moves, the placement will be obvious, a positive edge hold that accepts the throw of the hook, where the base of the hook provides great stability against the rock as well. What you're trying to do is achieve a three point contact using the point and base. If you get less than this, the hook can shift around more, which in most cases is fine but can be a problem if the hook is located very precisely.

Although there are blind hook moves, often the closest you will get to this is high stepping and feeling the rock with your fingers. When you've done a lot of climbing you tend to get an instinct for where you will find a hook placement and so know where to feel (on sandstone you'll often see two scratch marks from where the base points of previous hooks have rubbed against the rock).

Hook or Book, Sea of Dreams

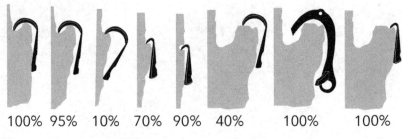

100% 95% 10% 70% 90% 40% 100% 100%

Matching the correct hook to the placement is vital.

Nevertheless it's always best to eyeball any placement first, meaning getting up high on your aiders. Once you've found it, use your finger to see if there is a hole, as even on flakes there will often be a sweet spot for the hook to latch on. When hooking flakes, I prefer to have the interior apex of the hook on the flake to help keep it stable.

When setting your hooks make sure you match the hook to the hold, and most of all don't rush it, take your time, each move having the same care taken over it as the last. An attitude of 'it's good enough' very often leads to falls, as the hook pops off.

I find that I will use the same hook (pointed grappling hook) repeatedly, but if it's a major hooking pitch make sure you have your other hooks to hand. On major hooking pitches, I will clip my hooks into my lockers on my lanyards so they cannot be dropped, as they have a tendency to come adrift off plain gate krabs. I also try and always have hooks connected to my lanyards when testing or looking for the sweet spot. This approach has saved me a few times, when the gear I was on popped, sending me onto my hook!

Difficult Moves: On hard routes, you may come across edges that are sloping, a scary proposition. In such situations,

you need to look for lumps or depressions that may offer something for the hook to catch on, like a small ripple along the edge of the placement. As I've said before hooks often stay or pop due to micro features.

Sometimes a hook will not be held by the point but due to friction from the apex of the hook's throw, most often when using long but shallow hooks, such as a sawn-off Grappling hook.

In very extreme situations you might have to weight the hook in one direction or use opposing hooks. On one route I had to use a poor copperhead, pasted into the back of a flared sloping flake, to counteract the transverse force on a hook on a sloping placement (even on a sloping placement, most of your weight is held by the flake).

On most routes, such placements need rarely be made, as there will almost always be some enhanced edge, hole or dimple to hook.

Moving Without Testing: A big flake, dish or hole in solid bulletproof rock, that shows obvious signs that everyone has hooked it before, does not need testing. In such placements, such as a long flake you're going to use as a hook handrail, you can often simply hook and go.

When moving like this, especially when speed climbing, even though you're not testing don't just switch off. I've seen people hook along solid flakes only to hook some loose section and pull it off, or miss obvious hook slots in wafer-thin flakes and hook the edge and break it. When moving without testing, focus on where your other hook is and see your last piece as being integral to this one. A good example of this would be the long handrail flake on the third to last pitch of Zodiac. You can free climb along this flake but most - being knackered and overburdened - hook it.

Some will stand on a hook, take the previous hook off and place it ahead of them and repeat. A better option is to just shuffle them along, keeping your feet fixed to each hook. This way you've always got two hooks on at all time.

Non-testing should be avoided when a fall could be very serious, say after a long run out section as even perfect flakes can come off!

TESTING THE HOOK

So you're on a long sequence of hook moves, each one smaller than the last, do you just trust them? No - some form of testing is vital for harder aid. I'm a big fan of aggressive bounce testing, but with hooks, you need to take it down a notch and go for 'body weight and a bit' testing. The reason for this is that a hook is not designed for the extreme loading you might produce while testing, with even the strongest hooks, only having a safe loading of around 400 kg. Being aggressive could break or bend out your hook, get it to jump the placement or damage the rock. What you want to achieve in testing is to answer the following questions:

Is The Hook Sound? Basically, are you using the correct hook for the placement, not one that's too big or too small? Sometimes testing will see one hook shift when a body weight load is applied, or cause it to pop. Swapping between hooks, and having a good selection of hooks, is the best way to find the right tool for the job.

Is The Rock Sound? When hooking fragile or micro features you need to be careful about the rock failing when fully loaded, not good if you've just hooked for twenty metres. Be aware of cracks, microfractures and leverage (you can hook detached flakes as long as you only pull down). Being aware and a little paranoid is vital when climbing loose rock or rock that you know is fragile.

Moving Up: Once you're sure the hook is good, make sure it doesn't shift while you prepare to move onto it fully. Try imagining that you're balancing a coin on the top of the hook, and make sure you don't shift around and knock it off.

Progressing on hooks, from one move to twenty, is all about being aware; aware of how the hook works, how the hook interacts with the placement, and how your body weight is affecting these two things. The bottom line is if you move smoothly, you don't disturb your hook. The importance of this increases the smaller the hook and the smaller the hold.

Try to keep a constant tension on the hook by gently shifting weight from lanyard to aider, aider to lanyard, keeping all movements fluid and in-line with the pull. I've seen a few leaders fall when they've allowed the hook to shift in between placing and moving, or when they've been on a hook and leant too far sideways and pivoted the hook off. Remember, keep the load in line!

High Stepping: Getting high on a hook is more problematic than getting high on other placements as your centre of gravity is moving above the hook, creating different forces, with an outward pull often leading to disaster. The worst case scenario for a high hook move is to lose your balance and either fall back and pull the hook off, or pivot sideways and shock load the hook. The best ways to avoid this is to wear sticky boots (rock boots or wall boots with sticky rands), use two aiders, and make use of any free holds for your hands (having a chalk bag is ideal).

Cheater Hooks: You can hook edges or flakes out of reach by attaching your hook to the handle of your hammer, or at the end of a stiffened quickdraw, a little scary lifesaver if you can't find anything else. Having Velcro fixed to your hammer or cheater clip makes this much easier as it's possible to remove the hook once placed. Unfortunately, it's quite hard to judge what you've hooked, so take your time to test the placement.

Climbing Down Off A Hook: If you've moved onto a hook from another hook, and realise you need to step back, make sure the hook you left below is still in position as it's easy for it to shift, or even fall off. Committing to a hook you realise is bad and trying to reverse onto another poor hook is up there in terms of big wall terror, so avoid this by doing it right in the first place!

Lowering Off: In some situations, such as being unable to go on and having no other gear to lower off from you may be forced to use a hook as a lower off point.

Although this may sound scary, if you have a good flake to hook then it's pretty safe, perhaps more safe than lowering off micro wires.

BAT HOOKING

I cover bat hooking later in the drilling chapter, but it's a rather distasteful business where a small hole (and occasionally one that's far too big) is drilled into the rock so that a hook can be inserted for aid, either creating a placement or enhancing an existing placement.

This technique was originally intended for spanning blank sections of rock rather than placing multiple bolts or dowels, and involves a shallow hole drilled just deep enough to take a pointed hook, about 10 mm in hard rock. The problem with this is that if the holes are drilled too shallow, they tend to get worn over time making moves very tenuous (having a very sharp pointed hook helps).

In the past, bat hooking has been used to climb almost full pitches, and although for the first ascensionist it's not too bad, as it means they know how deep and solid the holes are, it's not great for those who come after.

Luckily, the use of extensive bat hooking has now become pretty frowned upon, and most climbers will span blank sections with rivets, but this is also pretty dubious. Nevertheless, you will often find bat holes, or "chicken" holes, where climbers have been unable to perform an aid move and have drilled a hole instead. Very often if placements have dried up, you'll find a bat hook somewhere, although it might take you all day and many scary top step moves to find it.

Chicken holes, where someone has drilled a hole to avoid some move they found scary, should always be avoided and ideally patched while cleaning the pitch (and reported on forums so you don't get the blame!).

ENHANCED EDGES

Another common feature on many routes are edges that have been enhanced (modified or improved by the use of a chisel or drill bit) to create a small hole or indent that will take the tip of a pointed hook. Sometimes this will be nothing more than a point worn down by the passage of so many hooks, but on any popular route, it's always worth searching with your fingertip for these sweet spots. If you're climbing a new route then whether or not to 'enhance' the rock, either with a pointed chisel or a drill, is something only you can decide. I guess it comes down to what kind of route you want to leave as your legacy, and how you'd like to be judged as a climber and human being, and non enhanced edges are always the best way to go. All I know is that I've climbed a few routes where there were far too many holes, and, if it was me, I'd have chosen to make such 'enhancements' as few and far between as possible.

TESTING

Testing with body weight loads helps get your mind to feel comfortable that the hook will hold and so helps keep you calm. This is how to test:

01. Place your hook as perfectly as you can, attached to your lanyard, making sure the tie-off is straight.

02. If possible keep your hand on the hook so you can feel what it's doing, and also to stop it pinging off.

03. Now slowly apply your bodyweight from the lanyard, or via your fifi

clipped direct to the hook's karabiner. If the hook is high, then climb down low on the piece you're on first, and if you're already on a hook be careful to always keep this hook loaded and ready to catch you if the hook above rips (just lift your feet off the lower aider(s) by 1 cm).

04. Begin to apply more than body weight by a slow bounce, feeling the hook flex as you do so.

05. If the next move is scary and thin, then hang for a moment and try and relax onto it.

Sideways Testing: Sideways testing is harder, and you'll have to use your feet in an aider to test but not being able to apply full body weight makes this problematic. In my own experience, I tend to have to go with making the best placement I can and then just trusting that placement. Some people advise using a hammer and funkness, (on traverses for example) but it's hard to judge what you're doing here and it could just wreck your hooks. Instead you could test the rock by some light tapping, and also tap the hook, once placed, in order to make sure it's set in the right location.

Mind Your Face: When testing, be aware that if a hook pops it will be travelling at high speed and it's sharp! Looking at the hook when testing is a good idea as you can see what it's doing, but don't look if your face is in line with your belay loop and the hook (the hook will travel in line with the force). Always wear a helmet when hooking, and keep your face away from its trajectory, wearing safety glasses or sunglasses.

Don't Drop Your Hook: As mentioned earlier, when standing on marginal gear it's worth clipping the hook, or hooks, into your free lanyard, as falling or fumbling as you're trying to find the right hook(s) can see it, or them, lost.

HOOKS AS PROTECTION

Will A Hook Hold A Fall? The answer is maybe, but if not you'll end up breaking the hook or breaking the hold or both! I've taken quite a few "daisy falls" (the classic term for a fall onto your lanyard) onto hooks, some set on holds an ant wouldn't bivvy on, and so far they all held! But what we're talking about here is should you leave hooks behind as protection?

On some pitches you may not encounter any bomber gear at all, just beaks and heads, but also some very solid flakes and edges that you can exploit. On the 'Hook or Book' pitch on the Sea of Dreams, which features a long hooking section, the only pro is a nest of poor heads near its end, which all fell out when I tried to clip them, but beside it was a very solid flake where I placed a bomber hook. To provide reliable protection in this type of situation you'll need the following components to make it work:

A Strong Hook: Most hooks are not strong at all due to their shape, throw, and metal thickness, the Grappling hook one you don't want to take a fall on. Stronger hooks include the Moses/Leeper pointed hook or Logan and older Fish Hook or Captain Hook, or large Vermin Hook (these are rare). These hooks all have a breaking strain of around 4 kN, although this is from anecdotal evidence, as no CE testing is carried out on hooks. Standard hooks like Cliffhangers and Grappling should be viewed as being body weight only. An alternative to a traditional hook would be to use a large bird beak (Moses Tomahawk or BD Pecker) or Ice Hook (cut down or full size). These hooks are stronger, due to their alignment to the force, and are cut from solid steel, rather than bent into a hooking shape. The downside is that they are designed to be hammered into cracks, and so tend to be far less stable and will need to be taped into position.

A Strong Feature Or Flake: In a fall, the force created by a hook under load on the placement is very high. When combined with the prising action of a hook this can lead to flakes being ripped off the wall or edges snapped off, meaning that this section might then be unclimbable.

For this reason, it's vital to check that everything you hook is strong enough, taking into account that the further out you are from the belay the lower the peak force (you might break a 4 kN hook two moves off the belay, but not a 100 kg cliffhanger 40 metres out).

If possible, create a multiple point anchor, equalising more than one piece of protection, so this force is spread between pieces and use scream aids. If you want to use a large or medium-sized beak as protection, you can increase its stability by taping two beaks together but have them spaced with a wire, so as to create three points of contact. This has the added benefit of also doubling their strength and stops the beak from flipping sideways.

Staying Power: The most obvious way to stop a hook from moving once placed is to gaffer tape it down. When doing this, make sure you put tape both on the hook and its base. On bigger flakes, a perfect fit may result in the hook simply staying in place (don't hammer a hook onto a flake,

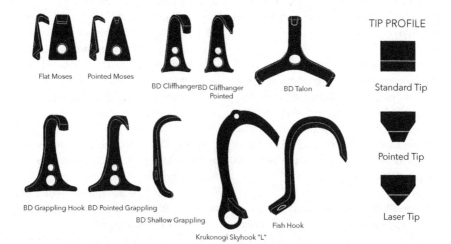

Flat Moses   Pointed Moses   BD Cliffhanger   BD Cliffhanger Pointed   BD Talon

BD Grappling Hook   BD Pointed Grappling   BD Shallow Grappling   Fish Hook   Krukonogi Skyhook "L"

TIP PROFILE   Standard Tip   Pointed Tip   Laser Tip

as it will probably just spring off). You can also choose to further increase the hook's resistance to being knocked off by weighing it down with other gear. On super small edges, a ball of Blu-Tack can lock a hook in place.

Personally, I have very rarely left a hook for protection, tending to trust my skill not to fall on long hooking sections. Nevertheless, you may one day find yourself on a pitch where, perhaps due to loose rock, skill is not the main factor. In these instances, knowing how to use a hook for protection can come in handy.

HOOK DESIGNS

Hooks come in many sizes and varieties, which is surprising when you consider how niche they are, with the users restricted to aid climbers and the odd free climber. All hooks are manufactured from high-quality steel, and although simple looking, they are in fact objects of highly advanced and well thought out geometry.

I will break hooks down into the following groups:

Micro Pointed: These are the smallest of the small hooks, their narrow tips able to hook edges with a surface area of less than a couple of millimetres. These were originally developed for the dubious practice of 'bat hooking' - drilling tiny holes in the rock into which a hook can be inserted. As I've said this was used for passing blank areas of rock, but was soon discontinued due to holes being hard to find by all but the one who drilled them, and was replaced by the use of rivets.

The first micro pointed commercial hook was the Pointed Leeper (now manufactured by Moses, with other designs by many others), which, although tiny, is a testament to the forging and design skills of Ed Leeper. When fallen on, most hooks will either bend out or break, but I've taken a full length "daisy fall" on a pointed Leeper, and it's held. Ed reckoned his hooks had a 1000 lb breaking strain (450 kg), way above that of a standard hook. It's for this reason, as well as its stability that I love the Leeper design.

Petzl makes a pointed hook too, and the Black Diamond Talon (a three-pronged hook shaped like a star) also has a pointed hook. Although both work well, I prefer the Leeper as it's smaller and stronger.

Vital for hard aid, it's standard practice to carry three micro pointed hooks (2 hooks plus a spare) on difficult routes, and advisable to carry one on most other routes, as they can be used to bypass broken rivets or bolts or chicken holes (holes drilled by cowards!), or even broken pegs.

Micro Flat: These hooks sit just above the micro pointed and are best typified by the Leeper Logan (now made by Moses). They are very small hooks with a tiny throw (distance from body to the point of the hook), but a wide flat 'grab' (area that touches the rock), two factors that make them very strong, and stable, the greater width paired with minimal 'throw' helping reduce bending under load. They are vital for hooking flat edges and executing difficult hook moves.

The Black Diamond Talon also features a Logan style hook. On very textured rock you may find that the tiny flat Logan doesn't sit well. An advanced alternative is the Black Diamond Grappling Hook which has its hook sawn off, creating a flat hook with a much shallower throw.

On hard routes, I would carry three Logan style hooks, usually a Leeper/Moses Logan, a sawn down Grappling Hook and a BD Talon. On easier routes, a Moses Micro Hook can usually work with these types of placements.

Standard: This is your 'vanilla' hook, the original do it all skyhook, the standard design being the Black Diamond Cliffhanger or Petzl P06 hook. These are designed to hook over flakes, and so

require a feature to wrap over, and are poor at hooking flat edges unless filed to a point. I find this style of hook - which is probably the most commonly bought - the least useful of all hooks, being scary and insecure on anything but hooking jugs. They are also the weakest hooks, and so I tend not to carry them.

Large: This is probably the new standard in hooks and is represented by the Black Diamond Grappling Hook, a hook that has a large shallow throw, which will hook small to medium-sized features, as well as fit into cracks and pods. The weight is higher than a standard hook, but it's much more usable and should be the main hook that most climbers reach for.

The Grappling Hook is also the hook most modified by hard aid climbers, with the tip filed more to a point, so that it sits in holes or divots in the rock, or cut down into a flatter throw hook. Another good hook is the Cassin Captain Hook size large, which features a tip that has already been modified.

On hard routes, I will usually carry at least four modified Grappling Hooks (2 hooks and 2 spares).

Monster Meat Hooks: This style of hook has become rare since Vermin and Pika stopped making hooks a few years ago, having produced a line of hooks that were large enough to hook a flake as big as your arm! These hooks were also very strong, and could be used both for progression (not that you'd need a hook that big, as you can just use your hands), and protection. Some people view the old Ring angle hook (a long angle peg bent into the shape of a hook) or the Fish hook (a solid metal hook that can be used as pro) as monster hooks, but these are really no bigger than Black Diamond Grappling Hooks. Luckily the Russian company Krukonogi now makes a large (50 mm throw) titanium hook that is very strong (5 kN) and light (55 g), and even features a fifi style hole in the top. This allows the hook to be racked more safely, and gives you a super fifi for 'spec ops' techniques. For hooks larger than this the only option is to use an ice hook or a Russian rock fifi.

MODIFYING HOOKS

The 'pointed cliffhanger' is probably the most commonly known modified hook, due to an illustration in Middendorf and Long's 'Big Walls'. In the illustration you have a standard hook that has the top filed to a sharp point, designed to be used in drilled holes. This hook is actually of little use as drawn in the illustration, and something a little less extreme works much better. The other hook is a Leeper Logan hook that has its point filed flat, the idea being that the slightly greater surface area will provide more 'grip' on flat edges. In reality, I think both styles have been replaced by the following two hooks:

Pointed Grappling Hook: This is the main hook all climbers should use. It will work on a wide variety of flakes and edges, and can still be used when hooking in super precise placements, especially routes with 'worn' hook holes. Trying to climb hard routes with a smaller pointed hook like a cliffhanger you often find that the throw is too short. To create this style of hook, simply file the point of the hook into a dull point (not sharp), removing the sides, leaving a 3 mm flat but rounded tip. A sharp point is less stable and creates much greater point loading - not good on soft rock.

Flat Grappling Hook: This hook is designed to work on flat edges and is super stable. It will also work in bat holes. To make one of these, simply draw a line at the apex of the hook's throw, and cut off the point of the hook a few millimetres beyond this. This will give you a hook that is almost totally flat, with a minimal curve at the point to help it lock down. Once cut, file the hook's point into a blunt point like the grappling hook.

Laser Hook: Some placements are very precise, or you want the maximum load going into the smallest point you can, with the hook loading one grain either way the difference between a hook that holds and a hook that does not. What you sometimes need is a laser hook, which you make by filing a pointed Moses hook as sharp as you can, but without reducing the actual length of the hook. This sharp point allows you to get the hook where you want it.

Hooks are best modified with a metal file and a vice but can be modified on the wall using the file on a multi-tool. You should avoid sharp hooks on sandstone as they can greatly increase the chance of fracturing the rock.

SLINGING YOUR HOOK

Some hooks come already sewn up with a nylon sling, but most don't, having instead a double or single hole through which you can thread a tie-off.

The standard procedure is to thread the hook with tape, something between 12 and 17 mm (1/2 to 9/16). I would advise not using flat tape, especially not 10 mm or 1/2 inch tape, but only the thickest tubular (supertape) you can force through the hole (use pliers to get the tape through). The reason for this is that flat tape may be adequate when brand new but soon loses its strength plus it has very poor wear resistance meaning the sling can break in a "daisy fall".

I don't use supertape slings as I find them bulky and instead just use 5 mm perlon cord or dyneema leaving a loop around 100 mm to clip into. The length of this loop is quite important. If it's too short you risk affecting the hooks ability to sit properly, as the hook may be forced out from the rock by your movement. Making the loop too long will improve the hooks stability, but could mean you end up losing vital height as sometimes an extra 10 cm is all that stands between you and a bomber placement. For this reason a loop of 10 cm tends to be about right (short quickdraw size). If you need to reduce this length, you can do so by re-tying the loop.

When tying your loop, the tape/cord should come out against the rock, not out of the hook away from the rock, as this would create an outward pull, which could prove disastrous when hooking flat edges.

I would also recommend colour coding all your hook tie-offs, so they're easier to spot, say blue for pointed Grappling hooks, red for Moses pointed hooks, green for Moses Flat hooks.

RACKING HOOKS

Hooks, as you can imagine, have a tendency to do what they do best, hook! Unfortunately, this means they also tend to hook when you don't want them to, a real problem when it comes to racking. They can also be very sharp and pointy, and having several clipped to the back of your harness can lead to a little bit of paranoia.

When racking, there are a few things worth considering:

- **Egg Basket #1**: Never clip all your hooks into a single krab. If you drop that krab, you drop all your hooks.

- **Egg Basket #2**: Try and keep hooks in sets, not in type, so a micro and large hook on a single karabiner, not two micro hooks on one karabiner, and your large hook on another. In all big wall climbing, you should build in redundancy as you don't want to lose all your grappling hooks with one fuck up!

- **Screw Up**: Keep your hooks on screw-gate krabs and try and avoid unclipping and dropping hooks when you unclip your hook locker.

- **Keep It Light**: Don't carry all your hooks unless you know you'll need them, but never leave the belay without one pointed grappling hook and a pointed hook or Talon.

- **The Hook Cavalry**: On hard routes, keep a spare set of hooks easily accessible at the top of your haul bag in case you drop the ones you have, as waiting for your mate to unpack the whole bag on a hanging belay rooting for a hook while you sweat it on a #1 head can be stressful.

- **Snag Proof**: When stowing hooks in your haul bag, keep them in a dedicated heavy duty stuff sack with clip-in loops both inside and outside of the sack so hooks can be clipped inside the bag. This will stop your hooks snagging all your other gear.

- **Hook Bag**: It's a good idea to store your lead hooks in a small pouch (like a chalk bag or vinyl ditty bag) on your

Russian Hook on Sea of Dreams

harness to reduce tangles. Make sure the bag features a locker. You can also use the same bag to hold your beaks.

RUSSIAN ROCK FIFI

A style of hook little known in the West is the rock fifi or ice hook, a flat steel ice axe that can be used as a sky hook or torqued into cracks, used in ice and mud or hammered like a peg. Although looking very odd indeed this is a very valuable tool, especially for adventure or alpine walls as well as hard aid.

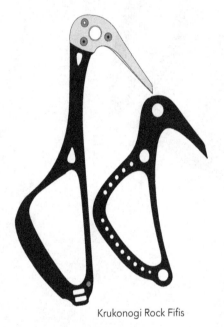

Krukonogi Rock Fifis

Although they look very antiquated by Western standards, these hooks kicked off a great deal of modern leashless axe development by pioneering both the idea of extreme handle angles and of making axes from a single sheet of steel. The problem with these hooks for a Western climber is that they look way too extreme, even old-fashioned, mainly suited to extreme routes in extreme conditions, but for hard aid on mixed alpine walls they're unmatched. The Russian hook can be used in the following ways:

Pegging: The rock fifi works just like a beak, and can be hammered, hooked, and hand placed anywhere where a beak can go, and can be both hooked up a pitch, or left behind as pro.

Hooking: For such a large hook the fifi can hook super small edges, as well as big flakes, and I've used mine on several very hard hooking cruxs. The very sharp pick of the tool and lack of a tripod base, but low loading position, mean that the hook can wobble around like an ice axe does but without walking off.

Cheater Hooking: The rock fifi, being very long, makes it easy to hook edges way out of your reach. Unlike using a hammer as a cheater stick, you can get a better feel for the placement as the hook scrapes around, feeling small holes and edges to hook.

Pendulums: The fifi is very handy on pendulums when clipped to your lanyard as it gives you extra reach and allows you to hook more easily, as well as torque or jam into cracks. Most of these placements will only be good for a sideways pull but can allow you the time to find something better.

Grappling Hook: When retreating down a wall, I've used a rock fifi like a grappling hook, throwing it down to snag on features in order to regain belays (it works well if you sling cord between bolts for it to catch.

Ice And Snow: When faced with ice or iced up cracks you can struggle if you

Fragile   Wide   Narrow   Micro

don't have the gear, but the rock fifi works amazingly well on ice, especially on very thin ice (the same design is used for ice speed climbing).

CAM HOOKS

Cam hooks are not technically hooks in the traditional sense, but rather long thin pieces of steel or alloy bent around to form a flat hook, like that of an open handed grip. By inserting the tip into a crack, and weighting it, the tip twists and torques into the crack and locks in position and can be very secure.

What cam hooks excel at is exploiting lost arrow cracks almost removing the need for lost arrows on most walls beyond the odd one placed for protection.

The nature of the cam hook often allows you to achieve a very secure placement in a traditionally poor location, such as a vertical expanding lost arrow crack, where neither cams or pegs provide anything you can rely on. This ability also increases speed as pegs neither need to be placed or removed.

A thorough understanding of how to use cam hooks is vital for all moderate to hard aid.

CAM HOOK STYLES

Micro: This is the smallest cam hook, designed to fit into the tightest of spots. Its small size means it has much lower strength than the standard hooks and can bend out if not loaded correctly, or while inverted, plus it only takes very thin low strength cord (get it swaged with #3 cable or use 3 mm dyneema). Despite this, this hook can be used in all sorts of interesting ways, going in spots where nothing else will go. It's also the right size to be stacked with other gear such as nuts or beaks and can be very useful as part of a beak stack (the meat of it). I usually carry one micro cam hook as part of my 'trick' gear.

Narrow (Standard): People either see this or the wide cam hook as the 'do it all' hook, but for me this alone is it, and I find it will go into most places I need it to, and having less severe a curve often fits into tight spots. It's strong, solid and reliable. When speed climbing I have one of these tied into each aider/lanyard and never set off on lead without at least one cam hook, two to five if it's a hard pitch. They work well in cracks that would usually take Lost Arrow pegs up to #1 angles. In fact, they do this so well that the need for pegs on all but the hardest routes has all but disappeared. On most routes I would carry three Narrow Cam hooks, two for leading plus one spare.

Wide: These are also workhorse cam hooks, and some climbers make these their standard, being thinner than the narrow hook. Their wider tip increases the spread of the load, but can also make it harder to find a spot that will take them, such as peg scars, and although they won't bend out on inverted placements the narrow cam hook inspires a little more confidence in my opinion. Many climbers will carry two wide hooks, but on standard aid routes I usually only carry one, preferring to use the narrow hooks instead. If the aid is harder, then as with the standard hooks, I'll carry three (one spare).

Force

Fragile Flake: This is a wide hook made from aluminium instead of steel, giving it a much better 'bite' on the rock. The width of the hook also creates less outward pressure on a flake than a wide or standard hook or even a camming unit. This final point was passed on to me by Ed Leeper over the phone, but I've never been able to find anything else about it, or the results of any testing. My own impression though is that it's true, and the hook's ability to tackle thin expanding cracks comes down to both its camming angle tip to tip, the grip of the alloy, and the ability of the cam hook to soak up any expansion to a much greater degree than

a small or medium cam. The downside is that these benefits created by a thick and wide hook make this the most specialised hook after the micro, only really fitting into thin flakes but not corners. Nevertheless I tend to always carry two of these on most routes.

SLINGING YOUR CAM HOOK

As with skyhooks, I never use tape sling with my cam hooks, and instead use either 5 mm perlon cord, or better still Dyneema. Dyneema cord may sound like overkill, but I've taken many falls onto cam hooks, and it would be a real shame to take a big whipper just because the cord snapped on a bomber cam hook!

Unlike normal hooks, cam hooks tend not to tangle with everything, and so can be racked normally on your harness. However, as with skyhooks it's still important not to stick them all on the same karabiner, as you could end up losing them all! If I'm doing more than a few moves I'll clip them to a locker on my daisies.

PLACEMENT

In order to set a solid hook you need a slot or crack that has two parallel sides, or parallel points at the top inside and bottom outside edge. If the crack or feature is irregular, try to pick a spot where the angles will allow the hook to lock solidly, trying it in both left and right orientation if the crack allows.

A cam hook will work in any cracks with the required angle, including horizontal cracks, roof cracks or flakes, and anywhere where you'd traditionally place a Lost Arrow peg. The hook works best if nice and deep (the curved tip fully inserted), but will also work if you can only get the tip in, just be aware of flaking.

The prime thing is to visually check that the hook is mechanically sound (having an engineer's brain helps). Ninety nine percent of the time a hook that looks good will be good.

In expanding cracks I tend to try and shuffle the hooks up without fully removing them, like a hand jamming crab crawl, as failure of the one I'm on means I fall back onto the other hook.

Beak/Micro stack

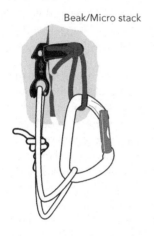

Leading On Cam Hooks: Cam hooks take a bit of getting used to. Beginners would be forgiven for thinking that either the hook will break under body weight, or that the rock will explode. However, very quickly you realise that these little pieces of flat bent metal are extremely strong, and can lock into cracks so well that you almost never have to doubt them.

Back Cleaning: Cam hooks are amazing for back cleaning and can turn a two hour nailing pitch into ten minutes of gearless fear, just moving the cam hooks along. When doing this for long stretches where a fall would be dangerous then consider using three cam hooks, each one connected to you. Two can be

clipped into your daisies while the third can be clipped into your lead line as a piece of pro (making your lead line a lanyard). This means as you move you will always have two cam hooks in the rock and the unweighted third hook will be held in place by the rope's weight.

Testing: Once you feel that the hook is good, give it some solid bounces to both check that it's set well, and also to seat it. Sometimes just jumping straight onto a hook can result in small crystals breaking, which can be a bit worrying as the cam hook 'pops'. Nevertheless, once you've got a handle on how a cam hook works, you can just place it, check it, give it one or two body weight bounces, then get on it. In all my life climbing I've yet to have a cam hook pop while on it (as with all aiding though, being slapdash is an invitation to a fall!).

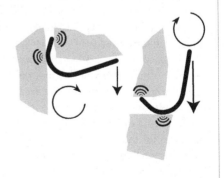

As Protection: A well placed cam hook in a vertical crack is good enough to hold falls as long as the cord is up to the job. The problem with using a cam hook for protection is that once you unweight a hook it will often just fall out of the crack. Some climbers make the mistake (often in panic) of hammering in a cam hook, in the hope that this will make it stronger, and prevent it from falling out. Unfortunately this often leads to the hook becoming fixed. To get a cam hook to stay put, you can either tape it into position, or try stacking it with a thin peg. Just the tip of a peg will hold the hook in place, and, once hammered out, can be easily cleaned.

Fixed Cam Hooks: You will often come across fixed cam hooks on routes, where the leader has hammered the hook and it's become stuck. I've never not been able to remove such a fixed piece. It does take time usually, but it's worth the effort. To remove fixed cam hooks try using the blunt side of your hammer to hammer under the apex of the hook, top and bottom, or even hammering in a lost arrow. The aim is to get it to come loose a fraction of a millimetre at a time.

PITONS

The days of the piton are almost over, the role of protection these days fulfilled by nuts and cams and sticky rubber, passive protection able to protect you on ninety nine percent of placements, and in most cases more securely and predictably. But what about that other one percent, where nothing else will do, that hairline crack or the beaten-out piton scar? This is where pitons come in, the second to last arrow in your quiver before you're forced to reach for the drill. So yes the days of climbers wailing on iron are pretty much gone, and even on the hard routes you

can often get away with a dozen beaks and the odd sawn off or small lost arrow, but you still need to know the tools of the trade and how to apply that knowledge.

BEAKS

Beaks are a piton for the 21st century, a state of the art piton concept that's highly effective, low impact, lightweight but with surprising lob stopping strength. Beaks should not be simply viewed as a hard aid tool, as even the smallest designs can provide considerable protection in all forms of climbing, being as effective hand placed as hammered home.

The western precursor of the beak piton was probably the Chouinard Crack N' Up, a 'clean' piton designed to hook into cracks rather than be hammered, but one that was too ahead of its time, ending up in the sale bin of climbing stores. But climbers took these nuts, and modifying them, found they could achieve both, having a piton that could be hammered but could also hook the placement like a nut, a strange hybrid skyhook, nut and piton all rolled into one.

At the same time the Soviet bloc were using various types of hooking piton that ranged in size, designed for use in both rock and ice and frozen grass. Called the "jakor", this piton gave the Eastern European climbers a real technical advantage on tough ground.

The first commercial beak design was the A5 Birdbeak, a tiny piton that redefined the possible, soon followed by the Black Diamond Pecker. BD moved things on by expanding the micro piton upwards in three sizes, with these larger beaks helping to counter the view that beaks were only for pure aid (like the RURP),

Moses Tomahawk

BD Pecker

Custom sling

Tie off

Mod

Mod

Wlodarczyk

Chouinard Crack N' Up

A5 Birdbeak

Cassin Iron Hawk

Krukonogi Small

Krasnoyarskt L v4

Krukonogi Mixt 2D" # 3

Krukonogi Mixt 2D" # 1

Krukonogi
Anchor Piton #3a

Krukonogi "SAP" or "Byak"

6mm 4mm

being adopted by winter and trad climbers and mountaineers.

The next big leap was the Moses Tomahawk, a refinement of all other designs, giving a solid, stable and predictable aid climbing tool for 21st century climbs.

Sizes: Beaks come in small, medium and large, with the medium size being the most useful as an all round piton, able to work in thin cracks and lost arrow placements when stacked. The small are the next most useful, especially on hard aid or as part of your 'escape kit', being light and compact yet able to get you out of sticky situations. The large beak can be useful to carry, but being big and heavy they're best held in reserve. Small and medium beaks will nearly always do the job, but a large beak when needed, is very needed indeed!

The Talisman Beak: No matter what route I'm on, be it hard aid, easy aid, or clean aid, I will always carry one small beak somewhere, on my harness or in a haul bag. On even clean routes, where all gear is fixed, very often you will come across a situation where nothing will work, you can't free climb around it, and the only alternative is to bail, drill, or get out the cheater stick. A good example of this would be on the third pitch of the Nose, where you can be faced with some strange pod that you can't free around, or on a clean pitch where a head has blown or a pin has lost its head. Here being able to use the beak like a hook can save the day.

Filed Micro Beaks: You can create specialised micro beaks by filing them down to half their size, creating the same pick profile, or more acute angles designed to do specific jobs, such as

being hammered into deadheads or into the most shallow of cracks. These micro beaks can come in very handy when faced with beaten out shallow placements, where a standard beak would be tipped out. To file these use a hand file and I would recommend having two filed pointed beaks on any rack, and considering shorter fat sawn-off beaks if you know the route has very shallow placements.

Thick Beaks And Angle Beaks: A standard beak is around 3 mm, but the Russian company Krukonogi also make a very thick (6 mm) titanium beak that works well in odd shaped cracks where you'd be forced to use stacked beaks or lost arrows tips, so is worth having in your tool box. They also sometimes make a kind of angle formed into a beak, but although I've carried it up several walls I've yet to ever use it, but then I don't place many angles anyway.

Placement: The trick to a standard beak placement is to take advantage of all its ways of locking into a placement by a hooking action, as well as being pinched and compressed like a standard piton, with the tapering hooked blade achieving a bomb-proof lock into the rock by way of several forces all at once.

First consider the beak's ability to hook and how it eliminates rotation under load like most other pitons, often the limitation of knife blades, which can shift when loaded. Very often you can place a beak by hand, then just seat it with a few taps of the hammer, old beak placements creating a lock for the next beak to key into. In some of these hooked placements you may fear the beak will fall out and stacking two or even three beaks together, or stacking a beak with a nut or leeper hook can create a tight little nest, plus two beaks nested and hooking into a crack give you double the holding power.

You should also view the beak like you would a nut, as most beaks feature some form of tapering blade, having a 'V' section when viewed end on (as with all gear it's worth spending time looking at, and playing with it, before you climb). This allows a beak to be set like a nut into a constriction, say a parallel crack too small for a micro wire (or where the cable would be too thick to slip into the crack), the beak placed just above the constriction or deviation, as you would a nut, with the beak's hook aiding the placement's strength further. Carrying a medium beak on your rack when free climbing helps you develop this skill, and there are many free climbs that can be tamed a little with a hand placed beak.

Beaks will also work in parallel laser cut cracks, working like a blade, creating a compressive force to hold it in place. But such cracks are rare and almost all cracks feature some form of constriction, deviation, jammed crystal or pebble.

In some situations you may need to use your heading chisel or a lost arrow to focus your blows on the beak.

Camming Beaks: Beaks can also be held in place by a camming action, with some twist rotating the head like you would an ice axe, and some designs feature a twist in the shaft of the beak to aid this, making then ideal for clean placements (some other minor twists are designed to simply aid placement in left and right cracks). The downside is that a twist can sometimes make placements in corners a little trickier as these come in left and right, so the bulk of your beaks should be straight and vanilla, maybe having one or two each of the twisted variety.

Horizontals: Beaks will work in horizontal cracks, and often you can place the shaft of the beak as well, making a very strong placement. If only the beak tip is inserted make sure you tie a tie-off through the head of the beak in order to reduce torque, which could bend or snap the beak in a fall. When placing a beak sideways take notice of the taper of the beak, as some beaks are flat on one side and tapered on the other.

Strength: Even the smallest beaks can withstand major falls, and I've taken full tether daisy falls and thirty foot falls all held by beaks, with medium and large beaks good enough for belays. Very often the weak link will be the cable, and on a BD Pecker for example the cable is only rated to 3 kN (brand new), much less than the beak itself. For this reason all beaks should have a 4 mm or 1/8 inch (#3) cable, sling or dyneema cord sling, or better still clip into the beaks with a small karabiner.

Testing: Once you've placed the beak it's often worth tapping it downwards with a few hard knocks inline with the force of pull, just to check it's seated well enough, and employ some solid bounce testing, as this can help seat the hook better into the crack or placement (rather than have it hanging up on a crystal). Due to their small size and cable they tend to provide good feedback to the climber's brain when testing, and tend not to produce time bomb placements in good rock.

Cleaning: Beaks are generally best cleaned with a few light upward yanks of the funkness device, and in many cases a simple hard tug on the quickdraw will pop them out. One thing to watch out for is over-driving the largest beaks into the crack when placing them, as they can easily become fixed, especially if the cable becomes damaged. If one of these large beaks becomes fixed you will need to create a pivot point between the shaft of the beak and the rock, maybe using a baby angle or lost arrow, slowly working the beak's blade out. Be very careful with small beaks not to snap off the tip by being heavy handed, remembering that these are precision tools.

Slinging Your Beak: Only buy beaks with wire cables, as this makes racking far easier, and if they don't have cables then get them fitted. Larger beaks work best if they feature a hole in the head big enough to hold a karabiner (if not, a 3 mm loop works) as this reduces the annoying tendency for the beak to hook your trousers and clothing all the time.

Rack: I would always carry at least one small and one medium beak on any route I climb, as they can be hand placed. On trade routes where the wall goes clean I would still carry 5 small and 5 medium, as you never know what you'll come across on any wall, and I've had to climb pitches on beaks on such routes after features have fallen off. On sandstone routes you will also often find placements where the original nut has simply worn out necessitating the use of a beak in its place. On hard walls I'd carry 15 small and medium, with 5 large, as well as a handful of filed beaks. Once you start using beaks you'll find they go everywhere.

Beak Bag: The best way to carry beaks, which are prone to snagging on clothing and everything else is in a small chalk bag sized stuff sack, ideally made from vinyl

or Cordura so the beaks don't rip it up. This bag needs a super beefy clip loop and should be secured with either a small screwgate or maillon. At the moment the best commercial bags would be Fish big wall beef bags (small) or rope access 'pod' style bags. I made my own bag that stores the beaks around the inside in pockets and also has room for a few RURPS, rivet hangers and other exotica I might need.

Manufacturers: Black Diamond, Cassin, Moses, Vermin, Krukonogi, Kop De Gas, Piotr Wlodarczyk, Krok

Stand Out Designs: Moses Tomahawk size 1 and 2

MICRO BLADES

Micro blades such as RURPs (standing for Realized Ultimate Reality Piton) have been pretty much replaced by beaks in standard thin cracks, but they still fulfil an important role on big wall ascents, being the best protection for shallow horizontal cracks, and when they are needed, nothing else will really do.

The original RURP design came about because it's impossible to tie off the very tip of a blade effectively, say a blade that only goes in less than the width of a fingernail, and the RURP really opened up a lot of ground that would have required bolts before. The RURP is really just the tip of a blade with an in built and highly effective tie off (the wire).

The most common micro blade on the market is the traditional old Chouinard/Frost design (made by Black Diamond and Cassin), that features a small swaged cable, and is by far the most popular and widely available. Next there is the flat cable-less designs produced by compa-

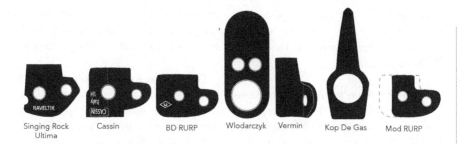

Singing Rock Ultima   Cassin   BD RURP   Wlodarczyk   Vermin   Kop De Gas   Mod RURP

nies like Stubia, Kop De Gas and Piotr Wlodarczyk, that work a little better in slightly wider cracks, with the Kop De Gas 'Pitonissa' featuring a clip in hole instead of a swaged cable.

In straight on vertical hairline cracks - for which they were designed - they have been superseded by the far superior beak, yet they still shine in horizontals and upwardly driven placements, where a beak is less effective, and so it's always worth carrying at least one on any big wall, and on hard walls carry at least two. In such placements it's vital that you tie a loop through the small hole in the RURP so that it isn't levered out.

Modifications: Although you may feel that a RURP is just about as small a piton as you'd ever need you might find that it's not! The now defunct Vermin micro angles were perfect for this, being about half the size of a RURP's blade, and suited to micro slots in horizontal cracks. Sometimes these small placements can be made with the RURP placed end on (filing the top of a RURP just a little can help this, but don't make it sharp as it could cut your rope!), or with a #1 beak placed horizontally, but a sideways beak isn't as strong as a cut down RURP. To cut down a RURP just file or saw the RURP in half and file it to shape.

Rack: I'll carry two RURPs on all routes, and double this on harder routes, using sideways beaks if I run out.

Placement: Micro pitons like RURPs should be viewed as micro blades, and require a gentle touch, plus an eye for a placement.

01. Insert 1/4 of the RURP into the crack, aiming for a uniformly constricting placement

02. Tap gently until 1/2 of the blade is locked in.

03. Now hammer harder, judging its strength by the force needed to set it fully in place. With a RURP you're balancing forcing the steel into the crack or bending the RURP, but hammering should give you some idea of its strength.

04. In some placements the piton can be hand placed and just locked in by your weight.

Strength: I've taken falls onto horizontal blades that only had one corner of the edge of the blade in, and so can attest to their strength when keyed in sideways. As for vertical placements this kind of piton tends to be working by being pinched by the rock, and so will always be marginal in a fall. The cable on the BD RURP is only rated at 3 kN which is a lower breaking strain than the RURP in a perfect placement so I would beef this cable up by having it re-swaged with #4 cable.

Testing: Always bounce test your RURP, making sure that the force is applied directly downwards below the RURP, not outwards.

Cleaning: RURPs due to their nature can either be easy to clean, or impossible if over driven (the RURP buried up to the swage!). They tend not to come free with the usual up and down motion, and sometimes yanking them with your funkness is the only option, or getting the tip of a chisel under one edge and prising it out. An over-driven old RURP will often break when you try and get it out, so take care.

Manufacturers: Black Diamond, Cassin, Stubai, Vermin, Reveltik, Piotr Wlodarczyk, Kop De Gas.

Stand Out Designs: BD RURP

BLADES

Blades or knife blades range in size from the slenderest 2 mm of flat steel (true knife blades) to the slightly more tapered, thicker and more solid blade (Bugaboos). Blades were once a crucial part of a climber's rack as no passive gear will do the same job, but as with all pitons, beaks have all but replaced them on all but the hardest climbs. Blades come in two main flavours; narrow (European) and wide (American).

The wide blades are what most people call knife blades, being flat with a slight taper, with two clip points, one in the blade, the other set at a right angle to the blade; designed to apply a torque to the piton and help it lock, plus allowing the eye to be clipped in tight corners. These pitons were designed originally for clean granite cracks, with the strength of the piton increasing with the thickness of the piton, with the smallest knife blades being very weak and easily bent in a fall.

The European blade, which tends to be narrower, lighter and in most cases much weaker, was designed primarily for aiding on limestone (you could view this as an Eastern alpine piton). In limestone, where placements can be much more complex, these can be very useful, but that's as far as it goes, and anyone looking for high strength should stick with traditional "granite" blades, with the Bugaboo being by far the most effective.

Blades have no in built "spring" to them - unlike an angle, nor the pound-ability of a lost arrow, and so are generally harder to place with total confidence. The only spring they offer is just like that of a knife, they will flex, meaning that if the placement involves deviations, then the piton may lock in tighter, but is mostly held by being compressed by the rock. Where this 'pinch' occurs and in how many places produces the strength of the placement.

The thinnest blades should always be treated with some suspicion unless placed in a horizontal crack, even in what appears to be totally solid placements, as in a fall they can easily bend, twist and pull out. One of the strengths of the longer pitons is that they work well in some expanding cracks, the longer pitons going deep into the crack and so having more opportunity to lock, with battered and bent blades working best.

Rack: These days I carry only a handful of blades and I can't remember the last time I placed one, using medium and large beaks instead, finding the large beaks better (although heavier). I will

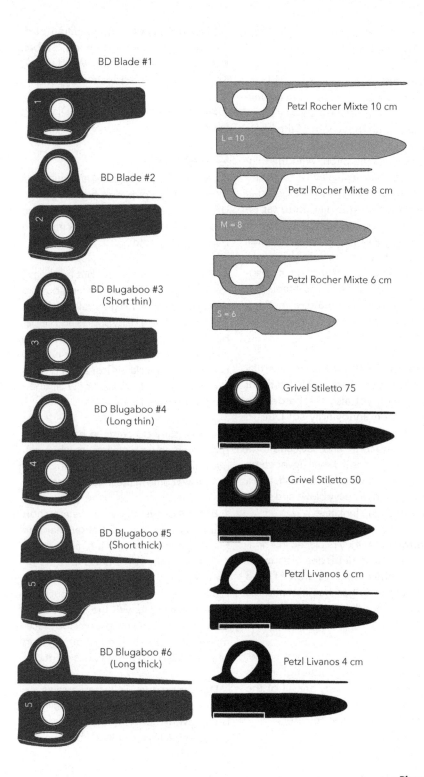

BD Blade #1

Petzl Rocher Mixte 10 cm

L = 10

BD Blade #2

Petzl Rocher Mixte 8 cm

M = 8

BD Blugaboo #3
(Short thin)

Petzl Rocher Mixte 6 cm

S = 6

BD Blugaboo #4
(Long thin)

Grivel Stiletto 75

Grivel Stiletto 50

BD Blugaboo #5
(Short thick)

Petzl Livanos 6 cm

BD Blugaboo #6
(Long thick)

Petzl Livanos 4 cm

carry one #1 and one short medium (#5) and a long medium (#6) bugaboo.

Placement: When placing a blade it's even more vital than normal to make sure you achieve the most mechanically sound placement, with the length of the blade inserted before hammering dependant on the taper of the piton. With the thinnest blades you can achieve a solid stick with anything from 1/4 to 1/2 going in before hammering, while more tapering pitons should be inserted 1/2 to 3/4. Listen closely and you will be able to tell when the piton is no longer going into the rock and being compressed. If possible I set the eye at the top as it feels that I get more twist and torque, something to take notice of when tying the piton off with a sling.

Cleaning: Of all the pitons you may place, blades can be the most difficult to place well, yet also the hardest to remove, often annoyingly so! Due to their shape very often they will simply pivot back and forth, and back and forth making it appear as if they'll never come out. Generally persistence pays off, and a combined effort of heavy blows and some hard yanks on the funkness.

Testing: Unless they're placed in a horizontal crack, test all blades, no matter how good they look. It's a bit of a no brainer but the longer the piton and the greater the taper, the stronger the placement should be.

Racking: Due to their uniform shape, blades rack very easily, although this is only the case when they are all of the same orientation (throw in a left angled blade and this won't be the case).

Manufacturers: Black Diamond, Camp, Cassin, Grivel, Simond, Stubai, Petzl, Kop De Gas, Piotr Wlodarczyk, Krukonogi, Climbing Technology.

Stand Out Designs: Black Diamond Long Bugaboo

LOST ARROWS

Lost Arrows (or king pins) are solid steel pitons that can provide a high degree of strength when well placed, and range in size from that of a thick blade (4 mm) to a baby angle (10 mm).

They pound very well, but are heavy for their range, and for anything but big wall use, climbers will generally stick with lighter pitons like baby angles and bugaboos. The smallest cams and cam hooks have removed a great deal of the need to carry these, with classic lost arrow pitches like the Nipple on Zodiac now climbed entirely on cam hooks.

Where they do come in handy is for protection on such pitches, or when you have piton scars that only a lost arrow will fit. Arrows come in the following designs:

Baby Arrows: Baby arrows are short stubby arrows that are lighter than the full length versions, and are much easier to place - without the need for a tie off - and remove, and are perfect for trade routes, where cracks are beaten out (they hand place well), with the short thin (4 mm) baby arrow going in old blade placements and the wedge (10 mm) going where the old lost arrows once went.

Daddy Arrows: Full sized arrows are of use primarily on hard big wall climbs, being overly heavy for alpine or winter use, and generally replaced by nuts and

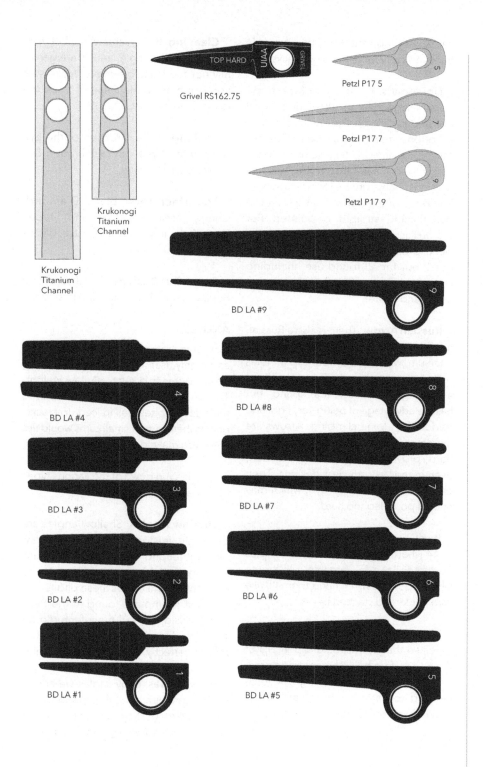

Krukonogi Titanium Channel

Krukonogi Titanium Channel

Grivel RS162.75

Petzl P17 5

Petzl P17 7

Petzl P17 9

BD LA #9

BD LA #4

BD LA #8

BD LA #3

BD LA #7

BD LA #2

BD LA #6

BD LA #1

BD LA #5

cams, although the long thin arrow is handy to carry for expanding cracks.

Universals: A variation of the traditional Arrow has an offset or twisted eye and is called a "universal." Universal pitons are more European (Eastern Alps), and aimed at limestone climbers, as a universal eye tends not to work so well in straight corners found in granite. The body of the arrow can be found to be chiselled (straight) or pointed. For big wall use a chiselled piton works best, working better when only the tip can be used, but for all round use, including alpine and winter, a pointed piton is more useful and lighter.

Russian Arrow: There is also a Russian hybrid angle design manufactured from Titanium, with three or four clip in holes drilled along its length. This piton is not a true angle as it has no real 'spring', but has the advantage of being very light and perfect for alpine climbing. Arrows are extremely strong, and can be pounded hard, providing very solid protection, even in the very smallest designs. Their only weak point is their eye, which may crack if pounded too hard.

Rack: On trade routes I'll carry two #1 to #4 (short thin, medium and thick plus wedge) and two #5 (long thin). On a route where I don't think I'll need them I'll use cam hooks and stacked beaks.

Placement: Most arrows have a good taper, so the piton should slip in 2/3 of the way, before being hammered home. As with all pitons, try and judge the force needed to hammer the piton home, rather than just the noise of the piton.

Cleaning: Being somewhere between a blade and an angle, arrows are generally not too hard to remove. Make sure you hammer on the spine of the piton rather than the eye.

Racking: If the direction of the eye is alternated you can rack around five arrows on a karabiner.

Manufacturers: Black Diamond, Camp, Cassin, Grivel, Simond, Stubai, Petzl, Krukonogi, Faders, Blue Ice, Climbing Technology.

Stand Out Designs: Grivel Top small pointed Sabre, Black Diamond Lost Arrow

ANGLES

Angles are bread and butter pitons, and highly useful, having a high holding power but with a relatively low weight. They are a boon for winter climbers, as their design bites well in iced up cracks, going where nuts or small cams would rip. They also make good makeshift spoons.

Here is a run down of the various types of angle:

Shallow Angles: Shallow angles are the angle version of a thick lost arrow, only lighter and with more spring, and are very useful for hard nailing. At the moment no one makes these pitons, but the best example is found in the Peck piton (designed and manufactured by Trevor Peck), which are highly valued as they fit perfectly on top of a baby angle.

Baby Angles: Baby angles are one of the best pitons around, being short, light and very strong. They have a good spring and can have a very high holding power.

Bong

BD Angle #5

BD Angle #4

BD Angle #3

BD Baby Angle #2

BD Baby Angle #1

Shallow Angle #1

Camp Baby Angle L

Camp Baby Angle M

Camp Baby Angle S

Bong

Krukonogi.com

Krukonogi channel piton Shveller

Kop De Gas Shark M

Kop De Gas Shark S

Sawn off BD #5

Sawn off BD #4

Daddy Angles: Full sized arrows are of use primarily on hard big wall climbs, being overly heavy for alpine use and winter use, being replaced by nuts and cams.

Sawn Off Angles: On big wall trade routes it's well worth sawing down both baby and daddy angles so they can be placed in piton scars (either hammered or hand placed), and they could be viewed as one of the few piton types still required on trade routes. I would highly recommend using a vice and a high quality metal blade for cutting down your angles, and don't be surprised if you go through a blade for each piton (ideally get someone who can machine cut to do them for you). Lengthwise as a rough guide cut the pitons at the halfway mark and file down the sharp edges with a hand file. You can also buy pre cut angles from Kop De Gas and Grivel.

Bong: The largest angle (and the largest piton) designed for the widest cracks and off-widths has all but been replaced by big cams and now is only of interest to those keen on collecting climbing memorabilia.

Rack: I will usually carry two of each size of baby angle, then two #3 sawn off angles, then one #4, #5 and #6 (sawn offs).

Placement: An angle piton has a certain degree of 'spring', and what you're aiming to do is create three points of contact between the rock and the spine, and both edges of the piton. For a solid placement slide the piton into the crack so that only 1/3 to 1/4 is left sticking out, and then hammer it home until the eye is flush with the rock.

Testing: Generally the act of placing it will give you enough information to judge the strength of your angle, and the more you place the more you'll be able to judge how good they are. In a horizontal crack or piton scar you can generally just tap them to seat them then weight them (or just hand place).

Cleaning: Due to a pronounced taper and their 'spring' angles tend to be quite easy to remove, something best done by a few hard blows backwards and forwards until they lose their grip, at which point they can be 'funked' out. Sawn offs in piton scars can be trickier, but due to their keyed in nature (they fit into an existing hole), the trick is to place them lightly, then funk them out.

Racking: Angles, due to their width, can be a real pain in the arse to rack, taking up a lot of room on a karabiner, and so a good tip is to tie short loops of 3 or 4 mm cord through the eye of the piton, so they can be racked in bunches. When leading, all my angles usually sit somewhere in my tag bag or haul bag, with sawn offs removed when I know I'll need them.

Manufacturers: Black Diamond, Camp, Cassin, Grivel, Simond, Stubai, Petzl, Krukonogi, Kop De Gas, Piotr Wlodarczyk, Climbing Technology.

Stand Out Designs: Black Diamond baby angles, Edelrid small V pitons.

Z-PITONS

Z-pitons are from the same family as the angle, only with an extra bend, and like angles they have a very positive spring, and are light for their size. They excel when it comes to stacking, allowing either one or two angles to be nestled together securely.

Russian Route on the Eiger North Face ©Neil Chelton

Designs: The current default Z-piton is the Grivel Onda, which comes in two thicknesses; shallow and deep, and in two sizes; long and short. Of these the long and short shallow Ondas are by far the most useful, either used alone, or stacked. It's also worth mentioning that Ed Leeper produced a very exotic version of the Z-piton that had no eye, but instead had two holes drilled into the body of the piton itself through which a loop of cord could be threaded. This created a load point within the crack itself. This was a great stacking piton for hard aid, but of no use beyond that, plus it was virtually impossible to clean if even slightly over driven.

Rack: On most routes I'll only carry one short Leeper to use for stacking.

Placement: A Z-piton has more spring than an angle, and due to its larger width care should be taken that all the possible contact points are in play. Try not to overdrive your Z-piton, as the gripping action of the piton will make removal difficult. If you find that the piton is a little too small, simply insert an angle into one of the kinks in the piton and hammer in to stack (Z-pitons can also be stacked with blades or arrows).

Cleaning: Clean as you would an angle.

Racking: You can sometimes nest Z-pitons together, which allows you to get more pitons on a karabiner, but may also affect your ability to find the right piton, so climbers may find tying a short loop of cord through the eye works better.

Manufacturers: Grivel.

Stand Out Designs: Grivel Onda.

WOODEN PITONS

In the early days of climbing, when there were no commercial pitons, wooden pitons were used in place of angles and bongs. They were home-made from various hard and soft woods, anything that came to hand, and used on many hard early climbs, especially those with wide cracks. These days wooden pitons are only really used on limestone walls, used in strange holes and often stacked together with soft or hard pitons.

Designs: As with most hardware the need for huge pitons has disappeared beyond blocks used for stacking with cams, and so most wooden pitons range from small wedges of wood the size of your finger, to pieces the size of a large box of matches. These pitons need to be shaped into both shallow and steep tapers, with a hole drilled in the end large enough to take a thin dyneema sling or 5 mm cord (you will usually be clipping the other piton, not the wooden piton, when stacking).

Rack: On a hard limestone wall you may want to carry a good selection of these pegs, as they will often become fixed or damaged.

Placement: This piton works the same as any other piton and can be used as a straight piton, hammered into a hole or crack, deforming as you hammer it in, or used as a wedge and stacked with hard or soft pitons. Due to their softness you can also hammer sharp pitons such as blades or beaks directly into the wood to split and wedge it.

Cleaning: These pitons will often end up fixed.

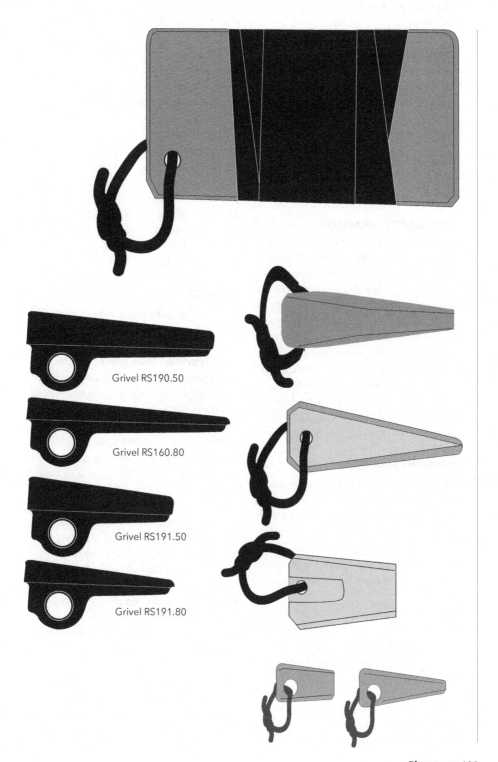

Grivel RS190.50

Grivel RS160.80

Grivel RS191.50

Grivel RS191.80

Racking: Rack these like any other piton.

Manufacturers: These are home-made but the Spanish company Kop De Gas does offer a pack of beech blocks for stacking.

THE HAMMER

Hammers come in all shapes, sizes and weights, yet all do the same job - only some do it better than others.

DO I NEED A HAMMER?

I would always carry a lightweight hammer on a big wall, even one that goes clean, as you never know what you might find. Even on a clean trade route a broken fixed peg, ripped out rivet, or disappearing feature can stop you in your tracks without a hammer and a few basic things to hammer in. Even on routes like the Nose I would always carry a lightweight hammer for cleaning, both my own gear as well as other people's, with bounce tested offset nuts becoming easily fixed without some solid taps with a hammer.

USING THE HAMMER

A hammer's effectiveness comes about both due to the length of its shaft and the weight of its head. Lightweight hammers found on ice axes for example are effective due to having 50 cm of leverage, while a short lightweight alpine hammer of the same weight requires more energy.

When using any hammer it's always best to let the weight do the work, beginning with short directed taps to set the piece, then harder strikes, keeping a loose grip.

Try and avoid holding the hammer closer to its head unless you're doing delicate work, and if your strikes get sloppy then try placing your thumb on the shaft in order to gain more stability.

Unless you pound nails for a living, extensive hammering can prove quite fatiguing, and it's vital to hammer in a relaxed style and take your time.

Tight Spots

Sometimes you will not be able to hit small striking surfaces on beaks or RURPS due to the nature of the rock, or if your hammer is worn out (its edges have become rounded). In these situations you might need to switch to a chisel to direct the force of your blows just where you need them.

HAMMER TYPES

I'll break hammers down into the following types:

Improvised Hammers: The improvised hammer isn't really any hammer at all. It's a stone age experience where you're forced to bash one object against another, generally requiring a great deal of effort (and sometimes pain), with little result, yet with a great deal of damage being done to the objects you're bashing together.

Unfortunately for the modern climber, who comes to a loose fixed peg that needs to be hammered home for example, the reduction of heavy and clunky hardware is not an advantage. Hammering a peg with an old school Chouinard Hex 11 is actually pretty effective when compared with doing the same with a Wallnut 10.

Nevertheless when it comes to an improvised tool to hammer home a peg you are forced to use whatever you have at hand; karabiners, large nuts, your head.

Salawa Alpine Hammer

A5 Hammer

BD Yosemite Hammer

Petzl Caritool

DIY Hammers: The late, and very great, Sean 'Stanley' Leary got his name by forgoing the classic and heavy El Cap big wall hammer by using a hardware store Stanley hammer instead.

This of course is fine, as both are for pounding nails of one kind of another, and a hardware store hammer can be bought for ten percent of the price of a big wall model. What such hammers often lack is the ability to be used with a funkness, or a blunt end for heading, or a clip loop.

Most important of all, most of these trade hammers have round hammer heads which can make placing or cleaning beaks or RURPS (your bread and butter pitons) very difficult in right angled corners. But for most users of such hammers the routes they are climbing will probably require very little, if any, hammering anyway, so this option might be a sound one.

Alpine Hammer: These hammers are generally lighter then a big wall hammer and most often built more like an ice axe than a traditional hammer, some having short ice picks, while others have a more traditional blunt 'heading' pick. Weight is important in these designs as they're for infrequent use, and so most have an alloy shaft or one piece nylon shaft, with a compact steel head riveted on.

This style of hammer sits comfortably on the harness until needed, reducing weight compared to a big wall model, and yet is fine for testing gear, placing pegs and cleaning. The downside is its lower weight makes it less effective for hard cleaning, drilling and copper heading, where often a bit more meat is helpful, although this is actually only marginal. If your hammer features an ice pick this can allow you to do basic dry tooling with the hammer, using it like a sky hook, and of course makes cleaning out icy cracks easier than with a blunt hammer. You can also use the axe as protection or for progression when placed in the ice, and more then once I've been forced to semi dry tool up a section of a route with just an ice hammer and my mountaineering boots, wishing for two axes and crampons.

If you cannot find an alpine hammer to suit your needs then it's easy to make one from an old technical ice axe. Just cut down the shaft and shorten the pick, adding grip tape and a hole for its leash. These days, where passive gear does most things, and the only pitons regularly used are beaks, I think the alpine hammer is the way to go for most walls, greatly reducing the weight on your harness.

On hard alpine nail ups, where you need to do both technical nailing, and mixed climbing, I usually take one lightweight hammer and a pair of axes each, with the leader using the hammer on aid pitches, and the second using their axe hammer to clean the gear. This system gives three hammers for the team - a good bit of redundancy in case one is dropped.

Big Wall Hammer: The big wall hammer is the dedicated tool for hammering, and generally features a wooden shaft to reduce vibration on the hand, a square head for hammering into corners, and a blunt chiselled side for precise placements and copper heading. All wall hammers should also feature a cleaning hole in the head, for use with karabiner chains and funkness devices.

The ability to deliver a large focused force is a real advantage in heading, either when used with or without a heading chisel, being far more effective then the alpine hammer in moving that soft metal around.

As with all wooden handled tools, make sure the head is secure, and if a little rattly just leave overnight in some water. A wooden shaft can also be a little hard to grip so add some wide finger tape (alpine hammers usually have rubber or textured grips).

THE HAMMER LANYARD

For technical climbing you need to connect your hammer to yourself somehow, both to eliminate dropping it while placing or cleaning gear, or in a fall. This connection should also be full strength as there are times where this cord might need to be tied off, with the hammer used as a nut or torqued like an axe, meaning 5 mm cord (or dyneema) or full strength tape.

There are several ways of setting up your lanyard, all with their pros and cons.

- **Classic Lanyard**: The most common system is for the hammer to have a cord or length of tape that leads from the bottom of the hammer shaft to a sling, which is worn around the shoulder. This system is simple and effective, and doesn't get too tangled. The downside is that it's still possible to drop the hammer, say if the sling is accidentally removed when racking up at belays, plus it offers a possible strangulation point, and at least one climber has died due to getting hung up via this cord (all climbers should always carry a knife for such emergencies).

- **Fixed Lanyard**: With this system the end of the hammer lanyard is clipped to a racking loop on your chest harness via a small maillon, or screwgate karabiner (a maillon is more secure and lighter). I fix the maillon to the top of my shoulder on my right hand side (I'm right handed), requiring the shortest length of cord possible to rack the hammer. This system makes it impossible to drop the hammer, and with the added benefit of a much reduced strangulation risk.

- **Sprung Leash**: Instead of using a piece of static cord an alternative is to use a sprung steel lanyard, the type used to secure chainsaws. This means the lanyard is always short and stays out of the way.

HAMMER RACKING

There are three ways to secure an unused hammer. Very often climbers simply let it hang via it's lanyard, pulling it up when needed. This of course is simple and quick, but having a heavy object swinging around always seems to be asking for trouble, especially in a fall. It can also get tangled up in the rope; get jammed in cracks or gear, and just creates a noticeable drag on your chest harness.

Another option is to fit a hammer holster (ice axe holsters do the trick) on your harness. If doing this make sure the holster is made from soft nylon, so it doesn't dig in when sleeping in your harness. A holster is usually best placed behind the hip, where it won't snag with the rack.

The final option, and one that I use, is to clip the hammer off to the chest harness, with a karabiner, where it can be quickly accessed (always try and clip it in such a way that it won't hit you in the face in a fall). Attaching your hammer this way to the chest harness means you can also have a shorter lanyard as I've said (compared to attaching it to your waist harness for example). Try and use a karabiner that is easily identified as the hammer krab when clipped in with the rest of your rack. Others ways of racking your hammer include:

Hammer Hook: Often when doing a lot of hammering, when drilling or heading, you can end up having to keep dropping or clipping off the hammer in order to use both hands, which wastes time. A way to avoid this is to add a small hook on the chest strap of your racking harness made from bent wire into which you can hook the head of the hammer. This could also include nylon tool karabiners such as the Petzl Caritool or Climbing Technology Hammer Lodge.

Hammer Quiver: The Russians use a system that replaces both the hammer hook and the need to rack the hammer, by having a pocket sewn into the back shoulder of their chest harness. This is kept open by stiff webbing or wire and the hammer is simply slipped in and out, like an archer getting an arrow.

HAMMER CARE

With all hammers it's vital they are up to the job, and so it's vital to keep an eye on all parts, including the area between the shaft and the hammer's head (a BIG stress area). Although it may sound odd, anecdotally wooden hammers seem to stand up better to hard use than alloy shafted hammers, and I know quite a few climbers who've had their well used alloy shafted hammer's head snap off. As already stated, if you find your wooden hammer's head is feeling a little wobbly, then it's

worth leaving the head submerged overnight in a bowl of water, as this expands the wood and locks the head into place. When the head of a hammer becomes beat out and rounded off, something that takes about ten walls, then it's time to replace it.

THE HAMMERLESS DELUSION

In the '90s passive gear got so good that big wall climbers began making a big deal about doing walls 'hammerless', which in many ways was a good thing, as it made people take up a bolder challenge rather than just nailing. But often the reason these routes went without having to place a single piton was that every crack was full of fixed gear and no pitons were needed. No matter how good you are you will always find a move that can't be climbed with anything but a piton, most often a beak - even a hammerless one, and so it's a fool who goes up on a wall with neither hammer nor pitons unless they do so with utter certainty they're not needed.

PITON TECHNIQUE

Most modern climbers are brought up using non aggressive, passive protection; nuts and cams, or simply clipping bolts, so placing pitons using a hammer, is not at all natural. What does go in people's favour is that placing pitons, unlike trusting cams and tiny brass nuts, is instinctual, the idea of bashing a lump of metal into a crack in order to create some life saving connection with the rock. As with all climbing techniques you need some basic understanding of physics and engineering, forces and levers, fulcrums etc.

The Protection Spectrum

Lay all your pitons out on the floor in a line, starting with the thinnest pieces, maybe a beak tip and RURP blade, and working up to the largest you have, probably a sawn off angle or a wedge Lost Arrow. Pick them up one after the other, handle them, look at them and imagine them slipping into cracks and holes, how they would lock, cam or jam into place.

Next take your normal rack of nuts and micro wires, plus small cams, and lay them out next to their equivalent sized pitons. What you'll find is that there is no equivalent to the smallest sized pitons (knife blades, RURPS and beaks), but as the crossover begins, where bugaboos and thin lost arrows match your passive gear, you are comparing a solid chunk of steel with a tiny alloy or brass nut, or the smallest cam, the contact surface no greater than that of a fingernail.

This signifies the importance of such pieces, both filling a gap in your spectrum of gear where nothing else will go (well apart from a bolt!), as well as also providing far greater (but more destructive) protection in place of the smallest gear you have. If you free climb and skyhook up twenty metres of loose ground and come to a thin crack do you want to place a micro brass wire or a three inch knife blade or size three beak? 1 kN or 5 kN?

As the pieces increase in size so does the strength of the opposing passive gear, a size 0.5 cam now stronger, faster and more desirable than an angle piton. This is an important exercise, to see how pitons and passive gear overlap, as it teaches you that in many cases pitons are pretty much redundant, and should really be the last resort, but that there is also a spectrum where pitons are the only way to go.

Nevertheless, passive gear is always faster to place, less destructive to the rock, and quicker to clean, and you should always endeavour to use up all such options before reaching for the hammer.

PITON PLACEMENT

How a piton stays put depends on its shape and design. It is held in place while loading (be that you sitting on it, or you taking a huge fall onto it), by one or several mechanical forces. Think of your piton as a lever, like a see-saw, with you on one end and the mountain on the other.

- Now imagine a flat blade piton with a slight taper, with no right angled clipping hole, hammered into a laser cut vertical crack, the crack uniform in width. As the piton gets thicker it will begin to be compressed by the rock, the piton's hammer tone changing as it is compressed into the space, the piton perhaps even deforming a little under your hammer blows.

- If you can hammer the piton all the way to the eye you can apply a downward force to it and the small contact area that holds the piton in place will resist your force. Here the contact area is the fulcrum (the pivot point), and the closer you can get the load to the fulcrum the better.

- If the crack only gripped the tip of the piton deep inside the rock then the strength would be much lower, and the load would be a greater distance from the fulcrum.

- Now let's change that piton to one with a second traditional clip in hole. Now we are applying some torque and twist to the piton, like an ice axe locked into a parallel crack and we have a much stronger placement, having two forces in play.

- Now let's make that zigzag, and place the same piton in a section that is at 40 degrees, now we have compression, and twisting from both the angle of the piton and the angle of the clip in loop, making it stronger again.

- Let's also make the crack irregular in diameter, varying from 1 to 4 mm, with the interior equally irregular. Now you can have multiple pinch points or contact points, the lever action blocked by constrictions all along the piton's length, meaning that no compression is needed to keep the piton in place.

- Now set that crack horizontally and the piton is locked in tight by any force but an outward pull, the piton hammered simply to hold it against the forces of gravity or the tug of the leader's rope.

Selecting The Correct Size Piton: All pitons have some form of taper, and the meat of the piton (two thirds down the length of the piton) should be considered the piton's optimum size when used as protection, as this should place the load as close to the pivot point as possible, the eye close to the rock. This is not to say that a piton that only has 5 mm of the tip locked into a crack and tied off is not effective and won't hold a fall, but only that this type of placement is less predictable, which is the name of the game on lead! Try and get into the habit of looking at your pitons like you do your rack, knowing the spectrum of sizes, from micro beaks to chunky lost arrows.

Preparing The Placement: Before you begin to place any piton you should first quickly assess the area into which you'll be placing it. A piton is basically a wedge, and hammering a wedge into a loosely bonded layer of flakes may end with the

whole area breaking apart, endangering both you and your partner. Even in solid cracks you may have loose sections, and the ideal placement will be a splitter crack in a piece of boilerplate rock.

On winter walls, or big adventurous climbs, you should watch out for frozen or compacted dirt or clay, which will take a piton easily, but will provide very low holding power, the load slowly destroying the placement while you're on it. Dirty placements are best cleaned out before placing any form of protection unless they're more ice then mud, then using a large beak is the best form of protection.

The one bonus with angled pitons is that they tend to bite well in icy cracks, something that isn't the case with blades and arrows, which can seem good but only be held in by ice, which will melt when compressed.

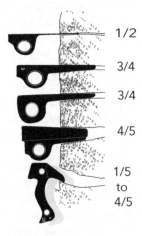

| 1/2 |
| 3/4 |
| 3/4 |
| 4/5 |
| 1/5 to 4/5 |

Depth Guide (before hammering)

The Best Piton Placement: Again consider the forces that will be allies to your piton, the aim always to secure a mechanically sound placement, one that is not dependent on the grip of steel against rock.

A solid piton placed in a horizontal is always the king of placements, with a knife blade crack leading across a roof (upside down nailing) being by far the worst (well after an expanding roof crack!).

When placing a piton scrutinise the placement and see if there is any mechanical advantage to be had, like placing a piton between two constrictions. Think of your pitons like you do your passive pro.

Also, when placing a piton you should always ask yourself how it will be removed, for example a piton hammered into the very top of a corner is very tough to get out as it can only be struck in one direction.

Setting The Piton: A perfect piton that slides in three quarters of its length, and is pushed in hard by hand, may have enough grip to hold even before the hammer blow.

Most climbers will aim to have both hands free, placing and holding the piton with finger and thumb, while tapping with the hammer until they can pound hard on it. It's at this point you will often discover if the piton is too small, as the few taps may set the piton deep and up to the eye long before it has time to really grip (you must feel some resistance). If the piton is working more like a passive nut, being locked in place, any kind of resistance should be enough to hold it in place.

If you have to place a piton one handed then things can be a bit trickier, and often you may need to jab it in place and hope it stays put, maybe using the heel of your hand, or fist to get it to stick. In some cases you may want to keep the piton clipped to you, and some climbers employ a leash that they clip their pitons to (your tether chain will do the job). This technique is crucial in loose or expanding rock or super

hard aid, where anything being placed should be clipped to you. When placing a piton try and judge in the first two or three taps if it's going to fit, and don't be tempted to hammer harder in order to make it fit.

Hammering Home: With the piton set you should get your fingers away from it and start striking it in even strokes, letting the hammer do the work, aiming your blows so the force is directed straight down the line of the piton. Hitting a piton off the line will cause it to shift position, and resetting it back on course repeatedly will reduce the effectiveness of the placement.

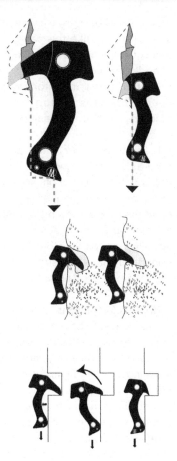

The Tone: Listen to the noise of the piton as you are hammering. The tone should rise, not fall, as it is being hammered. If the tone remains the same then either the piton is too small or the crack or flake is moving, not the piton. It's almost impossible to cover tone in words and instead you just need to go out and hammer on pitons.

Speed Over Strength: When you first start placing pitons there is a tendency to overdrive them, and use pitons that are too big for the job. This results in gear that will end up getting fixed in place, or waste many minutes and cause much frustration as your partner tries to get it out. On most big walls your actual piton rack (beyond beaks) will already be slim, so losing gear like this can have serious consequences. Again you need to consider the mechanical effectiveness of the piton, and some pitons will simply need a few taps to stop them being plucked out, making cleaning a doddle.

I tend to only carry short pitons and tend to be able to judge what's good, and what's good enough, simply by the sound and not testing, and like a piece of art the trick is knowing when to stop. In wide cracks it's sometimes possible to actually place pitons more like nuts, just using their shape and size to lock into a crack, or even used tip to tip.

Hard vs Soft Pitons: In the early days pitons were soft, bending and conforming to the placement as they were driven. As a result they were very hard to remove, meaning that much larger numbers of pitons were needed for big routes. The introduction of hardened steel pitons, like the lost arrow, meant that fewer pitons were needed as they could be cleaned and used again and again. The main downside of soft pitons is that they have a much lower pull out strength, even when they have conformed to a crack, and are really only of use to those aiding on limestone, as they can slip into funny shaped cracks. If you're doing a big limestone wall then take a mix of hard and soft pitons.

Piton Scars: Piton scars are both a blessing and a curse. They are a blessing as they often offer the opportunity to place a clean piece of pro instead, or give a place for the piton to lock in, basically being a hole in a piton board. Due to the way such pitons lock in place, and the need to stop the scars getting bigger, it's well worth only lightly setting your pitons, treating them almost like clean gear. If you find the scars are blown out and nothing fits then you will need to stack pitons, or use a piton stacked with something else such as a cam hook.

CLIPPING

Once a piton is set in the rock you will need to attach it to the rope. For this you can do several things. Due to the fact that a piton tends to be solidly locked in the rock, an extender designed to stop it being plucked out is not really necessary, and so in some cases the piton can simply be clipped to the rope with a single krab. But in most situations the path of the rope or the orientation of the piton's eye, means you will need to use some form of extension.

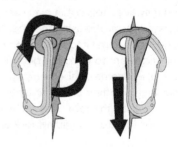

- **Quickdraw**: The easiest of course is to just use a standard quickdraw, and on most climbs this is fine. When clipping a karabiner to the eye of the piton, you need to ask whether you want the force to be applied to the eye of the piton, creating a twisting force, or to the spine of the piton, achieved by clipping the karabiner through the eye and around the piton's spine. This is not so important with your own pitons but can be a vital choice when it comes to fixed pitons.

- **Sling**: If the piton is set in an awkward spot then it may not be possible to clip a karabiner through the piton's eye and so a sling or tie off will need to be used. This tends to be a sewn or tied 30 cm sling simply larks footed or looped through the eye (a basket hitch) and secured with a karabiner. This system works very well on big walls, halving the number of karabiners needed in securing pitons to the rope. Some climbers question the lark's foot as a method of attaching a sling but in this situation it is very secure. I tend to always use thin dyneema slings for this job as they have no knots to come untied, are very strong and cut resistant on metal bars, and when used as a tie off can put the load very close to the wall.

- **Screamers And Scream-Aids**: On marginal placements it's well worth using shock absorbing slings, both for the added security they bring, and more importantly the big psychological boost!

TIE OFFS & KEEPER SLINGS

Pitons that aren't placed to their full depth - meaning the eye is proud of the rock - need to be tied off in order to reduce leverage. Strong skinny dyneema slings (8 or 10 mm) work best for this, and personally I would avoid using classic skinny 12.7 mm (1/2 inch) flat or tubular tape (the old school favourite), as these can be very weak, perhaps as little as 2 kN when knotted and larks footed to some sharp and gnarled piton, meaning a solid piton may well fail due to a weak sling.

A few lengths of 12.7 mm tape can be handy to carry to act as keeper slings to tie piton stacks together (so they aren't lost), but not for full strength protection. If you're using scream-aids then these come fitted with pre-sewn tie offs.

The four main methods for tying off are:

- **Lark's Foot**: This is simple, fast and effective, and works with all pitons, plus a tight fit is easily achieved. Due to dangerous loading of slings that have been larks footed together, this technique has fallen a little out of favour, but when employed with pitons is very valid. Best of all it can be tied with one hand and is easy to untie. If you need more height then you can tie a knot close to the larks foot in order to gain a little more height. Instead of a larks foot you can add a few more wraps and make this into a prusik knot so as to have more of a grip onto a piton that is angled upwards.

- **Clove Hitch**: Very secure and simple to tie, this is a great knot that can be tied one handed with practice. The only downside is that it's slightly harder to get the pulling point directly against the rock.

- **Sliding Knot**: This system is designed to be used as an alternative to a Lark's foot, with a noose being formed that locks down on the piton. In practice I find this fiddly and ineffective, as it's hard to get the knot to cinch tight. But of all three systems this does put the pulling force directly against the rock, and so has the lowest leverage.

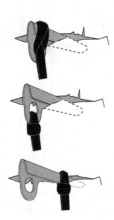

- **Rivet Hanger**: Another option, and one that has the lowest leverage of all when faced with very marginal gear (pitons where only the very tip is gripping the placement), is to use a rivet hanger, ideally a cinch rivet hanger. To do this you need to orientate the piton slightly upwards (tip down, eye up) if possible, so your weight presses the cinch hanger cable into the wall, and/

or prusik a sling onto the piton and push this forwards to keep the cable locked in against the rock, taking the other end of the sling and passing it through the pitons eye and back into the krab on the rivet hanger, so as to act as a keeper. It's important to remember to always use keeper cord or sling in this type of situation as otherwise you are at risk of losing the piton if it comes out of the crack.

Keeper Slings: As stated, with all tie-offs there is a risk that if the piton pulls out then it may slip out of its sling and be lost, and so adding a second tie off to the eye of the piton is often a good idea, and I tend to carry several loops of 5 mm cord for this task.

STACKING

Sometimes, once you start hammering your piton in, you'll find that it fails to bite or sit properly in the crack, meaning it's too small. If you don't have anything bigger what do you do? This is where stacking comes in, which is where you increase the size of your piton by stacking it with another object, maybe another piton, maybe something else like a nut or cam hook. The actual need to stack pitons in shallow placements has been pretty much been removed by cams, nuts and cam hooks, but still it's a skill you should be aware of.

Speed team on Aurora

The king of stacking is the Leeper or Z-piton, with its grooved faces allowing angle pitons to be slipped in alongside it. These can work well in wide but shallow placements that are too shallow for cams, with the tip of two or three pitons being locked in place around a central leeper piton. Flat pitons like arrows and blades can be stacked together, but care should be taken, as they can't lock in place like angles and Z pitons, and having low friction surfaces they can slip apart easily if placed in vertical cracks, so loading both pitons is important.

One piton that's stacked quite a lot are beaks, as often just tapping in a second beak beside the first will help to secure the primary piton and stop it wobbling around, or create more of a compressive force to aid the hook of the piton. When stacking it's always a good idea to tie off all the pitons together, especially when cleaning, as if the matrix fails you'll lose the whole lot.

You can improve stacked gear by using other items like nuts, hooks, cam hooks or even small blocks of wood, or non-climbing hardware like a nut tool or even a rock. Yet again we're trying to build a solid and mechanical placement, but also perhaps making use of camming actions as well, such as a cam hook stacked with a lost arrow, or a nut held in place in a very shallow crack by the tip of a piton. With all these things it's vital you remain creative.

PITON SPECIFIC TESTING

How you test a piton, or even if you bother, comes down to several factors.

You Just Know It's Good: Experience will tell a climber if the piton is good, feeling the resistance of the rock

with each blow, the tone of the piton, the angle and orientation of the crack. The classic example of this would be a baby angle placed in a deep horizontal crack. All it would need is a few taps to set it, and the camming action would mean it was bomber. With this kind of piton you can feel and hear it getting tighter and tighter. The same would be true of the right size beak hooking into an obvious perfect placement. Place it - get on it.

How Strong Does It Need To Be? For aid placements you can often get away with a crappy piton you wouldn't trust as a piece of protection, and instead just go on instinct, or perhaps pure luck. This would be the approach on a speed or alpine route where you'd be happy to fall if luck was not in your favour.

What Would Be The Outcome Of Failure? On a hard aid pitch, where you're creeping onto a beak, or an alpine face where you and your partner's life depends on a single baby angle it's vital that you know 100% how good the piton is.

Hammer Test: So you've placed your piton, and you think it sounded good. Now - holding the hammer loosely - let it drop onto the piton in the direction of pull. Does the piton shift down or rotate? A few hard blows in the direction of loading will tell you if it's good or not.

Funkness Test: If you're carrying a funkness device you can clip this into the piton and apply a greater force, only this time in the actual direction of pull, by giving the piton some hard yanks downwards. I've only ever used this technique for testing dodgy and uncertain pitons when traversing away, as the actual force is hard to judge.

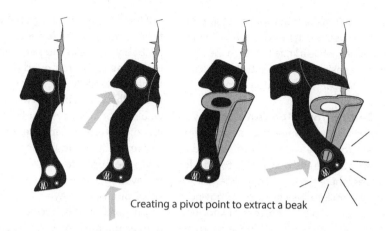

Creating a pivot point to extract a beak

PITON SPECIFIC CLEANING

Being able to bash in a piton is nothing if you can't also remove it. Leaving gear fixed for parties may seem like you're doing them a favour, but fixed pitons soon turn to junk and so any climbing team should endeavour to avoid placing pitons that cannot be cleaned.

When it comes to removing a piton there are five deciding factors:

How Hard You Hammered: If there is anything that teaches a climber how to place a good piton it's trying to clean the pitons they've placed. Only when hammering out a piton do you get just how well – or poorly – it was placed. The great climbers of the past could set a solid piton with just a few deft blows, blows that would set it solid, yet allow it to be quickly removed by the second. The bottom line is the more you wail on a piton, the harder it'll be to remove it.

How Heavy Your Hammer Is: A heavy hammer makes lighter work of removing a piton (just try removing a piton with a nut tool), but skill plays a big part still, after all if you were to use a sledgehammer you'd find that your pitons would

simply break under the strain. I tend to find if the piton was put in with a light hammer then it can be removed with one.

The Quality Of The Rock: Soft rock will disintegrate under the considerable forces involved in piton removal, while solid rock will remain stubbornly diamond hard. This has a bearing on how hard you hammer a piton, and its length, hence in solid rock you require less pounding to place a piton, and so it should be easier to remove, and vice versa with soft rock.

The Position Of The Piton: A badly placed piton can be almost impossible to remove, say a piton placed in a tight hole or pod, and so this comes down to good leader skills more so than cleaning skills really. Poorly placed pitons will need to be funked out or prised out with the hammer.

The Type Of Piton: Soft alloy pitons are much harder to place and are best avoided, as they can become fixed very easily, while solid steel pitons will be able to take a huge amount of productive pounding. A piton like an angle that is sprung, has three points of contact, which will make it harder to loosen, but once loose this type of piton will come out easily, while a knife blade on the other hand is easier to loosen initially, but tends to be harder to completely remove.

Getting The Piton Out: Just as you would with any piece of protection, first check for the easiest way to remove it, looking above and below, side to side, for places where the crack may widen allowing the rock to lose its grip. Removing a piton tends to be a process of knocking the piton backwards and forwards, backwards and forwards, as it slowly emerges from the crack. The greater the taper the piton has, the easier the piton is to remove, with the worst designs being knife blades, which will seemingly just simply move backwards and forwards in the crack without going anywhere. In expanding cracks removal can be very difficult as the rock will not let go, with the crack gripping onto your piton for dear life (something you unfortunately don't feel while actually climbing such features). In these situations often placing just the tip of one larger piton can open up the crack enough to allow it to lose its grip on the original piton, while for less tapered pitons you just need some patience.

Soft Clean: When cleaning, first try and move the piton with the extender, or tie off attached, before you start hammering, just in case it's been hand placed or lightly tapped in (pieces like beaks can often just be ripped out using their quickdraw). If that doesn't work then remove the extender from the piton - so as not to damage it while hammering - and give the piton a few hard blows to see if you can remove it. If after a minute of this you don't seem to be getting anywhere then up your game.

If the piton is remaining totally jammed then it must be keyed into the crack, probably in an existing piton scar, meaning it has to be removed by applying force outwards (the leader should have known this would be hard to clean and so would hopefully have just lightly placed it). To do this you can give it a few taps to remind it you're getting it out, then using the opposite side of your hammer, try levering it, placing the pick or narrow spike through the eye of the piton, jolting it hard until it budges. Be careful here as the piton may spring out and be lost forever.

Some pitons are just stubborn and need several minutes of intensive hammering, slowly softening up the piton until it eventually yields and pops out.

Fumble Cord: For heavy duty cleaning it's worth employing a fumble cord that can be attached to the piton as it becomes loose, as it's very easy to drop a piton in the last stages of cleaning. This can be a short (60 cm) length of 5 mm cord with an old karabiner clipped into the end, and attached to the hammer, or a longer cord clipped to your harness or chest rig. You can also use your funkness in the same role.

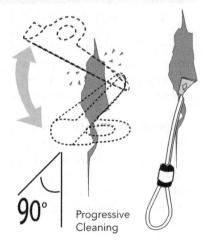

90° Progressive Cleaning

Progressive Cleaning: Pitoning is a dirty business and removing pitons doubly so, and in a perfect world we'd always use a clean piece of pro instead. Progressive cleaning aims to make this a possibility, and is a way of 'creating' a clean placement for future parties.

To do this hammer a piton upward in a vertical crack, then back down to its perpendicular position, and repeat. This should create a bottoming out slot that will take a nut with time.

When using beaks in sandy rock you should also not destroy the placement when cleaning, creating a solid notch for future beaks to hook.

Paint 'Em: I would recommend all pitons be sprayed so that they can be easily identified as being yours and not fixed in placed as this will notify the cleaner that the piton may or may not come out. Once, while trying to climb Tangerine Trip in a day, my partner, who was unused to big wall climbing, just left all the pitons in!

The Funkness: The most useful device for cleaning after your hammer is your funkness device (the term funkness was coined by John Middendorf in order not to offend anyone with its original nick-name) - a short length of thick wire with a loop at each end. This can be employed in several ways, and for big walls that involve nailing it can be indispensable. The funkness is usually set up with old battered screwgate karabiners at each end (these karabiners will get trashed), with one karabiner being clipped into the hammer's head, and the other into the piton. A screwgate is used as it's not uncommon for the force to cause either the piton or the funkness to unclip and be

lost. The funkness is then jerked, creating a static loading on the piton, allowing a cleaner to yank the piton up or down but most usually straight out, breaking the grip of the rock over the piton. It also has the advantage that the piton is clipped to the hammer via the funkness, so can be dropped, and generally I will clip the funkness into every piton while cleaning anyway so as not to lose the piton when it comes out (you can clip the other end to your hammer leash). When cleaning with a funkness be aware of the huge forces involved as you yank the gear, and always consider the trajectory of the piton if it was to spring out, and as always wear a helmet and protect your eyes.

Using The Body: A very effective way to remove pitons when they seem to be held in the rock, moving up and down but not out, is to attach the funkness device to your belay loop, and then position yourself so - using your legs - you're pushing away from the placement, pulling directly outwards on the piton. Now start hammering. Jerking with the hips and hitting the piton will generally remove even the most stubborn pitons.

Makeshift Funkness: A funkness needs to have no dynamic properties, allowing the full impact of the hammer to be transferred across to the piton, hence slings make poor funkness devices. The best option if you find yourself without a funkness is to create a string of karabiners, only be aware that the forces generated - especially on a cross loaded krab - can cause krabs to break.

FIXED PITONS

Fixed pitons are a feature - or should that be fixture - on many climbs, and tend to be viewed by many as a bonus. The problem is that it's often hard to judge the strength of the fixed gear, for example does the eye of the piton extend from a stonking angle three inches long, or a stubby sawn off the size of your little finger, and is it brand new, or corroded with rust just out of sight?

Here are a few things worth considering when clipping fixed gear:

History: Always visually check the piton before trusting it, looking at both its age, type, and current condition. Having some understanding of who makes pitons, and who used to make them, helps, as finding a Clog or Peck angle not made since the 80's may well signify it could have been there awhile, not to mention homemade pitons bashed out by hobby blacksmiths.

What Lies Beneath: Be aware that although the eye of the piton may look fine, within the damp confines of the crack the body of the piton may be little more than rust. This is especially true when climbing on sea cliffs, a place you will often find fixed gear, and reason enough not to either leave gear fixed or trust what's there.

Location: You cannot know what's going on inside the rock, but you may have noticed rusty piton stubs elsewhere giving you a clue.

The Eyes Have It: Is the eye of the piton intact or broken? I've clipped several fixed pitons only to find that the eye was broken and flexing under my weight. If it's at all suspect then tie off the piton by looping a tie off around the body/spine of the piton, not the eye itself.

Solid Piton But Weak Cable: There is an abundance of fixed beaks on a lot of walls, mainly large ones. Until the beak's blade becomes weak with rust the weak link will be the cable, with the cable on some beaks being pretty weak already (e.g., BD). This means that you may have a very solid beak, so solid it won't come out, that ends up failing when the cable snaps. For this reason I would always clip directly into the beak, either by adding a sling or karabiner, or tying my own cord through the beak if that's not possible. If the beak has been placed tight into a corner it might seem impossible to get it out, but by hammering the pointed side of your hammer between the beak and the wall, or a thick lost arrow, you can usually make some space. Another option is to hook the clip point with a hook.

Is It In Fact Fixed? There are many reasons why a piton may be left behind and yet be far from solid. Often people can hammer out a piton but simply forget to take the piton with them, meaning it's simply sat there waiting to fall out when weighted.

Freeze Thaw: Hot weather expands metal and cold weather shrinks it, the greater the difference between summer and winter temperatures, and the longer pitons have been up on a climb without being climbed on, the greater the caution needed. Pitons with some spring in them such as angles seem to be more prone to freeze thaw, while hook style pitons that you find fixed always seem good to go.

Cleaning Fixed Gear: Some people are just crap at removing pitons, maybe because they didn't have a hammer, or they just unclipped the rope and forgot, or even assumed it was a fixed piton in the first place, but as I've said just because something is fixed does not mean you should necessarily just leave it there. As with a piton you've placed, eye up how it was placed and try and use all your standard cleaning skills to get it out. A stuck piton will generally be stuck because it's been placed in a tight spot that doesn't allow the piton to be loosened (requiring funkness cleaning), or is being pinched by an expanding crack (often the case with knife blades). As with normal cleaning, a good hammer and funkness device will clean most pitons, while a beak requires the pivot technique. Beyond this you will need specialist gear beyond the rack of normal climbers, and only really of use to people cleaning up routes. These items will include lump hammers, chisels and crowbars.

BOLTS

The knowledge of how and why bolts and rivets are employed on a big wall is of vital importance, whether you're making a first ascent or the hundredth ascent. All teams will attempt to keep the number of bolts and rivets to an absolute minimum - the hole count - knowing that to over drill will both reduce the difficulty of their route as well as undermine how others view their skill as climbers. The knowledge of how to drill bolts and rivets is not only vital for first ascensionists, but also for big wall emergency and self rescue, as bolts and rivets may need replacing, or new ones may need to be placed, to bridge the gap between missing features and blank sections.

WHY NOT GO FOR NATURAL BELAYS?

The natural belay is always the most preferred belay as it's fast to build and take down and does not require invasive drilling. The problem with natural belays is that very often they require key pieces of equipment that may be needed on the next pitch, or may have been used already on reaching the belay. The Nose for example could feature all natural belays using just wires and cams, but this would mean a doubling up of gear and extra weight.

Another factor is that by bolting belays you aid a retreat, vital on very steep lines as well as popular ones. If The Nose was cleaned of belay bolts then retreat would probably be impossible from high on the wall, a whole rack needed to safely get everyone and everything down in one piece.

There is also the problem that very often natural features do not make ideal belay positions, that creating a belay in a vertical crack bunches up everything and everyone, where two bolts set a metre apart does not. There is also the safety factor of drilling into solid rock rather than trusting flakes, cracks and features that can - and have - proved to be unsound. The deaths of Finn Daehli and Hans Christian Doseth in 1984 on Great Trango has been put down to catastrophic belay failure while descending, a crushed cam evidence that the rock may have moved or broken away.

There is also something in the neatness and construction of a route, to make very long technical pitches that lead to perfect belays that are ideal for camps and hauling, the bolts part of the artistry of the leader.

ETHICS

Climbing big walls is primarily about searching out the impossible, using as little as you can to ascend the hardest, blankest walls you can find. The second you get out your drill you are admitting some kind of moral defeat, and so drilling is viewed as one of the most serious actions on a wall, so consider the following points:

Murder Of The Impossible: Messner's rage against the 'murder of the impossible' was a rage against the bolted direttissima, where hundreds of bolts were placed, by both hand and machine, in order to scale the blankest walls, turning a high skill game into DIY. Routes like the now de-bolted compressor route on Cerro Torre were great examples of man's arrogance and hubris, but such climbs have also served as an example to excess, a valuable message that success at all costs, costs too much, costs your reputation, costs the route you create, and costs the mountain, its walls littered with piercings.

Should We Drill?: So the first question we need to ask is; is this necessary? Well the answer on many big walls is yes. Due to the huge loads involved, the black nature of the rock, the lack of gear to create highly complex natural belays when they can be found means that bolted belays are pretty much a necessity. As for lead bolts or rivets, if you're creating a route that's a work of art then sometimes it is necessary to link small features together when climbing new routes, or drill blank sections when a feature is ripped off the wall. On most new routes a hole count is kept and this is set beside the climb to determine if massive bolting was justifiable, as with enough drill, bolts and battery power anything can be climbed.

Big Wall Junk: The world of bolting and drilling is a very complex one, big wall bolting even more so, with a long, complicated, and often murky past, leaving behind tons of crappy and dangerous bolts and hangers. In the past climbers used what bolts they could find, or make, as well as homemade hangers sawn from bits of steel, iron or alloy. These time bombs were often deadly even when they were placed, and although ancient, even now you can come across junk protection like this on popular walls. Some people feel that crap gear is part of the game, that when you come across a machine head rivet and you don't know if it goes in 30 threads deep or only 5 then that's OK, it gives the pitch spice. But the first ascensionist knew, they placed the junk, so it's creating false jeopardy, like planting a field full of mines then asking someone else to walk across it. The same goes for a whole pitch of bat hooks, again scary, but not so much when you're drilling them, know where they are, know how deep they go.

If You Drill It Fill It And Fill It Good: And so instead of this cheap skate approach of the past, climbers are now taking the issue of bolting routes more seriously, using high end, high strength and long lasting hardware that will last decades, if not centuries. The idea of placing shoddy mystery machine heads has been replaced by using stronger button head bolts that are tested and their length easily judged, or 8 mm stainless stud bolts, hardware that can be viewed as full strength.

The Weight Of A Bolt Is On Your Shoulders: Placing time bomb bolts, or bolts drilled with the wrong sized bits, or the wrong bolts in the wrong rock type, can lead to the death or injury of future climbers. You are personally responsible for any anchor you create, morally and also potentially legally, so you cannot be slap dash, flying by the seat of your pants, making it up as you go along. Like shooting a gun, you must have your shit together and know every step of the process.

Be Respectful: It's vital that climbers take the time to fully understand what the current thinking is on bolts in their area, both how bolts should be used and what bolts work best. For example a climber was killed in Australia when an 8 mm bolt pulled out as he aided on it, leading to a fall that cut his rope (and also maybe saved the belayer, as the belay bolts could also be pulled out by tugging on a quickdraw). In this situation climbers from another country had used bolts that would have been ideal on granite, on very soft sandstone, meaning the bolts were time bombs.

Adding Holes: Adding any new holes to an already established route is wrong, as the route was made the way it was for a reason. Drilling to make it easier is not acceptable, and 99.99% of the time there is a way on unless something else has changed. I also think adding bolts to belays is wrong, but rebooting and updating bolts is advisable as long as the old bolts can be removed, and not just yet another bolt added.

If rivets break the old idea was 'like for like', but you're not going to place another crappy alloy dowel when you break one, but rather an 8 mm bolt or 1/4 button head. On hard walls there is always enough scary climbing to keep your attention without trying to make the rivets hard and scary as well.

If you feel a bolt is needed, say a head placement has been destroyed or a flake has broken off, then you are adding something extra to that route. The opportunity to go down and contact the first ascensionist is not really an option

and leaves you with a dilemma; do you place a bolt and reduce the grade of the pitch (an 8 mm bolt in the middle of an A4 section will make it much easier), or do you drill a deep bat hook hole and maybe make it harder, or do you trench a new head? Of course there is no real answer as each one is problematical. If you're on a Bridwell route and he'd found a blank section he'd have done one of these three as well, but in the 21st century what do you do? The moral answer is you're drilling so you should fill it with a high quality bolt, but the moral option might just be a get out of jail card.

What I set out below is not a general coverage of all bolting techniques, covering every kind of bolt out there, but what I feel is the right way to go for big wall climbers today, some of which may be a little controversial.

HAND BOLTING GEAR

I'm not going to cover power bolting here as it's beyond the realm of classic big walling, and instead focus on hand drilling. The beauty of hand drilling is the fact it's a monumental pain in the arse, as well as hands, shoulders and biceps. This means that no one is going to go on a Warren Harding bolting bonanza and instead will keep bolting to an absolute minimum.

Bolting is an art, especially if you're talking about the bolting of free climbs with power drills, but here we're talking about big wall bolting, which tends to be hand drilled and kept as simple as possible. I will cover the tools for drilling first and then the bolts and rivets:

Drill Bits: The technology of rock drilling has advanced dramatically over the

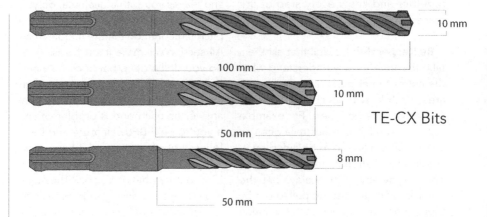

10 mm

100 mm

10 mm

TE-CX Bits

50 mm

8 mm

50 mm

last few decades, with climbers in the past having to file and modify rock bits for hand drilling, some placements eating up several broken bits before a bolt could be sunk.

These days we have SDS bits that are ideal for drilling holes in rocks and better still are the ideal design to slip into drill holders. SDS bits come in many sizes, metric and imperial, and it's VITAL that you match bolts to bits (for example, US bolts will not work with Euro drills). SDS bits come in long and short sizes and the short ones are of the most use to climbers, plus having your driver closer to the rock makes it easier when high stepping.

There are quite a few people making SDS bits but I would stick to Hilti and avoid cheap bits you find in hardware shops, or Chinese eBay bits as more often than not the carbide tip will just fall out! The best bits to buy feature an X style carbide (TE-CX) tip rather than a single carbide tip as this gives you more cutting power, and both SDS and SDS plus bits will fit any holder.

The wear rate of bits varies dramatically depending on the skill of the climber and

the hardness or softness of the rock, but as a rough guide I'd be conservative and go for one high quality 10 mm bit drilling 10 holes, although for some you will get five times that many out of it. Never have only one bit as they can get dropped, broken or stuck, so always have at least two in your bolt bag.

On a wall your default bit is the 10 mm short SDS, as this will do you 10 mm bolts, emergency bat hook holes and drilled edges. For new routes you will want to add 8 mm bits for rivets or 8 mm bolts, and drilled edges.

Modified Bits: In the past climbers would take standard high speed bits (HSS) and file the tip to a chisel point, as a standard bit was pretty ineffective at chipping down into rock. This has continued for some, with the SDS bits also being modified, the aim to achieve a more effective and speedier bit. My thinking on this is that people like Hilti know more about drill bits than I do, and although hand drilling is not quite the same as power drilling, they're manufacturing bits that balance out speed of penetration, low binding/sticking, and

Petzl Rocpec

bit longevity. When you sharpen a bit to a chisel point yes you do get a faster hole, which could be important for bolting on lead, but the bit dulls much faster, and on a wall you're often not able to be filing and taking care of your bits. And so for general use I would stick with high quality unmodified Hilti TE-CX bits.

The Driver: The driver is the bit holder and handle for the drill, the bit inserted and locked in place by a sprung catch or sometimes a collar or Allen bolt. The holder tends to have a rubber grip that helps in twisting and protects your hand from the hammer, as well as having some way of attaching the driver to yourself via a wrist loop (this loop should always be clipped into a keeper sling /cord). The driver tends to feature a steel insert in the handle as a striking surface to stop the end becoming deformed, and there is often a little play in the bit to help the bit 'bounce' as it's struck. All SDS bits feature a universal base diameter meaning one bit should fit into any holder, and the Petzl Rocpec driver also features an insert that allows an 8 mm self drive bolt to be used as well.

Blow Tube: This is used for blowing the dust out of your holes, and although not vital is good to have, especially if you're using longer bolts in soft sandy rock. This tube tends to be a short length of flexible plastic tubing that is narrow enough to fit in your bolt holes. Make sure you tape a clip loop on your blow tube so you can keep it close when drilling.

Bolt Bag: This is an important piece of kit and holds your bolts, hangers, driver, blow tube and bits. This should ideally be a bag designed for purpose (Yates make a very good bolt bag, with Petzl and industrial companies offering other designs), featuring a bomb proof clip loop, one handed draw closer, internal pockets and bit holders. Attaching a long cord or sprung leash from your bag to your driver can reduce the risk of dropping it, and any drill bit changes are best done with the driver inside the bag. Bolts and hangers are best separated into stuff sacks inside the bag, with only enough carried for the day's climbing if doing a new route.

Hammer: I've covered hammers elsewhere and I guess it doesn't need saying that a hammer is an important part of drilling holes. Some climbers think a very heavy hammer is needed for bolt drilling, but I find a medium hammer works well and is less tiring, which is vital when drilling high above your head.

Spanner: You will need a good sized spanner that will allow you some torque on the bolt's nut, and make sure it has a lanyard taped to it so you don't drop it. If you drop your spanner then bolts can be tightened by hand but view these pieces as passive protection until you're able to tighten the bolt.

Brush: A small stiff brush designed to clean out drilled holes is worth carrying if you want to do a good job, with the Fixe bolting brush being a good example.

Spares: Always carry spare nuts, washers and hangers (stainless), as well as some rivet hangers and wire cinch hangers (thick and thin). These should be both metric and imperial. I would carry one of each of the following nuts threaded onto a piece of cord; 8 and 10 mm, 1/4, 3/8, 1/2. Another piece to carry is a Petzl 8 mm self drive hanger as these are often found on belays for portaledges or as chicken bolts (there is one on the triple cracks on the Shield), although they can be hard to spot, as the hole is flush to the wall. Removable bolts (Russian or Petzl) may also be worth carrying if teams have used these in the past.

HARDWARE

The bolts a climber might place on a big wall may be different to the bolts a climber may place on a sports climb. The reason for this is that a big wall will get very little traffic, in fact a sports route might get more ascents in a day than a big wall climb gets in a year, or a century!

The standard for bolted sports routes is the glue in bolt, which will last for hundreds of years, and after that the 12 mm five piece bolt, both able to handle endless use without degrading. But these bolts are always placed using power drills, not by hand, and with the gear and conditions needed to place them perfectly (they are rarely placed ground up).

On a big wall you'll be placing a bolt by hand and often in extreme situations, maybe while hanging on some skyhook or funky head, and so you don't have the time, the energy, or the balls, to drill a solid 12 mm five piece. Instead you go for super strong hardware, but hardware that's appropriate to the climbing, lighter and quicker to place, and still lasting for a hundred years, but only for routes where the traffic will be light.

I'm going to cover the primary bolts that may be in your tool box.

Bolts - Hard Rock

These bolts are suitable for granite, quartzite or limestone.

<u>10 mm Stainless Stud Bolt Short (66 or 70 mm)</u>

Although you can place 12 mm bolts, such bolts are best saved for trade routes that get tons of traffic, where many rescues take place, and people have the time to drill them. For everything else the 10 mm stainless expansion bolt is the default belay and lead bolt, being very, very strong and long lasting.

The basic concept for anyone who's not seen one of these is that you drill a 10 mm diameter hole to a depth halfway down the threaded section of the bolt, insert the bolt, place on its hanger and nut and tighten. As you tighten the bolt the expansion collar binds on the bolt's shaft and locks it in place. In good rock this provides a very strong anchor suitable for the highest loads.

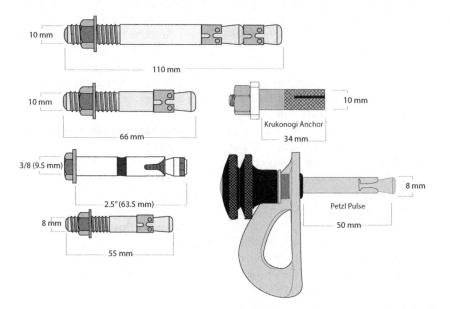

10 mm

110 mm

10 mm

66 mm

Krukonogi Anchor
34 mm

10 mm

3/8 (9.5 mm)

2.5" (63.5 mm)

8 mm

55 mm

8 mm

Petzl Pulse
50 mm

Usage: Belay and lead bolts
Strength: 25 kN (15 kN pull out)
Drill Bit: 10 mm SDS

3/8 Powers Power Bolt Short (2.4 inches)

This is the standard US big wall bolt, and is both high strength and long lasting, and easier to remove when re-bolting, although I expect these bolts will last 50+ years anyway. When using powers bolts you should always use the washer, placing it between the hanger and the nut.

Usage: Belay and lead bolts
Strength: 20 kN (21 kN pull out)
Drill Bit: 3/8

8 mm Stainless Stud Short (50 or 55 mm)

This is what I view as the modern 'alpine' bolt, or modern rivet, being very light, small and compact and quick to drill, while still providing a good level of protection on lead (10 kN which is the

same as a climbing nut). Unlike self drives or button heads the quality and component parts of these bolts is assured and will last for a very long time if matched to the correct stainless hanger. If alloy hangers are used on an alpine wall then these should be removed to avoid corrosion, but a Moses Stainless steel hanger only weighs 24 grams, meaning bolt and hanger weigh only 50 grams, so just do the job right.

Usage: Lead bolts and rivets
Strength: 10 kN (10 kN pull out)
Drill Bit: 8 mm SDS

Petzl Pulse 8 mm Removable Bolt

Removable bolts have been around for a long time but they have either been inappropriate due to the need to drill a deep 12 mm hole, or in the case of non commercial designs, because they either fell out or broke while being used, or became fixed when loaded!

The Petzl Pulse is the first practical

removable big wall bolt, and is a game changer for big walling, the 8 mm hole being easy to drill and the bolt itself being high strength.

The removal of the bolt removes the problems of both corrosion and basic wall junk, and offers the chance of having a virgin pitch free from rivet heads and hangers. Being full strength you can get high on these pieces when drilling rivet ladders (which would become hole ladders), with a small rack being used both for protection and progression.

The downsides with such removable bolts are that if you were to retreat you would need to use up your supply of bolts, plus you will need to supply a detailed description of pitch lengths and bolt counts, as finding empty holes can be a very tricky business, especially under snow and ice.

Personally I would stick to 10 mm bolts for belays and use these for lead bolts, hanging portaledges, and rivet ladders.

Usage: Lead bolts.
Strength: 15 kn
Drill Bit: 8 mm SDS

Bolts - Soft Rock

In softer rock a longer bolt is advisable, and by long I mean as long as you can get (a glue-in is the ideal but you'll not have that option on a big wall) as the surface strength of soft rock can be very poor, especially if saturated. In very soft rock even these bolts may fail to lock in place, the rock compressing instead of the expansion sleeve, meaning the bolt is 'wobbly' and may even be pulled out with the fingers, creating a torque anchor little better than a drilled angle (where a hole is drilled and an angle peg is hammered into it). The difference between a long

10 mm stainless bolt and a drilled angle is the bolt will retain its strength much longer. All bolts in sandstone should be viewed as highly suspect, no matter how much of a trade route you are on, and so should be equalised and backed up with cams and nuts.

12 mm Stainless Expansion Long (100 mm+)

Usage: Lead bolts and belays
Strength: 30 kN (28 kN pull out)
Drill Bit: 12 mm SDS

1/2 Powers Power Bolt Long (3.75 inches):

Usage: Lead bolts and belays
Strength: 30 kN (26 kN pull out)
Drill Bit: 1/2 SDS

BOLT HANGERS

Bolt hangers come in many styles but if you're using a mixture of sizes then you can use a larger hanger on a smaller bolt, meaning carrying 10 mm hangers for both 10 and 8 mm bolts, but using a washer if you have to put larger hangers on smaller bolts.

Walls can often take years to get a second ascent and so I would also always add a washer in between the hanger and nut to give it that extra little grip, and always check hangers are tight when climbing. Standard twist hangers are the style mostly used on walls, with bolts placed on belays either left plain, or if you think it'll become a trade route you can have ring hangers or leave maillons fixed to them.

Overloading hangers can be an issue and Raumer make a twist hanger for aid climbing and big walls called the Alien (27 kN / 57 g), that features two clip in holes rather than the normal single clip in point.

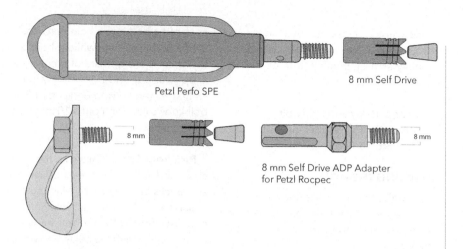

Petzl Perfo SPE

8 mm Self Drive

8 mm

8 mm Self Drive ADP Adapter
for Petzl Rocpec

8 mm

Lightweight Hangers

Most hangers are made for either industrial applications or for decades of intensive use, able to be fallen on perhaps a hundred times a day for years on end. On a big wall you may only see an ascent once a year, or even less, meaning that a full weight 33 kN hanger, three times the strength of the bolt it's hanging from might be overkill. Lightweight hangers for 10 and 8 mm bolts, often described as being for caving or canyoneering, are ideal for big walls. For example the Petzl Coeur 10 mm hanger (22 kN) weighs in at 65 g while a Kop De Gas Montsec 10 mm (20 kN) hanger weighs only 20 g, meaning a saving of 900 g if you carry 20 hangers in your bolt bag, a significant amount if you're carrying it.

SELF DRIVES (SPIT)

Self drive bolts are a dying breed of bolting tool. Designed originally for caving they are an integrated drill bit and bolt, a toothed point chipping away the rock surface until the whole bolt is buried into the rock. At this point the bolt is removed and a cone inserted into the end and tapped home, expanding the bolt's tip and locking it home, at which

point the driver is removed and a hanger replaces it.

This is a very simple and light system and was the default method for decades on alpine walls. The system is fast (I can drill a self drive in 10 minutes in limestone) and light and easy to master, with all the parts cheap and easy to buy. The only problem is that the bolts themselves are shit!

The combination of steel bolts and alloy hangers means they corrode badly, and I've seen self drives that literally flake to dust when you go to clip them. They are also weak (some have pulled out at 3 kN), the actual integrity of the bolt down to an 8 mm nut that only screws into the body by about 10 mm. The cone system is also problematic, as in soft rock you can fail to achieve full expansion, and I've placed self drives in poor rock that could be pulled out by hand and were only held in place by torque of loading.

One major risk when drilling with these self drives is that if the driver becomes untwisted just a few turns (easy to do), you can snap off the threaded tip of the driver, rending it and all your bolts worthless (unlike an SDS system).

As you can guess I'm not a big fan and would like to see this system disappear mainly as it's just not future or climber proof.

Usage: Belay and lead bolts
Strength: 15 kN (0 kN pull out)
Drill Bit: The bolt

DRILLING THE HOLE

To drill a hole in rock is never that easy, but it's also never that hard and simply requires the tools, the time and the patience.

Bolt Metallurgy: Before you start drilling make sure you have the right hardware. You should only use stainless steel bolts, ideally from recognised climbing companies such as Fixe, Petzl, Powers, Kong, Raumer, not cheap plated Chinese bolts off eBay. These bolts should also have all parts matched, so all stainless steel, from hanger, nut, bolt to washers, as mixing and matching, say a plain steel washer, alloy hanger, coated nut and stainless bolt will lead to a corrosive mix. Remember that you're creating a work of art here. Don't be cheap.

Basics: The basic principle is; hit the drill bit, turn the drill bit, hit the drill bit, turn... etc. When you hit the bit you're making a hole, when you turn it you're removing the debris from the hole and resetting the bit's cutting edge, taking the bit out now and again to blow the hole clean and see how far - or not far - you've gone. The real art comes from digging a bit more into detail, such as how hard do you hit, how often do you turn, when do you blow the hole clear?

Pick Your Bolt And Your Bit: Make sure you have your bit and bolt matched as to put a bolt into a hole that's too big is highly dangerous, while a hole that's too small is a big waste of time! Try and keep your bits and bolts clearly marked so that someone who ends up drilling a bolt knows you can't put a 10 mm bolt in an 8 mm hole!

Pick Your Spot: Make sure the rock is clean and solid and at least 30 cm from any cracks or other bolts. Make sure the rock is flat and not in a depression as this may interfere with the bolt hanger or even interfere with the belay, and you can check this by placing your bolt hanger on the rock before you start drilling.

Pilot Hole: Place the drill bit at 90 degrees to the rock and give it some hard strikes to create an indent to start. It's vital that you begin very carefully and make the first 5 mm clean and create a sharp starting hole. Once you feel you've set the starting hole you can speed up.

How Hard? The art of drilling the hole is to understand that you are not drilling away like a power drill does, or smashing the rock, but instead chipping the hole, each strike of the hammer breaking a few grains of rock away, like you're a sculptor, each twist positioning the focus of the drill somewhere else.

Look at the tip of an SDS bit. It's pointed and chisel shaped, each blow focusing down the driver to the bit and down to that tiny point, the tip of the spear. If you hit too hard you'd destroy your bit, your driver, your hammer and your hand, as you're basically just hitting the wall with your hammer. Tap too lightly and the bit will not be able to break the grains of the rock apart and you'll never drill any kind of hole.

Instead what you need are hammer blows that are up to the job of chipping the rock, and that are sustainable and rapid, the death of a thousand taps, not one bit breaking blow. When you start off you should be able to judge the right kind of hammer blow you need by looking at how the surface of the rock reacts to the bit.

How Many Taps? The number of taps before the drill is rotated is important as what you want is for the bit to chip away as much rock as possible but without binding, drilling a slot into which it sticks. You also need to factor in rhythm, as it's the huge number of small taps that will get the hole drilled. I tend to vary between 5 medium taps then twist, and two hard taps and twist, it comes down to what suits your style, but as a guide you want to be getting about 60 strikes a minute.

How Many Twists? The twist is both changing the position of the bit so it has fresh rock to cut as well as allowing the bit to remove some of the rock dust inside the hole, which can cause the bit to bind and stick. When it comes to twisting, try and imagine the face of a clock. You insert your bit and imagine the long chisel running vertically from 12 o'clock to 6 o' clock. Now twist the drill around the clock in hour intervals, so a twelfth of a turn at each turn.

How Often Do You Remove The Drill? You tend to remove the drill to blow the hole clean or to check the depth to see if you can stop drilling and bang in your bolt. The natural movement will remove quite a lot of the rock debris, but blowing the hole clean every few minutes gives you a chance to rest your hands (have your blow tube close if you've

got one). If you don't have a blow tube then you can spit on the end of the bit and clean the hole out this way. As for depth, it's a good trick to put an elastic band on your bit and position it for the depth you're aiming to drill (or pre mark it with tape), as this reduces the number of times you need to take the bit out and check the hole (one good thing with self drives is that they have a mark on the driver which shows when you've hit the correct depth).

How Deep? When hand drilling a stud bolt you will be tempted to drill the hole short and call it good - don't!

A stud bolt requires a full depth hole in order for the stud to expand the end cap, meaning that if you only drilled to the bolt's first thread then tightening the bolt would not engage the stud at all, and you would only have an unsightly passive bolt, like a piton hammered in a hole. Having all the threaded parts sticking out makes clipping karabiners more awkward, can be a snag hazard for haul bags lifting from the belay, and a hazard on lead bolts, as falling into them or over them can cause nasty puncture wounds.

If you want to drill a shallow hole then make sure you drill to at least a depth that will take 50% of the bolt, but ideally the whole length of the bolt, minus the hanger, washer and nut. This means once tightened you will only have 3 mm of threaded end showing. In reality hand placed bolts tend to be placed in shallow holes.

The Drill As Pro: Sometimes you might be in a position where you are on a time bomb piece, and trying to drill a bolt, rivet or bat hook feeling the seconds counting down. If the piece you're on fails, you'll fall onto the drill handle, which is clipped into you somewhere, which will probably see the bit bend and break. If you're desperate and just need to keep calm and keep drilling, then you can attach a #2 or #3 rivet hanger to the bit, and try and keep it as close to the rock as possible, clipping your daisy chain into it as short as you can. If you fall, and the drill is in the hole, you have a small chance of being held by the bit.

Placing An Expansion Bolt: Now you've got the hole, it's time to place the bolt. The following is for the standard stud bolt:

01. With the hanger, washer and nut screwed onto the bolt, tighten the nut until it's a few threads from the end, but not flush, as you don't want to damage the nut or threads when you hammer the bolt into the hole, hitting the end instead.

02. Making sure the hole is clean, insert the bolt, pushing it in as far as you can by hand, which should not be far. If it slides in easily then you have a problem as you've perhaps used the wrong bit, or if in soft rock your drilling has created too large a hole.

03. Once pushed in, hammer the bolt home until the hanger touches the rock. The bolt should go in with some resistance but should not require major bolt bending force.

04. Make sure the hanger is orientated correctly, and begin to tighten the nut, turning it until you are unable to tighten any more (do not use the hammer to hammer on the spanner).

05. If the hanger is off centre then tap it back into place with your hammer. You're ready to go!

Practise, Practise, Practise: The first time I had to place bolts on a route I was a third of the way up a new route on the Troll wall, solo and in winter. I was using bolts I'd never used and a system that was straight out of the bag. Mid pitch, hanging from a sky hook I tried to place an 8 mm button head bolt, whacking on the driver for all my might, thinking at the time that this was a game of violent penetration.

I'd only ever placed one bolt before, a self drive in a small rock in a car park, so was pretty much clueless, the articles I'd read giving me just enough knowledge to be dangerous to myself. When the hole was finally drilled I fished out the button head bolt and began to tap, the tip going in tight, millimetre by millimetre, until it got to the bolt's thicker part, the part that would need to be compressed to lock it into the wall. At this point it stopped moving, and so I hammered a little harder, but instead of going in it just bent over like a cheap penny nail. I tried to drill three more bolts on that wall, and all went the same way, a bent middle finger towards my lack of preparation and overconfidence, and in the end they were my undoing, the dream and the wall undone by a simple lack of skill.

It is vital that all big wall climbers have a basic understanding of how to drill, how to rivet, how to place a bolt. This of course should not be done on any crag but on small rocks and boulders in your garden (a rock that won't rock around and move when being drilled is ideal). A granite rock is ideal for practice but any good sized block is fine, and you should practice with different drill bits, hard and soft, fast and slow, to get an idea how it works. If you're climbing in a new location, such as on sandstone walls or strange alien granite, then consider just drilling a hole somewhere to test how fast and easy it is as this may affect your choice of line, as some rock can be hard like steel while others are soft as sand. Once you've place a bolt and rivet try taking them out again, another skill you may need.

NEW ROUTING

If you're planning on doing a new route then how many bolts should you bring? Well if weight is not a problem, but you aim to climb very long pitches to keep the hole count down, then think about one 10 mm bolt for every 20 metres.

This means for an El Cap sized wall you'd start off with fifty bolts, giving you an average of a two bolt belay every forty metres, where in reality some belays would be natural, while some would be longer or shorter, or only feature a single bolt. For rivets this would depend on what kind of wall you're looking at climbing. For a big wall like the Nose you may not need any lead bolts or rivets, but for some futuristic route you might want to take fifty 8 mm bolts.

Of course these are traditional bolt numbers for traditional belays, and instead you might want to employ a mix of removable bolts and 10 mm bolts, perhaps only having one 10 mm bolt per belay and an 8 mm removable bolt, and bolt ladders using 8 mm removable bolts with a few 8 mm bolts as protection, cutting your bolt load by over half.

Belay Bolt Positioning: Always place bolts with total focus on their practical positioning. Placing bolts at head height when standing on a big ledge may be easy for you, but not practical for the hauling later on, the haul line running over the lip of the ledge. Would higher belay bolts be better (on a narrow ledge), or would a belay placed off the end of the

ledge be more practical (you can place extra bivvy bolts on the ledge later)?

Think about where the bags will be coming up when hauling, and ideally you want to position bolts where the bags will be free hanging all the way. A great example of bad belays and good belays is the Peanut ledge on Zodiac, where you can set up two different hauls, one where the rope is running down a slab (easy to set up but horrible to haul), while the other has the bags free hanging the whole way (harder to set up but easier to haul).

Remember you're creating a work of art here. If you're drilling bolts or rivets for a big portaledge camp (2 portaledges), remember that unless you want them to hang side by side (ideal, but not easy to drill for unless you have a natural ledge to stand on), then having the second ledge bolt placed a little over half a ledge away, and hanging that ledge a little lower, is fine (as stated, drilling bolts six feet apart on a blank wall isn't easy!).

Where To Bolt Your Belay: I would advise that leaders try and bolt at the very end of their ropes, making pitches as long as possible. This increases the sustained nature of the climbing, reduces the hole count, and makes hauling faster. Often this will not be possible, as features will come up mid pitch that demand a belay be taken, so try and factor these into your plan, say having two thirty five metre pitches instead of one sixty metre pitch then a ten metre one to a ledge. When picking an actual spot to drill take into account the follow details.

Are You Drilling Into The Mountain? Bolts must go into the heart of the mountain, not just into its skin or some flimsy flake or feature. Be very aware of just what it is you're drilling into as it's easy to end up with everyone hanging on some house size flake that's only attached by a skin flap of rock. As with expanding or loose rock use your hammer to check that features are sound and check around for hairline cracks.

Where Does The Next Pitch Go? If you're pushing a hard line and the next section is twenty feet of birdbeak tips, do you want to be belaying right in the leader's fall line when you could have had a belay just out of the danger zone? A fall into space is much safer for everyone than having someone smash into your head or having a haul bag check your fall.

Is It Loose? Loose rock is the biggest danger to everyone on a wall, both leader and belayer, so if it's possible having a belay set out of the danger area is vital. If you're climbing a crack and need to drill a belay, going left or right of the crack might mean the difference between life and death.

Roofs Are Good: A belay set under a roof provides protection from storms and runoff, rock fall, and sun, and so is an ideal place to build a belay. This must be balanced with the next pitch, which may have to be shortened due to the drag of crossing a roof.

Is It Classic? Some belays are just meant to be where they are, and can be counter intuitive, such as the space station on the Sea Of Dreams, situated on the lip of a roof, so your legs hang down, your knees banging as you haul. It's a stupid belay, but also funny and memorable.

Ledges Are Always Good: Any ledge, no matter how small, is always welcome on a wall, be it king sized or foot sized. Just remember to drill your bolts high enough so you can stand on it when hauling (you can lower your haul point but you can't lift up a belay).

How Many Bolts Does A Belay Need? In good rock, two bolts should suffice, as a single 10 mm bolt should be strong enough to hold the whole team, so two provides some redundancy. Bolts should be placed around a metre apart so that the belay can be kept as uncluttered as possible, but if a metre is too difficult, then just drill the second bolt as far away as you can comfortably drill.

For bivvy belays you will need three bolts in order to spread everything out, with two being for the belay and the third being for the portaledge. This third bolt can be a modern rivet, but a bolt is better. Remember you may have two portaledges hanging from that single point (backed up from the belay).

If you're climbing capsule style and can make a mixed belay with one bolt and one piece of trad gear, then do so, as you will then be able to fix ropes to the bolt as you progress and reduce the number of bolts used on the climb.

EMERGENCY BOLT KIT

An emergency bolt kit us carried by climbers on walls where they may find rivets or lead/belay bolts have been damaged or are missing. This kit is usually carried deep in the haul bag and stays there unless all other options are exhausted.

The size of the kit varies but a good kit would include:

- 1x Heavy duty bag with clip in loop
- 1x Driver (Petzl Rocpec)
- 2x 10 mm SDS bits (50 mm)
- 2x 8 mm SDS bits (50 mm)
- 2x 10 mm short SS bolts + hangers
- 5x 8 mm short SS bolts + hangers
- 1x Blow tube

This is the bare bones of a bolt kit, with the 10 mm bolts used for belays and the 8 mm bolts used to replace rivets (the fact a rivet is missing probably means someone fell and ripped it out, so maybe a full strength 8 mm bolt is advisable), or add rivets to span a feature that may have fallen off (5 rivets plus two main bolts and the odd drilled edge should span most blank features on existing routes).

An even lighter kit can be put together using a long SDS bit without a driver, the handle formed by wrapping thick finger tape around the shaft of the drill bit (attach a 3 mm clip loop via prusik knot around the bit, then taped over). This kit is small enough to fit in a small pouch in the main haul bag pocket and would comprise of:

- 1x 8 mm SDS bit (150 mm)
- 5x 8 mm SS bolts + hangers.
- 1x Blow tube

If using an SDS without a driver you must be careful not to drive it too hard with your hammer and clean the hole regularly, turning the bit after each strike.

BOLT REMOVAL

The more obscure the route the higher the chance of coming across some junk bolts, and so it's important to know how to remove and replace them. It's beyond the scope of this book to talk about full on bolt removal practices, but rather practi-

cal bolt removal. The simplest specialist tool, say on a wall you know you will be replacing bolts on (i.e., you have bolts to replace old bolts) is a tuning fork.

This is a long thin lost arrow with a 12 mm notch ground through its centre. By placing the tip between the hanger and the rock and hammering on it you can get the bolt to pop out of the rock. If you don't have a tuning fork then a long thin lost arrow without the slot will also work, but you may have to wiggle it out several times and tap from different sides (make sure you have the lost arrow clipped off to something as it can easily spring free when being hammered on).

Some bolts such as Cassin bolts can often be pulled straight out of the rock with a funkness device or tapped out with a hammer. Petzl self drives and spit bolts have very low pull out strength but can suffer from their soft alloy hangers deforming, so having an 8 mm self drive bolt fitted to a small steel hanger makes this easier.

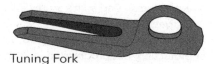

Tuning Fork

To repair holes in the rock (if you leave a hole someone may well fill it with some other junk), then use epoxy putty, ideally sealing the hole with rock dust to make a neat job of it.

RIVETS

Rivets will be encountered on many moderate to hard big wall climbs, most often being a small hangerless machine bolt, alloy dowel or button head rivet. They should not be confused with bolts! They will be commonly used to span a blank section of rock, linking crack systems, or dozens crossing a desert of nothing, placed instead of bolts to save time, weight or cost. Although best viewed as bodyweight placements, they can - and often do - offer you the most secure protection on a very hard pitch. Knowing how to identify and maximise the strength of rivets is vital on hard aid, as well as understanding the ethics of placing your own.

RIVET OR BOLT?

First of all there is really no such thing as a 'rivet', but rather a spectrum of hardware that begins with industrial fasteners made from aluminium, designed for holding signs to walls, and ends with glue in bolts, one rated to three tonnes, the other at, well… the weight of a metal sign. A rivet, in the case of a 1/4 button head, could be viewed as a lead bolt, being rated at 8 kN, while a 'bolt' could in fact be a 5/16 (that's around 8 mm) machine head bolt of undefined length hammered through a 25 kN bolt hanger (set up your hauler on this single bolt and you could have problems). And so it's a grey area where rivets end and bolts begin. I view a rivet as a drilled placement designed not for protection, but progression, a stepping stone, with any protection it might offer simply being a bonus.

RIVET IDENTIFICATION

Rivets, historically being improvised protection, come in many forms, with strength varying dramatically. A common rivet, and the old standard, is the short 5/16 x 3/4 steel machine bolt, bought from hardware shops for a few cents, then hammered into a shallow 17/64 hole (5 to 25 mm deep), creating a non-mechanical bolt or 'bashie' piton. These are easy to spot as they will have a hexagonal head,

but care is needed not to confuse them with power bolts.

Another far too common rivet is the Z-mac, which looks like a button head bolt (but it is not), being manufactured from zinc coated aluminium not steel, meaning it is weak and prone to fractures and bending. These rivets can be identified as they have a steel nail inserted into the head of the rivet (this is hammered home to expand it), and the rivet itself will often look like a time bomb, bent and a little deformed through heavy use.

An even worse rivet is the feared aluminium dowel, placed by climbers such as Harding, Porter and Bridwell. These were either commercial industrial dowels, or cut from lengths of bar, and were hammered into a shallow hole, the end mushrooming as it was bedded down. These are very weak to begin with, don't hold any hanger that well (cinch hangers work best), and become bent and fatigued over time. Climbers have made matters worse by hammering such rivets upwards to make them more secure, which only leads to further fatigue.

You will also come across many improvised and low strength rivets, steel and alloy bars, Cassin and Japanese bolts, or weak small diameter bolts, often without nuts or hangers or both. All non standard rivets should be viewed as suspect and treated as you would A4 protection.

Luckily the new standard is the split shafted button head concrete rivet (usually 1/4 inch, but also 8 mm), which are strong, easy to place, cheap and long lasting. These are easy to spot due to their button head shape (double check it's not a z-mac though).

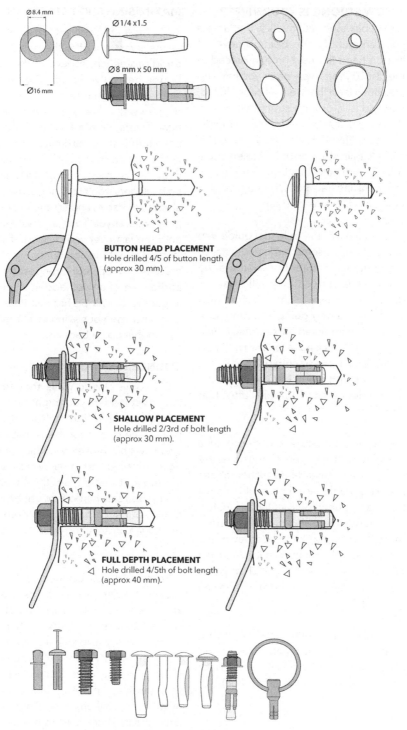

Ø8.4 mm

Ø1/4 x1.5

Ø16 mm

Ø8 mm x 50 mm

BUTTON HEAD PLACEMENT
Hole drilled 4/5 of button length
(approx 30 mm).

SHALLOW PLACEMENT
Hole drilled 2/3rd of bolt length
(approx 30 mm).

FULL DEPTH PLACEMENT
Hole drilled 4/5th of bolt length
(approx 40 mm).

Left to Right: Dowel, Z-mac, 3/4 Bolt, 1/4 Bolt, 3/8 Button, 1/4 Rawl Spike, 1/4 Button,
1/4 Button with washers, 8 mm Stud Bolt, 8 mm Ring bolt.

HOW STRONG IS YOUR RIVET?

One big issue with rivets is that unless you can identify it as being a new 1/4 button head (by new I mean placed in the last 20 years), very often you have no idea how deep the rivet has been drilled, how old it is, or if it's structurally weak. This means that you're forced to blindly trust your life to protection that could be a 22 kN train stopper, drilled deep into a solid 30 mm hole, or a bodyweight only, soft, bent and fractured DIY alloy rivet just going in a few threads deep.

Your eyes are the only real guide you have, as well as some basic understanding of human nature. For example the first rivet leaving a belay will often be drilled very shallowly, either a short rivet used (maybe only going in 5 mm), or a long rivet hammered into a shallow hole (the rivet will stick out a long way). This is because the leader is emboldened by the belay beneath them. But the next rivet will be deeper, and the one after that deeper still.

One way to judge the depth of a machine bolt is if you cannot see the thread, only a thread-less section of bar, meaning the threaded part, which must be long, is buried deeper (unfortunately many long rivets also have full length threads). A button head rivet, even the shortest length (about 30 mm), is strong enough as long as the split shaft is not exposed or the hole is botched, and can be trusted.

I would advise all rivets should be treated with caution and respect and never viewed as bolts (i.e., don't back clean and view a rivet as protection).

MAXIMISING RIVET STRENGTH

On hard aid, with lots of beaks and heads, rivets can offer the possibility of good protection, especially if it's a 1/4 button head. I've taken forty foot falls where all the gear ripped down to the rivet, as well as daisy falls onto machine head rivets, where failure could have been terminal. To maximise the strength of the rivet always use solid rivet hangers if you can, or the thickest cabled hanger if rigid hangers won't fit. Using screamers is always advisable, and try and avoid skipping rivets, as you'll only increase your fall onto the last rivet you clipped. If you're worried about running out of rivet hangers, then use up your strongest hangers at the start of a rivet ladder, where the impact force will be highest (less rope out), and use your skinnier hangers or nuts higher up (or back clean).

BOUNCE TESTING

On some classic walls that feature long rivet ladders you might find every single rivet is different from the one below. The reason for this is that almost every rivet has broken over the years and been replaced - often badly. It's a sobering thought that a rivet, this thing that offers you a safe harbour, might be a time bomb, but such paranoia is perhaps a good idea on anything but a 10 mm bolt ladder.

So should you bounce test rivets? Well first it depends if you have a bolt kit to replace a broken rivet, or a cheater stick to clip past it. Without either you'll be stuffed if you break a rivet, meaning a retreat. My own preference is not to bounce test rivets, but to just climb very carefully up them, clipping every rivet if I can, so if one fails I'll not give an unnecessary shock load to the one I fall on to. The only time I would bounce test a rivet is if I judged it to be questionable, and in a position where failure could be terminal, say a bent Z-Mac at the end of a long section of hooking. Here I would do a bodyweight+ test, rather than a full bounce test which could break the rivet and leave me stranded.

DRILLING RIVETS

I've covered the ins and outs of drilling holes in the bolts section, so as you can probably guess by now, the speed of placement is the reason why rivets are placed as opposed to bolts, well that and cost.

Speed is important if you're drilling rivet ladders to link features, with some routes requiring dozens and dozens of rivets to be drilled, perhaps even hundreds. With a good set up and some skill at bolting, a leader can usually drill a rivet in under twenty minutes, half that if you're only drilling very shallow holes for machine head rivets, half that again if you're drilling sandstone.

The trick to rivet ladders is the ability to get high and drill high, which can be very tiring (stiff boots are important). If you're trying to keep your hole count down then top stepping and drilling at arms length might work for two or three rivets, but make that twenty and you'll be toast. Drilling short small diameter holes (1/4 or 8 mm) is doable, while 10 mm is not, and so often getting high and drilling at shoulder height is more sustainable.

Some would argue that perhaps the age of rivets is over, that first ascensionists must create more future proof routes, with any drilled placements being good for half a century.

A more progressive approach is to simply use full strength hardware in any hole you drill, meaning only ever placing 10 mm or 3/8 stainless bolts. This approach is laudable, as the placing of sketchy machine heads is creating artificial jeopardy, as the first ascensionist knows how far it's drilled, but not those who follow, unsure whether this rivet could hold 10 KN or 1 KN, while a 10 mm bolt is a 10 mm bolt.

This approach might be best for some routes but on hard long new routes carrying hundreds of full sized bolts and hangers would be crazy, as well as very destructive to your arms and bank balance (free bolts and a power drill would be the answer). And so lighter, cheaper and easier to drill full strength rivets, for linking and ladders, and camps have their place, as well as replacing broken or missing rivets.

If a rivet was to fail while repeating someone else's route, say a classic like Mescalito, and you have a bolt kit, what do you replace it with? It is always best to respect the first ascensionist, and place something appropriate, which translates as a 1/4 buttonhead for a broken machine bolt, z-mac or dowel, not a 10 mm stainless bolt. If what has broken could be defined as a standard lead bolt of the day (5/16 button head with a Leeper hanger), then this should be replaced with a modern standard lead bolt (10 mm or 3/8 stainless).

STANDARD RIVETS

Below are what I would define as being the current standard for new rivets.

1/4 x 1 1/2 Powers Button Head

These have become the new standard rivet, replacing machine head bolts, being a simple carbon steel split shank with a mushroomed head primarily designed as an industrial anchor for concrete. The strength of these is around 9 kN, and they are light and easy to drill (1/4 SDS bit) and cheap. A 1 inch version is also worth considering for very long rivet ladders. For European climbers there is also the 8 mm Fixe button head, but I'd stay clear of these as I've had a few problems with them in the past, with the steel being too soft for hard rock (they bend!). When drilling the hole you need a hole deep enough to allow enough room for two washers and a hanger, which is about 1 inch deep (mark the correct depth with tape on your bit). A good way to avoid placing it too deep is to place your two washers and a rivet hanger on the rivet before you hammer it home, stopping before the rivet hanger touches the rock.

Usage: Rivets or lead bolts
Strength: 9 kN (7 kN pull out)
Drill Bit: 1/4 SDS (8 mm SDS for Fixe)

8 mm Stainless Stud Short (50 mm)

This is what I would view as the current alternative to the ¼ button head, and an easier bolt to find for climbers outside of the US (including non metric bits). This style of 'expedition' or 'alpine' bolt is very light, small and compact and quick to drill with an 8 mm SDS, while still providing a very good level of protection on lead (10 kN which is the same as a climbing nut), working both as a classic rivet and as a lead and belay bolt (this means you

only require one set of hardware to do both). Unlike the button head, the quality and component parts of these bolts is more assured (they are fall protection, not just industrial fixings), and will last for far longer if matched to the correct stainless hanger, nut and washers (stainless steel versus the button head's carbon steel). If you wish to use these as hangerless rivets then just leave the nut and washers in place, or use a Moses stainless steel hanger, which weighs only 24 grams, meaning bolt and hanger weighs only 50 grams.

Usage: Lead bolts and rivets
Strength: 10 kN (10 kN pull out)
Drill Bit: 8 mm SDS

OTHER RIVETS:

5/16 Machine Head Rivets

I will cover these here for completeness, but would not recommend their use. This is the old school rivet, a 5/16 machine bolt, with length of around 5/8 (this can vary, and real body weight machine heads can be 1/4). A hole is drilled with a 17/64 bit and then the bolt is hammered into the hole until it bottoms out, the head left sticking out with just enough space between the head and wall to allow a rivet hanger to fit over the head. Some people file the threads down or smash the threads down at the tip in order to allow a fast initial bite, but of course this reduces the pull out strength on the shortest rivets. The sheer strength of these can be very high, with a long stainless rivet placed deep in granite being good for over 10 kN, but a fraction of that for the smallest rivet going in only 5 mm (5 threads!). So with good quality steel rivet hangers these can either hold very big falls or pull out in your fingers, and

Rivet Ladder on New Dawn

for everyone bar the first ascentionists it's hard to tell which. For non US climbers, an 8 mm stainless machine bolt placed into an 8 mm hole will work in the same way, although it will have a much lower pull out strength (it seems impossible to get fractional metric bits and machine bolts).

Usage: Bodyweight rivets
Strength: Varies from 10 kN to body-weight or less!
Drill Bit: 17/64 SDS

WASHERS

The current approach when placing hangerless rivets, such as a 1/4 button head, is to always place two washers onto the rivet. This is so that a cable or solid rivet hanger has more purchase, as in the case of solid hangers the use of small karabiners does not guarantee the hanger cannot fall off. A second advantage is that when the button head needs to be removed and replaced, the internal washer protects the rock when a 'tuning fork' is employed, the outer washer stopping the head of the rivet deforming. The kind of washers needed require an outer diameter of 16 mm and inner of 8.4 mm (M8 washer), US size: OD:11/16 OD / ID 11/32, so they slip over the rivet and accept a 'Lucky' style hanger (check before taking them on the wall).

RIVET REMOVAL

Rivets can be removed the same way as bolts and can be very easy to remove, with the machine head rivet often just being removed by a few taps with a thicker lost arrow (used to pry the hex head out from the wall), or impossible if they're long, leading to the hex head breaking. 1/4 button head bolts are now placed with hangers or with two steel washers, making it easier to remove them, otherwise the button head just

gets mangled. 1970's alloy dowel bolts can be much harder to remove and often require more specialist equipment, and can be so weak they'll simply break when you try and pull them out (or just hang on them!). Be warned though, if you pull out machine head rivets you may be shocked how little they go in, some only by a few threads!

RIVET HANGERS

Rivets traditionally are placed without hangers and so require you to loop or slip a hanger over them, the hex or button head keeping the hanger in place (hopefully). The reason for this is more to do with misinterpreted tradition I think, i.e., that's how it's always been, rather than any real logic.

Harding's rivet ladders were made using aluminium dowels that could not take a normal hanger, and so climbers just followed his lead, placing their own rivets the same way, often with little concern for those who'd come later, or that a route's lifespan could extend over millennia. The upside for these early climbers was it was cheaper to use hangerless junk and required less stuff to be carried on a first ascent (Harding would have required several hundred hangers for the Dawn Wall for example), plus a single one piece rivet, such as a stainless machine bolt, is less prone to corrosion due to mixing and matching metallurgy (the use of washers on button heads could be a problem in this regard, compared to plain button heads). Rivets that have employed very lightweight hangers, such as the classic 1/4 SMC hanger, often crack, creating a time bomb (always check lightweight hangers), meaning the rivet may be sound, but the hanger is not, creating a weak link in the system).

There is also the fact that a rivet can be very hard to spot while leading a pitch, unlike a rivet ladder, which can make the pitch more challenging and interesting, and avoids a 'clip up'. Having climbed a route like Tangerine Trip before it was re-bolted, and experienced A5 rivet ladders (miles of downward bending dowels), then climbed it since, with every full strength rivet having a hanger, I'd say the hanger-less rivet gives a pitch much more spice.

The only way to use rivets is to employ rivet hangers, which come in three types; flexible wire cable hangers, solid hangers (sometimes called RP hangers), and improvised, all having pros and cons. The solid rivet hanger is much better than a wire hanger in all departments apart from flexibility, but often a rivet is placed in a position where a solid hanger can't be used, or has been hammered too close to the rock for the thick metal hanger to slip over the head of the rivet. For this reason, you should always carry a mix of hard and soft rivet hangers.

CABLE HANGERS

Wire rivet hangers are made from differing cable thicknesses, anything from barely body weight 1 mm (3/64) wire (122 kg) to lob stopping 4 mm (5/32) wire (1157 kg). The first rivet hanger I ever bought was some 1 mm cinch hanger, the cable basically what you'd use to re-wire a cam with! We thought it was the bomb and used it on the Shield and Pacific Ocean Wall, and looking back it makes my blood run cold, the strength of the thing not even body weight. We were so dumb we put blind trust in that stupid hanger.

Cable thickness is obviously vital and you need to get the biggest cable you can on the rivet. This does not mean that you end up carrying 4 mm rivet hangers as you'll be using solid hangers on any rivet that allows such a monster rivet hanger to be used, and so instead wire hangers are only employed when the rivet is too tight to the wall for a rigid hanger.

This means that your meat and potato wire hanger will be the #2 (2.38 mm / 454 kg / 4.45 kN) and #3 (3.2 mm / 907 kg / 8.89 kN) wire hangers (these strengths are for a single strand), with only a few #1 (1.5 mm / 174 kg / 1.71 kN) hangers being carried for very tight placements. You can buy #4 hangers (4 mm) for use on belay bolts but I think this is overkill and you'd be better to use a wired nut or two #3s side by side. One last note is that there is some debate whether or not the sharp threads of a machine nut could cut into and weaken the strength of a cable hanger, one more reason to go for hard steel hangers over cable if at all possible.

Quality Control: Some rivet hangers are made by climbing companies such as Fish, Cassin or Yates, while others are made in garages and on picnic tables, with the quality ranging from very high, from people like Bryan Law, who has the tools and skills, to clowns hand cabling with gear designed for fishermen. One cable and swage may look like another, but is the cable matched to the right swage, and has it been crimped with the right sized press, or even crimped at all? What if you've picked up one of these time bomb hangers and it ends up going on that one rivet that's keeping your spine in one piece in a monster fall? This leads to an immediate problem in that there is an issue of trust here, you may buy good hangers from a reputable source, but very soon you add in junk you find along the way. For this reason, I would:

- **Buy Quality**: Only get your wire hangers from people you trust, and personally, I would exclude some companies! For my money, I would only buy rivet hangers from Fish, Bryan Law or Yates.

- **Mark Your Own**: Make sure you know what is yours and what is the junk you find on your travels. There are time bomb rivet hangers out there and just because you find it on the floor doesn't mean you should use it! Spray or mark all your hangers and throw the rest in the bin.

- **Test Your Hangers**: This might sound a little paranoid but giving all your rivet hangers above size 1 a test is a good idea so you can feel a little bit more relaxed about using them. After all, there's enough reason to be scared as it is! Do this before setting off.

Once you've worked out the thickness you need to think about the two main designs of wire hanger:

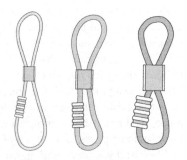

Classic (Closed Loop): The standard wire rivet hanger is made from a short loop (less than 100 mm) of cable, with a sliding sleeve designed to be slid up to lock the wire on the rivet. In reality, the slider tends to slide down and must be taped if you want it to stay put (or tied in place with thin cord), but often just the weight of the quickdraw is enough to keep the hanger on, especially if you use a screamer sling (recommended). The best thing about the loop is that you're getting the most strength out of the cable (the strength is reduced by the tight bend around the rivet), with strengths being around #2 = 4 kN+ (small wire strength) and #3 = 9 kN+ (full-sized climbing wire). The bottom line is stick to #2 and #3 hangers as protection and keep #1 for progression only.

Cinch (Butterfly) Hanger: This is a variation of the loop hanger, having a design that, when one loop is weighted it causes the loop to lock down tight around the rivet, making it ideal for keeping your rivet hanger put, which is especially important if the rivets lack heads (such as with alloy dowels or nut-less bolts). The downside is that these hangers seem to have got a bad rep due to strength problems, with the wire pulling out of the swage of some hangers, but having fallen on them myself, I would view this as being down to a bad batch of swaging, not a problem with the overall design. As the load is coming onto a single strand of wire the strength will be 50% of a looped hanger, but even so a #2 will be good for 2 kN (same as a microwire) and #3 for 4.5 kN (medium wire), which is fine for progression and also for protection as long as it is not critical.

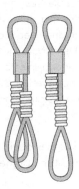

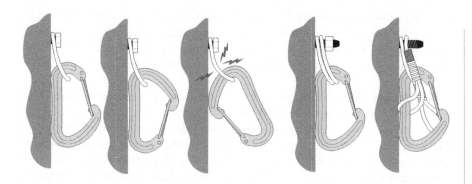

Correct orientation and doubling up hangers on hangerless bolts.

This loss of strength means I would avoid carrying #1 cinch hangers. One bonus use of cinch hangers is their ability to lock tight onto anything that they can be threaded onto, meaning they can be used to exploit broken or damaged cables on nuts and heads, or even used as tie-offs on micro placements, where you want the leverage reduced to a minimum. The self-adjusting nature of the cinch can also be used when you have gear that is very close to each other (such as heads stacked in a seam). To do this just invert the cinch. If the hanger becomes stuck then just yank on the unweighted side of the cinch.

Mix And Match: Don't forget you can put more than one hanger on a rivet or bolt, or mix and match, with a full strength loop being held on with a small cinch hanger for example and both being clipped (just be aware of leverage). This is the best approach if you need to achieve the highest strength possible for belay bolts that lack hangers, with a rigid hanger being secured via a cinch hanger if the nut is also missing.

Cheater Cinch: A very handy gadget is the cheater cinch, a cinch hanger with a 30 cm stiff extension wire swaged onto it, allowing you to reach out of reach rivets, bolts or even pegs. This should feature a clip in point close to the business end, so you don't lose any height, which will make the next placement harder.

Fixed Cable Hangers: One thing you often come across are loop or cinch hangers that have become fixed by a scared leader hammering on the piece's alloy cincher collar, usually to make sure they can't fall off. Such pieces can end up fixed for decades, growing weaker and weaker, and so can be a time bomb. I tend to always chop off the old hanger (use the tip of a beak) and replace it.

KEYHOLE HANGERS

The solid rivet keyhole hanger, made from stamped steel, is a micro bolt hanger, designed to slide over the head of a rivet or button head, the karabiner then helping to keep it locked on. Strength is very high, higher than the rivets themselves, and they are also more dependable than cable hangers, neither failing due to flaws or falling off once you leave them behind (or affected by sharp rivet threads). When using solid rivet hangers be aware that you can create leverage on some rivets that could see the rivet pop off in a fall! Match the hanger and karabiner (and its orientation) to the placement. The keyhole hangers come in two main types:

'RP' Hanger: This style of hanger originally came from Australia where climbs were put up with hangerless 'carrot' bolts (basically, a long machine bolt sharpened to a point and hammered into a hole, leaving the hex end sticking out). The original RP hangers were made by the late Roland Pauligk, who also invented RP nuts, and I guess both did a great deal to push the boundaries of free climbing. Formed from a stamped sheet of stainless steel these hangers are rated around 20 kN and so are stronger than the rivet. The best thing about this design is that the karabiner tends to lie flat against the rock in the same way as when clipping a traditional bolt hanger. At the moment the Moses stainless steel 3/8 is the only commercially available RP style hanger.

use of a lower strength wire cable hanger. Being a little softer these can often be tapped onto rivets but just be careful not to prise the rivet out!

Doubloon: A very specialised little rivet hanger for the connoisseur of dodgy rivet ladders such as you'll find on the Dawn wall, being a bent steel washer with sewn, tied or cabled sling, designed to hook into a single thread or fingernail thickness rivet stud. Fish sell one with a sewn sling, but you can make your own by getting a large 10 mm washer and filing one side of the hole, so it's sharp enough to catch on the dead rivet.

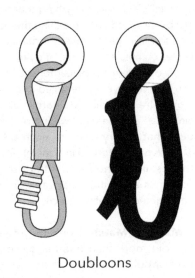

Doubloons

Lucky   RP

'Lucky' Hanger: This design, created by the now-departed Spanish brand 'Lucky', is a simpler and lighter hanger, and one that orientates the karabiner perpendicular to the rock and is weaker than the RP style (around 10 kN). Why not stick to the RP hanger then? Well sometimes a Lucky hanger will go where an RP won't, the next step if neither works the

Keeping Hold Of Your Hangers: All hangers should have a loop of 3 mm cord, or a swaged loop, threaded into them, so you have something to hold onto when cleaning, as they are very easy to drop! Also, mark your hangers with spray paint so the cleaner can identify them from hangers that are fixed.

Carrying Your Hangers: I tend to carry a mix of hangers at all times, having more in my haul bag for longer rivet ladders. On an oval on my harness I'll carry the following;

2x RP	1x #3 Loop
2x Lucky	1x #2 Cinch
1x #1 Loop	2x #3 Cinch.
1x #2 Loop	

A wall can use up a lot of hangers, plus they're easily dropped, so if the topo specifies X number of rivet hangers, I will usually carry twice that amount, 50/50 cable and keyhole, as on some routes you won't be able to use just keyhole hangers.

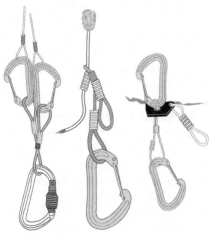

Expanded use of rivet hangers

Improvised Hangers: What do you do if you don't have any rivet hangers? Well, the obvious choice is to slide down your nuts and use the cable, although this is harder these days as many nuts are glued in place. Small wires tend to work best (Wallnut 00 etc.), and you can get a bit more length with a wire than a loop or rigid hanger. If reach is needed than you can thread two wires together, but this can create an even longer distance on the next move, setting you up for quite a struggle. Instead, using a cheater rivet hanger or a cinch rivet attached to your hammer is a better bet. If you run out of options you can use the swage on your beaks if you're desperate, or slings or prusik loops.

HEADS

I've left heads until last as they are probably the most distasteful tools at a climber's disposal, often being a short term and destructive fix. Nevertheless it's vital that all big wall climbers understand how to work with heads, even if they never place one.

Out of all the techniques and dark arts of big wall climbing the one that scares the bejesus out of people, even more than hooking, is copper heading. The very idea of bashing a lump of aluminium, copper, or maybe lead into a crack or corner and making it strong enough to take your weight - well that's some big wall magic trick.

In reality heading is far from being a black art, and like pegging or hooking, is simply a way of using a tool to achieve some mechanical advantage over the rock. By understanding the head, the tools needed to place them, and how each interacts with the rock, you can see that it's not trickery, just a skill like any other.

It's also not really known outside of big walling that heads are ethically dubious, being destructive, leaving trash behind (the head), and often robbing a good placement from a future skilled climber, if used without thought or skill. Heads should be viewed the same way as lead

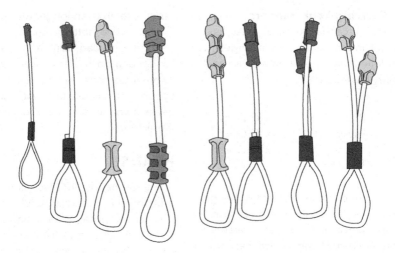

bolts, rivets and holes, as being a last resort, and thankfully improvements in cams, nuts, beaks and cam hooks have dramatically reduced the need for heads.

GETTING YOUR HEAD 'ROUND HEADS

A head is nothing but a swage of metal (a hollow barrel) designed to be used to crimp two wires together, that is swaged to a single strand in order to make a nut that costs pennies and is also very light-weight and short. Here are a few points worth thinking about:

The Head As A Nut: If we left it just as you would a nut what you'd be dealing with are cheapskate nuts, their downside being that the metal used is much softer than on traditional nuts (lead being the softest, then alloy, then copper), and not the ideal shape to create a good contact, although strength wise, in a perfect constriction they'd be close in strength.

Unlike a standard nut you'd have the advantage that the wire is half the length (as well as half the weight), meaning you can get higher than you can on other gear (people often overlook the fact that heads can do double duty as wires). But again in anything but a perfect constricted crack placement the climbing nut will sit better. But here is the advantage of the head over the nut - its size and shape is not fixed.

The Custom Nut: The softness of the head's 'nut' means that you can change its shape in order to fit the placement. This can vary from hammering your head flat so as to slip into a slot, or creating a bend in it to match a cracks deviation, right through to literally pasting the nut so that it grips or presses against every grain of the rock like a limpet. Sure an alloy climbing nut can be hammered to fit, but nothing is as easily fashioned to perfection as a head.

There Is No Magic: It is vital when attempting to use a head that you "get" what it does, otherwise you may falsely believe that magic is in play and proba-bly come a cropper. What is needed are some tools, a selection of heads, time, patience and skill.

Copper, Alloy Or Lead: The strongest head is one made from copper, but this fact also makes it harder to shape and fit, while the softest head is lead, which is one step up from blu tack. The alloy head is a fine balance of the two, being easy to shape and paste while still being strong.

With copper, the shape, once made by hammer and chisel, will be more resistant to being deformed in a fall, and also holds the cable within it with more security. But what point is there in that if the copper is not able to create the shape needed to lock into the rock's weakness, while an alloy head can. A lead head is very easy to mould, like using bubble gum, creating a perfect caste of the crack, but if fallen on you will simply see the wire pull straight through. What to use comes down to a balance between how effective you need the head to be, balancing shaping with strength.

On an easy aid pitch you can get away with a dicey head or two, as you'll have good gear close at hand so ultimate strength is not that important, but on harder aid your life may well depend on the security that a single head may offer, so it's vital you choose wisely. If you're placing a head that is going to perhaps stand between you and a hospital bed then I would try and place a copperhead, but if that placement required some major pasting then perhaps I'd go for alloy instead, maybe even lead if progress (not falling) was more important than protection.

Most climbers carry 70% alloy heads, with the rest made up of copper and maybe one or two lead heads.

Double Heads, Sliding Heads and Equalising Heads: Most heads feature a single swage, but double heads feature two, important for #0 and #1 heads, giving you double the holding power (that's holding power with a small 'h'), well, if you can place both heads. These work very well in very tight seams, but can be problematical in general placements.

A sliding head has one fixed head and a second loose head that slides up and down the cable, giving more flexibility in placement. Yates have a design where you have two equalised heads, which adjust automatically, but again such a head is of more theoretical use than practical.

All can serve a purpose, and there may be that one placement where nothing else will fit, but the standard head is best for 99.9% of the time.

Heads For Protection: When I first started big walling I never clipped heads as I had no idea how I'd place my own head if any of them ripped out, meaning I had some big run outs. If you're doing a trade route and have a short section of heads, or a single head (Zodiac for example), set between good gear, then I would leave the heads unclipped, or only clip the biggest head, and leave the rest. If you take a fall and rip out the head, it is going to take time to replace, so just clip and go. On harder routes with long head sections I would clip every single head, no matter how small, as you never know what will stop you on hard aid. I will often equalise two or three heads with a cordelette mid pitch, adding a screamer to provide a nest of heads. Yes one might pull, maybe two, but not all three when the load has already been

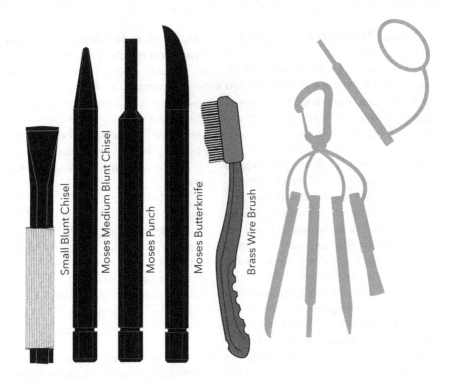

Small Blunt Chisel

Moses Medium Blunt Chisel

Moses Punch

Moses Butterknife

Brass Wire Brush

taken by two heads that had taken your body weight already.

HEADING TOOLS

The tools needed to place a good head range from just a hammer's blunt nose, to the old staple of a lost arrow, to various chisels. Here I'll cover a modern tool kit, leaving out the hammer and the lost arrow, as the hammer tends to be too imprecise and can damage the rock, and many will have a chisel, not a lost arrow.

Medium Blunt Chisel: This is your basic heading tool, a standard 16 mm (5/8) cold steel chisel with the tip blunt so as not to cut into the head and damage the cable. The weight of the chisel is important and I would go for chunky rather than slender unless it's for alpine walls where the weight you have to carry is more important. Make sure the chisel has a wrist loop and wrap with finger

tape to make it easy to grip, with the best commercial design being the Moses 5/8 chisel.

Medium Pin Punch: My favourite - the 6 mm (1/4 inch) pin punch has a smaller circular head, creating a very focused impact point allowing very precise head placements vital for harder heading. I file the sharp edges of the tip of the chisel to make it harder to cut into the head. Again make sure it has a wrist loop and is taped and I would recommend the Moses 1/4 copperhead punch.

Small Blunt Chisel: This is a 10 mm (3/8) cold chisel used for #1 heads.

Head Hammer: A heading chisel weighs around 150 to 200 grams, but a big wall hammer weighs maybe three times as much and can be used like a heavy blunt chisel, the force of the

hammer blow transferred very effectively through into the head, sort of blasting the head into the rock.

Butter Knife: This is used to remove heads, either your own, broken heads, or heads that are blocking clean placements. You can make your own (a chisel designed to remove mortar from bricks that's been sharpened works), but the Moses butter knife is recommended.

Wire Brush: A short super stiff brush, designed for removing rust (not a soft bouldering toothbrush), is handy to clear away crud. Add a clip loop.

Heading Bag: Keep all your heading kit in a heavy duty stuff sack, including a small set of heads on a small karabiner, comprising of:

2x #0 copper	2x #2 alloy
2x #1 copper	4x #3 alloy
2x #2 copper	

You can also include a few double heads (all other heads will be stored in your haul bags). I would not carry this kit on me at all times, and instead just carry a few heads in my hook/beak bag along with the 16 mm chisel, which can be handy for placing beaks.

HEAD RACK

How many heads do you take on a wall? Most topos will recommend the number of heads the first ascent team carried or placed, and so tend to be vastly out, such as '100 heads'.

In reality, on most existing routes that have not been cleaned of all their heads, you may get away with placing no heads at all, or if it's hard then maybe 10. As mentioned, the huge leaps in cams,

nuts and beaks mean that many old head placements can now be utilised by passive gear, heads being used for the really hard stuff, where heads are broken or stripped.

On a new route this is still pretty much the case and I've done A4 climbing where what would have been a head fest in the past ended up being climbed on hooks and beaks, plus the odd bat hook, creating pristine hard climbing with no fixed junk.

Here are some very rough examples of head racks for different routes:

New Route Or Hard Repeat

10x #0 copper
15x #1 copper
15x #1 alloy
15x #2 copper
15x #2 alloy
15x #3 alloy
10x #4 alloy
3x #1, #2, #3 circle head

Hard Trade Route

2x #0 copper
2x #1 copper
5x #1 alloy
5x #2 copper
5x #2 alloy
5x #3 alloy
2x #1, #2, #3 circle head

Classic Route

1x #1 copper
1x #1 alloy
2x #2 copper
2x #2 alloy
3x #3 alloy

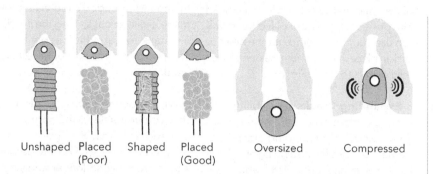

Unshaped   Placed   Shaped   Placed   Oversized   Compressed
          (Poor)   (Good)

THE PLACEMENT

So now we've got the tools we need here's a rundown on making a head placement.

Evaluation: Remember that a head is not magic, it needs something to work with, something to hold it, restrict its movement, or something for the head to exert force against. Try and imagine that instead of a little lump of copper or alloy you've got a tiny little climber attached to the wire. How is he going to cling to the rock? If you use your little man's body like a nut you can just jam him in a constriction, but then why not just use a nut or cam for that? What about in that parallel shallow slot, too shallow and wide to take a beak, or stacked beaks? Stick your mini climber in there and he'll try and jam his body in, like he's climbing a chimney, back and foot, applying an outward force to hold himself there, maybe finding the odd hold or high friction spot to further assist. So let's try that with a head.

Cleaning: Your climber is going to struggle if that slot is full of muck and loose rocks and flakes, so start by scraping and brushing it clean. If it's a dead head then clean it out and brush all the rock dust clear.

Pick A Head And Form It To Fit: Find a head that looks as if it has the best chance of fitting, erring on the larger size. Think about what shape it needs to be to fit like a custom nut, or how it will need to be compressed into the space in order to hold. Now taking into account the shape of the placement use your hammer to shape the head. When doing this you need to decide if the cable will be sitting in or out of the wall. In all cases you want the cable to be as close as possible to the rock so the force is applied straight through the head, with no pivoting. The only exception is if the head is going into a pod or slot you may want it coming out of the front side, so as to reduce leverage. The most usual shape you will want to create is flat on three sides, angled to match the placement, with two sides in contact and one for hammering. If you're wishing to apply an outward force on the rock (a compressed fit), then make sure the head is a little bit too big to go into the slot (think how a fat person jammed into a chimney is harder to budge than a skinny person).

Place It And Paste It: Take the head and place it where you intend it to go. In the ideal placement this custom nut will almost work without hammering, and this should be your aim when shaping. In easy placements with medium sized heads you can simply use the blunt end of your hammer to set and lock the head into position. For harder placements you can use your hammer to get the head to stick in place initially, then use one of your cold chisels to do the rest.

Expanding Cracks: The ability for a head to conform when hammered makes them handy for expanding cracks, the softness of the alloy also being an advantage over smaller nuts. First hammer the head so that it's got two flat tapered sides, like a nut, but not so flat as to undermine the swage's strength. Now, using the chisel, place the head into the crack, ideally into some kind of constriction. What you're trying to do is have the head compressed by the rock. The need to use heads for expanding cracks has been reduced by the availability of cams hooks, especially the fragile hook.

Working The Head: Starting in the centre of the head and working out, use your chisel to bash the head into the rock, the aim to have the inside of the head pushed into a perfect reverse image of the placement. If you don't use enough force you'll tap away and the head will look good, but when it rips out on testing you'll see the back side is almost untouched. Gradually increase the force, working outwards, but not so much as to destroy the head, or break the bond between head and cable. Like a piece of art, the trick is knowing when to stop.

Lead Heads: Due to the softness of lead heads you cannot use a sharp chisel and instead need to used the blunt side of the hammer, or use the flat end of the chisel.

TESTING

Once you feel the head is solid give it a few taps on the top and bottom to see if it rocks around or stays solidly in place. In John Middendorf's big wall book he made a joke about sniffing the head, and if it stank to get off it (people took this literally!). Now you can bounce test the head.

When bounce testing heads it's vital that you understand the nature of that placed head, that the swage that was crimped to the cable is now deformed and is probably no longer applying the same hold over the wire. For this reason when testing you should aim to stick to a force applicable to the head. For example, a #0 head has a breaking strain of between 70 kg and 120 kg (depending on wire used), more than most climbers weigh when racked up. I would consider a #0 as a balance head, and not intended to be fully weighted, so why give it a full on bounce test when you know a heavy test will just see the wire snap? Instead on a #0 I would apply a static body weight load and no more.

Now if it was a #1 head, you're looking at cable strength of around 200 kg, so it should be able to hold your weight if placed well and the swage has enough hold of the cable, but that's it, and aggressive testing will see the wire ripped through the deformed swage. I would test this by applying a body weight+ test, not an aggressive bounce test, so the head should not rip. If I wanted more protection maybe I'd place two heads and equalise with a sliding X or tied off sling and test a little harder.

Once we move into #2 heads we're using cable and head sizes that could well provide full strength protection, with a cable strength of 400 kg or 4 kN. Here I would apply a very solid test, the same with #3 heads (900 kg/9 kN), bouncing the head aggressively, but not repeatedly.

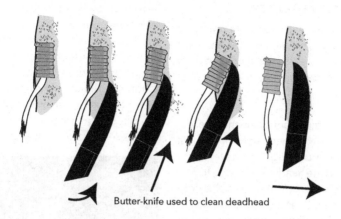

Butter-knife used to clean deadhead

What must be avoided with all head testing is slowly pulling the cable through the head, with each bounce further weakening it. The result is you bounce test it for five minutes, pulling the swage through the head, then get on it feeling happy and the wire rips!

On really hard aid, where you don't trust your heads, maybe a mix of #1 and #2 heads, I will often use three lanyards. I will stand on one head, I will have my body attached to the next head, and I will be clipping the next head. This way if any of the heads are time bombs I will only take a small (or no) fall onto one piece, the aim to keep moving that top lanyard up as fast as I can, so that I'm on three pieces at all times.

CLEANING HEADS

Heads are notoriously difficult to clean and most teams will leave their heads fixed for future parties, as the need for a head often means there is very little there anyway. If you choose to remove heads it can be hard work, and may end up destroying the placement, so think carefully before reaching for your butter knife. Here are the tools you may need:

- **Funkness**: Sometimes, especially with large heads, you can use your funkness to yank out the head. Don't yank too hard, but rather employ short sharp shocks. Be careful not to break the wire or rip the wire out of the head.

- **Chisel**: You can use your chisel in many spots by hammering it under the side of the head, then levering it out, or folding over a head that has had the cable ripped out. You can also use a pointed chisel to chisel the head out.

- **Beak**: You can hammer a beak in behind the head, or into the top, then use this to lever out the head.

- **Butter Knife**: The butter knife is by far the most effective way to remove a head, being a standard chisel with a curved blade ground into it. To remove a head insert the tip into the top or bottom of the head, curved side in, and hammer away until it catches (you need to keep the tip nice and sharp). Once locked in, hammer on the top of the butter knife to prise the head out. Sometimes you might have to do this several times to pop the head.

WHY REMOVE HEADS?

One of the main reasons for removing a head is that you can perhaps replace it with a better head, one that's not rusty or has damaged cables, or is just better full stop.

This is an important point and one less experienced climbers suffer from, just clipping and praying. You never know who placed the head you're trying to use, their skill level, or if they had the right gear for the job, and if you follow someone who knew what they were doing you'll really understand the craft of it. The confidence to look at a placement and think "I can do better than that" comes from experience, but once placed and tested you might feel it was worth the effort.

A secondary factor is that heads are often placed where modern clean gear will go; cam hooks, micro wires, offset cams, hand placed beaks etc, and so being able to get some ancient 'cow head' out of a crack is handy. Make taking heads out part of your training, putting them in, testing them, then getting them out again - and without damaging the rock.

FIXED HEADS

Long sections of fixed heads will be something you need to deal with on many walls, meaning you'll have to get used to creeping up on fixed heads. It's here I've experienced my biggest fears and falls, including a huge plunge off the second hardest pitch of the Reticent wall (graded A4+ which means I should be dead!) when a #0 head pulled two moves from the end of the pitch (sending me almost all the way back level with the belay!). Over the years my approach to

heads has changed, with the way I deal with them being modified by experience, often breaking many of the rules I set myself in order to stay safe on a wall (aggressive testing). On hard aid I treat all heads with the utmost respect, while on speed climbs I'll just switch off my brain and clip and go. Here are some ideas on how to deal with fixed heads:

Rusty Troll Wall deadhead (cable broke, leading to 10 metre fall)

Deadheads: Deadheads are heads that have lost their cable, perhaps because the cable has snapped off in a fall, or ripped out during testing or attempted cleaning. It is generally safe to assume that if this is the case then the head itself must be very well set. After all, if it wasn't, the fall or testing would have pulled it out. These deadheads can either be cleaned out using a butter knife (a slow, tedious affair), or exploited by hammering a small beak just above them, so that its blade pulls down on the head (see modified micro beaks). Using this trick can save a lot of time and can be

Beaks used to exploit deadhead, including filed beaks

vital when you have deadheads in spots where removal would see the placement destroyed.

Don't Judge A Book: Some heads that look bomber and well placed are time bombs, obviously only staying put for the person who placed them, by some force greater than our understanding as climbers! I've seen perfect heads that came out in my fingers or popped on the first bounce test, while others that looked like wall scrap, corroded and nasty, held factor 2 falls. Learning to place heads, especially ripping out heads you've spent an hour placing with the first bounce, will teach you that even if a head looks great, it can easily stink.

Not All Heads Are For Hanging: On the harder routes you may come across 'balance heads', #0 heads placed to hold the leader in check, giving them the extra reach to get a better piece higher up (their feet/weight being primarily held by a lower piece). These heads will look terrifying if you come across one that's fixed, and will live up to that reputation if you try and weight it fully.

Time Bombs And Booby-Traps: Some climbers set bad heads on purpose to fuck up people who just clip and go, especially cheat stickers! These will be heads that look good but are not good at all (some climbers such as Jim Beyer also tape their fixed heads so as to stop them being cheater clipped).

TESTING FIXED HEADS

No matter the age, how solid it looks, or the number of lard asses you know who've passed over it, never trust a fixed head. Treating all heads as suspect will go a long way to limiting the chances of a fall, but don't go too hard on them!

Eyeball Them First: Take a look at the head before you jump on it. How well is it placed? How rusty are the wires? Is the head corroded (if it's green it's been there a while). Can you see the end of the wire at the bottom of the head? Damaged or rusty wires tend to be a big cause of failure, with a single strand of wire able to hold around 5 kg (try and do the maths), when you've got half of them rusting off on a #2 head it's probably going to snap under your weight, meaning it needs to be replaced. My rule of thumb is that if something weak and crap is also rusty it's going to blow when I'm on it, and so far it's always been true (they did blow and I did fall).

Testing The Head: Unless you are on a very long string of heads, I would go for the skyhook style of test when it comes to fixed heads, being bodyweight plus a bit. This should tell you that the head is good enough for a careful and well executed move, but perhaps not a fall.

To do this I usually clip in my lanyard, weighting the piece with my full body weight (holding my lower piece as a backup). Once I've hung on it for a second or two, I'll increase the force slightly (with a small bounce or by pushing back on my harness), until I feel it's going to hold.

This approach works well when it comes to passing short sections of fixed heads, as over-testing could lead to an adequate head being ripped out, resulting in time wasted, and potentially a worse placement (old trenched heads). Note: On big sections of fixed heads (Aurora for example) I would probably give the bigger heads a full bounce test, just to convince myself I would survive a fall!

Moving Up: On fixed junk, and hard aid, the trick is to keep the force of your body moving level so as not to exert a high peak force on the gear. This means moving fluidly. You need to keep all your gear untangled, and have your spare daisy ready to clip the next piece as soon as you can, both to increase speed (the quicker you get off fixed heads the better), and as a backup to the piece you're on blowing.

ETHICS

Heading is viewed as being at the core of hard aid with all young tigers dying to bash those heads in. In reality modern hardware has reduced the need for about 50% of heads placed in the past, with offsets, micro cams and beaks taking their place. This means that a head should be viewed like a lead rivet or bolt, and only placed when there is nothing else.

Beyond that there are some other ethical considerations.

Manufacturing Head Placements: There might come a day when you're faced with a blown out head that cannot be replaced, especially a tiny head set within a small feature, like small flare in a corner. Here you've got a dilemma. If you can't climb past it you will need to drill a rivet, bat hook, or make your own head placement by trenching. This is a tricky moral dilemma, but many a hard wall was climbed with trenched heads in order to maintain the grade. Trenching is basically chiselling or drilling a channel/trench into the corner so as to create a slot into which you can compress the head. One way to do this is to drill two shallow 8 mm / 1/4 inch holes one above the other, then hammer the head. On really small #1 heads you will need to use the edge of your chisel or sharp butter knife to chisel out a groove, which should be narrower than the head, but a little deeper.

Bat Heads: This is a variation of bat hooking and trenching, where a hole is drilled and then a head inserted and hammered into place. The strength of these is strong enough as the head is being pivoted, but once the cable breaks you're left with a crappy lump of alloy or copper in a hole. Using bat heads will not only destroy the pitch but also your reputation. The only way to use a head like this is as a passive nut in a hole or pocket, as being round they will go where a squared nut won't, keying into the hole (just don't hammer it in any way).

KARABINERS

In the early days of big wall climbing the default krab of the big wall climber was the oval. These krabs were big, heavy and often not that strong when compared

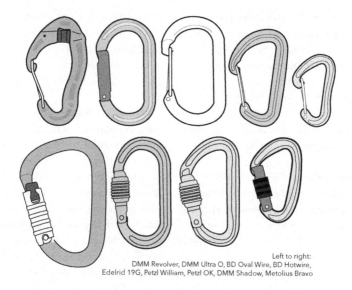

Left to right:
DMM Revolver, DMM Ultra O, BD Oval Wire, BD Hotwire,
Edelrid 19G, Petzl William, Petzl OK, DMM Shadow, Metolius Bravo

to a D shaped krab, but they were cheap, often army surplus, and didn't shift or snap when loaded.

Then the introduction of the wire gate krab started a revolution in karabiners, with a move towards lighter and lighter krabs being possible without a corresponding loss of strength (as had been the case with 9 mm bar krabs in the '80s). Forged bodies, keyhole noses and leaps in what climbers would accept as functional and practical sizes has seen the weight of karabiners come down in some cases by 50%.

Now we have full strength karabiners that weigh 19 grams, with the average being less than 30 grams, important numbers when you consider just how many karabiners are carried up a route.

The Big Wall Karabiner: There is no one style of karabiner for wall climbing, and due to the need for a vast army of krabs, often the perfect krab is any krab you can find. If you can be more discerning, then weight is the crucial aspect as

you could be carrying up to a hundred krabs on a hard wall, meaning kilograms can be shaved off your rack with the right krabs.

My ideal karabiner for hard aid weighs between 19 to 25 grams, meaning I can carry three krabs for the weight of one old school krab. Black Diamond, Petzl, Camp and Edelrid all make micro krabs that are ideal for wall use.

For less than extreme walls, where you will be free climbing and using guerrilla techniques, a standard sized krab works better, as it makes clipping a little easier in extremis (on hard aid you'll have two hands, while on easy aid you often only have one).

Number Carried: A big wall can eat up your karabiners, seeing you finish some pitches with only your belay device left, while on other pitches you can finish with almost all your rack unused. On a standard wall you will probably want to be carrying around 15 to 20 quickdraws and alpine slings, meaning about

40 karabiners. You will also have one on each cam meaning at least another 20, but maybe up to 40 or 50. Then you have racking krabs for nuts adding maybe 1 to 5 more, plus krabs to hold beaks, pegs, heads, rivet hangers, adding another 10 to 20. And so for a standard wall I would aim at getting together around 100 krabs, plus half that again for a harder wall.

Large Lockers: These are your large HMS krabs, ideally forged, used for masterpoints, belay devices and self rescue (vital for the Monster Munter knot). On a wall you will need one per belay kit, plus I would make sure each climber had a personal large HMS as their belay device krab. The beauty of such krabs is their capacity to hold many knots and hitches, only at the expense of weight.

Number Carried: 1 per belay kit (usually 2 belay kits per team), plus 1 per climber.

Standard Lockers: These are your classic D shaped medium karabiners, high strength but with a more limited capacity to hold knots, often only a single clove hitch or two or three bights of rope. These are good for secure connectors that will not be called on to hold too much, connecting haul bags to each other for example, ledges to haul tethers, or as guide belay device auto lockers. Although smaller than the HMS, these krabs are still easy to use, making them better than micros for clipping gear under a haul bag.

Number Carried: I would work on each climber being allocated five standard lockers each (not including their aider lockers), then two per portaledge (one on the ledge and one on the ledge's haul bag), and three per haul bag (one on the

suspension, two for under it), plus one per belay rig. On a normal wall such as the Nose, with a three person team this would give you around 20 lockers, while on a harder wall this would go up to 30.

Micro Lockers: These are screw-gate versions of micro plain gates, and although small and light, are really only good for the smallest of loads, only just able to handle a single clove hitch when using a large rope. These are ideal for where you want security but at the lowest weight penalty, and make good lockers for such things as racking ascenders, your prusik loops and as the tie off to your zip or haul line when pre threaded through your PCP. The downsides are they are fiddly and can be easy to fumble, or be hard to clip into large slings or ropes, making them unsuitable for general tasks.

Number Carried: I would allot three per climber and add another 5 to 10 for the team for various tasks.

NOTES ON KARABINERS:

Distinctive Krabs: It's worth having a handful of very distinctive and colourful krabs in your rack in order to identify key pieces. For example I keep my nut tool on a bright yellow Kong wire gate whose shape and colour is unlike my other krabs, meaning I can both see and feel it when I need it. The same approach can be used for hammer krabs, offset nuts, ascenders, each item easily identified on your rack, both by feel and by sight.

Looking After Your Krabs: Before each wall wash and lubricate your karabiners, as well as make sure they are marked as your own (with tape, paint or via a Dremel).

Damaged Krabs: Karabiners can become damaged on a wall quite easily, with big falls on pegs or bolt hangers making small nicks in the smooth load bearing areas of the krab. If these become very worn you can end up either weakening the krab or damaging the rope, so after each wall go through your krabs to check they're OK.

Loose Krabs: It's always worth carrying six loose krabs, chained together, as these will be used when equalising pro and at belays. Other loose krabs are kept at the belay. If I run out of draws near the end of a pitch I will begin to cannibalise karabiners from cams on my harness.

MAILLONS (QUICK-LINKS)

These are ideal for connections that require the highest degree of security but do not require constant clipping and unclipping. 10 mm alloy maillons work very well, being light but strong (better for cross loading than a karabiner). It's worth adding a wrap of finger tape to the locking barrel to aid in untightening (you can use another maillon as a spanner if need be).

SOFT SHACKLES

These are less well known in climbing, but used a lot in sailing and paragliding, offering a very strong but flexible connector. Most commonly made from material such as Amsteel, the cord has a spliced eye in one end and a diamond knot in the other, with the knot being locked in place once inserted into the eye (use rubber bands or whipping cord to keep it in place). Places where you might want to use a soft shackle include places where twisting can be a problem, such as your top pulley connector in a Chongo 2:1 or your PCP.

QUICKDRAWS, SLINGS, TIE OFFS, AND EXTENDERS

A big wall eats up karabiners, especially lockers, and on even a moderate wall you will have around 100 snapgates in your rack on cams, draws and other gear, and at least 20 lockers. How many draws you need on a wall depends on how hard the route is, as on a wall like the Nose you run out a lot of pitches, meaning you could probably get by with ten draws, while one pitch on a climb like the Sea of Dreams might require thirty! In either case it's pretty vital that you don't run out, which means having a flexible system, with a good base, then the ability to scavenge and cannibalise.

SLING AND EXTENDER LENGTHS

On a big wall you are always trying to have gear that is multi functional and adaptable to many different placements and situations. Take the humble 60 cm ("4 foot") Dyneema sling. This one sling can be used for the following:

- 60 cm sling for slinging spikes
- 60 cm extender
- Equalising sling
- 30 cm alpine extender
- 20 cm alpine draw
- Larks footed into piton
- Basket hitch to a cam
- Cows-tail into your belay loop
- Prusik
- Abseil tat
- Bandolier
- Foot-loop

This adaptability is important in all aspects of what style of draws, slings or tie offs you carry on a wall, which can range from a dozen to close to fifty for big gnarly nail ups. Below I'm going to go through the basic types and styles of equipment carried.

Short 'Sport' Quickdraws

I'd class these as being between 10 cm to 18 cm and sewn closed, and designed for general climbing. Being short and sewn they can only ever be used as quickdraws and nothing else. If the wall has a lot of free climbing and you're using double ropes than there is a place for 18 cm draws, as they remain neat on your harness and don't dangle down too far, but on long complex pitches with a single rope you're better switching up.

Number Carried: 4 to 6.

30 cm Sewn Slings

These are sewn open in a loop and can be clipped up as 30 cm quickdraws or made into short double loop 15 cm draws. This flexibility in size means it's possible to adjust where the krab sits, say if at 30 cm it is running over an edge, by shortening it you locate it properly. A 30 cm extender, being open, can also be extended easily by clipping in another 30 cm or 60 cm sling, something not so easy with more sporty draws. Being open also allows the extenders to be larks footed, clove hitched, basket hitched or threaded through gear, or slings, or even used to equalise two pieces close together (say two heads that are placed one above the other). Skinny dyneema works best, but with lightweight krabs the rope krab can spin into a cross loading position, so I always use a rubber keeper, like a Petzl 'string' on this end. On hard nail ups I might forgo making these into quickdraws, but instead carry them in bunches of ten, with the krabs chained beside them.

Number Carried: Unless I'm climbing a route like the Nose where I know there will be a lot of back cleaning, and so very few extenders used, as a minimum

I will carry 15 30 cm slings, and bump this up to 20 if on hard aid. This might sound a lot but on a really hard aid pitch you might have one piece every metre for fifty metres (or longer), meaning you end up calling on all your draws, slings and screamers. Another reason to carry more than you need is that you will end up dropping quickdraws.

30 cm Tie Offs (Keeper Cords)

These are 30 cm loops of tape or cord that are tied, and used on hard aid where you might be stacking gear, used as keeper cords, untied and threaded through all your pieces or fixed gear (like RURPs or beaks that have lost their wire). They are also viewed as being more disposable then sewn slings and so are traditionally left at lower out points. My personal preference is to use cord tie offs as I feel they are more robust.

Number Carried: I will carry an assortment of cord and tape made into loops between 20 and 30 cm. As a guide I would carry:

- 1x 30 cm loops of 2 mm Dyneema (SWL 120 kg)

- 4x 30 cm 3 mm Dyneema (SWL 375 kg)

- 4x 30 cm 4 mm Dyneema (SWL 490 kg)

- 4x 30 cm 5 mm perlon (SWL 550 kg)

- 1x 30 cm 5.5 mm Dyneema (SWL 1800 kg)

Note: All Dyneema cords need tying with a triple fisherman's knot.

60 cm Sewn Slings

These are vital on a wall, and are usually made into alpine draws. A good trick when speed climbing or where you only have a two bolt belay, is to just make a belay using two 60 cm slings, bringing them together to create your master-point, which means you have no knots to untie (remember any knot added to a sling is making it weaker).

Number Carried: I will take between five and ten 60 cm slings on a wall, with four to six being used as alpine draws.

120cm Sewn Slings

I find these less useful on most walls, and find carrying more 60 cm slings and just doubling them up is more flexible, but they do have their uses. These are of most use for making long extensions to far off pieces, such as under roofs, so as to avoid rope drag, and are also good for making mini equalised nests of gear on hard aid.

Number Carried: I will take just two 120 cm slings (unless I know the ground will be highly complex), using linked 60 cm slings or my cordelette if I need more.

240 cm Sewn Slings

These are nice and compact on your harness and are great for complex natural belays, and some climbers will prefer these to bulky cordelettes if that's what they're used to. The downsides are that you won't want to chop them up for rap anchors, they are much more limited for self rescue (you cannot create releasable knots in a sling), and they can be harder to untie when heavily loaded.

Number Carried: One carried by each climber if they don't want to use a cord-elette, or if this is what they're used to using. One spare for the team.

240 cm Cordelette (Personal)

Each climber should carry a cordelette on their harness, both for belays and for self rescue, and a hundred other things, plus have one spare for the team.

Number Carried: One per climber plus 1 spare for the team, min diameter 7 or 5.5 mm Dyneema.

240 cm Super Cordelette

For big teams (3+) I would go for a beefier version of the 7 mm cord-elette, using full strength climbing rope between 8 and 9 mm. These would not be carried by the leader, but sent up with the belay kit.

Number Carried: 2

RACKING YOUR SLINGS

I would avoid carrying any slings over your shoulder as they provide another hang hazard and invariably get hung up on hooks, beaks or your hammer cord. Instead try and either make slings into alpine draws, or clip them in twisted bunches and rack them (having multiple colours of slings makes them easier to sort). Some climbers rack their 60 cm slings on a single krab and clip it into the shoulder of their gear sling, then through them over their back. My own preference is to twist them up and clip them off to my harness.

FIXED SLINGS

Treat all slings you find as being highly suspect, even if they look brand new. A new sling could have been used to bail on, with a rope pulled through it melting the dyneema or nylon. If you come across dropped slings I'd also advise caution, as they might not have been dropped, but rather thrown away off a route. Nylon is heavily affected by UV light and its strength decreases rapidly. This means if you see a fixed sling try and avoid cheater sticking it, but rather climb up and replace it as the first ascensionist did. The most common place to find such slings is on lower outs and pendulum points (something unnecessary if you use a cleaning cord), often with several pieces of marginal webbing larks footed into one another and just creating wall trash. All such slings should be viewed as suspect and cut away and replaced by a krab or maillon. If cutting fixed slings and tat loose, be very careful of your knife near your loaded rope.

INSPECTION

After each wall inspect all your slings for nicks and damage, easily done when hammering a peg for example. In the future your life might depend on that sling.

SHOCK ABSORBERS

One of the most important things to understand on a big wall are peak forces and how they relate to the breaking point of your safety chain (rope, krab, sling, beak, rock etc). I cover this in fall dynamics but it's vital to keep peak force as low as possible, which can only be done by spreading that load over the greatest length of time, so force ÷ time. In the climbing safety chain the rope is the main stretcher of time, its dynamic qualities acting like a big sponge, the skinnier the better. How else can you add more time to this equation? One method is to use screamer slings, slings that are designed to rip apart when heavily loaded.

How Do They Work? Most screamers take a long sling then slowly fold and stitch, concertina-ring it down to about a fifth of its length. Each stitch is rated to around 2 to 2.5 kN, so body weight, and if loaded will break, closely followed by the next, and then the next, and on and on until the load drops below 2 kN, ideally having absorbed 4 - 8 kN of force. Now if you have a screamer sling clipped

into a #1 copperhead that is only body weight, then activation will never happen, as the head will rip before the first stitch breaks. But make that a #3 head, that has a potential holding power of 3 kN, and a screamer may well tip the balance in your favour.

Getting The Most From Screamers: The most important aspect of screamer use is to always use wire gate karabiners or lockers, as the vibration from the ripping action can make solid gates 'flutter'. A second way to maximise their performance is to use DMM Revolver karabiners on the rope end, as these further increase the rope's ability to travel dynamically. It's worth noting that the higher you go on a pitch the more rope you have out, meaning the rope can absorb more of that impact force. This means that screamers are best deployed earlier rather than later, with standard draws and slings working as well once you're halfway up the pitch.

Screamer Types: There are two main screamer types, general and hard aid.

General ripper slings are designed for ice climbing, and marginal but still solid gear (micro wires, fixed pegs, old bolts). The most common examples of this type of screamer are the Yates Screamer and the Petzl Nitro 3, and both work well.

The only dedicated aid screamer, designed for bodyweight gear, is the Yates Scream Aid. This small screamer activates at 1.5 kN and features an integrated tie off loop as well as double clip loop, allowing you to test without activating the screamer. The downside of the scream aid is its full strength is only 7 kN (when ripped open), and it only absorbs up to 2 kN, so should only be used for

Screamer slings on Sea of Dreams

small heads, hooks, dowels and size 1 beaks.

All screamer types can also be clipped sequentially, with one general screamer clipped into a scream aid for example.

Number Carried: On a trade route I'd probably not carry any unless I knew there could be marginal fixed gear (such as crappy fixed heads), old bolts and rivets. If this was the case then perhaps I'd take 3 general screamers and 2 scream aids. For harder walls I will take a lot more, perhaps as many as 10 scream aids and 10 general screamers, even more if the route was super spicy, using these early in the pitches.

Do They Work? There are all sorts of tests out there showing that these devices work or don't work, or work a bit. Often these tests are biased towards one area of climbing, such as ice climb-ing, where screws are so strong in reality that screamers are not necessary. Other tests show that in trad climbing the skinny half rope does all the work anyway. But none of these tests are looking at big wall climbing, where long complex pitches with dozens of placements can result in the rope's ability to absorb shock being reduced, or where the ropes used (10 mm+), are far less dynamic than a 7.5 mm rope. Having taken falls onto screamers clipped to marginal gear (heads, hooks, beaks), and seen a partial activation (half the stitches ripped), I can only think that they do work, and are a crucial part of the whole safety chain. Another perhaps more important factor, is that there is a huge psychological element in using these slings, looking down at a long string of them below you as you beak and head upwards. Often aid is more about the mental than the physical, the kilo Newton less important than a string of sewn nylon lucky charms.

FALL FACTOR	ROPE IN SYSTEM	FALL DISTANCE	IMPACT FORCE TO CLIMBER	IMPACT FORCE TO ANCHOR w/out SCREAMER	IMPACT FORCE TO ANCHOR with SCREAMER & SHORTY	IMPACT FORCE TO ANCHOR with ZIPPER/ PETZL NITRO
2	10m	20m	9kN	9kN	6kN	3kN
1.99	10m	19m	8.9kN	15kN	12kN	9kN
1.7	10m	17m	8kN	14kN	11kN	8kN
1.5	10m	15m	8kN	13kN	10kN	7kN
1	10m	10m	6kN	11kN	7kN	5kN
.5	20m	10m	5kN	8kN	5kN	2kN
.33	30m	10m	5kN	7kN	4kN	2K
.25	40m	10m	3.7kN	6.3kN	3kN	2kN
.125	40m	5m	3kN	5kN	2kN	2kN
.1	40m	4m	2.8kN	4.6kN	2kN	2kN
.05	40m	2m	2.3kN	3.8kN	2kN	2kN

CHEATER STICKS

Cheater sticks as the name implies are cheating…but sometimes they can come in very handy, bypassing ground when you find yourself out of your depth, or when you have to retreat (Note: No party should ever embark on a steep big wall without some form of cheater stick).

The problem with having a fully functioning cheater stick (rather than a makeshift one that needs to be dug out and put together) is that it robs you of the chance to push yourself on hard aid, bypassing moves that you may be able to do, but dare not. Often it's only doing such moves that enables you to progress in aid climbing.

A second problem is that making cheater stick moves can put you in harms way, as often it's hard to test a far off piece, meaning you may end up falling anyway, and sometimes a very, very long way. The one time I remember really finding a cheater stick a lifesaver (in retrospect), was hooking past the big loose flake below the roof on Iron Hawk. Having hooked half way up it, I suddenly heard it groaning, with the sound getting louder as I weighted my first cam. Terrified I backed off the cam, and used my stick to clip a rivet higher up. Of course I felt guilty at the time, but when a year or so later the flake fell off and nearly killed the leader and belayer I felt a little more justified in my actions. I've also used a cheater stick on a winter ascent of the Nose, to clip the bolt at the top of a very icy Texas Flake. The problem with cheater sticks is that yes, you can overcome some impasse (physical or mental), but once you do it your mental fortitude will crumble, and the next impasse may not be cheatable. Another factor is that on very

Karabiner / Hook
fitted to cheater stick

hard aid it's vital you put in the effort, as you're creating a foundation of moves, pro and understanding of how the pitch is playing out, which is lost if you start trying to cheat yourself up a pitch.

TYPES

Cheater sticks come in all sorts of shapes and sizes, with most being modified poles, and a few being designed for just that role. Here's a run down of sticks in order of reach and function.

- **Dedicated Cheater Stick**: A few companies make these, designed for sport climbers, featuring karabiner holders that allow the krab to be kept open, close and detach. The downsides with these are they're quite heavy and expensive if you're only going to use it in an emergency.

- **Avalanche Probe**: This is a very light-weight and compact option and one I prefer. To employ this you will need to rig up something to clip onto the end, and tape open the karabiner. Once clipped the stick will remain attached until you unhook it.

- **Portaledge Fly Pole**: Most fly sheets have a pole these days, and although bendy, they can make OK makeshift cheater sticks (halving the pole and taping together will give a shorter but stiffer cheater stick).

- **Trekking Pole**: Many climbers carry a ski pole for the approach and descent, and these can be used as makeshift cheater sticks pretty easily, often just by taping a krab or hook to the end.

TECHNIQUE

So you have a cheater stick that you can snare some distant object with, but what next? Here are some options:

- **Lead Rope**: If you're clipping a bolt or something 100% secure then you can just clip your lead line in via the cheater stick, then just yard yourself up the rope. The downside of this would be if the piece was to fail you'd fall a very, very long way.

- **Haul Line**: Works the same, but you won't fall as far. To use this you will need to clip the end of the line from the back to the front of your harness.

- **Aider**: This is the best option, as it allows you to test the gear as well. To do this clip a line of aiders together, then after testing via the aiders climb up them.

- **Knotted Sling/Cordelette**: Create a line of large figure of eight knots up the rope or sling, then aid up these (if the knots are too small they'll pop out under load).

ETHICS

Using a cheater stick when climbing, unless it was used on the first ascent (several routes feature cheater stick hook moves), pretty much robs you of any bragging right, and will also destroy your reputation if anyone sees you doing it. Reaching for a stick is always the easy way out, so make sure it's buried deep in your haul bag, for emergency use only.

HEIGHT MULTIPLIERS

Here are three non-cheater stick methods of adding a few extra inches (not all climber are the same height!):

Stiff Draw: A not quite cheater method, much beloved by the short, is a stiff quickdraw, a quick way to get around moves that are just out of reach. To make one of these just insert a length of stiff material (clothes hanger) between the two strands of a 30 cm draw, then tape it in place, as well as tape the top karabiner so it stays in position. Some people tape open the top karabiner, but I tend to use Velcro to keep it open.

Kong Panic: This is a dedicated stiff draw that comes in 30 and 45 cm lengths, and features a top krab that can be locked open, but locks down again when weighted. This is a must have piece of gear for all big wall climbers. I would also recommend adding Velcro to the top karabiner, as well as the top of the sling, so nuts, hooks and rivet hangers can also be used.

Hammer: My favourite reaching tool these days is my hammer, as it's always at hand, is very solid, and doesn't feel too much like cheating. To set up, glue an inch of soft sided Velcro just under the hammer head, then wrap a long narrow (1 cm) strip of hard Velcro around this. Using

Stiff draw and stone stack used on first pitch of Prodigal Sun

this Velcro you'll be able to attach krabs (gate held open), wires, hooks and rivet hangers, and this method has proved a life saver for me many times.

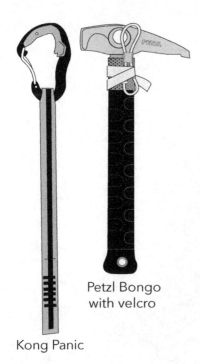

Petzl Bongo
with velcro

Kong Panic

RACKING

Unless you're speed climbing routes with only a skeleton rack (two sets of cams and a few nuts), then you're best to employ a chest harness. The pros of a chest harness are many:

- **Access**: Having your rack high allows you to more easily check out what gear you have, as well as have some items more forward than is possible with a waist harness. You can also clip off gear to the front of the chest harness, and have items ready for the next move right at your fingertips.

- **Organisation**: A typical chest harness will have more racking real estate, with

the classic Yates chest rig featuring four large racking loops, two bandoliers and numerous other clip points, allowing you to fine tune your racking.

- **Drag**: Many big wall pitches can be very long, which when added to a very heavy waist harness, can lead to your harness being pulled down. By lifting the weight up to your chest this becomes less of an issue.

- **Top Stepping**: A chest harness can be used to pull your upper body into the wall.

ORGANISING YOUR RACK

The big wall rack will generally be split into three parts; the primary 'active' rack the leader is using, the secondary 'reserve' rack, and the tertiary 'support' rack.

Primary: This can either be everything you think you might need for the whole route, say micro wires to Camalot 4, or what you need for just the pitch, say just heads, hooks and micro cams, or only what you need for the first third of the pitch, just hooks and rivet hangers for example. Which option you choose comes down to how big your overall rack is, and also how hard the climbing is. For a route like the Nose or Lurking Fear your rack will only be a little larger than a free rack, so it's possible to carry most of it, and doing so saves time, especially if short fixing and climbing in blocks. On a hard wall your rack could weigh twenty kilos, with dozens of pitons, heads, hooks, four sets of cams etc, meaning carrying the lot is not an option. And so your primary rack should be kept to a weight that is manageable and won't slow you down, with the zip or haul line used to replenish your rack from your secondary rack at the belay.

Secondary: This rack is kept at the belay and needs to be easy to access (so not buried deep in a haul bag). The best method for this is to clip a spare daisy chain between two belay points and clip your rack across it (avoid using anything attached at only one point, or stringing a sling between two points but clipping the gear into both strands, as both these methods could lead to you losing your whole rack, and this has happened!). This secondary rack will be stowed in the haul bag in between pitches. Another option, if the spare rack isn't too large, is to rack it on a second chest harness (remember again that racks should always be clipped to the belay by two points, never one), and have the second jug wearing it, racking the gear they clean on this as they go. This way when they get to the belay, they have everything needed to both replenish the primary rack, and prepare for the next pitch. This is important if short fixing, or if you want the leader to set off before the haul bags arrive (the secondary rack is not in one of those bags).

Tertiary: This lives in your haul bag, and covers gear you might not need, or only need on one pitch. This includes your bolt kit, large cams, spare beaks, Lost Arrows and sawn off pegs. It's best to put each type of gear in its own stuff sack (pitons, beaks, cams), within a larger easily identified bag with a full strength clip loop.

FINE TUNING YOUR GEAR SLINGS

As with your free climbing racking, honing your big wall chest rig comes down to personal preferences, and often this can change depending on the route style or rock (it's best not to be too dogmatic, but instead adapt to each route or even pitch).

When racking, it's important to try and balance things out, and of course have gear that's used regularly around the front, less used gear at the back. It's not necessary to stick to the free dogma of everything having its own karabiner, but instead treat your cams like you do sets of nuts, clipping the less used pieces into one karabiner. For example I tend to carry my offset cams on a single krab (one full set per krab), as well as my C3s and smallest cams (black and blue Alien), viewing them as more 'trick' gear.

When it comes to hooks and cam hooks I try and reduce the chances of losing them all by making sets, so one locker containing a BD Grappling hook, narrow Cam hook, and a medium beak (for hand placing), with another locker having the same, swapping out the beak for a BD Talon. The idea is to reduce the cramming of your racking loops, which just leads to frustration. I'm also a fan of colour coded karabiners, both for my cams, as well as everything else.

ZIPLINE

This is a thin rope, most often a thin half rope, designed to pass gear up to the leader, avoiding the full weight of the haul line, which can feel considerable at the end of a long pitch (the total weight of the lead line is spread out over all the protection, but the haul line is just free hanging).

On some pitches, you might start off with almost nothing on your rack, and have gear sent up every ten or so metres, or take enough for the first half of the pitch, then replenish from the rack at the belay. The gear that's sent up most often are quickdraws and cams, as it's better to start with fifteen draws rather then thirty.

It's best if the second knows what you might need beforehand, so they can sort it out at the belay, shouting down something such as "I'll need as many krabs as possible" in plenty of time, gives the second time to strip down other gear to send them up, or dig into the haul bags for extra gear.

How Much Gear To Leave Behind: The famous big wall climber Warren Hollinger always advised having enough gear on your harness to deal with anything, as on hard aid you might not be able to wait for the right piece to come up. If taking this approach then fit that 'do it all' rack to the rock type. On granite this would probably be at least one of every piece from a beak up to a Camalot 2 (you can often find odd, hidden, big cam placements on even blank looking cracks). You should view this as being a pear shaped rack, with two or three pieces between 0.5 to 1, two of each smaller piece down to beak size, but only one of each piece above, such as just one Camalot 2 and 3.

Pulling Up The Gear: Unless the rack you're pulling up is super heavy, you can do this hand over hand. When clipping in the rack to send up avoid overloading a single karabiner, such as ten cams clipped into one locker, and rather tie an overhand knot with a large 60 cm bight of the rope, and clip each piece into it, using the loop like a sling. When it arrives,

the leader can put it over their shoulder, transfer the gear to their harness, then untie the knot and send the rope back hand over hand. If clipping individual items I tend to avoid clove hitches, as in small krabs there is the chance they can unclip themselves, and just tie an overhand instead.

Dropping The Rope Back: Once you've retrieved your gear, don't just drop the rope, as this can lead to loops snagging on flakes or falling down into cracks and getting stuck (never allow rope loops to enter cracks). Instead slowly feed it back down to the belayer, who can feed the rope back into a rope bag or hank it onto a sling.

Emergency Lead Line: It's best to run a dynamic zipline, something between 8 and 8.5 mm, as this allows you to switch it over as your emergency lead line, say if your lead line got chopped by a rock. It also allows you to switch into a two rope system if you fear that your rope could get chopped, tying into the zipline, and having the belayer put both ropes on belay. If doing this before you reach the middle mark of your zipline then you can just use it to pull up the haul line and clip this into your harness, and if more than half way, pull up the whole zipline with the haul line clipped to the end, then slide down the end of the zipline via the haul line (clip it in with some gear to weigh it down).

Lurking Fear

LEADING

So now we've covered the placements, let's look at how you will use them to climb a wall. Due to the complexity here I'm going to start with the lead rope, and build up from there, covering your lead gear (aiders and lanyards), then move on to how to employ it.

THE LEAD ROPE

There are few pieces of gear that get as much abuse as your lead rope. Yes a piton may get a hammering every now and then, but your rope is constantly moving through belay devices and karabiners, over rock and sharp edges, being crushed by ascenders, frozen, soaked and dried, and left in the sun all day long. At the same time your rope is your life line, both as a leader and a second, and is the one piece of equipment whose failure will invariably be fatal. Your rope is the Jesus nut of a climb and a life.

BIG WALL ROPE BASICS

Here I'm going to cover the most important aspects when choosing a rope.

Diameter: Due to the hard life a rope receives, in most cases you want a thick sturdy rope, which in the past was 11 mm, but these days is somewhere between 10 and 11 mm. Thinner single ropes can be used, between 9 and 9.9 mm, but they tend to wear a little faster and be stretchier, which although is good for falls on hard aid, is not good for ascending. The actual difference between a 9.5 and 10.5 mm may actually be more psychological than physical, as a rock that chops a thin rope will also chop a thicker rope, the same when the rope runs across a sharp edge and is cut. Sheath damage seems to occur the same on both as well, but in all cases a thicker rope has more heft to it, more fibres, so if it does get damaged (core shot or broken sheath), meaning a 50% loss in strength, the remaining strength will be greater on a thicker rope.

Length: The standard length for all ropes is 60 metres (or 200 feet), but personally I like 70 metre ropes as they allow more free rope both for fixing pitches and short fixing, and if it gets chopped you might have enough to still lead on! This also allows you to cut off the ends of ropes when they become damaged (from fixing or hauling on your lead line). I have also used 100 metre ropes when natural belays were very hard to build, allowing me to climb very long pitches (important if you have to deal with big snow slopes, which are not conducive to big wall anchors). With this system you could also do 100 metre abseils, which also helps when covering difficult alpine ground.

Extending Your Lead Rope: If you find you're running out of lead rope and can't make the anchor, the only option is to extend your lead line by joining your lead line to your haul line (join with a double fisherman's or butterfly knot). Once this is done you can self belay, safeguarding yourself via a clove hitch to a HMS on your belay loop or by using your ABBD (always clip into a backup knot as well, rather than trust your life to a single karabiner). This method also works if you end up having so much rope drag you can't move (the lead line becomes fixed).

Impact Force: This depends on how much your rope stretches in a fall, which in most cases will be around 30%, the thinner the rope, the greater the stretch and the lower the impact force. As we saw with shock absorbing slings, the stretch of the rope is reducing the peak force, spreading the force over time.

When you fall onto a steel cable the impact force is huge, with a corresponding peak force, enough to break bones and gear. With a static rope the impact force is very high (up to 15 kN forces possible), but aimed at not being terminal, as in the rope should not snap (but your gear may). A lead rope on the other hand is designed from scratch to give a long soft catch, like an elastic band. Most falls will only generate around 8 kN on your top piece when using a dynamic rope.

Ideally aid climbers on bleak aid would climb on a skinny 8 mm rope, as this would produce the lowest impact force (most stretch), but this would be offset by it being terrifying to climb on, not playing well with sharp things for example. Also, the amount of stretch could see you hitting things you'd miss with a thick rope. The most important aspect of a low impact force is evident when climbing on marginal gear, such as heads, because it's vital that if you do fall, you apply the lowest force possible. Unfortunately just having a stretchy rope does not mean it will be as stretchy as it needs to be in a fall, unless you know how to use it.

The Dynamic Advantage: Most climbers see extending gear as simply about reducing rope drag, which is important, but on a hard pitch this is also vital in getting the most stretch out of your lead rope. Every deviation in the rope, every edge the rope goes over, every badly extended piece that zig zags your rope, the higher your impact force will be. This is because you'll not be gaining the maximum stretch from the rope, each little kink stealing some away. It's for this reason you should always reduce drag as much as possible, even if it means putting long slings onto your hardware. Yes it's scary putting a 60 cm sling onto a solid nut instead of a 10 cm one, but get ten metres higher on a line of beaks and heads and you won't care. On this point, you should also get out of the habit of taking in the slack when the leader shouts "watch me" on bleak aid, as the more rope out the better (within reason of course!).

The Dynamic Disadvantage: Counter to the above, you might also find yourself in a situation where you're climbing on good gear above a ledge and want to avoid too much rope stretch. Such sections will tend to be short and so you can use your single lead line as a twin rope, clipping both strands into each piece of gear. Once you want to switch back to a standard system, then just untie one strand of lead line and have the belayer pull it back through the pro to the belay.

Tired Ropes: Ropes can lose their stretch over time, with falls, ascending, rapping, and general wear and tear slowly stiffening them up. The ends will generally lose more stretch than the middles as most falls will be held with the first five metres on each end. For this reason I like

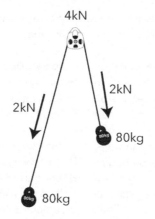

4kN

2kN

2kN

2kN   80kg

2kN

80kg

PEAK FORCE ON TOP RUNNER

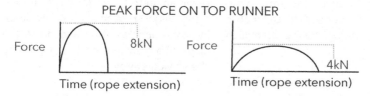

Force

8kN

Time (rope extension)

Force

4kN

Time (rope extension)

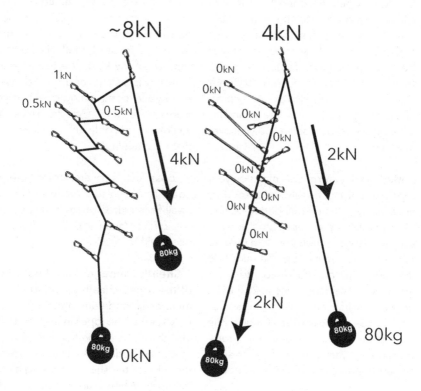

~8kN

4kN

1kN

0.5kN

0.5kN

4kN

0kN
0kN
0kN

0kN

2kN

0kN

0kN

0kN

80kg

2kN

0kN   80kg

80kg

80kg

2kN

80kg

80kg

to start a hard wall with a newish rope, and will swap ends after any big fall.

Dry Coating: Having the fibres of your rope coated helps keep the rope in better shape, reduce wear, as well as stop it freezing if you get caught in a winter storm. This last point might seem irrelevant if you're climbing Californian walls, but believe me, when your rope begins to turn into stiff wire on the last pitch of a wall, you're in some deep shit. When all of a sudden you can't belay, can't haul, and ascending is almost impossible (and terrifying to boot), it doesn't matter what pitch you're on, the top is a million miles away.

Pro Ropes: There is a big difference between ropes designed for a leisure climber, who goes to the wall once a week, and those designed for guides and heavy users. These ropes will always be more expensive, featuring better technology and coating, with tougher sheaths, and ideally also bonded cores. These ropes will not kink, freeze, and be a hazard, but should serve you well over many walls.

Markers: Having middle marks on your rope is important, but always check they are actually in the middle before setting off, and that all your ropes are the same specified length. If not, then trim them to size, and again make sure the middle is the middle. It's also handy to add other marks, such as a double ring at 20 metres on each end for example, using something like Beal rope marker. This gives the belayer more of a clue how much rope you have left when you ask (they can actually just measure to the 20 metres point).

ROPE SAFETY

Here I'm just going to cover a few important aspects of looking after your rope.

Ropes Don't Snap: This is a good thing to remember. No matter how big the fall, or how heavy the climber, the rope will not snap.

Unfortunately though, ropes can be chopped very easily, or be cut or abraded when loaded over sharp edges, especially if the rope saws along an edge (a fall around a corner, where the rope runs down an arete for example). To understand this just take an old piece of climbing rope and saw it up and down the edge of a rock and see how easily the sheath wears away.

For this reason you should always be acutely aware of sharp edges or acute deviations in the running of the rope, where the force of a fall will stress the rope over any kind of edge (sharp or blunt), using slings and quickdraws to keep your rope running direct to your higher pieces (if you suffer from rope drag you're also probably suffering from ropes that wear out fast).

Loose rock is covered elsewhere, but again it's down to directing your rope away from places where it's exposed to falling rocks (and not pulling off rocks to begin with).

Sheath Damage: You should think of the rope's sheath as being like the muscles around your intestines, in that they keep all the ropes innards together. The sheath holds the fibres in place, so that when loaded they all load together, the tube of the sheath focusing all that strength. When loaded over an edge this tube does flatten out, but the core and sheath are still loaded as one. The sheath construction is also designed to handle abrasion much better than the core, whose strands are much more delicate and slick.

Once the sheath breaks apart the inside, the core strands are exposed and so are vulnerable, and tend to spread out when loaded over an edge. For this reason it's vital to keep the rope's core inside the sheath. On average the sheath will provide 20% of the rope's strength, so if you can see the core through a small section of the rope you should be able to make a judgment on how much strength has been lost (10% of the sheath damaged will equal a drop of 2% in strength for example).

On the ground, any such damage would mean the rope would be retired, but not when you're five days up a wall.

If the damage to the sheath is less than 50%, then I would wrap some finger or sports tape around the damaged section, binding it quite tight. Make sure this is no more than 5 cm wide, otherwise it can jam in belay devices, and avoid duct tape, as this will stick and cause major headaches. You should also try and avoid stressing the sheath by abseiling, lowering or hauling, and when rapping the route always make the damaged rope the 'pull' strand, as this means the higher sheath load is on the other rope (ideally rap on your haul and zip lines instead).

Bonded Sheaths: Several companies now offer ropes that feature a core and sheath that are bonded together, the best example being Beal Unicore. This creates what is in effect a single rope, rather than a core rope and sheath, meaning if the sheath snaps or is damaged it cannot break, but stays attached to the core. For free climbing I'm not sure how important this is, but for big wall climbing it's a game changer, as it dramatically improves safety in all aspects of big wall climbing.

Spare Lead Line: If heading up onto a very big and committing route some climbers like to have a backup lead line. This can be an extra rope, perhaps a little lighter in weight, as a replacement in case the main line gets damaged. To increase its usefulness this can also double as a lead line, or for fixing (ideal if climbing capsule style, where the risk of damaging a lead line is often high). If you use a 10 mm dynamic haul line then this can be switched to become the lead line, the damaged line becoming the haul line (passing any knots).

Double Rope Technique: The use of double rope technique is rare in big wall climbing (more to do with most big wall technique coming from the US than anything else), yet it is a system worth adopting on very dangerous or loose climbs. Here it's best to employ two light single ropes (8.7 mm to 9.5 mm), or a thick and thin rope (9.5 mm and 8 mm), allowing at least one to be climbable on its own safely. The leader should have a primary lead line clipped into the majority of gear, and their second rope used as a backup in case the first is cut.

When using a double rope technique you will need to employ a lightweight zip line otherwise the total weight will get too much, important if you're mixed climbing on an alpine wall (using free, aid and winter skills). Cleaning a pitch like this can be tricky as some gear will be on one rope, some on the other, meaning both leader and second must be very experienced (the leader must be able to foresee problems for the second). The Russians often use a double rope system and get over its pitfalls by avoiding hauling, with the climbers ascending the rope with their loads instead, generally on a static line.

Climbing On A Chopped Rope: If your lead line becomes heavily damaged, but you have no choice but to climb on it (you're using a static haul line), then your only option is to rope solo pitches, as this does not require the rope to run through the protection, tying the damaged section of rope out with a knot (butterfly knot).

TYING IN

Most climbers will simply tie in as they do when cragging, but personally I would avoid using a bowline, and stick to a figure of eight knot, due to the length, the knot will be tied, (I've found a bowline can come a little loose over time). Care should also be taken when climbing on new ropes, especially dry coated ropes, as these can be quite slick and come adrift (use a double fisherman tie off).

Overhand Knot

When climbing with thick ropes your figure of eight knot can end up being quite bulky. An alternative is to tie in with an overhand knot instead, which is much less bulky. Strength wise it's the same, and I find both as easy to untie.

Competition Knot

This is a variation of the overhand, but instead of feeding the tail back through the overhand knot (rethreading it) to complete it, you feed it from the direction the rope is travelling, meaning instead of a classic bight, you get more of a loop. This knot is easy to untie and low bulk.

Double "German" Bowline

Sometimes it's not the knot that's bulky, but the stopper knot, which also invariably comes undone. An alternative is the double Bowline, which secures the tail with the knot itself, and so is super secure, but very easy to untie.

Chest Harness Tie In

One aspect of falling that's important to know when big walling, is that often it's easy to flip upside down in a fall, the weight of your rack pulling you down. This can be alarming in a big fall, and fatal if you hit a ledge. For this reason it's best to keep your rack weight as low as possible, using your zip line rather than carrying everything. Another option is to tie into your chest and waist harness with your lead rope, as this will keep you upright in a fall. The best way to do this is to first tie into your chest harness with a bowline with plenty of spare tail, then pass the tail through your harness and back up out of the 'hole', 'around the tree' and back down the 'hole', finishing it with a double fisherman's knot on the down strand. This places the knot around chest height so it shouldn't hit you in the face in a fall. The downsides are it will need to be untied when you hand over the rack (depending on chest harness style).

AIDERS

The aider, or ladder or etrier, is at the core of all aid climbing, literally your stairway to heaven (or to hell!). Being able to move smoothly using aiders is vital, as well as knowing when to use them and when not, switching between aid and free and the grey area in between.

AIDER HISTORY

The first climbers who used aiders were the pioneers of big wall climbing in

The author on the Parkin route, Mermoz, Patagonia ⊙ Ian Parnell

the Dolomites, using loops of rope with wooden steps threaded onto them. In those days climbers did not use prusik loops or ascenders and instead climbed up by the same method as the leader, meaning the leader had to leave an aider on each and every piton. These ladders were also used like leg loops as the climbers only had ropes tied around their waists, and so sat in the steps as well.

The introduction of prusik loops, and then early ascenders such as the Harbler, Jumar, Clog and Petzl, made the need to carry more ladders less necessary, and two or three aluminium stepped aiders became the norm, clipped to a fifi hook for fast retrieval.

Meanwhile over in the US the post WW2 glut of army surplus nylon webbing saw climbers make ladders out of tape instead, creating lighter aiders, using them on walls such as the Nose and Half Dome's Regular Route. These tape aiders became iconic, with their offset steps, and so when people began to sew aiders they just sewed them up in the same design, not realising that design was only the way it was due to the need to tie knots.

Troll were the first people to see that a nylon ladder aider was the way forward, creating an easy to step into aider that did not tangle with itself, with steps having a rigid top section to act as a spreader. This design was taken up by Yates and others (Fish, Metolius, Custom Runouts, Cassin), creating the modern aider, a mix of old and new.

LADDER STYLES

Classic 'Etrier' Aiders

These are the aiders you see in all the classic pictures, with offset steps, often used in pairs. The flaw in the design is that they tend to twist and tangle up more than ladder aiders and just aren't neat when using a two aider system, with steps bumping and overlapping. Their only saving grace is that they tend to use less material, meaning lightweight alpine models are much more compact than ladder designs, making them better for routes where you only need minimal aider time (the Black Diamond Alpine aider is a great example).

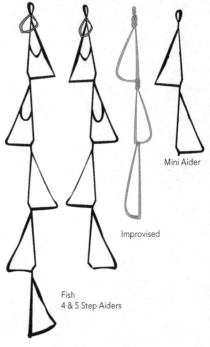

Mini Aider

Improvised

Fish
4 & 5 Step Aiders

Vanessa Kirkpatrick using Yates Speed ladder aiders on Prodigal Sun

Ladder Aider

For me this is the standard aider, and it's all I use unless going Russian style. This style of aider is very neat and tidy and does not tangle easily, and two pair well in two aider mode. Most important is that they're easy to step in and out of.

Make sure if you buy a ladder aider for full on aiding, you get a model with a spreader bar at the top (Yates, Fish, Custom Runouts), the one exception being the Metolius Pocket aider, which for its weight, bulk and cost is one of the best aiders you can buy for moderate walls (I've used a pair of these up to A4).

Rigid Aiders

Although rare, rigid aiders should not be dismissed, and were used by the late great Xaver Bongard and by Silvia Vidal. Using dyneema cord and threading on alloy steps (Raumer make these) creates a very solid system, meaning you have more feel for what's going on, especially when testing via the aider. You can also make your ladders long or short, and put the steps where you want them.

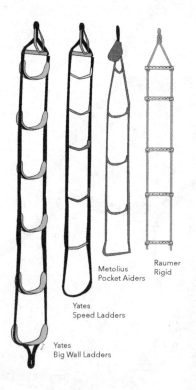

Yates
Speed Ladders

Metolius
Pocket Aiders

Raumer
Rigid

Yates
Big Wall Ladders

I used rigid steps on Iron Hawk, Lost in America and a solo of Aurora and found they worked well. Downsides are that they batter your legs leaving them very bruised, cannot be racked away in a small package, and can get jammed into cracks quite badly. I found they were also only good for aiding, not cleaning, and clanked around when climbing, making me sound like C3P0. In the end I dropped one by accident and had to switch to some Pika ladder aiders and I never went back after that. But I think what I like about the Russian system is that it has that very rigid feel like this old school set up.

Alpine Aiders

Although they come in both classic and ladder style, alpine aiders are aiders designed for less intense aid, especially for mixed routes and classic guerilla style (French Free), but use a set of these on a three hour lead, and you'll understand how much a little bit of extra comfort weighs. The skinny webbing is only comfortable for short periods of time, and can be agony in rock boots unless all your nerve endings are already shot (but in rigid alpine or plastic boots they're OK). What these aiders work well as are as sub aiders, matched up with a full weight aider to create a three or four aider system.

Improvised Aider

If you don't have a dedicated aider and come across a section of aid, then you need to improvise an aider.

To do this take a 120 cm sling (or a 240 cm if you have one) and first tie a small overhand knot in the top, creating the aider's clip in loop.

Half way down the sling tie another loop into the sling, only this time make one side of the loop larger than the other, creating a step that will stand out when the bottom is weighted. This is your top step.

Below this you will have a loop on the bottom of which you should tie another overhand knot, making it offset from the very bottom so that when it's weighted the bottom loop will still stand out as well. This is your mid step.

Next larks foot a 60 cm sling into the bottom overhand knot, making sure that the sling's bar tacked section is at the very bottom of the sling so that it keeps the step open. This is your bottom step. The bottom step can be left out but to do so means that you're going to have to be very gymnastic and will probably only end up wasting energy and time.

If you're embarking on a route that may require a big descent, then it may be worth making an aider out of tubular webbing beforehand, so that it can be untied and used as abseil tat when no longer needed. If you use tape for rap anchors make sure it's sound and isn't damaged, something easily done when aiding in crampons.

AIDER NOTES:

Comfort: This is the most important factor when getting an aider you'll spend many hours in, and it's fairly obvious what's going to be comfortable and what's not, the wider the step the better. But just as super chunky harnesses are still like torture devices within an hour of hanging in them, so are aiders. Lead for eight hours in your approach shoes and you're going to feel some serious pain.

The problem with foot pain is not just the pain itself, but also the fact pain is a distraction and a drive to rush to get the move done, which is not good on hard aid. For this reason, when climbing walls where I will be standing in my aiders for many hours, I wear very stiff wall boots (Sportiva Trango).

How Many Steps? Another very important aspect of your aider is how easy it is to step into your the steps, with longer, multi step aiders being better for hard aid. When you're doing very long reaches with a short aider you can find the bottom step is too high to step into to test your gear, or even to just step into, forcing you to climb up your bottom aider and do a top step move to get over onto it. For this reason, hard aid climbers tend to go for longer aiders, seven or eight steps, matching these with shorter aiders if they go for a four aider system.

Aider Strength: Most aiders are made from full strength webbing that is heavily bar tacked, and when new, an aider is maybe the strongest piece of gear you have. This means that you can clip into an aider anywhere when climbing up, clipping your fifi into steps or the grab loop. Personally though, I think safeguarding yourself with an aider is a bad habit to get into, say clipping a lanyard into one, as aiders can get unclipped and switched around a lot on a belay, and this could lead to you being disconnected from everything.

Longevity: Given how strong aiders are, they will outlast you, and most aiders only get replaced when you drop them or they get chewed by wall mice.

Aider Shelving: When you're dealing with a chaotic belay or bivvy, an aider can make a good spot to sort out gear, clipping off your rack into different steps, such as; beaks and hook on top step, then wires, then small cams, then big cams for example. When setting up your portaledge it's often good to clip an aider that hangs down beside your end of the ledge, and use this to clip off your personal gear before sitting down. This way, when you get up in the morning you can just rack it all back on again instead of getting your stuff mixed up with your partner's.

Racking Your Ladders: Racking aiders properly is vital if you're free climbing, or on approaches and descents (it's always good to have a ladder handy on complex descents), as they are real trip hazards, plus they will snag and tangle on anything. To rack simply pass the grab loop (tape loop at the top, which you should never grab) through every other step (alternate steps), then clip back into the main plain gate. To release the steps just unclip the grab loop and all your steps will drop out - great if you need to switch quickly from free to aid.

RUSSIAN AIDERS

The Russian aider system is a big departure from the US and European systems, but one that lends itself to the types of climbing Russian teams have excelled at, i.e., big gnarly walls. The Russian system feels more like an industrial approach to technical climbing, and can feel clunky if you're used to a two aider method, but I find it a very good hardcore system. If I was to push the aid climbing/bomb disposal analogy, the Western ladder system is like defusing a bomb in a t-shirt and a butter knife, while the Russian system is wearing full Kevlar body armour and using sonic screwdriver.

BASIC CONCEPT

The Russian system has two parts, the foot stirrups and the aid trees. The foot stirrups are strapped to your ankles and below the knees, and feature a small metal hook that sits close to the inside of the leg. The aid trees are long slings that feature paired metal rings every 30 cm along their length, and these are attached to your lanyards. The metal stirrup hooks are hooked into the rings to climb.

Set Up

The stirrups usually feature a full strength adjustable strap that goes around your foot, then a lighter strap around your ankle, then another full strength strap around the top of your calf. The hook part is rotated just inside the knee. The best method to keep the hook in place is to use a rigid knee pad, drill a hole into the plastic, and have the hook hooked through this, keeping it up and in position (it would also be easy to have a Velcro strap going from a knee pad down to the stirrup). Stirrups come in left and right and it's worth clearly marking which is which. The aid trees are set up in pairs on your lanyards, one long and one short on each, ideally alternate colours.

TECHNIQUE

Once you see the system it's pretty obvious how it works, and there's not much of a learning curve. The main point, like with aiders, is to get high as quick as you can, which with this system tends to be the second to last rings, the top rings saved for higher steps just because your knees are more locked in as you get closer.

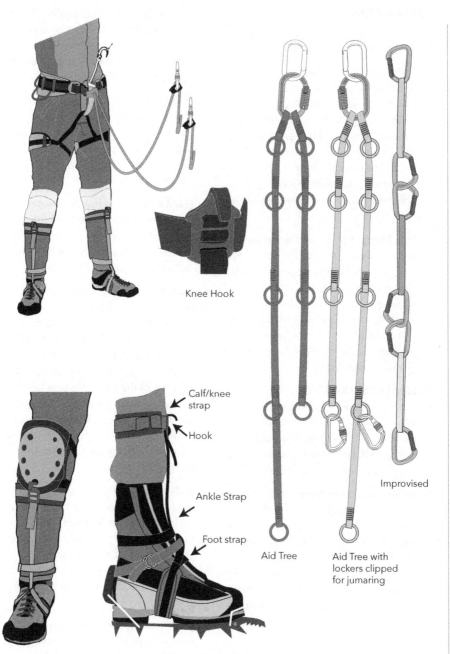

Knee Hook

Calf/knee
strap

Hook

Ankle Strap

Foot strap

Aid Tree

Aid Tree with
lockers clipped
for jumaring

Improvised

Russian aider with hook inserted
through hole in knee pad

Aider matched with crampon

ADVANTAGES

Here's a rundown of the stand-out benefits of the Russian system:

- **Balance**: When you're standing in an aider, you are trying to stay in balance on your feet, which means on steep ground where you're forced off balance, you need the extra support of a fifi hook. With the Russian system the strap around your upper calf helps to balance you, even on steep ground. This means that you rarely need to use a fifi.

- **Top Stepping**: This balance advantage allows more stable high stepping, with the stirrup hooks able to be clipped directly into high pieces, even wires, slings or tie-offs. This means most Russian aider moves are made comfortably around the level of the second, or a little below the top step, in a two aider system.

- **Step In And Out**: With this system you can easily go into aid or free instantly, especially if you are not using your aid trees, but just hooking into slings and quickdraws. This is a boon for free climbing or ice or mixed climbing.

- **Crampon Compatible**: Standard aid ladders do not play well with crampons, which get tangled up in, or cut, the webbing easily. With the Russian system you wear your crampons over your stirrups, meaning the webbing is protected, and you can easily switch into ice mode, important when hooking up on verglassed rock, as the crampons can bite into the ice.

- **Locked In**: When rope climbing and cleaning, you can clip the second lowest ring of your aid trees into the foot strap of your stirrup (avoid clipping it into your knee/calf strap),

meaning your foot stays in position and can't slip out. This also comes in handy when hauling, and when using a Frog system, with the bottom ring clipped into both foot loops.

- **Hard Bounce**: It's possible to use the aid trees to achieve a very static bounce test, either with your foot, or by using the aid tree like a lanyard, a good approach if using dynamic lanyards.

- **Hard Aid**: Having four aid trees means the system works like a 4 aider system, only with far less bulk or weight. This makes the system very stable for hard aid, as both feet are balanced.

- **Compact**: Having to wear stirrups can be a bit of a chore, making you feel like a linesman or lumberjack, but this is offset by the lower bulk of your four aid trees, compared to two, three or four aiders. The aid trees can be racked by clipping all the rings into your lanyards locker or plain gate, taking up the same room as a couple of slings. If switching to free climbing they can also be thrown over the shoulder to hang down the back.

- **Extendable**: If you want to extend your aid trees, perhaps because you need to do a very low test, well below the piece you're on, you can switch your lanyard down from the top into one of the tree rings, and then add a quickdraw or sling to the bottom ring.

- **Redundancy**: If you lose your aid tree you can easily improvise as mentioned above, with quickdraws or slings, or make ones out of cord or a spare daisy chain.

- **Ultra High Stepping**: There aren't that many tricks you can do, but if hooking directly into the placement with your hooks leaves you short, you can clip (or larks foot) a hook into your foot loop, and hook that into the gear.

DISADVANTAGES

- **Industrial**: Once you've used the Russian system you realise how much more freestyle the two aider system is, making it closer to free climbing on the aid to free spectrum. This means that I would not use the Russian system on easy routes or trade routes, opting instead for a lightweight system (Metolius pocket aiders), as the freestyle approach just makes climbing more fun. But when things get hard, gearing up with the Russian system can be a little like gearing up for battle, which can help with your psych.

- **Slower**: The Russian system is a precision technique, like playing chess, and is slower than just cranking up on an aider. This means that the system is really only appropriate for hard aid, especially if you're doing a lot of free climbing, the stirrups getting in the way when crack climbing and basically affecting flow.

- **Flipping**: Having hooks clipped to your legs creates the possibility of being flipped if you fall, the hooks catching on a rope or gear. I've never had this happen to me, but I've been told this is a risk, although this needs to be offset by the fact there is less risk of breaking an ankle with the Russian system by getting it caught in an aider step.

- **Ring Snags**: Maybe once on every wall I'll get one of my tree rings jammed in a crack, stopping me in my tracks, although again this can also

happen with ladder steps as well.

- **Hang Up:** Another minor but scary issue can be when the hook does not clip around the ring, but instead somehow balances on top of it for a second. These means that it will suddenly pop, either on or off, which can be scary and also hazardous if on marginal gear. Once you are aware of this issue, you tend to be more thorough in placing your hooks, and in over 200 pitches wearing Russian aiders this has only happened to me twice.

- **Cost:** You can buy two alpine aiders quite cheaply, whereas a Russian system, hand made, with titanium rings and dyneema is going to cost considerably more.

LANYARDS

I've decided to make the bold move to not use the normal terms 'daisy chains' or 'daisies' too often in this book, but the catch all term 'lanyard' instead. The reason for this is that these days there are so many different styles of 'daisy' being used, from adjustable cam lock slings, Personal Anchor Slings (PAS), rope lanyards, to old school daisy chains, that the term 'lanyard' seems more appropriate and less confusing.

WHAT IS A LANYARD?

A lanyard is fundamentally a connector. It joins you to everything else - belays, gear that needs shock loading to test, ascenders, haul bags and lifelines. Another way to view lanyards are as extra arms, making you a quadropus, helping you to juggle all those big wall plates.

MINI HISTORY

In the past, climbers left their aiders free or had them attached to themselves via a thin piece of cord. Once clipped into the next piece, the climber would use their rope to haul their body up, the belayer giving tension to hold them in place. This technique was slow, hard work for both belayer and leader, and also increased the load on the protection.

Cavers had been using 'cows-tails' for years, a length of rope with one long and one short connection, using this to clip into belays and ascenders and so leave their hands free. And so climbers began to make their own cows-tails, made by taking a length of tape and tying knots along its length with offset loops to clip into.

Now climbers could clip directly into their gear and aiders, saving the belayer the effort of supporting them, and also reducing the load to just the leader, not the leader and belayer!

LANYARD SPECS

How Many Lanyards? The standard is two, one for each ascender, one for each set of aiders, one acting as the back-up for the other when clipped to belays. For alpine or guerrilla aid one lanyard is most often employed, as one takes up little space and can be used for many other things in a standard free climbing system. For hard aid having a third lanyard can be useful as well as having a mix of static and dynamic lanyards, so you've a choice of which one to use. This third lanyard can be used as a tether when placing gear so as to avoid dropping it, clipped into a drill, hooks etc.

Lanyard Length: A common mistake climbers make is to have lanyards that aren't long enough, which means they come up short when making long reaches, reaches that always seem to be life or death. The imagined ideal length is from harness belay loop to the tip of your fingers, and your actual reach is further extended by your lanyards karabiners, doubly so if using a lanyard locker as well. In reality this ideal length always seems to be compromised by the lanyards being tangled, again something that always happens when it's a life or death clip. This means that you need to sort out tangles, and also that longer lanyards give you a little more length to tangle. Another problem with lanyards that are just right, is that on hard aid, you often need to drop down below the piece you're on, something not always possible if high stepping. For this reason I would recommend the longest lanyards you can get, with 115 cm being the minimum for a 6 foot climber on easy aid, and 140 cm plus for hard aid. You can also buy extra long lanyards or 'super daisies' up to 180 cm from companies like Fish.

Lanyard Materials: Lanyards can be made from nylon tape, Dyneema, or climbing rope. What your lanyard is made from will dictate if it is static or dynamic, with nylon or rope being dynamic (15%-30% stretch) and dyneema or spectra being static (think steel cable). If you're taking a fall onto a lanyard, then a dynamic lanyard will absorb much more of the impact force, but if you're bounce testing a #2 head then a dyneema sling will provide more positive reinforcement that it's solid, the force you're applying going into the placement. Dyneema also has an advantage in that it's far more robust and stronger for its weight. A skinny 12 mm dyneema personal anchor sling is as strong as a chunky 16 mm nylon daisy chain, an important consideration when you want low weight and bulk on your harness.

Lanyard Strength: The security of your lanyards is vital as often your life will be hanging from them - at belays, when attached to your ascenders, or when taking 'daisy falls'. Climbers seem to make an assumption that all lanyards are 'full strength', but this is far from true. Strength varies greatly from one design to another, with some lanyards I've used best described as body weight only, and some I'd not trust to hold an unruly dog. Another factor is, as with all climbing software, there is a very big difference between a new lanyard and a faded and battle scarred lanyard, with the strength of nylon slings dropping off steeply after just one hard wall.

Before I look at each type of lanyard in turn it's worth digging down into the dirt of this subject, as too many climbers just see the word 'full strength' or '22 kN' and assume they're good to go. First off, the moment you larks foot a sling you're reducing its strength by anything from 30% to 40%, with Nylon being stronger than Dyneema in this regard. So let's assume any 'full strength 22 kN' tape or rope lanyard is actually 15 kN for starters, while those that are not full strength (adjustables) maybe even weaker. Next you should view a single bar tack as having a strength of 2 kN for a shear load, but less for a tensioned load, and so treat anything with less than five bar tacks as bodyweight only. Below I will cover the strengths and weaknesses of each design in turn.

LANYARD DESIGNS

There are many different designs of lanyard, but they can be roughly divided into those made from tape and those made from rope.

Sling

Tape is something climbers get. It's cheap, comes in many colours, and is easy to sew and manufacture.

Daisy Chain: This is the most common design of lanyard, and the big wall default, featuring multiple pockets sewn along its length created by two or three bar tacks per pocket. Tape width varies between 12 and 18 mm, and comes in both nylon and dyneema.

The daisy chain is such a classic item, few climbers really stop to think about just where the design comes from, which is nothing but an evolution of those nylon slings with knots tied along its length. I must have gone through ten sets of daisy chains and although I took many falls onto them (factor 1 and 2), and broke many bar tacks and pockets, I never broke one. Now I tend to only use them for racking gear.

Although sewn into multiple pockets, a daisy chain should be viewed like a regular circular sling, and so has a minimum strength of 22 kN end to end, but reduced to 15 kN once larks footed to your belay loop. The weaker bar tacks can break apart under very aggressive bounce testing, or in falls, but the loss of a bar tack will only create a larger loop.

The main strength related danger (illustrated in the diagram on the next page) comes from pilot error; the climber cross-clipping a karabiner between two pockets side by side, so that karabiner is only held by the bar tacks between the pockets. Rip out the joining bar tacks and you are no longer clipped to anything.

If you want to retain your full loop strength at all times then get into the habit of shortening your daisy chains with your fifi or a separate karabiner.

As with many classic pieces of big wall gear I personally feel that although the daisy chain has served climbing well, it has been superseded by far stronger and safer lanyard designs.

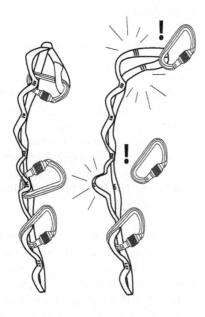

Personal Anchor Sling (PAS): This is a multi looped sling like the daisy, but one where each loop is independent of each other and full strength. The design came about due to the inherent weakness with bar tacked pockets on a standard daisy, where cross clipping could be lethal (bar tacks go, then so do you), and clipping off short was never full strength (22 kN), but rather a series of weak loops you could zipper out. By using linked full strength (22 kN) loops, the climber can clip in anywhere, have no issues with cross loading, and even have other

climbers use their PAS as an anchor point (actual end to end strength is 15 kN if larks footed to harness). The downside with the standard PAS is that it's too short as an aid sling for anything but guerrilla aid or free walls. Standard PAS are made by companies such as Metolius, Black Diamond and Grivel.

Multi Loop Daisy (Super Daisy): This is one of my favourite designs, a longer wall specific PAS, which although a little bulkier than a daisy chain, makes up for it in many other ways. Even when using adjustable lanyards, I will often carry one Super Daisy, as I can be assured of its strength. The Metolius Ultimate Daisy chain is the best model on the market.

Adjustable Cam Lock Sling: In the '90s this design became very popular, with the Yates adjustable daisy being the most popular design, with a long length of webbing adjusted in length by a heavy camming buckle, designed for industrial tie down straps. This setup allowed the climber to winch themselves up onto the gear as well as fine tune their position, a boon on awkward slots and squeezes (it's well worth carrying a set for such pitches). Drawbacks include the webbing wearing out very quickly, sometimes in just one wall, leading to dreaded sling creep, or cuts in the tape caused by bounce testing, which greatly reduces the sling's strength. Another problem is twisting, and it's important to get into the habit of running the tape through your fingers to untwist it before clipping into a piece, otherwise you will not be able to cinch all the tape through the buckle. You also need to keep an eye on the buckle release lever, as even slight pressure will drop you. Pros with this style of buckle is that it can be both tensioned and released under load and makes a fifi pretty redun-

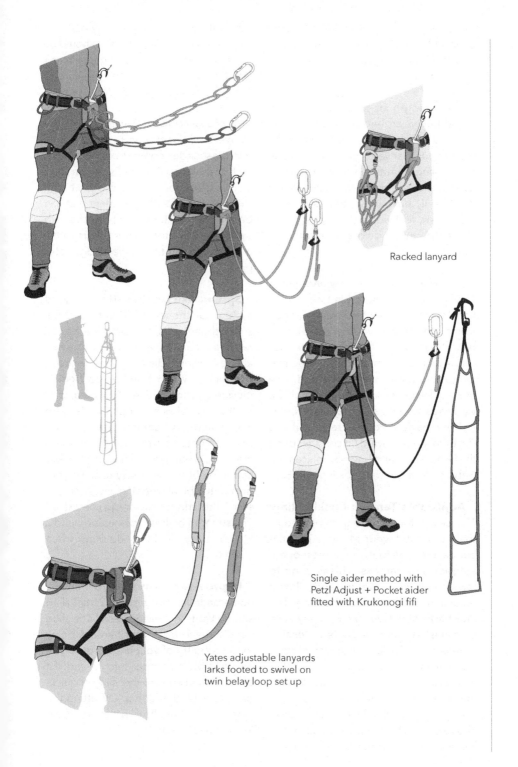

Racked lanyard

Single aider method with
Petzl Adjust + Pocket aider
fitted with Krukonogi fifi

Yates adjustable lanyards
larks footed to swivel on
twin belay loop set up

dant, this offset by the fact that more time is wasted if you're constantly tightening and then releasing your lanyards with each move.

The strength of these slings when brand new is around 6 kN, due to the crushing nature of the buckle, as well as the fact such lanyards break the golden rule of slings that they should always be used as a loop. This means such lanyards would only be barely adequate when brand new, and would soon drop below a strength that would guarantee your safety.

Personally I've taken very hard factor 2 falls onto new adjustable lanyards, so hard that the cam buckle inverted (rather than cut the sling, which is good as I'd not be writing this now if it did), but even so I still never trust them. Once they begin to fur up and get worn they slip, and once they slip I expect their strength should be viewed as suspect, and they could break if shock loaded. For this reason, if you like this style of lanyard I'd consider using the Fish design, and buying replacement webbing for each wall (costing only $5).

Adjustable Tension Buckle Sling: This design forgoes a big chunky industrial buckle in favour of a two part flat buckle, the type found on most modern auto locking harness. This is done to lower bulk, cost, weight and allow a reduction in the width of the sling. The drawbacks of this design are many, such as it's just about impossible to tension or release under load, but worst is that the narrower webbing is even weaker than a cam lock buckle. How weak? Well this style does not even really warrant a strength rating, with the old Petzl Quickfix and current Metolius Easy Daisy rated less than 1.5 kN. These are not conserv-

ative ratings, but dangerously real. For this reason any design like this should be avoided (if not banned outright), as their remit is so narrow that they are sure to stray into dangerous end use.

Micro Ascender: A variation of the above two designs is to use a small micro ascender compatible with tape, such as the Kong Duck or Ropeman Mark 2. This gives you a more compact high strength method of adjustment that can be matched with narrow high strength webbing. Strength wise this is a grey area, and I would put this in the dodgy category.

Sprung Axe Leashes: This is a good system for those who don't need full strength lanyards, but simply a way to retain their aiders, and works well when alpine or winter climbing and you need to quickly switch from aid to free. A modern sprung axe leash system, with built in swivel, also stops tangles and is very light and compact, and can be switched onto ice tools quickly for mixed climbing. Getting the right length is key and it might be necessary to build your own with tubular webbing and elastic, or switch the larks foot up onto a chest sling. The strength of these leashes is around 2 kN when new, and they do break when fallen on.

Improvised Lanyard: To make a homemade lanyard take a 120 cm sling and tie knots in it every 20 cm. The sling should reach from your harness belay loop to the tip of your fingers once you have a karabiner clipped into the end. If it doesn't, then add another sling or quickdraw to extend it further. Offsetting the loops just a little will make it easier to clip in and out of them.

Rope

Using rope, over tape, in your lanyards offers several advantages, the biggest being rope can not twist like tape, and is also more robust and dynamic, a major improvement in safety. I feel that rope is the future of lanyards.

Rope Lanyard: This design is best demonstrated in the Petzl Connect Adjust (9.5 mm) or Evolv Adjust (7.7 mm rope), featuring high strength dynamic cord adjusted by a high strength rope friendly forged torquing buckle. Unlike an adjustable cam lock or tension buckle sling, this design can employ any 7.7 to 9.5+ mm cord (I've used 7 mm but it slips), allowing you to create your own system, or replace broken/worn cord. A custom system can be tied directly into your waist and leg loops (saving your belay loop), allowing you to cinch up tight, as well as giving you extra length and the opportunity to beef up the cord.

The Evolv is the dedicated double aid lanyard and although great for easy or trade walls, lacks the beef for heavy use, and the sheath on the one I had stripped after approximately 20 climbing days. This was primarily caused by bounce testing. For heavy duty walls I would custom make a system using 9 to 9.5 mm rope.

Downsides include the fact you cannot release the buckle under load, only cinch it tight, and that a dynamic rope makes a static test impossible. This is overcome on hard aid by carrying a dedicated testing lanyard such as a static Ultimate Daisy.

Another drawback is that being a long length of cord these lanyards are harder to rack away compared to daisy chains or PASs, and knots need to be tied in them for racking. This problem can be reduced by tying a micro 2 mm prusik in to the end of the cord, or just tying a knot onto the cord for racking.

Strength wise Petzl do not provide a rating but it is in the region of 15 kN.

Micro Ascender: This is the same as the sling version, using a Kong Frog or Wild Country Ropeman, only this system tends to work better here, as micro ascenders work better on cord. The ideal cord for this is between 8 and 9.5 mm, and being a self build means you can create the length that's right for you. When tying a stopper knot at the end of each strand of rope, tie in a small loop of 2 mm cord to act as a clip point for racking. I've used this system in the past, where I needed something that would not freeze up like tape adjustables do, and found it worked very well, and many climbers have tinkered around with this style of system. Strength wise this is the same as using a jumar, although many micro ascenders are designed to slip around 4 kN.

Cord: This is the old school way, with just a strand of 3 mm cord linking you to your aider, usually tied into the top hole of a fifi attached to the aider. This system was designed so that you could pull up the aider once you left it, or even for it to lift off by itself if you were busting into a free move. The downside is of course this is not a lanyard but just a retaining cord, and any fall onto it would see it snap, but using 3 mm dyneema (995 kg breaking strain), or drilling your fifi for thicker cord can help.

Sans Lanyard

Some climbers don't use lanyards at all when aiding, a risky approach as any piece that rips while bounce testing may result in the loss of both the piece and the aider. I would class this technique as being one for big wall masters, like chopping arrows out of the air with a samurai sword; requiring great skill and awareness of what will and will not hold. Often the climber who uses this technique will carry a single lanyard, such as a PAS, for testing, for belays and to use with an ascender, making use of slings or their rope to maintain the two points rule.

LANYARD APPRAISAL

As you can see, there are many options open to big wall climbers regarding lanyard choice. The majority use daisy chains, but this is down to tradition more than functionality.

For me the primary concern is strength because I neither want to die, or take a huge fall due to a lanyard snapping. I guess many would scoff at the idea of being killed by both your lanyards failing, but I can think of several situations where my life hung by my two lanyards (factor 2 leader fall onto a belayer only clipped in to the belay by two adjustable lanyards, or a fall onto your ascenders if a pendulum point fails while cleaning). I also want a system that is robust, gives me good extension, and can test gear effectively.

The two systems I like are the PAS systems (two Metolius Ultimate Daisy Chains) or the Petzl Evolv (with rope beefed up to 9 mm), used in partnership with a single Ultimate Daisy.

"DAISY FALLS"

The term 'daisy fall' means to fall directly onto your lanyard and is something that should be avoided or mitigated at all costs, due to the dangerously high impact forces created. In a drop test a 120 cm dyneema sling will break in a factor 2 fall with an 80 kg weight. Several climbers have died or been injured in just such a scenario, when clipped in with a single sling to a belay, they have climbed above their clip in point and fallen, breaking the sling. Of these, the most infamous is the death of Todd Skinner, who took a short static fall onto his daisy chain when abseiling onto an anchor, the force great enough to break his worn out belay loop, causing him to fall to his death.

In the real world daisy falls are lower than factor 2, as some of the force is transferred through the harness into the body, the chunkier the body the greater the shock absorbency (offset by the higher weight). A real world example of such a dangerous fall would be top stepping on a piece, then transferring over onto the higher placement only for it to fail after you fully commit, sending you down onto your lower piece clipped to your lanyard, the fall twice the length of your lanyard. If you compare this to a leader fall onto a belayed rope, you have more dynamic rope out in the second case, and in most cases the belayer will be lifted up, the force being further absorbed into their body, the overall effect to smooth out the peak force.

In a daisy fall the only real give is the compression of the climber's body, the gear, karabiner, lanyard, belay loop, legs and waist loop having very little give, creating a severe spiked peak force. Such a force can break wires and cables, twist or deform pitons, nuts or cam lobes, or break linking karabiners or the lanyard itself. In such a fall, becoming 'detached' like this can be lethal if your lanyard is your only connection, or if the piece you've broken in the fall is the only good piece in a string of psycho placements. This latter scenario is the main concern when aid climbing, especially on hard aid, where a fall can create a domino effect that can strip many pieces.

Mitigating Daisy Falls

So, especially on hard aid, the leader must mitigate this happening. Here are a few ways to reduce the risk of a daisy fall:

- **Testing**: The aim of testing is to reduce the chance of a fall onto the gear below. Test well and you should almost eliminate daisy falls. Good testing technique also limits the domino effect of gear failing during the test, all of which is covered in the testing section.

- **Shorten The Fall**: As soon as your waist is higher than your lanyard's attachment point, you need to be shortening your lanyard, either by using some form of fifi, or adjusting the lanyard's length if it's adjustable.

- **Clip In The Rope**: Getting into the habit of clipping in the rope as soon as your waist is level with the piece may not reduce the impact on the daisy (unless you ask the belayer to take the rope tight), but it does mean you're clipped to the piece if the lanyard fails. If you feel you might fall, but cannot unclip your lanyard, then get your belayer to take you tight.

- **The Safety Illusion**: A leader must overcome the idea that being clipped in to the last piece with their lanyard gives more security then just being clipped in with the rope. Try and think of it like a short strand of steel cable versus a thick strand of elastic.

- **Unclip As Soon As You Can**: The sooner you have the rope as your safety net, rather than the lanyard, the safer you'll be.

RACKING YOUR LANYARD

You can rack a lanyard in a few different ways, such as passing it through your legs and clipping it to the back of your harness, or wrapping it around your waist. The first method can be painful if the lanyard somehow becomes loaded by accident, while the second is a recipe for disaster, as invariably when you clip gear into your harness it becomes cross clipped with your daisy lanyard, meaning you can't unclip it. The best method is to simply clip the lanyard into its end krab twice in its length, and clip this onto the side of your harness. This makes it short so it won't get under your feet, yet allows it to be quickly unclipped.

CONNECTING YOUR LANYARDS TO YOUR HARNESS

There are a number of ways to connect your lanyards to your harness, as well as a few ways not to do it.

Larks Foot To Belay Loop: This is the best method to employ and gives you a good strength connection (around 15 kN). You can just larks foot each lanyard in turn but a better way is to bind the two larks foot knots together. To do this, larks foot one sling, and while still loose, larks foot the second but also pass it through the first's loop. This way when both are tightened they wrap around each other. The reason for this approach is that it creates a single point from where both lanyards start, which reduces tangles, and allows you to just reach down to one point. You can also add your fifi cord to this combined larks foot, but personally I tend to leave this floating on the belay loop.

Larks Foot Legs And Waist: In the old Middendorf big wall manual this was the method shown, a set of daisy chains larks footed directly into the waist and leg loops, bypassing the belay loop. This method is designed to get closer to the gear and create a more direct link. In reality what happens is that the larks foot just crushes the waist and leg loops, making it feel like you're hanging in your harness 24/7. If you do not feel like this then maybe there is something wrong with your harness, as the rise should not be long enough for such a method to feel anything but uncomfortable.

Double Belay Loops: I've seen some harnesses that have double belay loops described as allowing a lanyard on each loop. This of course is just marketing crap, as very often it's vital that your lanyards focus down onto a single point. By splitting this you open yourself up to all sorts of problems.

Swivel: This approach takes the tangle resistant swivel mounted ice axe leash idea and up-scales it for serious big walling, larks footing your lanyards into a full strength climbing swivel, either sewn or connected into a belay loop. No one makes anything like this, so you'll need someone to make one up for you, or get a Petzl Micro swivel that can be opened and closed (via an Allen key), and slip this onto your own, or a secondary belay loop. The advantage of this system is that the lanyards almost never tangle and so retain their full length at all times, with cord lanyards being even more tangle proof. The primary downsides are weight and extra bulk on the front of your harness, as well as adding further distance between you and your placement. I've used this system on two harnesses and I like it for hard aid, especially pitches where there is a lot of traversing. The issue of distance is not a problem if you make good use of your fifi hook.

LANYARD KARABINERS

If your lanyards are your arms, then what you clip to the end are your hands, and so require some careful thought.

ROLE OF THE LANYARD KRAB

The primary role of the krab is to connect you to the gear you're aiding on, so you can test it and weight it, as well as safeguard it from loss if it fails. A secondary role is as your connection to belays, ascenders, haul bags and life lines. This means that you need a strong connector that is easy to handle and will not snag, and is large enough to take multiple pieces of protection, as well as ideally being able to be locked.

LANYARD-AIDER CONNECTION

Some climbers go for a krab on their aider and a krab on their lanyards, and clip these into each other, allowing some small autonomy between the two, but in action the two are rarely separated. The role of the lanyard clip is to connect aider and lanyard together so as to avoid loss of the aider when left hanging in space, falling etc.

HARD POINTS

Whatever links your aiders to your lanyards becomes a 'hard point', something that when loaded is easy and quick to clip in and out of, unlike daisy pockets, grab loops or quickdraws. This hard point should always be the first point of call for your fifi hook, especially if you want to climb quickly and smoothly. I call this 'metal to metal', the idea being to always use your body, climbing up your ladders, with this as your aim, not cinching yourself up inch by inch.

FIFI OPTION

Attaching a fifi to your aider will usually require it to be tied on with cord, or the aider unpicked and resewn. Another option is the Krukonogi Ladder Hook, a small fifi that can be quickly slotted on to any aider. By adding a small loop of cord to the top hole of the fifi you can just clip in your lanyards instead of using cord.

SINGLE KRAB OPTIONS

The following is a run down of lanyard krabs and their combinations.

Plain D Shaped Krab: This is the old school favourite, just a wire or plain gate krab clipped into the lanyard with the aider clipped in as well. A large krab works best as it might be called on to clip into multiple ropes, and one with a low profile keyhole style nose does not get hung up when unclipping.

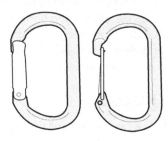

Oval: An oval karabiner has an advantage in that both lanyard and aider sit in the very bottom of the krab, and are not pinched into the tight radius of the D krab. These oval krabs also tend to be high capacity and can be clipped without having to tilt the krab at an extreme angle (as is the case with very hooked D shaped krabs). The most important factor, and one vital for the single, double or triple aider system is that when one oval is clipped into a second oval they do not shift and 'snap' like D shaped krabs. This use of two oval karabiners in fact replaces the old school method of carrying thirty or forty ovals for fear of this issue. For me this is my preferred method. The Black Diamond wire oval is very light and strong, but suffers from a hooked gate, while the DMM Oval has a shrouded nose.

Screwgate Locker: A locker is always needed on the end of both lanyards for belays, ascenders etc. so this method just replaces the plain gate with a locker. The screwgate is screwed tightly open and used like a normal karabiner, only being screwed closed for belays, ascenders etc. Using a large sized locker, such as a HMS gives you a great deal of working space, and this can also be used as a grab handle. The drawback with this system is that screwgates are fickle things on walls, and I find when using ascenders they often come undone and so need constant vigilance (not a bad thing).

Twistlock: A single action twistlock gets over the problem of security, in that it's always locked, and with practice opening and closing one handed when clipping in and out of placements requires no more effort than with a plain gate. Nevertheless few climbers find this method useful.

Push Lock: This method sits somewhere between a plain gate and twistlock and uses a Petzl Vertigo, a krab designed to provide greater security than a plain gate, but open and close easier than a twist or screw gate. To achieve this the krab locking barrel is simply pulled down to open, and then springs back to close and lock. This style of semi locker is designed for via ferratas, where the user is constantly clipping in and out of placements. The Petzl Vertigo also has the advantage of being high volume, very strong and having a keylock gate. The main drawback I've found with this system is that it does not work well with the Petzl lanyards, as the lanyard and aider get too pinched in the bottom of the krab (but it works well with standard lanyards).

DOUBLE KARABINER METHOD

An alternate approach to lanyard krabs is to use a double krab system, a security locker connecting aider to lanyard, with a 'clipper' plain gate used for clipping into placements. This option gives you total security from loss of aider, and by using twistlocks you know you're always locked into belays and ascenders. For this approach it is best to use an oval twistlock and oval plain gate, so that any part can be clipped into another part without shifting. If you use a large locker then this can also act as a grab handle, and gives

you more room if you want to clip gear in direct to the locker (say when leapfrogging, so as to eliminate dropping gear), but this comes at a weight penalty.

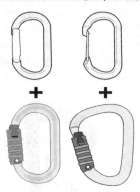

LOSING INCHES

One issue some flag up with the double krab system is that by adding a large locker to your system you are losing the height of that krab, something that could be an issue where every millimetre counts (when high stepping and searching for an edge to hook for example). In reality it is very rare to ever actually use your very top step, and most 'top stepping' is done in the secondary step unless you're in slabby ground. What this means is by adding an extra karabiner the top step actually becomes more usable. A secondary factor is that having two krabs gives you two hard points, which can help when high stepping. If you do find yourself maxed out and need a few more millimetres to clip that fixed head, then simply unclip one aider into the plain gate.

FIFI HOOKS

A fifi is an integral part of aid climbing, used to quickly connect oneself to gear or slings, and so provide a sort of third hand that holds you in place for a short length of time. For both hard and easy aid, fifis are invaluable and they need to be mastered to make your movements both less taxing and safer. I am going to lump all such short term connectors under the term fifi, but there is a large variety of connectors, with most climbers constantly switching from one to the other. In this book when I use the term fifi unless it is specified as a fifi hook, it can also be a karabiner used in the same way.

FIFI HISTORY

As I've mentioned before, in the past, climbers were held in position by their belayer locking or pulling on the rope, creating that third hand. But as climbers tackled steeper and steeper walls in the Dolomites this proved ineffective.

And so climbers began taking the small fifi hooks from the tops of their alpine aiders, designed to ensure the aiders could be quickly pulled off placements, and attaching them to their harness instead. Now all they had to do was hook their fifi and then sit back and rest, saving both the leader and belayer a great deal of stress.

This technique soon found its way over to Yosemite, where it fitted in well with the new knotted and sewn daisy chains. Unlike chunky oval krabs which were hard to slot into webbing and whose noses would hook and snag, fifis just went anywhere.

ANATOMY OF A FIFI HOOK

A fifi hook is a question mark shaped climbing tool, usually small, and generally stamped out of a sheet of steel, or forged out of alloy. It has a large hole at the bottom for connecting to one's harness via sling or cord, and large enough for a karabiner, and a smaller hole at the top for connecting a retrieval cord or pig's tail. Its basic function is to

hook into gear and take your weight. It offers very little strength and, due to its open shape, requires a great deal of care when used as it will likely fall off as soon as it becomes unweighted. Some climbers use a karabiner instead of a fifi as they find it more secure, with a keylock krab working best.

FIFI HOOK CORD LENGTH

The length of the cord or sling between you and the fifi is important and I feel many get this wrong and have it too short, meaning they're left scrabbling around for it in between moves (the tape on a BD fifi being a good example).

The simplest method is to just larks foot a 30 cm dyneema sling into the fifi, then larks foot it into your belay loop, giving you around a 25 cm connector. You can also make your own fine tuned connector, and my preference is for dyneema cord, as a lot of force can go through the fifi.

Belay Loop

Tip: One of the best ways to get two differing lengths of fifi connection is to pass the fifi through the gear you want to hang from, and then hook the fifi back onto your belay loop, thereby halving its length (as shown in diagram on previous page).

THE PULL CORD

The fifi hook's retrieval cord can be either a small loop, or a single strand of cord tied at either end with a sliding double fisherman's knot (3 mm perlon). The cord is used to pull the fifi off a placement easily, but many users don't realise this, meaning they fiddle around with their fingers in order to pull it off. Using a loop also means you can clip the fifi out of the way, but I personally prefer a single strand about 10 cm in length. The Petzl fifi has a system that has a slot running through it that helps to stop accidental unhooking by the pull cord, but this is really only of use for solo tagging as the hook is too weak for remote hauling, even if doubled up.

ADVANCED CONNECTION

You can buy a double fifi set up, where the sling has a fifi at the end, and also close to the larks foot, giving you two options. In reality I find this two fifi system is unnecessary, and instead prefer a system where I have a fifi at the end of the cord, then a Petzl Spirit clipped in to the knot joining it to the belay loop. Why not just clip this karabiner into the belay loop? Well being clipped into the cord allows it to twist, something not easy to do when clipped to a belay loop. With this system I use the fifi for fast action, and the krab for security, when top stepping. Also on hard aid you often need two short connectors, clipping off the piece you're on and the piece you're testing.

ADJUSTABLE FIFI

There are several adjustable fifis on the market, with the Kong model being the most common and simple. These are attached to the belay loop with a length of soft 7 mm cord, can be easily lengthened and shortened, and are well loved by their fans. You can also make or modify adjustable lanyards (cut down a full length Yates adjustable daisy for example), but these tend to be two long when adjusted down, with buckle, webbing and karabiner just adding more bulk.

High on Suser Gjennom Harryland, Troll Wall

ALFIFI

The alfifi is an adjustable length fifi, and it utilizes a cam buckle and 1" webbing. It is girth hitched to your harness as a body weight positioning device. It solves many of the problems with using adjustable daisies for body positioning. The main problem with adjustable daisies is that they are not releasable under load. This is critical when using them while top stepping. The Alfifi is easily released under load and allows you to extend the fifi to the perfect length needed to top step comfortably. Adjustable daisies require you to release the buckle and extend the length, let go, grab the krab and release it, then you might have to grab the buckle again to extend the daisy further, then grab the krab again to clip it. With the Alfifi you grab the buckle, press the lever to extend the webbing while removing the hook and moving it up to the high piece. It's all done in one fluid movement, making things way easier, smoother and faster.

Fifi Limitations: Although I've taken factor 2 falls onto my fifi and it has stayed in one piece, I've seen plenty that have ended up looking like bananas!

The main danger is that you forget to secure yourself adequately and end up hanging from your fifi. In 2000 I made a stormy ascent of Zenyatta Mondatta in April. One morning I climbed out of the portaledge to sort out the rack, which I did while hanging from my fifi 400 metres off the deck. It was only when I climbed back to the ledge, yarding on assorted slings and aiders, that I realised I wasn't tied in and had, in fact, been trusting my life to a cheap bit of alloy.

The Black Diamond fifi seems very strong, while the Petzl model is much easier to break due to its cut outs (it is also very sharp).

AIDING SYSTEMS

So now we have covered the component parts of what you will need to employ to aid climb, let's talk about how they fit together.

BASIC PROGRESSION

You aid up a climb by working through the following steps:

01. Place gear.
02. Attach lanyard with aider attached.
03. Test gear (optional).
04. Climb up aider.
05. Free hands up by hanging on fifi, (not always necessary).
06. Place next piece.
07. Repeat.

This is pretty simple stuff, but within it there is a lot of complexity. How many aiders do you have? How do you test gear? What if you can't find the next piece? Below I'm going to cover the main systems of ascent. As I've already mentioned, when talking about aiders, lanyards and fifis, these are general terms and different types can be employed (a quickdraw instead of a fifi for example).

ONE AIDER METHOD

The one aider system is the one I use when alpine climbing, speed climbing or employing guerilla aid methods. It requires very little gear, and is ideal for improvisation (makeshift aider and lanyard). It can take a little while for people to get this one aider and one lanyard system, but the basic principle is that your lanyard goes first, acting as a third arm, holding you while you move up the aider, which you use to move up the lanyard further. So move lanyard, rest on the lanyard, move up aider, climb the aider, move lanyard, rest on the lanyard, etc. This method is one worth learning if for no other reason than you'll have a fall back plan if you drop one of your aiders.

Step By Step

Putting the gear in is not important here, so I'm going to go through the process as if climbing a line of bolts.

01. Clip a quickdraw into the first bolt.
02. Clip your lanyard into the bottom krab on the draw.
03. Clip your aider into the top karabiner.
04. Climb the aider until you can clip in your fifi and rest.
05. Clip in the rope.
06. Place quickdraw on new bolt above.
07. Unclip the lanyard and clip this into the bottom krab on the new quickdraw.
08. Climb the aider below until you can't go any higher.
09. Tighten/shorten your lanyard (or switch your fifi from the quickdraw to the lanyard).
10. Rest on your lanyard.
11. Remove aider from bottom bolt and 'clip up' into quickdraw above.
12. Climb the aider until you can rest on the new bolt.
13. Repeat.

With this system the aim is to be able to unclip the lanyard easily each time, meaning you don't want it to be jammed by the aider or fifi. The best way to do this is to keep the three parts separate, so lanyard in rope end of the quickdraw, aider in gear end, fifi into the gear, etc. In reality, there tends always to be some juggling of what's weighted, but you just need to be adaptable.

NOTES:

Metal To Metal: The ideal with this system, as with all aider systems, is to avoid creeping up the lanyards, and instead move up efficiently from one piece to the next, your fifi going from one hard point to the next (into a karabiner, bolt or gear). This approach, the 'metal to metal' mantra will save you a great deal of time.

One Aider Testing: With the above method it's best to test via your lanyard before fully committing and clipping up your aider.

Sideways: The only place where such a system falls down is where you have a lot of traversing, and so it's good to have a second aider available. Saying that I have climbed some tricky hooking pitches with one aider, so it can be done.

Fifi Variation: A Euro style version of this adds a fifi hook to the aider, attaching this to you via a length of cord (3 to 4 mm dyneema ideally). I would recommend a cord long enough so that the fifi hangs below your feet when free climbing. With this method you can't drop your aider, plus the narrow fifi can slip more easily into your gear. This method allows you to step off your fifi and then have it lift off automatically - a real boon for mixed free and aid climbing.

TWO AIDER METHOD

This is probably the default system, and the beauty of this system is that it's half as heavy or bulky as a four aider method yet still gives you many of the advantages when the aiders are clipped together, and like the one aider method, promotes movement (with the four aider method you can end up just mincing around on all those steps). The only real disadvantage of this system is when things get harder, when maxed out on your top steps, as being offset makes them a tiny bit less stable ('tiny' can mean a lot on an A4 lead). As a follow on from that, once you've made that top step move it can be very 'balancey' to reach down and get that second aider up (using a third aider can help), which is why the three aider system was invented. Saying that, when I soloed the Reticent I just used two aiders.

Step By Step

Again this demonstration takes place up a line of bolts, and when I talk about the 'aider' I am talking about the aider, lanyard and linking karabiners as one unit.

01. Clip the first bolt with a quick draw. When placing anything but cams it's best to always set up the next piece ready to clip, even though you will not clip in the rope. This means if you place a wire for example, you clip in a quickdraw. The reason for this is that once you're about to leave the piece you do not want to have to unclip totally in order to clip in a draw, as to do so exposes you to a longer fall if the new piece fails.

02. Clip your aider directly into the piece. You are now directly connected to the piece, which means it cannot be lost, important when using marginal gear. Clipping high, and not into the quickdraw, will allow you to get higher.

03. Test the piece. This is done via the aider or via the lanyard.

04. Clip your second aider into the first's linking karabiner. If you're using a two karabiner system, then clip one oval into the other. Now you have two aiders to climb, each step a little offset from the other.

05. Climb the aiders. Climb up carefully until high on the piece.

06. Clip in your fifi to the top aider. Now you can relax and scan for the next placement.

07. Clip a quickdraw into the next piece. If you have to step high you can, using both aiders.

08. Reach down and take the lower aider and clip it up into the new piece. This may require a little balance, but you can hold onto the quickdraw above when doing so.

09. Test the gear. Be aware that if the gear fails you do not want to shock load your current active piece.

10. Clip the rope into your current piece. You should never be clipping the rope any higher than your waist when aiding. Your lanyard is your connector, and pulling up loads of rope only exposes you to a longer fall, and also makes extra and unnecessary work for your belayer.

11. Climb up onto the new piece. Sometimes this can be made easier by stepping on both steps, but be aware

Vanessa Kirkpatrick using the Two Aider Method in Zion

where your feet are in case the new piece was to.

12. Rest on your fifi. Ideally you want to go 'metal to metal', but if it's very steep you can clip into - or shorten - your lanyard. It is also vital that you learn not to hang off your arms, but employ the fifi at all times necessary.

13. Reach down and clip your bottom aider from the lower piece into your higher piece. Now you have two aiders to stand in again.

14. Repeat.

This is the simplest, most effective method of aiding on any type of terrain and is the core of aid climbing progression.

THREE AIDER METHOD

This is the same as above, only you have a floating third aider that lives either on your harness, ready for use, or is clipped off onto one of your main aiders. This is used to overcome a problem on harder aid, when high stepping, in that it can be very hard to balance on one foot in order to reach down and unclip your aider. By using a third aider you can have a very stable platform set up, with your other aider and lanyard ready to clip once you get high. Metolius pocket aiders or Fish or Black Diamond alpine aiders all

work very well in this method. Another advantage of a three aider system is that you always have a spare.

FOUR AIDER METHOD

This was the old school standard, and how I climbed my first few big walls. The advantage here is that you're always standing in two aiders, making top stepping much easier. The problem is carrying four full size heavy duty aiders up a wall can feel very cumbersome. Worse still, get in some serious wind or updraft and you're in for a real mess and tangle. And yet for really hard aid, especially drilling rivet ladders, it does create a good platform, so should be in your bag of tricks.

TWO AND TWO HALF AIDER METHOD

This is a speed system that sits between the two aider and four aider method, allowing you to step high without the weight or tangles. With this you simply cut down, or make your own short two step aiders, matching each with one full sized aider, thereby creating what is in effect a four aider system when top stepping, but without the weight or bulk. This allows you to climb up the full length aider until you can step into both and then stand in balance, which fosters getting higher than normal, and increases speed.

RUSSIAN AIDER METHOD

I've discussed this system already, but to recap - the Russian system employs four very light 'trees' that you hook your leg loops into, creating a four aider system without all the weight or tangles. It is also possible to employ a two or one 'tree' system, and a one 'tree' system using a fifi hook arrangement is great for full bore mixed action.

TESTING

Being able to judge the security of your next piece of gear is one of the most important skills of the aid climber. This skill both stops you taking a whipper, and reduces the terror of leading. Get testing right and you open up the hardest wall. Get it wrong and you won't go far at all, or you'll go all the way!

A PERSONAL JOURNEY

On the first wall I did I knew very little about bounce testing, just some stuff I'd read in a small big wall manual. This told me that I had to step into the aider and bounce up and down, which sounded easy while sat at home, but not half way up El Cap. In reality I'd place a piece of gear, and not really trusting the piece I was on, half heartedly weight the next one, afraid if I pulled it out the shock would make the one I was on fail too. This approach meant that even bomber nuts and cams, things I'd feel were train stoppers while free climbing, now seemed like time bombs. Each and every lead was just a long drawn out journey into absolute fear. By the time I reached the belay I'd feel like I'd had a death sentence commuted.

The error is easy to see, that by failing to make sure the first piece was bomber I

undermined the next, and the next. This came to a head on the head wall of the Shield, the crux, where not only did I not trust anything, I was also back cleaning, having only a few cams that fitted the beaten out peg scars. Oh and we were trying to go hammerless. Reaching up to a good looking head I clipped into it, unclipped from the piece I was on, and started up the aider, my heart in my mouth. Then, to my horror, I could feel the wire pulling through the swage, a fraction of a millimetre at a time, until BANG, it ripped and I was off; a big head first plunge down my first big wall.

More walls followed, and bit by bit I got my head around it, testing each placement with more force, Pacific Ocean Wall, Iron Hawk, Lost In America, teaching me the importance of building confidence in each piece. Looking back though I think a great deal of this confidence did not come from testing, but from understanding the gear, how it worked, how to get the most out of it. I realised that by rotating a cam one way or the other I could either have a junk placement or something that could hold a fall, that the tip of a RURP could hold as much as a long lost arrow. Often I was testing, but not fully, using skill and an eye to tell me what was good and what was not, well skill, eye, and luck.

Then when I soloed Aurora, my fifth wall, I found myself on a route that demanded the highest security, where you could not afford to fall. Here, alone on long pitches of heads and hooks I learnt the art of testing, testing gear to break it. I made a shift in my head from "please don't pull out" to "I'm going to pull you out you bastard". My job was to yank it out, most often using my daisy chain, the best way to statically shock

load gear, and if I could not? Well I just had to move on.

This robust method was then further tested on other walls, loose walls, where aggressive testing would break the rock, or open it up. I realised that being too rough could break edges, or pull cables through heads. On these walls I had to adopt a mixed approach, softly, softly at times, hard at others. I learned to balance the eye and the knowledge and skill with the brute force.

In the end I realised that testing gear requires many notes.

WHY TEST?

This is not such a stupid question really. Testing gear is the way of finding out several different things. First of all you're testing the piece to see if it will hold your body weight, which will be around 100 kg with all your gear on. This can be achieved by simply hanging off it. If it fails a static body weight test then it's no good. In reality you apply more force than body weight, and just the act of climbing up onto the piece creates further forces, as well as the weight of the ropes and their drag. And so what you're trying to test is body weight plus a bit extra. This would be a speed climber's aim, not really needing to know if the piece will take a fifty foot whipper, but just whether or not it will let them past. Next comes the ability for the piece to hold you if the next piece should fail while testing it, your body coming back down hard onto this piece. Can it hold that? Next and last is can this piece be viewed as 'solid', which means it can hold the force of a falling leader.

TESTING PSYCHOLOGY

When testing gear you're playing a long game with the rock, each placement a move, each move tested to see if it was correct. Like chess, if you rush it, are slapdash, you'll lose. What losing translates as can be anything from a piece ripping out as you begin to climb it, sending you down onto the last piece, to this last piece also failing, to a piece failing when high on it, creating a larger force on the gear below. On really hard aid this game of chess can become more like defusing hundreds of tiny booby traps, trying to gauge the right move based on many variables, testing just one tool in your tool box.

TESTING SCENARIO

Your first piece of gear from the belay is a top step move to an old rusty RURP, its cable bent and twisted and frayed. Beyond it there are just heads and hook moves all the way to the belay one hundred and fifty feet away, a big ledge to break your legs if you blow it.

Here are two approaches to this problem:

Non-Jenga Approach: You top step as high as you can and clip the frayed wire, knowing others must have trusted it, so it should hold you too and if it breaks maybe you won't break your legs because surely all those other climbers wouldn't have risked that. Once on it you realise you need to top step from it to reach a #1 brass head. As you sit there and contemplate the move all you can imagine is the cable breaking, and the sound of your body hitting the ledge.

Jenga Approach: Instead of focusing solely on the obvious high RURP, you look around and spot a possible beak tip between the belay and it. It's shallow, but you have a filed down beak that fits in pretty well. Once placed you get down below your Jesus piece on the belay and bounce test it hard. Knowing it's solid you climb up and get eyeball to eyeball with the RURP. The cable is junk, but the hole is visible, so you use the tip of a beak to cut away the cable. Now you have a choice to replace it using 3 mm dyneema, 1/2 inch webbing or by threading it with a #0 rivet hanger.

You go for the dyneema, and then give it a hard test, clip it off with a Yates Scream Aid sling, and step up. Feeling confident now, you see that below the #1 head there is a deadhead where you can get a beak tip. You place it and test it, and test the head above. Both are solid and so you equalise them with an 'improved' sliding X tied with a 60 cm dyneema sling, then clip in another Yates screamer.

As you can see in the first example, the one most new climbers could relate to, the approach is one of fingers crossed, while the second demonstrates crossing the Ts. The former can work, especially on trade routes, or for speed climbing, but as the climbing gets harder, the risk becomes greater, especially as you get onto dangerous ground where you must not fall. Worst of all the former style of climbing is mentally exhausting and terrifying, leaving the leader feeling like they're out in the middle of a frozen lake in a thaw.

The latter may look overly paranoid, treating the whole pitch with utmost care, but this approach leads to a very safe and confident lead, a professional lead and also a faster lead. If a fall does happen,

which it can on hard aid, then the leader has left behind a string of placements, some nests of gear, that they know will hold them. If you climb like this, then the confidence it brings you allows you to rapidly move onto harder and harder pitches. I guess what I'm really saying is that hard climbing is not about dealing with hard or dangerous moves - that's easy - it's about dealing with hard or dangerous thoughts. Jenga thinking is the best way I've found to scale the mind.

FORCES

It's vital that you understand both the forces a climber can generate in bounce testing as well as what forces your gear can take.

When teaching testing I always begin by tying a loop of 2 mm perlon cord and getting my students to weight it. Now a loop of 2 mm with a double fisherman's knot is rated about 100 kg, and by carefully creeping onto it the loop will hold the climbers weight, but not if they move around, stress or shock load it. Now I get them to bounce test it, and one hard bounce breaks it. This tells you that if you can give a few hard tests to something then it should hold your weight.

Now I tie a loop out of 3 mm perlon, which will hold about 200 kg, which will be roughly equivalent to a perfect #0 head. Now the student can hang off this easily, and can swing around. Now I try and get them to break this using both bounce testing on their aiders and via their lanyards, something few people can do. This gives the student an understanding of the value of a hard bounce, that it means they can feel confident that the piece is safe to get onto.

On the flip side of this, if you were to try testing with a funkness device it's not unknown for the forces involved to break karabiners or wires, telling you that the force you are applying is beyond the margins of what is needed.

TESTING TECHNIQUES

In the following descriptions X stands for the gear you are testing and Y is the gear you are currently on.

Body Position: Before we get into the nitty gritty, it's vital when testing that you don't expose your gear to larger forces than necessary, especially on hard aid (just think of it as undermining the good chess moves by one failure). What you need to focus on is what will happen if X fails and you fall onto Y. For example, I've had partners testing a poor piece by getting fully onto the aider clipped to the piece and jumping up and down like a cowboy. Here they've not considered what will happen if X fails, which will be a hard daisy fall onto Y, which could rip it out. By having the rope clipped in to the gear you can add some small shock absorber into the system, but you'll still be falling onto Y with your daisy. Instead you need to hedge your bets and use your body as that shock absorber. To do this always keep one hand and one foot on Y, your arm ready to take the shock, your foot ready to step back into the Y aider.

Aider vs Lanyard: In the past, books used to just say test everything by standing in the aiders and jumping up and down, but I find the lanyard is a much better way to test gear. The reason for this is that with a lanyard test (or a 'daisy test'), you're stable on the piece below and are less afraid of a failure, so can be more aggressive. Dynamic lanyards such as rope lanyards and cam lock slings make it harder to create a solid static load on the gear, and so on hard aid I often use a third static lanyard such as a long PAS, finding this allows me to do a harder test. One other issue to be aware of with standard sewn daisy chains is that hard testing can and does break the bar tacks on pockets, which are only rated at 2 kN, which is one reason why looped PASs style lanyards (i.e. Metolius Super Daisy) are better.

Watch Your Face: When testing be very aware of where gear will go if you pull it out. This should be in direct line with the load, but if your chin is in line with your lanyard or looking up from your aider, then that could be into your face or forehead. Wearing a helmet is vital, and wearing sunglasses or safety glasses is recommended, but even with these, keep your face clear.

Visual Test: This non test is just a judgement call by you the leader, that the cam is set well within a clean crack for example and therefore does not require testing, a common approach when leap-frogging up perfect granite cracks. This can also apply to more complex placements when speed climbing, just placing them well and getting on them. If I'm not 100% sure I'll give the placement a body weight test, or bounce, just to make sure the load is inline. One place I would test perfect placements is at the end of a run out or hard aid pitch, where you find an A1 placement and feel inclined to just jump on it. One out of a hundred placements like this will fail for no reason, some unseen loose skin over the rock, or fractured section, causing the gear to fail, and sending you down the wall.

Gut Instinct: Sometimes you cannot test a piece, and cannot visually check it either, and here you'll need to go for gut instinct — or luck. Sometimes you may have a cam that must be placed blindly around a corner or behind a flake. In these situations it's always best to hedge your bets, and place a few cams of varying sizes to be sure one is correct, such a green, yellow and red Alien.

Bodyweight Plus: This is a good speed climbing test, and is best done with your lanyard. Just clip into the gear you want to test and sit on it for a second, then give one hard test. On a hook the plus part of the test can be done by just pressing down with your body, and often you can see the weight going onto the device by the hook flexing, or the karabiner opening up a little.

Crescendo Test: This is like the bodyweight test, but builds up to a very hard test, maybe over five bounces. This is ideal for pieces you need to be sure will not fail, perhaps on a run out section.

Low Test: On bleak aid you may find yourself on a piece that you've tested but don't fully trust, such as a bat hook or tiny head. Here you might be afraid of any extra force on the piece while testing the next one. In these situations you can create a little top rope style test, where you clip X, then climb down until you are below Y, so that any failure of X will create minimal impact. This style of testing requires long aiders or longer than normal lanyards.

Terror Testing: You will come to a point on hard aid — or easy aid if you're doing it wrong — where you're so scared you cannot move. In Psychovertical I call this the 'Fearometer', where the terror sends you into the red. One way to deal with this is solid testing, but even then that's often not enough. If this happens just sitting with all your weight on X while below Y for several minutes can help lower your fear to a level at which you can climb up.

Sideways Testing: Testing gear off to the side can be quite tricky as it's hard to get all your weight onto X without fully committing to it, and is usually done via your aiders. On some pitches, such as the great roof on the Nose, you're doing a visual test, and with gear like cam hooks you can usually tell they cannot come out once committed to. On more bleak terrain a low test can put you in a better position to judge the security of the placement, and with the rope clipped into Y you can almost have a top rope, testing, then climbing up to place the next piece.

TOP STEPPING

Top stepping, getting as high as you can on the piece you're on, tends to be done mainly in the second steps, and is vital at all grades, even easy routes. Often being able to get super high, as high as your grab loops, allows you to get A1 placements in A3 terrain, sewing the good hooks, cams and nuts, and avoiding the A4 gear. Once you get up to A3 it often becomes the key to progress. It is one of the most important, albeit scarier, aiding techniques, and in the case of bleak aid, also one of the most hazardous! It plays a part in climbing fast, as getting high on a piece comfortably allows you to place less gear.

DO YOU NEED TO TOP STEP?

Top stepping is a vital skill, but one that is not useful 100% of the time. If the only possible next placement can be reached from the third step in your aiders, there's not much point cranking up to the hero loops. So before you start moving up in your ladders ask if you need to be using all the extra energy? If you do need to get a bit higher check first is the step you're on (usually the third step), as high as it can be? If you're running a two krab system on the top of your aiders (locker plus oval), you can just clip into the highest position you can (into the clip loop of an Alien rather than its sling for example), gaining you an extra 10 cm. A counter intuitive option can actually be to drop your aider (clip down from the clip loop into the cam's karabiner), so you lower the second step meaning you're not so high above the piece, and making it easier to stay in balance.

FIFI METHOD

As in rock climbing, just an extra inch of height can make a big difference, and so getting comfortable moving up out of your lower steps is crucial. The main technique used to move up with confidence and stability is balance, then when this can't be maintained, tension. Balance comes from moving carefully, using any holds that you can (having chalk is handy), but on very steep ground this can be tricky. In order to move up onto a higher step on tricky ground like this, simply pass the fifi hook through the karabiner at the top of your aiders (or the one attached to the gear) and hook it back into your belay loop, thereby shortening it. This shorter length loop (about 15 cm), will allow you to step into the next steps, and create an upward pull on the gear/aider krab (one step below the fifi was pulling down). Using your legs, core muscle, and the stretch/give of your harness you should be able to hold yourself in balance with your waist above the gear. Of course the danger of this technique is that the fifi hook is only held in place by tension, and a lack of concentration will see you fall - not good on hard aid. If you're using

an Alfifi you can achieve the same effect, but being adjustable, it allows you to fine tune your position.

Alfifi Method

KARABINER METHOD

A more secure method is to clip a karabiner to your belay loop (or use the more advanced fifi method), and clip this into the placement you're on (where you clip it allows you to further adjust your position). If this is too short (you can't stand

up), then extend this with a second or third karabiner (for very high steps). This creates a very solid chain that will not come adrift if you need to drop back down again. There have also been occasions when I've clipped a karabiner into my leg loop to stay in position, but this is hazardous, as falling back would see you spin upside down.

Two karabiner method

FEET

Top stepping is very hard on your feet, and I find solid boots help, with continuous top stepping leading to feet so sore they become debilitating. One important tip is feet positioning, locking your heels together and splaying your feet so as to create a tripod position.

RUSSIAN AIDER

I find the Russian aider method much easier for high stepping, putting you in about the level of a step and half from the top for very little effort. For really high steps you might need to clip one knee strap directly into the gear (cable on a beak for example), but this can be very sketchy and balancey (wearing rock boots can help).

HERO LOOPS

When you're forced up into the grab loop or plastic stiffener of your aiders you're in your 'hero loops', which can be very scary (and nearly impossible), on anything off vertical. One way to step into these loops on steep ground is to employ a less than body weight 'balance' placement that only holds your body in position, something like a #0 head or poor beak. This allows you to make almost body weight spans and is often the key to very hard aid.

TOP STEP TESTING

It is very hard to test gear when standing in your second steps, so unless it's a hook or an A1 placement, you should test it low on the piece you're on (from the third step), which will mean you need to extend it (most lanyards will be too short), best done by clipping in a 60 cm dyneema sling, then bounce testing it. If you don't test it and you fall, you'll be taking a factor 2 onto your lanyard, which could break the lanyard, krab, or rip the gear - not good on bleak aid.

EASY OPTIONS

One final point. Remember that getting a placement just 10 cm higher can make a difference, so don't overlook a placement that's within reach, like a head 10 cm higher.

LESS NOT MORE

Lastly, always remember Bridwell's view on the subject, that on hard aid, where one failure could spell disaster, you are better with twenty bomber pieces rather than a mixed bag of forty.

TRAVERSING PITCHES

Many climbs feature pitches that traverse, usually at an angle, but sometimes horizontally, or even downwards.

The most important thing to stress is that you need to focus on the cleaner here, that they will need to lower off each piece then reach back to clean that piece when on the next one.

This means all pieces either need to be about one metre apart, or placed within one metre of a fixed piece. A good example of this is the Great Roof on the Nose, which is sometimes fully fixed, and others only partially. If the leader only clips the fixed pieces as protection then that's fine, as the second can simply lower off each in turn. If they leave pro on either side of fixed pieces the same applies, as the second can just unclip these pieces and lower off the fixed piece.

When this falls down is say a horizontal crack (such as the Knifeblade Traverse on Iron Hawk, or the second pitch on Zodiac), where the leader leaves a cam two metres from any other piece of gear. Here the second has to either just leave it behind when they lower off it, or try and unweight it while on it and take a big swing.

Some pitches that traverse backwards and forwards can give the second the opportunity to down climb and retrieve the left gear below them, but usually you just want to either back clean fully, only clip fixed pieces, or stitch it up.

LEADER FALLS

The harder the aid, the less you want to fall, but it's important to come to terms with the idea that sooner or later you will, and that when you do, you've done your best to make it safe.

CONSEQUENCES

The first thing when leading is to be able to spot dangerous falls, where you can fuck yourself up, or worse. These can often be more likely on easy walls, when you are being sloppy, than on hard walls, where the ground is often steeper and more blank (think easy rock climbs vs hard sport climbs). The sweet spot of safety is around A2+ to A3, where it's hard enough for you to take it seriously, but steep enough to allow some big whippers. Once you get into hard A3+ and up, you begin to get hard aid above bad landings (ledges, corners and pinnacles). Being a safe climber does not mean being happy to fall, or being blind and fearless, but rather making the judgement about what the outcome will be, and then reducing the chance of that outcome being realised by all means possible.

SAFE FALLS

This kind of fall comes so fast, and ends so quickly, that you won't even notice it until it's happened. Sometimes you'll fall onto your lanyard and be so startled you'll not feel the shock, while other times you'll fall so far you'll be aware how far you're falling.

When you take a safe fall it can take the edge off the climbing a bit, as well as focus you to be less sloppy. I've seen the latter with many gung ho partners, who were a danger to themselves, just trusting bad gear, but who - after a few falls - got with the program. This learning process of falling, and why falls happen, is important, as to still be flying by the seat of your pants on hard aid could be terminal.

DANGEROUS FALLS

Very often a big gear ripping fall off an A4 pitch will be far less dangerous than a slip a few metres up from a ledge, say climbing off Camp Four on the Nose for example, where climbers can hit the ledge and break their legs up. When you're leading you should always remain aware of what you could hit and the consequences of a fall, as this will inform you if you can cut corners or not. It's also important not to expose yourself to hazard by caring about what people might think of you being 'safe', on both hard ground and easy. My experience is that often we can't choose when we will fall, falls most often coming on ground we don't expect (on A1 not A4, 5.6 not 5.11), meaning you should never lower your guard.

Very often I've climbed run out pitches and forgone gear thinking I'd find something else higher up, only to find nothing. Experience tells me that it's all too easy for the hero moment, running it out, to come undone by one broken flake. Very often a climber will be 100% focused on a hard pitch, then switch off on easy ground, only to pitch off there and hurt themselves. Falling is also not always the main danger, rather what you could pull off with you when you fall, and what that might hit.

WHY DO CLIMBERS FALL?

Hard aid is not sport climbing, you don't get better by taking loads of falls, you get crushed, and no one will climb with you. The idea is that good testing should limit the chances of a fall being taken, and looking back at the falls I've taken, many were caused by rushing and not testing properly, while the others were caused by rock failure. In the past I think I used to climb a little quicker, while now I'm slower, I take my time, and enjoy making the unsafe and marginal, safe and solid, but that takes care. I think you can divide the most common falls into the following categories:

Insta-Falls: When aid climbing, most falls happen so quickly you don't even know you've fallen until you've stopped, unless they're really big, and even then it's out of your control anyway. This is the reason why ABBD devices are ideal, as the chances are your belayer will be asleep when you whip eight hours into your pitch.

Time Bomb Falls: Good testing should eliminate this kind of fall, and they often happen when you know the gear is bad, or you fail to test it, the gear holding just long enough to hold you, but no longer. Very often these falls are caused by being lazy, that you know that head with a broken and rusty cable will not hold, but you trick yourself into thinking it will. Then BANG you're falling. Rock quality can also play a part in this, as soft rock can disintegrate while being loaded, and often such rock has a time limit. Examples of this would be micro brass wires in very soft sandstone, which will slowly cause the placement to fail (placing a wider alloy micro such as a 00 wallnut might give you more time). The more you climb the more you get a sense of what's a time bomb and what's not.

RETREATING OFF BLEAK AID

There might come a time when you're forced to down climb from a very hard aid pitch, the main cause often being you've gone the wrong way. In such situations just down aiding is not an option, as the gear will often be very poor. Instead you need to lower off your high point, but do so without leaving all your gear behind. If you did this the traditional way, of lowering off and stripping the pitch, you would be really exposed, because if the lower off gear failed you'd take a huge fall. Instead use the following method:

01. Create a lower off point with a karabiner (not a sling). If this piece is bomber than a single piece is fine, but if marginal, try and make an equalised lower off with your two highest pieces.

02. Clip your haul/zip-line into your belay loop, then into the lower off.

03. The belayer will lower you on your haul/zip-line, while taking in the slack on your lead line. This is best done by clipping the haul/zip-line into a belay device, and keeping the lead line on an ABBD.

04. Begin to lower slowly so as not to shock the system, the leader taking out each piece they come to.

05. If you run out of haul/zip-line (the leader is lowering further than 50% of its length), then the climber will have to create another lower off, then unclip and untie the haul/zip-line, pull it down from the top lower off, and continue.

06. The advantage of this system is that the leader is always on belay, meaning if the lower off fails they will only take a smaller fall (otherwise a twenty metre lower off exposes the leader to a forty metre fall).

An important detail here is that if you're on a piece that will only hold 100 kg and you lower off it, then the load is doubled (your weight, plus the weight applied by the belayer), which could cause the gear to fail, hence the need to create a solid nest of protection.

FIXING MID PITCH

There sometimes comes a point when you can't complete a pitch, due to darkness, bad weather, or you're just too scared. In this situation you can't just down climb like you would on a free route, as you might be too high, or the gear will be too bleak (you don't want to re-climb that rope tomorrow when it's only clipped through a #1 head.

Instead you should first create a solid belay via the protection you have. On a very hard pitch this would be achieved by equalizing your three highest pieces with your cordelette, creating a masterpoint below the lower piece (you will need to down climb each one, with the lead line clipped in to the highest piece, giving you a top rope as you build the anchor).

Once you have your masterpoint you should clip your haul line (or zip line) into this using two lockers, or a locker and a plain gate karabiner back to back. Two krabs are used because if the belay fails while descending your life would be held by a single shock loaded lockers, so why not back it up? Now you should clip your lead line into the locker with a Butterfly knot, and attach your belay device or ABBD to the haul line (zip-line). If using a belay device make sure you use a backup Prusik as well, and increase the friction if on a thin zip line. While clipping into the rope the belayer should secure the lead line (tie it off to the belay masterpoint).

With all the weight on the haul line the leader now unties from the lead line and abseils down. If the belay above fails they will be falling onto lower pieces - while rappelling - which cannot happen, hence the need for a solid belay. The following day the climber ascends the rope back to the belay, re-ties into the lead line, clips into the haul line, unties all knots and continues up, leaving the three equalised pieces as a super runner.

ROPE TRICKS

Here are a few tricks you may need on a wall:

PENDULUMS

Not all walls feature pendulums, and not all pendulums require pendulums, some done just with tension, but this is an important skill to understand as it's also vital for retreat.

Pendulum Safety

The most important aspect of penduluming is that your lower off point is 100% secure, especially if you back clean the pitch as you lower off, as a ten metre lower out could see you take a twenty metre fall! It's also vital that the point is solid as your second will end up having this as their top anchor.

The Pendulum

Before you lower down make sure everything is ready, your aiders etc clipped off and out of the way. If you need to snatch an edge or feature have a skyhook ready on a lanyard, or gear you know you will need (such as a Camalot 4 for the King Swing). Having rock boots on is often a very good idea, as well as chalk, and a light rack.

TENSION TRAVERSE

This is a variation of the swing, and requires very good communication, as often you want the rope to be fed out by the centimetre. Again having rock boots on is important, but you can also tension off hooks, using vertical edges to get to where you're going. When tensioning try and keep talking to your belayer to avoid suddenly getting dropped (this has happened to me several times when people think your silence is a signal you no longer need a tight rope!).

ROPE TOSS

This can help to span sections of blankness, using a large nut, hook, or loop to snag some far off object. Unless you're good at throwing it might take some time and perseverance, but it generally pays off.

FREE CLIMBING

If you're very strong then you might be able to free climb a wall bottom to top, but if you're not, then you're going to have to just do it as free as can be. More often than not, your free climbing ability on smaller climbs may well come up short when you double the weight of your rack, throw in a heavy lead and haul line, and a few bad nights sleep, not to mention early starts and late bedtimes. Add in exposure, heat and long pitches and often climbers, even great climbers, tend to find that 5.9 is their limit. On the other hand, it's easy for climbers to get too stuck into an aid mentality, and just stick with it, aiding easy ground that's actually well within their grade, even in approach shoes. Getting out of this mindset is vital for easy to moderate aid. If you intend to free climb then it's important that you get into the right mindset, get the weight down, wear your best rock boots, and use a zip line rather than a haul line etc.

ROCK BOOTS

Most teams will take at least one pair of rock boots on a wall, and these should fit the best free climber and be fitted for the appropriate climbing. This means a good quality pair of rock boots (like Sportiva TC Pros) that can climb well, and yet still be worn most of the day, not a big baggy pair of rock boots you can walk down from the summit in. Wearing a thin pair of socks can help comfort, fit and reduce stink, as well as making them a little warmer on cold days. If your sights are set on something hard and free, then you will probably need to bring a few pairs of boots. If you're tackling colder alpine walls, then you need to think about your feet and fit rock boots to wear with thicker socks, or use insulated boots, such as the Boreal Invernal, or heated socks.

AID TO FREE / FREE TO AID

If you need to go into free mode here are a few methods:

01. While standing on one aider, stow your second aider and lanyard.

02. Place your fifi direct into your piece, freeing up your lanyard.

03. Place your feet in position to climb.

04. Stow remaining lanyard and aider away.

05. Flip fifi hook off and start climbing.

If you have to climb off a placement, and cannot simply reach down and unclip your lanyard/aider (you can throw this over your shoulder until it can be stowed), then use a sling as a makeshift foot loop to step off.

Of course the simplest method is to have the belayer take you tight on the lead line, while you put away all your aiding kit, then launch into free climbing.

Sometimes you might not have your rock boots on, so will need to put these on while hanging on your last piece (also make sure you have your chalk bag, crack gloves etc).

GUERRILLA AID

First of all, what is guerrilla (or Gorilla) aid? In the past, this style of climbing was unkindly called French Free, which translated as 'anything goes' climbing, otherwise known as cheating. Technically this tends to be a spectrum between full free and A1 climbing, aid climbing that can be done with a minimum.

This type of climbing is most often found on mixed routes, where there is aid and free - or 'as free as it can be' climbing, where speed is the key, freeing what can be climbed quickly and frigging the rest. This style of climbing is also of great use for alpine climbing, which is the reason why we have the term 'French Free', the pulling on pegs and fixed gear necessary to nail those guide book times, rather than taking turns on the rope to try and free one single move out of many.

GUERRILLA RACK

The rack for A0 climbing is, of course, the same as for free climbing, but there are a few things worth thinking about. Having longer open draws that will take a hand allows you to use them like an axe wrist loop, or grab loop. Larger top clipping karabiners that will take three fingers also help, and some krabs are much easier to hold than others. Cams such as the Totem have slings that can take the hand easily and are much simpler to hold and pull on than standard looped units. When using all such gear be aware of the dangers of inserting hands and fingers into loops, as falling onto fingers threaded through a cam's loop can break them, or worse, and ideally being able to 'let go' is best.

GUERRILLA CLIMBING TECHNIQUES

Most of the techniques involved in guerrilla aid are like street fighting, just what works at the moment, and so there's very little formal stuff to learn. But the fundamental principle is to pull, stand, tension and yank your way up the pitches, lowering the free climbing grade to the point where you can keep moving up. The second you come to a free climbing impasse you flip into guerrilla aid mode. Aiders, fifi hooks and lanyards are held in reserve as much as possible, deployed when needed, and then racked away again when the problem is dealt with.

The basic approach is best termed as 'cheating', for example stuffing in a cam, grabbing it like a hand hold, and pulling up until you can reach a good hold and keep free climbing. You need to get over your resistance to step on pegs, bolts, even your partner's head, to move. The lower pitches of the Nose are a good example of guerrilla climbing, where you don't need to go into full aid mode, but instead, just be more ethically relaxed!

If one A0 move leads into another, you're best to clip in your fifi hook, and try and climb on your fifi, half free climbing and pulling in so you can get your fifi into the next gear. Without a fifi you will need your partner to give you tension on the rope, or tension yourself up on the rope, pinching the rope to hold yourself in place. This, of course, can be far harder than just free climbing, and if it goes on too long will exhaust the leader, but is necessary if the free climbing is beyond you, and speed is an issue, as it's far faster than aiding the pitch. Very often you'll be forced to bust some hard free move where there is nothing else, so it's best not to get bogged down onto pure guerrilla mentality. Remember your motto is 'Free as it can be'.

GUERRILLA A0+

There will come the point though when it's best to switch to aider and lanyard, perhaps a longer section of pegs or rivets, where hanging off your arms will take longer than just getting out the aid kit. A good example of this would be the Glowering Spot on the Nose, easy free climbing broken up by a short section of micro wires.

Classic guerilla ground on pitch five of the Nose

ROPE CLIMBING

On most big walls one of the make or break skills a climber needs to develop and work on is the ability to climb ropes. Get this simple skill set wrong and you'll soon ground to a halt, and furthermore make those missteps in the wrong order and you could well end up dead. I can remember climbing one pitch on El Cap that had racked up at least two deaths by ascender failure, an awkward downward traverse on your ascenders (yes you may have to go down as well as up!), and marvelling at just how much skill was needed to stay safe, juggling ascenders, an ABBD, lowering out, pulling yourself in.

When it comes to seconding pitches, once you know how to climb a rope with a pair of ascenders you can imagine you've got it dialled, but then you come to a pendulum, or maybe a horizontal traverse, gear every few feet, and you come up short again, leading to either failure, some nasty scare or accident, or some seat of your pants make do technique just to get the job done. On this last one, I know of one team who on climbing the Pacific Ocean Wall on El Cap, found they lacked the skills to clean long sketchy A4 traverses on junk heads and hooks. Unable to think of a better way they elected to have the second just use a knife to cut the tie off on each piece, taking some monster swings, the knife flashing in his hand. They only stopped when the swashbuckling cleaner stuck the knife in his leg, after which they sharpened up the can opener and used that instead!

WHY CLIMB THE ROPE?

In an ideal world the leader would climb up the rock with hands and feet and the second would do the same, as we do on free climbs. This approach is fast and simple and relies on our hard-wired monkey skills to just pull. Where this begins to fall down is when the leader is climbing a pitch that takes everything they have, maybe some awful offwidth nightmare, and is beyond the skill of the second, meaning they'll end up dogging their way up over many falls. Another reason is speed, as an able rope climber can climb a rope in a few minutes, and use very little energy, saving this for the next lead if leads are to be switched.

On aid pitches in the past, the leader would leave aiders hanging from each piton, meaning the second had to climb the pitch as the leader had, only on a top rope, taking pegs out (or leaving them if they were soft pegs), and bring the ladders with him. It was only when people began using prusik knots, and then mechanical ascenders, that the second could more easily climb a rope, which sped up the whole game. On harder pitches, a leader can take half the day to nail and hook the thing together and is probably not keen on then sitting on the belay for another few hours while their second does the same on a top rope.

Even if pitches are to be climbed traditionally, led and followed without ascenders, it's still vital to have a solid bombproof understanding of rope

Vanessa Kirkpatrick cleaning on Mescalito (note excellent use of back up knots)

ascending, as it's the key to the wall's primary highway - the rope.

Even on climbs you will still often need to jug fixed lines, descend and climb lines when climbing from a fixed camp (think Tommy Caldwell on the Dawn Wall), as well as go back to basics when your ass is on the line, jugging someone else's (or the mountain rescue team's) lines in a storm.

On any big climb the ability to climb a rope without killing yourself, or wishing you were dead due to your gut busting lack of skill, is a keystone of self rescue, be it with handled ascenders, prusik loops, or just shoe laces. As I said, the rope is a highway you need to be able to navigate in many ways - up, down, left, right. Lack the skills to do this and you can get into big trouble.

ROPE CLIMBING 101

So the basics of climbing a rope is that you're going to use a device that moves in one direction (up ideally, but sometimes down), then locks tight once weighted. We'll call this an ascender. Unless you have a petrol driven rope climbing machine, you'll need two rope ascenders - one for your feet and one for your body. To climb the rope, you'll weight your foot ascender (by stepping in your aider attached to it for example), push up your body ascender, weight it (by simply hanging from your lanyard attached to it for example), move your foot ascender up, and repeat, moving up about a foot at a time.

ASCENDERS

I'll cover the technical stuff here, the stuff you'll climb a rope with, using the catch all term 'ascender' as that's what this software and hardware functions as.

SECONDARY ASCENDERS

Before getting into the primary ascenders, I'll just cover some things that can be used as makeshift ascenders for emergencies or 'now get out of that' tools. When would you need these? Well the obvious one is if you drop one or both of your ascenders (you find many ascenders at the bottom of El Cap), or if you find yourself hanging in space - perhaps after a lead fall - with no way of getting back up the rope (often you will leave ascenders behind when leading to keep weight/ clutter down, or only have one set for the cleaner). The bottom line is you should always be equipped for some system of rope climbing.

Human Hand: The most basic rope clamp you have is the human hand, which can work really well on very thick gym style ropes, but is pretty crap on even thick nylon ropes, attested to by the number of burnt and ripped apart hands I've seen over the years! It is possible to descend ropes without any tools, by way of wrapping the rope around your body, but climbing one is impossible unless you're on a slab, using the classic Batman technique of hand over hand. 'Batmaning' like this can have its place in guerrilla style climbing (anything goes), or as a last resort, but it's seat of your pants stuff, and finding you can't hold on after yarding ten metres up the rope will have you shouting for some real superhero intervention.

Prusik Loop: This is your bare bones ascender, a 1.5 metre length of 5 or 6 mm cord (on a wall you'll be using thicker ropes so 6 mm is better) attached to the rope in varying ways, with the auto block (French prusik) and Klemheist being the best two knots to learn for all round use (plus for self rescue and protection on raps), with the Bachmann knot also worth learning (this uses a krab as a handle, speeding things up considerably).

All climbers venturing onto big walls should have some actual experience climbing ropes using each of these knots, even if it's just climbing a tree on a rainy day, as it's vital to both know how to use them, and their limitations. Knowing how hard it is to climb a free hanging rope with two prusiks (when you've lost your ascenders) could well help you avoid losing them in the first place, as it's desperate.

You should always carry your prusik loops with you at all times, even when sleeping in your harness, as they can get you out of sticky situations (having sewn loops, such as those made for tree surgeons means you don't have bulky knots that will dig in). If you find you don't have any prusik loops, then of course you can use slings instead (be careful using the Klemheist on skinny dyneema slings, as they can slip), but cord tends to be better, mostly because a prusik loop is a prusik loop and so doesn't get nabbed for other duties.

Whenever you trust your life to a skinny bit of nylon, always back yourself up by tying into the rope as often as you can. One major advantage of soft ascenders like this is that they can be cut with a knife, but they can also be used like a knife. If you need to cut yourself out of a loaded rope or sling just untie the prusik loop and wrapping it once around what needs cutting, use it like a wire saw. By moving the cord rapidly you'll cut through even an 11 mm rope in seconds (one reason why you never want your moving haul line running over your weighted lead line!)

Guide Belay Plate: You can use your guide plate in auto lock mode to climb a rope. Used in conjunction with a second ascender, it can feel a little bit more secure, but is still hard work. When using it for ascending, it's best to use as round a blocking karabiner as you have, to aid the rope's movement through the device. Like the prusik loop this will probably always be on your harness, and so practising using it as an ascender at least once is worthwhile.

Micro PCD: These small devices such as the Wild Country Ropeman series, Kong Duck and Petzl Tibloc are far more effective at climbing ropes than a prusik loop for only a little extra weight (a Tibloc weighs only 39 grams), plus they're more secure and safer to use. Although better than prusiks, these devices still cannot replace ascenders for full on rope climbing duty, as they are small and fiddly. They should only be seen as backup devices or for self rescue. They can also be employed in lots of other roles better than prusiks, such as setting up light haul systems or parts of heavy weight Z hauls (the PCD on a 2:1 pulley system), when tying down portaledges in a storm, and for many other bits and pieces. For this reason I tend to always carry at least one micro ascender on my harness, along with two prusik loops. As with all such devices covered here, the user should take the time to play with the device before using it in anger, as devices like the Petzl Tibloc require some skill and the correct matching with karabiners to work effectively.

Micro PCP: Using locking haulers such as the Petzl Micro or Pro Traxion to ascend a rope again comes under the heading of emergency tools, but it's good to remember they can do double duty. When ascending, they are ideally used on the waist (but can be used as the foot grab just as well). The Petzl Micro Traxion is an incredibly versatile tool, and weighing in at only 85 grams it is light enough to carry instead of a micro PCD, or with one, as it both climbs ropes very well plus is perfect in a Z pulley.

ABBD: An ABBD such as the Petzl GriGri (other ABBDs are available) is the most commonly used belay device on big walls, and is a crucial component of the big wall climbing system, but it can also be used to climb ropes. The 'sport' ascender set up has the ABBD acting as the ascender on the waist, with an ascender used above it for the foot, the climber pulling up with one arm and then pulling the rope through the ABBD then sitting back. This system is popular for sport climbing as it allows the climber to switch to abseiling mode quickly, simply by unclipping the ascender.

I've heard climbers who've lost an ascender and switched to this set up claim they like it better than a two ascender system, but they must either have short memories or be way too strong. Pulling up with one arm and then pulling the rope through the ABBD can be very tiring, and although fine for maybe ten metres, soon begins to bite when used on a whole pitch, and even more so if it goes on day after day.

I can remember watching Adam Ondra jugging fixed lines on El Cap this way, the only rope climbing technique he knew, and although fast on pitch one, several ropes later he looked buggered, meaning he arrived very late at his high point and pretty wasted. It was only when someone showed him how to ascend Texas style that he zoomed up the ropes, taking minutes to climb each rope.

Tip: If you do employ this ABBD system, you can make it a little easier sometimes by running the rope up from your ABBD through a karabiner on your ascender, allowing you to pull down on the rope, not up, including some slight pulley effect in the process.

PRIMARY ASCENDERS

These are your main tools to climb ropes and will probably come in the form of a set of handled ascenders, but can also be chest or foot ascenders.

Handled Ascenders

These work by way of a cam that allows the rope to pass through the device in one direction but then locks down tight when the rope tries to reverse its course. This cam is usually locked in place by a safety catch that keeps the rope captured in the device. The climber attaches themselves to the device via either a clip in hole at the base of the handle, or directly into the handle, with a secondary clip hole found at the top near the cam, which can be used to either add a secondary rope capture (stopping the device from unclipping from the rope, but not stopping the cam from disengaging), or as a higher primary attachment point. Ascenders come in left and right models, the primary difference being that when the user is holding the right ascender in their right hand they can see the cam, vital for safety, as well as manipulate the cam with their thumb, vital for speed. ascenders

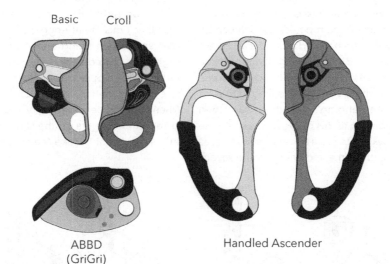

Basic   Croll

ABBD
(GriGri)

Handled Ascender

can be used in the opposing hands but you lose quite a lot of functionality.

Chest Ascender

This variation of the handled ascender is used for the Frog system of ascending, and is attached between your harness and a chest sling or strap. Due to being fixed in place this style of ascender is by far the best for pure vertical rope climbing, and is the standard for industrial and caving technique (Single Rope Technique or SRT), where the rope hangs down with only a few belay points or non. When used in conjunction with a handled ascender, or better still with a handled ascender and foot ascender, a free hanging rope can be climbed almost without effort (almost!) once you have your system dialled. Unfortunately this highly effective rope climbing system falls down when faced with highly complex pitches that need cleaning, where the pitch is traversing or includes lower outs.

On such pitches the Frog system becomes a tangle, and a battle with the chest ascender's cam and safety catch,

the climber forced to clip into gear they would otherwise just ascend past and clean. When climbing Iron Hawk with a partner who used this system, which had served him well on many 'easy' walls (where the rope ran straight), the rope popped out of his chest ascender at a tricky point, his top ascender catching him! For this reason I would only employ this style of ascender for fixed rope expeditions, or when you're fixing very high on a wall, say you've got many free hanging ropes to climb, as the extra weight of a chest ascender will save you a great deal of time. It's also worth noting that you can use a handled ascender as a chest ascender by clipping the handle to a krab between your legs and waist loop, then clipping a sling into the top of the ascender. Being longer it's not quite as effective, but is still better on free hanging ropes than a Texas style system.

Foot Ascender

This is a tiny little ascender that fits on the inside of your foot by way of a strap and is used for 'rope walking', a technique really only employed in major caving expeditions, allowing the climber to save a great deal of energy, pumping their leg on the rope, it's used in combination with a handled ascender and chest ascender. Being very lightweight these ascenders can be very handy on some walls where you'll be dealing with a lot of free hanging ascending, say when climbing in teams of 3+, where someone always has to jug a free hanging rope, as this allows time and energy to be saved.

where the sweet spot is between taking it off and just not having it engage with the rope (I call this "feathering"). This is best seen as the cam being either fully disengaged and locked back, safety lock open, and just being pulled away from the rope by a few millimetres, the lock still in place. When teaching people this I try to get them to keep their fingers off the safety trigger unless they want to take the ascender off

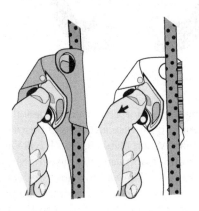

Cam feathered (cam, not trigger, is moved)   Removing Cam (trigger, not cam moved)

THE CAM

The heart of the ascender is the cam. It is usually made from steel so as to resist wear and tear, with teeth designed to bite, and a light spring that keeps it locked on the rope, even though it is the action of the ascender being weighted that locks it down. The climber must be familiar with their ascender's cam and trigger, able to operate these with one hand, able to unlock and remove the ascender from the rope in one easy action (to pass gear for example), and then put it back on again. The cam must also be operated with one thumb in order to lower out or down ascend, again vital skills, meaning the operator needs to understand

the rope, keeping it on the cam (which tends to have a thumb depression). You can practice this by sliding the ascender easily up and down the rope by way of the cam, and when practicing ascending it's good to ascend both up and down the rope.

ROPE CLIMBING SYSTEMS

Now we know something of the tools, let's look at how we can use them. Rope climbing can be broken down into two main styles; the Texas system and the Frog system, with each having further sub systems, such as rope walking. Of these styles, the most appropriate for big wall climbing is the Texas system so let's start there.

TEXAS SYSTEM

This system works via two ascenders, one in your right hand and one in your left, with one for the foot (so you will most likely have one of your aiders attached to this one) and one for the body, with both ascenders being attached to the harness (via your lanyards) so as to offer some redundancy, vital when removing an ascender from the rope.

To climb the rope, the climber will usually use one aider on their bottom ascender, stepping up on this in order to weight the bottom ascender, and push up the top (body) ascender, then sitting back on the top ascender in order to weight that so they can push up the bottom one, and on it goes.

On less than vertical terrain however, the climber may use an aider on both ascenders (making both top and bottom ascenders 'foot' ascenders as opposed to the top one being a 'body' ascender). This is ideal for slabby ground, the climber 'stepping' up the wall relatively effortlessly in small steps.

The default method though is the one aider method (as big walls tend to be mostly the wrong side of 'off vertical' for the 'slabby' method!), which for a right handed climber will be right ascender in right hand attached via your lanyard to your harness, with left ascender attached with other lanyard, with an aider attached to the left ascender for your left foot. The crucial thing here is the set up, getting the distance right between the right ascender (which in this case will be the top ascender) and your harness. Get it too short and you'll not be able to push the ascender far enough with each stroke, make it too long and you'll end up hanging from your arms.

Set Up

This is best done by actually hanging from the rope. Hanging fully from your top ascender (via your lanyard), you should be able to reach the cam/safety trigger on the ascender. Once you've worked out what the length of your lanyard should be, try and remember where this ideal point is, either by counting the pockets of your daisy chain or PAS, or by marking the point with tape or a rope marker. A rule of thumb on length is to keep it shorter on slabs and longer on vertical ground.

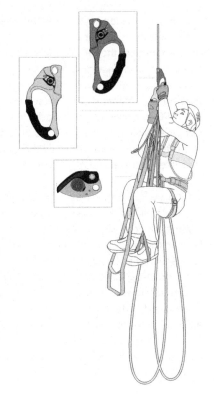

When adjusting the length with adjustable lanyards, you can fine tune this as you go on, but if you have to adjust the length at the far end of your lanyards (e.g., if using a daisy chain) with a single krab, then to adjust will mean you're forced to unclip from the ascender.

Instead, use a second screwgate attached to your belay loop to adjust the length so even if you need to unclip this and clip it into a different pocket of your daisy chain for example, you're still attached to the ascender. The length of the bottom ascender's lanyard is less important, and should be set so that when this lower ascender is pushed up under the top ascender, the lanyard is not too slack. The reason for this is that when you remove the top ascender to pass gear you could fall back onto your lower ascender, so you don't want too much slack there.

Your foot position in your aider attached to the bottom ascender again depends on the steepness of the terrain, but the baseline is that when hanging fully from your top ascender, with your bottom ascender pushed up against it, your knee should be at 90 degrees to your body, meaning when you step up you'll be able to push the top ascender roughly the same distance as the length of your lower leg.

On free hanging ropes, I often switch my foot to a higher step in the ladder, so my bottom ascender is closer to my waist, kind of rocking into it so I can push my top ascender as far as I can, but this takes some practice. On slabby ground I might switch to a lower step, and as previously mentioned, attach an aider to my top ascender as well, meaning I have an aider for each foot. I would then make smaller movements and kind of step up the wall in baby steps.

If the ground changes mid pitch (from slabby to vertical or overhanging), then be prepared to take off the second aider again (or at least throw it back over your shoulder), as otherwise it just gets in the way.

FROG SYSTEM

The frog system needs a chest harness, sling, or strap, to work effectively and requires some thought to work perfectly.

01. You begin by attaching your chest ascender via a karabiner that goes through your leg and waist loops (the same way your belay loop does). This is done as it's vital to have your chest ascender as low as possible, and the ideal krab is a semi circular karabiner such as the Petzl OMNI (or you could use a 10 mm delta maillon).

02. The chest ascender is then attached to the chest harness via another D shaped karabiner, or via a strap that is fed through the top hole, or even a loop of bungee cord. The most important thing to remember is that when you get the chest system set tight you should be somewhat stooped over, as this will make the system more efficient.

03. Now connect your handled ascender to your harness via your lanyard with an aider or foot loop attached (the lanyard acts as a back-up, the aider used for traction). The correct length of this lanyard is not critical as your body is always hanging from the chest ascender.

04. Clip in both ascenders and then once you've taken up all the slack and are hanging from the chest ascender, put both feet together into a step of the aider.

05. Trap the rope between your feet.

06. Push up the handled ascender, allowing your feet to lift, letting your legs splay like a frog.

07. Using both your arms as leverage, rock your body over your feet and press your body up (you progress via your

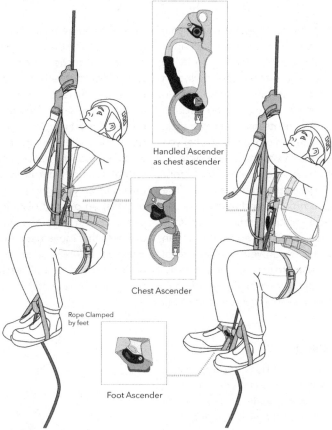

Handled Ascender
as chest ascender

Chest Ascender

Rope Clamped
by feet

Foot Ascender

Frog method with a Croll

Frog method with chest
mounted ascender

legs, not your arms). As you splay your legs, your feet will clamp down on the rope stopping it moving, and allowing the chest ascender to slide up the rope (do not pull the rope through with your hands as you'll lose 50% of your pull strength).

08. Once your legs are straight sit back immediately on your chest ascender.

09. Push up handled ascender and repeat.

A rope walking system adds a foot ascender to one foot, with gives you further push power as you climb.

CLIMBING THE ROPES

Now we've covered the basics of setup and gear I'm going to break it down into the different scenarios you'll face while climbing ropes.

FUNDAMENTALS

When climbing a rope you need to visualise how you are going from rapid movement to rest, the movement pressing your legs to lift your body, your arm moving your ascender up at the same time, then the rest happening when you lean back and weight this top ascender. The ability to coordinate feet, hands, and ascender, and so execute the movement part all together and quickly, reduces your fatigue window. This window - if left open more than a second - sees you moving your body up the rope, then trying to balance and push your top ascender up in fits and starts, maybe sitting back on it before it's gone its maximum distance. The faster you can move the quicker you can stop. When you stop, you slide up your bottom ascender with its foot-loop/aider and get ready to move again. The actual time moving and resting can be measured in microseconds, but that is what's happening, as no ascender can move unless it's unweighted. It is vital when ascending to fully trust your ascenders so you can sit back on them easily and relax, otherwise your hands and arms will take the strain.

FREE HANGING

This is the most basic rope to climb, be it hanging from a cliff or out from an overhanging big wall. By learning to climb ropes using a free hanging rope first you'll quickly learn the basics as you'll have no advantages over the rope apart from your body and skill with the ascenders, with nothing to press against in order to get purchase (as you will have on vertical walls or slabs).

As I've said, the ideal technique to use to tackle a free hanging rope would be the Frog system (in most caving/industrial set ups ropes are set so they do not touch anything), but most readers of this book will probably not set up for this system, but if you are, the trick is to take it slow and don't burn out. As with all ascending techniques, often multiple small movements that are sustainable will get you to the top faster than a sprint approach, as ascending is pretty cardio intensive, with arms and legs moving simultaneously,

as well as some major body tensioning going on. With the Frog system just take it slow, and focus not on how far you've got to go, but rather on making each move as efficient as possible. Try and imagine where the energy is going and make the most of it, for example pressing down inline with the rope rather than out with your feet will get you moving a little further. Going 'full frog' with your heels pulled up to your groin may get you the greatest amount of distance when you push out, but your legs are not used to doing such a movement and will quickly get tired, whereas 'semi frogging' might not get you as far with each movement but is easier to maintain.

Placing your hand over the top of the ascender helps when using the Frog method

For the Texas style I'd recommend considering using one handled ascender as a chest ascender, but if not, then again just take it slow. This idea of moving and resting is most valuable when ascending free hanging ropes, as a lack of anything to press against makes it very tiring,

A gripped John O'Connor leaving Camp 6 on the Nose

meaning those micro rests in between movement are vital.

With the Frog system you can finesse your way up the rope, but Texas style requires a more gymnastic approach, and I tend to find longer movements are easier than shorter ones, as there is a huge amount of body tension involved while on free hanging ropes.

With longer movements in mind, I set my top ascender as long as I can (making sure I can reach the trigger/cam), then have my foot one step higher than usual in my aider, and after taking in the slack, slide up my bottom ascender until it's as close to my top ascender as possible (so your hands are almost inline), then I rock into my aider, pulling hard on both arms (not just my top ascender). As you press up with your leg and pull with your arms there will be a dead point, which is your moment to move up, and at this point you should snap that top ascender up as hard as you can, getting that top daisy chain tight so you don't lose any height. In that split second when you sit back on your harness, use that slight downward force to help you fire up your bottom ascender, and repeat. On a free hanging ascend take plenty of rests and enjoy being up high.

OFF VERTICAL

If you've done some practice on free hanging ropes, then you'll find that having something to brace against makes the whole thing much easier. On vertical walls, or even slightly overhanging walls, having your feet and knees against the wall allows you to stand more erect and so inline with the rope. If the wall is plum vertical or slightly overhanging you're best using the same Texas style with one aider on your bottom ascender, and this setup will work fine on any ground, from vertical to overhangs. The change comes when the wall dips back even just a few degrees, allowing the rope to lie a degree off vertical. Now when you stand upright you will be able to stand in balance (you cannot be in balance when the rope is at vertical as it pushes you off balance). This means you can now use more leg and less arm, and by adding a second aider or foot loop on your top ascender you can begin to step up the wall, using your arms to hold you upright.

The lower the angle the less arm power needed to stay in position, and you'll be surprised just how little arm power is needed when you find the correct balance point. When trying to find this sweet spot play around with your foot position a little, as switching from instep to forefoot can help put you a little more in balance. If your pitch is switching between slab and vertical, and maybe free hanging, then it's best to stay with just a single bottom aider, as two can become a little bit of a pain, and switching systems more than once during a pitch is too time consuming.

SLABS

Climbing slabs can either be as easy as going for a walk, or like a battle to the death. By stepping high in two aiders, one on each ascender, you can step up very quickly, climbing a whole pitch in less than a minute, no weight on your arms at all, the main skill the rapid shift of weight from foot to foot. Small steps work best, the same way that steps on stairs or ladders are small, yes you could have steps one metre high, or ladder rungs waist height, but you'd soon get very tired! If you try and do this with one aider, the angle can lead some climbers to

struggle with their balance, making them fall over or lean too far back or forward.

ASCENDING NOTES:

Possessed Ascenders: When you're climbing with novice big wall climbers they often see the ascender as having a life all of its own, that it just jams on the rope and won't move out of spite. In fact an ascender is a stupid bit of metal, it only locks when it's weighted, and so on every occasion you just say "lift up your foot" for example and unweight it, and the ascender suddenly lets go as well. If using two aiders, one on each ascender, it often takes climbers a while to get their hands and feet coordinated, meaning they're lifting up one foot but pushing up the opposite ascender, one reason why it should always be left ascender, left hand and foot and vice versa.

Easy Running: One important skill a rope climber must master is how to rise the bottom ascender without having the end of the rope lift up with it, that annoying thing where you see someone holding the rope below you while you get higher, or forcing you to reach down and pull the rope through the ascender (the rope always pulls through your top ascender as you're weighting the rope).

As you go higher and the rope gets heavier this is no longer a problem, as now the rope will feed through by itself, and the thicker the rope the sooner this will happen. So what's the trick to ascending without this problem from the beginning of the pitch? The answer is cam control, being able to pull back the cam just a tiny bit (but not take the ascender off - remember you are not pressing the safety trigger) as you push up the ascender. This allows the rope to pass

through easily. This skill is a vital one to master as each time you tie a backup knot it will be as if you're starting on a fresh and unweighted end of rope.

Jammed Cams: The cam of an ascender needs to travel forwards a centimetre or so for it to disengage, meaning that if the ascender is rammed tight against a knot you may have trouble getting it off. For this reason always leave a finger's room between the cam and anything you find fixed on the rope that can't back up! If your ascender does get jammed it will eventually come off but you'll need to prise and twist it to try and force some slack out of the knot.

Two Handed Technique: A handled ascender only has space for one hand but very often you'll need to use two, especially on free hanging ropes or when using the Frog system. To use two hands, use the correct hand in the handle (right hand for right handed ascender), and then wrapping your thumb and forefinger around the rope, pull down on the top of the ascender. This has an extra advantage in that it gives you a little more reach but also puts your body closer to the centre of gravity, which needs to be as close to inline with the rope as possible.

Keep It Light: It's very common for climbers to wish to burden themselves with gear when ascending, stuff they may need on the next pitch, hardware, maybe a pack or a rope tied to their back. On a slab you can ascend heavily laden relatively easily, but on anything else you need to be as light as possible. Remember that every extra gramme is being lifted by your body, a great deal of it on your arms. A good example of this is when climbing as a three, how the second has to frequently jug the free hanging haul line and will often be bringing a second lead line. Having a 10.5 mm rope hanging off you as you go feels OK at first, but very soon your arms will be screaming, and so a lazy approach is always better, just hauling stuff afterwards on the rope you're climbing, or using an alternative. Again remember one of the universal laws of big wall climbing is to be lazy!

Ascending With A Load: If you're forced to ascend a rope with a heavy pack or haul bag here are some tips. First, avoid wearing it on your back unless you're on a slab, with a slab being anything where you can keep your weight over your feet (so your legs do the work). Once you get onto vertical or overhanging ground, attach the bag to your harness via a locker through your leg and waist loops (not your belay loop). When hung this way you can use your legs to lift the load each time, but it won't interfere with your top ascender, allowing you to move and rest, move and rest. It tends to be best to hang the load below your feet if you can. Russian climbers use this technique to great effect on complex ground that cannot be hauled, and it can be used when moving haul bags over unhaulable terrain, such as bushes or hanging boulder fields.

Feet In Place: One thing that people find takes a while to master is keeping your feet in your aiders or foot loops. Some aiders feature an elastic band sewn under the aider step, allowing you to flip this out and over your foot, and if your aiders lack these it's easy to just sew one on. Some aiders that can double as dedicated foot loops may include a strap that runs over your foot (this needs to be somewhat elastic to stay put), and are designed for major ascending. The one issue with these is often being able

to take out your feet quickly is useful, as some free climbing can help when ascending and cleaning, allowing you to step left or right, plus step into different steps quickly. My own preference, built up over many kilometres of ascending, is to just apply a tiny bit of pressure down with my foot as I push up my ascenders, not so much as to lock an ascender, but just enough to keep my foot in place.

SAFETY

Climbing ropes can expose the climber to death or serious injury. As with abseiling your life is literally hanging by a thread. It is vital to follow some basic rules in order to stay safe, as well as not cut corners.

The Two Points Rule

This is repeated throughout this book I know, but it's one that's broken at your peril! Make sure you have a minimum of two points of attachment to life at all times. When ascending, this means two ascenders clipped to the rope. The second you unclip an ascender you will break this rule unless you've take action, such as tying into the rope. There is always that temptation to skip this, but I know more than one person who did just that, took an ascender off without tying in short, then clipped it back in, and took their bottom ascender off, only for their top one to pop off! In each case the climber fell to the bottom of the rope, in one case a sixty metre fall! Many climbers have hit the ground in this situation before the rope went tight, or not being tied in at all, have gone all the way. Keep that in mind!

Tying Into The End

Being tied into the end of the rope

you're ascending should not be seen as a safety measure, more something done as good wall manners. Many climbers have hit ledges before they reached the end of the rope when they've messed up, but having the end makes great sense for lots of other reasons besides safety. If you know where the end is, you won't have it fly off into a crack for example, plus it's vital to have the end for lower outs etc. But this does not count as one of your two connectors!

Tying In Short

Your primary way to add more security is to tie into the rope as you climb. This does double duty as it both lowers the distance you fall if you fuck up, as well as reduces the amount of rope that can blow around and get stuck or hung up (which can be very dangerous as well).

How often should you tie in? Well this depends on how often you're unclipping an ascender, and the result of a fall each time. As a minimum I tend to tie in four times, as this means falls will be shorter, but I'm not adding tons of knots to my harness and slowing everything up. If it's windy and the ground is complex then you may want to add many more knots, so the loop is never too long, or even stow the rope in a rope bag as you climb, adding and taking off back up knots as you go.

The best way to tie in short is to just have a big screwgate on your belay loop (clipped at the bottom of the belay loop underneath everything else so it does not interfere with your lanyards), clipping your rope in with simple overhand knots.

This use of multiple backup knots by the second climbing the lead line, clipped

in one after a time into a big locker, also means the rope can just be clipped in at the belay, ready for the next pitch, one knot unclipped at a time while belaying.

THE RUNNING BACK UP

One of the great leaps in safety, as well as making cleaning easy, is to use your ABBD as a kind of running knot, the rope running through it by itself, or pulled through as you go. Unlike a cam, this type of device can take a dynamic fall and will not damage the rope, and will actually slip a little, lowering the impact force. When using a running backup you should still add backup knots, but you will need less, unless it's very windy.

The best thing about the running back up is its simplicity. The belayer is already using the ABBD, and as soon as the rope is 'fixed', all they need to do is pull the rope tight through their ABBD, and take their weight off the belay, allowing their ascenders to be clipped in. Now all they have to do is strip the belay and climb the rope.

SECURITY KARABINER

A common technique is to clip a karabiner into the head of the ascender, so as to stop the rope from escaping from the device. Some climbers always do this with both ascenders, but if it is to be used then it is only required for the top ascender. The problem here is that every time the ascender needs to be removed, so does this karabiner, which slows things up. And so I would advise to only use this when climbing fixed ropes where no back-up knot can be tied, or when cleaning and the rope is angled at 45 degrees or more. An important issue is that you must be 100% sure the karabiner is enclosing the rope when clipped through the ascender. Failing to do this can actually result in the

Karabiner locking rope in

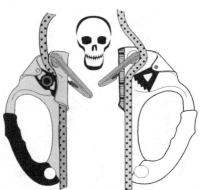

Karabiner locking rope out

rope popping out of the ascender when weighted.

CLEANING

Now we come to the real make or break of big wall climbing, not just the ability to climb a rope, but also how to take out the gear. This may sound simple, and on a straight up vertical pitch it can be, just moving up the rope and taking out the gear as you go. But the second the gear moves around that vertical line, the rope going left and right, or the pitches become overhanging, you'll suddenly find you can no longer just unclip the rope from your karabiners, each one loaded. How you deal with this is one of the main skills many climbers lack.

PASSING UNWEIGHTED GEAR

When the gear is unweighted the best approach is to ascend up until you can touch the karabiner, then unclip it, then move up until the gear is at hip height. Why? Well trying to take out gear that's above you wastes energy, can be tricky and awkward, and increases the chance of you dropping it. By moving up a little you can see the gear more clearly, and when out, you can quickly move it to your harness for racking. If a hammer is needed you'll also be hammering with

the hammer below your shoulders which saves energy.

PASSING SLIGHTLY WEIGHTED GEAR

If the karabiner on the protection is slightly weighted, then sometimes you can rest on your top ascender, grab the gear with one hand and use the other to force the rope out, then move up and take out the gear. This approach removes the need to take an ascender off the rope, and so is quicker, but if you find it a struggle then you need to move onto the next technique.

PASSING A LOADED KARABINER

If your weight on the rope makes it impossible to unclip the rope from the gear, then do the following:

01. Ascend up until your top ascender is an inch from the gear.

02. You can see you will need to remove an ascender to pass this gear, so check that you are backed up as discussed. You might need to take in some slack on your ABBD or add another backup knot to the karabiner on your belay loop.

03. Bring your bottom ascender up below

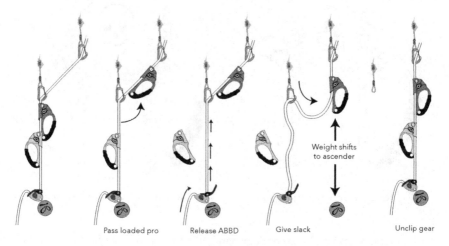

Pass loaded pro   Release ABBD   Give slack   Unclip gear

Weight shifts to ascender

ABBD Pass

the top one.

04. Balance on your bottom ascender's aider, either holding on to your bottom ascender, or the rope above the gear (remember that a loaded rope is like a solid hand hold).

05. Using your thumb, press back the safety trigger on the top ascender's cam, unclip the cam, and remove the ascender from the rope (all this must be done with only one hand).

06. Clip the ascender back in above the gear, and push it up as high as you can.

07. Now sit back on your top ascender and take your weight off your foot ascender.

08. The rope going through the karabiner will now go slack unless the rope is at a very acute angle. Simply unclip the rope, move up a little and take out the gear.

REMOVING GEAR WHERE ROPE IS AT AN ACUTE ANGLE

In this scenario you do as you did above, but find that as you weight your top ascender your bottom ascender is sucked up and jams into the karabiner, meaning you can't move it, or unclip the rope. You will come across this on traversing pitches a lot and it can be a real killer. The wrong approach that's often taken, sometimes out of desperation, is the climber clips an aider into the karabiner in order to unweight their ascender, or hangs off the gear with their fifi hook, but often the bottom ascender will remain jammed, but if not they can unclip and pass the gear. This approach, even if effective, is very slow, and can also be unnecessarily scary or even dangerous, as you're exposing yourself to a fall if the gear rips out, creating a shock load on your rope with your ascenders - not good.

I will now cover two techniques to deal with this problem, and both need to be mastered.

The ABBD Pass:

If you're running an ABBD running back up you can also use this as a highly effective method to pass gear, which although a little slower than the more advanced

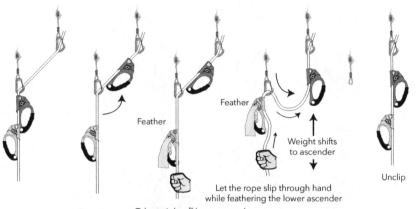

Feather

Feather

Weight shifts
to ascender

Unclip

Let the rope slip through hand
while feathering the lower ascender

Pass Pro

Take weight off lower ascender
by pulling with hand

Hand Pass

method, is much easier to master. To use this you do the following:

01. Move both ascenders up to the gear, top one an inch from the karabiner, bottom one as close to the top one as possible.

02. Stepping on your bottom ascender aider take in all the slack on your ABBD, positioning yourself as high as you can, the aim to be able to easily reach past the loaded karabiner.

03. Remove the top ascender and pass the gear, pushing it high up the rope.

04. Now just lower out with the ABBD until all your weight is on your top ascender again.

05. Step up a little on your ascenders, and reach over to unclip the rope from the gear and take it out.

Hand Pass

This method requires more skill, but is much faster, and just requires manipulation of rope and ascenders. Here is how it works:

01. Ascend up to the gear as usual, top ascender about an inch from the kara-

biner, bottom ascender just under top.

02. Weighting bottom ascender pass the gear (remember to make sure you are tied in short to the rope as a backup before you do this).

03. The bottom ascender will want to get sucked into the karabiner as you begin to sit back.

04. To stop this from happening, as you weight the top ascender, pull hard on the rope below your bottom ascender. This is your breaking hand.

05. With your weight on the top ascender, and your hand pulling the rope, the karabiner and bottom ascender are between the two forces.

06. Taking your free hand, thumb the trigger on your bottom ascender (remember don't take the cam off or press the safety trigger), and with it not engaging the rope, let some rope slip through your breaking hand.

07. You will now find you lower out until all your weight is on your top ascender, and the rope is slack through the karabiner.

08. Unclip the rope from the karabiner and push up the bottom ascender, move

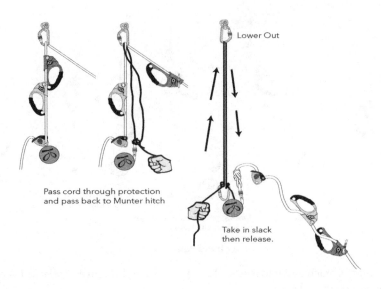

Pass cord through protection
and pass back to Munter hitch

Lower Out

Take in slack
then release.

up a little, then remove the protection.

Once mastered you can use this technique on even quite long lower outs, the loop still being attached to the gear giving you a hand line to pull yourself back over to get the gear out.

LOWER OUTS

I would class a lower out as something more than just passing gear, maybe when the rope is running at more than forty five degrees to the next piece. When you come to these very acute angles I think it's important to clip a karabiner through the hole in the head of the top ascender as you weight it, as the acute angle means your safety may not have clicked on fully (quite common) and you can twist the rope out of the ascender. If you add this karabiner, remember, as I've said, it's vital that both the ascender *and* the rope are 'captured' in the karabiner, as it's actually very easy to just clip the ascender and

block out the rope.

LOWER OUT CORD

Mark Hudon invented the lower out cord as a way to simplify lowering off fixed gear, or gear that had to be lowered off before moving up and swinging back. This comprises of a length of 6 or 7 mm cord around 10 to 15 metres long, carried on your harness (you can also use an untied cordelette). To use, tie one end to a karabiner on your belay loop with a clove hitch, then pass the cord through the piece that needs to be lowered off (don't pass it through nylon, as it will melt and damage or even break the nylon). Now reattach the end via a Munter hitch (or Monster Munter) to the same karabiner, creating a loop that can be used to lower out from. You can pull yourself tight with this loop so as to take the tension off the ascending line, unclip it, then slowly lower yourself out. Remember that you can only lower out half the distance of your cord as it's a loop. Once you've lowered out just pull the cord through the lowering point and repeat for the next piece. This lower out cord can either be a dedicated piece of kit stowed in a bag on your harness for example, or simply your lower out line for your haul bag.

PENDULUM POINTS

When faced with a pendulum point, where the next piece of gear is a long way off, or even below you (such as when seconding the pitch off Dolt Tower on The Nose if the leader has not back cleaned), you should take it very slow and steady.

The first thing to do is secure yourself to the lead line below your ascender and ABBD with a screwgate. This is done due to the possibility of ascenders being highly stressed or twisted during the lower out, and becomes your primary backup knot.

Now you have two options:

BIGHT LOWER OUT

Use this method if you judge the distance of the lower out to be less than one quarter the distance of the rope you have below you to play with:

01. Untie any backup knots.

02. Feed or clip the bight of rope through the lower out point.

03. Clip the loop that is returning to you through a locker.

04. You now have 4 strands of rope, forming a rope pulley system.

05. Pull on the free strand on the loop until all your weight is on the lower out point (you can do this by hand as your weight is reduced by the pulley action of the rope).

06. Unclip your live rope from the fixed piece.

07. Begin to allow rope to feed out into the loop, lowering yourself down under control.

08. Once your weight is back on the main rope, unclip the loop from your harness locker, and pull this through and free of the lower out point.

09. Continue on up.

RAPPEL LOWER OUT

If you're not confident you have enough rope to lower out using the above system (for a five metre lower out you need twenty metres of rope), then use this system:

01. Untie all your backup knots (apart from the new primary backup) and untie from the end of the rope (you are hanging from two ascenders and the primary backup knot).

02. You will now have a very long length of free rope below your primary backup.

03. Take this free rope and thread/clip this through the lower out, and attach it back to you with a belay device.

04. Take in the slack on this loop you have formed until all your weight is on that lower out.

05. Unclip your lead rope (this might now be pointing downwards to the next piece).

06. Begin to lower yourself slowly until all your weight is back on your ascenders.

07. Take off the belay device and pull the rope through the lower out point.

This last method is more foolproof than the first, as sometimes it's hard to judge how much rope you have, and coming up short can be dangerous (leading to a very big swing). The cleaning cord achieves the

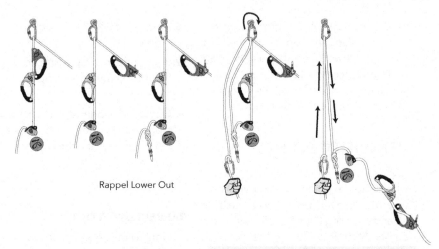

Rappel Lower Out

same results, but is not applicable for very long lower outs.

LOWER OUT POINT SAFETY

It's worth pointing out that when lowering off such a point you are fully trusting this piece (or loop of ratty cord or sling in some cases), and that if it was to fail when the next point is lower, this could be very hazardous. If possible always lower off a hard point like a karabiner, or make sure the leader has replaced a bad piece or backed it up before you get there. If failure of a lower out cannot be ruled out, then I try and make sure all my weight is on my ABBD, not my ascenders, as the ABBD is OK with a high shock load, while the ascenders are not. To do this I will bring both ascenders down so they are just above my ABBD and are unweighted (I have my primary backup knot as well, so I've got my two security points). This is also a point worth considering when cleaning very scary traverses, where ripping gear can send you falling onto your ascenders (say you're climbing up to a very poor head, then the rope goes right for ten metres with no gear). Here I would try and make sure my ABBD is going to take the fall, not my top ascender, and would do this by keeping my lanyards long, and sit back on my ABBD rather than my bottom ascender (yes this is paranoid, but when your life hangs by a single thread, paranoid is good).

FIXING ROPES

Ropes are fixed for many reasons. Most often fixed ropes are used as a way of delaying departure and committing to the wall, meaning less water and food is needed, and you can spend one more night around the camp-fire. Ropes can also be fixed as a way to avoid hauling over difficult ground, and on steep walls often you can make one huge free hanging haul rather then several more problematical hauls. For expedition walls, or walls where you wish to play your hand cautiously, the capsule style approach of fixing up from solid camps requires a good understanding of fixing, both to get your ropes where you want them, as well as stay safe while travelling up and down them.

ETHICS OF FIXED ROPES

Many climbers will fix one or two pitches, both to get a head start and to reserve their route. In Yosemite ropes

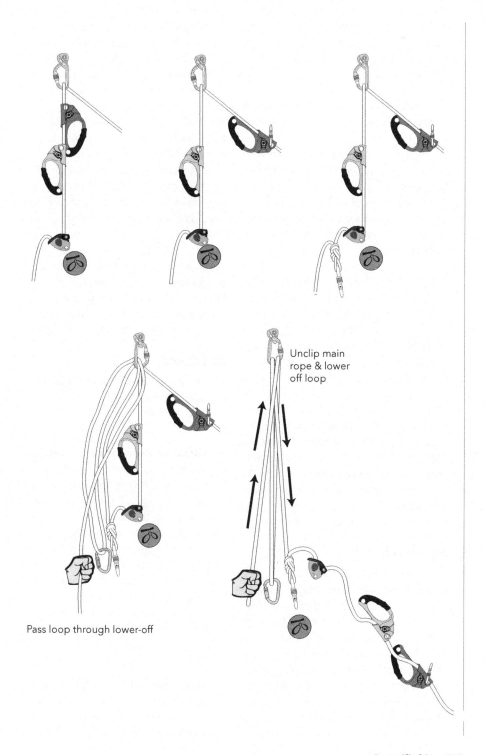

Pass loop through lower-off

Unclip main rope & lower off loop

should not be left for longer than 24 hours, although ropes often are, and ropes left for weeks, or months, or years (beyond established fixed ropes), will be removed.

Some climbers feel that fixing pitches is cheating, that you should just start at the bottom and climb, but it's best to be pragmatic, as some routes are just best climbed that way when hauling (the Nose for example). When fixing pitches on routes with a lot of traffic, I would leave a note with the date the rope was fixed, contact info, and when you intend to blast off.

Beyond Yosemite, fixed ropes can be important if you want to climb the wall without hauling, such as many of the walls in Zion. Fixing pitches combined with a very early start can allow you to do a route in a day that you would otherwise have hauled on.

On alpine walls fixed ropes become more important, especially when dealing with tiny weather windows (Torres del Paine for example). Where capsule style ends and siege style begins is a tricky question, and it's for each team to decide. Just make sure you're not simply using fixing as a replacement for commitment.

BELAY POINTS

When securing ropes to belays it's best to secure rope ends to belay points, so you have no rope joints mid pitch. This is not always possible if you're trying to stretch your ropes up a wall. The only knot that should be used at all points is the alpine butterfly as it can be easily untied no matter how often it's been weighted. If you have multiple belays you will not be able to create a fully functional belay at every point due to a lack of gear. Instead make sure the highest belay (your working belay) is solid and equalised (multiple anchor points), and then treat all other belays below as sub belays, each one tied into the other and supported by each other. With this system each sub belay will be one piece (ideally a bolt), with the rope secured via an alpine butterfly. When securing both ends of the ropes (bottom of top strand and top of lower strand) always tie them together and make all excess ropes secure. You should have no tail ends hanging down or loose strands to confuse the climber. To join ends at the anchor you can simply clip both ropes into the same locker, or tie them together. A good way to do this is to tie an alpine butterfly with your bottom rope, then thread the top rope through this, creating a double alpine butterfly.

RE-BELAYS

A re-belay is a point that lies between the actual belay points and is used to achieve the following points.

- **Abrasion Resistance**: If you have a sixty metre rope going all the way down the cliff face, going over multiple edges, you will get some abrasion, perhaps to the point of separation if it's there for a very long time or used by very inexperienced climbers (who tend to bounce up a rope). To avoid damage over the whole rope, and reduce stretch to shorter sections of rope, you attach the rope to several other points on the way down, creating mini belays that will take the weight off that section of rope.

- **Ascent Speed**: By breaking up the ropes into smaller chunks than one full pitch, you can have several climbers climbing one pitch at a time, which can

Climbing a fixed rope while 'capsule style' on the Troll Wall

really speed things up (it can take an age to get three climbers up the fixed ropes to Sickle Ledge on the Nose for example). Of course the downside is that it also takes longer to get down the rope, so it's best to keep these re-belay points to a minimum.

- **Eggs And Baskets**: By breaking up the rope into sections that can be more easily checked, you can see the next section of rope, vital if your ropes may have been damaged or cut by rock fall. Start up a fixed rope left two months ago that stretches way up out of sight and you're in for a scary trip, but if you can see each section first, this will take some of the fear out of it.

The best place to make a re-belay is where you can place solid protection and where there is a stance. This allows the descending climbers to simply untie the alpine butterfly, step onto the stance, then retie above their ABBD or belay device and continue. If re-belays are used on steep ground with no ledges then the climber will need to pass the knot traditionally, either using their ascenders or by clipping in and out of the re-belay point. When ascending the rope the climber simply passes each knot as they would gear, either tying into the rope as they pass or clipping into the knot (so as to stick to the 2 point rule). When climbing the ropes for the last time, the last person up should remove each belay, untie any knots and then move on up to the next.

ROPE TENSION

When setting the rope always make sure there is enough slack in the system so the rope climber can tie a knot on the rope as a back up if need be (when passing re-belays for example), or tie out a damaged section.

FIXED ROPE SAFETY

When climbing up a fixed rope you will not be able to tie into the end or tie in short at any point, or use an ABBD, meaning you will only be hanging off your two ascenders. There are a few ways to add more safety, such as attaching a Prusik loop above your top ascender, but I think that it's not necessary, and the best insurance is to simply clip a karabiner through your ascenders top clipping point (capturing the rope remember, not just the ascender).

JOINING ROPES WITHOUT A BELAY POINT.

If you're forced to join two ropes where there is no belay point, on a blank slab for example, then there are many ways to do it; double fisherman's, rethreaded figure of eight or butterfly knot. One knot that works well is the standard overhand knot, with the tails left long and tied off with a figure of eight knot (more secure than a double fisherman's knot). This works well for the same reason it works well for abseiling in that the overhand knot flips away from the rock, reducing wear on the sheath, with the loop formed by the figure of eight acting as a solid back up clip point. If you plan on hauling your bags up on these joined ropes then I would switch these knots out for a rethreaded Alpine butterfly or a traditional reef knot backed up by fisherman's knots (remember to have tails about a metre long for passing the knot when hauling).

HEAVY TRAFFIC FIXED BELAYS

If you're forced to fix a rope on a belay that gets a lot of traffic you can sometimes end up having krabs either taken by accident or down right stolen (one very good reason to have all ropes tied into one another). One way to avoid losing lockers is to tie the rope directly into belay bolts, via a rethreaded double bowline or butterfly knot (not easy to tie), or consider gaffer taping your lockers so they can't be confused as being someone else's. On such routes, don't leave your ropes fixed for more than a day as you may find they'll get some heavy traffic, with people zipping down them with little care leading to melted sheaths as well as abrasion or even outright loss (some see fixed ropes as being 'free ropes' so beware).

BEWARE OF KILLER ROPE ENDS

A major killer of unwary climbers is where a knot is tied joining two ropes, or a rope is secured to a belay, and a long tail is left hanging. The unwary climber can easily misidentify this tail as the next strand of rope, clip into it, and rap off the end! For this reason all rope ends must be tied into the belay with a figure of eight, or left short enough not to lead to such terminal confusion.

EDGE PROTECTION

I tend to avoid using edge protection unless I'm on a seriously heavy duty fixed rope mission, maybe just wrapping a rope bag around the rope if it's going over something really nasty. I tend to prefer to use re-belays instead, and have all climbers skilled up so they don't damage the rope when ascending.

Ropes are damaged by the sawing action of the rope moving backwards and forwards, and a skinny dynamic half rope can be cut through to the core very quickly by a careless climber, and cut in half unless they understand what damage they're doing (a broken sheath tends to give ample warning of death).

For this reason the best defence against rope/edge damage is for everyone to know how to ascend a rope with care. What often makes this harder is when climbers over burden themselves down with kit, like carrying a rucksack on their backs, or a heavy camera or a full rack, leading to them lurching up the rope. If you're on a slab you tend to not have to worry as the rock is taking a good deal of your weight, but on a free hanging climb, where the rope is running over an edge high above, well you're going to have some problems.

To protect an edge you can add some gaffer tape to the edge to kind of reduce the abrasive friction, but this only works well if the climber is good anyway, plus it's messy and creates trash. You can add tape direct to the rope, which you may need to do if it gets worn, but this makes a sticky mess of the sheath, and can see it stick in belay devices. Wrap around rope protection provides the best method, but this needs some practice setting correctly. This is done by securing the rope protector via a Prusik, allowing it to be pushed up and out of the way as you pass a sharp edge. Once bypassed this can then be pushed back down into place. Remember that if the rope is going over multiple objects, or even gear (if cleaning), the effects of your climbing will be spread over many points, whereas if it's going over just one, then that wear will be focused. Also keep in mind the more stretch on each side of the wear point the more movement you'll have, one reason why the rope can often run without damage one metre from the belay on a sharp edge, but get rubbed badly twenty metres down.

As I've said previously, the chances of

a rope snapping are very low, especially if you're using static ropes (10 mm is the wall standard, with 9 mm better for alpine walls), the real danger being side to side movement or 'sawing'.

DAMAGED ROPES

If you climb walls long enough, you're going to come across damaged ropes you have to climb, that damage varying between the humble core shot to the complete separation of the rope's sheath. As I've mentioned I would only take bonded construction ropes if I had a choice, but you may not have a choice, or find yourself using old fixed ropes or other climber's ropes. Core shots may seem scary at first, but they're not so bad (remember the sheath is around 20% of the rope's strength), and can either be patched up with finger tape or tied out with an overhand or butterfly knot. To be honest damaged ropes seem to be part of the game so it's something that you may have to deal with, as halfway up a wall you can't do anything much about it. If you're climbing the rope and the sheath of a traditional non unicore rope breaks apart, which will usually happen as you get closer to the damaged section, you will plummet down the rope as the sheath slips over the slick core, something you won't forget in a hurry. If you've tied in to the rope, the sheath will bunch up and you'll stop eventually, but if you have no knot then you may slide right off the rope (the melted rope end may (may!) cause the rope to bunch up though). Why I mention this is that if you see any sign of the core through the sheath on the way up or down a rope you need to deal with it before it goes that far.

THE APOCALYPTIC SCENARIO

So what do you do if faced with that apocalyptic scenario of hanging from some bunched up sheath, several metres of pure white core above you, no option but to get past it? First of all tie into the rope if you can, and if you have any way of getting a belay from another rope, then do so, placing gear if possible. Now all you can do is begin to ascend up on the rope's core, taking care that the strands are located as well as possible under your ascender's cams, tying in all the way if you can (remember that the core is still 80% of the rope's strength). One way to try and maintain the loose core's structure, and increase your safety is to attach a classic prusik loop as close to the top of each ascender as you can (clipping into the head clip-in point), and so doubling up your attachments to the rope (the ascender will push the knot up as you push them). Now take a deep breath and climb!

GROUND ANCHORS

When using fixed ropes always secure the end of the rope to a solid object so it doesn't blow up onto the wall, and ideally pull it out and away so the rope is not touching the rock (it's also less likely to attract attention). Don't pull the rope super tight because the rope will shrink a little bit once it's left for a while, and shrink a lot if left for a long time in the sun. If you're in bear country you can secure your bags to an ascender on the rope, then haul the rope back away from the wall until it's safe (bears are pretty tall when they're standing up, so keep it high!).

Max Biagosch cleaning the Great Roof on the Nose

HAULING

A long time ago I had the pleasure of teaching two top climbers, one of them one of the best in the world, how to haul, their aim to make a free ascent of El Cap. I had them up on an overhanging route down at the local climbing gym, space hauling a bag full of bottles of water. One guy huffed and puffed to get the bags moving, while the other acted as a counterweight, and by the time they'd raised the bag ten metres they were toast. "It won't be as bad as this?" one of them asked, sweat dripping from his zero body fat frame. Taking a moment to make some calculations - four people, five days water, a ton of food, portaledges, hardware, bivvy gear - "it'll be much worse" I replied. And it was.

Almost everything on a wall can be done in a lazy style, and again, if it's hard then you're doing it wrong. The one exception is hauling, which, unless you've got the time to switch to a compound pulley (two, three or four pulleys in your system), is going to require some work, for some the hardest days work of their lives.

Hauling, for both the small and light, and for the lazy or inept, is often the crux of the wall, that old 'the bags were too heavy' often given as an excuse for bailing. But let me say here that heavy bags are no excuse to turn around, and that moving them is just part of the fun.

In this chapter I'm going to focus on moving objects from point A to B, be they nothing but a small haul bag containing supplies for a one day ascent, or a ton of gear for a big team on a very big wall. It's important, as in every chapter, that you learn both the basics and the advanced stuff, as both tend to complement each other.

WHY HAUL?

I guess the first thing to ask is why haul at all? Well firstly, on a big wall you tend to be in an environment that is pretty damn committing, much more so than an alpine face, which you can rap down in a few hours. This means you'll most often to make sure you have all that you need, which often means heavy stuff you can't do without, namely water. A person can climb for several days on starvation rations, or no food at all, but take away the water, or reduce it to survival levels, and you'll grind to a halt. Secondly, on a big wall you may well not be able to retreat easily, meaning you need full on storm gear, including heavy duty sleeping bags, ledges, winter clothing, and then there's your food. Once the weight gets to the point where it's impossible to carry on your back, which is one day's worth (you can ascend with maybe two day's water in your second's pack, but that's all), your overall weight increases as other stuff gets added, like music, speakers, twenty litres of wine, the usual stuff.

BEING GOOD IS VITAL

Get hauling wrong, or be slack or weak in your systems and you'll not get far, and worse still you'll expend more sweat, energy and blood than you can ever imagine. Get it right, learn the systems,

Space Hauling two weeks supplies on Ulvetanna, Antarctica.

be sensible in what you bring, and you'll also expend more sweat, energy and blood than you can ever imagine, only you'll get to the top for your efforts! Being confident in your ability to move things up a wall, that work ethic, is often what sets teams apart from the ones that succeed and the ones that make the abseil of shame. Very early on in my big wall climbing I met the great Valley climber Singer Smith, a gnarly soloist built like a jockey. "How do you haul a month's food on a Baffin wall?" I asked. "Just keep adding pulleys" he replied "and when the bags get stuck just add some more until the stitching rips".

HAULING 101

Hauling is moving objects, some very heavy, from one point to another, from belay to belay, almost always upwards, but not always (you will sometimes need to haul from a lower out, or haul bags along a line). The weights involved mean this must be done in a safe and systematic manner with the highest level of security, both due to the value of what is being lifted (all your water and storm gear for example), as well as the possibly catastrophic result of failure (people have died hauling, as well as broken bones).

MECHANICAL ADVANTAGES

It's vital that you have some grasp of mechanical advantage as well as mechanical disadvantage before going on any wall. By 'grasp' I mean the most basic of understandings, a practical real world understanding rather than classroom knowledge. Yes it's nice to know what W=Fs means, but will it help you haul 200+ kilos with just one foot? The way I think about mechanical advantage is that it's a juggle between energy used to lift, distance lifted and time taken to lift. For example with a 100 kg load using a 1:1 system, in 60 seconds by applying 100 kg of force on the rope you can lift the load 1 metre. With a 2:1 the same load is only lifted 50 cm in 60 seconds, but this only requires 50 kg of force, while a 3:1 only requires 33 kg of force to lift the same weight, but only lifts it 33 cm in 60 seconds. Scale these figures up and you're looking at 50 minutes to haul a load 50 metres with a 1:1 but 2 hours and 30 minutes for a 3:1 (if these figures are flawed then please just imagine me leg hauling 200 kg with a stupid ignorant grin on my face). Understanding the trade offs, and how to adapt your systems to take into account terrain, body weight and changing loads is paramount in rationing out your energy on the wall.

BASIC HAULING RATIOS

Before getting into the 'how' let's just cover the different mechanical advantages you'll be learning.

1:1: Now this is the most common method of hauling, where an object is lifted by applying a force equal to the load, with each metre of rope pulled lifting the load one metre, meaning as long as the force can be applied without becoming exhausted, it's the fastest and simplest method. On a wall the simplest version of this is a climber on a ledge pulling up a rucksack hand over hand, using muscle power to lift it. If the rucksack weighs 10 kg then this method is the most energy/time efficient, but if it weighs 50 kg then your arms will soon run out of energy, plus you won't be able to let go and have a rest. This of course is mechanically neutral.

1:1 Redirect: Imagine you get a job as a bell ringer, but find that instead of

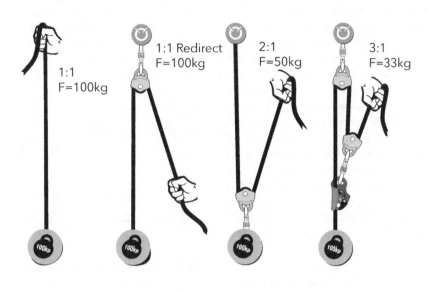

1:1
F=100kg

1:1 Redirect
F=100kg

2:1
F=50kg

3:1
F=33kg

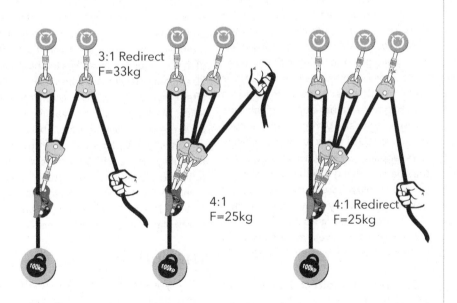

3:1 Redirect
F=33kg

4:1
F=25kg

4:1 Redirect
F=25kg

standing at the bottom of the church steeple, with the bells on top, pulling ropes down, the bells are at the bottom and you have to stand in the steeple pulling the ropes up. How crap would that be! Pulling down is always easier than pulling up as gravity is on your side, your body weight being added to the pull, rather than using your muscles. People often think that in a classic haul system you are gaining some mechanical advantage by the pulley, where in fact it's still a 1:1 system, but the pulley is just acting as a redirect. In reality you have less than a 1:1 ratio, as the pulley, no matter how efficient or large, will always rob you of some of that lifting juice (with a pulley that is 80% efficient the climber must apply 125 kg of force to lift 100 kg, so creating something more like a 1:1.25 system).

Now if a 75 kg climber sits on the rope a 70 kg load will begin to raise. But what if with all this hauling the climber's weight drops to 70 kg? Well now the load is equal so the climber must apply some extra force, using either their legs or their arms to pull the rope through the pulley, or by pulling on the up strand simultaneously in order to tip the balance. In this perfect world what happens if we add a haul bag to carry that object, which rubs up against the slabby rock as the climber is hauling? Well more force then needs to be applied. So what if now we double that load to 140 kg? Well the climber can try and employ more muscle power, get upside down and try squatting it out, their feet on the bolts, but it's no good, 1:1 is not going to work unless more energy can be applied, or the load can be reduced.

2:1 and 3:1 Redirect: Now we start to create real mechanical advantage, adding in an extra pulley and a redirect (2:1), or two extra pulleys (3:1), or even

more. Now that climber can reduce that heavy load to below their body weight.

4:1 or 5:1: This is typically the limit for big wall mechanical advantage, usually found in industrial rigging systems for rescue, with a complex multi pulley rigged up to piggyback on the main line and using 4 pulleys, or 4 pulleys and a redirect pulley.

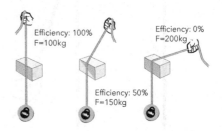

Efficiency: 100%
F=100kg

Efficiency: 0%
F=200kg

Efficiency: 50%
F=150kg

MECHANICAL DISADVANTAGES

What's most important with these systems, as with all mechanical advantage systems, is that just as all forces applied by you are magnified (70 kg of weight pulling on the rig creating 140 kg of force on the load), so too are the inefficiencies multiplied. For example, if with each lift of the 2:1 your rope grab lifts the haul line 30 cm, but you fail to pull the system tight after each reset, and your load strand is a little slack by only 5 cm, you'll lose 10 cm on each lift, maybe more. This is one reason why the whole set up, from how the pulleys are attached and able to twist, to the cord used, is so important. You're trying to create a Formula One hauling system. The bottom line is to be an efficiency Nazi in all complex hauling set ups.

THE PULLEY

Everyone thinks they know what a pulley does, but most tend to have little clue just what it really is, how it works or how it came to be what it is. First off, a pulley wheel does not make a load lighter, it is not a machine in itself, it cannot make something magically lighter. Chuck a rope through a pulley the size of the moon and you will still not be able to lift the world.

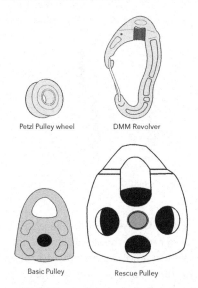

Petzl Pulley wheel   DMM Revolver

Basic Pulley   Rescue Pulley

The first pulleys were not pulleys at all, just ropes thrown over tree branches or maybe the masts of small sailing boats and used as a redirect for the force of the person below using muscle power and weight to lift an object. As that tree branch became smoother and the bark rubbed off, and was lubricated with sap, the load began to feel lighter.

These redirects were one day made from blocks of wood (the sides of the pulley are called the block), bronze or steel pins inserted to create an axle to further reduce the friction of the rope, that axle soon made more efficient still by the adding of a wheel, drum, or sheave over it, perhaps to reduce wear on the expensive metal.

Soon people realised they could create machines with these pulleys, linking them together, so that one man could not only lift his own weight, but that of two men, then four, then with as many pulleys and time as he had, maybe even the moon.

The first major use of pulleys in big wall climbing came in the post war years when climbers began to tackle the big walls of Yosemite, the heat of such walls meaning more water was required than on walls in the Alps. People like John Salathe and Anton Nelson, Chuck Pratt and Royal Robbins and Warren Harding and Bill 'Dolt' Feuerer took maritime pulleys and created prototype big wall hauling systems, most often simply utilising the leg haul. As weights increased, with climbs like the first ascent of North America Wall, and harder and longer routes such as the Dawn Wall, The Shield, Mescalito and Zodiac, the size and strength of the pulleys also increased. Early or cheap pulleys featured an oiled axle on which the sheave rotated, but such designs were no match for heavy loads, and soon sheaves featuring enclosed roller bearings were introduced, making pulleys highly efficient.

WHAT YOU NEED TO KNOW

As I've said, a pulley is not magic. So first off, remember that no matter the size of the pulley, when used alone, the load will never be less than what it is, but can be more.

Efficiency: The main factor in any pulley is its ability to redirect the force running through it, with those designed to add the smallest amount of friction and resistance being the best. This must also be balanced with its weight and size when carried up the wall.

Sheave: This is the technical name for the pulley wheel, and should be the only part of the pulley that comes into contact with the rope. The efficiency of the pulley is partly the result of the sheave diameter and the way the sheave is able to rotate on its axle. This rotation is achieved either by a bushings or by sealed ball bearings. Bushings are made from a smooth nylon or metal cylinder rotating on a lubricated axle, and although strong and simple are not as efficient as a sheave running on ball bearings. The complexity and weight of a pulley with bearings tends to make them more expensive and many companies will offer a design in both types, with the bearings version often identified as being a pro model. A sheave running on bushings will often be 70% efficient, while one running on high quality bearings will surpass 90%, vital when hauling the heaviest loads.

Pulley Strength And Safe Working Load:

Pulleys have huge forces going through them, twice that of the load (it takes an equal force to raise an object, so double the weight is on the pulley) so make a note of their strength and safe working loads (SWL). A Petzl Oscillante for example has a breaking strain of 15 kN, but only a safe working load of 4 kN. What this means is that although the alloy side plates will not break until around 1500 kg, the plastic sheave will deform and stop working at around 4 kN. This SWL is different on a PCP as the unit's cam will damage the rope long before the sheave is put under any pressure. For example a Petzl Pro Traxion has an overall strength of 22 kN (strength before the whole unit buckles and breaks), and a sheave SWL of around 8 kN, but the SWL of the cam is only 2.5 kN. This strength should be rationalised by understanding that a good quality metal pulley, ideally running on ball bearings, will be strong enough for any load, and it is the cam or ascender that it the limiting component of the system.

Multi Directional: Beyond standard pulleys that are clipped off at the top, there are several models that have suspension holes at the bottom as well, used to clip in other pulleys or ropes, or to secure the pulley closed. This bottom clip point is called the 'becket' and is vital for more complex compound pulley setups.

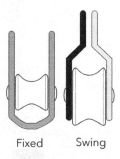

Fixed   Swing

Fixed Or Swing: The side plates of a pulley provide the strength of the pulley, creating a solid platform and foundation for the sheave, and a home for your locking karabiner. The designs of the side plates can be split into two primary versions; those that are fixed, with the side plates usually made from a single piece of bent or forged alloy, and those that are in two parts, allowing the plates to swing apart in order to place the line over the sheave. The fixed design tends to be stronger but requires the correct karabiner in order to have the sheave properly aligned with the load (an oval karabiner works best), but this also allows for the possibility of more advanced methods of piggybacking other krabs or slings on the main locker. A swing cheek design is more common, and will work with any style of karabiner, although an oval is still the preferred locker. One advantage of some swing pulleys is that if the plates are set close enough they can also act as Prusik minding pulleys, the plates stopping a Prusik knot from being sucked into the pulley, creating a soft PCP.

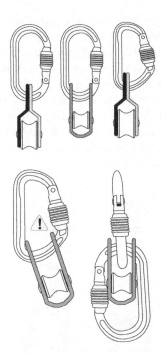

ATTACHMENT

The pulley can be attached either by a hard link, such as a locking or plain gate karabiner, or a soft link, which allows the pulley to twist and adjust to the direction of the force. These links can be as simple as a single or double loop of cord (Dyneema or 7 mm+ perlon), or a sewn sling, or sailing soft shackle.

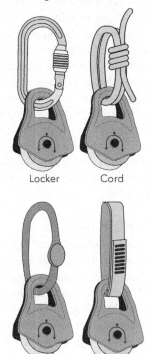

Locker   Cord

Soft Link   Sewn Sling

WHAT PULLEYS TO USE?

Beyond the PCP covered here, a big wall team should always carry at least two small light (sub 200 gram) highly efficient (90%+) pulleys, used as a backup in case the main pulley is dropped or breaks, for pick ups and for setting up 3:1 systems. These small pulleys can also be used in lieu of a full sized PCP for pulling up the main belay kit, and one micro PCP like the Petzl Micro Traxion (85 g / 28 mm sheave) is ideal for this double duty (as it can be used as an ascender as well). The other pulley should be non PCP as such pulleys do not work well as the bottom pulley in a 3:1 (the cam will constantly lock when resetting). There are many suitable non PCP pulleys like the Petzl Rescue (38 mm sheave /185 g) and Mini (25 mm sheave / 80 g) or DMM Pinto Rig (16 mm sheave / 111 g), or any small/medium pulley from companies like Eiger, CMI, Rock Exotica, Camp etc.

DOUBLE PULLEYS

These pulleys feature two pulley wheels built into the side plates, with the best models having a becket on the underside, allowing more complex systems to be built. These pulleys are primarily designed for industrial and rescue use, but can be very handy if you're tackling a major objective with a big team, being vital for 4:1 and up systems.

THE PCP

I use the term PCP to cover Progress Capture Pulleys, as the term hauler or wall hauler can become confusing when the climber is also the hauler. The PCP is the focal point of your hauling system and requires real understanding, even a bit of empathy, in order to use it effectively. In the past a simple pulley was used, as large as could be found (the CMC rescue pulley being the standard), with an inverted ascender clipped below it to hold the rope each time the rope was pulled through. These days we use an integrated PCP, where the ascender's cam is integral to the unit, making a much more compact and light system. I will cover an old school set up first, which is worth knowing about, even though most climbers will use the modern integrated design today.

OLD SCHOOL PCP

The old school traditional PCP system, unlike the modern integrated design, was most usually built from a medium pulley and a handled or basic ascender. The pulley would be clipped to the masterpoint with an ascender attached beside it via a short sling, or in the case of a smaller pulley, via a karabiner. Once set you would usually add a little weight to the head of the ascender to keep it in position and weighted down. The overall strength and function of the system was probably higher than is possible with even the largest PCP, as you could employ very large rescue pulleys. This system is one that you should study and learn as it can come in handy, especially if you drop your primary pulley.

I've also used this in the past with super sized pulleys when loads were very high (when climbing in big teams), as it was stronger and more effective than the integrated PCP at the time (Rock Exotica/Petzl Wall Hauler), giving you a little more confidence when you've got three people space hauling. These days the modern PCP like the Petzl Pro Traxion is more than strong enough to take these loads, and most climbers should switch to 2:1 or 3:1 systems rather than look for a heavier pulley.

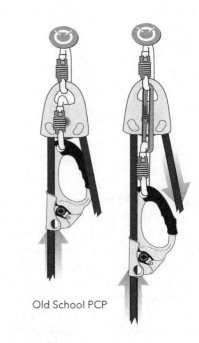

Old School PCP

PCP MODELS

There are several companies making Progress Capture Pulleys, including Petzl, SMC, ISC, and Kong, some for climbing and others for industrial use. I think the two best models at the moment for big wall climbing would be the Petzl Micro Traxion and the Petzl Pro Traxion mark 2, taking into account their availability, size, cost, bulk and weight. These two devices are both big improvements on the older Mini Traxion and Pro Traxion mark 1 (the Micro is much smaller than the Mini, yet has a bigger pulley, while the mark 2 Pro is just stronger and better featured for safety), offering primarily greater strength, function and ease of use. The best thing about the new Pro Traxion is that it features a closure system that allows the rope to be inserted and removed without taking it off its karabiner (so less risk of dropping), and a safety lock that reduces the chances of the two plates not being locked into place before you start hauling (which can lead to failure or the rope jumping out of the device!). A few things to think about with all these devices are the following.

bearings will not have the load spread over them equally. In the worst cases you can actually damage the pulley, with the pulley itself rubbing on the side plate (it's bad enough hauling without grinding down your pulley as well!). Whenever you haul always pay close attention to the orientation of the pulley.

Back Up Your PCP: The amount of force going through the PCP can be huge, and in extreme cases can lead to failure (I've seen old A5 haulers twisting under the load). For this reason always use the clip hole in the bottom of the Pro Traxion as this will stop the plates coming adrift, locking them in place (and acting as a further safeguard to the safety lock). This does not have to be done with a locker, and you can fix this karabiner to the position with a keeper cord for just this job. Another back up when dealing with big loads is to simply clip a quickdraw from the suspension point to the rope - peace of mind when space hauling with two people hanging on the rope.

Petzl Micro Traxion

Kong Block Roll   Petzl Pro Traxion

Correct Orientation: One aspect of all PCPs is that they need to be matched correctly with the right karabiner, more often than not an oval. The reason for this is that the PCP and its inbuilt pulley must remain in-line with the load being applied to it. Have your PCP slightly tilted in the bottom of a D shaped karabiner and you'll lose efficiency, as the pulleys'

Locker Or Not? It seems a no-brainer that the PCP will live on an oval locker, the Petzl OK (70 g / 25 kN) being the best (screw gate not twist lock), but there are some advantages to a plain oval krab, such as the Petzl Owall (68 g / 24 kN) or DMM Ultra O (61 g / 25 kN). A non locking krab is easier to clip in and out of your rear haul loop and once loaded by the haul line there is no way it can jump from the master point, and so is something worth considering.

Keep The Rope Running Out: When orienting your PCP you want the rope to ideally run out from the device away from the wall so it runs direct to you, rather than against the wall. If this is not possible the whole unit will have some twist to it when hauling.

Always Removable: Always clip the PCP into the masterpoint krab via its own krab, not direct into the masterpoint. The reason for this is that once the bags have been docked and backed up the haul line needs to be removable and the PCP taken off the masterpoint to be brought up to the next belay. If you have the PCP clipped in direct to the masterpoint krab, this can be impossible (some loads can make it impossible to open the masterpoint for example).

PCP Fuckwittery: One thing I've seen more than once is climbers clipping a PCP, like the Pro Traxion, upside down (yes!), with the bottom safety hole being clipped into the anchor! Luckily, if you do this, you should realise something is wrong as you won't be able to engage the PCP's cam, but with some more fuckwittery maybe someone can, leaving the rope then jammed in the PCP once the weight of the bags is on it. If this was to happen the only option would be to set up a second hauling system and using a rope grab lift the bags enough to disengage the first PCP and get it the right way round.

SAFETY

Hauling is potentially one of the most dangerous aspects of big wall climbing,

with several fatalities caused by failure to secure haul bags to belays, incorrect use of PCPs, and overloaded hauling components breaking, not to mention many, many near misses. When hauling you need to think about the huge loads being moved around, and hanging from your belay. This translates to ultra caution in all parts of your hauling system and interaction with bags, haul lines, docking cords and pulleys. If you rush and make a mistake, drop a load or have it shift where it's not wanted, you can easily kill someone or yourself. I try and teach climbers to view their bags as dangerous creatures, like a great white shark, rhino or raptor that is in their charge. The ability to keep them calm and under your control comes down to paranoia, foresight and heavy respect for the damage they can do.

THE WEAKEST LINK

The weakest link in the hauling system is the cam on the PCP, which due to its compressive action, crushing the rope, should be viewed as having only a safe working static load of 500 kg. Although the pulley itself may be able to take 30,000 kg, anything above 500 kg, and you will begin to damage the rope, ripping off the sheath, then eventually cutting it completely. So can you haul 500 kg loads? Well no, to be safe you should keep big wall loads below half of this, so around 200+/- kg, which is also defined by rescue teams as a 'rescue load' (two climbers (2 x 70 kg) and stretcher plus equipment). Remember though that this is for one strand of rope, so when space hauling for example you may have close to 500 kg hanging from the pulley, but divided on either side of the pulley, only half hanging on the PCP's cam. If you think you might need to go above 200 kg, perhaps a four person team on a grade VII wall, I would advise going for a double hauling system so as to reduce the weight on all components, and make all ropes a minimum of 10 mm (rescue teams only use 11 mm ropes).

EVERY ACTION...

Remember, before you do anything, such as untie a docking cord, pull the haul line tight through a PCP, or untie a backup knot, work through what will happen next. I know people who released docking cords and had their haul bags simply crash down the wall, and have heard the infamous story of the team on the Nose whose bag fell from the anchor and broke their 'death triangle' belay, sending all three to their deaths. Before you do anything remember that every action has a reaction, so make sure you know in advance what the result will be of each action you take on a wall.

THE HAUL LINE

The haul line is not really any particular kind of rope, but a catch all term for any rope that is used to lift something from A to B, and can by anything from 5 mm dyneema cord to chunky 11 mm static rope. These ropes also get used for double duty, as fixed ropes or even as lead ropes if the primary rope gets damaged. Of all the ropes you use, the haul lines get the most abuse, over-loaded, ground through PCPs and ascenders, and for pitch after pitch, wall after wall. Here I'll try and break down the haul line into its important attributes so as to fully understand what rope you might need.

HAUL LINE SPECS

In order to get the right rope for the job you need to weigh up a lot of options.

Strength: This is a good one to start with, as this has a direct impact on how you approach everything on the wall. The simple figure is that all static ropes need to pass a minimum strength test of 18 kN for a half rope (9 mm) and 22 kN for a single rope (10 mm). Added to this, both ropes must be able to take at least five factor 1 falls without breaking, something that is good to know if one day you drop a haul bag to the end of the line. In practice, the strengths of these ropes is actually much higher, perhaps by as much as 50%, the same with falls, with a 10 mm rope able to take over ten factor 1 falls before breaking. These initial figures should be viewed more as safe working loads (SWL), and translated more easily in terms of hauling, a 9 mm static rope will hold 1835 kg and a 10 mm will hold 2243 kg. In reality no big wall haul line will ever be asked to hold such a static load due to the inherent weaknesses in the system (a 1800 kg load is what you have cranes for!), this strength only ever required in that aforementioned doomsday scenario of the bags becoming detached from the belay and taking a factor 1 fall onto the anchor.

Length: The haul line should not be any shorter than your lead line, and ideally either 60 or 70 metres in length. This is because if running pitches together it's obviously a good idea that both ropes are the same length! Saying that, a longer haul line can be very useful as it can be used as a lowerout line (see 'Lowerout Line'), as well as give you more rope to play with when fixing ropes, the down-side being the overall weight of longer ropes (important for alpine walls). You also need to make sure people know the ropes are mismatched when abseiling.

Bonded Sheaths: As with lead lines, having a 'unicore' style rope provides a huge advantage, both in terms of strength robustness when hauling, but also when using your haul line as a fixed line.

Static Or Dynamic: There are pros and cons of using either a dynamic or static rope which must be assessed by the climber, with the conclusion being dependent on the route.

- **Dynamic Pros**: The main advantage of having a dynamic rope as a haul line is that you then have a spare lead line in the system, in which case the haul line must be a UIAA certified single rope, important if your lead line should get damaged. A secondary benefit is if your haul bag should come adrift off the anchor and fall the full rope length, the shock load on the belay will be much more dynamic – which could make the difference between a nasty shock and finding yourself at the bottom of a very deep hole!

- **Dynamic Cons**: A rope's dynamic properties does lower the efficiency of the haul system compared to a static line (although in my experience once all the slack has been taken in tight to the bags and the rope is loaded, it actually has much lower dynamic properties than you would imagine). Dynamic climbing ropes are also not as tough as static ropes, or as strong, with the sheath being designed for more industrial use rather than the leisure market. A dynamic haul line might only last about half as long as a static haul line.

- **Static Pros**: Stronger, tougher, and obviously static, which makes hauling a little easier, especially when doing a Z haul. If you want the maximum life out of a haul line then it has to be a static. Fixing a static rope is also far safer, as there will be minimal stretch making ascending far safer if the rope is running over any sharp edges. It can also be easier to pull down a thick lead line on abseils using a static rope.

- **Static Cons:** Cannot be used as a lead rope if something happens to your climbing rope, and is dangerous to fall on, applying dangerously high forces.

Diameter: The diameter of your haul line depends on the expected wear and tear, the load it's expected to take and the amount of routes you want to get out of it. These are the typical haul line diameters.

- **Super Light (5 mm Dyneema/Spectra/Titan or 6+ mm Trail/Rap Line)**: This type of haul line is used for very light loads, loads so light that the second may actually climb with the sack for speed if possible. The rope is also used for rapping with the main line, or as a static zip-line. This diameter is most appropriate for free or speed walls where weight is crucial, and hauling will be very light or non existent. If you want to haul, make sure the rope works with the pulley system you have.

- **Lightweight (7 to 9.5 mm Dynamic or 8 to 9 mm Static)**: This is a good system for short multi day or alpine walls, being lightweight (important if free climbing), low bulk, and OK for moderate loads up to around 100 kg. Using a skinny half dynamic rope means that fixing can be risky as they aren't great when being repeatedly ascended unless the team are very skilled, especially if they are passing

Forest Altherr using a 2:1 haul on Moonlight Buttress

over sharp edges, but if you're only hauling on it it's OK. A better dynamic alternative is a full strength skinny single rope (9 to 9.5 mm), which is not only stronger, but can also be lead climbed on and is a much safer line to ascend. Lightweight statics are designed for alpine use and expeditions, can be found in 8 or 9 mm, and are very effective ropes for both hauling and fixing (the go to ropes for capsule style), but they work best when employed by climbers who are highly skilled at ascending and fixing ropes etc.

- **Full Weight (9.5 to 11 mm Dynamic or 10 to 11 mm Static)**: This is what you should be using on most walls, with the length of the route and abrasiveness of the rock dictating the diameter and type of rope used. With the thicker ropes it's well worth employing a tag line rather than trailing the rope, as the weight can become considerable, with a 10 mm being the max diameter you'd want to have clipped to your harness. The thicker static ropes are also perfect for heavy use, fixing, and super heavy hauling. If employing a three person speed climbing system then the haul line should be of this weight, as it may often have to support the weight of both the bags and one team member, with one climber ascending the haul line on every pitch. For me the standard weight big wall haul line would be the 10 mm static, but if you think you may encounter some dangerous ground, where the lead line may be cut or damaged, then a dynamic 10 mm gives you redundancy, serving as a backup to your lead line.

FALLING ON A HAUL LINE

The nightmare scenario for a leader is to have their lead line cut, causing them to fall on their haul line. In most cases the haul line is simply fed into a rope bag and attached to the haul bags and to the belay with the backup knot (without a backup knot you'd be falling onto the docking cord, which would probably break). This means in a fall you would most likely fall a minimum of 60 metres, but probably far further, maybe twice that if you fell from the end of a pitch.

Now a static rope is designed to take a dynamic fall without killing the climber or breaking, but we're talking a major and dangerous fall here, and not one you'd be whooping at the end of. If you're climbing ground where the lead line could be cut then you probably need to be running a two rope system (see 'Leading'), or at least running a dynamic tag line or haul line. If you want your dynamic haul/tag line as a backup, then tie into it as you would a rope, as taking a fall onto your rear haul loop (or gear loop) may be worse than death!

The leader should always communicate with the belayer what they are doing so that they can belay them with the haul line as well, or at least clip off the haul line short (just tie an overhand knot and clip this in and tie another when the rope goes tight). I only know of one fatality from a haul line fall, the climber falling to the end of the rope when their lead line was cut by a loose rock, but this death was probably caused by the climber clipping the haul line to their chest sling rather than their harness.

HAUL LINE AS SECOND LEAD LINE

If you are worried your lead line may be compromised, then you can clip your haul line into protection, but this will make a full haul impossible, and the haul line will need to be un-clipped by the second, a difficult thing to do if the pitch is traversing. You can make unclipping easier by using a very long extender or sling, but it's really best to avoid doing this unless you're convinced your life is in jeopardy.

As the lead line tends to deviate around the pitch, while the haul line goes direct, if on running pitches together you come up short on the lead line, you might be able to get to where you're going with the haul line. To do this you should tie the lead line to the haul line via a rethreaded figure of eight (make sure you don't lose your lead line in the process), then belay yourself on the haul line (using a clove hitch) until you can reach where you're going.

KEEPING THE LINE UNDER CONTROL

When leading I hate it when the belayer just lets the haul line slip out of the rope bag, meaning I've got extra metres hanging on my harness, which can be quite heavy if you're using a 10 mm static. Instead try and give the leader only the rope they need, having it clove hitched off at the belay (this will also act as a back-up if the lead line breaks). On windy days the belayer should also pay extra attention to this, as coming close to the end of long pitches (Changing Corners on the Nose being a good example), you can have your haul line whipped into nearby flakes.

CONNECTING THE HAUL LINE TO THE HARNESS

The climber's end of the haul line can be finished off with just a simple overhand or figure of eight knot. This can then be clipped to the rear haul loop on your harness via a locker, simple and straightforward. A neater alternative is to use a barrel/scaffolding knot (breaking strain: 65% to 75%) as this reduces the excess bulk at the connection. Most climbers clip their PCP into the rear haul loop along with their haul line, but this puts one of your most valuable pieces of gear as far away from you as possible, making it much easier to drop or fumble. For this reason I often clip my PCP closer to the front where I can see it more easily.

I would recommend that the locker at the end of the haul line is both large and distinctive, so that it's easy to un-clip from the back of the harness without fumbling, and can easily be located on the belay when it comes to taking it up the next pitch (the leader's end always stays the same, as the other end is always attached to the bags). If you don't have a distinctive PCP locker then use tape or spray paint to make the locker easy to spot (an odd shaped krab is best as it can be felt more easily when doing the reach around).

PRE THREADED PCP

A better system is to pre feed the haul line through the PCP (although obviously this is not such a good idea if you think there is any chance you might take a fall onto the haul line, as previously discussed), and use a non locking karabiner to clip the haul line end either into the haul loop or into the PCP's locker. On reaching the belay you will unclip the haul line karabiner first and pull it through the PCP and clip this onto the belay (high on the side the leader will lead the next pitch from so it's ready), then un-clip the PCP and clip this to the master point, the whole system designed to avoid dropping either haul line or PCP. With this system you can forgo having a locker as your rope end karabiner, as it's already backed up by the PCP's krab.

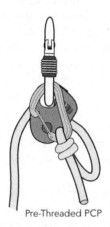
Pre-Threaded PCP

FORGETTING THE HAUL LINE

Sooner or later you will find you've forgotten the haul line. This can be avoided by having a set of pre lead checks, such as: "On belay - check - haul line - check". Usually the error is noticed when the leader isn't too high, meaning the leader can send down a loop of lead line to retrieve the rope (on bleak aid you will need to create a belay). If the error is discovered too late to retrieve the rope, and the leader can reach the belay, then the second will have to clean the pitch and bring up the haul line end, then rap back down the lead line, release the bags, and climb the lead line again (yes this is a ball ache).

SIMPLE HAULING

This covers a series of techniques, some very simple, used for very light hauling (these could be considered as 'alpine hauling' techniques). These techniques

are designed to be used with either no equipment, or simply the gear the leader will already be carrying. One of the main uses for this type of hauling is when the leader pulls up a tag bag via their tag line once at the belay, the tag bag having the haul line attached, as well as all belay building kit and haulers, which can be surprisingly heavy.

Hand Over Hand: By far the simplest and low-tech solution, this requires nothing more than a pair of hands and some muscle power (ideally you need to be wearing gloves). The downside with hand over hand is when you start pulling up a bag, say a tag bag or rack bag, you'll find that the bag begins to feel heavier and heavier. One place this can lead to you getting unstuck is when pulling up gear while leading, as you're increasing the load on what you're hanging on, not good if it's a time bomb. Hand over hand is worse when free climbing, you have to use one hand to pull and your teeth to hold the rope. I was once stuck in a bomb bay chimney with no protection for miles and was forced to pull up a power drill with my haul line. Within a few minutes it felt as if I was hauling up a haul bag, screaming and shouting down to ask what they hell they'd clipped to the rope. By using a shoulder or body belay with the rope you can have a rest, but in most cases it's better to use one of the following techniques.

Karabiner Redirect: In order to gain some more control on the rope, clipping the rope through a karabiner above you creates a crude fixed pulley. As mentioned previously there is no mechanical advantage, but it affords you the ability to rest. Use the thickest and roundest karabiner you have and if you're pulling up gear mid pitch pull it up on a piece of gear above the one you're on. Having a few DMM Revolver karabiners with a built in pulley can help this process, although only with light to medium weight loads.

Alpine Clutch (Garda Knot): Using two matched karabiners (same model) you can create a clutch, where a rope will run one way but not the other. Avoid using screwgates as the chunky gates can block the correct positioning of spines, and be aware that the clutch does not offer 100% security and that the rope needs to be monitored to stop it escaping. The friction of this knot makes it only suitable for lighter loads. This knot works best with one hand pulling up on one strand and the other pulling down on the other.

Locking Munter: This is a cool knot, that unlike the Alpine Clutch does not require matched karabiners to work, and is more secure. By adding a karabiner to the classic Munter hitch you can make a clutch knot, that will only run in one direction. Like the alpine clutch, this knot works best with one hand pulling up on one strand and the other pulling down on the other.

Guide Plate: Using a guide plate in auto locking mode is the most obvious way of setting up a simple hauling system. Using a large round bar karabiner aids smooth movement of the rope,

and like the above methods, having one hand on each strand of rope (lifting up and pulling down) works best.

Handled Ascender: A simple method where the ascender is clipped into a locking karabiner with the rope running through the ascender and around the karabiner, and could be viewed as a pulley-less hauling system. Unlike the previous few methods you can pull the rope through with both hands and this can work quite well if you have light loads. You can also improve this system by playing around, by adding a second karabiner to create an alternative redirect, and making this a DMM revolver further increases the efficiency of the system. If you have a small back up/emergency pulley, then you can easily create a PCP instead.

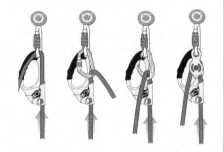

Belay + Prusik: If you run your rope through a belay device (in non guide mode), and then use a prusik loop attached to the rope, the belay device stops the prusik locking as you pull the rope through (like a prusik minding pulley). Unlike the guide plate you can use both hands on the rope more effectively so it is more efficient.

Micro Ascender: Micro ascenders like the Petzl Tibloc or Kong Frog are ideal haulers, as they're light, 100% secure, and allow two handed hauling. If you've got two micro ascenders, or one micro and a handled ascender (or GriGri or belay device), you can use the micro as the locking hauler, with the second device used to pull the rope through the device.

Micro Traxion: Although technically one level up, the Traxion is such a 'do it all' tool, and is so lightweight, that it should always be on a climber's harness. This of course is by far the best way to haul anything, from light bags to pretty heavy multi days bags. When leading, this device can be placed on the gear you're on, or above or below, but above will make hauling the easiest.

HEAVY DUTY HAULING

In this section we switch up a gear to the meat of most big walls, moving loads that weigh around body weight, to loads that weigh the same as a small family car. The techniques range from simple, with very little gear needed, to highly complex, with multiple pulleys being employed. I would advise all big wall climbers to have a thorough understanding of techniques beyond 1:1, especially 3:1, as even on easy routes you might find yourself out manoeuvred by the rock, the weight, or both.

CLASSIC 1:1

So now we get to the meaty stuff, the proper hauling. The default setup is the 1:1 haul, most usually employing a PCP.

Basic Principle

This is the standard hauling set up for big walls, and is the core technique and foundation on which following more complex systems will be built. The 1:1 system I'll cover below gives the best balance between energy and time, and is what most climbers will use on most short to medium length walls, perhaps employing a 3:1 or space hauling early on when the bags are at their heaviest. The techniques covered, such as how to pull the rope should be employed in all other types of hauling.

1:1

Component Parts

All you will need is a PCP and your ascenders, the size and function of your PCP depending on the size and style of wall.

Set Up

01. Having set up the belay, the climber (hauler) takes the end of the haul line and clips this off to the top anchor on the side the next pitch will lead off from.

02. They unclip the PCP (which is still clipped to the haul line) and clip it into the masterpoint, with the hauler oriented correctly.

03. Checking the cam is engaged, they will begin to pull in the slack. This is a vital form of non-verbal communication between team members, as the constant movement of the haul line, without the lead line moving, tells the belayer the leader probably has the haul line through the PCP and is safe and at the belay (the belayer does not need to take them off belay).

04. The climber continues to pull the rope through the PCP. The reason for pulling the rope through the engaged PCP is that if, in a worst case scenario, the belayer released the haul bags during this time, the load would come onto the PCP, not the climbers' hands.

05. As the rope comes tight to the haul line backup knot, the belayer unclips this, and the rope is now running free to the hauling point on the bags.

06. The hauler will feel the rope go tight.

07. If there is no way to communicate, the moment the rope goes super tight to the bags, the bags should be able to be released. But ideally Steps 8 and 9 will occur.

08. The hauler shouts down 'Ready to haul.'

09. The belayer unties the docking cord, releases the bags, and shouts 'Haul when you're ready'.

10. The bags swing clear and the belayer can now set about stripping the belay

and cleaning, while the hauler can begin to haul.

11. When going through this process remember that nothing can be done until the bags are off the belay, so it's down to both climbers to make this happen.

2:1 HAULING

So you're maxed out, maybe because the bags are too heavy, maybe because you're too light. The easiest thing to do is a 3:1 or classic Z haul, but maybe you want something faster. The following method comes in many forms, and under many names, the most common the Chongo Wall Ratchet (Chongo popularised the system in the 90s). It's also known as a pig haul (due to it piggybacking the haul line), but whatever you call it, it's a great technique to know and master, so be able to build your own 2:1 rig.

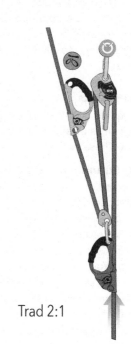

Trad 2:1

Basic Principle

A 2:1 would traditionally require you use a rope twice as long, the rope attached at the belay, going down to a pulley on the bag, then back up, with a Change Of Direction (COD) pulley on the belay. Of course this isn't the way to go, both due to weight concerns, and the fact you would lose a huge amount of efficiency over such a distance. Instead what you want is a 2:1 system that has both the minimum of stretch in it, so that every centimetre pulled lifts the bag a centimetre upwards (well half that, so 5 mm, as it's a 2:1), and that the lowest friction is achieved, using low diameter cord and high quality pulleys. You then set this lifting rig beside the haul line and lift the haul line, not the load, a rope grab used to move the line up with each action of the 2:1, the slack pulled in tight on the haul line's PCP before each reset of the 2:1. Using this system the hauler reduces the weight of the bags by roughly half, at the cost of lifting at half the speed, which is a very good trade off, as a 70 kg person will take twice as long to lift 100 kg, than 50 kg anyway.

Component Parts

The 2:1 requires both the highest quality parts as well as careful selection and employment. These include:

- **Hauling Strand**: This is a 4 metre length of cord or sling, and can either be thin static cord (6 or 7 mm) or standard 5 mm dyneema (wears out fast), or a specialist cord such as Sterling 5.9 mm Power Cord or 6 mm TRC cord (the best). You can also use a thin dyneema sling (8 or 10 mm), or the tail of your haul line if you want to make up a 2:1 on the fly. One end of the cord is fixed at the top of the system while the bottom end is free. To avoid losing your pulleys I would fix a rap ring via a double bowline at one end as this will jam in the pulley wheels and stop the system falling apart. This will also be used to clip into. If you don't want to use this, simply tie a big knot in the end and adjust your position using a clove hitch.

- **Pulleys**: These need to be two high quality pulleys with the largest diameter that is practical to carry.

- **Rope Grab**: You can just use one of your own ascenders, but having a dedicated small Petzl Basic or chest ascender (Croll) fixed into the system works best, running smoothly and creating redundancy if an ascender is lost, or for use with the frog system. This can be moved down at each stroke by hand, or weighted with some large gear, leaving your hands free to pull up each time.

- **PCP**: The PCP used here will be your full size PCP, as you will probably switch over to 1:1 hauling once the bags get lighter anyway, or employ it in 3:1 or space hauling. If you want to create a 2:1 system but only have two pulleys, then you can use your PCP as one of those pulleys and replace it in the system with a guide plate, ascender, auto-lock Munter or Garda knot.

- **Lockers**: You will need a locker to join your ascender to your pulley and I would go for a 10 mm Alloy Maillon (25 kN) and a small micro locker to clip the system into your master point.

- **2:1 Bag**: It's best to have the whole system pre built and stowed in a bag ready to be deployed.

Set Up

There are a number of ways to set this

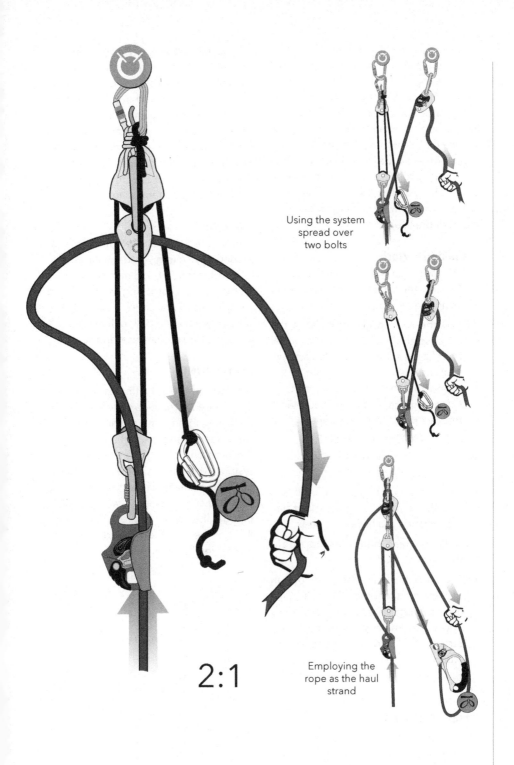

Using the system spread over two bolts

2:1

Employing the rope as the haul strand

up and it's actually a very simple system when you're able to spread out and separate the top pulley, hauling strand knot and PCP, but often this is not possible. One important feature is that the system has to be able to auto align to the load, meaning that a non rigid connector works best, such as a rope loop (5 mm dyneema or 7 mm cord). I've given a number of set ups here and it's best to try each one as variations in what pulley you have will make or break each set up.

Making It Work

The basic idea is simple and obvious:

01. Clip into the hauling strand via a locker using the rap ring or a clove hitch.

02. Pull the rope grab tight down the rope, so the hauling strand is super tight (using some force helps achieve this). You can also add weight to the rope grab to achieve this, such as some large cams, freeing your hand, but this tends to be less effective at creating a tight hauling strand.

03. Squat down, pulling the hauling strand down, raising the rope grab.

04. A slack loop will be created in the haul line above the rope grab about half the distance you have dropped.

05. Pull the dead haul line loop tight through the PCP.

06. Step up (pull yourself up on an ascender attached to the dead haul line), pulling down the rope grab as you do so, making sure the hauling strand is locked tight once you're stood up.

07. Repeat.

EMERGENCY 2:1

A variation of the 2:1 should be learnt for a scenario where you drop your PCP and have no extra pulleys, as a 1:1 haul from just a karabiner is probably impossible unless the bags are super light. This works the same as the above system but has no pulleys within it. Instead the system runs on karabiners (use the largest and most rounded krabs you have, but ideally use something like two DMM Revolvers), using cord (from cordelette) or via a thin sling (cut a 120 cm sling to make a 240 cm single strand sling).

Set Up

Have the load hanging from an auto locking device (e.g., guide plate, ABBD, inverted ascender), and then create a 2:1 system using a cord/sling as the hauling strand, with karabiners replacing the pulleys. After each pull, pull in the rope on the locking device, reset and continue.

3:1 HAULING

Although the 2:1 offers some benefits in speed it can be a system that suits the climbing nerd more than the practical minded, with many not willing to take the time and effort to get the perfect system (when only a perfect system will do). Instead many climbers simply switch between a 1:1 and a 3:1, with the latter being a little slow, but requiring only a third of the effort, and so ideal for the heavier, earlier days on a wall.

3:1

Basic Principle

The set up for a 3:1 is the same as most climbers have already learned for a z pulley rig for crevasse or self rescue, with 2 more pulleys being added to the system on top of the PCP, reducing the force needed to raise the load by a third, but at the cost of taking - on paper - three times as long as a 1:1.

Component Parts

As with the other systems the greater quality the pulleys, the better, and an eye to efficiency in everything is vital.

- **PCP**: This is still the core of the system and is set up the same as in a 1:1, with the 3:1 built around it, meaning if after starting a 1:1 you find it's not working, then it's easy to switch to a 3:1.

- **Pulleys**: You need 2 small to medium pulleys and I find that a PCP like the Petzl Micro Traxion is ideal for the top (sub) pulley in the system, as it keeps the whole system very tight, but any pulley will work. When setting up the Micro Traxion make sure the rope is running through it as it would in haul mode, otherwise the cam will lock with the pulley on it.

- **Rope Grab**: You will need a rope grab at the bottom of the system and in most cases this will be one of your ascenders. You need to make this weighted so that it resets itself down the loaded haul line when the system is reset, and adding one or two large cams will achieve this.

Set Up

Let's imagine we have a 1:1 system already set up and the haul bags hanging from it. Now we realise we need to switch to a 3:1, perhaps due to the effort required, or due to the bags arriving at an area of rock that's increased the friction, e.g., a slabby section.

To do this you will:

01. Clip the dead strand (unloaded strand) of the haul line through a pulley and clip this into an ascender.

02. Clip the ascender to the loaded rope creating your rope grab.

03. Take the dead rope from the rope grab and clip this into either a second pulley or ideally a micro PCP, and clip this into the bottom of the main PCP via it's lower connection point, making sure the ropes are not twisted, and will run cleanly.

Making It Work

01. Let slack run through the pulleys (disengage the micro PCP cam), so that dead rope lowers down the rope grab as far as you feel is needed. Make sure you don't lower the grab so far as to lose sight of it, or where it might get hung up or jammed.

02. Lock on the micro PCP's cam and take in the slack.

03. Now begin to haul, either by squats or by ascending the rope in place (so the rope moves but you don't).

04. When the rope grab reaches the micro PCP, release the micro PCP's cam and allow the dead rope to re-enter the system and allow it to reset again.

SUMMIT SET UP

If you need a 3:1 to haul over a slabby summit you can forgo the 3rd pulley, and just pull away from the load.

JAG 3:1

An alternative 3:1 system if you're using a Petzl Jag is to use the two double Jag pulleys to create a 3:1 system - a good move if you want to switch down from a 4:1. This works best if the Jag pulleys are all using oval lockers.

4:1 HAULING

A 4:1 system is probably only of use to the lightest of solo climbers climbing the largest of walls, or grade VII ascents with big teams. With this system I've hauled loads close to the safe limit of my system by leg power alone, but this comes at the cost of hauling four times the rope! Therefore, you could assume such a system to be slow, but I find it so easy once you nail the reset (don't be greedy with how much rope you suck up), that it can actually be quite fast. The system below is a system that can be broken down from 4:1 to 3:1, then 2:1 or 1:1 as the load becomes lighter, or up to 5:1 by inverting the system and adding a redirect.

Basic Principle

There are many ways to set up a 4:1, with a myriad of tools available, ranging from 4:1 kits where everything is included (Rock Exotica Aztek, Petzl Jag or DMM RPM), to using double pulleys and locking double pulleys (Petzl Jag Traxion). Any system for big wall use will be a piggy back system, used in partnership with the main PCP. Of the current systems the most appropriate are two Petzl Jag pulleys, made up into a system, rather than buying a 4:1 in kit form.

Component Parts

Unlike other systems this setup requires specific components.

- **PCP**: This is still the core of the system and is set up the same as a 1:1.

- **Pulleys**: Here you will use two Petzl pulleys, the Jag and Jag Traxion. These are highly efficient yet compact double pulleys with the Jag Traxion also able to be used as a single pulley (the Jag can be used as a pulley but it does not orientate 100% correctly

inline). The Traxion version is a PCP and can be used as a stand alone PCP, or as a rope grab.

- **Hauling Strand**: This fulfils the same role as the 2:1 hauling strand but here we use 8 to 10 metres of 8 or 7 mm static cord (this can double up as your lower out line), or the end of the haul line itself (ideally a static haul line). The strand should be tied into the Jag's becket with a bowline, so as to make it easy to untie when the system is being stripped, or when the strand is required for something else. This knot also creates some form of damper, reducing the risk of jamming both pulleys together, the far end knotted to avoid the loss of the pulleys.

- **Rope Grab**: An ascender or dedicated ascender (Petzl Basic style). This can be weighted but with this system I find hand, or foot, pushing down after each reset works best.

- **4:1 Bag**: It's best to have this set up and all connected together at the start of the route, and then break it down as you progress, as you need to switch down to 3:1, 2:1, etc.

Set Up

01. With the bags hanging from the PCP, you are going to create a pig system like the 2:1, but one that is 4:1 instead.

02. Set up the 4:1 as seen in the diagram, with the Jag Traxion at the top, and clip this into the bottom clip point on your PCP.

03. Make sure all cords are running straight and not tangled around each other.

04. Clip the 4:1's rope grab onto the loaded haul line.

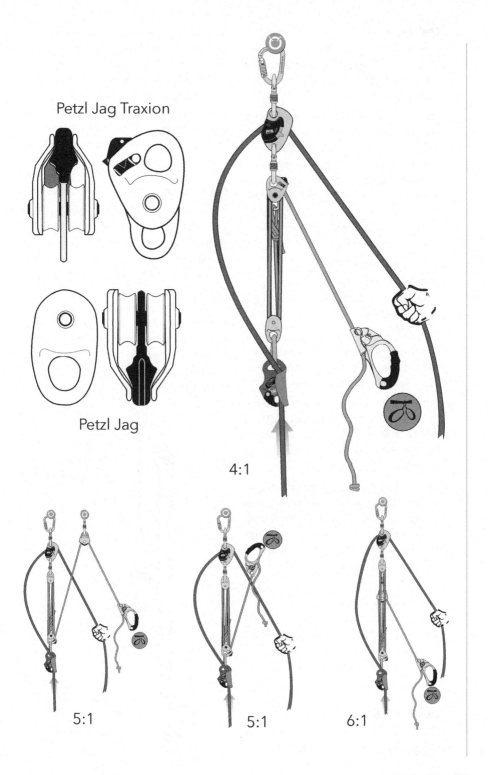

Petzl Jag Traxion

Petzl Jag

4:1

5:1

5:1

6:1

Making It Work

01. Set yourself up so your head is level with the PCP, with one foot standing in one aider, your body held in position with your lanyards.

02. Release the cam on the Jag Traxion and push the rope grab down as far as is possible with your hand. To do this you may need to pull some cord back through the Traxion (having the ropes neat makes this easy). Ideally when the ascender is as low as you can hand push it the end of the pull strand will come tight on the Traxion.

03. Click the Traxion cam on.

04. Clip an ascender with foot loop attached into the hauling strand of the 4:1 and begin leg hauling.

05. You should find it very easy to leg haul (change legs every now and then), and very quickly you will find the two double pulleys lock together.

06. You must now pull the haul line through the PCP before resetting (once the rope you have hauled becomes heavy enough it will start to pull through itself).

07. To reset, pull down with your jumar to release the Traxion's cam, then feathering the ascender, pull the rope grab down, the rope running back through the ascender. Once reset clip back on the cam and haul again.

Stand Alone

You can use this 4:1 system without a second PCP using a guide plate or ascender to hold the haul line after each reset, saving you the extra weight and bulk.

Downsizing

Once you find that the load has decreased you might want to switch to a 3:1 system, using the haul line directly through the pulleys, and this is easy to set up, with the Jag Traxion now acting as the PCP. When you do this simply untie the load strand from the becket and stow this for later use. Lighter still, and you can switch down to a 1:1 system, just using the Jag Traxion as the sole component of the system.

5:1 AND UP

If you find you need to further increase your pulling power, and are using a 4:1 system, then it's possible to increase your power by several methods. The easiest is to invert the 4:1 system and add in a directional to make a 5:1 (you can do it without a directional as long as it's viable to pull away from the load, something most likely when pulling your bags onto the summit, which is also the time you might need such pulling power due to horrendous friction).

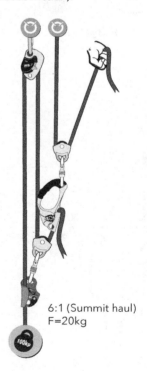

6:1 (Summit haul)
F=20kg

HAULING THE ROPE

So we've covered how to set up differing systems, but what about the meat of it, the actual pulling of the rope through the system, which no matter if it's 1:1 or 4:1, is going to get those damned bags up. So let's assume the bags are hanging from your haul line forty metres below you, the rope fed through whatever system you're using and locked tight into the PCP cam. Now your job is to pull that rope around that pulley inch by inch. This can be achieved (attempted) by the following methods:

Leg Haul: Unless you're hauling shopping bags, or using a 4:1, then this isn't going to lift anything, and is only ever of use for pulling up a tag bag.

Squat Haul: This is more effective. Here you will squat down, using your body weight as a counterbalance to the bags, the heavier you are the better it works. Seeing as your hands can't hold such weight as your bags the dead rope is connected to your harness either using an ABBD or ascender.

I tend to like to get the ascender as close to my body as possible, so that I can get the most height each time I stand up, so clip the locker through my leg and waist loops rather than belay loop. The best thing about using an ABBD such as a GriGri, is that you can pull the rope tight through it each time you stand up (like you're taking in the slack). You can also improve this by clipping the dead rope through a high point and using this both to pull yourself back up, and pull in the slack (even better if someone else does this for you). An ascender is good too, but you'll need to use your thumb to allow the slack to be taken in each time

you stand up. This style of hauling is good for light haul bags, or heavy climbers. Like rope climbing, sometimes small mini squats, taking in 30 cm of rope, are better than dead squats, where you'll use more energy pulling yourself up.

When setting up for this, try and pay attention to where your feet are, ideally on either side of the loaded rope, and your body, which should be dropping in line with the loaded rope, so your rope is running correctly around the pulley. Also try and make sure you have something to grab and pull yourself up with, and an ascender clipped into the belay for example can make a great grab handle.

Tug-Of-Wall: Here you use your arms to press out against the wall, maybe even your legs, like a tug-of-war, using both weight and brawn. For me this kind of hauling is inefficient and tiring and I would just switch up to another ratio, from 1:1 to 3:1 usually.

Power Walk: This approach can be very effective and fast, but requires some balls. Attach yourself to a back up rope (your lead line extended out as far you dare go), then transfer both ascenders onto the haul line and cast off, doing a kind of power pull down the wall (imagine you're a strong man pulling a bus). Pulling yourself down the wall with the help of the loaded rope can really break the back of the job. Once you've reached the end of your safety line you jug up and repeat. Be very careful doing power walks as the bags get lighter, as just your body weight might be enough of a counter weight, and starting with some hard pulls can see the bags flying up the wall and you flying down the wall! In these situations you might want a brake man at the belay making sure the ropes do not run out of control, as just a gloved hand can be enough to have some control over the ropes.

Pulling Up On The Live Rope

It seems odd that pulling up on a rope loaded down with 100 kg plus of weight can make any difference at all, but in fact this can have a dramatic effect. What you are most often doing is creating a further mechanical advantage in your system, as you are not really lifting the bags, but using the weighted rope as an anchor to pull yourself down against the weight of the bags, your muscles in your arms and hands just helping to close the distance. If you have a spare climber they can attach their ascenders (inverted) to the loaded rope and pull as well, which can be very effective. Remember that very often the load and the pull are very close in weight and force, and so just a small amount of extra energy added to the system on your side can tip the balance in your favour.

AGGRESSIVE HAULING

I've seen a lot of climbers be super aggressive when hauling, literally having some full on frenzied fit, even hanging upside down yanking at the rope like their lives depend on it. Such aggression is a waste of time and energy, and instead - as always - a cool head is required. Upping the system can take the strain out of it, plus bouncing hard is neither good for gear or the human body (you do not want a hernia on a wall!).

SPACE HAULING

This is a great technique used to get very heavy bags up as quickly as possible, taking a third of the time as a 3:1 but with only a little more work than a 1:1. The basic idea is that a second climber acts as a counterweight to the bags, dropping down the wall as the hauler hauls, jugging up every ten metres or so before going down again. If your bags are super heavy then you may even elect to have two climbers acting as counterweights, but you must always factor in the safe working load of the cam on the Pro Traxion, which is 2.5 kN (so let's say a static load of no more than 200 kg on each side before you risk rope damage, the device itself having a strength of 11 kN).

Set Up

The most important aspect of space hauling is to keep everyone safe, as unlike with normal 1:1 hauling, where the hauler is attached to the belay, here the second hauler (the weight) is only hanging from the haul line, and so are the bags, with everything hanging from the PCP. The danger here is if the rope was to break or the pulley fail the 'weight' would die. For this reason the 'weight' should always be backed up by a second rope, ideally the lead line. The 'weight' is most often the cleaner anyway (who is likely to be already tied into the lead line, and set up on arrival to go over to the haul line). If you can't use the lead line, then the zip-line will do (if it's full strength), or the haul line (even a static is designed to take falls without breaking). The following are a few factors to consider:

Drop Length: You are best to only drop down as far as is easy to ascend up again. If for example you're on an overhanging wall you could drop the full length of the haul line, the bags lifting all the way to the belay. But then you'd be faced with a full overhanging pitch to ascend back up. If on the other hand the first five metres allowed you to touch the rock, then doing multiple five metre drops would be faster overall. Each time you drop you will come tight on your safety rope, then come back up, allowing the hauler to rest as well.

Power Walking on the Nose

Matching Ropes: When you first start dropping you might not have that much dead haul line, if the climber ran a couple of pitches together for example, or the haul bags were re-tied in short and the rest of the haul line used to lower them out. In this case, when you drop, the haul line will be very likely to go tight long before your safety line does, resulting in your bottom ascender becoming inverted. This is dangerous as it means you are really only relying on one piece of protection (your top ascender) until you sort the problem out. So to avoid this happening in the first place, just be aware of it, and early on in the space hauling, shout to the hauler to stop before you reach the end of the haul line, so you can ascend the rope again. Later, when the bags have come up a bit and there is more dead rope, it will no longer be an issue, as whatever you are using as your safety line will come tight to you before the haul line does.

Backup The Backup: Your PCP should have a clip loop at the bottom with krab inserted, but you can add more back up by clipping a quickdraw from the loaded rope to the master point as an extra back up.

The Rope Master: The hauler at the belay will find that the counter weight makes hauling very easy, and simple squat thrusts will see the bags rise. Due to the rope being loaded you cannot use an ABBD, and instead will need to use an ascender, clipping it to your belay loop.

Getting Close: When the bags get close to the PCP, get the 'weight' close to the belay, so after tying off the bags they can help release the cam on the PCP.

Imbalance Warning: As with the power walk hauling technique there

comes a point when the haul bags might be lighter than you think, perhaps rising faster than is healthy for everyone, especially the 'weight' guy on the rope.

DOUBLE HAUL

The double haul is one way to deal with really large loads on a wall, splitting the bags in two and lifting them one at a time. This approach is not only a good way to deal with huge loads as it makes them manageable (it's faster to haul two 100 kg loads than one 200 kg load), but is also safer, as it creates lower loading of crucial components of the system, the cam acting on the rope being the most important (see Hauling Safety).

APPROACH

For the double haul you will of course need two haul lines. These can be a mix of lines, and early on you can just use your haul line and zip-line if you want a split system. For major grade VII walls you will want to have two dedicated haul lines that are easily identifiable (untangling 120 metres of rope that looks the same can feel like a Sisyphean task), and these may well be used for fixing as well, getting your monster loads up to a camp using a double haul, then going capsule from there, switching to a single haul from then on. Having a mix of static and dynamic ropes can also give you some redundancy and on the Reticent I actually switched ropes depending on the pitches, with a 10.2 and a 9.5 mm rotating from haul to lead line depending on how low an impact force I needed, with a 10 mm static hauling the big loads. Two haul lines are not clipped to the back of the harness, but pulled up by either a third rope, or one rope is pulled up, then the end of the main line sent back down this (weighted and clipped in), to give two haul lines. You can haul the bags one load at a time, with the first load going up, then the second, or you can release them at the same time, so that the second can start cleaning.

SPLITTING THE LOAD

If you're climbing in a team then you will want to split the bags into the primary and secondary loads, with the primary having the rack, belay stuff and some water, and hauled quickly, while the secondary can hang and be hauled while the next pitch is being led.

TECHNIQUE

If you're hauling one load off the belay at a time, then hauling is the same as 1:1, the haul line put into the PCP one after the other, but having both loads released and then hanging at the same time needs a different approach. First off it's best if you can create two masterpoints set on either side of the centre of the belay, so the bags have room when they arrive, but often you won't be able to do this, so it's vital to try and keep everything neat and tidy. Below is how I would do this:

01. Arrive at the belay and set up standard belay with master point.

02. Pull up haul lines via zip-line (hank and secure zip-line).

03. Secure the ends of the haul lines to the anchors, one left and one right. This is important in case you fuck up with the transfer from a fixed line to a hauling line.

04. Take one haul line and attach it to the PCP and clip this to your master point with a locker and pull the rope tight to the bags, making this PCP ready to haul.

05. Take in the slack on the second haul line, tie a tied off Munter hitch (Munter Mule) and clip this into the master

point with a locker. Make sure it's well tied off! The one downside with this technique is that you will have two loaded elements on your master point, that can cause the PCP to not align properly. As an alternative you can attach this second haul line direct to a bolt via a tied off Munter.

06. Both bags can now be released.

07. When the first (primary) bag reaches the belay it is secured off to one side (docking cord attached to the belay point), leaving the masterpoint free for the next bag.

08. Now you need to get the loaded haul line into the pulley.

09. Clip an inverted ascender from the master point to the haul line (use a sling or strand of haul line).

10. Release the Munter hitch and allow enough slack to run out so all the weight is on the ascender, plus enough to pass into the PCP. Tie off the Munter.

11. Clip the rope into the PCP, lock the cam, then untie the Munter and give yourself enough rope to haul.

12. Haul away.

13. When the secondary bag arrives, this is either secured to the master point, or direct to a belay point opposite to the primary bags, but being heavier it's best to leave them hanging on the master point.

AVOIDING STUCK BAGS

Getting your bags stuck on a wall is a constant problem, so here are some ideas on how to avoid this in the first place.

Jam Reduction: Make sure that your bag or bags are streamlined in every way possible, with the top of the bag packed with soft stuff and its straps and tie downs creating a rounded bullet shape, not a wide mouthed shape. Remember that your suspension straps form a kind of 'point' and will help the bag move over some obstructions, but not if the edges of an unsecured bag's rim are sticking out.

Bag Train: On overhanging walls you can hang your bags all at the same level, creating a big bunch of bags, but not on slabby or complex terrain. Here you need to create a train of bags, with the biggest bag driving it, with all cord or loops secured. Remember you need to create a bullet with no edges so that it has the best chance of sliding over any obstructions.

Use A Haul Cone: This looks a little like one of those things pets wear when they've had an operation. Haul cones are made from a sheet of 2 or 3 mm poly-ethylene and form a cone shape that stops the top of the bag catching. This approach works very well on snow and ice as well as complex terrain, but should not be considered 'the' solution to stuck bags, just a way to reduce the chance of it happening. The cone is secured using four bolts with wing nuts on the inside (so you can stick it in your haul bag when approaching and descending).

Bag Husbandry: This is the best way to stop bags getting hung up, and is done by the cleaner staying level with the bags as they are hauled. If the haul is direct then this is easy, just grab the bag when it gets stuck and pull it clear until it's hauled past the problem. If the haul is not direct then the cleaner should remain attached to the haul bags with the lower-out line or via the haul line tied in short (so the cleaner has the end of the rope and the bags are tied in further up

the rope). If the cleaner is way above the bags, but within reach of the haul line, then often just pulling sideways on it will see the bags shifted. When doing this it's vital that the haul bags are never directly above the cleaner as they can knock rocks down, plus make sure that the haul line is not running over the lead line.

Use Your Eyes: When leading try and look around you to see where the bags might hang up, and where choke points might be. If you're given a choice of belay points or the ordina-tion of the rope, say at the top of a big wall, remember that the haul bags don't have to travel the same way you did.

STUCK BAGS

If a bag does hang up and you can see it you may be able to work out what the problem is, but very often you'll be blind, plus such annoyances often happen in the dark, hauling up to your bivvy for the night for example (when you've got the least amount of energy to sort it out). Here are some tips and ideas:

Feel The Force: First off, when haul-ing you need to build up a feel for the bags, know when they are moving and when they are jammed. If you don't have this and just keep hauling and hauling, getting that haul line tight as steel cable, you may well make things worse, welding the bags into a crack or slot. Also when you really increase the load you stress everything, and yes sometimes that force may see the bags suddenly shoot up and be freed, but often at the cost of something break-ing! The use of major and destruc-tive force should be your final option.

Instead, as soon as you feel the bags are not moving, evidenced by the additional effort needed to haul, you should stop and begin using the techniques below in order.

Jiggle Them: Often, as you feel the bags begin to get hung up, by making short hard pulls out from the wall on the haul line, maybe also shaking the haul line with your hands, you can wobble or jiggle the bags around the obstruction.

Deviation: Another option is to get under the loaded line and using your feet against the wall, push out the haul line with your shoulder or hands. This can help change the direction of the rope just enough to get the bags moving again.

Try Again: A very effective method is to lower the bags just a little, by setting your hauling ascender low, then thumbing the cam on the hauler as you pull, and letting some rope run back through. If you lower just half a metre and haul again very often you'll see the bags come up this time.

LOWERING THE BAGS WHILE HAULING

Fully loaded bags may have to be lowered for some reason while hauling (distinctly different from lowering bags while in retreat), which can be harder than it sounds if they're very heavy. If a 70 kg climber using a 3:1 system, finds they have to lower the bags down, so clips in their belay device and unlocks the locking pulley, they may well get sucked up into the pulley, maybe losing control in the process. If the bags are easy to haul by one person then just replace your hauling ascender with a belay device or better still an ABBD, and while pulling in

a few centimetres, unlock the cam and begin to let the rope out, ready to lock the cam when necessary (it's a good two person operation, as one arm is often needed to brace against the wall). But what if the load is too heavy and you can't just release it and lower? Here is something you can try.

01. Secure the haul line coming up from the bags with an inverted ascender attached to the masterpoint via a releasable cord or sling (see Knots).

02. Allow the weight of the bags to be taken onto the inverted ascender.

03. Take the haul line where it exits the hauler and secure it via a large HMS with a tied off monster Munter knot.

04. Remove the PCP.

05. Release the inverted ascender via the releasable sling until the weight comes fully onto the Monster Munter.

06. Take off the inverted ascender and begin to lower the bags slowly.

SLAB HAULING

Hauling on slabs can be very tricky, and having a second climber walking the bags up helps a lot. Another technique that can work well when 1:1 hauling at the top of walls for example, where you can get bushes and rocks and small overhangs, is to haul from the bags. To do this you go down the haul line (backed up to another rope), and haul the bags as you physically pull them up, yanking, dragging, and lifting, all the while hauling on the rope.

Another technique is the pick up, where you take off the bags one by one and haul them individually. This is an important technique when pulling up bags from the bottom of a haul bag train, or when you're faced with complex ground and just want to haul the bags one after the other. It's obvious how to achieve this, but good communication is vital.

If you're hauling your bags up an area of very slabby ground, say on the final pitches, or easy ground, then sometimes you can haul level with the bags (remember to stay clipped to another rope though), say ten metres down from the belay, pulling the bags with your hands while also pulling on the haul line. Ideally you need to be hauling at the belay, with a second climber doing this, but often your bags will get close to you then get stuck, so this is one way to proactively sort this out.

PASSING KNOTS

This is a vitally important skill for a big wall climber, because to do this wrong can be either very dangerous or open you up to a nightmare of clusterfuckery, but also because, once mastered, this skill allows you to do monster hauls, missing out belays. I have used the following method to do a single 400 metre haul using several ropes, doing in an hour what would have taken a whole day going from belay to belay.

The basic problem is this; you have two ropes joined together by a knot that cannot pass through your PCP, meaning they need to be untied somehow without losing your haul bags in the process. Now there have been several ways to achieve this, but the one I'm going to describe now is the simplest and safest.

First off, you need to join all your ropes with a knot that will not end up welded shut by the weight of the bags. The easi-

est knot for this is the simple reef knot finished with a double Fisherman's knot, the old school standard we used to use for joining abseiling ropes before the overhand knot. Now the crucial part here is that the tails of these knots has to be about a metre long (actually this is only true for the tail of the lower rope, but making them both long removes the risk of making the wrong rope long). Even when heavily loaded the load will only ever be taken by the simple reef knot, meaning it's easy to untie.

A better option, but one that people find harder to grasp, is to use a butterfly knot. To do this first take one strand and tie a water knot, then thread the other strand through this, creating an overhand with a bight. Now tie a butterfly knot with a large loop with this overhand knot in its middle. This knot is safer and easier to untie.

01. As you haul up your bags you will eventually reach the knot joining both ropes.

02. Stop hauling when the knot is a hand width from the pulley (don't jam the knot into the pulley!).

03. Now take your ascender and using a sling as an extension, clip this in the inverted position onto the active haul line below the knot, and secure the sling to the master point or a bolt.

04. Pull on the haul line again and as you begin to take in that last little bit of slack on the line, release the cam on the PCP, and let the haul line go backwards until all the weight is now on your inverted ascender.

05. Make sure there is some slack in the rope where the knot is located, and return the PCP's cam back into locked position, so your haul bags are secured

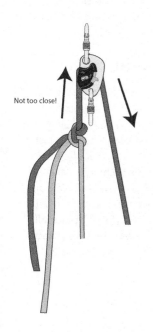
Not too close!

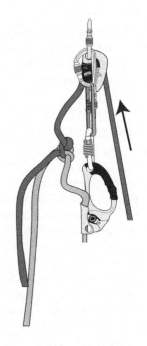

Passing a knot

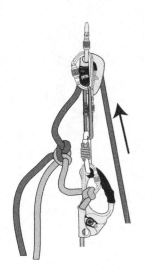

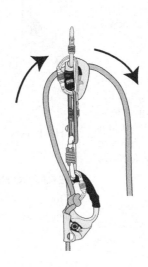

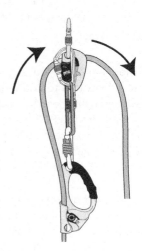

by both the inverted ascender and the PCP's cam.

06. Now locate the tail of the new active haul line and tying a figure of eight into it, clip this to your master point with a locker. This secures your haul line in case you have a failure in the inverted ascender or the PCP itself.

07. Now untie the knots joining the ropes.

08. Pull the now redundant rope out of the PCP (secure this end so as not to lose the rope), and opening the PCP insert the new haul line and close and lock the PCP again, remembering to lock the cam in place. If you're using a 2:1, 3:1 or 4:1 you will not be able to easily open the PCP (a 2:1 and 4:1 actually make passing knots very easy though), and instead must simply insert the rope end, but you can add a fail safe knot before the rope end.

09. Pull in the slack and unclip the backup knot and set up to haul, removing the inverted ascender as soon as all the weight is hanging from the PCP again.

10. Haul away!

The main error you may find is that you've forgotten to add enough tail to your next haul line, so you cannot feed the rope into the PCP. To deal with this you'll have to lower your PCP down to the point where the rope can be fed in as above, which is easily achieved.

It goes without saying that throughout all of these steps, make sure each action is done carefully and thoughtfully, with a good dose of "what will happen next...?".

PROTECTING JOINING KNOTS

When tying ropes together and hauling, on low angled terrain in particular, your joining knots can become very abraded, and so should be protected. This can be done by simply adding an old school plastic bottle to knots.

LONG LINE HAUL

A long line haul is where you leave the bag hanging from a fifi or taped open karabiner (the cargo hook), and simply lift it off the belay remotely, the bags just sitting there unattached. This of course is a highly dangerous technique, and is used when you wish to bypass a belay, or when hauling many pitches at once, most often when capsule style climbing (all your lead and haul lines used up as fixed lines meaning you can't haul normally).

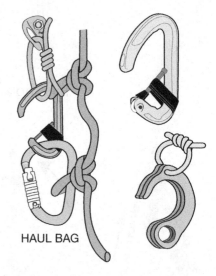

HAUL BAG

THE CARGO HOOK

The bags are hung from a hook from a single bolt or piece of solid protection, either through some strong cord or webbing, or through a leaver karabiner (cord is often better as the karabiner needs to be orientated correctly). This is the 'release point'. The strength of the cargo hook needs to be beyond doubt, and must be fully thought through and

Alwyn Johnson hauling onto the summit of Zodiac

pre visualised before you commit the bags to it (you will lower your bags into position via the docking cord). The easiest system is to use two fifi hooks (I use BD ones) side by side (two are used for strength), threading 5 mm dyneema cord through their release holes and clipping them direct to the haul bag strap's locking karabiner (the weight of the bags will be held by this cord). This is your cargo hooks lifting loop. Another option is to use a keyhole karabiner with the gate taped open, and a 30 cm sling Prusiked onto the top radius of the krab.

Method

01. Attach the haul line to the bags as usual.

02. Attach your cargo hook of choice to the haul bag's suspension point (karabiner or swivel), via a Butterfly knot as shown in the diagram.

03. Create the release point, which, as mentioned, is most usually a loop of thick cord.

04. Transfer the bags over to the release point by hooking the cargo hook into it by lowering the bag via the docking cord.

05. Make sure the release point can't become fouled in the cargo hook (by getting caught up with the rope for example).

06. Pay close attention to how the haul line will lift the cargo hook off the release point.

07. Remove the docking cord and stow it neatly away.

08. Remove all the belay, including all back ups, leaving the bags on their hair trigger.

LIFTING

When it comes to lifting, all you do is pull the rope slowly until you feel it go tight to the bags, which will actually be tight on the cargo hook. Begin the haul and the bag will lift up off the belay and swing clean.

BACK UP

You can create some kind of backup using a slippery hitch, which will come untied when you pull from above, but will lock down if the bags fall off. To do this you need to be very proficient in tying the knot, and I would tie and re-tie several times before using it.

WORST CASE SCENARIO

This of course is the bags falling off the belay, but really this isn't going to happen, not if you take care, and don't hang the bags off a single fifi hook.

The second worst thing would be for the bags not to lift, or get hung up (if the haul line is pulling in the wrong direction for example). This would mean you have to return all the way back and sort it out.

Once, while using this system, this time to avoid two poor belays (I left the haul bag on belay one, and climbed up to belay four), I began to run out of haul line, meaning the weight of the bags might end up hanging off me while on lead (unlikely due to their weight!). How did I get out of this? I made an intermediate anchor from two cams, untied and tied my haul line into the end of the lead line. Then I pulled up all the slack on the lead line and rope soloed the last five metres. Once at the belay I then had to haul five metres of lead line, pass the knot, then haul the haul line.

LOWER-OUT LINES

On traversing pitches you will need to lower out your bags until they're in line with the next belay, otherwise they'll swing down and smash into the rock, breaking your stuff, especially water bottles. On some routes you may need to do a lot of lowering out, while on others none at all (a little swing is no big deal, and the docking cord can be used as a very short lower-out line). There are two methods of lowering out.

DEDICATED LOWER-OUT CORD

A dedicated lower-out line would be 20 metres of 6 mm cord carried in a stuff sack. To use this you would:

01. Attach the end of the lower-out line to the haul bags strap's karabiner.
02. Clip the line into a high belay point or into the master point using a monster Munter (a Munter hitch can do, but seeing as cord is so thin a monster is better).
03. Wait for leader to shout 'ready to haul'.
04. Untie backup knot on haul line.
05. Shout 'haul away' and wait until the haul line begins to lift the bags.
06. Untie docking cord and lower the bags out on that slowly until the weight goes on to the lower-out line.
07. Slowly lower out the bags until the end of the lower-out line runs through the monster Munter.

HAUL LINE LOWER OUT

With this method, you simply tie the haul bags off short (back them up before you do this so you're not just relying on the docking cord), and then use the now free end of the haul line to lower out the bags. This eliminates the faff of dealing with a separate skinny lower-out line.

To do this you need to first be sure you've got enough rope. Before the leader has taken in any haul line slack, tie an alpine butterfly into the haul line, giving you the maximum amount of rope possible, and clip this into the haul bag's suspension point (the locking karabiner attached to the bag's straps).

You will need to unclip the old end knot first (unless you are adding another karabiner to the system). As stated, make sure you back up the docking cord before you do this, using a sling to connect the bags to the belay for example, as you never want the bags hanging from the docking cord alone!

Undo the backup, and you should now have a long length of haul line to play with.

Clip this into the belay via a Munter hitch, and release and lower out the bags as previously described.

SIMUL LOWER OUT AND HAUL

Sometimes you will see that once lowered out, the bags might get stuck, perhaps the lower-out leaving them under a roof for example. If having the bags a little higher will avoid this problem then consider hauling the bags up while still on the lower-out line, the haul line at an angle, and the lower-out line paid out as the bags rise. This way the path of the bags can be somewhat controlled from the belay until the lower-out line runs out.

EXTENDING YOUR LOWER-OUT LINE

There often come times when you realise your lower-out line is too short, forcing you to just let the bags go earlier than you intended - which is never good. Another option is to extend out the lower-out line, using either a cordelette or your lead line. With the former just untie it and tie it onto the end of the lower-out-line with an overhand knot, then lower it out using a Munter hitch, allowing the knot to slip through. You can add more cordelettes if needed. If using the lead rope then clip a karabiner into the end of the lower-out line, then lower this out via a loop of lead line. Once you're out of lead rope (as it's a loop you can only lower out 50% of the rope you have), just unclip one end and pull it through to retreat it. If you realise this is going to be a problem then it's best to employ a mix of techniques, using the haul line as lower-out line as well.

TYROLEAN TRAVERSE

There will come a time when you need to get the bags from A to B but neither is in line, say A being horizontal to B. In these situations you could lower your bags from A via a monster Munter, and have them hauled in at the same time from B, but often the competing forces can cause all sorts of headaches. Instead it can be better to set up a Tyrolean with your haul line, then clip your bags in one at a time and send them across, lowering from A and pulling them over from B. Problems that can occur include a twisting of the bag and the lower-out line, but the possibility of this occurring can be reduced by hanging each bag from a sling (the sling takes up the twists) larks footed to the straps. Also secure bags with two lockers back to back.

THE HAUL BAG

The way you transport all your big wall junk on a wall is via your haul bags, designed to be both simple and cheap, and as indestructible as possible. If the

lightweight alpine pack is the pro French cyclist of gear, then the haul bag is an American wrestler, and be it one wall or ten, that bag is going to give all its got to get your crap to the top.

WHAT SIZE?

The best advice I was ever given by anyone regarding haul bags was 'buy the biggest bag you can', which at the time was an A5 Grade VII, which did me proud on about fifteen El Cap routes, its life coming to a premature end after being thrown 800 metres from the Dru, the bottom blowing out when it hit the ground (I forgot to leave the lid open).

Since then I've had several haul bags, from Fish, BD and Metolius, plus some homemade jobs. The sizes have ranged from massive to day pack size, and each worked well for what it was intended for. Below I'll break down the bags into the general sizes available and the purpose of each.

BIG BAGS

Examples: *Fish Deluxe (150 litres), Metolius El Cap (157 litres), BD Zion (145 litres)*

These are the load movers of big wall climbing, able to do multi hour, multi day, or multi week walls. Big stupid brutes, if packed well, like an alpine sack, they'll carry enough stuff for a three man team for a three day route, enough for the Nose, with two bags best for anything over three days. The big downside with these bags is often their depths, and short people should think about putting all the bottom items in a separate bag inside the haul bag and having a pull cord running up to the lid (water bottles are fine as they stand up about a quarter

Vanessa Kirkpatrick humping a load down, Zion

of the bag's height making them easy to reach down for). A wider bag would be easier to get into, but creates more bag to get caught up when hauling.

MEDIUM BAGS

Examples: *Fish Grade V (85 litres), Metolius Half Dome (125 litres), Grivel Large (90 litres)*

These are sub bags, and being such, can often be neither big nor small enough. They are really for climbers who want bags to fit their height, so small men and women. A medium bag (the Fish Grade V bag is 7 inches shorter than the Deluxe) carries better on a small frame, which can be important during arduous approaches and descents, and is easier to reach into on the wall. If you only ever did five day walls and you wanted a bag all for yourself, then these are good, but for anyone else just go large.

SMALL BAGS

Examples: *Metolius Quarter Dome (69 litres), BD Touchstone (70 litres), Grivel M (60 litres)*

These bags make very good haul bags for speed ascents, or day bags for multi day walls, being small and easy to carry, but big enough to carry water, rack, ropes etc. As a day bag they can be used as the rack bag, hauled up on the end of the zip-line with the haul line attached.

MICRO BAGS

Examples: *Fish Atom Smasher (40 litres), BD Stubby (35 litres), Metolius Sentinel (46 litres), Grivel Small (30 litres)*

The larger micro bags can be used for speed climbing if you want to carry it on your back, and they haul and pack well,

but work best as day bags for bigger groups of bags.

ALTERNATIVES

'PAINTERS' BUCKETS

Carrying a rigid plastic bucket/container allows you to haul items you don't want crushed in the main bag, such as fruit and veg, hummus, chips etc. These buckets are very light and cheap, and can be stowed inside your main bags when being carried up and down, and to and from the climb. Many of them come with a metal handle that tends to be very strong (it's designed to support the bucket when full of water), but these can also be cut off and webbing added. Make sure you have a keeper cord from your lid to your bucket.

HAUL BARRELS

When it comes to both packing and hauling you cannot find a better piece of kit than a large (120 litre) plastic chemical barrel (as used on expeditions). These barrels move amazingly well on any terrain, especially slabs and snow slopes, having the smallest contact area possible due to their barrel shape. When a hauling cone is added these become even better, seemingly impossible to hang up anywhere, and stuff can be thrown in and taken out without worrying about items pressing against the outside (being stiff they're also easy to access while on the wall).

These barrels are lightweight, cheap, can be found anywhere, and are watertight on the wall and when being transported. The downside with the haul barrel is how hard they are to carry around, requiring either a webbing harness to be added (used by canoeists for portering barrels), strapping onto a frame pack, or cobbling something together, such as a belay seat with a bolt passing through the wood into the barrel and locked with wing nuts. None of these allow the barrel to carry loads and so the barrel tends to have to be carried up almost empty and carried down empty, making these barrels really only suitable for major walls where access isn't difficult.

Setting Up The Barrel

The barrel needs to have two hauling straps added, and these should be made from two lengths of 40 to 50 mm webbing (seat belt style webbing), bolted into the top of the barrel. Use short round headed bolts (8 mm), with washers on the inside and outside, doubling over the webbing where the bolts enter the barrel. I would also consider reinforcing the inside edge with a glued square of HDPE (high density polyethylene, used for making the haul cone). You can improve the design by having one haul strap and making the other from a single strand that is adjustable, using a metal quick release buckle (this will allow you to release the strap when gaining access). The lid needs to be secured with a keeper cord threaded through a drilled hole, and I would ditch the metal locking ring and add two cross straps instead (or you can remove the whole lid, and rivet on a cordura lid instead). Add at least one clip in loop on the bottom of the bag with 7 mm cord (pass the cord through 7 mm drilled holes and then through washers, tying the cord into a loop).

HAUL BAG ANATOMY

The haul bag is a very simple beast, and even the top of the line versions, with all the bells and whistles, are not much more than flexible trash cans. Here I'm going to go through the basic parts of the bag.

Body: The body of the bag is most often made from heavy, and I mean heavy, duty vinyl, a material very hard to sew, so keeping the shapes simple, like a trash can. Some bags have sealed seams while others are stitched, others having that stitching covered to protect it from abrasion. The material is waterproof but in heavy weather they take on water from the lid, so anything you want to keep dry needs to be in waterproof stuff sacks (sleeping bags and spare clothes for example). I'd also write your name inside and outside the bag as I've had bags go for a wander when other climbers thought they were theirs, even from high points on walls.

Hauling Straps: All haul bags feature a two strap system used to haul the bag, some going all around the bag while others just attached at the top. These straps are either the same length or slightly offset, the idea being it's easier to unclip one strap this way, so as to access the contents of the bag when on the wall. One mistake many make with offset straps is to attach their docking cord or sling to the long strap, which can make it hard to unclip the short straps krab, which can still be under tension. Hanging the bag from the short strap fixes this problem.

Hauling Strap Tab: In some bags you'll find a small tab at the base of one or more of the straps. This has several uses, but none of them are to be the sole hang point of the bag on the belay, as the tabs themselves tend to be only sewn on with a few bar tacks (at least one haul bag has hit the deck due to one of these ripping out). What they're actually meant for is securing the tension straps on top, or for taking some of the weight of the bag in order to create a rounded opening (but again, the bags should never be hung just from this, and should stay clipped to the docking cord and backup knot). When used properly like this you are getting around the problem that the straps are sewn into two points, and so when hanging from those points they pinch the bag's top together making access difficult. By clipping into a single point the bag will hang more open (you can do this by lowering the bags onto a sling clipped into this tab, having an adjustable sling permanently attached, or clipping in a rope/cord and doing a mini haul until all the weight is on the tab).

Closing System: Haul bags vary in how they are closed, from simple nylon storm style (like on a stuff-sack or rucksack), to roll tops. Neither one or the other is better, but all should be secured as well as possible, and not allowed to bulge out and get worn.

Closure Straps: Some bags have two locking straps that hold down the contents, while others have a spider's web design, with a long strap that zig zags around the bag. The twin straps are very neat and fast but often the spider straps, feeding into each other, can be more effective, and tend to be clipped off with a small karabiner. The main thing you are trying to achieve with any such top closure is to create a bullet shape, with the sharp upper edges of the bag pulled in rounded (sharp edges will catch on roofs). This is one reason it's good to not over pack the bags and why two half full bags are better than one crammed bag.

Pocket: Most bags feature some kind of internal pocket, and this is a good place to stow small items you might want in a hurry, without having to go digging. I tend to break any of these kinds of items

that don't fit in the pocket down into a number of smaller stuff sacks, so I don't end up losing stuff when searching for what I'm after.

The pocket will tend to contain items such as the following:

Wag bags	Notebook + pen
Leatherman tool	Waterproof marker
Head torches	Cord
Head torch batteries	Cargo hook
Camera batteries	Spoon
Sunscreen	Duct tape
Spare topo	Finger tape
Phone	Whistle
Small first aid kit	Condoms

Bottom Straps: All bags tend to feature bottom straps that criss cross the base of the bag. One misnomer is that these are full strength and can carry big loads. Yes they can when the bag is new, but after the stitching becomes worn they soon lose their strength.

I've experienced these straps breaking first hand, in my case sending the haul bag clipped to the bottom and a portaledge crashing down the face. For this reason I'd avoid fully trusting these straps for anything over 10 kg, using them instead for lighter items (poop tubes and portaledges).

A second problem is that hanging full weight haul bags under another bag squeezes each bag above, making it hard to do anything, and so I often stick to a heavy top bag and very light bottom bag if possible (on a big wall your bottom bag often becomes your trash haul bag). If you want to clip heavy things to the bottom they can be attached but they're best backed up with a leash cord running from the hauling point and down to the bag, then clipped onto a separate strap.

Clipping in and out of these bottom straps can be a major pain in the ass, especially when hanging upside down, and a better way is to larks foot a 60 cm sling through the straps and clip things into these, or clip a big HMS into the straps and clip into this with other lockers, or tie a loop of 8 mm cord with an alloy rap ring as your clip point.

Carry Straps: Bags either have carry straps that are fully removed and stowed inside the bag, or straps that can be tucked inside the back of the bag. The level of comfort these straps provide when carrying the haul bag on your back varies enormously, with some being thin and skinny (Metolius) while others are thick and chunky (BD and Fish), the thinner straps designed to make them lower profile when stowed, but at the expense of carry comfort. All have pros and cons, but whatever system you use, none make haul bags anywhere near nice to carry, and any load carrying is always a bit of a nightmare. One big problem that crops up is people losing the webbing parts of their straps, and one way to avoid this is to always feed them back onto the buckles on your straps before storing (having a metre of 25 mm nylon webbing in your repair kit also helps). If you do lose a strap than a quickdraw can act as a replacement. Oh, and expect to have that comedy moment at least once of packing your haul bag but forgetting your straps are still inside!

BAG REPAIRS

Fish always recommend using Plasti-Dip to protect the stitching on a haul bag, as it becomes damaged and 'grinned off' while hauling. This is probably a good idea, but the design of haul bags means that even when badly worn they tend to stay secure, and the only way to kill a haul bag is to blow out the side seam, which I've only seen when the bags have fallen many hundreds of metres (and even then sometimes they don't split). The main place for concern is badly worn spots, as they can allow water in, or small items to fall out, and these should be repaired by coating in Seam Grip, then adding gaffer tape on the inside and outside of the bag. Pay close attention to all straps also, as a very worn nylon strap, or one that's nicked or cut, can rip apart when heavily loaded.

GETTING YOUR BAG TO THE WALL

Load carrying to a wall can be one of the most crushing parts of big wall climbing, and in some cases, such as when scrambling up or down slabs is involved, can also be the most dangerous. The loads involved in climbing any wall are huge, with water being the bulk of it, but also ropes, food, hardware, portaledges adding up to a spine crushing load.

For this reason I would advise ferrying your load in loads that can be carried comfortably, and a good standard weight to go for is between 25 kg / 30 kg or 50 to 60 lbs (legal limit for a Nepali Sherpa is 30 kg), depending on size and fitness. Go above this on the approach and you will not only tire yourself out before even setting off, but you expose yourself to twisted ankles, damaged knees or a hernia.

Body weight and gender should play a part in what load you carry, with women typically (but not always) tending to find slightly smaller loads less injurious (women have a lower bone and muscle density) for example.

Some approaches can also involve technical climbing, and these should be split further, and having a three person team allows one person to shuttle loads while the other two fix pitches. Be careful of scree slopes and talus, and boulder hopping, as your total weight is much higher than normal, so rocks and boulders that may not ordinarily move, can often shift under you. I'd also make sure you've got good quality approach shoes, or ideally boots if you have them, and walking poles can make or break the approach - or a leg!

Timing: It's always best to get your loads to the start of the wall in the early morning when it's colder, and in the dark is even better. Stripping down to shorts and t-shirt even on cold days will help keep you from melting down. Getting an early start will also get you to the route first.

Strategy: I will often carry in all the hardware and anything else within my load limit on the morning of day one, then lead and fix as many pitches as possible. Then I will go back and either bring up the rest of the stuff in the evening and bivvy at the base, or come up the next morning. Some climbs I've done have required multiple trips up to the base, getting everything ready to blast off.

Helping Hands: Having just one single person willing to carry even a small load, maybe just a rope or two can make a big difference, and having five is even better! Some climbers pay other climbers to carry their stuff for them, and carry it down as well. I'd not be so quick to judge such people, because although it is cheating, really it's all cheating, and climbers getting old and with poor knees maybe deserve a break (plus it adds something to the dirt bag economy).

PACKING FOR THE APPROACH

Having a 150 litre bag the size of a dustbin, filled with 30 kg of water on your back can be quite an ordeal, and that's when you've packed it right! Pack it badly and you'll make the hell twice as hellish, the bag moving around with every step, or slipping over at 45 degrees, and edges of badly packed items pressing uncomfortably into your back.

People tend to either be bottom heavy or top heavy packers but personally, after years of carrying stupid loads, I'm a top heavy person (below your shoulder level that is, as it always has to be light above that to avoid the haul bag tipping over at crazy angles!). Whichever you are, with such large capacity bags, the most important thing is to keep the weight close to your centre of gravity.

First off get all your heavy stuff together, which will be rope, rack and water, and maybe your ledge. If you have a belay seat, or anything long and rigid (e.g., portaledge) then slip them inside and close to your back to create a flat rigid frame/panel. Now either place the bag flat on the ground (straps facing down) and begin to add the heavy stuff close to your back, or stand up and create a dense/heavy area close to your back and pack it close with softer and lighter items.

Try and have your rack packed in bags, with cams in one, nuts in another, pitons in another. Being a top heavy packer I often put slings, webbing items and clothing in first, then slowly add in the heavy stuff, creating a wedge that ends at my shoulder level, with stuff like water, pegs, hammer and ropes going in high. You will have a lot of dead space above

Humping a 40 kg load into the Troll Wall with a 400 gram pack

the weight, and you want to fill this with lighter objects such as sleeping bag etc. As stated, I always try and stop adding weight above the shoulder strap, as it will make the bag top heavy and unstable.

Top Strap

Running a sling down from the top of a bag that's packed high, and pulling down and forwards on this while walking, can marginally increase your comfort as well as aid stability.

Using A Big Pack

A haul bag is designed to be hauled up a wall first and carried second, and so it does a good job of A but not of B (don't let companies make you believe they've cracked this with comfy straps). If you're only carrying your bag to the base of the Nose on El Cap this isn't a problem, but if you're having to ski twenty miles, or climb tough and challenging wilderness terrain to get to the base of your route, then it is. A large rucksack on the other hand is designed for moving loads and not hauling, so often it's worth using this for most of the heavy lifting, taking your haul bag up last.

The ideal bag for this is something very large, an expedition pack (80 to 100+ litres), with dedicated packs such as the Berghaus Expedition, Wild Things Andinista, and Cilogear 60L worksack being ideal as they can be stowed inside a haul bag easily afterwards. For real heavy duty users bigger and more carry focused bags may be preferred, and some, including those made by companies such as Kifru, designed for a military and hunting market, feature both huge capacity and strength, plus the ability to use the carry system alone, like an old school framed pack, allowing the haul bag to be carried on the panel.

In the other direction, in the past I've used a very lightweight (500 g) rucksack, just a bag with straps and 38 mm nylon belt without any back padding, for shifting loads, and then used it as a rope bag on the wall, or stuffed it in the bottom and used it to ferry loads down, a great approach when there is more than one bag person.

The usual male/female/body weight variations in load carrying capacity previously noted can be offset a little by the use of better load carrying gear, and so this should be considered for wilderness walls for mixed teams.

PACKING FOR THE WALL

When it comes to packing a haul bag, how you pack it depends very much on how many bags you're packing, as on big routes you may have four or more haul bags, but on some it'll just be the one. As with any packing the aim is to have what you want where you want it, and not what you don't want getting in the way. As a rough guide I'll break down how you'd pack a typical three day haul bag for two people into its primary levels:

First Class: This is the top of the bag, the prime real-estate, where the stuff goes you'll need (or might need) to get quickly, such as spare rack, storm bag (containing waterproof top and bottoms), one or two medium sized bottles of water (nalgene with clip loops), some snacks, belay jacket, taking up the top 30 cm of the bag. All stuff is best held in stuff sacks, so it can't tumble out, and can be taken out and clipped off when you need to go deeper down to search for something else (you don't want to be balancing vital kit on your knees as your dig around).

Second Class: This is where you put the bulk of your stuff, but stuff you probably won't need during the day, including your sleeping bags (in dry bags), sleeping mats (inflatable), first aid kit, food bag, camping equipment. Things like spare clothing and your bivvy bag can be used to fill in the gaps and pad this area out.

Steerage: This is where your water goes, packed in tight, with bottles being fished out each night for that night's tea and for the next day.

Bilges: This is the very bottom of the bag, the dead zone, and here lies all the stuff you won't need until you get to the top, or things you want to make near impossible to get hold of. Here lies rubbish, haul bag straps and belts (tied together), the bolt kit, wallet and keys.

TAMING THE CHAOS

Inside the rim of the bag you'll often find clip in loops or racking loops, and these are handy for clipping off stuff sacks. It's worth having lightweight (but strong and secure) mini krabs on all bags, with the large BD Micron (9 g) being the standout design, but flat wire gates being much cheaper. A daisy chain or knotted sling or cord can also be larks footed into the bag, with the most important bits clipped at the top (food bag, important rack bag) and less important stuff as you go down. The bottom line with all bag related chaos is the stuff sack.

LINING THE BAG

It's vital that when you pack the bag you create a smooth profile free of lumps, bumps or edges, as one hard edge can lead to a hole in your bag within metres of hauling. How to reduce the possibility of this happening is to pack the bags

well, and keep any hard objects away from the edges, and also have some form of lining or barrier between the contents and the vinyl.

Back in the day, books would tell climbers to line bags with their foam sleeping mats (cut to fit around the inside with a little to spare), but this was never that satisfactory, as they would take up too much room and be almost impossible to get out without unpacking the whole bag, plus the foam would bind with everything, making it hard to push items down into the bag.

Instead I would recommend all climbers line their haul bag with something stiffer. This can be achieved with something as simple as cardboard, a big cardboard box flattened out and taped, but this tends to get wet and smelly pretty quickly. Corex plastic sheeting (stuff house sale signs are made from) works well, but is a little thick and heavy, and needs to be cut in the correct plane (channels going vertically).

The best material of all is 2 or 3 mm HDPE. Just cut the material about 30 cm short of the rim of the bag so that the bag can be cinched into a bullet shape (line it to the rim and it will be rigid like a coke can). If using this sheeting, drill 10 mm holes about 20 cm in from each corner, and every 30 cm along the sides, so you can clip this off on the belay if you need to take it out, or thread cord or slings for using it for other jobs, as a makeshift sledge or stretcher for example, a wind or sun break, or clipped into the suspension of your ledge to deflect rock fall! In hot weather the polyethylene will become much softer but still provides a great solid barrier between the bags' contents and the wall.

MULTI BAG STRATEGY

On bigger and longer walls it's often best if each person has their own haul bag, as this makes it easier to get what you want when in the portaledge, rather than asking someone to "pass me…" all the time. When doing this it's best to try and keep an eye on how much water each person is drinking, as it's easy to keep dipping into the bags only to one day all come up empty! When you have your own bag each you need to have one a day bag as well, leaving the other bags sealed up, or hanging under the day bag when hauling, ideally not to be accessed until the end of the day.

Compartmentalizing: On monster walls you might be hauling three or four bags, and so here it's even more important to have some kind of system so as to avoid searching through multiple bags. To do this break down your bags into Week One and Week Two, with week one bags on top and week two bags underneath (as well as week three and four perhaps!). Hang these bags from two full strength cords, using one of them to do a mini haul in order to get it up to the belay for transfer of kit into the main bags. Make sure all food in weeks 2+ bags is suitable and won't go off or be crushed, but add some treats as well so you've got something to look forward to when you haul up this resupply.

All Your Eggs: As with everything on a wall don't make the mistake of putting all your eggs in one basket, unless you only have one basket! If all your water is in one bag and the bottom blows out you'll lose everything, so better to have it spread over at least two. This way you have more of a chance of overcoming bag problems, even if only in the form of a well hydrated honourable retreat to go and buy a new haul bag!

SECURING THE TOP STRAPS

On the wall you will always need to be able to unclip one of your haul bags' straps in order to get in and out of the bags more easily. As mentioned most bags are designed to have offset straps to make this easier. But in practice, especially when using very heavy haul bags, unclipping a strap and accessing the haul bag can be quite a job, as you're often trying to lift the weight of the bag with one hand (using your foot to lift the bag makes it a little easier). Here are a few things that can help:

Cam Buckle: You can pick up one of these metal camming buckles easily (e.g., from eBay or from motor shops - they're used in roof rack straps) and use it to make a very effective strap for the purpose involved (an old worn out adjustable lanyard chain is also ideal). Larks foot or tie the webbing cam strap to the haul bag strap, then clip a small karabiner (keyhole works best) into the metal buckle end and clip this into the suspension locker, rope or swivel. This allows you to quickly tension and release tension on the bags, and also easily clip the bag open by clipping this strap over onto another piece on the belay. With this setup you may want to tie a knot in the haul strap to create more distance over which to tighten.

Cord: This is a simple option, using a 70 cm length of 5 mm cord. Simply tie this into your strap and then tie the other end into your suspension locker via a munter mule knot. If there is no room for a munter knot (perhaps if the ropes are tied in directly to the bags), then simply wrap the cord around the haul line tie in knot.

Micro Ascender: Using a micro ascender such as a Ropeman, Tibloc or

Kong Duck you can make a variation of the cam buckle system, using a length of rope through the device, and clipping it off to the hauling point. If you make this cord long, say 1 metre, you can also use it to transfer the bag between anchors, as you can clip off the ascender, then yard in the rope, taking the load off the docking cord.

CONNECTING THE HAUL LINE TO THE BAGS

There are many ways to create a suspension point - the point where the haul line connects with the load, and which method you choose varies depending on whether you're hauling one bag (the suspension point can be clipped into the bag), or several (you need to create a multi suspension point). The basic fundamentals of attachment are very similar however. Here are some connection methods:

Tie Them In: This is the simplest and most secure way to attach your bags, as it almost totally removes the chances of the bags coming adrift, cross loading or detaching from karabiners. When tying in your bags it's vital that you tie a knot that can be easily untied after heavy loading, which means not a rethreaded figure of eight! The reason for this is that all rope ends need to be able to be freed at any time, as this is the only way to deal with tangles and general belay husbandry. The best knot is the rethreaded bowline or straight bowline, as it's a simple knot that's easy to untie after loading, and the load is spread over two strands, which reduces wear on the rope and haul point. An alternative is the rethreaded alpine butterfly, but this is difficult to tie!

Clip Them In: This means adding a locking karabiner so you can remove the line without needing to untie anything. The best knot to use is an alpine butterfly, as it can be easily untied, with the best krab a medium to large D shaped krab or forged HMS, as too small a locker can be hard to unclip and can get snagged when other things are clipped into it. When using a locker be very aware that you need to avoid cross loading, with all the weight coming onto the gates. Try making the bight of the butterfly very small and tight around the locker.

DMM Compact   Maillon (Quick Link)

Maillon: A high strength but compact option, where cross loading is not an issue, is to use a 10 mm alloy maillon rapide, but this has the drawback of being quite a small link, so it's not always easy to clip other things into it (such as your belay seat).

Shackle: The large DMM Compact shackle (35 g / 26 g) allows you to attach a hard link to your straps, or as a link to a swivel or Micro Traxion.

Swivel: A swivel can be added to the system. This reduces the twist of the haul line when hauling on slabs, and also makes it easier to spin the bags on the belay. The swivel can be attached by a locker on either side, or tied in on one side (double loop of 7 mm cord or strap, or rethreaded bowline on rope), or on both. The swivel also gives you a secure closed loop into which you can attach other gear, or larks foot in a docking cord.

DMM Axis   Petzl Micro

There are many swivel models on the market, with the DMM mini swivel (46 g / 26 kN) being nice and light, but lacking the small Axis swivel's (118 g / 36 kN) strength and room to clip in karabiners or ropes. Another style of swivel is the open swivel, with the Petzl Micro (75 g / 23 kN) having the ability to be attached directly to your haul bag straps, and thereby removing a link in the chain. Other swivels are available by many other manufacturers, with Rock Exotica Nano being a good model.

Note that all swivels have a working load limit at which point they will stop rotating under load and become fixed. This tends to be 3 kN for small ones and 5 kN for larger, which means all will be capable of handling most big wall loads (it should also be noted that even when fixed these swivels are still stronger than the karabiners or ropes holding them).

Rock Exotica SwivaEye   DMM Sidewinder

Swivel Locker: This is an integrated swivel attached to a high strength locking karabiner and perhaps is a good balance of everything you might need. The rope is best tied to the swivel with a rethreaded bowline or rethreaded alpine butterfly knot.

PCP: One system borrowed from soloing is connecting your bags to the rope via a PCP (Progress Capture Pulley) such as the Petzl Micro Traxion, as this allows far end hauling (where the bag is lifted at the bag end as well as the belay), which can be handy if hauling on slabby terrain, allowing the cleaner to lift the bag over obstructions without assistance from the hauler. If using a PCP then always tie off the rope as a backup to the PCP as the cam can release accidentally, and if using this with a swivel make sure the backup knot is clipped to the rope side of the swivel, so that the rope does not become tangled as the bag spins around.

PCP

DOCKING THE HAUL BAGS

Once you get your bags up to a belay you need to somehow park them, ready for the next pitch, and enabling you to free up your PCP. You'd think the obvious answer would be to just tie them in with the haul line, but of course that's not going to fly, as you'd not be able to get the weighted knot open when it came to hauling the next pitch.

The other option, and one used for years, was to clip the bags into the belay with a sling, daisy chain or a lanyard. This has a few problems, such as the pocket of a daisy chain isn't that strong (plus it would also be easy to cross clip pockets in the rush and crush of the belay), and an adjustable lanyard is far too weak all round.

A bigger problem is the whole weight would be hanging off the sling or lanyard locker, and if the next pitch was off to one side then the bags would not be raised allowing you to unclip, but instead would only create more force on the locker. In the past, to overcome this, the lower-out line would be used to create a mini haul, pulling the bags up a little in order to unclip, but it was a real pain in the ass.

So what was needed was a system that could be 100% secure, and also adjustable and easily releasable.

THE DOCKING CORD

The docking cord appeared in the '90s and pretty much revolutionised the parking of haul bags, doing away with slings and mini hauls.

The docking cord varies in the type of cord used and the way it's set up, but the classic is a 6 metre strand of 7 mm cord (10 kN) or 8 mm cord for mega loads (12 kN). The length of the docking cord can be shorter (4 metres), but longer cord allows it to be used as a very short lower-out line, and longer is better if using a swivel in order to give you more rope to play with.

The cord is then tied around the shortest haul bag strap (this allows the bags to be opened more easily once hanging as previously stated), or if using multiple bags then into the swivel. The knot used to tie the cord to the haul strap/swivel/locker is important as the loading on the cord is considerable. You can tie the cord in with a figure of eight knot but the knot will get so tight you'll probably need to cut it off. You can also larks foot the cord onto the strap (tie a figure of eight in the middle with a small bight), so you can take it on and off. A very good method to use is a double bowline, as this is strong but can be easily untied after you get to the top of the wall.

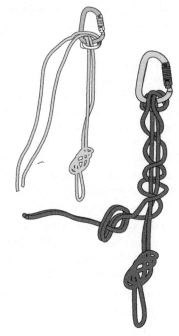

One note is I would always make sure that this cord is highly visibly different to any other cord, say some very bright yellow or red accessory cord, as this will reduce the risk of it being untied by accident.

Using The Cord

With the docking cord fitted in place, as the bags get near to the PCP, it is fished out, making sure it is not wrapped around anything, but goes direct from bag to masterpoint. Then the following steps are completed.

01. Tie the docking cord into the master-point with a munter hitch (you will need to practice this if you've not tied a munter hitch into a karabiner before, as it's preferable to be able to do this without opening or closing the master-point).

02. Take the two tail strands and wrap then in opposite directions around the loaded docking cord strand five times, the loaded strand acting like a maypole.

03. Take the ends and tie them together with an overhand knot, then a second knot. NEVER tie the bags off with a quick release knot, but something harder to untie, as a quick release knot can be easily pulled by accident. The reason for two knots rather than one is the same as having a fail safe on anything that can kill or injure.

04. Release the PCP cam and allow the bags to weight the docking cord (taking the strain on an ABBD device or an ascender, allow the rope to slip back through the pulley).

05. Tie a fail safe knot in the haul line and clip this in before releasing the PCP fully.

FAIL-SAFE KNOT

You'd probably not feel that happy hanging from the wall on a single 7 mm docking cord tied off with a Munter hitch and neither should you think it a good idea for your bags.

Docking cords can fail or become untied by accident, especially if there are multiple cords tied to the belay, so make sure they are always backed up.

This is achieved most easily by clipping the haul line close to the bags after they are docked with just a figure of eight or overhand knot, and untying this once the haul line is threaded into the pulley on the next belay before the bags are ready to be hauled. An alternative knot to tie is a slippery hitch or slippery clove hitch, which allows the knot to be untied by the leader pulling in the haul line.

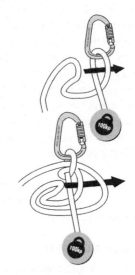

RELEASING THE BAG(S)

To release the bags, make sure the fail safe knot is untied first, then making doubly sure the haul line is through the PCP at the next belay (always wait for the bags to be hauled up a little to confirm this), untie the two overhand knots and allow the docking cord to feed through the Munter (keep your fingers clear of the Munter as it will pull them off!). If you're using a lower-out line this can be tied into the ends of the docking cord if you wish via an overhand knot, as this will travel through the munter once under load.

Why Two Strands? Having two strands gives you more to hold onto (7 mm x 2), some small redundancy, and allows the cord to be tied off in a manner that works better than a traditional munter tie off, in which the loop can be hard to release (remember that most munter tie offs are not loaded). Also by larks footing on the cord it can be un-larks footed off easily.

Single Strand: Instead of two strands you can go for a single strand, but I would use a minimum of 9 mm rope for this, so you can control the rope well, and make sure you learn how to lock off a munter hitch correctly with a munter mule.

KNOT PROTECTION

Your knot will need some kind of protection while on the wall, and although a heavy plastic bottle will work, the best method is a heavy-duty fuel funnel. With any knot protector, remember that if you re-tie the bags in short to use the tail of the haul line as a lower-out line as previously discussed, you will need to push the knot protector up the rope first and tie the new knot below it. Otherwise it will no longer be protecting the knot for the next haul, and if you don't spot the error, could slide off the end of the haul line and be lost. Your knot protector should have a loop attached to the bottom and be clipped into the haul bag straps, so it does not travel up and down the rope, or get dropped when the haul line is unthreaded from it.

MULTIPLE BAGS - VERTICAL TERRAIN

On very steep walls you can haul all your bags together, like a raft, with all the hauling points being at the same height (poo tube and portaledges underneath),

making it easier to get into the bags on the wall (having all of them on one swivel means you can rotate the bags at the belay to get the bag you want to access away from the wall). This approach, although a little crowded, is much easier to deal with at bivvy time, as no bags are hanging low down, requiring a pick up.

The Parallel Multi Suspension Point

When hauling multiple bags you can try and clip all the hauling straps into a single large locker, or have several lockers jammed into a swivel, or tied in, but often you're better tying a multi suspension knot, which acts as a connector between your haul line and your bags. This connector is made from a long length of 7 mm cord, pre tied while on the ground, with the primary loop being used to attach the haul line (a swivel can be threaded onto the 7 mm cord removing a link) as well as the docking cord (rather than having that on a single bag), and loops coming off it to attach each bag. First tie a triple figure of eight knot giving you three loops and leaving two long tails, then rethread both tails through the figure of eight and so create a double looped bight at the top. This is where you'll clip your haul line (or thread the swivel). Try and make the bag loops about 30 cm long so that the bags hang together well.

MULTIPLE BAGS - SLABBY TERRAIN

Making a train of bags works best on slabby terrain, as it creates the smallest profile, and if one bag can be cleared of an obstruction then all will tend to follow. The downside is that lower bags will need to be picked off one by one at every bivvy, unless you use lower bags for food and water for higher up the wall.

Having a long chain of bags creates more problems than you might imagine, as you want the load to be going in-line through all your bags, so top bag hanging from suspension point, then each bag clipped one into the other, like a long train or haul bag centipede. In reality though this creates a huge load on the top bags' bottom straps, maybe too much, plus you're faced with having to go down and pick off every bag at bivvies, or at least the top two bags. Ideally you want a system where all the bags are on the rope, and yet will allow you to take them off one by one as you haul, so that you can just keep hauling up one bag after the other. There are a few ways to do this:

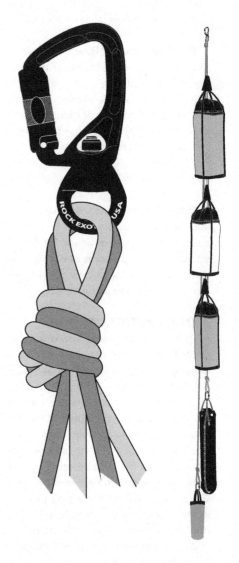

Butterfly Chain: I've used this setup for a mammoth eight bag chain (6 person team with 14 days stuff!). It's achieved by tying each bag into the haul line via its own butterfly knot. When the haul bags reached the belay each bag had its own docking cord and back up sling, and as it reached the PCP I'd dock it, lower the line onto an inverted ascender, untie the butterfly knot, then haul up the next bag and repeat. The following day each bag would be tied in again with butterfly knots and released one after the other, the top bag being the designated day bag. The downside with this technique is that you end up using some of your haul line, but as you always tend to have lots of free line it's not so bad.

Spider's Web: Tie multiple strands of 8 mm rope into a swivel or large locker creating multiple strands of rope. Each length of cord is tied into the pulley at the centre of each piece, so you have a knot with two strands (tails) coming off it. Match the length of these tails to the number of bags, so if you're hauling a chain of two bags plus ledge and poo tube:

- First bag clipped in short to strand A (or direct into swivel).

- Second bag clipped into other side of strand A so it hangs below first bag.

- Ledge bag is clipped into B cord so it hangs below second bag.

- Poo tube hangs on longest B cord strand.

The end result should be each bag is hanging clear of the bags above and below each other.

DAY AND TAG BAGS

Attaching small haul bags to your bigger bags depends on how you're hauling, but if you're using a dedicated small or micro day bag then it needs to be on top and easy to get at. On steep walls you can just clip it into the suspension point, but when the bags are hauled in line, I'll often attach it to the rope with a French prusik and push it up the rope until the base is clear of the other bags. When the prusik gets to the PCP I'll push it down to the level of the other bags, or unclip the bag from the haul line and clip it into the belay.

SUSPENSION CORDS

Suspension cords or 'keeper cords' are used to hang items beneath the primary bag(s), such as your portaledge, poo tube or small bags. These are made from 7 or 8 mm cord clipped/tied/larks footed into the suspension point and allowing items to be fished up hand over hand, without going down below the bags to get them (which can be a gut wrenching operation).

The bags can be both left free to hang or be clipped into the bottom of the primary bag, the latter method best in high winds as it means everything stays clipped together under the main load (wind can easily whipped up a poo tube or painters bucket and land it on your head!

I will often tied my cords direct to each item, meaning I don't have to worry about fumbling and dropping them when moving them up to the belay.

Try and have different colour cords and keep them only a little longer than your bags otherwise they'll swing around wildly.

ADVANCED TECH

I've already covered a lot of topics that could have been included here, such as hooks, heads and beaks, but such things can be found on trade routes, and so I thought I'd simply focus on techniques you might need for going beyond the rational here!

EXPANDING

Expanding or 'expando' rock is one of the scariest things you'll come across on any climb, just the germ of that thought, that something is expanding, enough to utterly undermine your confidence. Thankfully, cams have eliminated much of the scariness of expanding flakes, meaning climbers often don't even notice the feature they are on is elastic, the expansion absorbed by the cams' lobes, something a piton cannot do. Nevertheless it's vital that you know how to deal with such features.

WHAT IS AN EXPANDING FLAKE?

Imagine a large sheet of thick wood that is secured to a wall with many screws, but along only one edge. The sheet would be totally secured to the wall, and yet you would be able to pull the unscrewed edge away a little with your fingertips. If you jammed a coin under this edge it would be held in place by the forces of the screws holding the wood in place, but if you pushed in two coins, one on top of the other, a few centimetres higher, the first coin would drop out. An expanding flake, or expanding feature, works like this, in that it is slightly elastic, the degree of its elasticity depending on many factors, such as its thickness (some flakes can be paper thin), it's size (the distance from its edge to where it is attached plays a role in this),

and its shape (some flakes defy gravity and seem to be attached by far less than you'd imagine would be needed to keep them attached). Each of these factors decide just how dangerous an individual move is.

LOOSE OR EXPANDING

The main thing to focus on when climbing such features is the difference between a solid attached feature that has some elasticity, and a loose or completely detached feature. I've learnt to my cost, that when you tackle such features as if they are expanding they can often just break off, and that an expanding feature, if pushed too far, can become a loose feature and break. How you determine this difference comes down to experience.

BASIC TECHNIQUE

Before we get into this it's worth pointing out that the term 'expanding' covers a spectrum of stuff that moves, and if tested you'd find that a great deal of the rock you apply weight to, moves to some degree. This is one reason why we place cams at 50% of their range not 95%, but here we're talking about the climbing features on the more hazardous end of the spectrum, where a shift of 10% could see you fall and rip all your gear out.

◄ Short fixing, on a speed ascent of the Triple Direct.

The way to climb such features is to work out how much they expand and then try and move along them with the least amount of placements possible. It's really the game of spinning plates, the solid piece you're on being undermined by the next piece you place, as it opens up the rock as in the previous coins example above. In the past, when using pegs, you'd be standing on one peg, hammering in the next, when the one you're on would just blow, but these days cams have pretty much removed that problem.

Now often the issue is how much expansion there is, as stepping on a 00 cam with only a few millimetres of range may see it open up, while a size 1 cam, that has its cams 90% retracted will have plenty of room as the crack expands. The basic technique then requires you first of all work out how expanding the flake is, whether that's by hammering a piton, or placing a cam or a nut, and seeing how the force effects the rock, then rolling that knowledge into each placement you make thereafter.

Hammer And Eyes: The best way to work out what's going on is to use your hammer to test the rock, hitting it to see how it sounds, a high note being solid, a low note meaning it's not. Then use your eyes. Why would a solid, thick flake, be expanding? Look around, maybe you'll notice a fracture running through it, meaning it's semi detached from the wall. Very thin flakes, the thickness of a porcelain plate, can have some flex to them, or break if they are flexed too much, but it's rare for such features to be uniform, with the rock thickening up as soon as you move away from the edge, meaning deeper placements are more secure. Taking the time to use your eyes and hammer can allow you to know that a

cam placed 30 cm higher is good, where 30 cm lower is terminal.

Keep It Tight: When climbing an expanding feature you need to be clipped in tight to your next piece at all times, so that if the one you're on fails as you begin to weight the next one, there is a chance the next placement will hold your weight. Adjustable lanyards make this easier to do, but careful use of a fifi works just as well. You can also try the fixed copperhead method, of trying to spread your weight over multiple pieces, feet on one piece, body on another, weight also on your next piece.

Get High: If you have a four metre expanding section, the ideal situation is not to place gear at the bottom, middle and top, but to place a single place in the middle and try and bypass it as much as possible, the idea to always step high. The more gear you're placing, the greater the risk you'll cause your house of cards to collapse.

Free Climbing: Sometimes you can do some free moves to bypass an expanding section, or climb it guerrilla style, half freeing and half weighting the gear, the idea to keep the weight low and reduce the force on the placement. In other situations, just freeing a section can be easier than trying to aid it, some gnarly A4 pegging up an expanding flake becoming a 5.9 layback.

Forces: I've not really talked about the actual forces involved here as it's a highly complex area, and what you get in a lab. Pulling a cam in a straight crack with everything aligned, is very different on a wall. The basics are your body weight is doubled by a cam or a cam hook, less so by a fragile cam hook, and even less by a nut, but all such things depend on a great many variables. Whether you have a masters in physics or a certificate in business studies, you'll be equally baffled at the black magic of why one piece holds and another does not. And so instead it's worth setting some practice experience on the ground to see what will hold and what won't. To do this, try and play around with big blocks of talus, placing gear between a small block and a large one. Practise placing cams and cam hooks, and then nuts, and you'll see the blocks will often move under the load of a cam, but not a nut or fragile cam hook.

EXPANDING PLACEMENTS

Cams: As I've said, cams tame most expanding cracks to the point you probably don't even realise they're expanding at all, but as the cracks become smaller and smaller their ability to absorb the movement becomes more limited. It's best not to bounce test expanding flakes, but rather to watch and monitor, and with cams that means weight the cam and see what it does, applying a slightly higher force than body weight to check the cam will stay secure when you place the next one. If in testing, the cam expands to within the limit of its range then stops, then this should be replaced with a larger cam, as ideally you want it to have some chance of holding a fall and not just umbrella opening. For this reason always try and place the largest cam you can, and remember that cams with cam stops might work like a nut if they umbrella out.

Cam Hooks: Once cams become really small they lose their edge for expanding pitches as they might not be able to take in the slack of the flake, or if you fall on them the cam will just rip anyway. In such situations, most often Baby Angle or Lost

Arrow cracks, using cam hooks makes a scary pitch feel like A1. All cam hooks are very useful but the best of all is the alloy fragile hook, as its thickness and width mean it has a great deal of stick and cohesion, as due to being wide, it exerts a lower force on the rock (lower than a cam). Often you can just leapfrog the hooks up a crack placing pegs or nuts every few metres as protection (this is what I did on the infamous Gong Flake when I soloed Aurora).

Pitons: The classic technique is to hammer in a piton at the start of an expanding section to take out some of the slack, then use passive gear above, and this is still a good idea as long as you're sure it's not just loose or detached. Climbing a whole pitch on pitons only happens if you cannot use cam hooks, but most often it will be a mix of the two. With a piton you need to think of it more like a cam, or a nut, than simply something that exerts an outward resistance. If you can slot a long thin lost arrow into a spot between two constrictions, or above a constriction, and clip the eye, you will be creating a camming force as well as a blocking force, the constriction resisting the rotation of the pin. Some climbers advocate having the pin with the tip pointed slightly down so as to resist twisting, but really it's all about the shape of the rock around it, as sometimes a pin will lock in with the tip pointing up. By hammering in the peg you are also getting it to be pinched by the flake.

Nuts: Nuts work well in the right spot as they create more of a downward force against the feature, creating less creep, but you need the nut to have enough taper to take in any movement. Sometimes you can tap in the nut a little bit to open up the rock and have it pinched. The larger the nut the better and if you were looking at either using a small brass micro or a knife blade, then I would go for the blade.

Heads: A copperhead can be used both as a copperhead and as a nut. As in normal cases, the idea is to create a custom fit, so you might flatten and taper the head to make it more nut shaped, then use your chisel to hammer it deeper into the crack where it might find a solid place to seat. In some cases you can find a head that's too big to go into the crack, then hammer it in (using the hammer at first, then a chisel), so you're really making the flake eat it (also don't forget to exploit any natural constrictions to further improve holding power).

Hooks: Don't have tunnel vision and miss out on features that can be hooked to either side of the crack, or in the crack itself, perhaps a broken off chunk or hole (on some walls climbers have broken holes in paper thin flakes and hooked these). If you can get out of the crack onto something else you can always place something tight and solid without fear of the gear you're on popping.

Slider Nuts: Some climbers like ball nuts for expanding rock, but few carry these anymore, and for pure progression a cam hook is way more reliable.

Nut And Piton Stack: A nut and piton stack is very similar to using a ball nut or nut stack, but in expanding climbing it seems to create very little outward force, probably due to the forces being spread out between the peg, the cable, and the nut, with both an active and passive force. Where this works well is in very thin features, thinner than a cam hook, using a combination of alloy or brass micros or small heads, and stacking these with a

#3 beak. When using this technique you should find a nut that just fits into the crack, then place the beak beside it, but with the nut inverted, tapping in the beak so it binds with the nut, causing the two to lock together. The idea is that the greater the force on the nut the greater they lock together, failure coming when the crack expands to the point the nut slides past the piton (which tends not to happen due to lower outward forces). This is a very advanced technique which needs to be practised, but can come in very handy for very thin expanding sections.

CLEANING
Due to the elasticity of such pitches cleaning can sometimes be difficult, and I've lost a few cams over the years that have become squashed behind flakes. If you've placed any pitons then the passive gear needs to be taken out first, so that means if you placed a piton to open up the crack this will be the last piece you take out, even if that means down jumaring to get it. If gear becomes very stuck, be careful not to bring the the flake down on your head by being overly aggressive in trying to remove it.

LOOSE ROCK

Loose rock is one of the more dangerous aspects of big wall climbing, from dealing with large detached features on otherwise solid pitches, like boulders sitting on ledges waiting to topple, to large areas of tottering, hanging and stacked madness. The dangers when facing loose rock range from falls caused by rock breaking, or impact injuries to the leader, belayer or people on the ground, to life threatening injuries, missing body parts, cut ropes or cataclysmic annihilation of whole teams.

IDENTIFYING LOOSE ROCK

The key to climbing loose rock is identifying the problem before it's too late, and if the piece of rock you're on is breaking under your weight then you've probably failed at this. Experience will tell you what is solid and what is not, and very often it's the misidentification of which is which that leads to problems.

If you get good at looking, then you should be able to see what's going on, both by looking at the route at the granular level, and the bigger picture. Looking at a wall from the ground you will be able to make out large weak areas, where big sections have broken off, fracture lines, layers of weaker rock, big black concave sections of cliff with bands and layers of different rock. As a rule, it seems anywhere where you get big roofs tends to be a sign that something big has fallen off, while slabs or vertical walls tend to be more solid, that is unless they've simply become eroded by the rain. The ground below a route also gives you signs, with things like smashed trees, rock fragments lying on top of larger boulders, tons of rock dust covering large areas, obvious indications of loose rock above.

On closer inspection look out for fractures, chalky impact marks, or rocks that are just stacked up there waiting to topple, flakes that are simply balanced or boulders balanced on ledges. In all these situations you need to climb as if you're taking a stroll through Jurassic Park.

RULE #1 STAY CLEAR

It's always best to stay clear of loose rock, to neither touch it, nor go near it. It's just trouble. This does not simply mean you, but also your ropes and haul bags. You must always be aware of these other elements, haul line, bags, backup loops when jumaring, as even on solid trade routes it's possible for there to be hanging flakes and blocks on either side of heavily trafficked pitches, ready to snag the lax or unaware. But what happens if you don't have a choice?

TACKLING THE LOOSENESS

So you're climbing a route that involves some or a lot of looseness and choss, maybe because there is a short section of bad rock, or bad rock is your thing. Here are some things to think about.

Handle With Care: Treat all loose rock like you would an old World War II bomb you might find in your garden, be it big or small. A small flake can take off a finger, slice a rope, or kill your belayer, while you can ride one the size of a kayak without a scratch. Treat all loose rock with respect and if you can't avoid touching it, then try and understand how to work around it or work with it.

Forces: Remember that gravity should have made sure that the rock is able to withstand a direct pull but that's it. Stick a cam behind a detached block sitting on a sloping fracture line and the force of the cam can be its tipping point, making the block move and fall. Layback a pillar that's detached at the base and it might weigh fifty tons but it will fall like a tree. Some features are simply keyed into place, held up by other loose pieces, like big wall Jenga. Break any link between these pieces and the whole lot can come down.

Work Out What Is What: Very often you can find good solid gear by working out what is 'the mountain' and what is not the mountain, what's attached and what is not. Paying attention and not being slack is the way to go, not just jamming in a cam where it seems like the right place to do so. Very often on hard routes you might come across a large fragile feature that just seems to hang there and you have no idea how someone could climb it, that dangerous little voice in your head telling you they did and so can you. But then you spy a hook move to the side, or realise if you top step you can avoid it, or swing around it. If it looks too dangerous to climb then it's probably been avoided by everyone else.

Use Your Hammer: As with expando climbing, make good use of your hammer in determining how solid the rock is.

PROTECTION

Like expanding climbing, you need to be thinking of the forces applied and place the right gear, placing nuts instead of cams, or hand placed pitons, getting high and getting through these loose areas fast.

No Pro: Sometimes you need to make a choice between placing gear that might hold but might also cause the rock to fail, bringing down big rocks or flakes on you and your partner, or not placing gear and risking a big fall. In these situations you might choose the latter, and forgo any protection at all, even if aiding, just going from one careful piece to another, knowing that a short hard fall onto a lower piece is more hazardous than a longer fall into space. On some new routes I've ended up doing A4 climbing on beaks when there was the possibility of A1 climbing within reach, big stacked blocks, but blocks which I felt would all collapse if I even touched them - or not. Why take the risk when you have something safe to climb? The no pro route is high risk and should only be taken when you're looking at death blocks.

Think Of The Second: Another no pro factor is that maybe you could put a cam behind a death flake 'just in case', but not weight it or fall on it, but what happens when your second starts ascending on the rope, and the cam becomes loaded?

Strength In Numbers: If you're looking at smaller scale choss, stuff that's not going to kill anyone, but is just choss, like bands of poor sandstone or alien mystery rock, stuff that seems to have the consistency of old bone marrow, then here you want strength in numbers, placing everything you can, with long pegs and beaks being ideal, the idea being that hopefully something will hold you.

Making It Work: Very often you will find yourself climbing rock that is mobile and not attached to anything, that can be moved with your fingers. This type of climbing is like climbing through the rubble of a fallen building, where you need to somehow find some strength in the chaos of it all. Here you need to not only work out what force your cam applies to the rock, but what forces the rock applies to the rock around it. For example you might find a crack that is full of fractured flakes of rock, stacked up together, that look impossible to use. And yet if you think about it, as the force is applied to the loose flakes these will press into one another, like books on a bookshelf, and you can achieve an effective placement, making what in effect is a stack, only using a cam and the pieces of rock.

Locked In And Locked Out: Even in the most terrible rock you can see that a long peg hammered into a horizontal fracture line, say in multiple small bands of weak rock, cannot create enough force to literally explode the rock, that there are millions of tons of rock both above and below it, but where a micro cam would, or

Large expanding and loose flakes on the Troll Wall

a small nut that does not have the weight of the mountain on its side, but is working on the granular level, with grams of rock the difference between a disintegrating placement and something that might hold.

Weigh It Up: Very often you will be faced with a block of stone, or a flake, and have to work out if you can climb it safely, either free or aid. You know it is totally detached and so must decide if the force you're going to apply will move it, moving it not being what you want to do. A rough rule of thumb is that a one foot square lump of granite, limestone or sandstone weighs around the same as a person (about 70 kg), and that a cam will apply twice your bodyweight. What does that mean? Well it means a block the size of a microwave will weigh around 130 kg, and will probably move if you stick a cam behind it, while a block the size of a washing machine will weigh around 500 kg and will not. Of course this is a very rough guide to such things and many other factors come into play, and you must develop as sharp an understanding of choss dynamics as someone going into flattened buildings. This means that you need to factor in many variables, such as that a cam might hold behind a loose microwave if the friction between it and the rock below it is high, or if you place it at the sweet spot, not where the block will just pivot. Try and think about the dynamics of a 0 cam placed under such a block and a long thin lost arrow, in that the cam may well lift the block enough to pop, but the lost arrow will not be able to create enough lift from your body weight to lift the stone.

Spread The Load: In very marginal rock, where you are forced to aid fragile features, you can try and spread the load, and this can be done literally, by setting two pieces together, say two cams, and making a sliding X, or by using a balance piece, with you standing in your hero loops on a piece below and just using a poor piece for your upper body, the force going through that low enough to hold as you reach for something that will take your whole weight.

Free Climbing: Free climbing allows you to climb more lightly on loose rock, only pulling or pressing down, and is often the best way to climb loose sections, sometimes the only way. This means wearing rocks books is very handy on loose sections, as you can often just do some tension off a piece, or climb guerilla style, half free and aid, spreading the load. If you're climbing on this kind of rock it's best if you have some experience of such climbing beforehand, knowing how to spread your weight, what can be pulled on and what can't, the basic rules being test everything and tread lightly.

Micro Choss: Choss comes in many forms and sizes, and I would include mud, dirt and gravel in this category. This tends to fill up cracks and act as a kind of cement between bigger blocks, and in winter can be very climbable, with beaks or axe picks going into it like old chewing gum. Very often you will find that on chossy routes you can have great nut placements that are chocked up with stones and pebbles, and some hard cleaning with a hammer (having one with a pick is best), will create a perfect placement.

Sand Choss: Another kind of choss that is sort of choss on a micro scale is mudstone, sandstone that seems to lack the stone, and various strange anomalies that look like talcum powder. This stuff looks like stone from a distance but close up turns out to be barely stuck together particles of something or other, most often than not the consistency of nightmares. To climb such rock requires some out of the box thinking. If you have a crack then you're lucky, but take care as in such rock nuts can pull through or cams can bite into the rock deep enough to fail (one reason why sandstone cams have wider lobes). Often you will find there are blank sections and these can either be bolted or riveted (use long 110 cm+ bolts), or often you can just hammer a beak directly into the rock and it can make its own crack. On existing choss routes or routes with choss bands, they will often be marked as going clean, but such fragile features can break off or dissolve in the rain. Here you can end up with flared holes or pockets, where you might fit two cams of a Totem, a Tricam, Hexentric or some kind of piton stack.

Mystery Rock: Sometimes you come across rock that should act like all the other rock but does not. If you're a geologist maybe you could tell what it is, but as a climber it's just a problem. In Antarctica I came across granite that was so weathered by freeze thaw that its entire surface was covered in scabs, meaning there was almost no feature that could be pulled on with any trust. Even the cracks were full of these scabs, meaning you could only climb them if every placement was cleaned first with a hammer. The crystal structure of the rock was also strange, being so large that when you were beaking, the beak was only held between two crystals the size of a penny, meaning the placement could suddenly fail. The same was true when bolting, as care had to be taken not to drill into a single crystal, otherwise the bolt would be weakened (and in the case of self drives you could just pull them out by hand). Such mystery rock appears now and then, from a strange plug of sandstone on Tangerine Trip, to the acid rock of Suser Gjennom

Harryland, and it's good to be able to modify your style to climb it, treating it with care, respect and suspicion.

BELAYS

There isn't that much you can do about rock fall, but this should be taken into account when setting up belays on loose pitches. Setting belays under some kind of cover, or out of the fall line, is vital, and on new routes this could mean drilling anchors off to the side of the line you're climbing. Long pitches can also help. If you think rock fall is going to be a problem anyway, the belayer should try and seek some kind of protection, and this can be improvised by getting under anything solid, like a belay seat, rope bags, haul bags. If you can haul up the bottom of a haul bag to another anchor you can get the bag to lie horizontally, which can provide a very effective choss umbrella.

DOUBLE UP

If you're heading onto ground you know to be loose and dangerous then you should consider using a double rope system, as this doubles your safety margin both in terms of falling onto suspect rocks, but also in terms of rocks falling and chopping your ropes, which can be easily done when climbing choss. This tends not to be used on most big walls, outside of Russian teams, a fingers crossed approach being employed instead, but one that often seems very irrational. If going for a double rope system (such as two very thin 9 mm single ropes), make sure you use a skinny zip-line as well.

TRUNDLING

Pulling off loose rock is all about the possible consequences; are you going to make things safer for others, or put others in harm's way? If you're on some wilderness wall then kicking off a hanging flake that will miss everyone is fine, but do this on the Nose and you could kill someone, if not a climber, then some kids with their mum and dad at the base. Sometimes too, what looks like it's ready to go won't go, but will just be made more perilous, and so it's often best to just leave things as they are, or get the second to try and kick the crap off. One time trundling is definitely worth doing on a wilderness wall is if you're coming back the same way (rappelling the route), as this reduces the chances of rockfall later on.

SPEED CLIMBING

There can be few things more rewarding than climbing fast and light on some huge big wall, a wall that maybe took you a week of sweat, fear and toil to climb the first time. Climbing quickly, with no haul bags to deal with, or ledges and bivvies, just climbing fast, fast, fast is up there as one of the most masterful moments of any climbing.

What is best about speed climbing is that although fitness and experience play a part, just knowing a few tricks can turn a three day route into a one day route, cutting out all the fat of a big wall ascent. This ability to move quickly and remove the clutter of climbing also translates into longer routes and is especially good for alpine walls.

There is quite a lot to cover here, but I must stress that these are advanced techniques that require the highest level of skill and judgement, and could very easily bite you if you don't know what you're doing, speed climbing full of tales of big whippers and near death.

LEADING

Climbing fast is not really about climbing fast, not when you're moving up many hundreds, maybe thousands of metres of rock. It's about fundamentally just not stopping or fucking around, but simply keeping the momentum up. Often going hell for leather will just see you in a tangle of aiders and lanyards, with gear dropped or you taking a whip!

Instead of this you should think of all the stuff you do when not moving, sorting gear, thinking about the placement, putting in gear, taking it out, testing, testing again, taking selfies. Another thing to think about is how long it takes you to get sorted to leave the belay, how long it takes to make a new belay, tie knots, how long you sit there considering the size of the universe as your partner slowly cleans the pitch.

Removing or reducing the time spent on these small (and large) things is really where the war of speed is won, the little battles, a belay made in 10 seconds flat (butterfly knot into one bolt - done), a cam placed already on the aider, you up in your top steps in 5 seconds - done. You twenty metres up the next pitch before your partner has even reached the belay, ten metres more by the time he's hauled your light haul bag.

Very often if you break down all the time leading and all the time belaying, and faffing, and remove that you'll find you half the time required, a 33 hour push ascent on some route that usually takes six days really not fast at all once you factor out 60 hours of bivvy time, and 60 hours of belaying.

MENTAL APPROACH

It's easy to say that speed climbing is a mental game and ignore all the other stuff, like fitness, skill, efficiency, experience and balls, but I really think it is about making that switch in your mind. I know I've climbed some pitches faster than I've made some placements on my first big wall, and know without doubt some speed climbers could have lapped me on El Cap four times over while I led just one pitch.

Of course taking your time is vital on hard aid, or when learning the business, but you need to switch into a special mode for speed, and add a little more gutsiness, a little more daring, into the mix. Imagine you come to a line of fixed heads. Can you imagine just clipping up them like they were bolts, or you're on a via ferrata? How about being unsure if something is 100%, but just getting on it anyway?

As with all mental aspects of climbing you need a solid base, the ability to know that those heads are good, that that blue alien won't rip, that a cam hook placed like that might seem imperfect but once you load it, won't come out. It's all about confidence, skill and judgement, the eye, as often you might be hanging from a single piece of gear many metres - or tens of metres - from your last bit of pro.

FREE CLIMBING

Being able to free climb quickly depends on how confident and comfortable you are, how tired you are, how much rope drag you have, how knackered your feet are feeling. With a lot of rope drag, running three pitches together, but climbing several grades below what you can usually manage, you're still moving, still got momentum. The best thing about free climbing is that you can master the art of speed anywhere, climbing multi pitch routes faster and faster, learning to

master how to extend your gear so as to make those linked pitches less of a grind. Being able to integrate free climbing with short fixing, with your partner ascending really frees things up, and allows you run two pitches into one. Again the thing to focus on is not some mad crazy dash, but a slow and methodical movement, where you don't fall, place solid but spaced gear, and having a kind of a soloing head but with a rope.

FRENCH FREE

As with standard leading, the ability to switch between aid and free is vital, as you're racing the clock, not the grades, and if a quick yank on a green alien saves you thirty seconds or a fall, then go for it. Being able to French free and avoid using aiders and lanyards is vital on low angled terrain (such as the start of the Nose), as any sticking feet in aiders is slow, and often painful. Again this is a technique you can practise by trying routes a grade harder than you usually climb.

AID CLIMBING

Speed climbing when aid climbing is really just a state of mind, and it's amazing how fast you can climb once you just switch off some bits of your head while switching on others.

As with all speed climbing it's more about momentum, and making those judgements, such as do I step high to save time, or make an easier placement where I am, saving the time needed to get high?

A few ways to speed things up include:

Fixed Gear: When you get to fixed gear, pegs or heads, you should try to quickly make a call as to whether it's solid or not, by both giving it a quick once over with your eyes (is the peg's eye broken, is the head's cable rusty), and by knowing how much traffic it's had. If you think it's good then you can give it a mini bounce then get on it, or just get on it, and get off it quickly. Always be on the lookout for booby trapped gear, where something isn't fixed at all, like a sling that's fallen down the face and is stuck in a crack, as often failure of one piece when speed climbing will see you take a big whip! I try to only clip fixed gear that's super trustworthy and stick to pro I know is good, cams and bolts, as I don't want to take a twenty metre fall onto some peg Warren Harding placed. If testing heads just do a body weight and a bit test, then get on and off it fast.

Hard Fast Test: If you want to have more confidence in your gear then do one really hard bounce test with your aider, then get on it.

Avoid Death By Inches: A lot of aid climbers climb up their aiders one step at a time, or make little mini moves with their fifi hooks, or are constantly hanging off their adjustable lanyards. On the latter point, every time you adjust that lanyard requires you to then un-adjust it, which when done hundreds of times, all adds up. And so, when speed climbing, the aim should always be to perform as few acts as possible, just clipping your fifi on once and that's it, but ideally not at all, using hand holds and cracks to balance and move up.

Crack Jamming: Practise moving fast up easy cracks by having a cam on each aider, just stepping up on the bottom one, sitting back on the top one, and repeating, but not leapfrogging them as usual. This takes some practice getting your feet and lanyard's length right, but once mastered is a real time saver.

Mini Racks: When aiding and back cleaning, you'll soon notice that very often you put in a piece by removing it from your rack, then do the move, then take it out and put it back on your harness, and repeat again and again, with pieces around size 20 mm being used over and over again. If you can remove the taking on and off your harness part of the process, you can be maybe 50% faster, and this can be achieved by making two mini racks that live on your lanyards. These would include your primary cams, usually something like a green, yellow and red alien, plus a wire rivet hanger, cam hook and pointed grappling hook. All these are either tied into a small loop of 7 mm cord (small as you can make it), or clipped into a twist lock karabiner. None of these pieces can be placed as pro, so it's best to carry two of each size on your harness as well, and place these when you feel it's time to leave some pro behind. With this setup you can almost lead some pitches without placing any other gear, just clipping bolts or putting in gear as if you were free climbing.

Go Nutless: Nothing slows things up like a stuck nut and so try and stick to leaving cams behind as gear, or place nuts as protection as if you're free climbing but without weighting them and making them fixed, instead just giving them some hard yanks. Often when speed climbing, I'll only carry half a set of wires, but four sets of small cams, maybe more if you add in offsets.

Draws: On some speed climbs I'll try and place as little gear as possible and instead clip bolts and pegs and stick to draws rather than gear, carrying more draws than usual.

Get High Quick: When aiding people tend to creep up the aiders one step at a

Short fixing with three climbers and haul bag

time, but in speed climbing you need to be rocking up, getting that leg high and getting up there in your upper steps.

Mini Aider: It's very important that you get the most height as you can from your gear, but you probably don't want to be dragging up four aiders for top stepping or clipping aiders into each other, instead just getting high, placing gear and going. One way to make this easier is to make a mini sub aider, just two steps that match your main aider, which helps force you up to the top.

Cam Hooks A-Go-Go: You cannot climb fast unless you're down with cam hooks, can place and clean them fast, and trust them. Some pitches that might have required an hour or two of careful pegging can be climbed in a quarter of the time by just back cleaning cam hooks, such as the Nipple on Zodiac, or making one easy hook move, like on the Great Roof, can save time messing around with cams.

Intermediate Aiding: A very good way to milk each placement is to get high on the piece you're on, place the next piece, but instead of testing it or clipping it, just use it as a hand hold, stepping into your top steps and placing a piece even higher. Once placed, clip in your lanyard, step across into your next piece and reach down and unplug the bottom and intermediate piece while hanging straight armed.

Cheater It: Having a stiff draw, or better still something like a Kong Panic, that allows you to reach fixed gear or belays, saves you lots of time.

Nail It: Spending ages trying to fiddle with micro wires wastes time when you could just hand place a beak, and do you want some A4 nut or an A1 piton when you've run the rope out twenty metres. Even on clean routes the odd beak can be vital to a fast ascent.

Bust It: Having shoes on that allow free climbing is a great way to climb pitches fast, as you can often bust the odd move here and there, stepping up and mantling onto good holds and bypassing crappy hooks. Also make sure you've got chalk. The downside is if your feet get toasted you'll not be able to step up high in your aiders, so always make sure you've got solid shoes as well.

Keep It Light: There's no point carrying a Camalot 4 up sixteen pitches of aid for that one offwidth crack on pitch 17, or those sawn-offs for that single move you might make if the fixed gear is missing. Instead leave this gear with the second, and allow them to bring it up and save some of your energy.

Organisation: Having what you want where you want it, and when you want it, is vital for speed climbing, as missing one cam can make turn a five second job into a five minute one. Try and have a system that you stick to, and resist the temptation to hastily rack gear anywhere, but keep it where it's meant to be.

STRATEGY

Speed climbing strategy boils down to what route, where to start, who's going to lead what, where handovers will be, and what time you'll start and hope to finish.

What Route? It's always best to know the route you're trying to do first, and few people do one day ascents of routes they've never done. The first time I climbed Zodiac it took us 4 days (albeit we were a team of four including a disabled climber), the next time it took two days, the time after that 17 hours, each ascent having less and less unknowns. Routes like the Nose require all sorts of tricks which can shave hours and hours off an ascent, but need some practice, with many climbers aiming for a sub 10 hour ascent doing many training laps up to Dolt, allowing them to be catapulted quickly up onto the climbing they're not so fast on, but with time saved from below to waste working it out.

Where To Start? I'm a big believer in starting at the bottom of a route, rather than stumbling through boulder fields at 2am, preferring to bivvy close to the start, the bag packed and rack ready to go. I find this less stressful, and it allows for more sleep, as you can just get up and go and don't have all that 'have we got everything?' at the truck in the dark, your brain frazzled. For bivvying at the base you just need light sleeping bags and mats, and some extra food and water, so little real weight, and it allows an easy evening approach and chilled out start. You can often leave your bivvy stuff at the start and pick it up afterwards (having someone camp with you and take your stuff down is best), or take it with you up the route, so you can bivvy at the top, instead of trying to get down when knackered. For others they might want to stay in their tents or vans, in warm beds with hot bodies, and just set the alarm an hour or two earlier.

Who Leads What? Break down the route into blocks, with a two person team maybe doing half each, or maybe a third each while fresh then subdivide the last third again when you're toast. Doing the NIAD you'd want the better free climber to climb the first half of the route and the faster aid climber to climb the second half, while on a pure aid route with a three man team you might want the fittest climber to be jugging the haul line.

Hand Overs And Transitions: It's best to try and hand over on a ledge, or somewhere where the leader can get their breath, have a drink etc, with Dolt tower being the most classic spot, maybe even somewhere you can take your shoes off! Sometimes when the leader is on a roll you should just let them run and run, and keep the second(s) fresh. Just be on the lookout for the tendency for the second to become resistant to get into the lead, especially if they've not done any day walls before. Just having your second climb a single pitch or two can make a huge difference.

Timing: A fast team can often start in the cool of the morning and get to the top in a day, but I cannot stress how much being tired is amplified by climbing into the night. You can be almost there and feeling OK, but with nightfall comes a slowness and uncertainty that can be crushing, with a malaise that can make you feel like pitches have been run together, just going on and on, when really it's just you who's been wrung out. One approach to this problem is to start in the evening, when the sun has yet to set, and climb right through the night when you're at your freshest, and into the morning. The drawback with this approach is often you'll have been awake all day psyching yourself up, but then if you can't sleep anyway, why not start the route now? Having tried this a few times all I can say is it's a pretty good system if it works out, but there is nothing worse than seeing the night come on twice without going to sleep, the 36 hour ascent soul destroying.

WHAT TO BRING

Haul Or Carry: On some speed climbs you might just carry a small day bag each, carrying everything each of you needs, two litres of water, a jacket, some gels and bars, meaning no hauling is required, and the weight is low for both the leader and the second. On other routes, the second can carry extra water, maybe two or more litres to refill your bladder packs at a certain transition. If you jug with a small or micro haul bag then you can switch between hauling and carrying it on your back, say hauling on the steep overhanging terrain, but not on the slabs (the higher you get the lighter the bag becomes). Full on hauling from bottom to top allows you to bring lots of water, as even a generous supply is easy to haul compared to a multi day load. Hauling also allows you to throw in more clothing, emergency bivvy kit, and some tunes!

Food: As in any high end sport performance, it's important to nail your nutrition both before you climb, and on the climb, as it's vital your energy level doesn't dip due to a deficit in calories (as it will already be in deficit due to climbing non stop for hours on end). Food wise it's often best to stick with what you know, be that gels and bars, or sandwiches and wraps, but I'd recommend trying to make time to eat at least once an hour, some food, some drink. I would avoid having too much sugar as it'll make you crash, and save any caffeine for the end of the climb, those chocolate covered espresso beans or caffeine gels for the dark hours of the climb, if you need them.

Water: I've jugged up Lurking Fear with ten litres of water on a roasting hot day, only to get to 'Thanksgiving' ledge with nine litres left, probably expending more energy than was necessary. Trying to do the Triple Direct in a day we only had the water in our bladders, counting on the wind to come up before we got blasted by the sun and darkness to come on a before we'd drank the last of it. Speed climbing is something that is a balance of many things, and due to the high level of 'being on it' required, I'd try and avoid running out of water, and always err on the side of caution, going for 3 litres each unless you know for sure you can do it with less.

Clothing: People have speed climbed walls naked, some in just a pair of shorts, but for most people, it's a good idea to think about what you'll need to wear. The obvious answer is that you need something to protect you from the sun and the rock and the cold, so long sleeves and long pants that can be rolled up or folded are best.

Even on very hot walls, once the wind gets up, it can get pretty cold, especially when sat at the belay. When night comes on you can get very cold, as your body will be lacking energy too, with clothes maybe damp and dirty with salt from your sweat. On a few walls I've had all my clothes on and thought I'd have a micro nap while I waited for my partner to jug up to me at a transition, only to wake up shivering, knowing I should have kept moving around.

For this reason I always try and have enough clothes to both keep me warm while climbing, and while static, such as a light belay jacket (you can take a full weight belay jacket for the second).

The choice of waterproofs is a personal one, and if no bad weather is forecast it's your call, but if there is any chance at all, then take full shell (lightweight non breathable running shells are good for emergencies), as you'll be naked to the weather and wasted if you get hit by a storm (I know one famous climber who almost froze to death on the Nose in a snowstorm wearing just a Hawaiian shirt).

Emergency Bivvy Kit: Before I finally climbed El Cap in a day I had several near misses, where I got close but ended up being so tired we had to stop and bivvy, sometimes more than once. These bivvies varied from curling up in a shivering ball on the hard granite with just a fleece on, sitting in your belay seat with your legs in your bag (yes you can bivvy on a belay seat!), to having a cushy half mat and light sleeping bag.

Going with nothing means you probably won't stop and sleep on the route unless things get really bad, and will have to keep going down once you reach the top, unless it's warm and you can sleep in the sun. This approach gives you some incentive then, to not be weak and stop, like swimming across a lake without armbands, it's sink or swim or "travel light, freeze at night".

A better approach is to take enough stuff to make at least a stab at some comfort, some insulation to go under your body, and something to keep off wind and trap a little heat. First of all, think about what insulation you already have to stop conduction from laying on the rock. The rope is of course the best insulator, and should be carefully snaked to make a mat. After this you have your haul bag or pack, which you can also stick your feet into (foam on the bottom), and even plastic bottles will give you some insulation when most of the air is expelled. The super light folding mats you get inside alpine packs are really good for this, as they take up very little space and insulate well when placed on rock (have a clip loop on them so they don't blow away), and two 3/4 mats used to line a haul bag are best of all.

For the upper body of course, a sleeping bag is best, and one bag can be used for two people like a blanket, but this assumes you have a ledge big enough for two people to curl up on. I once had to bivvy with this one bag solution on Lunar Eclipse, but found the ledge was long and thin, meaning one person got the bag, while the other got the bivvy bag. Luckily here we had a bothy bag as well, and I was able to stuff this loose and scrunched inside the bivvy bag in order to stay warm (like homeless people do with newspaper).

As a base level of emergency kit I'd go for a bothy bag, as they can keep you quite warm with two people sat inside (and alive in a storm), even more so if you have a sleeping bag to drape over your legs. If you can add in a bivvy bag each for more warmth and have some warm layers this can be good enough for mild weather. Snuggling up together is also a good option, and the warmth of another person cannot be overstated, especially if you're the giver not the taker.

NIGHT CLIMBING

Learning to climb in the dark, to feel confident and not intimidated is vital, as often you'll be starting in the dark, finishing in the dark, or maybe even climbing right through the dark!

Head Torches: A good quality head torch is vital, with brand new or fully charged batteries, not some you 'think' are good. If you're starting in the dark and going into the dark you can easily zap your batteries, and there's a big difference between a bright beam and a dull beam after 22 hours. I would always say to carry your spare batteries in a head torch, and make sure you have at a minimum one spare torch per team, as head torches are very, very droppable (have a clip loop going from your head torch to your helmet). Having run down all my batteries on both torches I had once, I can tell you having no light on top of a wall is pretty much a survival scenario, you cannot muddle through, and you will have to stop until it gets light.

Micro Naps: The ability to catch '30 winks' can make a huge difference, as if you push it long enough you will begin to nap unconsciously, only realising you were asleep when you wake up, like falling asleep at the wheel. The military teach that just sleeping 15 minutes every four hours allows sustained action over many days, and in a three person team, allowing one person to doze off on the belay is the ideal. Once, when soloing Aurora, a speed team came through, doing a push ascent that ended up taking two days. By the time they reached me they were wasted, and as the leader led the A4 crux of the route in the dark, his two teammates hanging on my belay, I woke up to find everyone was asleep, well apart from the leader. If you find that you're getting slower and slower, and maybe unable to climb safely (falling asleep mid lead is OK if you're aiding, but not free climbing), then consider a team nap, stick on your clothes and snuggle up for 15 minutes. One thing you should not do until you reach the top is slip into REM sleep (45 min - 120 min), as you will wake feeling far more exhausted than you would after just sleeping for 15 minutes. Just for the

record, the record for staying awake is around 264 hours (11 days), so think about that when you watch the sun rise for a second time.

Night Swimming: Be aware that at night the rock can change, things come out, strange creatures, frogs and bats and silver fish. Things are different. Another factor is that as the rock begins to cool at night, moisture will often condense on it, making it slippery, important to know if you're free climbing. Darkness can also affect you and your teammates mood, and slow the whole thing down, which isn't so bad if it makes you safer.

SPEED CLEANING

Speed cleaning is the same as normal cleaning, only faster. Here you will tend to have less gear to clean, which can make ascending the rope a little harder as it will often be free hanging. Where you win and lose is having your shit together, so that the second the leader shouts 'rope fixed', you're leaving the belay. Leaving your ascenders on your aiders means you can just clip the top ascender on, pull yourself tight on your ABBD, sit on that and strip the rest.

Racking: As you clean, try and rack everything in size order, with all nuts and non cams going on a separate krab and stripped of quickdraws. It's worth clipping draws into bunches, one into the other, maybe five at time, meaning you can just hand over bunches of draws at the belay, rather than one draw at a time.

SIMUL CLIMBING

Moving together is one of the traditional ways to speed things up, used originally on alpine routes where time is always ticking.

Emergency bivvy using a hammock on Lurking Fear

On big walls the technique can also be employed when free climbing, allowing the team to move over long sections where neither the leader aids or the second uses ascenders. In my own experience this has often been at the bottom and tops of walls, where the angle changes, but you don't want to employ short fixing.

On really easy ground, 3rd class, or scrambling, then moving together with some protection placed between you is often good enough, maybe shortening the rope (then both climbers should take kiwi coils), so that rope drag is not an issue (easy ground leads to more drag).

But what about when the climbing is harder, where you could fall but are fairly sure you won't? Well here you can employ a progress capture device (PCD).

PCD Belay

A PCD is any device that allows the rope to run in one direction but not the other, so anything from a handled ascender to a Micro Traxion. In this case we are really talking about the smaller PCDs such as the Petzl Tibloc, Kong Duck or Wild Country Ropeman, which are ideal, with other devices such as the Micro Traxion also working well (plus you'll probably already have one of those with you). The use of a PCD as a belay is an advanced technique and so requires the highest level of skill in order to not actually increase your exposure to dangerous falls. As with all such techniques you need to practise this before using it on actual big walls.

BASIC PRINCIPLE

With this setup the leader sets off, and when they reach the belay instead of bringing up the second climber, they attach a PCD to the rope and clip this in,

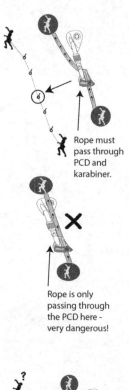

Rope must pass through PCD and karabiner.

Rope is only passing through the PCD here - very dangerous!

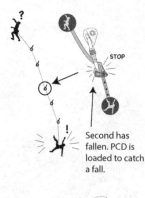

Second has fallen. PCD is loaded to catch a fall.

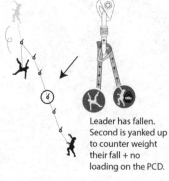

Leader has fallen. Second is yanked up to counter weight their fall + no loading on the PCD.

and then continue to climb. The second now follows, with the rope passing up through the PCD. If the second falls, the PCD locks on the rope and holds them, and if the leader falls, the weight of the second acts as a break as usual, with no load coming onto the PCD. Using this system it's possible for both climbers to move together for many hundreds of metres, placing a PCD at each belay point.

PCD Anchors

The anchor has to be multi directional, (the leader might fall before they place their next piece), and will ideally be a single bolt onto which the PCD is clipped, but due to the fact you will be placing gear all along the route, and it is really acting as a runner for the leader and usually only taking the load of a falling second, you can go for a single solid piece, such as a solid cam, tree or fixed piece.

Clipping In The PCD

Make sure you familiarise yourself fully with the PCD, how it works, how it doesn't work. Some PCDs require a particular style of locker to work correctly, otherwise they will not lock on the rope, with the Tibloc working best for example with 10 mm round bar krabs (not I-Beam style), such as the Petzl Owall. When clipping this into the rope make sure the rope not only passes through the PCD but also through the karabiner, so the karabiner takes the load of a leader fall rather than the device (which may fail or even chop or damage your rope). Once clipped in, double check it's running well and then start climbing.

Shortening The Rope

You'd imagine that having the leader climb sixty metres, making an anchor for the PCD, then moving on, would be the best way to employ this system, but in reality this causes far too much rope drag, poor communications, and variations in speed, with the leader often on very different terrain to the second.

In real life you want the leader and second to be a standard pitch length apart, which tends to be more like 40 metres, as the leader will not have too much drag then, and there won't be so much stretch in the rope the second will drop too far if they pop off.

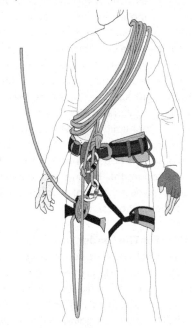

To shorten the rope, the second can either just take coils (kiwi/alpine coils), and clip into the rope, or do the same but leave their belay device on, ideally an ABBD, after their knot (using a clove hitch allows the knot to be unclipped one handed). Using an ABBD means that if they find they're on a crux move but the leader stops moving, perhaps because they're also struggling, they can pull some slack through on the ABBD, and take in their own rope. This also allows the second to batman up the rope if need be, taking in their slack, or put the leader on belay by making a belay, dropping the coils, and belaying as normal. When taking in rope on an ABBD be careful to keep full control of all long loops, otherwise they're bound to get snagged.

Care For The Second

When leading you should try and imagine where your second is in relation to the climbing you've just done. If you can see them below doing some hard moves you should make sure you keep moving to take in the rope, and if that's not possible then you should just pull in the rope until they're over it, then move on. Remember you are effectively being belayed by your second, with their bodyweight acting as a counterweight to yours, so you can climb pretty much close to your limit, but just try and keep your second informed about what you're doing, as you don't want the second to run on ten metres behind you, creating loads of slack in the rope, as you're climbing the crux moves.

Care For The Leader

The most dangerous thing you can do as the second in a simul team is to run on too far, allowing slack to build up between you both, as a fall will shock load the PCD, maybe damaging the rope, plus it is exposing the leader to a greater fall (would you want to be leading the crux on a pitch only to look down and see 10 metres of slack at your belayer's feet?).

SHORT FIXING

Of all the speed climbing techniques, the one that really cuts down the time is short fixing, a system whereby you pretty much eliminate all waiting at the belays, often the time spent there only a few seconds before you move on. The ability to short fix comes down to a very high level of partnership and communication, speed of rope ascending and self confidence to rope solo pitches, and so is a combined system of speed. Here I will cover the two main systems, the single rope two person team, and the double rope three person team, but first start with the concept.

Basics

Short fixing removes the need to wait for the second to arrive at the belay and begin belaying, or starting their lead, by the climber simply pulling up some lead rope, fixing it to the belay, then belaying themselves up the next pitch as the second ascends the one below. On reaching the belay, the second puts the leader on belay, and unties the rope allowing them to climb as normal. If gear is to be transferred, it can be pulled up on a zip/haul/rap line, or a loop of rope sent down, or just pulled up on the rope if no gear has been placed.

Fixing Short

When you arrive at the belay you first need to pull up as much rope as you think you'll need to get you to the point when the second will arrive. If you're looking up at some 5.6 free climbing then you might want to pull up all the rope you have, giving you perhaps twenty metres to play with. If on the other hand you're facing some hard nailing or technical climbing, then maybe ten metres will do, as this will be quicker and give the second some rope if they need it for lower outs etc when cleaning. It's best not to have to deal with too much rope, but then there's little worse when speed climbing than sitting waiting for the second when out of rope.

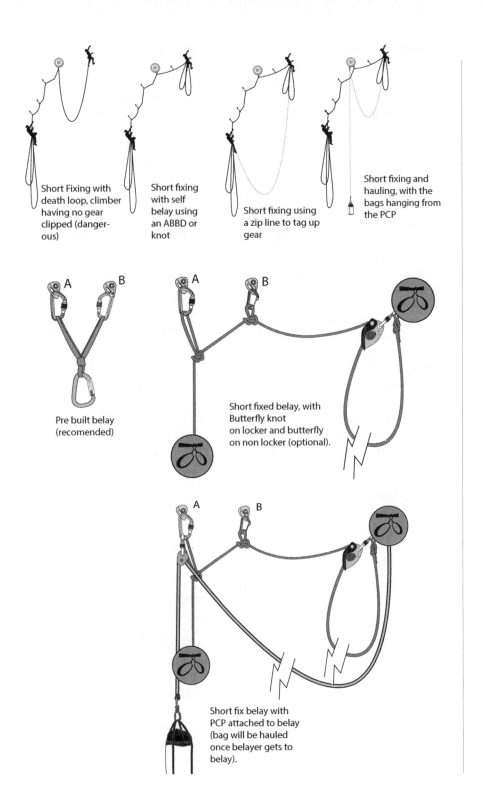

Short Fixing with death loop, climber having no gear clipped (dangerous)

Short fixing with self belay using an ABBD or knot

Short fixing using a zip line to tag up gear

Short fixing and hauling, with the bags hanging from the PCP

A B

Pre built belay (recomended)

A B

Short fixed belay, with Butterfly knot on locker and butterfly on non locker (optional).

A B

Short fix belay with PCP attached to belay (bag will be hauled once belayer gets to belay).

Fixing The Belay

How you attach your rope to the belay depends on how close to the bone you want to go. As you're only fixing a rope to be ascended and potentially hold a 2:1 fall then two bolts are good, and you can set up a two krab, 120 cm sling and locker belay point as you would normally, and can have this belay set up and pre tied and ready to go. An alternative is to forgo the sling and just clip the fixed line into bolt 'A' with a butterfly knot (easy to untie after loading), and then again into the second bolt, bolt 'B'. The beauty of this setup is the second, on reaching the belay, can clip their own rope into bolt 'B', put their belay device onto the rope, and then untie the butterfly knot on bolt 'A', clipping into both with their lanyards and aiders, and taking in the slack between the leader and belay (or leave leader to belay themselves while they get set up). If speed is all you're interested in then just fix the rope with a butterfly knot to a single bolt and keep on chucking, one bolt acting as belay (for factor 2 fall) and fixing point.

Self Belaying

How you self belay at the start of your pitch depends on how good and how confident you are, and how sure you are you won't fall.

- **Death Loop**: If the next pitch is a big bolt ladder or a scramble up some ledges, then you might just lead with a big death loop between you and the belay, kind of free soloing, but with a rope. If you've got some hardish free climbing then unfortunately this is one of the only ways to climb without straining against knots or jamming belay devices, but this approach is best avoided unless you're supremely confident.

- **Figure Of Eight**: The next option is to use a figure of eight (or overhand) knot to belay yourself, just tying it a few metres along the rope and leaving the death loop hanging down, or tie a series of knots so as to control your loop a little (vital in windy conditions, where a stuck loop ten metres away will really slow your day to a stop). This is a good technique as it's fast and easy.

- **Clove Hitch**: You can get some fine adjustment by tying a clove hitch on a HMS krab and just paying it out as you go (by clipping a krab into the knot you can use this to pull through slack with one hand). This is a better approach if the climbing is actually hard and you want to feel you're not running out the rope.

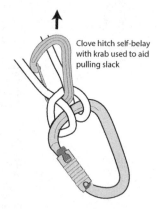

Clove hitch self-belay with krab used to aid pulling slack

- **ABBD**: If you want to move without having to pay out knots, and especially if you're free climbing and don't want to be feeding out with one hand, then using an ABBD can make it a little easier. I would highly recommend anyone who wants to use an ABBD should first practise rope soloing beforehand, so they know it's limitations and its advantages (there is no drag).

The most crucial aspect of the ABBD is how much slack you have between the device and its backup knot. If there's too much, then the weight of the loop will cause the ABBD to catch, while too little and it'll run out too fast. The backup knot is usually an overhand knot clipped to the belay loop (a backup knot is used, as an ABBD is not designed for self belay), but you can run the rope through a PCP, allowing you to pull through slack as you climb.

The limits to actual free climbing with this method are considerable and speed free climbing tends to be done by someone soloing on a death loop, with an ABBD only used for climbing fast on aid and easy free. The hardest free pitch I've used an ABBD on was 5.9R, where fifteen metres up, without any gear, the leg retainer tab caught in the cam of my Micro Traxion, pulling it off the rope, and so all the backup loop dumped itself.

The basic thing is if something can fuck you up, it will fuck you up! For a fuller grasp of rope soloing please read 'Me, Myself and I'.

Back On Belay

It's vital when you reach the belay, the second puts the leader on belay quickly and BEFORE they untie them from the belay, something that is often done the wrong way round, with the fixed rope being untied, then fed into the belay device, meaning a fall during that moment between untying and getting the leader on belay, would be to the end of the rope!

HAULING

You can haul with this system by the leader attaching a PCP into the belay and pulling through an equal amount of haul line as lead line, the belayer knowing that when the lead is fixed then so is the haul line. They then release the bag, and can haul it when they reach the belay, using an ABBD to belay while hauling. If the ground is more complex than the leader can haul before soloing off. Due to the haul bag being much lighter when speed climbing, maybe even just a few kilos of water, hauling is always fast.

COMMUNICATION

Try and keep all communication simple, with one signal that says the rope is fixed, with a yelp or monkey call being a good signal, and hand or arm signals good if it's very windy and you can see each other. If you can't hear or see anything, but the rope runs out fast (but not fall fast), then stops, give it a minute, then apply some force to see if the rope budges. If it seems fixed, it probably is.

CLIMBING AS A THREE

A three person short fixing team is a great way to climb fast without getting beat up. With this system each person only has to climb one third of the wall, and you can play to different skills, with the best free climber doing some parts, the best aider others, and the third climber making sandwiches. If you're climbing into the dark the third climber can also have a sleep, which can really keep things fresh.

To climb as a three you need to have a haul line that can be safely ascended, such as a static 9 or 10 mm. When the leader fixes the rope to the belay they pull up as much haul line as fixing lead line, then put it through the PCP (so the climber is ascending the rope held by the PCP's cam) making sure to also tie it off (Butterfly knot) to the belay in case the PCP's cam fails. The third person then ascends the haul line with the haul bag hanging from it (remember the bag is very light when speed climbing so this is OK), so the third person and cleaner are all moving, and in fact everyone is moving. Once they reach the belay, they set up to haul, and put the leader on belay.

Getting Gear

When short fixing, you tend to carry a rack and a half, and place as little gear as possible, just enough to be safe and to allow your second to ascend easily. Ideally you can lead through without needing to wait for gear, so knowing what's coming up is important, saving the vital gear. The easiest way to get gear is via your haul/zip line, clipped into a loop by the cleaner as soon as they get there, and pulled up when you've got time. Some climbers just carry a short line for pulling up gear, maybe 20 metres of 5 mm cord (their lower-out line), leaving one end tied to the belay, but being up a wall with only one rope is never a good idea, even if your rap line is in the haul bag.

3 PERSON SPEED TEAM

Before short fixing was invented, the way walls were climbed fast was with a three person speed team, which I will cover here as it's still a good way to climb walls fast, and can be adapted to short fixing or standard ascents as well.

Basic Principle

With the 3 person speed team when the leader reaches the belay they pull up the haul line and a second lead line with their zip line, then the third climber climbs this second lead line as fast as possible, the second climber lowering out the haul bags, then cleaning the pitch. Once at the belay the third climber leads off on the new lead line and zip line. In this way the only down time between leads is the time it takes for the third climber to climb the rope.

Pros And Cons

The standard system requires an extra lead line, and also a haul and zip line, so four ropes, whereas short fixing only needs two. An advantage over short fixing is that the new leader is fresh, and being belayed by the first climber, can lead the whole following pitch before the second climber has cleaned the previous pitch, very likely if the next pitch is a free pitch. This approach also keeps putting fresh climbers in the lead, but then that can also be a drawback, as often once 'in the game' it's best to keep the leader going for a block or two. One problem that can occur is that the leader runs out of rack, so hauling some extra with the haul/second lead line is a good idea. This system is very good for hard aid, where the leader is maybe not into doing two death pitches back to back as they would short fixing.

Variations

A more up to date version of this uses longer ropes, such as 70 metre lead and haul lines, and at the belay the leader pulls up as much rope as they can, so they have maybe 20 metres of lead and haul line. The third climber is then lowered out with the bags, jugs the haul line, and begins leading on the rope ends, while the old leader hauls and belays and the second cleans the pitch.

With this system you dump the extra ropes and some of the complexity, but the leader might run out of rope before the second arrives, so it's maybe only good for harder aid. You can also include a second lead line that the third climber jugs up with, the haul line being fed out to them as the bags are hauled (but then on hard aid it's best to have a zip line, so maybe the savings made are not worth it).

Matt Dickinson on an attempted one day ascent of Tangerine Trip

THE WALL

In this chapter I'm going to cover topics that are applicable to the multi pitch world of big walls.

BIG WALL TEAM STRATEGIES

So how are you going to get up this wall? In a team of two, three or four?

Two Person System

This is the classic big wall set up, two climbers, a haul bag, a lead line and a haul line. This is how they ascend:

01. Climber A leads trailing the haul line, and belayed by climber B.

02. On reaching the belay, climber A hauls while climber B cleans the pitch (and minds the haul bag where necessary and possible, helping it over problem ground and freeing it when it gets hung up) using their ascenders.

03. Once the haul bag and both climbers are at the belay, climber B begins leading the next pitch.

Pros And Cons: On the pros side, climbing a wall in a two man team is

very simple and requires minimum gear. However the speed of the team is dictated by both the speed of the leader, and the time it takes to haul and clean each pitch. The pioneering of short fixing was a way of eliminating this dead time, as it meant the leader could begin the next pitch immediately, rather than waiting for the second to arrive and the bags to be up.

Three Person System

This is a great system and has many advantages over the two person system.

01. Climber A climbs, belayed by climber B and C.

02. When A reaches the belay, climber C ascends the haul line.

03. When climber C reaches the belay, climber B releases the haul bag.

04. Climber A hauls while climber B cleans, and climber C prepares to lead.

05. Climber B arrives at the belay and passes the rack from the pitch to climber C, then belays them on the next pitch.

Pros And Cons: I really like a three person team, as it is very low stress, the loads you have to carry on the descent are less (you have the same hardware as a two person team), and you can deal with problems more easily. Best of all, on a hard wall you only need to climb a third of the pitches (although sometimes your third person will just be along for the ride). With this method it's worth carrying a few extra primary cams if you want to start leading before the pitch is cleaned.

Variations: See Speed Climbing in Advanced Techniques.

Four+ Person System

It's rare to climb in very large teams, but it can happen.

01. Climber A climbs, belayed by B, while C and D wait.

02. Climber A arrives at belay.

03. Climber B begins to clean, but leaves end of lead line fixed to belay.

04. Climber C ascends haul line trailing a second lead line.

05. When C reaches belay climber D releases haul bag.

06. Climber B arrives at belay and passes rack to C, then belays them on the next pitch with the new rope as A hauls.

07. Climber D climbs lead line, which now becomes the spare lead line for the next pitch.

Pros And Cons: This is for a 'party wall' and can be fun, but means everyone gets minimal leading. I've used this system with five person teams as well.

Variations: This system can have tons of things bolted onto it, integrating speed climbing techniques and capsule style. For example, instead of climber C bringing up a new lead line (which can be tough), climber A can just pull up some lead line to belay them on until B arrives. D also does not have to wait for B to get off the lead line if B rebelays the lead line (butterfly knot on cam) as they ascend, meaning both can be on the rope at the same time. If the pitch is traversing though, it is vital that D (the last climber up), has enough lead line to lower themselves out from the belay. Alternatively C can leave gear clipped for D to clean. A capsule style approach would leave all the hauling to C and D, with A and B doing all the leading (swapping each day). With this approach you will need at least one extra rope to fix, so A and B can leave one fixed line between belays (C climbs fixed line with haul line, D lowers out bag, then climbs same line as C).

Strategy Notes:

How Many Pitches?

On easy walls you can of course climb many pitches in a day, the speed pretty much the same as when free climbing if you get your shit together. On harder walls of A2+ and above you should aim to climb four pitches a day, meaning most walls can be climbed with four or five bivvies. On harder walls just climbing two pitches a day can be as much as you can handle, which means, when adding in the easy pitches you always find along the way, most hard walls will take around seven to ten days. Doing even pitches has the advantage that the same person leads each morning, while the other ends late, meaning you can divide the route up for morning or night climbers.

Timings: It's always best to start when it's cool and finish before it gets dark, so getting up at sun up is a good idea, and ideally get the leader up and leading asap (you can have a leisurely breakfast while packing up).

Pushing It: If you're doing a non speed ascent, but need to get to the top at a certain time (work or flight) then set a rigid pitch per day rate, and stick to it, even it means you're climbing into the night. I was once invited to speak at Banff and was still on El Cap the day before my flight, having decided to try and squeeze in one more wall. If I'd climbed one less pitch on any number of days that week on the wall I'd have missed my flight.

Block Leading: This works well as long as the climbing is not too stressful, with one leader climbing two or more pitches before handing over the lead. This technique works by making the most of the leader's momentum, plus the leader will be rested after waiting for the second to clean the pitch (while waiting they can haul, semi haul, or leave the bags to the second to deal with if the ground is super steep).

BELAYS

On a wall, be it a trad belay or a bolt belay, your belay is like a small island of safety, a safe harbour as you sail across the wall, and so it's best to be a good harbour master! Here I'll go through both basic and advanced techniques to do with belays, some of which overlap with Hauling and Placements chapters.

A free climbing belay may never be tested, beyond the belayer leaning against it to rest their tired legs, but a big wall belay always gets tested, and tested hard. The forces applied on a standard wall are pretty big, with things like hauling, your partner cleaning, you sat on the belay twiddling your thumbs, a factor 2 fall, all meaning many hundreds of kilos, with just the static load for example being around 300 kgs at one time. Scale that up to a harder wall, with three team members and ten days water and kit, space hauling as the second cleans, and you're looking at maybe 500 kg, stressing every part of the belay. Now throw in storms and flying portaledges, stripping a pitch to the belay in a fall, or teams passing each other out on a wall, and you can have some crazy forces in play. There is nothing more terrifying than being on a shield of rock, you and your bags hanging from some vintage junk hangers, imagining at any moment the belay might rip.

S.E.R.E.NE

I've experienced a whole gamut of belays, from A6 belays made from a matrix of bird beaks and micro nuts on poor limestone, and expanding belays (where cams shifted once the weight came onto them, with some popping or inverting as the crack opened up), to bolt belays so solid you could hang a battleship from them! On all these walls I've always tried to conform to the S.E.R.E.NE standard.

- **S (Strong):** The belay must be solid and provide 100% security, even if some of its component parts are marginal (it is the 'masterpoint' that must be strong, not necessarily the 20 pieces it is drawn from!).

- **E (Equalised):** In order to achieve this strong belay you must equalise everything.

- **R (Redundant):** Belays must contain more than one piece to allow for some failure.

- **E (Efficient):** Speed is important, especially on speed ascents, but not at the expense of safety.

- **NE (No Extension):** If one or more pieces should fail the belay must remain solid - no shock-loading.

Does A Belay Need To Work For An Upward Force?

On a bolted anchor this of course is unimportant, as the belay is multi directional, while on a trad belay it is also often unnecessary, as the weight on the belay will be considerable. If the belay could be judged as being marginal (many poor pieces that only work in one direction (such as small nuts and beaks), then try and incorporate some upward placements, so as to secure the masterpoint from being yanked upwards.

The Role Of The Belay

With a free belay, its purpose is to act as a secure anchor for the belayer to bring up the second (holding both their weights), and then withstand a factor 2 fall onto the belay, achieved via the S.E.R.E.NE standard.

On a big wall the belay has more demands put on it, including:

- **Hauling Station:** The big wall belay must allow one or two climbers to raise and dock the haul bags, and be strong enough to withstand a factor 1 fall if the bags become unattached.

- **Safeguard The Cleaner:** The cleaner's rope will be fixed to the belay, so it must allow the cleaner to ascend the rope safely.

- **Belay Station:** It needs to allow the belayer to belay the leader on the next pitch and must be able to withstand a factor 2 fall.

- **Bivvy Station:** It needs to allow the safe suspension of portaledges.

Belay Components And Tools

Before I get into the belay set up let's just look at the parts of the belay first, both the hardware and software, and the points of interest within the belay. This will need reading twice as it's highly complex with lots of overlapping info.

Masterpoint And Its Locker

The masterpoint is where you draw the strength of your belay to a single point. This is where the highest load will be applied, both when hauling and then when hanging your bags. This is where all the action is. In most cases team members will not hang directly off the masterpoint, moving a little higher instead and hanging from the anchors on either side via their lanyards (it's best if the belayer can reach all parts of the belay, including the top anchors). The only time the team would be attached and hanging from the masterpoint would be when the belay is marginal. The high loading on this point means that you need to use a very high strength link here, and you have a number of options:

- **Naked:** Here you simply clip into the loops formed by your sling or cord, removing the need for any extra piece of gear. Although simple, the drawback with this is that your PCP and other krabs will bunch up, often making it impossible to unclip karabiners that are no longer loaded (say your PCP after you've tied off your haul bag). This approach is perhaps fine when very light hauling is being done (speed ascent), or no hauling at all, just the fixing of ropes, but otherwise I'd go for a hard point.

- **HMS (Open System):** A HMS locker is the ideal shape for this task as it has plenty of volume for karabiners and ropes, plus its smooth curve stops karabiners shifting, clicking or becoming jammed, with the loaded krab always pushing the others out of the way (unlike with a D shaped karabiner). I would pick a hot forged large HMS auto locker with a very high strength open (8 kN+) or closed (22 kN+), the open strength vital when you are forced to open it when fully loaded, with the DMM Boa (25 kN/86 g), BD Rocklock (87 g / 24 kN) or Petzl William (27 kN / 90 g) being ideal, and I would go for a twist lock over a screwgate. Also make sure the locker has a gate limit, so that it can't be over tightened when heavily loaded and become impossible

to undo. Although your masterpoint locker can be opened, it's a good idea not to open it, but rather clip other karabiners into it, so your PCP is clipped in with its own locker for example, as is the belayer's rope, so that anything can be removed without being jammed in by anything else (the only non karabiner going into the masterpoint locker will be the docking cord on your haul bags).

- **Rigging Plate (Closed System):** A very light and strong alternative to using a HMS is to create a closed system, where nothing can be opened, only clipped/tied into. This is created by using a small rigging plate (the DMM Bat Plate XS (35 g / 36 kN) works best due to its rope friendly nature), with the cordelette pre threaded through it and tied. This gives you three primary clipping options on the plate for, A: PCP, B: belayer's rope, and C: docking cord, with the clip hole also taking karabiners (as well as the loops). The benefits of this system are, it means a small package on your harness, with the cord pre threaded and tied (works well with 240 cm of 5 mm Dyneema), and it should ensure jammed ropes and krabs do not happen. If using a two bolt station you clip two arms into one bolt, and the third into the other. If you want less rope, then tie out the knot with an overhand knot. Once you have the correct position, then tie an overhand into the cord isolating the rigging plate. You can further improve this system by threading a large alloy anchor ring (DMM 26 mm anchor ring 30 kN / 39 g), and tying this out of the main overhand knot, creating a closed clip in point on top of the shelf. The total set up weighs around 170 grams. The use of a plate can also make the setting up of 2:1 and 3:1 pulley systems a little simpler.

The Shelf

This is the area above the masterpoint knot, the separate strands of the belay, clipped into so as to free up the masterpoint, which can become cluttered. Climbers wanting to secure themselves at the belay should consider the shelf as an option, to avoid overloading the masterpoint or bolt lockers, and this is also a good place to clip in belay seats or rack bags. If you're hauling a belay kit then consider having two dedicated shelf lockers (one for each kit), the lightweight HMS being the best, or the pre threaded anchor/rap ring.

Fixing Point

This is where you attach the lead rope leading up from the lower belay, securing it, and so fixing the cleaner's rope so they can climb. This can be clipped to the masterpoint (traditional method creates a separate masterpoint to the hauling masterpoint), but I would clip it off to a solid anchor to one side, so offline from the haul bags/haul line. It should ideally be clipped to the highest solid piece on the side where the next pitch begins, so the second can just start leading off from their ascenders (this will save a great deal of time). The forces here are low (body weight) to zero (if rope is fixed to last piece of protection also via a Butterfly knot), and the rope will also be backed up to the masterpoint, as well as tied to the leader. If you want optimum organisation then have two small specific 40 g +/- lockers, one on each belay kit. This will remove the chance of the lead rope being clipped onto something that cannot be unclipped later.

Anchor Points

These will usually be the bolts on the belay, which will generally number two or three bolts, and most will feature large hangers big enough to hold two lockers. If you're just moving up the wall and the belay is good then just clip two bolts, as the third is probably for a portaledge (if climbing as a three then clip all three). On a trad belay you may have multiple anchor points of varying strength, and this often requires the equalising of several sub anchor points (body weight), to create a single anchor point, several of these equalised further to create the masterpoint.

Anchor Point Karabiner

Using large HMS locking karabiners is the ideal, as they give you plenty of room to clip into, and avoid other krabs becoming jammed into a tight bottom radius. The drawback is that this style of karabiner is heavy (90 g), but the smaller HMS karabiners (50 g) work too. Non lockers can also be used, such as the super light 19 g krabs, but you should avoid clipping anything into them apart from your belay components (this also applies to micro lockers). If using non lockers then I would advise against stripping these from your quickdraws, and instead include your anchor point krabs in your rack kit (having 1 large HMS, 1 small HMS and 1 micro locker is a good compromise).

Cordelette & Slings

The type of cordage or slings you use to create your belay varies depending on the type of route, team size, expected loads and anchor complexity. On speed climbs, often you never really make a belay, you just clip into a bolt with a locker, tie in an alpine butterfly and you're good (the rope is fixed), while on fast walls (alpine style, like the Nose or Lurking Fear), then a 120 cm sling is fine, just tie an overhand knot and you're done. If you're moving fast then you can also pre build your belays, having a 120 cm sling with a small locker on each end (40 g lockers work well), and a light but strong HMS tied in already (or a pre-tied rigging plate). For most walls though, the cordelette is ideal, as it allows a fair degree of adjustability and flexibility, with the height of the masterpoint being more adjustable than with 120 cm slings. What kind of cordelette you use depends on how you employ your belay kit:

- **Belay Kit:** The gear you will carry with you on a wall for setting up belays needs to be light and able to do the job. It's a good idea to have the gear to set up a two bolt belay ready, without having to strip off karabiners from your draws. My recommendation would be a minimum of a 240 cm (16 foot) 8 mm/10 mm dyneema sling, or 7 mm cord or 5 mm Dyneema cord, with 240 g+/- lockers and a large masterpoint HMS or rigging plate.

- **Belay Kit Bag:** This is an alternative method where the leader carries no belay kit, and simply pulls the haul line and belay kit up with the zip line. The bag contains everything the leader needs, which can be a cordelette as above, or longer (300 cm/20 foot) cordelette made from 8 mm cord, and three lockers - masterpoint, shelf and fixing locker. It's also worth having an extra cordelette in the bag, plus water. When using this method. I will also send up the belay seat and perhaps a rope bag to stow the haul line when the leader starts hauling.

Using The Lead Line: An alternative to using a cordelette is to simply use the lead line.

The advantages of this are:

- Less to carry.
- Stronger.
- Knots are easier to untie.
- More dynamic.
- You tie yourself in by default while building the belay.

The downside is that you are using up part of your rope, say three metres, so six metres at both ends, which can be a problem when climbing long pitches or when linking pitches.

Now let's put all these components together:

Traditional Big Wall Belay

The old standard belay set up was to create two separate masterpoints, one as the hauling point, the other for fixing the cleaner's rope. This setup no doubt came about when belays were a little more dubious, and is less necessary these days, with a single bolt as strong as an entire old school belay. Downsides of this traditional system include needing two cordelettes, extra karabiners, and the unnecessary complexity of it, with the load of the cleaner actually being low and also static. For this reason I'd resign this one to the bin.

Modern Belay

The modern big wall belay creates a single masterpoint and is designed to be as simple as possible, while also being as strong as possible. Here is an example of a leader setting up their hanging modern belay:

01. Leader arrives at two 10 mm stainless bolts with a small foot ledge six feet below.

02. Leader clips their lanyard into right bolt and hangs from this.

03. Leader removes cordelette from back of harness and taking the two small lockers (A and B) clips each one into a bolt, leaving cordelette clipped to locker on left bolt.

04. Leader pulls up several metres of slack on the lead line and ties alpine butterfly knot into rope and clips this to left bolt with locker A. This is the anchor point for the cleaner's rope. This should ideally be the bolt from which the leader will climb on from, so they don't have to climb over the bags.

05. Leader now takes lead line and clips it into last piece of protection used to reach the belay (with alpine butterfly), so that all the weight of the cleaner is held by last piece, not the belay, stopping the rope getting in the way of hauling.

06. The leader now clips the cordelette into locker A and B and draws it down to create an overhand knot that creates a masterpoint five feet above the ledge.

07. Leader attaches the masterpoint karabiner to the masterpoint.

08. Leader clips his lead rope into the masterpoint leaving enough slack to haul and move around the belay, depending on his lanyards as his primary connection points (he can use a locker to do this, or clip directly into the masterpoint, or simply tie into it with a bowline on a bight).

09. In a traditional climbing situation the leader would now shout 'safe', but not on a big wall unless it's easy to talk.

10. The leader now takes the karabiner clipped to the end of the haul line and fed through the PCP, and pulls it up and clips it high into locker A, which is attached to bolt from which the leader will leave the belay (this reduces the chance of forgetting the haul line).

11. Now the PCP (still attached to the haul line), is removed and clipped into the masterpoint.

12. The haul line is taken in through the PCP until the haul line comes tight on the back up knot on lower belay.

13. When the backup knot is untied by lower belayer they know that this is a signal that the haul line is **IN THE PCP** and the leader is secure (do not haul up all the haul line, **THEN** attach the PCP).

14. With the backup knot now untied below, the leader hauls the rope tight to the bags, making sure PCP cam is engaged, and shouts "Ready to haul!!!!".

15. If belayer is unable to hear the leader shout "ready to haul" they should view the haul line being pulled tight to the bags as the signal to undock the bags. Belayer waits one minute, shouts "bags away", **THEN** undocks the bags and lowers them out.

16. Now the belayer is free to break down the belay and start cleaning, as the lead rope is always secured before the haul line (worst case scenario is leader forgot, and rope comes tight on masterpoint not top piece of gear or top bolt, and worst-worst case scenario is rope comes onto leader's harness).

17. The leader can have a little breather, have a drink and get set up to haul.

18. The belayer strips the belay and ascends the rope, and cleans the pitch, the rope coming onto the left bolt (out of the line of the haul bags) when they remove the rope from the final piece of gear.

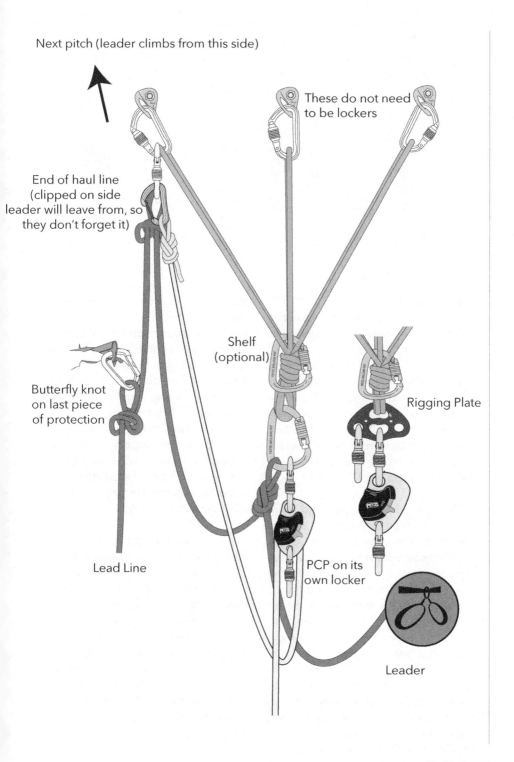

Next pitch (leader climbs from this side)

These do not need to be lockers

End of haul line (clipped on side leader will leave from, so they don't forget it)

Butterfly knot on last piece of protection

Shelf (optional)

Rigging Plate

Lead Line

PCP on its own locker

Leader

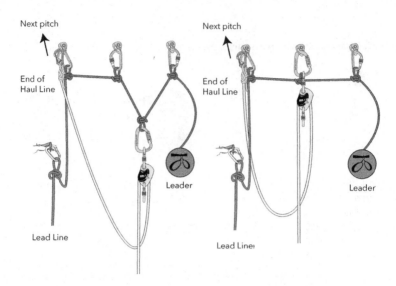

Next pitch

End of
Haul Line

Leader

Lead Line

Next pitch

End of
Haul Line

Leader

Lead Line₁

Banshee Belay

A modern bolted belay will have two or three full strength stainless steel bolts featuring solid hangers, everything rated at a minimum of 20+ kN (don't confuse a 44 kN hanger as meaning the bolt is 44 kN, and instead assume all modern anchors are 20 kN). In such situations why would you go to all the fuss of fretting over equalising everything, all that faff with slings and cordelettes when you can belay off a single point?

This is a good question and there are times when it might be a good idea to bypass convention and go for a non-equalised option, perhaps hauling direct from one high bolt, fixing the lead line to the other. Hauling from a higher bolt, rather than a lower masterpoint created from two, can make hauling a little easier when hauling onto a ledge, but less so than you'd assume, as the masterpoint will be in the same line. When speed climbing you may also want to bypass convention and just fix a rope to a single bolt, plus when belaying you do spend most of your time hanging off just one bolt. But such rule breaking

must be matched with a healthy paranoia, that 'what if' that keeps us alive. Modern bolts are religiously tested, but those who place them are not. Holes are botched (drill bits too big for the bolt), or bolts are left untightened or not effective in the rock type (I've seen countless junk bolts in sandstone). I myself have placed one bomber bolt only to find I could wiggle it back out due to the large crystal structure of the rock. There is also the issue of bolts that were not bolts at all, just machine headed bolts hammered into a hole, a 1 kN bolt in a 30 kN hanger!

For this reason I would not recommend direct belaying unless the leader is 100% sure they can identify the quality/security of all bolts (such as Yosemite trade routes). Instead, climbers should treat any fixed gear with some small (or large) suspicion as nothing is unbreakable or unfuckupable. So always follow the S.E.R.E.NE standard in your systems, and spread the load around so any gear failure is not terminal (what I'm saying is it's best to just stick to the current belay set up!).

Mescalito belay

Natural Belay

Setting your own belays using trad gear is one way of learning how to place solid gear and get it all working together, and I often think this is one of the best cross-over skills a big wall climber can take into trad or alpine climbing. When using what features the rock offers up, you are often not afforded nice inline horizontal belay points, where you can spread your gear out, but rather gear placed in cracks that mean a bunched up belay. When setting such belays try and use gear that will not be needed above, and any route that requires trad belays must take this into account, meaning more nuts, cams and pegs (this is one reason for bolted belays, in that such routes require just a lead rack). When setting natural belays take the following into account:

- **Loading:** When the load comes onto your gear, it can create some large forces, and often it can be very hard to create perfect equalisation with your cordelette, so more force comes onto some pieces rather than others. Really small gear, such as micro nuts or the smallest cams might break under the strain, perhaps not due to being overloaded (remember that a small micro only has a 200 kg loading), but because the rock flexes, small cams inverting and breaking, something you won't face with larger nuts, cams or pegs.

- **Egg Basket Cracks:** Be very aware that putting four bomber cams in a single crack is relying on that single crack as much as the four cams, and ideally you want four cams in four cracks! Cracks, by their very nature, are weaknesses in the rock, and so you need to spread the gear as far as you can. I've seen people place five cams

in a roof crack to form a belay, not noticing that the back of the crack was not the wall, but a thin skin of rock that flexed once the weight came onto it. If you're forced to use a single crack or feature, check it's the mountain, not a flake or feature that might move under the loading (several times I put pegs into horizontal cracks, only to find they were just blocks sitting on ledges).

- **Pitons:** Using your big pegs, like baby angles, big beaks and lost arrows, is a good way to achieve solid anchors and save your pro, plus they tend to have a calming effect on the belayer.

- **Cramped Belays:** If the belay is set in a vertical crack everything can get very cramped, even with a two person team. You can try and reduce this by hanging the haul bags lower, attaching their docking cord at the limit of length. This will make it easier for the cleaner to get onto the belay, where they should be placed on belay straight away and move up onto the top piece of gear. If the belay is very cramped and you have a big team, your other member(s) can stay on the previous belay until it's OK to come up (if using a zip line this will be when it's time to haul up the haul line). This approach works well when you're going from a very good ledge to some abysmal bivvy (but don't leave a climber alone who'll get lonely and freak out!).

Marginal Belay

The idea of having a marginal belay might sound like a misnomer on a big wall where you have so much weight, or A6 territory (A5 climbing with a belay that won't hold a fall), but if you're climbing alpine walls or repeating routes, and don't have a bolt kit (bad idea), then you may well come across such belays. Marginal belays come down to two types; bolted and trad.

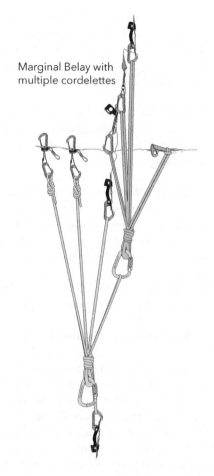

Marginal Belay with multiple cordelettes

piece. The main thing to look for are shitty hangers, old weak designs (SMC or Leeper), or alloy or steel hangers that have corroded. The bolts should always be 'good enough', and actual bolt failure is rarer than hanger failure, and is most often caused by improper placement or incorrect matching of bolts to rock type (short stud bolts placed in sandstone for example). So very often you might have some crappy tin hanger that could break under body weight (Leeper hangers can break around 200 kg if they have stress fractures), but that has a pretty strong 1/4 button head bolt running through it, which un-corroded will be good for at least 500 kg. Here you might be able to slip a #3 rivet hanger or dyneema sling around the back of the hanger, and bypass the hanger. The same applies to Japanese ring bolts, which although consist of a shit hanger and a short bolt, might give you an extra 100 kg if you bypass the ring that's been bent into an oval.

- **Marginal Trad:** On a trad route you really need to find at least one bomber piece, then build out from that, with two less bomber pieces, then four or five bodyweight pieces, then bring the whole matrix to a single master-point. The better you are at sniffing out gear placements and understand-ing the strengths and weaknesses of gear, the more able you are to create a solid belay. For example, a large Black Diamond Pecker, well placed, with a dyneema sling threaded through its clip hole (instead of 2 kN fixed cable), could be as strong as a bolt, whereas a bugaboo in the same place might not be, due to the shape and mechanical action on the rock.

- **Marginal Bolted Belays:** On a marginal bolted belay you might find yourself faced with bolts of dubious vintage, with weak hangers, machine head bolts or homemade anchors. As ever having some grasp of anchor history (or even archaeology!) helps sort out what's what. If someone else has passed this way you might find one good bolt, and so build up from that, but again you need to make sure that everything is equalised and the greatest strength squeezed from each

BELAY NOTES:

Is It Worth It? Ask yourself this before you shout that the rope is fixed, and your mate starts ascending and hauling begins. Consider the outcome of the belay ripping, but also consider that you're gambling with your partner's life as well, that "don't fall off, the belay is shit" moment. Unless it's life and death, you need to talk about going on with the rest of the team, or try and out think the problem, not just put the gun to your head and pull the trigger hoping the chamber is empty.

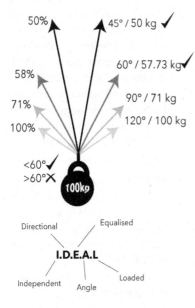

Don't Settle: I've seen three people and their bags hang from three Japanese ring bolts that were not only old and bent out, but also crazily weak already, having a pull strength of only 300 kg (they look like 12 mm bolts, but taper down to 8 mm, and only go in around 15 mm!). What made this worse was just to the side of them was a bomber crack, where you could build a very good belay, the bolts obviously placed long ago before people had a good selection of cams.

So if you've got a shitty belay, look around for some way of boosting it with trad gear, and don't just think "oh everyone else trusted this belay", as you might be the one team whose luck runs out.

Test It All: On a marginal belay bounce test everything, and make sure it will be aligned in the direction of the pull of your belay.

Create A Web: A cordelette is the best way to bring together a large number of pieces, but often the belay might be too complex for this, with pieces too far to reach the arms of the cord. Here you can often create little nests of gear and clip these together with 120 cm slings, then integrate these with your cordelette.

You Determine The Belay: Often on routes that have notoriously bad belays you might find that this reputation was born in an age where protection was not so sophisticated as it is now. Beaks and micro cams and wires can offer up protection were nothing else would once go, but you just need to look. Another factor is people will make do with a shitty belay, and then the first runner is bomber, or the last piece of pro just below the belay. There is nothing wrong with creating a belay from high runners, or low, equalising it all with your ropes, long cordelettes etc. All that matters is you have a good solid belay.

End Of Your Rope: If you've come to the end of your rope and have still to find a belay then, either the rope is too short (some climbers have 70+ metre ropes), meaning you'll need to climb on with your haul line tied into your lead line, or you've climbed past the belay (easy to do at night in particular), or the belay has been removed (8 mm self drives could have been unscrewed by first ascensionist for example). When repeating a route you always need to try and think like the first ascensionist, hoping they weren't crazy. This means that pitches stop on ledges or where hauling can be done well, or climb to the top of features. Digging into the history and background of a route should inform you of how it would have been climbed, for example a French team would probably use 8 mm Petzl self drives and pitons, whereas an American team would place bolts and rivets, a Russian team using removable 10 mm bolts.

The A6 Trick Belay: One way to create the illusion of an A6 belay, one that won't hold a fall, is to run pitches together using your haul and lead line while soloing, all the gear left in the pitch below, then that pitch pushed up as far as your haul line will go. A full 60 metre pitch is a long way, a 70 metre one even further. So if you come to a belay that comprises of just two 1/4 button heads someone might just be playing a trick (and if not, you're best not following their lead!).

Bypass Haul: If you don't want to overload a marginal belay then you can leave the haul bags on the belay below and haul from the next one, bypassing the marginal one. This of course requires more rope, but if you're on a big alpine wall you should have this, or at least a lead, haul and zip line. To bypass haul, once the third belay is reached, the belayer would need to descend the haul line back to the bags and set them up on a cargo hook system (two fifis or karabiner), then return up the haul line and attach this to either the lead line or zip line, then haul the bags two rope lengths. The bags could be left already set up to be hauled remotely, but being attached means you have some small hope in hell if the belay above rips!

BELAYING

When belaying, you are there to keep the leader safe, plus facilitate a situation where they need something sent up to them, and good communication is crucial. For example if the leader sees they'll need a Camalot 4 soon, or more beaks, they need to ask beforehand, so the belayer can have the gear organised and ready to clip onto the haul or zip line.

The belayer can move around, say drop down to get stuff out of bags, or unstick ropes, while keeping the leader on belay, but don't fully trust your ABBD, or your leader not falling while your hand is off the rope.

Always have some kind of back up to the ABBD, or your belay plate, either by giving some slack and tying off the device or tying a large overhand knot into the rope. Belay devices can easily get fouled or snagged on fifi hooks or slings, so it's vital to be a little paranoid.

Big wall falls can sometimes by very hard on the belayer, especially in bleak aid, where falls can be very long (full pitch!). Aid falls will also tend to happen without warning, meaning the belayer cannot brace for a fall. What this means is that often the belayer can be accelerated upwards until they are checked by their lanyards. This of course can be very dangerous. And so it's important that the belayer always wears a helmet, as well as gloves (even with an ABBD).

Advanced Belay

Most climbers will belay from their belay loop, extending themselves from the belay, meaning in a big fall they can be slammed into the rock, a real possibility if you're trying to create a frictionless protection chain (so as to exploit the dynamic properties of your rope fully) .

In the past this lifting action was seen as being a way to reduce the impact force, that the lifting belayer was a damper, but I'm not convinced. I know nothing about engineering but having taken many falls and stopped many falls, some very large, I wonder if the load on the top piece is in fact increased by lifting the opposing weight of the belayer, rather than being attached to a fixed point. This point has been reinforced by many solo falls, where the rope was fixed, versus belayed falls.

The best way to belay on bleak aid would be a body belay, but this is not practical, as the belay also needs to have some kind of auto braking action (vital on a busy belay).

The best method I've come up with for bleak aid is to feed the lead line from your ABBD through a Munter hitch clipped direct to a bolt or your strongest multi directional piece. With leather gloves it's possible to allow some rope to slip through the Munter hitch, with the ABBD acting as a backup further down the rope (you can simply pay out rope via the ABBD and the rope will pass up through the Munter). This means you will have two modes of belaying, passive and active.

Passive will be hands off the ABBD but with a back up knot tied in the rope somewhere (while sorting the rack etc.), and active would be a few metres of slack payed out from the ABBD and the leader being belayed via the Munter. With the passive system the catch will be static while the active gives the opportunity for a dynamic catch (backed up by the ABBD).

Another advantage of this system is the Munter stops the belayer being ranked up, and so creates a fixed load point.

This may sound like a complicated system, but on hard aid the leader may only be moving ten or fifteen metres an hour, so the added drag of the setup is acceptable, and the Munter can be clipped out at any time.

A variation on this technique is the employment of the Edelrid OHM, which reduces the loading on the belayer, but with the downside that it's just something else to carry.

CLIMBING OFF THE BELAY

When the leader is leaving the belay they will probably still be tied on from cleaning the pitch, but it's worth checking as I know of two climbers who set off with only the haul line clipped to the back of their harness!

Get them on belay, and have them move up to the highest anchor as a jumping off point (this is a good spot to check they have everything). When carrying their belay kit (and not hauling it) they will now remove the PCP from the masterpoint and clip it into the karabiner on the end of the haul line which is clipped onto the top bolt. They will then clip the end of the haul line plus PCP to their harness, ideally running the haul line through the PCP first to limit the chance of dropping anything. If using a zip line instead of the haul line, then the same approach is used, only you might only take a PCD such as a ropeman, or a micro PCP.

Having the haul line or zip line ready on the bolt where the leader is leaving reminds them to take it! If this is forgotten, then hopefully someone realises the error sooner rather than later in the pitch, as a loop of rope will need to be dropped down to recover it.

THE LOWER BELAY

When you think the leader is close to the end of the pitch you need to start prepping to go yourself so time is not lost. In no particular order, this could include:

- **Close Up The Bags:** Put everything that can go in the haul bags in, closing them tight, so nothing will snag while hauling. Ideally have what the leader might need while belaying on top (or ready to be attached to the zip line), such as water and food and maybe the belay jacket, with rack bag underneath, and ghetto blaster under that.

- **Put Away The Belay Seat:** Attach the belay seat to the haul bags or get it set up to be pulled up on the zip line. Getting off the belay seat also allows you to get your body ready to move after being on your ass for four hours!

- **Double Check Your Ropes:** As soon as the leader starts pulling up the haul line you want it to run free until it gets close to the back up knot, which should be untied as the rope becomes tight. Remember this is safe, because the leader will be pulling in the slack through the PCP (ideally). Often you might need to unclip the haul line from the haul bags to bypass any tangles, and this should be done early,

as doing this in haste can lead to the haul bag not being clipped back in! Remember the number one sentence that needs to be avoided on a wall is: "Hang on a minute!", as ropes are untangled for example. Also remember to back up the bags if doing this so they are never hanging solely from the docking cord.

- **Have Your Ascenders Ready:** Ascenders need to be ready to go. It's now that you might find you don't have them, so will need to find them or make other arrangements.

- **Get Your Shit Together:** Remember you might have frozen your arse off, but once you start climbing you'll sweat your bollocks off, so take off extra clothes and stuff them in your day/haul bag, or clip them to your harness.

- **Dump The Weight:** Get rid of any rack or junk off your harness and put it in a haul bag, where it can be accessed later. You do not want to start ascending with loads of hardware as you'll be picking that up when cleaning anyway. All you should have is your hammer, funkness, nut tool, the belay kit you'll be taking apart shortly, and your rope tools; ascenders, belay device etc. Remember the best way to lift a load on the wall is on the end of the haul line.

Taking The Belay Apart

Once you've released the haul bags you are free to go, and in front of you there should be the belay slings (or cordelette), masterpoint, lockers, lead rope bag, belay bag, and not much else. Here is how you'd leave the belay assuming you are belaying with an ABBD, and are attached to the belay with two lockers on your lanyards, plus tied in to the master-point or off to a bolt:

01. Take in all the slack on your ABBD until you're hanging from the rope, not your lanyards (remember that unlike a trad belay, the leader does not pull in all the slack, just enough to move around).

02. Take off the lanyard lockers one by one, clipping them into the rope via your ascenders. Remember you will also need one or both of your aiders attached to your lanyard locker(s) depending on the nature of the pitch you are about to ascend.

03. Unclip or untie your rope from the belay.

04. If you have a very long length (loop) of rope you can clip it off short. If it's very windy you can stow it in (or leave it stowed) in the rope bag, and keep stuffing it in as you climb the rope (you will have to restack when you get to the belay above).

05. A variation if you have to lower out a long way from the belay is you clip or tie in short (bowline on a bight), then untie the end of the rope and use this to lower yourself out.

06. You'll now be free of the belay, and can take it all apart.

07. It is best to get into the habit of always breaking apart knots on your slings and racking everything ready for the next lead.

08. Now you are free to clean the pitch.

BELAY NOTES

There are a few things that can make life easier, and more fun, on a belay.

Ship Shape: When on the belay you should get into the habit, and get everyone else into the habit, of keeping everything as neat and tidy as possible, ropes hanked or stuffed into rope bags and hung out to the side (haul line on one side, lead line the other), knots no longer needed untied, and tangles dealt with. Spare rack should be removed and either racked in one place, or put in your tag bag. The reason for being so anal on a wall is that it's good practice because a messy belay is a slow and dangerous belay, kit or people get dropped, or things get jammed and slow down the momentum. In high winds or a storm, which can come at any time, having ropes flying everywhere can be a disaster, and woe betide anyone who lets the haul line get snagged under the haul bags - that's a walking the plank offence.

Rack Bag: It's a good idea to avoid just stuffing your spare rack into the top of your haul bag as this most often leads to dropped kit when looking for other things. Try and keep it all together, or in specific heavy duty stuff sacks with clip loops on them, say one for pegs, one for wires, one for cams and one for other stuff. Have these clipped into the top of your bag so you can dig into them when you need to get something. If you're on a hard nail-up then consider carrying a small haul bag for just this job, using it like a day bag, carrying the rack (in its bag), along with spares clothes, food and water etc. This would be hauled attached to the main haul bag on steep ground, or could be pulled up on the end of the tag line with the belay kit inside it (for this the leader needs a micro Traxion or some kind of PCP).

Belay Racking: When the leader reaches the belay, they tend to take off their big wall chest/racking rig and clip this off between two anchors, so all the loops are easy to access. When the

Docked bag with slippery hitch back up

cleaner arrives they take the cleaned gear and re-rack it on this sling, then it's put on again for the next pitch. But there is often gear that's not needed, or not needed straight away, and this gets left at the belay.

Rack on the belay requires a system if gear is not to be dropped or missed when asked for, vital when tagging.

One of the worst things to do is clip off dozens of pieces into the cordelette, or anchor points, creating a traffic jam of krabs. Here it's easy to unclip the wrong thing, or find what you need jammed up beneath a loaded rope. Worse still is when a sling is used, clipped between two anchors and the rack is clipped into both strands, meaning if one is unclipped the whole lot slides off the end!

The best method is to always carry a multi loop racking daisy/cord, that you clip between anchors and clip the gear in to in groups, such as nuts; big, small, medium, cams, pegs etc. This sling is carried in the tag bag or haul bag, and the gear on it placed into the bag while still on the sling.

Pre Jesus Piece: If the leader has hauled the bags and stacked the rope, they can speed up the transition by placing the first piece of gear. When the second arrives she can be put on belay straight away and then move on up onto this first runner (while still attached to the belay). Off the belay they can rack up more easily.

Music: Having some music on a wall is great, and although this would have been the ghetto blaster these days it tends to be an iPod or phone and a mini speaker. Having the ability to listen to the radio helps to break up the monotony of your mate's collection of James Blunt albums, plus you can get some kind of idea of the weather, and for valley climbers you can't do a route without listening to The Hawk FM! Having a mix of audio-books and podcasts can also be great for killing time if you get stuck for a while, and even better is some TV or films. Such things might sound frivolous, but they can really help to depressurise a team, and can be the difference between sitting out a day waiting for good weather or going down because of boredom. Try and make sure all parts of your music system can be clipped in, and a small mesh bag makes a good Hi-Fi system, as everything can be clipped in nice and safe. Avoid using earphones on a wall as it's important to be able to hear your partner screaming.

Phone: A phone can be both invaluable and a real danger on a wall. With it you can get rescued, or call for help for other teams. You can stay in touch with the real world, even pretend to be at work. If you're online you can check the beta, email climbers to see what they think, plus get up-to-the-minute weather forecasts. The downside is that if people are expecting you to call, and you drop your phone, or run out of juice or phone reception, they're going to worry, and maybe end up ringing for a rescue. Also being in touch with people reduces the isolation, and takes your mind away from the wall - not good on many levels. I was once leading on a wall and heard the belayer talking to himself, only to find he was doing a live interview on the radio. "What do you want to say?", he asked, holding out the handset. "Get off the fucking phone!" I shouted down. If taking a phone, get the direct number for rescue teams and someone on the ground.

Umbrella: Sounds like a luxury? Not if you're climbing a wall in the summer sun! Having even a small umbrella can take some of the sting out of the hottest days, and takes up very little room (go for a small outdoor style model). Make sure it has a clip loop.

Spray: Another luxury? Guess again. Having a small garden spray filled with water can really cool you off, a fine mist speeding up evaporative cooling.

Solar Panel: If you're doing a long wall and want to keep everything charged, then a medium sized solar panel can work really well, especially if you have mammoth belay sessions. A word of warning though is that you will need some sun, something my solar panel sponsored partner found out on the Troll Wall in winter, 14 days of semi darkness not even able to power a robot's fart.

Book: A lot of people make the mistake of bringing a book on a wall, imagining themselves sat reading poetry on the belay, when really there never seems to be the time (or energy), even on all day belay sessions.

Dress For Belaying: On a really cold wall you can freeze your ass off, and even on a hot wall, once the sun goes around the corner and the wind picks up, you can get very cold indeed. Having warm clothes, like a belay jacket, and even belay pants, is a good idea, and remember to put them on before you get cold (once you get cold it's harder to get warm again). Mitts and gloves can also be vital, and on exposed walls you might even want to use a bothy bag to protect the belayer (I've heard of belayers sitting in a haul bag!). If conditions are this bad often it's better to just solo the pitch and let your belayer have a lie in!

Eating And Drinking: Having food and water at hand is vital, and your haul bags should always have both close at hand, your water ration for the day placed where it is needed. Having a water bottle, nalgene or bladder that you fill in the morning is the best approach, and then a stuff sack with bars, nuts etc. in it as well. The colder it is, the more food becomes important to stay warm, and on very cold walls fatty food like sausage is ideal, plus food helps pass the time. Remember that food and drink should come second to keeping the momentum going, and there will be more than enough down time to eat and drink once the bags are off the belay or the leader is on the sharp end.

THE BELAY SEAT

Unless you're climbing a wall in a day, or ledges abound, the belay seat is something you leave behind at your peril! Hanging in your harness for days on end can be a long journey into pain and some legs take months to recover. When sitting in your belay seat you can operate your belay much easier, get gear, tie knots, sort shit out. Belay seats come in five main types:

Wooden DIY belay seat, BD seat, and Yates fabric seat

- **Fabric:** This is the soft, stick in your pocket belay seat, made by people like Fish or Yates, and is good for short belay sessions, plus weighs nothing. This style of seat is good as a second seat, for when setting up a camp etc.

You can also get the soft belay seats that come in BD haul bags, which again are OK for half an hour, and better than nothing, but after that they'll feel just the same.

- **Wooden:** This is the classic design and can be either bought (BD) or made yourself out of a plank (marine ply 30 x 60 cm and some rope (add some foam to the seat). When making your own make sure the cord is long enough, being at least from your bottom to your shoulder (use 7 mm cord). Although heavy, inserting the seat down the back of your haul bag (either in the main bag, or in the slot for the straps), can make carrying a little more comfortable, oh and if you're desperate, you can take out the wooden board and use it to stack with a cam or pegs, make a fire, or use it as a cheese board (or chess board!).

- **Hybrid:** This is the BD soft seat but with a sheet of carbon fibre slipped into it, creating a very low weight and compact belay seat, important if you're carrying it any distance.

- **Hammock:** A hammock can make a great belay seat, clipped into a single point, with both nylon and mesh hammocks working really well. Mesh hammocks are tougher, and won't rip if you lie in one while wearing gear on your harness, while string won't either, but will entrap you like a net (take the gear from your harness first). The biggest downside of a hammock though is that it's so comfortable it's often hard to stay awake, so keep those backup knots tied in your lead rope to jam in your belay device if you nod off.

- **Mini Ledge:** This is the luxury of luxuries, a small folding portaledge, made by Metolius, Fish or D4. This would be best used for really heavy duty belay sessions, where you don't have a full sized ledge to lay on, or for alpine walls or speed ascents, where it might have to be used to sleep on (I spent 14 nights sleeping in a homemade ledge like this, so it is possible as long as you have something for your feet).

- **Portaledge:** A full sized ledge is of course the ideal belay platform. Again just make sure you don't fall asleep belaying. The downsides of using your ledge are that in windy conditions, the transitions from flagged to someone sitting on it, or unpacking and packing can be problematical for one person without some prior experience of the bucking bronco ledge. Having a wild flying portaledge can be both terrifying and dangerous, and it needs to be kept under control at all times, which means one corner must be clipped direct into the belay until someone can step into the ledge, and it should never just be hung from the suspension unweighted unless there is zero wind. If not in use, with the ledge clipped by its suspension, clip one corner into a high belay point and then jam the ledge behind your bags, sandwiching it between the bags and the wall. This should also be done if you're belaying a leader where they might fall onto the ledge, rather than past the belay, as yes, a low fall onto the bed might be like falling onto a trampoline, but a fall onto the tubing will not, and can destroy both bones and your ledge.

ROPE BAGS & MANAGEMENT

On a wall it is vital that you get a grip on your ropes, as more so than anything else on a climb, they are your greatest enemy!

Ropes, if left wild, will fly around and get tangled in everything, get stuck on flakes, wrap around haul bags, feed through holes and notches - basically fuck you up! And so it's vital that they are tamed at all times. This is ideally done using rope bags, but can also be achieved with good old rope management.

ROPE CHAOS KILLS

Accidents, and even fatalities, on a wall can be caused by allowing slack rope management, with loops trailing here and there. More than one climber has died due to clipping into what they thought was a secure fixed rope only to find it was just a loop hanging off the belay. When ropes are looped they can feel very secure when pulled hard, and seem OK to clip into, say when hanging under the haul bags and wanting to transfer from under the bags to another rope, but these mystery loops might not be secure at all. Keep all your ropes within sight and yourself and partners out of danger.

Rope Bags

A lot of climbers think rope bags are just more wall junk, designed to steal an extra buck or two from the newbie, when just being proactive is all that's required.

Well in some ways this is true, and good rope management can go a long way to solving the taming of ropes, but only so far. Get in a big storm or high afternoon winds or rain, or try to move ropes around when hanked into slings and aiders, and you'll soon see the limits of this technique.

Also factor in lead line, zip line, haul line, lower out line, then racks, bags, belay seats and bodies and very soon you're in a highly dangerous clusterfuck zone.

The humble rope bag gives you somewhere you can stuff ropes where they cannot be whipped by wind, or soaked, and can be moved from here to there, or stuffed into haul bags, without any care at all. They make life easier and are well worth those extra bucks in my opinion.

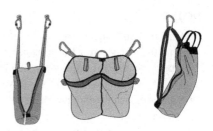

Rope bags come in a few styles:

- **Big Wall Rope Bucket:** This is the dedicated big wall rope bag, often featuring a tapered design, sometimes with a zipper which allows a wide opening that can be cinched down once the rope is in, plus multiple attachment points and beefy materials. I think Fish makes the best rope bags, but you can get these from several other companies too, including BD.

- **Extra Large Stuff Sacks:** Heavy duty stuff sacks with strong clip in loops, made by companies like Fish or Metolius, or homemade, can work well as rope bags, being lighter and more compact than big wall bags. The only drawback is that these bags do not hold open so well when stuffing.

- **'IKEA' Bags:** Light, cheap and heavy duty, these IKEA style bags (small masonry bags) also make very good rope bags, with the smaller ones being ideal, and the handles can be crossed clipped to keep them open when stuffing.

- **Haul Bags:** You can stow ropes in the top of your haul bags, but if you do this make sure nothing will come out as the rope feeds, with the other drawback being you'll need to go searching through the ropes to get anything else from the bags.

NOTES:

Stuffing The Bags: There is an art to stuffing the rope, vital for solo climbing, but for team climbing you just need to focus on getting it in fast and neat enough, as any mini tangles can be sorted easily. The best way to stow the rope in the bag is to have the bag low (you can clip it to your belay loop, or low on your aider), and run the rope in from a higher karabiner, using it like a pulley.

Have Both Ends: It's also good to always have both ends of a rope at hand when using rope bags, so when stuffing ropes try and always tie the end into the top first, then stuff the rope in over the top of it, as this means you don't need to go digging down for the other end.

Widowmaker Ropes: In the jungle you get told to always look up for dead branches or widow makers, that can fall on your head, and on walls you should be equally as paranoid about all ropes that hang above you. The greatest degree of rope management should always be employed at all times, with no loops or strands allowed to simply hang down.

Every Rope Should Be Clipped In: Why is this? Well there have been several deaths and accidents where someone decided to rap or jug on a rope they thought was fixed, only to find it was either just a loop, or worse, just a cut strand of rope hung up on a flake. I heard of one Russian team jugging a free hanging rope only to find it was just stuck to some ice! The need to secure rope ends is because often climbers will clip into a rope without realising they're attached to the wrong end, and weighing it, say to move off the belay, will see them take the long plunge over the side.

Not good! The bottom line is when you clip into something make sure it's attached to something else, and make sure each team member communicates just what can be ascended or rapped. To demonstrate this point I remember listening to two climbers topping out on Zodiac, always a clusterfuck ending it seems, each shouting backwards and forwards in the dark. At last I heard the leader shout "ROPE FIXED!", followed closely by, "NOT THAT ROPE!!!!!".

What this means is that all dead ropes (ropes not attached to anything) need to be secured away and identified as being dead, for example having ten metres of rope trailing from a rope bag and unattached to anything is very dangerous.

ROPE MANAGEMENT TECHNIQUES

Beyond using rope bags, you can use a number of other techniques, and some of these will be necessary even with rope bags, as ropes will need to be tamed when you have no bags to take them, such as when hauling your haul line or dealing with the zip line. Unlike a traditional multi pitch climb, you don't want to be looping the rope around you, but hanking it short and neat on either side of you, either to remain there, or to be transferred into rope bags when you have them. The number one rule for wall rope management is you should never allow rope loops to hang any lower than you can reach, especially not low enough to get caught around your haul bags!

Wall chaos, seven ropes, eight climbers, two bolts

The obvious choice for hanking ropes is to drape them through slings, but often these are in short supply on a wall, and so the next is your aiders, the rope looped through a step. The problem with this is the rope tends to get caught in the step, or you end up stepping on it or it just gets tangled with everything else. The haul bag straps or cordelette strands are a little better, but again tend to create their own kind of chaos. Tying knots in the ropes works well as each is just released as you need them, and you can have the loops a little longer with less fear of them feeding into one another. Secure each knot on a large HMS.

For me the best approach is to make the rope it's own prison guard, tying a large overhand knot in the rope below where it's clipped into the belay and then looping the rest of the rope into this, and once all looped you can secure it by wrapping the end around the loops to secure the lot. Once looped this way you can easily move the whole lot by unclipping the rope end.

PASSING PARTIES

The ethical aspects of passing are complex, but it's best to take a laid back approach to it when you're the one being passed. If you don't think your team is going too slow, then you could refuse, but if you can afford the time to let them pass, it's always nicer to not have another team up your arse for the rest of the route, their leader reaching your belay and tapping their feet while they wait for you to go. When a speed team are approaching you should definitely let them pass, as they will have no bivvy gear (I've been passed by the same team twice on the same ascent of the Nose). Such climbers may even start climbing up a pitch your leader is already on, which can be a bit alarming, and it's for you to call if someone is being unsafe (if two people are climbing the same pitch then it's best for the slowest one to just hang and let them pass).

Some speed teams are just trying to get to the top, so if you say they can jug your rope after the pitch is led they might agree to wait for that, and they'll be gone by the time your haul bags are up. If they're holding you up, you could ask them to fix a rope for you in return, which can actually be faster in the end.

If heavy teams need to pass each other this should be on a good stance or where you have a solid three bolt belay (you can extend out a solid belay to cracks to create two belay stations), as everything and everyone will be on one belay. This means you'll need two masterpoints, and a little trust between teams. I've had eight people (three teams), all on one belay, and in such situations it can be chaos, with ropes and things clipped everywhere, and you need to be super careful that nothing and no one becomes un-clipped by accident. It's important to keep your rack tidy (ideally in a bag), so nothing is taken by the other team by accident, as well as your ropes secured away.

At such crossovers it's often best for one team to stop and bivvy in order to let the other team get a head start. If you're passing parties it's down to you to look like you're another class of climber, be friendly when you arrive, and negotiate about passing. Sometimes, if the other team is slow, you can negotiate by offering them some water in return, or as above, offer to fix some ropes for them.

The bottom line for passing though, would be to try and avoid other parties as much as possible, and adjust your speed so as not to catch parties up, or be caught!

BIG WALL COMMUNICATION

A big wall can be a very tough place to give and receive commands. This can be due to several factors including distance - with long pitches often climbed, complex terrain - where you're hidden from each other, or weather - with high winds often an issue. For these reasons big walling tends to be very light on communication, with systems being necessary to be able to cope with total communication breakdown.

PRIMARY COMMUNICATIONS

If you can hear each other, you might use the classics 'slack' or 'take in' or 'watch me' from standard climbing, but really there is only one, and at a stretch, two commands.

- **"Rope Fixed":** This call covers a lot of information and replaces the usual "safe" or "take me off" or "at the belay". When shouted down this means that the belay is set up, the leader clipped in and safe, the lead line is fixed and safe to ascend and the haul line is fixed to the PCP. This signal will not come as a surprise as the belayer will have seen the haul line moving independently of the lead line as the leader was taking it in through the PCP. Although the haul line will also move upwards without the movement of the lead line, if the climber is short fixing or rope soloing to the belay, using the end of the haul line due to a: running out of rope, or b: too much drag. In both of these situa-

tions though the belayer will be forewarned.

- **Failure To Hear "Rope Fixed":** If nothing can be heard, but the haul line is coming very close to going tight to the back up knot, the belayer should assume the leader is at the belay and the rope is fixed. Tugging on the rope will not allow communication as it will be through the PCP, and instead the backup knot should be untied, and then once the bags begin to lift the docking cord should be released. If you're really not sure, then wait for the bags to lift before letting go of the docking cord, or rig the bags with a longer lower-out line, so they can't fall onto the leader if you've really fucked it up.

- **"Haul Away":** On hearing "rope fixed", the belayer can signal when they are ready to release the bags by shouting "haul away", and at this the leader will begin hauling in the last of the slack on the haul line. It is always best if you're the leader not to haul the haul line tight until you've shouted "rope fixed" but only snug, as this allows the belayer to make sure the haul line is free from everything else, and untie the backup knot once they hear the rope is fixed. Once the backup knot is untied, they can shout 'haul away', and untie the docking cord as the bag begins to lift.

- **Failure To Hear "Haul Away":** Here the leader should pull the rope snug, until they feel the backup knot, then wait a minute, then pull again. If they feel the extra rope coming up they know the backup knot is untied. Take it slow and take up the weight of the bags until you see the bags swing out.

SECONDARY COMMUNICATIONS

- **"Free Climbing":** This is important as the belayer will need to go from slow aid mode to something a little faster, and you're not going to want to hear 'wait a minute' in the middle of some mantle shelf move.

- **"Watch Me":** This is of course the same as any lead although on an aid route it might have less effect, most often just a roll of the belayer's eyes and the taking in of one inch of rope.

- **"I'm Going To Need...":** Informing the belayer that you're coming up to a beak crack for example allows the belayer to get the beaks ready, rather than the leader stopping and shouting down 'send up some beaks', then sitting there for ten minutes as the belayer digs them out.

Monkey Call: The monkey call is a low grunt that travels very well, especially early and late in the day, and can cut through night and wind and storm pretty well (a howler monkey can be heard clearly over a mile away). This signal is good for single communications such as 'rope fixed' or 'rope free' when used in ascent or descent. It is best that any monkey call be answered with a monkey call so that both people know they have been understood, vital when speed climbing or when descending in bad weather.

Keep It Simple: It's best to try and keep chit chat down unless you're climbing in very still weather, as talking all the time can make important and misheard statements sound like chat.

Keep The Belayer Informed: If you can see you'll be at the belay in three moves tell the belayer so they can get ready for the bags to be lowered, rather than just shout 'I'm at the belay' after an eight hour lead. The same is true if you think you might fall, as this allows them to take in that inch of slack!

NON VERBAL

If you know each other and have a good system then you might not need any verbal signals at all, but if you do rely on them you can try the following:

Radios: If communication is vital you can make use of small radios, but if you do, spend a few hours working with them beforehand so everyone knows how they work and can make sure they're on the same channel! It's often not appropriate to leave them on all day waiting for a call, and instead having a signal pre arranged to turn on the radio is a good idea, such as hand signals or a whistle.

Tugs: Tugging on the lead line or haul line can sometimes work, but it's easy for someone bounce testing a #1 head to appear to be asking for lots and lots of slack for example. Not good. Basic tug signals should be:

- **Single Tug:** Usually one big tug means 'slack'. Make a tug then wait a few seconds before you give a second one if needed, so as not to give the impression you're giving two tugs.

- **Two Rapid Tugs:** If you want the belayer to take in the slack or 'up rope' do some rapid double tugs two seconds apart.

- **Five Rapid Tugs:** Rope fixed.

- **Non Stop Tugs:** I'm shit scared.

Whistle: A whistle is very small and compact and can be used as above, but is best employed in single blasts and

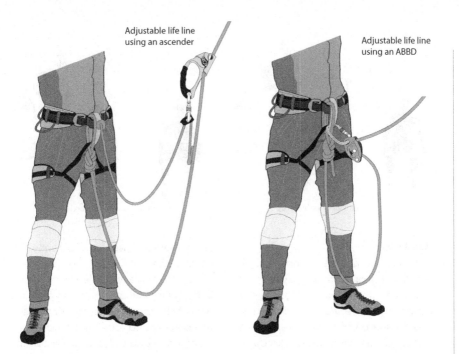

Adjustable life line using an ascender

Adjustable life line using an ABBD

no more, as it's easy for people on the ground to think you're in trouble (if you are in trouble you should blow six blasts with a one minute interval).

Hand Signals: If you climb a lot together you can come up with all kinds of strange hand signals, like flapping your arms means take in, or putting one arm out means you're almost at the belay.

LIFE ON THE WALL

The big wall working environment must be up there with working on the deck of an aircraft carrier or castrating bulls in terms of danger, with hypothermia, hyperthermia and gravity all conspiring against a safe life. The fact that with a big wall, the goal is generally to climb something only just possible, means it takes time, maybe one night, maybe thirty. Even if you're gunning for a one day ascent of a multi-day climb you still need to know how to walk the line in order to plan and carry out all that stuff

around the climbing. In this chapter I'm going to cover all the basic stuff involved in living on the wall, sleeping, eating and going to the toilet.

BIVVY BASICS

One thing I love about living on a big wall is how there is only climbing, and not climbing, but that not climbing is still climbing really, laid on a craggy perch or portaledge, wasted but happy, knowing that climbing will begin the second you step off in the morning. Bivvying is an art, and the more you do it, the better and safer you become. Really, like most climbing it's about keeping things simple, having a routine and being aware of risks and dangers. Get it right, and you can live like a king, get it wrong, and you'll feel like you're in the highest torture dungeon. Before I move on to the technical side of bivvies, sleeping on ledges and portaledge living, I'm going to cover some universal principles and techniques.

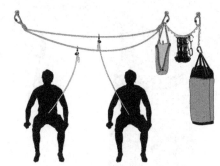

Life lines with lead ropes   Life lines with lanyards

Lifelines

When you're moving around a bivvy, be it a rock ledge or portaledge, you should always stay tied in with a lifeline, even on big ledges. I've seen rock crash down sending shards out like shrapnel and winds whip up portaledges like battering rams, plus countless slips and trips.

Not tying in and using a lifeline is never really about being competent, but about bravado, so stay tied in.

The best method to tie in is with the end of the lead line, and then adjust that end at the belay so you can move anywhere on the ledge, plus a little bit more.

Some people clip this into their harness with a locker, but I always tie in (usually using an overhand knot as this is less bulky than a figure of eight for example), as this means less 'stuff' at my waist when sleeping.

If you don't have one end, then tie into a bight of rope, but pay close attention to the following:

Lifeline Far Ends: This is one of those little details that 99.99% of the time is just being anal about safety, but where

being aware may well save someone's life in that 0.01 situation. On a complex belay where you have multiple ropes, slings, krabs, gear, haul bags, etc., all crowded in on each other, it's easy for someone to unclip the wrong rope - either your rope or someone else's. I've experienced this several times. This is a typical scenario:

A climber ties into the end of the lead line, then clips the other measured end in with a figure of eight. Later another climber, trying to sort out the belay, or scrambling to get some rope for an emergency, unclips this random mystery knot. Later the now disconnected climber scrambles down from the ledge to have a crap, congratulating themselves on how well measured out their rope is, not coming tight, until they realise they are unattached and could fall to the end of the rope (if the other end is even tied in!).

As I've said before, this can also happen when loops of rope are clipped into, where some random bight is grabbed and clipped without any idea if it's clipped to anything.

So how do you identify your primary connection to the belay? Well, I would try and only clip in 'life or death' krabs and cord into your masterpoint (haul bags or

Two very tired climbers on Dolt Tower

people) as a start, and keep everything else out on the boundaries, on strands, the shelf, anchor points or handrails. You can also help to identify your lifeline, be it clipped to the masterpoint, or more importantly when not, by tying an easily identifiable lifeline knot. For me, the best knot for this is a double 'rabbit ears' figure of eight, as it's easy to tie and cannot be misidentified as anything else (clove hitch, butterfly or regular figure of eight knot).

Adjustable Lifeline: So you've set your lifeline so you can move ten metres from the anchor to have a sneaky crap, but you don't want to fall that far in your sleep. The answer to this is to create an adjustable lifeline, shortening or lengthening your lifeline via an ABBD, PCD, PCP or Prusik. I hate to sleep with loads of junk on my harness so tend to clip this into both my lanyards so that this adjuster can lie outside my sleeping bag.

Handrail: A handrail works with your lifeline and can be a single strand of rope, but a multi strand loop is both safer and more practical, and is run from one end of a bivvy to another (ideally from bolts, or you may have to build a second mini belay). This rail is used to clip off all your gear to secure it, and is also used to clip yourself into instead of using a lifeline. Having a loop (two strands) means that one strand can be used for clipping off gear allowing climbers to move freely along the other strand. A loop is also safer, as if either anchor fails, the climbers are held within the loop.

Clip Loops

Remember you are climbing in a zone of high gravity and so everything you have must have a clip loop, from your spoon to your head torch, as anything that does not, and is just rested or balanced, invariably gets dropped. Things like sunglasses hung from cords should not be trusted, and should have cord taped in place, otherwise you'll find in the morning you just have the cord! Don't trust drawcords either as the knots tied in Chinese factories often come undone, seeing your nice warm sleeping bag sailing down to earth. Tie off all drawcords with your own knots. Also, don't trust zip pulls as a method of anchoring your jacket, as zip pulls break. Everything needs a clip loop, so these need to be tied, sewn and threaded everywhere.

STUFF SACKS

A bivvy lives and dies on stuff sacks, and having a good supply of medium duty bags with clip in loops sewn into them (big enough to get your hand in) is a boon for all bivvies. Try and have them different colours, so you know what's got what inside it.

Sleeping Bags

Unless you're going high and don't think you'll be there long, or going super fast with a perfect weather forecast, there is only one way to go in terms of sleeping bags for big wall climbing, and that's synthetic.

There are many reasons to use a synthetic bag on a wall, but primarily it's because they are tough and can take a lot of punishment and give you the greatest survivability. A synthetic bag can be ripped, melted, pissed and crapped on, food smeared, filled with sand and grit and talus, unzipped and used as a blanket over three unlucky souls, or clipped off and used as a sun shade. A down bag will not survive all this, it will rip apart and end up a sorry rag that needs dry cleaning and repairing, while a budget bag can be chucked in a washing machine and brought back to life, a battle scarred life, but life.

Your sleeping bag should have a heavy duty clip loop sewn into the bottom, where the zipper ends, with a long loop of 5 mm bungee attached to this for clipping into the ledge. Here are a few thoughts on sleeping bags:

- **Wet Warmth:** The greatest advantage of a synthetic bag is that its fibres retain far more warmth long after a down bag is nothing but two skins of fabric with a sludge of feathers in the bottom of the baffles. This is not to say that a wet synthetic bag is warm, but only that it will retain a significant percentage of its warmth (you can wring the water out, and it will warm up), probably about 50% of its rating. Cover your bag in a bivvy bag, and you will be able to sit out a night in full storm conditions and still function the next day, put that combo inside a portaledge with fly and you'll be able to sit out a week of bad weather. Where synthetic bags excel is for multi-week routes, where you cannot avoid but get your bag wet from moisture inside the portaledge as well as ice and water on or in your clothing. I've used a heavy weight synthetic bag for two weeks straight down to minus twenty, and at the end, the bag had ice chunks inside it the size of grapes, and yet was still comfortable. With a down bag, you'd have retreated long before.

- **Bag Ratings:** I always tell people they should equip themselves as if they were heading up on a winter ascent of the Walker Spur, not some sunny rock climb. This approach

means you maybe carry a few extra kilos of insulation, have a bit more bulk, maybe require two haul bags instead of one, but if you get hit by a storm, you will find the energy used to haul those extra few kilos the best you've ever spent. Having a winter weight sleeping bag means that on day three of being stuck in a storm, where everything is damp, you'll only be grumbling a little, while that team with the 'summer breeze' bags will be being rescued - or worse. Another factor is that what is warm on day one, when you're rested and fed and hydrated, might not be warm five hundred metres up, tired, running on empty, kept awake by the storm for two nights (remember that in the worst storms you will not be able to be rescued). I tend to ignore bag ratings these days and go more by weight, and would say the ideal bag for a big wall would be something around 1.5 kg (20° F/-6° C) for summer walls, and 2.5 kg (-30° F/-34° C) for winter walls. If you want to go for a lighter bag, then a 1 kg (35° F/1° C) bag is ideal, and this is a good option for speed climbing or two day ascents. If you're buying a sleeping bag to use on walls primarily, then buy a long bag if you're over 5' 6", as you may not be able to sit up inside a standard length bag with your helmet on.

- **Double Bags:** A good flexible system is to use a two bag system, with one summer bag used over a three season bag, and each used on its own. For example, summer bag on night one and two, three season on nights three to five, and both together for the rest of the route. An advantage of a double bag system for cold walls is that moisture tends to get captured in the outer bag (use the lighter bag on the outside), saving the inside bag. On this kind of wall, where rain is not a problem, I've often used a 300 to 400 gram down bag as a liner, with a four season bag as an outer. This might sound a lot, but after a few weeks I guarantee it will not feel like overkill. A further advantage of a two bag system is that if someone drops their sleeping bag, you have a spare, and in a survival situation you can zip bags to make double bags. This way body warmth can be shared. Left and right zipped bags allow the bags to be zipped together if the zips can be mated (go for same brand bags). If zipping bags together to create a double sleeping bag is something you plan to do on a wall however, make sure you test this works before you leave the ground as I have bought left and right zipped same brand bags in the past that would only zip together on one side, creating more of a double duvet effect than the double sleeping bag I was going for.

- **Blankets:** After many months of sleeping in portaledges, I became a fan of the synthetic blanket, either using a commercial or homemade blanket, or simply unzipping my sleeping bag and using it as a blanket. The reason I like this is that it's much less restrictive, especially when you have all your ropes and lanyards clipped to you. Having a blanket also tends to stop you feeling immobile, not wanting to move and sort out stuff, important if you need to deal with small problems before they become large.

Sleeping Mats

A big mistake climbers make is thinking they don't need sleeping mats when using portaledges, but anyone who's slept on a blow up bed or hammock will tell you, you do, as all you have as insulation is a thin piece of fabric. When sleeping on actual rock ledges, the mat takes up some of the hardness and chill from the ground. All mats should have a clip in loop, and my mats tend to have one at each end (using bungee cord), so they can be secured to the top and bottom of the ledge.

Closed cell foam mats are really the best way to go when sleeping on rock ledges, where there are many puncture hazards, and often just a three-quarter mat is fine, with your rope, shoes, knee pads being used to insulate your feet. An inflatable mat, especially a thick one, irons out the bumps on a ledge somewhat, but tends to have less 'stick', which is not good on sloped ledges.

On a portaledge, a small air mattress works well as it packs down small in your haul bag and provides a great deal of insulation, but you need to make sure you don't puncture them with nut tools clipped on your harness for example. You should always carry a repair kit for these mats (if you have no patches, super glue a circle of duct tape that is inverted - sticky side up - then once dry add another larger layer over the top). Air mats need to have clip loops duct taped to them, and securing them this way on both ends tends to stop the mats moving too much in a portaledge, where nylon on nylon can make them even more skittish. On major alpine winter walls, you should carry two mats, either both closed cell or a mix of the two.

If you need more insulation remember that many haul bags have a thin piece of foam inside the back panel. One little tip; draw a large chess board on your closed cell mat, and use karabiners and pegs as the pieces, a good way to pass the stormy days.

BIVVY BAGS

A big wall survival system is comprised of the sleeping bag, mat, portaledge fly and bivvy bag, and if you had to just take one of these, it would be the bivvy bag. The bivvy bag is used to slow the wetting out of your sleeping bag when used inside a fly, or to keep the wind off when sleeping without the fly. It also provides a little bit of extra insulation (+5° C).

I'm not a fan of half and half bags, with non breathable fabric on the bottom and breathable fabric on the top, as you need to place your mat inside the bivvy bag, which isn't always that easy when sat on a portaledge. Instead, I tend to use a cheaper XL sleeping bag cover (a bivvy bag without a cowl) where all the fabric is breathable and is cinched down into a drawcord.

Having an oversized bivvy bag is important as you need to get in and out of it in a confined space, and often you might want to get dressed inside the bivvy bag, plus you have more room to store stuff. A fully breathable Gore style bag with a cowl that you could sit under would be best, but no one seems to make these anymore (I make my own, which are easy to sew up). I would avoid any featherweight 'water resistant' bags, as these tend not to be effective in really bad weather.

On nights I don't expect to need a bivvy bag I still often sleep with my sleeping bag's foot section inside my bivvy bag so that I can pull it up quickly if needed. Again make sure it has a good clip in point. Oh, and if you think that 'water resistant' shell on your sleeping bag is enough, then try lying in the garden while someone sprays you down with a hose pipe to test the theory.

Tarp

A tarp might seem like a funny thing to take on a wall, but it can be very useful for all sorts of things and weighs very little. It can be used as a makeshift hammock on slopey ledges, windbreak, survival blanket, flysheet repair, sun shield, or as a tarp, strung between anchors for climbers without a portaledge, or used at the base or summit. If you have a ledge, you can often stretch the tarp between two anchors then hold it out by hanging water bottles in stuff sacks along the bottom edge. I've also strung a tarp between two portaledges so the doors could be left open in light rain (so used as an awning), and collected water with one. Get a bright coloured tarp (red) as this can be used to signal you need help, either hung from your ledge or placed on the ground to be seen by helicopters.

Bothy Bag

This lightweight bag, designed to take two, or four or more people, is a great little addition to any speed climbing kit, being surprisingly warm, and unnoticed in a haul bag or pack. One human being gives off the same heat as one bar of an electric fire, so get two inside one of these, and you'll not be as warm as two bars of an electric fire, but you might survive the night. These bags are also good to protect the belayers on long belay sessions, acting a little like a greenhouse, cutting out the wind dead. Make sure your bag has some heavy duty clip in points, as once they fill with the wind these things can get airborne!

PORTALEDGES

If big walling is known for anything, it's for sleeping in portaledges, those little flimsy beds that make flatlanders shake their heads and fellow climbers swoon at the idea of waking up, just a half a millimetre of Cordura between them and the abyss. The portaledge unlocks the hardest walls, allows the climber to live in the most inhospitable places on earth, to hang their whole world onto a small stub of steel.

A POTTED HISTORY OF LEDGES

Before the portaledge, people had to somehow climb from ledge to ledge, as they had in the Alps and the Dolomites, sitting and lying on anything they could find. Routes like the Nose were perfect for this alpine style of climbing, as it is broken up by some of the best ledges you'll find on a wall, and one reason for the use of fixed ropes was not to make things easy, but rather to link the places you could sleep together.

As climbers moved onto the bigger and steeper walls, such as The Muir and North America Wall, and the number and size of ledges were reduced, climbers had to suck it up. Hammocks were employed, strung between pegs, allowing something better than sleeping in your harness, but only just. The high point in this period was Warren Harding's 1970 ascent of the Wall Of Early Morning Light, where he and Dean Caldwell spent 27 nights on just about the steepest wall in the world with only a single point 'bat' (Harding's B.A.T. products standing for 'basically absurd technology'!) hammock each to sleep in. Few people were as tough as Harding, and so a better way had to be found, and in fact it already had, a year before, with Greg Lowe's LURP (Limited Use of Reasonable Placements).

This was the first portaledge, with a magnesium frame and built in flysheet, and perhaps as good or even better than ledges that came after it (it even featured a zipped poophole in the nylon floor). Having a rigid bed allowed climbers to fully rest and stay out of the weather, with the added advantage that sleeping bags did not become compressed by a hammock. In bad weather, they could now sit it out, where before it would be life and death (Harding almost died in such a storm on the South Face of Half Dome in 1970, being rescued by Royal Robbins).

The LURP was used on the first winter ascent of Half Dome's Northwest Face in 1972, by Lowe and Robert Kiesel, and should have ushered in a whole new era of big wall ascents. But climbers were dirtbags - the LURP was custom made - and so they soldiered on with B.A.T tents, with few LURP tents being bought and paid for.

Walls continued to be climbed Harding style, such as Zodiac, The Shield, and Mescalito, with some climbers playing around with junkyard prototypes, but mainly suffering it out, dreaming of soft flat beds through long, fitful nights. The nearest climbers got to something better was the use of 'submarine cots', rigid folding beds used in Camp Curry tents, a tubular frame with canvas roped into it. The problem was, unlike the LURP, which could be folded down, these ledges could not, and so were thrown off the wall after each ascent.

The first real commercially successful portaledge was the Gramicci ledge, made by Mike Graham, appearing around 1977 and used on walls such as The Sea of Dreams and the Norwegian route on Trango Towers, resigning Harding's B.A.T tent to only the most destitute and hard-core (or British). During this period big walling moved from the sport of the hard-core, to something anyone could do. The introduction of the Wild Country Friend and new smaller camming devices made by companies like Wired Bliss, as well as micro wires like the RP, opened up big wall climbing, and with this came an increased demand for portaledges.

Fish ledges appeared in 1984, made by Russ 'Fish' Walling, an ex-member of Yosemite SAR, a design building on problems he'd seen with the Gramicci design. Fish ledges were made from extremely robust 4130 chromoly steel tubing and had machined alloy corners and a very robust flysheet, something that came from Fish seeing how useless existing flysheets could be in a big storm, leaking or ripping apart in high winds.

In 1986 Jon "The Deuce" Middendorf started A5, making alloy ledges whose design innovation was to revisit the LURP design and create a fully enclosed hang-ing tent, with other innovations such as three person diamond flysheets (one climber hanging in a hammock under ledge), that could be anchored below to resist winds. These A5 ledges went on to climb some of the gnarliest walls on the planet, including the Polar Sun Spire, Great Trango and Thalay Sagar. At the same time climbers were still making their own portaledges, even as other larger companies entered the market, such as Black Diamond, Metolius and The North Face (who bought A5 in 1996).

The high point of portaledge appli-cation perhaps came in 2004, when a Russian team, using a larger four-man ledge, climbed Jannu's 2800 metre North Face over fifty days.

BASIC PRINCIPLES

A portaledge is a bed made from a rigid frame of steel or alloy tubing, designed to be either folded or slotted together to allow it to be carried to and from the wall, with most tubing fitting in machined corner pieces. Most (but not all) ledges hang from a single point, the masterpoint, from which four to six adjustable straps attach to the frame. Ledges vary in size from three-quarter ledges, to single, double and larger. All ledges are designed to be fitted with flysheets that either are deployed over the ledge like a parachute or enclose the ledge.

PORTALEDGE SIZES

Ledges come in a number of different sizes, each having pros and cons.

Mini Ledge

This style of ledge is somewhere between a large belay seat and a ledge made for dwarfs. Being neither one thing nor another, it's a very specialised item, and can be used as a single person ledge, with your feet resting on your haul bags (the Fish ledge has a bag your feet go in), or on your deployed flysheet. I've used a ledge like this with a fully enclosed fly for 14 straight nights, using the base to rest my feet on. You can also use this style of ledge for two climbers to sit on, perhaps on an alpine wall (it's lighter and smaller than squeezing onto a single ledge), and can be a lifesaver when there are no ledges anywhere, used as a super belay seat and emergency bivvy. None of these ledges come with a fly, so you'll need to use a full sized fly, or make your own out of tent fabric.

Models: Fish One Night Stand (3.8 kg / 61 x 121 cm), Metolius Gizmo (2.45 kg / 51 x 98 cm), D4 Trapezoid (3.6 kg)

Single Ledge

This is probably the standard ledge, giving one person a lot of room to do their stuff and having enough room for two people at a pinch (single ledges have the same components as double ledges, so are plenty strong for two as long as you support the centre of the long tubing). The single is much easier to put up than a double ledge, and it catches less wind while pitching, or when pitched, important in a storm, but offset by the ledge having less weight on it than a double (so swings and roundabouts). The real pain with a single ledge is that you need more wall real-estate when you have two or three climbers compared to one double ledge.

Models: Fish 5 Season (3.8 kg / 107 x 190 cm), BD Single Ledge (6.8 kg / 80 x 213 cm), Metolius Bomb single (5.2 kg / 76 x 220 cm)

the way to and from your climb. If I was buying a ledge, an Alpine Double is the style I would go for.

Models: Fish Double Whammy (4.2 kg / 107 x 198 cm) and Runout Customs UL (4.1 kg / 107 x 190 cm) and D4 Double (4.7 kg / 118 x 203 cm)

Deluxe Double

Although the Alpine is maybe the best design for big walling, the large deluxe or 'cabana' is probably the most popular ledge, and gives a lot of room for two climbers to live in, and on an extended alpine wall, or in a big storm, having that extra room might keep you sane. The downsides are these ledges tend to be much heavier due to the beef of their construction, plus harder to pitch requiring a spreader bar due to the strain on the long sections), and they catch a lot of wind.

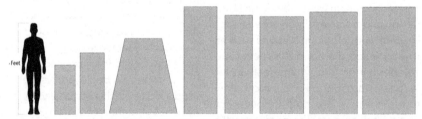

Left to Right: Metolius Gizmo, Fish One Night Stand, D4 Trapezium, BD Single, Fish Five Season, Fish Double Whammy, BD Cliff Cabana, D4 Double

Alpine Double: This is a small double ledge, or extra large single ledge, and is the most efficient system for a two person team with regards to weight, bulk, windage and price. Such a small ledge requires some toughness, and the ability to deal with being a little squashed, especially when buttoned up in a storm or on an alpine wall with the fly fitted, but this is made up for by less weight on

Models: Black Diamond Cliff Cabana (9 kg / 130 x 213 cm), Metolius Bomb Shelter (6.3 kg / 120 x 220 cm)

Double Parasite

This is a style of ledge that is no longer built by anyone but was an alpine double with a 6 point hammock fitted underneath, with the 3rd person slipping into this to sleep each night. This was probably the most efficient sleeping system

Troll Wall camp

ever created when the weight was divided between three climbers, and was designed for major alpine grade VII walls. Downsides with the design included a huge stress on the poles and a very clammy and drippy night for the climber on the bottom bunk.

Models: A5 Diamond (6 kg / 220 x 142 cm)

Triple Ledge

Russian climbers often use much larger portaledges then western climbers, with these extra large ledges accommodating three climbers laying down, or four climbers sitting (Russian teams tend to climb as a four). Made from heavy duty material, these are often assembled and fixed at the bottom of the climb, and then carried up the wall clipped to a climber (just hope it doesn't get windy). The only company making these ledges is Krukonogi.

Models: Krukonogi Triple (11 kg / 120 x 210 cm)

Quad Ledge

Eric Brand used a double decker on his ascent of Mount Thor in 1986, with one huge Cordura flysheet covering the whole shebang. (Heavy / big)

Improvised Portaledges

Climbers are an ingenious bunch, and I've seen many homemade ledges or 'ledgy' style things made to hang from a wall. Of these, the best examples would be Steve "Crusher" Bartlett's ascent of PO Wall using a strung up lawn chair, or the team I saw using rigid Yosemite Mountain Store signage that had been designed to 'look' like a portaledge, only at 1:25 scale. Often the ability to tinker around with fabric and metal, and think out of the box can produce some

interesting designs. One such ledge was a Russian design that used a budget double blow up mattress as the frame (it had two point suspension points which helped it work). But often, when time and materials are totted up, you're best to just look for a second-hand ledge!

PUTTING UP THE LEDGE

The effort required to put up a ledge is really what makes or breaks a portaledge design. Some are incredibly easy to put up, such as the Fish, D4 and old BD folding Sky Lounge, while some are good once you know how to do it, such as the Custom Runout UL. And then there are others that can feel as if they were designed only to frustrate and harass your small, tired climber's brain.

PRACTISE, PRACTISE, PRACTISE

Knowing how your ledge fits together, its little eccentricities and bugs, is vital when it comes to a quick deployment on a hanging belay. I would practise putting it together on the flat several times, working alone and with a partner, paying close attention to the order in which the pieces go together. I would then practise putting the ledge together with the suspension clipped into a tree or wall a number of times, as this affects the dynamics quite a bit. Finally practise putting it up hanging from the wall, both by yourself and as a team. The reason for putting up the ledge by yourself is that often one person will put up the ledge, either while the leader is above, or when the cleaner is yet to arrive, or when it's needed as a super belay seat.

Get The Ledge Up Early

I have a pet hate of setting up portaledges in the dark, as this seems to magnify the tiredness and difficulty many times over. I will always aim to have the ledge up even if this means the last pitch of the day is not hauled or cleaned, with the leader coming down instead to a ready-made camp.

Get It In Order

Knowing in what order everything needs to go, both in erection and dismantling, is vital. Here is the standard way most ledges go up:

01. Clip the suspension into an anchor point (you can move the ledge to a different anchor point later if needs be).

02. Remove from bag. It's best if the suspension straps are wrapped around the fabric and poles to keep it all together.

03. Lengthen all straps to their full length and remove any central divider straps (it's best practice really to do this before dismantling and packing away the portaledge, in which case ignore this step here as it will already be done).

04. Connect both long tubes together in the middles.

05. With the corners still disconnected, make sure no straps are twisted under the ledge, or the corner connectors are tangled with webbing.

06. The ledge should now hang like a closed stretcher, the long tubes parallel and the end tubes dangling down.

07. Make sure the ledge material is not rucked up and runs smooth along the length of the tubes.

08. With your back to the wall rotate the ledge so it's pointing out into space horizontally.

09. Insert one side of end tubing in its hole in the corner section (easy), then try and insert another end into the other hole (harder). To get this second end into place, both the tubing and the connector needs to be at a 90° angle. Check this by making sure the long poles are parallel, and not at a slightly acute or obtuse angle, often caused by the poles being slightly twisted. Get them in-line, and the tube will slot into the female section.

10. Tighten any tension straps on this end, not super tight, but enough to stop this end pole falling out.

11. Flip the ledge around, so the finished end is facing out from the wall and pull the fabric towards you, so there are no tight spots that will create acute angles (you just want parallels and right angles).

12. Insert next tube section into its end hole (easy).

13. Now comes the hardest part, getting the final end tubing to mate with the long tube's connector. Make sure the fabric has not slipped down the poles as this will create an acute angle.

14. Insert the end piece as best you can, and twist the ledge, and wobble the corner piece until you can get the pole end at 90 degrees to the hole. Now the tube should snap in.

15. Now flip the ledge around so that the inside of the ledge (reinforced side) is facing in to the wall, and the extended straps are facing out to space (inside straps are shorter).

16. Now tighten down all the bed tension straps.

PORTALEDGE NOTES:

Know Your Own Ledge: Knowing your own ledge inside out is the most important thing, and how much time you've spent practising putting it up and packing it away in different situations will determine how quickly and easily you can do both on the wall, especially when it's dark, windy, raining, and you're knackered. Different ledges have different little knacks and tricks to setting them up, so you may discover you need to adjust the above steps to suit your ledge. For example I find with my Fish ledge it's much easier to assemble if I connect all the corner parts first, leaving the centre connectors in the long tubing until last (the opposite to what I have suggested in this book).

Don't Hammer: Some people get frustrated when putting up a ledge and end up trying to hammer it together, which isn't clever with aluminium tubing, which is incredibly prone to warping and damage. If the connectors won't slot together, don't blame the tubing, maybe the straps have not been loosened fully, or the bed fabric has become rucked up. If you hammer the ends, you might not get them out again. The only reason to do this is if your ledge is bent or twisted, and in this case, once up, it should stay up.

Wind: If it's windy, then you will need to put the ledge up between you and the wall to stop it blowing around, maybe even wedging it behind your haul bags, or clipping some bits in while you work on others.

Keep Your Helmet On: Like a sail's boom, a gust of wind can make a portaledge a dangerous weapon, and I've had a ledge crack me in the head more than once.

Use Your Feet: When trying to create right angles in a twisting and buckling ledge stepping on one section of tubing

and holding it in position, and pulling with your hands on the opposing section works well.

HOW TO HANG THE LEDGE

Now your ledge is up, you need to hang it and get it the correct height. A lot of climbers make the mistake of seeing the suspension straps as being the primary way to raise or lower the ledge, but these are only for fine tuning. They should mostly be left long, as shortening them reduces space on the ledge, only adjusted to straighten out the ledge and make it more comfortable, to raise it into a short flysheet, or because the ledge is bottomed out on a rock ledge for example. The best way to get the ledge in the right place is to use its connection. There are two main methods, one fixed, and one adjustable.

Fixed

You can just clip your ledge direct into an anchor point, sling or the masterpoint, which is how most people always do it. When picking this point, take into account where you want your bed to be in relation to everything else, as once fixed it tends to stay fixed.

Adjustable

Setting your ledge on an adjustable connection point allows you to lower out the ledge if you find it's not in the right spot, or to raise it if it's too low. (Although you'll need to get your weight out of it to do this). This is achieved with an adjustable lanyard, that can be released under load, or an ABBD clipped into the primary point, the ledge hanging from the rope (tie this off when set), or by attaching an ascender to the rope and hanging the ledge from this. If you want to make your own adjustable portaledge lanyard just buy 2 metres of 25 mm (1 inch) polyester webbing and a 25 cm (1 inch) steel motorcycle buckle (make sure it is rated 800 kg+), the total cost about a quarter of buying an adjustable lanyard from Fish or Yates. The advantage of having an adjustable strap like this is that you can use this as a secondary clip point/lanyard when clipping the ledge from the bag, or around the belay.

WHERE TO HANG YOUR LEDGE

This is the killer point for portaledge functionality, where to hang your ledge so that you can access your bags, sort out your gear, and chill out. Setting up your home on the wall is about juggling lots of stuff, namely your ledge, your bags and perhaps other bags and other ledges. Before we get into the setup here are a few things to think about:

HANGING GEOMETRY

Think of a portaledge like a tripod, requiring three points of contact to be solid and stable. Less than three, and it's very unstable, more than three, and you'll end up having the weight shift from one point to the other. The three points are, your ledge's masterpoint and the two end corner connectors on the inside. This should be taken into account when positioning the ledge, as having a bulge of rock pressing into the centre of your long inside tube will create two points of contact (ledge's masterpoint and the section of tubing leaning against the bulge of rock), with the ledge constantly see-sawing around as it tries to establish 3 points. One advantage with the BD ledges is that they feature rubber bumpers on the inside which not only reduce wear on the ledge but help the ledge stand proud of the wall, and so aid this three-point stability.

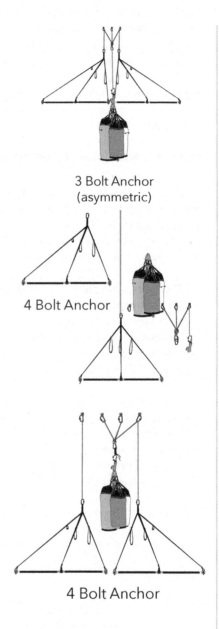

3 Bolt Anchor
(asymmetric)

4 Bolt Anchor

4 Bolt Anchor

ASYMMETRIC HANG

A ledge does not have to hang with the masterpoint at the very centre, creating a sort of isosceles set up, where the straps on each end are equal, but rather can be set up acutely, with straps longer on one side than the other in order to shift the masterpoint one side and the ledge the other. This is ideal when you're forced to hang the ledge in a tight spot, such as a corner or when the bags are crowding into the ledge. A ledge's ability to do this is based on the amount of play the ledge's straps have.

CLIMBING AND CAMPING ANCHORS

Another factor is the setup of your belay, as some are drilled for camps, having three or four bolts that are spread out, others will only have two bolts, while trad belays may be vertical. Here are some ideas for different scenarios:

Climbing Anchor (2 Bolts/ Single Masterpoint)

This is the hardest set up, as a sloppy set up here will see everything squashed up, a ledge pivoting on haul bags that are squashed and hard to access.

The trick here is not to be lazy and just make do, rather than put some effort in. I've had countless nights on walls where we were so tired we just threw up the ledge and crawled in, only to spend all night complaining how crap it was.

When you're tired or strung out, you tend to want to step down from the anchor into your ledge, not mess around abseiling into it, passing down bags, etc., but that's the only way to do it.

So here the trick is to extend out the camp, with the haul bags at the anchor, and the ledge hung below the anchor so that the bags are clear of someone sitting on the ledge. One climber climbs down into the ledge, and the other accesses the haul bags and sends down what is needed.

'Camping' Anchor (3+ Bolts)

These will usually have two or three full strength bolts, then a rivet or bolt further out, in line with the main belay.

On such a belay you want to set up your masterpoint as far to the side of the belay as possible, and dock your bags at this point also, so the bags are out to one side, leaving room free for your ledge.

Now you can either attach your ledge direct to an anchor point or create another masterpoint for the ledge, adjusting its position.

Unless the bolts are spread out wide or you have more than three bolts, just clipping your ledge to the furthest bolt from the bags will probably still see the ledge crammed in by the bags, and so it's best again here to extend the ledge's masterpoint down.

I often try and have the bottom of the weighted ledge close to the bottom of the haul bags, with the contents being decanted out by someone standing (giver) while the other sits in the portaledge (taker).

This also allows you to connect the edge of your portaledge to the bottom of your bags, making the ledge more stable, plus gives you access to the poo tube hanging under (way under!) the bags.

BAGS ABOVE OR BELOW

I tend to like to have my bags above the ledge if they won't fit to the side, but you can have them below, but this will require someone to jug down to get the stuff out or someone to press the ledge away from the wall while someone else hangs head first into the bags. One way

to reduce all the handing over of stuff is to put all the stuff in a day bag or rope bags and lower these off the main anchor, so they hang level with the ledge.

Side by side

Bags below

Bags above

the middle, but often this only occurs on camping belays you drill yourself or walls with heavy traffic (such as Zodiac).

In most cases, the ledges will be cramped if set at the same height, and so need to be offset (remember that ledges are triangles), with one ledge one metre lower allowing good room for both.

On climbing anchors, the ledges will need to be stacked one above the other, and you will need to use the haul line to extend these out, using a butterfly knot for the bottom ledge as the anchor point from where the ledge can be further adjusted via its adjustable connector.

HEAVY CAMPS

If you're making a camp on two bolts and have; four people, two ledges, haul bags, ropes, water, although technically you're fine, it can be a little unnerving when you wake at midnight and look up at your lives hanging by so little. Ideally, with heavy camps, you want to be sleeping on two sets of anchors, setting up the camp at an anchor, while the leader is pushing on to the next (having one less person on the belay also makes this easier). Once there, they should fix the lead, and haul lines then rap the haul line, leaving the gear in the rope to be cleaned tomorrow (why bring all that rack down to just carry it back up tomorrow?). Once down nothing else needs doing as the lead, and haul line is now fixed to the belay above, and so backing up the two bolt belay you and your camp are hanging from.

MULTI LEDGE POSITIONING

When you have multiple portaledges, the ideal is to set each one at the end of the belay, with the bags/masterpoint in

FINE TUNING

So you've got your ledge hanging where you think it'll work best, and now it's time to get it perfect.

SETTLING THE LEDGE

Once you've hung and set the ledge in the right spot, one person should get into it to make sure it's tweaked for use, tightening straps, getting it level. Often you want to rise the outside straps (the long straps), a little more, so you create a very slight rise on the outside edge, which helps keep everyone and everything in the ledge. Going down first means you won't be able to stay clipped to the belay, and so it's best to give yourself enough rope to move around, sleep, etc., then just adjust yourself to it with an ascender or ABBD or by tying in short. I tend to unclip my aiders from my lanyards and clip them to the anchor, so they can be used as ladders, important when setting the ledge low (sort of like ships rigging). Before going down to set the ledge, take off all your rack but make sure you have a least ten karabiners with you, which will be used for clipping in stuff sacks, boots, stove, etc. Once down on the ledge, you can clip into the ledge's masterpoint with your lanyard until you want to sit down.

GETTING SORTED

Once the first person is sat on the ledge, the second should begin to pass over the stuff sacks, and it's here that the vital importance of stuff sacks comes to the fore.

The main stuff sacks to pass down will contain sleeping bags, food, personal stuff, e.g., wipes, toothpaste, maybe clothing (belay jacket), plus stuff like your music, extra water for the evening, your stove. Each item should be clipped onto the ledge in such a way that it keeps the bed clear (you don't want a big pile of bags hanging in your face). Clip bags into the suspension straps, clipping those you need straight away closer. Here you will appreciate having daisy chains sewn into your suspension straps, and if your ledge lacks these then consider sewing some on. Avoid clipping multiple krabs into the same loop, strap or hard point, as this increases the risk of dropping items, and is just a pain.

I use a Fish heavy duty ledge that has multiple daisy chains sewn into the bed on the underside of the ledge that really helps keep things sorted, but even with these you can run out of clear clip-off points. Another way to increase your clip points is to tie loops of 5 mm cord into the outside ledge corners and middle, giving you extra clip points. I dismantled my ledge and inserted three open 10 cm quickdraws into these three points, and also use these as tie downs and as my primary flagging points.

Once sorted your partner can climb down and join you. It's best to sit with your backs against the wall and create some space between you, down the middle, where you can sort out food, stove, etc. with less risk of anything falling off (remember if it's not clipped in you'll probably drop it!)

GETTING SETTLED

Once you're sat down, go through the motions of taking off shoes, socks, knee pads, gloves, clipping them off so they hang down from the ledge (socks and shoes might need hanging from a long sling!). I will often take off my leg loops as well to let my legs breath, plus this makes it easier to go to the toilet in the morning. I also try and reduce the clutter at my harness, and might even take the harness off altogether and tie a sling around my waist or tie in with a bowline.

LEDGE SAFETY

Remember that you are sitting on a single layer of lightweight nylon, and that ledges can tip very easily when people get off, and so falling off the ledge is not unknown. For this reason, you need to keep your connections long enough to be able to sleep, but not so long that if you fall off, you'll end up a long way below the ledge. Always keep two Prusik loops on your harness, which you can use with your length adjuster to get back up if you do fall off. Always keep your helmet close at hand too in case of rock fall, and it's worth sleeping in it if there is any chance of being hit while sleeping (sleeping in a helmet is actually pretty comfortable). If you don't want ropes feeding into your ledge then you can clip a 120 cm sling from the suspension masterpoint or have a length of pre-tied cord tied into the masterpoint krab, and clip into this with your lanyards.

PORTALEDGE LIVING

There is nothing finer than portaledge living, and the longer you do it, the better you become at it. How to get good is easy, as life is simple and there are few moving parts, the main things to nail being sorting yourself out and sorting out your bowels.

Make sure you have all you need at your end of the portaledge, stored in a small stuff sack (your personal bag), so you don't have to go hunting.

This bag could contain items such as the following. In addition to these, make sure you have water at hand, and try and drink water before you go to bed and if you use your pee bottle.

- Book or Kindle
- Cheap watch
- Spoon
- Toothbrush
- Floss
- Spare spoon
- Spare Batteries
- Pencil
- Notebook
- Pan grip
- Lighters
- Spare socks
- Wet wipes
- Hand sanitiser
- Mug
- P51 can opener
- Cards
- Phone
- Earphones
- Pee bottle
- Spare topos
- Small sponge
- Sewing kit
- Repair kit
- Ear Plugs
- Spare toilet roll

TAKING THE LEDGE DOWN

Taking the ledge down is pretty much the same as getting it up - only backwards. Something to think about is that when you take the ledge apart, you want the straps to all be untangled and lengthened, and each part packed into the ledge as you want it to come out. I tend to release all straps (including tension straps), then place the end tubing inline with the long tubes (resting in the envelope of the bed). Then I break the long tubes, and letting the whole lot hang from the suspension fold the tubes together, then roll everything up together to be slipped into the ledge's bag. The last part is lengthening the connector, and clipping this into something, as you will use this like an umbilical when clipping the ledge in and out. There is often no need to rush taking down the ledge, as the leader can get kitted up, and climb off the ledge while the belayer is still in their sleeping bag, with ledges being taken down slowly as the leader leads off.

HAULING THE LEDGE

There are a number of ways to carry your ledge, including inside a haul bag, but most climbers do this one of the following three ways.

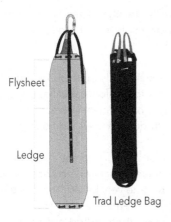

Flysheet

Ledge

Trad Ledge Bag

Improved Ledge Bag

As the ledge comes up to the PCP the top corner is unclipped, then the suspension point removed from the rope and clipped into the anchor, then the bottom corner unclipped.

Negatives for flagging include the fact the ledge tends to get a little more beaten up, and it's worth having beefed up webbing on the corners for this duty. Also, the fabric of the ledge can shrink in the sun over time, making it harder to take apart, and then assemble next time.

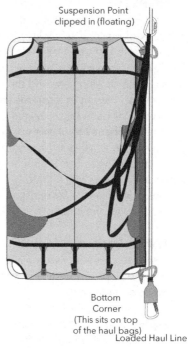

FLAGGED LEDGE

Top Corner (Floating)

Suspension Point clipped in (floating)

Bottom Corner
(This sits on top of the haul bags)
Loaded Haul Line

This diagram shows a ledge being flagged. You can see how the suspension and two corners are clipped into the haul line just above the haul bag's suspension point. The ledge will act as a 'flag' in the wind, moving freely from side to side around the flag pole (haul line).

Hang It: Stowing your ledge inside its own beefy haul bag and clipping this into the bottom of your other haul bags is the standard way to transport your ledge. This is partly covered in hauling, but always make sure your ledge is clipped in twice; once via the ledge's suspension point (clipped into the straps of its haul bag), and then again by it's connector/umbilical. Never unclip the bag and just hold it in your hand, as it's easy for it to disappear before you clip it in again.

Flag It: Flagging your ledge is a way of keeping the ledge up in between belays, saving time if you want to use it as a big belay seat, especially useful if you're a big team.

The ledge is flagged onto the haul line, the weight of the bags making the line almost rigid (the line is the flag pole, the ledge is the flag).

The ledge is attached via karabiners clipped onto the two long corners of the ledge, with the suspension masterpoint clipped in as a backup. The ledge will be floating now, but should not be affected by the wind, as it will just flag with it.

Improved Ledge Bag: One piece of gear that I make myself is an improved ledge haul bag, that is an oversized bag, big enough to take a ledge and fly when fitted, or just swallow up the ledge with the fly stowed above it. This bag has a cord lock closure at the top and the bottom, and once clipped into the ledge's suspension the bag remains there and is not taken off. To use just undo bottom drawstring and pull up the bag like a skirt, allowing the ledge to fall out. To take down just gather the ledge together (using its straps to retain it), then pull the bag back down again. My model was made from 1000 denier cordura, and could be made on any sewing machine.

FLYSHEET

The portaledge flysheet is the most overlooked piece of safety kit you own, sitting like a big lump of uselessness, taking up room in your bags, a pain to put up and take down again. And then one day you get caught in a serious storm, feel a waterfall pound down on the fabric, feel the wind barrelling like a truck before smashing into it, its icy fingers grabbing at its base, trying to peel it back from the ledge and kill you within the day. Yes, a flysheet is a pain in the ass until you need it, and then it IS your ass!

Flysheet Designs

Flysheets come in two main types, the simple deployable design and the enclosed expedition fly.

Deploy Fly: This fly is designed to live in its stuff sack and either be fixed in place when there's a storm, or attached but not deployed as insurance against a storm, or most often left in the bag when the weather is good. This style is usually made from heavyweight fabric and sewn in the most simple pattern possible, with some flys having welded seams or taped seams, while others need hand seam sealing. A draw cord runs around the base of the fly (usually with two cord locks), and some form of strap or clip loop may also be fitted.

This style of fly tends to be designed primarily for California, but has been used on many hard alpine walls as well, before the introduction of expedition flys.

Personally, I like these flys and have used them on some pretty hostile walls, and in some very bad storms. I like their simplicity, and the way they can be deployed then reefed out of the way when not needed. All such flys should have the ability to take a fly pole, and I would add beefy tie down loops around the fly every metre (make them big enough to take a large karabiner easily), as the ones fitted are often more for show.

Expedition Fly: A5 were the first to introduce these flys, mini tents that wrap around the portaledge, with doors fitted to both sides for easy access, and with the ability to secure the ledge down from updraughts. These flys are seen as being the default deluxe big wall fly, what pros and aspiring pros should use.

In reality, this style of fly is highly specialised and only suitable for sub-zero 'alpine' walls, as they can't guarantee water can't get blasted in through chunky door zippers, which a tied down deploy fly can. I've been on walls where my deploy fly, well tied down tight, with air allowed to move up through the bottom, has kept me and my partner dryer than someone in a state of the art expedition fly being forced to batten down the hatches, water getting blasted in through the zippers.

On alpine walls though, expedition flys excel, as they create a secure cocoon that

Eiger wall bivvy

can be kept warmer than a deploy fly, and keep out spindrift, which tends always to find itself blasted up into a deploy fly (waking up with an inch of snow over everything is a bad start to any day).

Tent Flys: Some climbers use single skinned tents of the Bibler style (models vary and most seem to be dropped from ranges quickly), as this allows them to use the tent for the approach and descent, sitting them on the portaledge and having the tent held within the ledges' straps. In practise, due to not being able to use the ledge's divider when using a tent fly, the occupants tend to get wedged in the middle, not ideal when there tends to already be far too much stuff in your fly on an alpine wall. Personally, I know that if I'm caught on a glacier I can dig in, build a wall around my single skin tent, but on a wall you have no protection at all, and so you're far more exposed. Having been stuck 1600 metres up a wall with a lightweight fly that's ripping apart, I would recommend going heavy every time, and just use a 1 kg bivvy tent as well for the approach and descent if need be.

FLYSHEET NOTES:

Flysheet Fabric: The fabric used on most flys is heavy duty PU coated nylon, 100% waterproof in all conditions, with reinforced areas in either heavy duty ballistic cloth or the same vinyl as seen on haul bags (better). These wear areas can wear through within a night if you scrape around a lot, and will scrape through in a storm, and so need constant monitoring and repair. Some people use custom made breathable flysheets, designed for alpine walls, which help to keep moisture down, allow a little more drying to be done, and tend to be warmer. The downsides of such flys are that they are much more flimsy than PU flys (often made from 3 ply fabrics designed for clothing), tend to get damaged easily, and cannot be trusted in really hellacious storms, so would only be recommended for walls where you could retreat.

Inside And Out: Flysheets are cut to have a shorter inside seam and long outside seam, meaning it's vital that you get it right when fitting the fly to the suspension. To avoid trying to work this out in a storm take a waterproof marker and write on each panel near the top what side is what, and then write inside beside the fly's reinforcing corner patches; 'inside left', 'inside right', 'outside left', 'outside right'. Also use different coloured cord on the zippers, so you know which goes up and which goes down.

Make Sure The Fly Fits! A lot of climbers seem to come unstuck by getting to their first bivvy only to find they have the wrong fly for their ledge; a BD double fly looking identical to a single for example. Also, people miss match ledges and flys, finding that they won't mate when it comes to a big storm, with flys that don't wrap under the ledge frame or have doors too narrow to get the ledge inside. For this reason, all ledge flys need to be easily identified by their brand and ledge style/size on the bag and should be tested before going on the wall. Many ledges have flys that are short, meaning they won't fit under a loaded ledge with the straps extended fully, something worth knowing beforehand.

Fly Repairs: Flys can get damaged in all sorts of strange ways, from hot stoves, to rock fall, to general incompetence. Any holes need to be patched as soon as possible. Short-term patches can be made with duct tape, sticking tape on both sides (so the duct tape sticks to itself). If you have seam-grip, stick tape on the outside, then add the Seam Grip to the inside, then cover with tape. In cold conditions, or to create super sticky tape, heat the tape first with the stove. The weight of the fabrics used on flys means you should not have to deal with major rips, but you should always keep your sewing kit handy, and patch repairs can be made with squares cut from stuff sacks.

Flysheet Poles

One of the most important little features of your ledge is the fly pole, used to create more space within the ledge and reduce flapping, which can cause you to get wet. The pole is also one of the most dropped items of big wall gear and should have a clip loop taped into each end, and a dedicated fly pole pocket sewn into your ledge's bag (so it doesn't fall out when pulling the ledge out). Another option is to sew a pocket into the ledge itself on the fabric beside the long tube section.

When the pole is fitted, be very wary of clipping too much into it, which happens when stuck in a ledge for a long time, as the strain of too many things (food bags, boots, etc.), can cause it to break (and a broken pole can rip your fly). Another issue is if one end comes adrift bags can slip off the pole and be lost. If you pre-attach some 2 mm Prusik loops along the length of the pole, then these can be clipped into for small items (spoon, head torch, music) and then moved around as you need them.

This pole can also be used as a cheater stick, but be warned, thin Easton alloy poles are designed for their ability to bend, not to be stiff, and so stick clipping with the fly pole can be very frustrating!

If you are hammered by a really big storm, your skimpy easton pole is going to be hammered and might break. For this reason, anyone heading onto a stormy wall should take a pole repair kit. If a pole breaks and you don't have a repair kit, you can bind and tape sections together using twine, thread or floss, then wrap in duct tape (or you can try and make a repair kit by taking the top and bottom off a can, then hammering the middle section flat, folding it over and covering it with duct tape to hide the sharp edges). Or you could take a spare pole, double poling the ledge. Also, don't overlook the other poles you might have, such as an avalanche probe, cheater stick or your ski poles, which can be used to brace out the fly, lashed into the suspension.

Hauling Your Fly

Most flys come in a heavy duty stuff sack, but don't assume that this means it can be hauled. Haul your fly, even on the bottom of your bags, and it will get battered and full of holes. Instead, the fly should be stowed low inside your haul bag, or make up a heavy duty vinyl micro haul bag for it. Some of the bags for these flys are designed to make the package look nice and small but can be hard to re-stuff when the fabric is cold and stiff, and I prefer a larger bag that can be squashed flat inside the haul bag.

Fly Storage And Admin

Don't stow your fly all squashed in its stuff sack. Instead, treat it as a sleeping bag, and stow it somewhere cool and dark in a pillowcase for example, making sure it's dry and clean before putting it away. Check it for damage and repair any holes or rub marks with seam grip and tape, and add seam grip now and then.

GOING SANS PORTALEDGE

Going up on a big wall without a portaledge can be bold unless you know you've got some little islands where you can dock your tired bones along the way. In the early days, it was these ledges that dictated which walls could be climbed. To be able to go from ledge to ledge requires skill, confidence and experience, and going without a portaledge as a novice team can create a large amount of stress and pressure, often resulting in a retreat. With a portaledge, you can stop anywhere, and often and even having a ledge for everyone to sit on can turn the tide.

On some routes where there are natural ledges, it's often still nicer to have a portaledge as the bivvy spots tend to be imperfect or downright grim (more like alpine bivvies). And so going without a ledge means you either need to be prepared to go all the way to the top, or retreat, or have the ability to make do or just take the suffering. Having been up on El Cap several times with almost nothing, just a single rope, rolling the dice, it's hard to quantify just how exposed you can feel at 2 am, 24 hours in, exhausted, the wall blank and overhanging, knowing you have to sleep.

Personally, I like to take some survival stuff on a wall, things that might keep me alive, give me some small comfort, maybe swing things mentally. This depends on the route, as going for a one-day ascent of the Nose or Lurking Fear that might just be a light fleece and a waterproof jacket, while on a one-day ascent of the Shield that would include a hammock, tarp, bivvy bag and belay jacket. As with all such lists if you need to ask what to take, then take it all.

LEDGE BIVVIES

Sleeping on a ledge saves you a great deal of hassle and expense, buying, hauling, and setting up a portaledge made redundant by a big (or small) spot of rock to call your bed. These rock bivvies can range from something as flat as your bedroom floor, where you can lie out with your teammates, to slopey, spikey perches the size of your foot. How you use these ledges, and how well you sleep, depends on how tough and how well equipped you are. Here are some thoughts:

Flatten Out The Spot: Very often climbers will just lie grumbling and making do with some crappy boulder-strewn ledge rather than improve it. Russian climbers, like boulderers, are well known for being experts in levelling out and terracing bad ledges, and it's a skill worth developing. Look at the resources you have to make things better, such as your haul bag, belay seat, large cams, ropes, water bottles filled and empty. If you have a liner for your bag, this can help flatten out the landing and don't be afraid to move rocks around (just make sure you don't drop any if there's any chance they could hurt someone).

Fix Down: Instead of putting up with some terrible ledge how about rapping 120 metres down to a good ledge with your bivvy kit then just jug back up in the morning? Are there ledges on routes close by you can reach? Having some beta of good ledges around the place can be vital, such as the good ledge on Triple Direct just a pitch below the crappy camp four bivvies on the Nose.

Sloping Ledges: Trying to sleep on a sloping ledge is a bit of an exercise, as even the smallest degree will make

Bivvy on Lunar Ecstasy, Zion

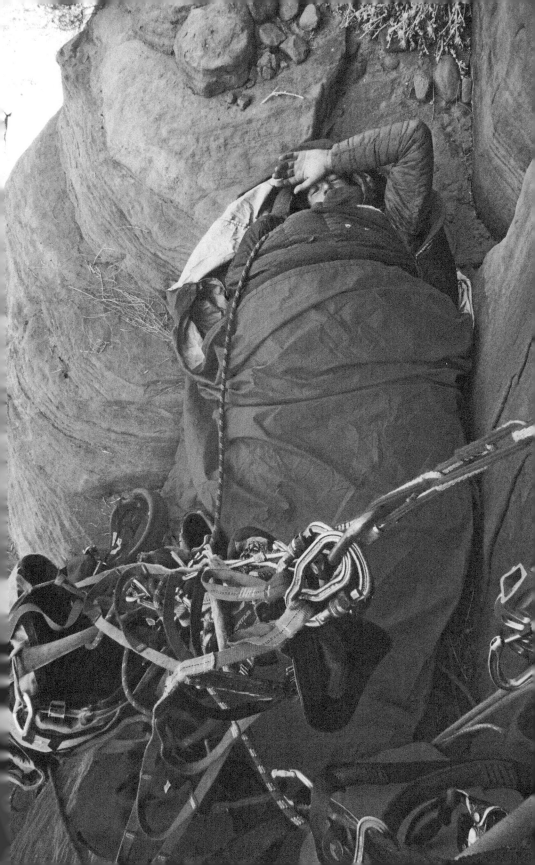

you feel as if you're going to roll off in the night. The trick is to secure yourself and your sleeping bag, which will need to be done by either blocking your roll (by lying against your haul bag or belay seat maybe), or securing yourself via slings. You can create a makeshift hammock with your sleeping bag by larks footing slings around something largish inside the foot, knee and chest section of your bag. If you find a small three-quarter ledge, it's best to lay with your feet raised, rather than sleep sitting up, as you'll invariably slip off if your weight is higher (sleeping with your feet raised helps you sleep). Having a hammock in these situations is perfect, as it can be used to make you feel a little cocooned and stop your rolling off, and if you don't have a hammock then a tarp or bivvy bag can be used instead, larks footing slings as you would with the sleeping bag.

Sitting Bivvies: Sitting, rather than lying on a ledge, is better than nothing, and you should try and make the best of it. Just being able to lean sideways onto something will make things a little more bearable, as will have something to support your feet, such as your haul bag clipped horizontally or your belay seat. Remember that a stress position is having your lower and upper back pressed against a flat wall, so it's best to lean forward or sideways. Wearing your helmet when sleeping is not so bad, and is better then sleeping without it if you don't have anything for a pillow, and crossing your arms gives your upper body some stability (plus you can hug yourself). If you want to stay sitting upright, tie a little loop of 2 mm cord onto your helmet and clip this into something to hold you upright (be aware here though, if you fall off the ledge you might get strangled by your helmet strap). These kinds of bivvies are always grim, no matter what you do,

and I would recommend finishing late and starting early, and if it's one consolation, once you're on night five of such misery it's not that bad, and you just toughen up.

LEDGELESS BIVVIES

The nightmare scenario, nowhere to sleep but unable to go on! This is the dreaded night in your harness you'd heard all about, which when it comes, is as bad as you'd imagined, but that's offset by the fact that within an hour of setting off again, the pain will have dissipated, and only the hardcore tick will remain. In such situations, people have done all sorts of crazy things with the aim of finding some small crumb of comfort, such as sleeping on the haul bag (if you clip the straps between bolts you can sit on the lid, or you can try and rise the bottom up and hang it horizontally).

A rigid belay seat can be slept in if you clip something around your chest to hold you up, and a hammock is worth its weight in gold, being either clipped between bolts, hammock style or clipped into a single point and used like a stork delivers babies. If you have none of these things, then you can try and avoid just sleeping hanging in your harness, by putting your feet in your aiders and creating a cradle using the ropes, looping it back and forwards under your body. Remember that exhaustion will help you get some micro-naps in between the pain, and think about poor Franz Romer, who spent 58 consecutive days sat in his kayak crossing the Atlantic in 1928, during which time he could only sleep while in the troughs of the waves.

WATER

A man's body is made up of between 50% to 70% water while a woman's is 40% to 60% water, about 47 litres for an average man and 33 litres for a woman, with the brain being 80% water. If this percentage drops by 2% you will begin to lose performance, creating a feeling of thirst, meaning if you feel thirsty you're already losing your edge. After this, you will begin to feel tired and lethargic, and get that feeling like you need to act but can't, and just roast instead. Once you drop by 4%, you will begin to get dizzy, develop a headache and your mouth will get super dry, your tongue will swell, and you will have trouble talking. If you have your wits about you, you will know that you are in deep trouble. Keep going like this, and very soon you'll be unable to do anything, and will drop into a coma and then die.

The Water Margin: So the question is; how much water do you need to survive? Well, the answer is highly complex, with factors like body weight, your metabolism, acclimatization to heat, exposure to the sun, physical work, clothing, all playing a part. Most climbers who've done a lot of walls seem to be able to get by with much less than the minimum, able to climb the Nose in a day with only a litre of water for example, while others can drink ten times that amount. For me, I would say that the minimum to take on any wall, if you don't know how much to take, is 3 litres or 3 quarts (a little more) per person, per day. That roughly means two bottles of coke (1.5 l) or 3 bottles of Gatorade (1 qt / 946 ml), but these are pure survival rations, not holiday rations. If you're heading up onto a very hot wall, in the height of the summer for example, or are climbing a wall 'holiday' style, then go for 5 litres each per day. This may be a little more than you might use, but being on a wall is no place to take bets on your survival.

Working It Back: Try to think about how you consume your water, for example; I have a 1 litre GSI Fairshare mug which I use for my granola + milk powder and a cup of tea (requiring about 750 ml of water) in the morning, and then my noodles and another cup of tea for dinner (another 750 ml), leaving me around 2.5 litres to play with (assuming I have opted to bring 1 litre more than my recommended minimum, so 4 litres a day), which I'll put in my 1 litre bladder twice, with some left over.

The Safety Margin: I have never topped out on a wall without any water, but I've come close, such as making ten days water stretch out to fourteen. I've also topped out with nineteen litres left. I would always take at least one full extra day's water, as this should be able to be stretched over two or three days, as the water consumed is never exact, and so all those extra quarter litres add up.

Tapering Water: If you want to nail how much water to take, say for an ascent of the Nose, you should work on a tapering allowance, based on a drop in temperature due to height, and less energy required to haul each day as the bags get lighter. On day one I'd go for 4 litres each, then day two and three take 3 litres, and 2 litres for the last day and the descent. Of course the downside of a more precisely calculated system such as this means, if you're too slow you'll blow it and really suffer, and just taking a little more water is the best insurance you can have for an ascent.

Water Monitor: Try and keep a log of how much water you have, both so you don't drink too much, but more importantly so that you drink enough. Get into the habit of getting bottles from your bag each night, using these for dinner, then filling up your bladder/water bottles for the next day, the extra going in the top of the bags. Try and use all this up otherwise you're just carrying dead water.

Dumping Water: If conditions are mild and windy, you can find that you're only drinking 2 litres a day, meaning that's 2 or 4 litres in credit, or 4 kg you're hauling for no reason. Dumping water is a risky business, and if you feel you can haul it easily enough, then do so, but if not then either empty it out and dump the crushed bottles in the bottom of a haul bag, or leave it on a ledge, writing the date and 'FREE WATER' on the side of each bottle.

How Little Water Can You Survive On? Wilfred Thesiger famously crossed the Empty Quarter (Rub' al Khali) in the Arabian Peninsula on only a pint of water (568 ml) a day. He did this by being well acclimated and staying out of the midday sun, often travelling at night, using camels, and wearing the right clothing.

The lesson here is that there is no set amount of water, although the books say there is, and that the amounts mentioned in this book are only a guide. If you think you're going to run out of water, then maybe consider not speeding up, like someone whose car is running low on gas, hoping to get to the next gas station before it does, but slow down instead.

Creating a shield from the sun with your haul bags, sleeping bags, bivvy bags, etc., sitting out the midday sun, and then moving in the evening, even through the cold of the night, might be a better bet.

If the heat is extreme, like the hottest summer days with no wind, your body might require up to 12 litres a day, not 3, and so you need to question if your route choice is sensible? Some routes feature corners that can be hidden in, and if timed well you can stay out of the sun, but others are just a roaring inferno from dawn until dusk.

Always Leave One Last Drop: When water is running low - the team supply or the water you have to hand on lead - then never drink the last drop, using it only to wet your mouth. Any thirst you feel will be magnified ten times once you know it's all gone.

Hot Water Bottles: If you have spare gas and you're cold, or a teammate is struggling, then make a hot water bottle using a Nalgene and stick this between their legs to warm their blood. This is also a good technique if your sleeping bag becomes wet.

Alcohol: There's a strong tradition of drinking on big walls, with beer, wine and spirits often being hauled up with the water. I've never been a big drinker and have tended to prefer to haul water and make tea my tipple, but each to their own. Cans of beer tend to puncture easily and end up making your haul bag smell like a nightclub toilet, while a gin and tonic cannot be drunk without ice, or a mojito without fresh mint, and so I tend to stick with whiskey or wine, red wine of course. Wine in boxes tends to carry well, but stowing it in a Nalgene bottle is best. I should also cover drugs while I'm at it. I've climbed a few walls with people who smoked a lot of dope, and I didn't like it, as really your life is in someone's hands who's on some spectrum of fucked up, and having someone taking tokes on a bong half way up your lead does not inspire confidence. I've also noticed a general increase in people being wasted in Yosemite wall climbing and would controversially put down a few deaths to

Aleks Gamme tucking into monk fish casserole on the Troll Wall

being high the whole time. Get stoned on the ground, not on the stone, and if you can't, then you have a problem.

Electrolytes: Electrolytes are like the oil in your engine, helping to make your body perform optimally. Allow these to drop, and you'll start to cramp up. Most often you will experience this when climbing hard and fast, such as on one day ascents of very long routes, the electrolytes you got from your dinner or breakfast sweated out. And so it's important to add some electrolytes to your personal water supply, best done by adding tablets. What brand you use is up to you as there are many different types on the market, but I'd check out proper sports shops, running shops especially, and see what they have. Try the tablet before you head off to make sure you like the taste, and often you don't need to use a whole tablet (some can be too strong), as you're not running a marathon. Another bonus of using tablets is that flavoured water is drunk more regularly. Adding salt to your food is OK, but not really advisable because electrolytes are more than just sodium, and having too much salt can lead to swelling in your hands and feet, and of course make you much more thirsty.

WATER TRANSPORT

How you carry your water on a wall is important, as leaking or dropped bottles can ruin your day. A lot of climbers spend ages wrapping their bottles with tape and tying on clip loops, which to my mind always seems to be a waste of time. It's rare that you can't find somewhere to stow your bottles (portaledge, stuff sack, rope bag), and wrapping your bottles just seems to waste tape, and I never really trust those little loops people add anyway. Therefore either just take the bottles as God or Walmart made them, or just tie a 3 mm Prusik knot around the neck of the bottle.

If you have a mix of bottles, such as 1 litre, 1.5 litre, and 4 litre, always put the smaller bottles on the outside edge of your nest of bottles. This way they protect the larger bottles from impacts, help milk all the room out of the haul bag (rather than loads of big bottles with big gaps), and if they do break in an impact, you'll only lose a smaller amount of water. If you're heading up on a sub-zero wall, and are taking water bottles with you, consider lining the bottom of the bag with foam, and use smaller bottles so that if they freeze they're easier to break up (cut off plastic, put ice in a stuff sack, and break it up by tapping it with a hammer).

Tip: You you stow the bottles upside-down on a sub zero wall the ice forms on the bottom of the bottles, not where the lid is.

Tip: If you're using easily crushable plastic bottles to store your water (I use 3.78 l supermarket bottles), when a bottle is empty, open the lid, crush it down letting all the air out, close the lid again and shove it in the bottom of a haul bag. Then when you get down, you can take off all the lids, blow the bottles back up again, and refill for your next wall.

WATER NOTES:

Personal Water: On some routes, I've left my water at the belay and only drank between pitches, while on others I carried a 1 or 2 litre bladder on my back, and just took little sips every five minutes. The former system probably meant water lasted longer, but maybe at the expense of dropping into that 2% dehydration zone by the end of the pitch, while the latter used up more water and meant I was carrying up to 2 kg extra on a pitch. I guess on balance, being hydrated and having water with you keeps you sharper and more alert, not thinking about guzzling down water all the time. Having a small bladder pack is also handy when climbing fast, short fixing, as you can stick all your other bits in there too, like a light top, windproof, head torch, etc.

Team Water: Team water should be stored in fit for purpose plastic bottles, and these should be between 1 litre and 4 litres, as having more risks losing too much water if it bursts or gets dropped (a 5 kg weight of water is easier to drop than a 2 kg bottle). The classic bottles are the 1.5 litre Coke, 1 litre Gatorade bottles or 3 litre bottled water, but of course, there are many different plastic bottles out there! Be careful not to buy the super cheap bottles as the plastic can be very thin, and avoid any bottles that have lids that cannot be replaced (pull off lids).

Water Bags: Water bags are really good for big walls, such as the MSR Dromedary and Ortlieb water bag, being tougher than they look, light enough to bring along on your trip (which saves time scrambling around for plastic bottles when you get there), and also featuring clip in loops etc. Where they really shine is that they take up 100% of the volume of the haul bag, increasing the volume left for everything else, so are ideal for walls where you want to take just one bag (The Nose for example). The 2 and 4 litre sizes are good. When you get home, make sure you dry out the bags and store them with the lids off. Oh, and practice use these bags before you get on the wall. (I've had partners who found operating the MSR Dromedary bags without spilling water everywhere difficult).

FOOD

Food comes in two main categories for wall climbing, the rock diet and the expedition diet.

Rock Menu

This typical big wall diet is one that's very simple and requires no cooking, only boiling water. In reality, unless you're stuck in a storm, food doesn't seem to be a big issue, as everyone is always busy doing something, so there tends to be no lunch beyond the odd bar, gel, or handful of nuts or sweets.

- **Breakfast:** This can vary from something as simple as a small tin of fruit, instant porridge, or granola mixed with powdered milk, to a bagel with cream cheese on it. With long hard days, it's good to eat something substantial here, and I'm a big fan of measuring out granola and milk powder, and sticking this in my cup and filling it to the top. This way I get a drink of milk and breakfast in one, sometimes forgoing a hot drink, saving that for later. Breakfast should be packaged up in days, so at dinner time you can grab the next day's breakfast and day food and store it in your personal bag for the morning, so you can just wake up and eat. Climbers addicted to coffee might want to have some chocolate covered coffee beans for breakfast too.

- **Lunch:** I will always keep some bars handy near the top of the haul bag, and in any day bag carried. When it gets colder you'll find that climbers and belayers begin getting more hungry, so this should be factored into your menu planning, with hard cheese, nuts, sausage and bagels good day food, stored in a bag in the top of the haul bag (a bagel can also be slung with a sling and sent up via the zip line).

- **Dinner:** Dinner can be a long or short affair depending on the time, and finishing early and taking your time is always great. I'm a bigger fan of bagels than tortillas, but both are great wall staples, as they can't get too damaged or squashed in the bags. Onto these, you can add a whole range of foods, but usually, the base is made of cream cheese, hummus or mayo (collect mayo sachets), then add another layer or two, with things like salami, tuna, ham, beef, chilli, pepper, baby tomatoes, creating a kind of Scooby snack. One or two of these is usually enough for most climbers. Having a few little tiny plastic bottles of things like sweet chilli sauce, pesto, Tabasco, plus salt and pepper is also good. Fresh fruit and veg like tomatoes can be taken up for the first few days and used up before they get too squashed and nasty, with avocados being great for day one and two. One thing I like to do if I want something warm is to put two packets of Ramen noodles in my cup, then pour in boiling water and let sit for five minutes. I then drink the liquid like soup, and then once I'm down to the noodles, I add a packet of tuna, and maybe some pepper. Other climbers take food like instant potato and mix this with soup, or couscous, and most supermarkets stock a lot of great alternatives to the old staple wall foods.
- **Supper:** Having stuff for after dinner is good, including tea, hot chocolate (hot chocolate sachets are a great addition to any wall), with some sweet and savoury bits like biscuits and fruit being popular.

FOOD NOTES:

How Much Food To Take: Try and work on a menu that is generous and gives you two extra days of food, but which can then be subdivided again. Very often some people eat more, and some eat less, and once on the summit, there is always food left over. When stuck in a storm you can reduce your food intake by half, and very often if you're dry, food is just a way to break up the boredom. Having a good supply of drinks and milk powder is always good, as they weigh very little but help raise the spirit.

Calorie Value: On a warm wall, you're probably never going to get hungry, and you seem to be able to live on fresh air and water most of the time, and I've done routes on nothing but a bagel a day. Just make sure there is always something to fill your stomach. On milder walls, the same applies but make sure you have more, and more fatty savoury stuff, like ham, salami, sausage and cheese, as the fats are good in the cold. The place you need to be more calorie wise is on major alpine objectives, where you may be climbing for more than a week or two, or even a month. Here, with extreme cold, and a lot of hard work and sitting around, I would aim for between 4000 and 5000 calories a day, adding butter and olive oil and fatty meat and cheeses into the mix.

Storage: Try and break your food down so you don't have one huge bag of food that weighs a ton and requires much digging around to find anything. Instead break it down into multi-day bags.

Rubbish: Include a rubbish bag in all your food bags and keep a few spare in the base of the haul bag. Plastic wrappings can be folded and stored inside empty tuna packets and meal bags, and all tins should be hammered flat, the idea to combine all rubbish into neat little packages that can easily be carried down. If you're on a wilderness wall, then try and separate out what can be burned and what cannot.

Vermin: Be very aware of vermin, mainly mice, on a wall or on the ground. Everything should be stowed away at night that might be of interest to mice, either hanging from the wall or ledge, or in stuff sacks inside the haul bag. Cups and bowls left out on a ledge that get heavy traffic will be visited by mice or rats, and more than once I've seen mice crap and/or a piss stain in my cup - not nice or conducive to good health (GSI cups with screw on lids are good for keeping mice out). If you're sleeping on the ground or summit, then hanging food can work (albeit not very well - I once hung a food bag from the branch of a tree beside a river in Zion, and woke to find the bag swinging around wildly. When I got it down and opened it a cartload of very happy mice jumped out!), but where there's a lot of animal action, consider using a bear proof container or stow food inside a large pan and put a stick or stone on top of it.

Designated Cook: It's best to have one person making dinner for everyone, so they have everything in one place, rather than passing bags of food, knives, wraps, etc. all over the place. Before cooking tea, the chef should clean their hands with a wet wipe and hand sanitiser.

BIG WALL STOVES

On some walls, a stove is a luxury while on others it's a necessity. If you're climbing light and fast then a stove is just something that requires more stuff, gas, a pan and lid, maybe something to hang it from, and so it's best to stick to cold rations and water. If you're going slower and heavy, then a stove can be a real boost to morale, and if you get stuck in a storm it can save your life. On a wall, there can be flat spots to stand a gas canister, but you're best to use a hanging stove.

HANGING GAS STOVES GAS

The ability to hang a stove from an anchor or inside your portaledge is a real boon, allowing you to brew up anywhere and at any time. The JetBoil style integrated stove is the ideal choice for wall climbing, being small, light and compact, yet able to serve up boiling water efficiently, for tea or coffee . I would avoid ever cooking anything inside a stove on the wall, only boiling water to be decanted into cups or dehydrated food bags. Most of these stoves come with hanging kits, which vary in effectiveness, some being good, some poorly thought out, and don't be afraid to make your own using cable and swages. The downside with the gas stove is that none of them are as dependable as a liquid fuel expedition stove, and once they stop working they tend to stay not working. Another strange problem with these stoves is how little heat they give off, which is one of the best parts of using a stove inside a ledge on an alpine route, helping to lift the spirits and dry stuff out a little. This can be achieved by simply leaving the stove running without a pan. The major drawback with all these stoves is that they give off a huge amount of carbon monoxide, which could be a killer if you don't allow ventilation.

STOVE BAG

All the stove parts should go inside their own stove bag, that will also contain a mug (ideally this will fit inside the pan), lighters, pan scrub (not necessary if you're only using it as recommended above, i.e., only to boil water), flint and steel lighter (will light stove when wet), and hanging kit. The gas should always be unscrewed from the stove when stowing.

USING A STOVE IN THE PORTALEDGE

Although it's always made clear people should not cook inside tents, in reality, you will be cooking inside your portaledge, either open or under your fly. The first thing to be aware of is how dangerous your stove is, both to you and your ledge. Get a hot stove close to the ledges webbing, and it'll melt them in a blink of an eye. Spill a pan of boiling water over yourself or your partner, and it would be the end of your climb. Here are a few tips:

- **Hang It:** A hanging stove will find its balance point, unlike a stove balanced on its cartridge on a belay seat between the two of you. Hanging also keeps it away from everything else. I tend to hang the stove from the funkness device to get it the correct height, but be careful of the karabiner getting super hot and melting your slings. Hanging it straight down with the suspension, via the hanging loop you often find there, tends to put the stove too close to the wall, and instead, you want to create a deviation by clipping a quickdraw from a suspension strap to pull the stove away from the wall.

- **Centre It:** The area of the ledge that moves the least is centre, inline with the suspension, and so it should

be hung here, both climbers on either side.

- **Hang It Low:** The stove should be set low, so you can see inside the pan while sitting, as having it high makes it hard to see what's going on.

- **Protect Yourself:** The person cooking should think about wearing their gloves when handling the stove, and when pouring water into cups, protect your legs by pulling your sleeping bags or bivvy bags over your legs (a damp bag is better than a 1st-degree burn).

When cooking inside your fly try and avoid a rolling boil, switching the stove off as soon as bubbles begin to form, as a rolling boil will just add tons of moisture inside the ledge, and moisture is the killer. Always have a sponge handy for wiping the walls of the fly when cooking, and a lighter or flint and steel striker at hand to re-fire the stove if it goes out (a damp portaledge will kill most lighters, so make sure you have a flint and steel). When cooking try to keep everything that can absorb moisture put away, stored in a waterproof bag or inside your bivvy bags. On winter walls I try and avoid cooking in the mornings, as the heat from the stove tends to melt all the frozen condensation, which then drips down on you. A better option is to fill a Thermos flask the night before or just stick with cool water and cold breakfast. If you're melting ice and snow, bring this in a large stuff sack and use a cup to add it to the pan.

CARBON MONOXIDE

Carbon monoxide (CO) is a major danger when a portaledge fly is deployed, as the very reason it is deployed means you're battening down the hatches and locking yourself in. CO gas will form at the top of the fly (where to stove is hanging) and slowly work down, meaning a climber sitting might be affected more quickly than a climber laying down. CO is called a silent killer, but having been poisoned many times, I'd say it's only a killer of the stupid. Any stove that's running inside an enclosed space, made from what is in effect a big plastic bag, should elicit some concern and wariness.

Signs of CO poisoning include headaches, weakness, sickness and general lethargy, and so you need to be venting clean air into your ledge long before you have any of these signs. It's also important to know that modern JetBoil/reactor style stoves that feature highly efficient heat exchangers also pump out a great deal more CO than liquid stoves like an XGK. This is caused by the flame being very close to the pan, and so not combusting the gas properly (but heating the water quickly). This is compounded when heating pans of snow or ice, which further induce CO production. What you need is a hot blue flame (indicating there is enough oxygen present for carbon dioxide to be produced), not a colder yellow flame (a sign CO is being produced). On the plus side a stove running without a pan, say to warm up your ledge, is pretty safe.

The distance between the pan and the flame is the crucial part, and anyone tackling a major alpine wall over a long period should look into using a liquid fuel hanging stove, or a non JetBoil/MSR Reactor hanging setup, where more room is created between the flame and the pan. This distance needs to be around 40 mm, and also don't forget that CO poisoning is cumulative.

With an enclosed fly, try and have the door open, and if that's not possible, at least keep the top sections open as much as you can, allowing a free flow of air to take the CO away. With a deployable fly you can often just secure the bottom up onto the fly pole, keeping the rain off, but allowing air in. CO is only slightly lighter than air, so doesn't really rise or sink

TOILET STUFF

"How do you go to the toilet?" is a question all big wallers get asked. Well, on an alpine wall you go where you want to go (not so on a big wall, where you need wag bags and poo tubes and I will talk about all that soon), but it's well worth taking it slow the first time if you've never taken a dump wearing your harness!

First make sure you know how to unhitch your rear risers. I tend to wrap these around my leg loops or pull them through my legs and clip the riser to my belay loop (this way you won't end up dangling your risers in your poo!). You can pull your trousers down with your leg loops still in place, but it's usually nicer to take them off, although that'll only be possible if you're on a ledge. To do this you tend not to need adjustable leg loops, and most people can slip them off. When buying a new wall harness make sure the rear risers can be operated easily, or if not then consider adding your own Fastex buckles.

HAVING A WHIZZ

Peeing on the wall tends to be a matter of making sure you remember to go, and on hot walls, you can often only go twice a day. Some people urinate into plastic bottles on the wall, to avoid ledges ending up smelling of piss (often they'll smell fine when dry, but stink when it rains), but I think as long as you don't piss on ledges or down cracks you should be OK unless you're on a mega-popular route (such as the Nose). Of course if you go down the plastic bottle route, once on the summit, pour the piss out! The most important whizz factor is to always have a piss bottle close at hand, as wanting to go all night will spoil your sleep (it's also important to keep a water bottle close, so make sure you can tell which is which in the dark). If you don't have a piss bottle, then a cup will do (chucking the piss over the edge of course), or half a water bottle or tin. For women, the only option tends to be to shuffle your bum over the edge (I've yet to find anyone who seemed skilled enough with a Shewee to use one in a portaledge). It's maybe worth saying that if you're planning on taking a dump, then it's worth having a piss first, as you don't want to be pissing in your wag bag.

POO TUBES (WASTE CASES)

Back in the day, climbers used to crap into paper bags from the grocery store and just throw them off, meaning the base of popular walls was covered in desiccated bags of human shit. The idea was people would come back later and pick them up, but often they didn't, meaning things got messy. Worse still, when climbing under another team there was the risk of being hit by a bag of human shit, the only thing worse being if they'd set fire to it as well (flaming shit bags they called them). Another problem was taking a dump into a small paper bag, someone telling me before my first big wall "you may think you know where your asshole is, but you don't until you shit into a paper bag". Luckily things have moved on a lot since then.

Although as I mentioned on some alpine walls most climbers will proba-

bly just take a dump down the wall (avoid crapping on ledges though), in most cases it's best practise to use a poo tube on any route that has a chance of being climbed by anyone else, and in national parks, it's a legal requirement.

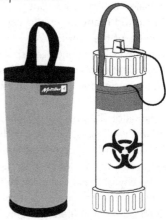

A poo tube is anything that you use to carry your poo in, and can be homemade, made from pipe, or bought, with the Metolius Waste Case being the most widely used (a mini roll top haul bag). I would avoid the solid poop tubes (made from a length of plastic drain pipe with a screw cap on one end and a glued cap on the other), as they're not easy to carry, can crack if dropped while being carried down, and can't be thrown in the washing machine. A soft case can be rolled up small when on the way to the climb, and strapped onto the top of a haul bag for the way down. You'd think carrying it down would be a problem, but your nasal passages tend to be battered by dirt, and so smell isn't that big an issue (plus you probably stink as well). I would advise you line your poo tube with a bin bag to stop them getting too smelly, and a little cat litter in the bottom can reduce odours further. Hang the waste case on a very long length of distinctive cord from the main haul point so that it can be pulled up quickly, then dropped out of range!

WAG/GO BAGS

Poo bags are different than poop tubes in that you poo in these bags, tie them up and then stow them inside the poo tube, disposing of them when you get down. Commercial wag/go bags are highly recommended. They consist of a heavy duty resealable plastic bag used to stow the poo bags and a large poo bag, meaning you can tuck it under your knees when squatting. This bag contains a gelling/deodorising powder in the bottom. You also get toilet roll and a wet wipe to clean your hands.

When using these bags avoid pissing in them, as you'll end up quickly filling up your waste case, plus you'll be hauling even more weight (human crap can end up pretty damned heavy without adding your piss in too). Once you've gone, make sure to shake the gelling powder around in the bag then squeeze all the air out before twisting up the bag and tying a knot, so as to make as compact a package as possible. Place the poo bag in the heavy duty outer bag and again squeeze all the air out.

I tend to stow wag bags in the top pocket of one haul bag in a stuff sack, and it's often worth carrying one in your bladder/day pack if you have one, just in case! Your wag bag contains a small sanitising wipe, but it's worth carrying a small bottle of hand sanitizer too, especially if you're a big team on a long wall.

HOW MUCH POO?

As a guide go for 0.5 litres (that includes wag bag, etc.) per person per day, so a Metolius Waste Case will do two people for eight days. If you find you're running out of space, then you can cut open water bottles and put wag bags in there, then tape them up and stow them in a stuff sack hanging from the bottom of the haul bag.

POO ROUTINE

It's important to establish a poo routine, where everyone dumps once a day (more than once and you've got too much food). The reason for this is you'll get this out of the way, and won't have people being distracted wanting a dump mid-day, or even mid pitch (I once took a dump while ascending, but I'd not recommend it). This also means that at the end of the day everyone is in sync, and that when people are in their portaledges, you'll not have someone crashing around looking for Wag Bags, trying to pull up the poop tube, taking a dump as you're eating your beanie weenies

ALTERNATIVES

Some climbers crap in paper bags and stow the bags in a heavy duty mesh bag hung far below their haul bags, allowing the sun to dry the bags out. Once on the summit, the bags are then burnt (I don't see this as being the type of bonfire you'd sit around talking shit, just breathing it!). I've never used this method but it sounds very green, although open fires are often illegal in many parks and will also soon lead to a lot of unsightly mess and damage. If you're going to have a crap, then carry your crap out. Another option already mentioned is to put your Wag Bags inside cut open water bottles that you then tape up and hang from the bottom of your haul bags, stuffing more poo bags in, and re-taping.

STAYING ALIVE

STORMS

Big wall climbing is not rock climbing or alpine climbing, where bad weather will result in a retreat back to the ground. No, on a real big wall you will most often not be able to go up or down in bad weather, and instead will be trapped, and have to deal with what is about to unfold. And what might unfold may be a little discomfort, a little wet maybe, a little cold, but something you get through fine, or it could be a fight for your life, the most terrifying out there experience you will ever have. It is vital you understand just how exposed you can be on a wall, looking down at the road, the tourists driving by, while fighting to survive, and with no way of being rescued in that moment. It is hard to describe how exposed you can feel in such a situation, forced to just take it, like lying in the gutter while being blasted by icy water minute after minute, hour after hour, sometimes day after day. When the storm is all around you, and water is everywhere, there is no down or up, only survival.

WHAT ARE THE CHANCES?

Some sailors can sail around the world without ever coming across a serious storm, while others just poke out of the harbour and get clobbered. Climbing walls is the same, and the longer and harder the wall, where your climb stretches beyond the weather forecast, the more you need to be prepared to face and survive such things even if they never happen.

THE SURVIVAL SPECTRUM

It is incredible how fast a person can succumb to hypothermia. One minute you're dry and warm, climbing up from camp six on the Nose, and then it starts to rain. You push on in your t-shirt, knowing the summit isn't far, just a few pitches, you're a mountaineer after all. You have a waterproof jacket and a fleece, but that's in the bag with your mate, plus you'll be at the belay soon. So you press on, your clothing wetting out, the wind blowing it cool. Your synthetic t-shirt should be warmish when damp, but it feels like cotton, water soaking your clothes, rain running down into your shoes. You try to ignore it, but you can't, your hands numb, your body shaking. "Send up my jackets" you shout down, seeing your mate looking equally dejected down at the belay. He sends up a fleece and waterproof, and knowing putting them over your wet top would be a mistake, you take off your top and tie it to your gear loop. The warmth is instantaneous. You pull up your hood and feel ready to get the hell out of there. You move on, but feel water running down your sleeves, wetting your arms, and then your body. Your legs now feel numb, your hands clumsy. A stream begins to flow down the wall, flowing over you, you are soaked again, and this time you feel even colder. You cannot go up, you need to act, you can feel you're slipping into hypothermia. Thinking fast you place an extra piece and somehow make a belay, tie in the haul line and lead line and prepare to rap back down to camp six.

Steve Bate nearing the summit of El Cap after soloing Zodiac.

But your fingers can't untie the knot, your skin all dead and slippery. Frantic you fish out your pen knife and cut the rope at the knot and taking real care not to panic, rap down the wall to camp six. Here you find things are just as bad, a waterfall crashing down on the ledge, your mate seemingly having given up the ghost, forcing you to shake him awake. You pull out a bothy bag and pull it over the both of you, and the change is instant, your brain begins to move again. You have synthetic sleeping bags and two bivvy bags, having taken this seriously, and manage to somehow get them out of the haul bag and get into them under the bothy bag, but everything gets wet in the process. You sit on the haul bag, the noise of the water on the bag deafening, and wonder if you should have waited and saved the sleeping bags from getting wet, but you know you were too close to hypothermic.

The summer weight bags had only just felt warm enough last night, the late September temperatures colder than you'd thought they'd be. Now the bag is wet it feels as if it has no heat at all, and the only heat comes from your partner's hip and shoulder pressing against you. You are so cold, in fact you've never been so cold, and you cannot think of doing anything but sitting there. You talk about trying to go down, but with your ropes fixed above you can't summon up the strength to leave the bag and ascend up there, the very idea of coming out from the bothy like a death sentence. Your forecast is three days old and as night comes on it begins to snow. As you wonder if you'll survive the night, and how long it will take to rescue you, if you can hang on that long, a few pitches below, on camp five, two guys smoke a bong and play cards.

THE DEADLY SPELL

The number one killer on a wall, beyond falling off it, is hypothermia, and so this should be the focus of much of your planning and preparation for the climb, as it's actually an easy foe to defeat. I've nearly died of hypothermia a few times, had my body temperature drop to the point I felt like I was dead already, and I would recommend all climbers experience this kind of deep cold, best achieved by cold water immersion (go swimming in the sea in winter). Knowing how it feels helps you to identify the onset of hypothermia, and arms you with a healthy fear/paranoia, as you know how hard it is to warm up once you begin to slip under its deadly spell.

HYPOTHERMIA FUNDAMENTALS

The human body has an internal temperature of 37° C +/- 1°, and once you allow your body to fall below that by 1° you are moving into hypothermia.

At 35° - 35.5° you will begin to shake involuntarily, your body trying to create some warmth by muscular contractions. This will continue until glucose reserves are used up, or the body temperature drops further. At 32° you stop shivering and you will become confused, seem drunk, make stupid or irrational choices and find easy tasks almost impossible. Blood may flow out from your core and into your limbs giving you unbearable hot aches, leading to clothes being taken off (often seen as a sign of suicide).

Below 28° C (severe hypothermia) you will drop into a semi coma and eventually die through organ failure, although 'looking dead' is no sign of being dead. I crossed Greenland with a guy whose friend, Anna Bågenholm, was brought back to life from a core temperature of 13.7 °C.

HOW HEAT IS LOST

The two main ways you're going to get clobbered are through evaporation (wet) and convection (wind), with conduction (touching) being an issue if you're lying in a portaledge without a sleeping mat.

Cold is really not the problem, as I've lived in total comfort at very cold temperatures (down to -50° C), and with the correct diet and clothing, it's not a problem.

Where you have issues are 0° C and up, where you get slush, hail and rain, and on a wall I mean RAIN! The human body will lose heat 25 times faster in water than in still air, something worth thinking about before committing to climbing up a waterfall, but in a real world situation, a climber tends to become wet, but not submerged (unless water is running through their clothes). Here your insulation will be compromised, but the insulation value of each piece of protection varies, say a cotton t-shirt vs a grid fleece top, synthetic belay jacket versus a down jacket. You will see figures like a piece of clothing will be five times more insulating, and this is down to the density/structure of the clothing and the amount of air it holds within its fibres.

HYPOTHERMIA REALITIES

On a wall you will not have a little thermometer sticking out of your mouth or arse, and so need a very practical approach to this form of potential death. The number one thing to realise, as you plan your defence against this killer, is that it can rob you of your ability to use your hands and fingers very quickly, and it will be that which kills you, blocking off your escape route (going up, down, or switching on your phone to dial 911).

The first stage of this is hypothermia in your limbs (your core can be 37° C, but your arms can be 28° C), where you quickly lose dexterity, your hands no longer your own, going 'stupid'. This is something most climbers have experienced while climbing in winter, on rock or ice, only here it's often more severe than that 'cold hands' or hot aches, more profound and debilitating. We are well trained as climbers to spot frostbite, but less so hypothermia in our limbs, as climbing, grabbing and holding axes, tends to be less dexterous than untying ropes, clipping in ascenders, opening stuff sacks.

Once you lose your ability to use your hands, you are pretty much in a survival or rescue situation, and all climbers should know how to descend or belay on a Munter hitch, as this is a good knot if you can't feed a rope through a belay device, and also works very OK on frozen ropes (getting a frozen stiff 10.5 mm rope into a belay device with frozen hands in a storm can be a Herculean task... I know).

This limb hypothermia is of course the first stage of frost-nip (surface freezing) and then frostbite (deep tissue freezing), both of which will make you a casualty (I've seen both on big wall climbs, including frost-nip on El Cap in April). Feeling your core temperature dropping is terrifying, and on a wall you can't run around and do star jumps, and are often forced to be static. Even if you're leading heroically, staving off deep cold by moving fast, your belayer is not, and it's not uncommon for a leader to come unstuck by a frozen stiff second.

HOW TO AVOID IT

The number one rule is 'stay dry', and if that's not possible then number two is 'stay as dry as you can'.

On a wall this translates to not exposing yourself to the elements, not trying to be that hero from the example at the beginning of this chapter, who climbs through the storm and makes it out the other side. No, be the guys playing cards under their flysheet before the storm arrives. The safe climber is the one who plays it safe, keeps the deck dry, because a losing hand now is one thing, being stuck on the ledge, cold and wet, but how do you know the game is even over?

A team that stops early and puts up their ledge, maybe fixes up from a sheltered spot, then retreats at the first sign of the storm, is more able to keep their powder dry when that storm lasts a week, where the rescue team cannot reach anyone, and the summer storm turns into a winter horror.

Don't feel it's a failure to keep one eye on the sky and a hand on your flysheet, as I've climbed with several people who had no doubt they were going to meet their maker, hugging their mate in their one synthetic bag, rolling over every half an hour because no one brought a mat, a waterfall crashing directly onto their ledge.

STORM NOTES

So, if you're going to survive and thrive on the wall, here are some tips:

- **Avoid Death Funnels**: A wall tends to contain certain areas that act as huge water collection points, with bone dry rock turning into a roaring torrent in minutes. If you get caught in such a funnel your chances of surviving exposed are zero, your chances within a portaledge slim. Identifying these spots on a route, either by looking at the wall beforehand, or checking beta or route lore, is vital.

- **Dress For Success**: I always tell people to take the same clothes on El Cap as they'd take on the Eiger North Face in winter, able to cope with wind, rain and snow, both while moving and static. This should include a full shell (wear knee pads to stop the knees wearing through), the jacket used to also keep the wind off you. Bring a medium weight fleece that will be warm when wet (fibre pile style fleece rather than a hard fleece), or a medium weight synthetic 'puff' jacket, or both. I always bring a heavy weight synthetic 'DAS' style belay jacket, and one set of standard base layers (long sleeved top worn as primary top) and one set of 'emergency' Brynje mesh underwear (very good in wet conditions). I also include a balaclava, fleece gloves and a pair of industrial waterproof latex gloves.

- **It's Never As Bad**: The wind and rain smashing into your flysheet is never as bad as it sounds, the wind half as strong, the rain half as violent. The dark magnifies the storm, and morning tends to always lift the spirits no matter how bad things seemed at 2 am. So don't sit there cowering. If you have good quality gear you should just enjoy the ride. If you've got ear plugs then stick them in.

- **Handcuffs**: No matter how good your waterproofs are, water will run down your sleeves, and then through your clothes. If you were really paranoid then you could carry a light kayaking

Bad weather and high winds on the Shield

cag with rubber cuffs, or get some rubber cuffs and glue them to an old shell jacket. Alternatives would be to tape your waterproof gloves over the wrists of your waterproof jacket (some people have climbed in Marigold washing up gloves like this).

- **Climb Stormy Routes In Stormy Weather**: If the weather has storms passing through don't risk trying to 'nip' up a wall that features slabs and major water courses, such as the Salathe or Lurking Fear, especially as the slabby nature means you'll take less storm gear. Instead go for the steep routes, the Leaning Towers, the Tangerine Trips or Virginias, and go prepared to climb in a more alpine or capsule style. Take it slow and go prepared for the worst.

- **Weather Or Not**: Get a good weather forecast and keep getting updates if you can. Sometimes you can be at the boundary of good forecasts and might need to check multiple forecasts. When they disagree, don't just go with the one that sounds like the one you want to be true.

- **Go Ready For War**: Don't put your life in the hands of a computer model, and instead go ready for bad weather and a worst case scenario. Even on a summer wall you could get some freak weather, and end up shivering away with 100 kg haul bags wishing you'd brought along 1 kg more of fleece

- **Sleeping With Your Fly**: The killer when bad weather is close is not being arsed to put your flysheet on, or have it set to deploy quickly, clipped into the top of the ledge. There is nothing worse than feeling that pitter patter of rain on your face knowing your fly is deep down inside one of your bag... somewhere.

- **A Roof Over Your Head**: Try and identify good spots to spend the night, ideally under roofs, but also in corners, where you can get some protection from the wind.

- **Wet Is Wet, Dry Is Dry**: Don't make the mistake of getting into a dry sleeping bag with wet clothes unless you feel the bag will not be warm enough without them. Try to change into dry clothes or take off all your clothes and get into your bag. Wring out all the water from your clothes and then lay them over the top of your bivvy bag, then add your shells over the top. If you stay there long enough they might dry out enough to put back on.

- **Zero Water Tolerance**: Once hunkered down in your ledge you need to try and keep everything as dry as possible, and one single drip can lead to utter disaster. Have your repair kit ready, and gaffer tape, and if the tape won't stay fixed try heating the tape with your stove first so it becomes super sticky. If you're getting drips then lay your waterproofs over your bivvy bags (this will add more warmth too), and try and avoid ever sleeping in your waterproofs. You can also use a tarp as an inner tent, by wrapping it around the ledges suspension (Just the top section might reduce condensation considerably). You can also lay the tarp over your bivvy bags (again this will also add warmth).

- **Burn It Up**: Running a stove, even on low, will create a very warm environment and will help to dry things off as well as lift morale. Leave the pan off the stove and make sure you have a blue flame. Heat up water in your Nalgene bottle and put this in your sleeping bag (between your legs is good), as this will also create a temperature differential and pump the moisture out.

- **Stock Up**: If you know you're going to be hammered, make sure you have everything you need in your portaledge, or close at hand, so you don't need to go out and get wet looking for stuff. Stuff sacks with a few days food can be hung over the side helping to tension out the fly

- **Lash It All Down**: If you're hunkering down, put everything you can away, with ropes and hardware put away in the haul bags, and the haul bags tied to the ledge, and the ledge fixed to the rock. If you can't create an upward anchor for real storm protection, then clipping one side of a ledge to a haul bag filled with 30 kg of water is pretty good, while clipping off a corner or two to gear is also better than nothing.

- **Leaky Pipes**: Many routes will have spots where you can see where there is seepage, with signs like black marks, thick plant life, and moss, and these need to be avoided for bivvies as they will often spout waterfalls.

- **Keep Your Ropes Dry**: Wet ropes will freeze, and frozen ropes are no use for anything. They are hard to ascend (you will need to clear them of ice), almost impossible to rap on (you can't pull them), and difficult to belay with. Your best bet is to wait for the sun to come out and melt them out, but of course it's best that they don't get wet and then frozen in the first place.

- **Fix**: If you feel you'll be in an exposed spot, then consider fixing up from a safe belay. For example, if you're under the big roof on the Shield, or the Great Roof on the Nose and have a bad weather warning, how about climbing up two pitches, or even three, then fixing your lead and haul line down. If nothing appears you can push on (learn how to use a cargo hook), and if it does you can feel smug.

- **The 384,400 km Pitch**: So you're almost at the top, with just a pitch to go. There's bad weather coming but you're dry and warm and safe, and it's only one pitch, so you rack up and go for it. I think one of the hardest pitches I ever climbed on El Cap was not on the Sea of Dreams or South Seas or PO wall, but the final 5.4 slab on Tangerine Trip. Wet and hypothermic, without socks or gloves, snow covering everything, I somehow dry tooled that last pitch using my knees and two cliffhangers, plus a frozen rope thrown to a loose rock. In that moment that summit could have been as far away as the moon. Bottom line - stay put until you know you can make the moon shot.

- **The Wall Will Always Be There**: The final word is the oldest there is. Don't risk your life or the lives of your friends by rolling that dice. If the weather is bad get out and go climb somewhere else. When you come back you'll be twice as psyched - what's more you'll be alive.

SHIT FAN

So all of the above assumes you've got your shit together, you're sure your gear is up to the job, and you've been a good boy or girl. But of course that's often not the way it goes. There are also the times when you get caught with no waterproofs, no ledge, no sleeping bag, in a waterfall, with ropes that are frozen. What then?

Armageddon Inventory: First off, you need to work out if it's best to go for fight or flight, basically do you have the kit to stand your ground and try and survive, or should you try and get down or up and hope to make it. If you're standing in shorts and a shirt and the hailstones are coming down, then you will not survive and so the only chance to live is to try and get up or down, with down being best. If on the other hand you have some kit and think you can make a go of it, and limit your exposure, then that's what you should do. Often it's 50/50.

Hasty Retreat: Speed here is vital, and although I would never recommend it, when your life force is running down to minutes, and you're soaking wet, you may need to do simul raps, making sure both climbers are tied to the end of the rope (with three climbers, use the Stone knot). When you get within three pitches of the ground see if you can tie your ropes together and rap the whole way down using a Munter Hitch (tie the ropes with overhand knots), allowing the knots to pass through the Munter. Once the storm has passed ascend back up and get your ropes.

Going Up: Escaping upwards is more risky as it takes longer and so makes you more exposed. I saw a guy once top out on the Nose, solo, who had no waterproofs, only a down jacket - oh and sandals. When he scraped his way to the top, no doubt ending the greatest epic of his life, he just tied off the lead line and walked off and never came back, leaving all his stuff behind.

The Ground Is The Top: Don't assume that reaching the flat ground on the top of your route is the end of your survival story, as often it's only about to begin. I've got to the top only to fall down slabs (I once slipped all the way down from the exit of Tangerine Trip to Zodiac in a snowstorm), fall through ice into rivers and lakes, get avalanched, and get benighted. When you get to the top you often have three dimensional weather, plus snow, a drop in your adrenaline, fatigue, and more often than not, night time to contend with. Try and pace yourself on the way down.

Powder Dry: If you are soaking wet and have no way of protecting yourself properly, say you're huddled under a flapping tarp, then consider not getting your sleeping bag wet, as this is the highest value insulation piece you have (think of it like wood for a fire). Instead of getting into it first, keep it in its bivvy bag, and use the bivvy bag like a blanket protecting the insulation. Try and squeeze the most insulation out of everything, and anything that stops wind or holds dead air (that crunched up topo in your pocket is technically 'insulating') is something that can keep you alive.

Foam Sweet Foam: Foam mats are highly insulating and can be cut up and stuck around your torso like body armour. And, as an aside, Ed Drummond famously used his Karrimat to stave off hunger by eating a section of it.

Spoons: Getting close and spooning your partner is one way to stay alive, and two wet sleeping bags used over two spooning climbers will give you a better chance of surviving than two wet climbers in single layer bags curled up in a ball. If you are caught out on a ledge where you cannot spoon, then sitting close together and wrapping the sleeping bags around both of you is the best option.

Battling through a storm on a very slow speed ascent of the Trip

Eat And Drink: In a survival situation it's easy to forget to eat and drink, but food is warmth (you need sugar in your muscles to shiver), and dehydration reduces blood flow to your extremities. Any fatty food will create more warmth, but avoid tea, coffee or alcohol.

Run For Help: If you can't get to the top, or get down, can you get some form of protection close by, or can you get help from anyone else? If someone is close by on the wall can you get them to lower down a rope to you, or can you reach them? A portaledge can take the weight of four people as long as you're very careful, and although you'll piss someone off by crashing their pad, it's better than dying. It might even turn into a party!

Retreat From Moscow: Survival trumps everything else, and you should be prepared to leave anything behind in a true life or death situation, including gear, ropes, haul bags. Get down and sort out the bill later.

Asking For Help: If you need to be rescued, then don't wait too long to ask, as making someone aware in time you're in trouble could mean the difference between life and death. Signalling with lights and the Y signal now might begin a rescue that sees you later picked off the summit with a body temperature of 33° C, within minutes of falling into a coma, rather than the alternative of arriving on the summit in the dark and the storm, with no one aware you're dying.

HEAT EXHAUSTION

As with all life threatening conditions, having experienced something like this helps you take it seriously, makes it less abstract, and I've both had heat exhaustion myself (solo ascent of Aurora) and

seen it strike partners (ascent of Iron Hawk).

THE SCIENCE

The body regulates its core temperature of 37° C by sweating (evaporative heat loss), but if this is not effective at keeping the body temperature optimal and it rises to 40° C, you will suffer heat exhaustion. This begins with feeling dizzy and generally unwell, then comes extreme thirst and nausea, followed by vomiting and unconsciousness, falling into a coma, and then death.

IN THE REAL WORLD

Heat exhaustion can affect you very quickly on a wall. Climbing with all your gear on in the full sun, with no wind, and on black rock, you are in an oven. Drinking water and having your body sweat this out can only do so much when there is no movement of air, or your body is covered in gear, harness, helmet etc. Very quickly you will feel like you're burning up, and if this was reversed, and you were so cold you knew you were going to get hypothermia, then you'd back up and do something about it, but often in heat people just think "I'll drink more", but that will not work. Very soon you begin to feel unwell, like you're coming down with something. You will feel weak, feel crampy, feel your body is burning up, creating a sort of 'heat panic'. You will begin to be aware you're thinking irrationally. You might become lethargic, and often a climber will lay on a ledge in the full sun, just getting hotter and hotter, rather than act to remedy the situation. You might try and drink more water, but then you'll feel sick and not want to drink, then throw up, losing the water you've drank. At this point everyone tends to get a reality check and something is done about it, but if nothing can be done, then you'll die.

As a guide, here is how you will experience a percentage rise in body temperature:

- **1% Few symptom**s or signs of any thirst present, however, there is a marked reduction in VO2 max.

- **2% Beginning to feel thirsty**, loss of endurance capacity and appetite.

- **3% Dry mouth**, performance impaired.

- **4% Tired,** Increased effort needed for exercise, impatience, apathy, vague discomfort, further loss of appetite.

- **5% Difficulty concentrating**, increased pulse and breathing, slowing of pace.

- **6-7% High pulse,** difficulty breathing, flushed skin, sleepiness, tingling, stumbling, headache.

- **8-9% Dizziness**, laboured breathing, mental confusion, further weakness.

- **10% Muscle spasms**, loss of balance, swelling of tongue.

- **11% Heat Exhaustion**, delirium, stroke, difficulty swallowing; death can occur.

AVOIDING HEAT EXHAUSTION

Being acclimated to the heat is vital, and someone coming off the plane from a mild climate and jumping on a desert wall is asking for trouble. Instead you need to allow your body to adapt, which it does by learning to sweat more effectively (to dump heat), but more importantly it gives you time to understand the sun's effects on you, and so adjust your physical expectations, dressing better, moving slower, getting up earlier, drinking more. It is possible to climb even super hot walls as long as you know you cannot fight your own physiology, and so make adjustments to limit your exposure.

These would include:

- **Dress Right**: Wear light coloured baggy clothing, that covers your whole body. Black fabric sheds heat faster, but on a wall you just want to reflect the sun's rays off you. Being baggy you create an air space between your skin and the fabric that is cooled by your sweat, so the actual air temperature is lower next to your skin.

- **Protect Your Head**: Keeping your head cool is vital, and you should wear a peaked cap under your helmet with a long neck/face shield that extends down your back, so that when you look down your neck is not exposed. This should wrap around and when worn with sunglasses should give you great protection.

- **Avoid Wicking Fabrics**: For normal climbing, wicking fabrics are ideal, stopping you getting chilly when you stop, but in extreme heat that sweat is what is keeping you alive and having it whisked away down the fibres is like syphoning off a firefighter's water. This type of clothing tends also to be closer fitting, which is not good. An ideal top is a tough oversized white/sand shirt (it won't stay white for long), and for your bottom half, baggy white (or grey, stone or sand) painter pants.

- **Drink**: Don't allow yourself to become dehydrated (2% water loss) as this will reduce your body's ability to regulate body temperature. Carry a bladder and keep it topped up, drinking a little regularly.

- **Spray It**: Instead of wasting water by pouring it on yourself, or drinking more than your body can deal with, use one of those small 500 ml / 24 oz plastic spray bottles to increase your evaporative heat loss by spraying your face and clothing. **Staying Alive / 405**

- **Bring Lots Of Water:** If you're climbing in super hot weather you don't want to be stingy with the H2O. If you don't feel like you can haul as much water as you need, then do another route. Remember that the survival minimum of around 2 litres a day (big wall minimum is 3 litres) is just that, and sticking to the minimum is not going to work on a sun blasted wall, being consumed in one or two pitches. On a really hot wall you need to be taking at least 5 litres - or more! Also remember to eat and add electrolytes to your water.

- **Only Mad Dogs**: Avoid the heat of the afternoon by stopping and having a siesta, protecting yourself with things like your sleeping bags, fly, tarp. Often the actual air temperature can be pretty cold once you block the sun - you hope!

TREATING HEAT EXHAUSTION

The only way to deal with heat exhaustion is to lower the casualty's temperature as fast as you can (yes you are a casualty) back to 37° C. First of all you need to get them out of the sun, then you need to cool their skin by wetting it out in the shade (pour water onto some clothing and keep their skin wet with this (keep their hair wet too)). You also need to keep them drinking, which can be hard if they feel sick. If you were on the ground then cooling in a river or shower would be ideal. If you are in the shade, then allow the casualty to cool before moving them, and if you move them only do so in small stages, allowing them to cool, and not overheat each time. If you decide to retreat with a casualty then either lower them or do a tandem abseil. If the climber has been sick but recovers, then you could choose to carry on, but avoid them being exposed to heat exhaustion again, as they will be more susceptible to further heat exhaustion, which basically translates as 'you're going down'. If they have lost consciousness or had any kind of seizure you should contact search and rescue and follow their instructions.

TRAUMA

Accidents can happen on big walls, and I've seen many rescues taking place, both for the living and the dead. Very often it's not the hard routes that prove dangerous, not the A5s or 5.13s, but the A1 and 5.9 walls, where the traffic is heavy and the ground below you rich in ledges. Having some ability to deal with trauma is important, as often rescue can be hours or days away. This section is not intended as a medical manual, but I will share some thoughts based on my own big wall climbing experience, which I'm sure differ from how trauma is approached by professionals, and EMS training for ground based casualties.

KNOW YOUR LIMITS

A fully trained paramedic with a fully stocked first aid kit would still be hard pressed to do much more than an untrained climber when intensive care is needed but out of reach, say a climber laying on a ledge with a spiral fracture of their lower leg. This is not designed to belittle paramedics but to give you confidence that even without training you can bridge that gap between someone dying and not dying. The person who swoops in on that rescue rope or arrives lights flashing, is really the tip of the spear, their job to stabilise the casualty long enough to pass them on to the emergency ward, who then pass them on to theatre, who then pass them on to intensive care. Standing on a ledge with your mate white

Ingeborg Jakobsen cleaning on Holstinnd, Queen Maud Land

with shock, his ankle twisted at 180° you need to know your limits, but also know that untrained or not, you are the only spear tip they have in that moment.

WHAT CAN YOU DO?

First off, before we get down to the nitty gritty, like I said you need to know your limitations when it comes to your ability to help, so if there is someone more qualified, or who seems more able, then stand back and let them take charge (and do as they say unless your own experience tells you they are a hazard). Having done a basic first aid course is a start, knowing how to perform ABC checks, CPR etc., and something highly recommended that could save a life someday. Someone who's done a wilderness first aid course or has been through the military might be one better, but not always. In the real world often the person with all the paper is not the one best able to save anybody.

IT'S NOT ROCKET SCIENCE

Keeping another human alive when they have a busted spleen or a broken pelvis, blood filling up their insides, is beyond anyone outside of a well equipped hospital. You might be able to carry out a tracheotomy with a pen when your mates broken jaw swells up, but probably this is at the extreme end of what an untrained climber can do. Instead you're only going to be able to do the basics, call a rescue, and hope their body can do the rest. Much of what you can do has nothing to do with training and more to do with common sense, so even if untrained get stuck in where you're needed.

FIRST AID KIT

You should have two first aid kits, one small and always close at hand and one larger and able to deal with major problems. The small kit should live inside your haul bag's top pocket, while your big kit should be stowed in a small easily identifiable dry bag inside the main bag.

Small Kit: This kit is basically for minor cuts and grazes, and should include:

1x Wide Elastoplast tape on a roll
1x Small folding scissors
1x Small tin of Vaseline
1x Paracetamol 500 mg
1x Duct tape wrapped around old credit card
1x Tick removal tool
1x Tea tree oil 30 ml

Large Kit: This is your main trauma kit and hopefully you'll never need it. I store mine in a military EMT pouch, giving me lots of space, and then inside a small red roll top waterproof bag. It should include:

1x SAM splint
1x Micropore tape (5 cm)
1x Zinc Oxide tape (5 cm)
1x Traumafix dressing
1x Israeli bandage
1x Vetbond Tissue Adhesive (3 ml)
1x Celox Haemostatic Granules
1x Compeed (mixed)
1x Imodium
1x Medical shears
1x Scalpel blade
1x Ibuprofen 400 mg
1x Ibuprofen 400 mg
1x Betadine Antiseptic 15 ml
1x Sudocrem 30 g
1x Miconazole cream 30 g
1x Amethocaine eye drops 5 ml
10x Safety pins (small and large)
1x lighter
1x Soap
1x Sharpie (small)
1x notebook
2x Ziplock bags

On an alpine or wilderness wall I might also include antibiotics and tooth repair kit and heavy duty pain meds such as Tramadol.

A TRAUMA SCENARIO

In order to go through the basics I'm going to describe a real world example of an accident and then go through each stage as I would approach it. You can use this as a guide for further reading or instruction or compare it to how you would deal with the same incident.

The Fall: Your partner is climbing pitch 15 while you belay them from a large ledge. Out of sight you hear him falling, the sound of his body mixed with the sound of rocks crashing. He tumbles into sight, rocks all around him, the rope coming tight as he hits the ledge hard, the rocks crashing on down the wall below.

Don't Panic: Yes something bad has just happened, your partner is injured or worse, but try not to react instinctively. Detach for a second and stay calm and make an assessment of what's going on, even if that lasts only one deep breath.

Stay Safe: Don't rush into something and end up as screwed up as the guy you're about to try and assist and maybe save. Make a risk assessment. Are there more rocks coming down? Have you got your helmet on? Can you grab something as a shield? Can you get to your partner? Can the climber get to you? Being a hero can work out sometimes, but two injured climbers are of no use to anyone.

Dying From Embarrassment: The climber begins to move, says he's sorry, looks as if he's about to get up. Don't let him move. The human brain has an incredible ability to be self conscious of its own stupidity, and allow embarrassment and shock to trump sense. I've seen countless climbers deck out only to jump up and tell everyone they're fine, rubbing their limbs, and shaking off the concern of others. Some of these climbers sat down when the adrenaline wore off, listening to people laugh at their close shave, only to drop down dead, at the bottom of the route or walking back to the car. What the human body is capable of in these situations is incredible, part of it is fight or flight response, and I've seen video of tanker crew running away from their destroyed tank on the stumps of their blown off legs. Do not allow people who have just taken a bad fall to move. Tell them to get a grip and lie still until the adrenaline subsides.

Dying From Overcompensation: So this person has just decked out, and then jumped to his feet, and you've been unable to get him to sit down. "I'm fine" he says, adrenaline fizzing through his bloodstream, hyped up, and super aware, a berserker's heart beating like a drum. He starts back up the pitch, shaky, off balance, sketchy, the adrenaline come down hard, all the life draining out of him just before he falls again and lands at your feet for a second time.

SPINAL CORD DAMAGE

It is advisable in all climbing falls you assume the climber has a spinal injury. This does not just mean a 'broken back', often caused by the shock of a fall running up the spine, which is not necessarily life threatening (I know countless people who have 'broken their backs'), but actual spinal cord injuries. The spinal column runs from your brain down to your lower back and ranges in thickness from 6 to 13 mm and can be damaged in several ways in a fall, stretched, bruised, compressed, severed or lacerated. This damage can be done by striking the rock, the rock striking you (rock fall), by broken bones penetrating your spine (broken vertebrate) or by falling onto uneven ground. A common injury is for the climber to hit the ground feet first and for the shock load to shoot up their spine.

The body is both incredibly strong, and very weak, and I know people who have fallen a thousand feet down a mountain and walked away, while others have fallen from a pull up bar and ended up para-lysed. A spinal injury can be fatal or life changing, and having met many wheel-chair climbers, I know that just one poor lift or turn of a casualty can stand between life and death or worse.

There is a lot of stuff written about dealing with probable spinal injuries, but rarely in a climbing situation, where you are not dealing with someone laying on flat tarmac, but hanging in a harness, on ledges or awkward stances, maybe hanging in space. Very often climbers are forced to make a choice between saving the spine or saving the climber, but at all costs you should try and protect both. This translates to keeping the casualty still and carrying out an ABC assessment without moving them, and keeping them warm and waiting for the SAR team to arrive if they are injured, who will be able to better deal with spinal injuries. I'm saying this now as it needs to be in the forefront of your mind when reading through the next section.

ABC

The instant you can get to your casualty you need to assess them and check their condition, calmly going through the ABC of keeping them alive.

A (Airway & spinal): First you need to check the casualty's airway is open so they can breath, this being the number one priority as they will begin to suffocate and die within 3 minutes unless you can open their airway. This means you ignore blood, broken bones and everything else. First, is the casualty talking, shouting or screaming, or do they respond to you talking to them?

- **NO**: If they are not responsive and are unconscious your number one priority is to make sure they can still breath. If they are laying on their backs the tongue can slip into the throat and choke the casualty (this is where the impossible "swallowing your tongue" idea comes from), or they might have other damage that is blocking their breathing (broken jaw, broken teeth). You need to check in their mouth, tilt their head back carefully, and pull their chin down to open up the jaw. If they are wearing a climbing helmet it could be exacerbating the situation by forcing the chin down and chok-ing them, and you can either choose to try and remove the helmet very carefully, or try and work with it on. If they are laying on their front or side they won't choke, but try and assess if their airway is open, without moving them. If you don't want to remove the helmet (injured climbers have been struck in the head after having helmets removed), or need to leave them, then try and carefully roll the climber onto their side and into the recovery position. When moving the climber in any way, their neck or spine, it's always best to have two or three climbers helping, the aim to minimise the chance of nipping or damaging the spinal column, rolling them like a log, moving legs and arms first (be aware that this might not be applicable with leg injuries and the casualty may need to stay on their back). But Murphy's law tells us there will just be you, meaning you'll just have to be super humanly careful.

- **YES**: If they can speak, then talk to them while checking their helmet (is it broken?) and ears, nose and mouth for blood or clear liquid. Check their pupils are responsive and equally responsive, if they are not they might have concussion. Ask them where they are, what day or year it is, what route they're on, if they know what has happened (this might give a clue of any injuries). They might have retrograde or anterograde amnesia and babble on, not even aware they've had an accident (again, having had a few head injuries it helps to understand the effects of smashing your head). Ask them if they feel any pain and if so, do they feel unable to move? Can they move their fingers and toes? Check their breathing and take their pulse (50-80 is healthy) to see if either is irregular. If you think they have concussion keep them still and warm and contact SAR, but if they seem fine, then chalk this up to a lucky escape.

B (Breathing): Now you need to check if the casualty is breathing. Put your ear to their mouth, or lick the back of your hand and hold it close to their mouth and see if you can feel their breath. They should be breathing around 15 breaths a minute (normal breathing rates are between 12 and 20 breaths a minute). If they are not breathing then you will need to check their pulse. If there is a pulse then begin mouth to mouth. If there is no pulse then begin CPR.

C (Circulation): So they are breathing and have a heartbeat. Is there blood, and how much is there? Don't be distracted by minor but bloody injuries, inadvertently ignoring major injuries. Someone struck on the head with a rock can bleed spectacularly, and it can be good for photos, but it's probably not going to kill them like a fractured leg. If they have internal bleeding, a very fast light pulse, there is not too much you can do, other than keep them still, and hope the SAR team can reach you before they die. Very often people with internal bleeding can seem OK, only to rapidly deteriorate and die. Try and lift the casualty's feet 30 cm higher than their heart to help keep blood flowing to their organs.

By now you should have your first aid kit (don't get it until you've made sure the casualty doesn't need CPR or mouth to mouth) and can use this to stem any blood by putting pressure on the wound. Military bandages are much better at dealing with major trauma wounds than crappy bandages you get in first aid kits, and you should familiarise yourself with the Israeli bandage and Traumafix dressings (learning what they do while trying to treat someone is not ideal). If you don't have enough in your first aid kit, you can use clothing and duct tape and make do. Don't try and stem blood flow with slings or cord unless the limb is missing (it happens) or you cannot stop the blood flow. If fingers get cut off, and you have them, then wrap them in wet wipes and stick in a ziplock bag, and try and get to a hospital as soon as possible.

SHOCK

I have a friend who saw someone fall and break their leg while crossing a bergschrund, and although seemed OK while they waited for SAR, just dropped down dead from shock, something few climbers seem to factor into how they deal with falls. Imagine the effect on your emotions if someone punched you in the face, now imagine your body getting a giant punch instead, smashing onto the rock, breaking bones, thinking you're about to die. In this situation, the body goes into survival mode and constricts the blood vessels in its extremities in order to force the blood into its core, and the casualty becomes incredibly fragile. They may appear unharmed, or may be relatively uninjured, but the effects - sometimes terminal - of shock overlay this.

Signs of shock include:
- Pale skin
- Blue lips
- Sweaty but cold
- Thirsty
- Confused or nervous

Anyone who has had a major fall should be treated for shock, which basically means keeping them immobile (don't let them lead off again, or 'walk it off'), and keeping their body temperature stable. Don't allow them to drink anything until you're sure they're OK, as someone in shock can often have trouble swallowing. Most of all, try and remain calm around them, talking slowly and being reassuring, and not saying stuff like "stay away from the light".

HEAD INJURIES

Head injuries are common on big walls, with loose rock always a hazard, as well as falling into the rock, flipping or falling head first when wearing a heavy rack.

Wearing a helmet is a no brainer, and that's what can happen if you don't wear one! A helmet is not foolproof against head injuries, but it can make a potentially deadly blow just injurious, or an injurious blow just a broken helmet and a stiff neck. As with spinal injuries and shock you should always be on the lookout for concussion or skull fractures.

A heavy impact on the head that causes a concussion (the brain being rattled inside your head) will present symptoms such as the following:
- Confusion
- Dizziness
- Lack of balance
- Double or fuzzy vision
- Memory loss
- Nausea
- Trouble remembering
- Headache

On a wall these symptoms will usually pass if the climber is allowed to rest for a while, but more serious symptoms should trigger a rescue or immediate retreat. These include:

- Changes in size of pupils
- Bleeding from nose, mouth, or ears
- Convulsions
- Distorted facial features
- Fracture in the skull or face
- Severe headache
- Slurred speech
- Blurred vision
- Stiff neck or vomiting
- Swelling at the site of the injury
- Persistent vomiting

Any kind of head injury can lead to bruising or swelling on the brain, and so the casualty should be closely monitored, as a mild concussion can rapidly worsen into something far more serious. Even a mild concussion can lead to postconcussive syndrome (PCS), which can be a tough road to go down, so if your symptoms continue even after a minor head injury, then seek medical advice as soon as you can.

SUSPENSION TRAUMA

A climber who is left hanging in space for more than ten minutes can be exposed to suspension trauma, which can be fatal. This is caused by blood pooling in the legs below the harness, with the heart pumping the blood into your legs but the harness stopping it flowing back at the same rate. If the climber cannot take their weight off their harness (stepping onto a Prusik or ascender), they will begin to sweat, become short of breath, feel sick and dizzy. The danger here is if a climber is knocked unconscious or is unable to get back onto the rock, and so they have to be rescued as soon as possible. Once back at the belay try and release the pressure on the injured climbers legs by laying them down on a portaledge.

FRACTURES AND BREAKS

Broken bones are common on big walls, with climbers falling onto ledges or swinging into corners, so it's worth being able to deal with them in some way. A broken bone is usually a reason to retreat, but if it's only a hairline fracture you might be able to carry out a self rescue after informing the local SAR team. More complex fractures and breaks (like compound fractures), are going to require a full on rescue and surgical treatment. If the casualty has a badly broken bone you should try and protect them from shock, keep them warm, and wait for the SAR team. If you feel that circulation is affected you may have to do something, as a limb can only survive a few hours without an adequate blood supply. If you have to do this, say the climber's foot is pointing at 180 degrees, then just pull the bones inline and the muscles should pull the leg inline (easier said than done). If a rescue is on the way then don't bother with splints and just protect the wound and stem any bleeding, but if not and you have to carry out a self rescue, then use your SAM splint and sleeping mats, fly pole, ski pole or cheater stick to make a splint.

THE SHITS

Walls are dirty places, with dirty climbers, and you should try and at least reduce the risks involved with this slightly by keeping your hands clean as well as knives and anywhere where food is prepped (a ledge on El Cap might have the piss and shit of several hundred climbers on it, as well as that of mice, bats and rats). Having someone come down with vomiting and diarrhoea is not good when you're sharing a portaledge, and will probably mean a retreat unless the body can fight it quickly, and you have something like Imodium. You will also find that Wag bags don't contain enough toilet roll for 'the shits' and so it's always worth taking one roll of toilet roll on a wall (this can also be used for cleaning up spills… food spills).

BODY ADMIN

Beyond major trauma on a wall you need to look after your body, and the longer the wall, the more you need to take care.

- **Teeth:** keep your teeth clean and avoid food that might get stuck in teeth and lead to infections. Avoid drinking very sugary sports drinks for extended periods as you'll get mouth ulcers. On wilderness walls carry tooth repair kit such as Dentemp and oil of cloves.

- **Hands**: Keep your hands clean and free from infection by cleaning them carefully with wet wipes each night as well as hand sanitizer gel. Popular walls are pretty toxic places, like I said full of human piss and crap, as well as rat and bat and mouse droppings, no good. You should cover any bad cuts with tape or glue with super glue, and try and reduce the damage with gloves.

- **Feet**: Wearing plastic boots or sweaty rock boots and dirty socks for days on end can lead to fungal rot, so try and clean your feet as much as you can, and on winter walls try and sleep in clean socks or bivvy boots, drying your feet and using anti fungal talc. Pay close attention to between your toes as athlete's foot can appear very quickly and be very irritating.

- **Eyes**: You need to protect your eyes on the wall, be that with sunglasses or clean safety glasses, the wall full of dirt, grit, metal and germs. Wash your face with a wet wipe every day and carry eye drops in your first aid kit in case you have any eye problems.

- **Nether Regions**: The army teach people to wash themselves with soap, their ass and bits, because if you don't you save up problems. This is doubly so if you're climbing in waterproofs for days or weeks on end, wearing a thick climbing harness. Cleaning yourself with a wet wipe every few days is a good idea to avoid crotch rot, plus it shows you're considerate to your wall partners - although on a wall 'smelly' tends to be relative.

- **Periods**: This often comes up, where periods arrive early, and for all the women on the team at the same time, caused by stress, lack of food, hard work etc, so always make sure female team members have the necessary kit for this.

RESCUE

Getting people out of deep caves many kilometres under the ground is perhaps the hardest task for a Search And Rescue (SAR) team, but snatching someone off a thousand metre overhanging wall maybe comes close. On a wall there are three outcomes of an accident:

SELF RESCUE

If you can get yourself off a wall safely after an incident this is the ideal. With a self rescue you are not exposing anyone to further danger or cost, or taking away SAR resources from somewhere else where they could be better employed. 'Pulling the pin' should only be done when you are sure you cannot remedy the situation, that it is out of control, or that someone is going to die or go through intense trauma in attempting to self rescue. Yes Joe Simpson carried out a self rescue but that does not mean it was the best option, only that he had no other choice.

How you carry out a self rescue comes down to how experienced and skilful you are, and the level of confidence you have to do it yourself. I know climbers who have retreated down major walls with broken bones by working as a team, able to do tandem abseils, multi rope monster Munter abseils etc. Others have had minor injuries but lacked the skills to help themselves and so extended their own misery, as depending on factors like your location, it can take a day or more for a SAR team to swing into action. When to pull the pin is a tough decision, but you just need to ask yourself if you're making things better or worse, slackening the noose or pulling it tighter? Here are a few things to think about:

Pan-Pan: If you can communicate with the SAR team, then do so. Tell them; your situation, who you are, how many you are, what you are wearing, how to stay in contact and who can be contacted on the ground. Giving SAR a heads up means they can start the process of stepping in, in case things do not go to plan. This is in effect a 'pan-pan', a signal given instead of a 'mayday-mayday', that a safety problem exists they should be aware of. Leaving it too late to contact the SAR team can mean the difference between life and death, plus SAR teams are normal working people, they like to do their work between 9am and 5pm, not in the middle of the night, so make the call, they'll thank you for it.

Saving For Your Funeral: A lot of climbers try and carry out a self rescue because they lack insurance, in the belief that to be picked up by helicopter will land them with a bill they can't pay. In many countries rescue is free, or very cheap when it's set against the actual cost, with the real cost being once you get to the hospital, which you cannot avoid anyway (unless you want to just pay for your funeral). If you have a broken leg then you're going to the hospital and crawling for miles is maybe not advisable. Having rescue and medical insurance is

advisable, after all you're not going on a beach holiday.

THE RESCUE

Can You Be Rescued? This is something you need to think about when going beyond the big wall flesh pits, as in many areas there is no way you can be plucked from the wall and you're on your own. If you can make it down maybe people or animals can be found to carry you out, but that's it. Having larger teams (3 or 4) allows you to carry out a self rescue more effectively and so is recommended for over the horizon walls. Here are some more thoughts:

SAR Are Not Firefighters: SAR teams are not sitting around in their climbing harnesses waiting for the alarm to ring so they can rush to your aid. Very often SAR teams are comprised of a wide range of people, doing a wide range of jobs and situated over a wide area. Getting these people together and working out what's going on, making a plan, and starting to work through that plan can take time. If you're on the West face of the Dru then yes, maybe the PGHM can get to you in 15 minutes and have you blinking on the ground 4 minutes later, but often not, and I know of climbers who hung on faces for days waiting for the chopper to come. And so don't assume that SAR is the magic bullet. They often can't operate at night or in bad weather, and it might take many dozens of people and helicopters to be put in position to get you down.

SOS: You need to tell the rescue team you need help, and this should be done by phone, and ideally you should have made a note of the SAR team's direct number, and on some wilderness walls it's also advisable to talk to them first, so they know you're there. If you can't use a phone, then having a Sat phone, EPIRB or 'Spot' style device is recommended. Carrying a small radio such as the Yaesu VX-6R or VX-3R allows you to communicate with the rescue team (in an emergency), as well as check the weather forecast by NOAA in the US. Without electronic means to call for a rescue then you will need to signal with a flashing light, and having an LED torch that flashes is ideal, or you can carry a small strobe like the West Marine See-Me 2.0 or ACR C-Light. You can also try signalling with clothing or write HELP with marker pen on your fly or a tarp, and make sure you know the international rescue signal of two hands up for 'YES' for rescue and one hand up for 'NO".

Short Term And Long Term Survival: As I've said, when you pull the pin you need to be prepared to wait it out. This means making yourself safe and comfortable and protected from further incidents. If you have a portaledge, put it up and conserve your food and water. Stay off your phone and conserve the battery and get ready to wait.

Do What They Say: I will not go into how you will be rescued, be it a long line from a chopper or a lift or lower as the SAR team are the experts. They will tell you what to do at each step of the way. Think of them like a cop with a gun and do only what they ask and nothing else, no rope throwing or bag tossing or selfie sticks. Don't make their lives more difficult and dangerous. They will come to you.

Prep For Rescue: Make sure all ropes are stored away, and everything is packed and lashed down tight. If you're in your ledge be prepared to break it down or clip it off to the belay. Get rid of all clutter and be prepared to ascend out or be lifted. If the rescue team is coming they might only rescue you, not all your crap, so make sure you get what you need to take, such as passport, wallet, keys, camera, and be prepared for the rest to be left behind.

Storm bound portaledge camp, Holstinnd

XS WALLS

The term XS comes from the British rock grade of 'Extremely Severe', which is a grade that covers any climbing that could be considered 'heads up' or 'engaging', also translated as death routes. Such walls are beyond the Yosemite holiday walls, but walls that are hard to get to, in alpine or high mountain terrain, where you will need all your skills about you. In this environment you are often faced with much more complex terrain, with both more complex approaches and descents, as well as difficult and dangerous climbing. In the alpine the rock will often be variable, from bullet hard granite to loose and terminal alien mystery rock. Here you might be dealing with slabs and overhangs, rock, and ice and snow, with both mild weather and extreme cold. In climbing, I think moving into the alpine walls requires the greatest amalgamation of a climber's skill.

GUARANTEED OUTCOME CLIMBING

There is a point where a face becomes a wall, where the severity, steepness, and difficulty means it cannot be climbed in pure alpine style, with just a pack on your back, and instead needs a more complex approach. By climbing with portaledges, haul bags, and fixed ropes a team can stay on a wall for over a month longer than a lightweight team, plus they can sit out storms, take their time, and stay safe. Steve House called this 'guaranteed outcome climbing', and I guess he was right, but then anything is guaranteed when you spend that much time and effort on it.

THE SAFETY FACTOR

Big alpine faces are dangerous, featuring many hazards, from rock fall, to bad weather, to simply taking the big whippers. Getting down is also equally dangerous, and for every single ascent of a hard alpine wall there are at least ten failures. You can spend a lifetime trying to get up these things in a pure style, maybe solo with just an apple in your pocket, but with age you see the other climbers are all dead, and there has to be a better way.

WHAT STYLE?

Pragmatic Style: By going big wall style up a hard face you are choosing not to take the easier option, but the other hard option. With a ledge and haul bags you will move slower, but you will be able to suffer through storms and cold where the alpine climber has had to retreat and is now tucked up in bed. You feel avalanches and wind rattle your fly for nights on end. Your sleeping bag will become mildewy from freeze and thaw. Your body will wither, and you'll give everything to reach the top - but if you do, then the struggle will be worth it. It is a great privilege to spend two weeks on a mighty face.

Alpine Style: Climbing normally, as you would on a sunny big wall, will work on most big walls, with the team going up one at a time, leading, following, hauling etc, putting up the camp each night, climbing as a team of two or three.

Mixed climbing on the Troll Wall, Norway.

Starting early and not finishing too late is the key to this style, and it's always best to have the ledge up before it gets dark, ideally with someone making water or getting the gear prepped as the leader finishes the pitch above.

Where this system does not work is on a wall with very bad weather, as the belayers are exposed to many hours of snow and wind, which can be debilitating to the body and the mind if it continues over many days. The alternative below is a good way to keep your team from being ground down by the wall.

Capsule Style: When tackling a big gnarly wall you can try and climb it like a normal Yosemite wall, as this is fast and efficient, and does not require any new skills to be mastered.

When I climbed the Lafaille route on the Dru in the winter of 2002, this is how we started, climbing through two weeks of terrible weather, freezing our asses off, hauling our bags in the dark, feeling like hunted little creatures. Then one day we found sixty metres of 9 mm static left behind by Lafaille on a ledge, and being dirtbags we took it. In the bad weather we started to do what we'd read about in Savage Arena, the capsule style ascent, having a camp then fixing our ropes up, two or three pitches, then rapping back down when it got dark. Almost straight away our work lives improved. Camp was always just ten minutes away. There was no more battling with frozen portaledges and frozen sleeping bags, hauling at midnight unsure how you'd find the energy to sort yourself out.

Right then on that route I was convinced of the benefits of capsule style when employed on hard climbs tackled by mortals.

Key Points:

Home Is At The End Of The Rope: When climbing hard and cold walls, or where an accident can strike at any time, having the ability to just rap down your lines back to your home is a huge boost to your safety. It's very easy to get close to hypothermia on these walls, but knowing you'll be in your sleeping bag in half an hour can help make that waiting bearable.

Camps: Fixing ropes from a fixed camp allows you to set up the best camps in the best spots, which often means camps under roofs or even in caves or snow holes. Here you can create a solid base from which to work on the route above, working up until you can get to the next good spot, or you run out of rope.

Back door: Having many ropes can mean you can fix down from quite high if things go wrong, or you have team or technical problems, and four sixty metre ropes can get you a hell of a long way down to the ground. Once on a wall our stove broke so we sent down its owner to sort it out, lowering him all the way to the ground. We then climbed on, but kept enough rope to drop down again, and that night he returned with a new stove and extra tea bags as well!

Days Off: If you climb in a team of three or four, then one or two people can take a day off each day, chilling out in the ledge, sorting out gear, sorting out dinner (melting water etc). In a four man team, two can sort out the hauling while the other two push the ropes up. You can imagine that sitting in a ledge all day could be boring, but it tends to be pretty chilled as long as you've got some tunes, a book, everyone's sleeping bag, and fuel for brews.

Only Bad Clothing: A big advantage of capsule style is that you can often climb in conditions you'd never tackle normally, wind and snow, as if things get too hairy you can just retreat back into your home.

Blue Collar: Capsule style is shift work, and you need to make sure you're up at the top of your ropes by first light, or as soon as possible each day. It's very easy to take a lax approach and sort of get into a big wall life where you think the food and fuel will never run out.

Stay Sharp: Being up on a wall so long, jumaring and rapping the same ropes dozens and dozens of times, you can let your guard down, and more than one climber I know has died from being sloppy in transitions. Keep to the rules of two connections at all times, use a prusik and re-belays, and take it easy.

The Big Lift: Once you run out of ropes you will need to haul all your bags up to the next high point, an exercise that can take a whole day, or just an hour. With the right system, space hauling for example, I've hauled a huge load of bags four hundred metres in about two hours. Ideally if the wall is steep, and you've strung out three or four ropes, then the bags should swing clear of everything. If not, then you'll have to haul pitch to pitch, using a cargo hook haul if you only

have one rope on each pitch. Make sure you know how to pass knots and keep all your ropes tidy.

The Selfless Lead: If you know how to rope solo then you can rope solo pitches in really bad weather, leaving the other team members in their sleeping bags, staying warm and resting.

XS LIVING

STAYING WARM

Alpine walls create a problem that normal alpine climbing does not suffer, in that everyone but the leader is static for long periods of time, which can lead to problems.

Clothing: Wearing standard climbing clothing for the conditions will keep the leader warm, but be prepared to get holes in your hard-shells if you're tackling chimneys and wide cracks. The real difficulty is for the belayer, who might have to sit still for many hours without being able to really generate heat. It is usually best to make one person designated belayer for the day and equip them for that task, wearing extra clothing, both their own and their leader's belay jacket. Having synthetic belay pants with full side zips are maybe not a luxury, but even wearing an extra pair of lightweight shell trousers will make a big difference (trapping another dead air layer). When cleaning or climbing your ropes strip down if you can to avoid getting your layers damp.

Hands: When leading in really cold conditions leather gloves will become stiff and useless and you will need a high quality pair of technical gloves that allow you to use even small gear without taking them off. Even with these gloves you will still get cold hands. Another option is to wear thinner softshell gloves and wear these under a pair of flip mittens, flipping them back and forwards as needed. Always carry a pair of full weight mitts on your harness as well for when the climbing is over, or if you drop a glove. Always bring plenty of thin spare gloves as they can wear out very quickly. As for the belayer, make sure they have the warmest mitts you can find, and heat pads can be added for the really cold days.

Feet: Keeping your feet warm on a big slow wall is crucial, and having cold feet all the time can easily lead to a need to retreat. I would go for the warmest boots I can find, the Himalaya double boots such as the Scarpa 6000 or 8000 or Sportiva G2 SM, Spantik or Olympus Mons EVO. Boots like these will get a real hammering, so be prepared to do some running repairs on the toe caps. Using vapour barrier socks will help to maintain the insulation of the socks over a longer period, changing into clean dry socks every night.

Face: When you're climbing capsule style you can often often end up in some pretty crappy weather and so face protection is a good idea to avoid frost-nip on your nose and cheeks.

XS BIVVIES

If you're heading up onto a big alpine wall you need to have the highest level of protection, enabling you to deal with storms, and keeping you alive, and in some small comfort for the climb. Some teams have spent over a month living in their portaledges, withstanding sunshine and storm, and so being able to thrive in such a habitat is vital.

SURVIVABILITY

The number one thing is that your flysheet and ledge are up to the task, and follow all the recommendations for storm protection, including heavy duty materials, tie downs and poles. Rocks, or even axes, ripping through a flysheet are not unknown, so make sure you have the kit to repair it too.

ENCLOSED OR NOT

People have climbed very hard walls with pull down flys but these days, hard alpine climbs are mostly done with enclosed flys, usually the Black Diamond Expedition flys, and these have so far stood up to some of the worst weather imaginable. The only real advantage of the non enclosed fly is that it is lighter and more compact, but such things don't mean much when you're looking down the barrel of a storm.

A FULL HOUSE

One of the hardest things to manage when alpine wall bivvying is the massive amount of stuff you will have in your ledge - big sleeping bags, clothing, food, big winter boots, maybe even an extra climber. It's important then to keep everything as tidy as possible and have a system for everything, keeping as much gear as you can in stuff sacks or moving it into your haul bags. Having each climber stick to 'their side' is the best way to have a routine. If you're using an enclosed fly you can stow bags under the ledge when you don't need them, and having a thin clip line running along the outside edge between the three straps gives you something to clip them into, otherwise they tend to disappear into the black hole. Try not to get into the habit of pushing rubbish under the enclosed fly as it will end up making your ledge stink, and

rubbish can blow away when taking the ledge down (along with spoons, socks and other stuff you'd rather not lose!).

GREENHOUSES

On very cold walls, when climbing capsule style, if there is any sun it will quickly heat up the inside of a portaledge. You can use this to dry kit or sleeping bags by leaving them out but secured to the ledge. To do this lay the bags open one on top of the other with the ledge zipped up tight, and make sure they are secured to something.

ICE SHOWERS

In sub zero temperatures there is often a big problem with frost, both from cooking (remember to avoid the rolling boil!), and also just breathing into your bags. When you wake up in the morning you will find you have a lot of frost inside the ledge which will rain down on you as you move or drip on you as it melts. This often seems to be something you have to deal with, but can be reduced by having some kind of airflow in the ledge, and happens with both breathable and non breathable flysheets. It's worth smashing off all this ice every time you get into the ledge and carrying a medium sized hand brush to sweep all the bits off the bed (this usually goes underneath the enclosed fly and builds up, and needs removing. Having a large brush comes in handy for brushing off all the snow on your clothes when you get back into the ledge or for sweeping snow off the rock in stormy weather.

CONDENSATION CURTAIN

In early wall tents, such as those used on the South Face of Everest and Russian bivvy tents, a lightweight inner tent is often used in order to create a condensation or hoarfrost curtain. Made from simple mosquito netting or the lightest breathable fabric or Pertex, this is loosely hung inside the ledge, stopping any ice that falls from landing in on you, as well as creating dead air and warming the ledge a little more (heat from the stove is not lost as quickly). No one makes one of these but they're easy to sew up and can be as complex as you want, anything from a full inner tent (attached to the pole, corners and suspension), to a simple piece of material wrapped around the top of the ledges suspension straps (most frost forms on the outside face of the fly. The top of the condensation curtain should not be closed, but open like a chimney to allow the moist air to rise out of the fly.

MAGIC CARPET TIE DOWNS

One of the most dangerous things that can happen to a ledge is for the wind to throw it around, smashing the ledge and the people to bits (and I've heard of ledges flying up above the anchor like a magic carpet). Some expedition flys feature the ability to secure the ledge from below by fixing lines down to an upward anchor point, either a bolt or a crack to one side. In an emergency you will need your haul line to do this and it is advisable to do this sooner rather than later if high winds are on the way, or you are fixing a camp on an alpine wall, as once the rodeo begins, your chances of getting out and sorting the problem are minimal. If you are setting off onto a wall where you will be securing your ledge, perhaps for a capsule style ascent, then take along four 4 metre lengths of 7 mm cord, bring the cords up from a single (or multiple) point and tension these at the fly corners via a Trucker's hitch (this means you can re-tie or re-adjust as they stretch). For non enclosed expedition flys, and ledges with deploy flys, you will need to rig up the bottom of the ledge without interfering with the bottom of the fly (which wraps around the bottom). In this case you will need to just fix the rope to the ledge somehow.

IMPACT PROTECTION

It's always best to try and set camps out of the fall line of your route, ideally under an overhang, or out on a steeper section of wall. Sleeping on a ledge that's being struck by rocks or ice is not conducive to good sleep, and can be terminal. If you find you're exposed to rockfall, you can try and create some form of overhead protection by hanging your bags above the ledge, or if you're using HDPE liners in your haul bags, take them out and attach them to the flysheet. Remember that most rock fall hits the outside berth on the ledge, so in high impact situations, you are best to sleep sitting up with your back to the wall.

TENTS INSTEAD OF LEDGES

On some walls you might be better to use a tent rather than a portaledge, especially if the wall features good sized ledges. A tent tends to provide much more warmth and comfort than a portaledge, with more room to move around being the biggest bonus. Also don't overlook the chance to make use of snow holes or caves on routes (a good sized snow hole can be hacked out with ice axes).

FLY WITHOUT THE LEDGE

If you find a snow ledge then consider using the fly without the portaledge, as the lack of straps can make a fly easier to live in. Just make sure the fly is secured down like a tent, and stuff sacks filled with snow make good anchors.

XS FOOD AND WATER

An expedition requires a lot more work, and often in much harsher conditions, meaning more calories. Also days can often be shorter, meaning dinner time is something everyone looks forward to, a bit of a lift to the day. For this reason it's vital that you nail your expedition menu otherwise you will be resigning your team to extra misery they can do without, which can undermine the whole climb.

Breakfast: Eating breakfast at 6am at minus ten can be a little grim, and so you need to fit the food to the environment. Using a flask makes great sense in such situations, and this can be done while still in your sleeping bag. On some walls we've gone away from a wet breakfast and gone for cheese and hard bread, but the main things are that it's easy to sort out, and you get the job done with minimum exposure to the cold (there tend to be few pancake mornings). It's always slow, but there's slow, and then there's slow.

Lunch: As with breakfast, it's often hard to eat lunch on such a wall, and bars and gels tend to be the easiest food to eat, but anything fatty, like sausage, tends to be welcome too.

Dinner: The best food for alpine wall dinners are freeze dried meals, as all that is needed is for water to be added, then the meal is left to cook itself, and these meals can be passed around easily, even between portaledges. In cold conditions you can stick the meal inside your jacket to warm you, just don't forget the food is in there and roll around! Having a long handled spoon is handy with these meals, as it allows you to dig to the bottom of the pack and stir into the corners. Try and avoid using food or meals you've not at least tried before, as some can be pretty nasty. Fats are important on cold walls and should be added to all meals, and I often take olive oil in a large plastic bottle (it goes hard so the bottle needs a large opening for a spoon), or sachets of butter. At the start of the climb people are often unkeen to eat butter or olive oil, but as the climb progresses this becomes a fixation.

Supper: In cold conditions you can take chocolate without fear of it melting, and small bars or packets of nuts are nice to have with a hot drink at the end of the day.

WATER

On big winter walls or alpine climbs, climbers often forget that you need the same as on a summer wall, maybe more if you're carrying dried food. They look up at this snowy wall and just think they'll get snow from ledges and save the hassle of taking water. In reality unless you've got some major ledges and a lot of snow, this approach does not work that well and you're best to bring what you need. Most climbers can't see the value of taking all the time and fuel to melt ice to fill water bottles that will only freeze anyway and so take just the ice. Ice is very dense but I'd work on a 2:1 ratio to be safe (60 litres of ice gives you 30 litres of water), while snow is pretty hopeless and is probably not worth hauling at all (you'd be better to melt the snow on the ground and haul the water refrozen in bottles), having more like a 10:1 ratio, meaning you'd need several haul bags full just to last a week. When hauling ice a standard bag works fine, and this can be hung at the bottom of the bags and ice decanted into stuff sacks each night. Water ration wise I'd aim for around 3 litres a day.

XS STOVES

Redundancy

On most walls climbers will use hanging gas stoves, but on very long and committing walls they can never be 100% reliable, and in the past I've had many problems with such stoves. When a gas stove stops working there isn't much you can do apart from poke a pin into the nozzle and hope, but often the problems are more complex than that. For this reason I would always bring a second micro gas stove along as a backup.

PROTECT YOUR CANISTERS

Gas canisters are fragile things, more fragile than water bottles, and so on a major climb, where you might have dozens of gas canisters, try and keep them in the centre of your haul bag. Also avoid using large canisters if possible, with nothing larger than 250 g, as to puncture something larger loses a lot of gas. Micro 100 g gas cartridges are OK, but you'll find you need to replace them more often which is a pain and they are probably the least cost effective option.

COLD WEATHER CANISTERS

Using a canister stove on cold walls can be problematic if the temperature is below freezing, with the gas being more and more useless as the temperature drops. Many of the cold weather tips don't work that well in the confines of a portaledge with the most common JetBoil style stoves, requires you to either warm the canister with you hands, hoping the ambient heat lifts within the fly, or create a heat exchange between the stove and the cartridge via a strip of copper. Try and keep your cartridge warm at night if you want an easy start to the next day, and you can also stick one under your layers while you set up for the night.

Ian Parnell cooking dinner on the Dru

BIG WALL CANISTER STOVE

The ideal big wall stove would probably be one you make yourself (as we used to do), using a gas stove that can have its canister inverted, and with a flame to pan distance that burns up all the carbon monoxide. Making something like this using a stove like the MSR Wind Pro II would be ideal, swaging up a pan into which another pan can fit. If fitting a pan, then consider one with a handle already fitted to make pouring water safer.

HOW MUCH GAS?

With a highly efficient system, a three person team should be able to stay within a 250 g cartridge per day when melting snow.

LIQUID FUEL STOVES

On major alpine objectives, where all the water must be made by melting ice, you may need more security than you can get with a canister stove, which I find can never be relied on 100% (fine for short routes, but not for long). Another problem is that on a multi week climb you will be carrying maybe half a haul bag of gas canisters! On such climbs I prefer to use something like an MSR XGK II, which has proven itself able to work for many months on end with only a small amount of maintenance. A liquid stove, running white gas or Coleman fuel, requires less volume of fuel, with one drawback being the fact it is a little messier to light, requiring priming (although once mastered this is not such a problem). A liquid stove is also not affected by cold, although plastic pumps need to be treated carefully in really cold temperatures (probably such temperatures would be beyond those found in climbable conditions). These stoves also give off a great deal more heat, making them excellent for use in winter to warm up your living space, a

downside of this being they are not as fast or efficient as JetBoil style stoves (which as a result do not warm your tent though).

HANGING LIQUID FUEL STOVE

There are several ways to hang a liquid stove, but no commercial options, with a DIY approach needed instead. In the past I've bolted an XGK onto the bottom of a large pan that I've swaged wire to, then fitted a smaller pan inside, having the bottle hung from a chain or loop of wire. Also consider using a smaller pan set up and rise the height of the pan in order to reduce CO output.

NON HANGING

If you can't rig a hanging stove, you can set the stove up on a metal tray, a stove base made from wood, or the wood from your belay seat. The drawback with this system is that the stove ends up being on one person's knees or set on the bed of the ledge and is prone to getting knocked over - not good in many ways, from wet sleeping bags to third degree burns.

HOW MUCH WHITE GAS?

The classic answer to this question is 250 ml (8 oz) per person per day if melting ice and snow and 125 ml (4 oz) if the water is liquid. I find this is more a guide's rate of consumption, cooking and melting snow for large groups, where fuel is plentiful and so is the snow. On a wall you're looking at more like 100 ml per day, with this being reduced further as you add team members (it does not take twice as much fuel to heat twice as much water), so working on 150 ml for two people and 200 ml for three is closer to a correct amount. Keep an eye on your fuel as having an excess can mean you can have more hot drinks and water bottles, and if you're running out then you'll need to switch to cold.

FUEL TRANSPORT

I would recommend all fuel be carried in metal fuel bottles (such as the red MSR bottles), rather than plastic containers or thin metal fuel canisters, and stowed in a dry bag (remember Amundsen had his fuel cans soldered closed!), as otherwise if the fuel leaks, you will not only lose fuel, but also contaminate everything else, from food to sleeping bags.

SPARES

Bring a spare pump and maintenance kit and try to know your way around the stove.

SNOW AND ICE

Unlike on a summer wall, you might come across snow and ice climbing, anything from an easy snow slope to get to the bottom to full on mixed climbing on the route. This means you need to be able to move on this terrain as well as protect and belay off it.

AXES

In a large team the type of route dictates how many ice axes you need. On some routes you may only need tools for the leader, the other members using ascenders, while on others everyone will need them, say perhaps because there is some down climbing on the descent, or stretches where full on ice climbing is needed, such as up approach slopes. Very often lightweight tools can be used, which can do double duty as a hammer for the second, with an adze coming in handy on many such routes.

CRAMPONS

Although you can get away with only one set of axes on many routes, I would recommend everyone has some basic crampons, both for the approach and descent, as well as when seconding some pitches, where to climb without them would have you slipping and sliding around.

SWITCHING BETWEEN AID AND ICE OR MIXED

This is the same as switching between free and aid, although it's often best to have your crampons and axes sent up rather than having them on your harness. On complex terrain you might have to switch between the two several times, and so here you'll want to keep your crampons on. In such cases make sure you get your feet in the right spot in your aiders as a sharp crampon point can slice straight through an aider's step, or a sling. The advantage of the Russian aider comes to the fore in such climbing, as you can easily switch from one system to another, giving some small clue into Russia's success on huge mixed walls like Jannu, Makalu and K2.

AIDING OFF ICE TOOL

An ice axe is basically a great big sky hook and a peg combined, and can be used as such on very mixed ground if you don't want to free climb, hooked and hammered and twisted like you would normally. A T or B rated axe should be suitable for this, and often you'll only do one move and then get back into free climbing or full aid mode, examples being hooking a chock-stone or placing the pick into an icy slot or crack. Axes are also great for clearing out cracks, and try and view them as multi use, with the hammer and adze or shaft all able to be employed for aid or free moves. It's best to always run the load through the shaft rather than trying to tie off the pick, as this places the load in the correct position for the pick to hook (tying it off will make it unstable).

RUSSIAN ROCK FIFI

If you're carrying Russian hooks, then this kind of mixed climbing is where they excel, able to climb anything you'd use a sky hook on, or go where a beak or blade would go, and also work like an ice axe. The ability for these hooks to climb thin dribbles of ice in corners is amazing, and I doubt the best climbers could free climb where these hooks can cheat their way up.

ICE PROTECTION

You should always bring at least one long ice screw and an ice threader on winter walls as you may end up needing to use an ice thread to descend. For routes that include more mixed terrain you will need to add a requisite number of screws.

ICE BELAYS

If you're going to hang your ledge or bags off ice screws, be aware that a loaded screw will often melt out while under pressure and should be monitored. Setting up a multiple V thread anchor and using this with the screws is much safer, and screws set in series, with one screw passing on some load to the next being safer perhaps than a traditional belay set

up (remember screws should be around an axe shaft apart). In warmer weather screws have a tendency to melt out as well, something to think about if you're fixing ropes off screws.

SNOW ANCHORS

Setting up a big wall anchor on snow is very tricky and is best avoided at all costs. When I've been faced with this problem I've opted to use very long ropes (100 m), so that I could get to rock. Also there is a very big difference between a belay anchor on a snow slope and an anchor you must haul from. Snow anchor tools like the DMM Deadman are not usually carried, but in an emergency you can create a deadman anchor with stuff sacks filled with snow, a small haul bag, or even by using your portaledge.

NON ANCHOR ANCHORS

Seeing as we're on the subject of dodgy anchors, often you will be called on to really think out of the box on a major climb, finding ways to build an impossible anchor, set up a crazy way to get you up or down the rope. Often these can be fun ways to pass the time on walls, coming up with problems, such as how to descend a wall when you only have one rope, or your ropes don't reach the next belay, or both ropes have knots in them. Anchors are another good variation on this, how to set up non anchor anchors, where you take away the tools. The classic non anchor anchor would be where you are the belay, using your body for others to jumar up on (I've heard tales of climbers making a belay on a hand jam), or belaying off a knot jammed in a crack. Such role playing is a good way to quickly do an inventory of everything, such as wide crack equals; boot, helmet, pan, water bottle etc. Often the strangest things can create very strong anchors such as a haul bag filled with rocks.

Wide cracks on Ulvetanna

DESCENT

This book is not meant to teach you how to rappel, but it's important to know how to get down from the top of a wall, or if you have to retreat, down the wall itself. Due to the weights involved and also the steepness of many descent routes, you should view getting down as being as complex and serious as the ascent, although often the descent can be even harder. There are many reasons to be descending a wall with all your gear. Here are a few:

RETREAT

Bailing off a wall, making that rap of shame, is part of the big wall game, that for every metre climbed to a summit, you probably have five getting down to the ground. Try not to take turning around as being shameful, evidence that you over-reached, but treat it as a learning experience, as even in retreat you're learning some good skills for later. At the same time, acknowledge the real reason you're descending. Don't come up with excuses designed to let you off the hook, such as 'we didn't have enough water', 'the bags were too heavy', or 'we dropped our topo'. No - these will not allow you to learn from the situation if the primary reason is a weakness in yourself.

The blaming of others, of things, is a very human response to failure. It's better to understand what was really to blame, such as just not being mentally or physically prepared, that you lacked the skills, or did not trust your partner or yourself. If you can be honest with yourself, and your partners, then you can set about remedying the situation, doing easier routes, building up a little more slowly. If you do this you will get up the walls you dream of doing. If you don't, you'll just end up doing nothing but bailing, and then wondering why? I would add to this that you should always keep the motto:

"Don't retreat in haste" foremost in your mind. I know it sounds like such a simple thing, to not retreat in haste, but this has served me well on several climbs.

The human mind is weak - we get scared and intimidated, dreams rapidly turning into nightmares. It's all too easy to take days to haul all your gear to that point, and all of a sudden feel incapable of going on. All you can think about is the ground, your head full of every reason why you should not be where you are, and non to stay. I was once guiding someone who was paying a fortune to climb a big wall, but who was so convinced he wanted the ground he did not baulk when I said he'd have to pay double to go down (but the second he reached the ground he was full of shame he'd been so weak).

Instead of going down, get out the portaledge, sit on a ledge, put on a brew, and some tunes, and try and reconnect with just why you're here. Look around you. Look how fucking amazing this is. Consider what you'll gain by sticking it out, compared to going down. Is a pizza and a can of coke worth the loss of a dream? A moments weakness can undo weeks or months of hard work, planning and preparation, a window squandered.

Tormod Granheim descending Suser Gjennom Harryland, Troll Wall.

Instead, take off your shoes and dangle your feet over the edge. Spend a night there on the wall, and see how you feel in the morning.

NON RETREAT

If things aren't going your way, say bad weather, illness, not enough water, then think about fixing down instead, as three ropes (lead, haul, zip) can get you pretty far. I've done this several times, and come back a week later jugged up, and carried on. Just leave all your water, food and gear at the high point and rap down with your sleeping kit (don't forget your car keys and wallet!). Another option if you're too high to do this, is to leave one bag full of water and gear and stuff you can afford to abandon and then rap down until you can fix to the ground, then come back and re-lead those pitches. As ever, when fixing ropes, try and think about your future selves, fixing the ropes in a way that will make it safe and fast to get back up again, meaning re-belays and edges protected.

DESCENT

Sometimes, especially on alpine walls, you might choose to descend down your ascent route, especially where going over the back with haul bags and ledges is not an option. If this is your plan then it's important you have fixed belays below you, ideally two bolts on each belay. Keep a note of fixed gear and features on the pitches you climb, so these can be used to get you to each belay station without major down aiding or just swinging in. On some routes you might want to leave some rope fixed to get over roofs or diagonal features (such as 5 mm cord lines), but so far I've never found this necessary.

This kind of skill is ideally learnt while bailing from routes, understanding swinging in and over to runners, rather than learning it for real, rapping down a thousand metre wall. If you have your sight on some major objective that demands such an approach, then perhaps climb a more moderate objective first and descend that, a route like Leaning Tower in Yosemite, being a good training ground.

GETTING DOWN

So now let's get into to the nitty gritty of getting you and your bags down from the wall.

Bail Preparation

So you're going down. First, you need to do what hot air balloons do to go up - dump some weight. This means getting rid of most of your water. You can either pour this out or leave it for someone else, which although littering, is one of the best forms of trash in the universe when you're dying for a drink. If you do leave bottles, write the date and 'free water' on them, and make sure they're secure, stuck in cracks or wedged behind rocks, otherwise they might be blown from the wall and kill someone. Work out what rack you will need for your descent, and what rack can be put away, making sure you keep everything you might need to down aid out, plus all your descent tools, including head torches. I would also try and pack everything into your haul bags, such as portaledges, poo tube, rack bags, so you only have single bags to deal with at anchors (anything hanging under the bag will invariably snag your ropes).

Top To Bottom

Getting down from a wall can be a big or small deal, with descents varying from sunny bolted stations every thirty metres with rap rings, to ice threads and drilling anchors at night in a winter storm. The skills needed are the same as with normal climbing, but with greater loads, both on you and on your anchors, and so it's more industrial. I have had to do double raps on some walls (rap with one load, jug up, rap with another), and some vertical descents can involve down aiding, especially walls that "cannot be retreated from". Getting down overhung walls is not always about full on down aiding, but instead just achieved by creating mini redirects with the rope, moving your ropes into line with the next belay. Here are some basic things to consider:

Recon By Rappel: One person should go down first with all the rack, as well as ascenders, belay kit, cheater sticks, PCP, with the ropes locked off with a stone hitch or butterfly knot tied into each rope in case they need to re-ascend. If possible, this person should not have a haul bag, or just have the lightest bag, as carrying one will make swinging in much harder (if not impossible). Keep the rope ends clipped into their harness so they can't blow away and get stuck, or whip off the ends (knots in the end of the rope are not good enough). They will slowly make their way down, swinging in, putting in gear, stick clipping, until they can reach the next belay.

Clipping In (Down Aiding): Clip into anything you need, to get where you're going, but don't go crazy, as the next person down will need to clean all the gear, which will be tough as they'll also be bringing down the heaviest haul bags. Using long draws makes it easier for the second to unclip. If you come across some proper aiding, then try and back clean as you go, as the aim is for the second person to rap down as easily as possible, not clean a whole pitch with a haul bag clipped to them. It's worth trying to maintain your swings, kicking out, etc., as it's easy to suddenly find you cannot touch the rock with your feet and just end up hanging there stuck (this is one reason why you use locked off ropes and no haul bag, so can jug back up if need be to re-establish contact with the rock). If the first person down had to bring down a heavy bag, this would reduce the amount of swing due to gravity. Just think of an empty child's playground swing compared to a swing with ten kids sitting on it!). If you have a cheater stick or ski pole then this can also be used to swing you in, by pressing yourself out a little.

Stick Clipping: Using a stick clip makes getting down far easier, but it's not just a case of clipping gear and then pulling yourself in. First of all, depending on the model of stick clip you're using (or if improvised avalanche probe/flysheet pole), you usually can't pull on the stick clip, as it'll come apart or maybe break. Instead you need to attach a long sling or length of cord (two cordelettes), to use as a pull in line. Also make sure your cheater stick is always secured to your harness via this sling/cord as they are very easy to drop. The business end of the stick needs a taped open keylock karabiner, with taped on sky hook. It's amazing what you can hook and pull on when hanging from a rope (you'll also be equally amazed how short a very long cheater stick can feel on an overhanging wall!).

Rope Toss: If you plan to descend down a wall you're climbing up, then leaving a rope loop between the belay bolts is a good idea. This gives you a good target for a rope toss, using a large skyhook clipped into the end of one rap line (it's also a good target for a cheater stick's hook). You can also just do standard rope tosses as well, aiming for spikes and flakes, just remember that such things might come off if you pull them!

Fixing Down lines: On very steep lines you can leave thin lines fixed to aid getting over the steepest sections, such as roofs or pendulums. Here you should fix something strong and thick enough to pull yourself over, with 5 mm cord being ideal. The main issue with this is that if you don't go down this way you're just leaving trash.

Alternative Ways Down: On a wall with many routes, you might not have to descend the route you climbed. By switching to another route, you may find the anchors are more in line, or the wall less steep. This is one good reason for carrying copies of topos for routes that are close to yours. Be aware that following bolt belays down a route you did not climb up might lead you to a dead end, as some routes traverse in, or pendulum down, with nothing below you but blank rock. This is one reason why doing a rap recon is always a good idea, as well as carrying a small bolt kit.

DESCENDING WITH A BAG

One of the core skills of going down is handling your bags, not just haul bags but any heavy bag. The first thing is you do not want it on your back! Next, you should not view the transport of this huge object as some small task, just whizz down and you're done. No, you need to have the right gear, then apply it with the right attitude. The gear you should have should include:

- **Helmet**: No matter how solid the way down looks you should wear a helmet, doubly so if you're the first down. Haul bags are big clumsy beasts and have a habit of knocking off rocks. If there is any chance of darkness catching you then stick your head torch on it too.

- **Prusik Loops:** You should always carry at least two prusik loops, one short and one long. Use an auto block on every single rap, and always try and attach it to your belay loop, not your leg loop (your belay device will be located higher than normal, leaving your belay loop free). The longer prusik loop might be needed to transfer the bag over to the rope if you need to escape from it.

- **Cordelette**: It's always good to have a cordelette with you for setting up hangs for the bag, plus they can be used as rap slings, prusik loops and releasable cords, or a makeshift docking cord. This can be clipped off onto your harness, or tied into the haul bag's straps in the form of a Purcell-Prusik with a locker attached, allowing you to fine tune the position of the bag a little easier than a docking cord.

- **Knife**: You need to have the ability to cut yourself out of some major cluster fuck, be that hair stuck in your belay device, or a sling caught around your neck.

- **Ascenders**: Having the ability to go both up and down the rope is vital, as you might need to come to the rescue of someone, or find you've gone the wrong way and need to re-climb.

- **Aiders**: Keep one handy for clipping to your ascenders.

- **Lanyards**: Vital for creating your Y-hang and for clipping in and out of belays. You should have one lanyard for yourself, and one for the bag (unless you're using the bag's docking cord), then one shared between you both, which will form a Y-hang. PAS style lanyards work best for creating the Y-hang, then daisy chains, but cord or sling lanyards will also work with knots added.

- **Lockers:** keep a few locking karabiners handy, both for increasing friction on your device and for clipping into bags.

- **PCP:** The PCP should be carried by the first climber down, and if you have a backup PCP this should be carried by the last person down. This can be vital for sorting out mistakes, as well as attaching the bags into a rope without the need of a rope.

Y-hang style abseil, as you would in a pick-up rescue, with you on one end of your lanyard and your bag on the other, the descender close to the middle. There are two methods of doing this:

Simple

01. Clip your belay device into the rope.

02. Now you need to attach the belay device into your lanyard (if it's a rope lanyard then tie a butterfly knot). If you make this attachment point at the centre of the lanyard it can often

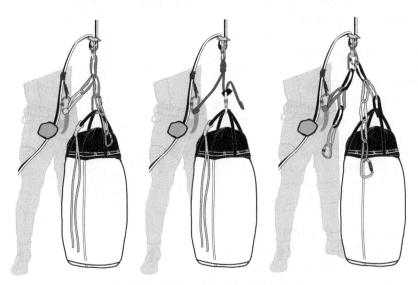

L to R: Simple, knotted lanyard and independent

HAUL BAG SET UPS

Unless your haul bags are super light (empty!), then you need to get them off your back, otherwise you'll invert, or find just going down a rope a Herculean task. Often, descents can require a great deal of hard work, concentration and problem solving, meaning you need a system that's relaxing to use, and the following system is designed with that in mind.

When rapping with your haul bags, you're best to employ a tandem/rescue/

03. end up too high (you need to be able to touch your belay device, doubly so if using an ABBD). Instead attach it to the lanyard in such a way that you have control of it (chest level).

04. Attach your lanyard into the haul bag hang straps in a position so that the base of the bag is not too low, so your legs are able to hug/control the bag as you descend (if you're using an adjustable lanyard then simply clip this into your bag's straps and fine tune the position).

The beauty of this system is that it's simple, and if you're using two lockers on your belay device, its also very secure.

Independent

Here you attach your belay device to the rope with two HMS lockers, then clip into these with a locker from your lanyard and one from the bag's lanyard (you can also use the bag's docking cord in place of a lanyard, allowing it to be removed without lifting). The up side of this approach is that each part can be more easily removed, the climber escape from the bag, the bag from the climber, the downside being more connectors, which will require greater monitoring.

DESCENT CONTROL

When rapping very steep ground with heavy bags, I would go for extra friction and wear leather gloves. To add friction feed the rope(s) around two large HMS lockers rather than one (unless you're on a low angled slab). This extra karabiner will also help absorb more heat.

Belay Device Or ABBD?

Having the ability to have your device lock off when rapping is nice, making an ABBD such as the Petzl GriGri popular, but such devices can be jerky, get hot (due to a small steel cam taking all the friction), become very hard to control over a long distance, and only work on single ropes.

The single rope issue can be overcome by tying a stone knot for the climber using an ABBD, then untying it for the last climber down, who uses a belay device. An alternative is to do a single line rap with the rope secured to itself with a locker, with a second rope (haul line), used to pull down the rope .

The issue of pulling back the handle of an ABBD can be magnified by using it on a Y-hang, as it will often end up in a high position. A belay device, on the other hand, is smoother to use, and the friction can be increased, with the auto-block being able to lock off the device as well.

Personally I tend to use my belay device more, especially when on suspect fixed ropes or anchors (where your nerves can't handle a jerky belay device), but will use an ABBD when forced to down aid, as an ABBD is always safer than a prusik loop.

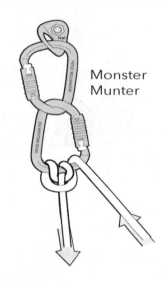

Monster Munter

Monster Munter

Another option, which is ideal if you're going down with very heavy loads (you cannot dump your water for example), is to use a Monster Munter on the Y-hang. The level of control is huge, and unlike a standard Munter, which twists your ropes, this double knot untwists itself. This can either be set up on a very large HMS krab, or two separate HMS krabs. When using it in this mode you must take great care that the live ropes are running over the spine of the karabiner(s), not the gate, for obvious reasons.

Ingeborg Jakobsen rapping with a haul bag down a 400m wall

Double Belay Devices

If you don't know how to rig a Monster Munter but need a high degree of breaking power then you can double up your devices, with a belay device at the Y-hang being fed from an ABBD on your harness (using a single rope).

BELAY TRANSITIONS

When moving down the wall with heavy bags, getting them on and off fixed belays can be tricky, and is a danger point, a heavy bag easily overpowering its master. The first thing to focus on is your safety, making sure your auto block is locked on, a knot tied in the rope, that you're clipped in, before trying to manhandle the bags. It's very easy to get to a sloping stance, and try and clip your bag in, lifting etc., and forget you're no longer holding onto the rope. Make yourself safe, then make the bag safe - not the other way around. On a hanging stance consider how you'll move the bag from hanging from a Y-hang to hanging on the belay. This can be achieved in many ways, and all should be understood, as each one can come in handy.

Muscle Way

The simplest option is to clip the bag off to the belay when you're just above it (a belay usually being two bolts, or a rap sling), doing so by either its docking cord (just tie an alpine butterfly or figure of eight into it), or a dedicated lanyard or sling. Once it's clipped in you can rap down until the weight is off you, and so you can secure yourself, then set about preparing for the next rap. With this set up you will need some muscle (a knee can help), to lift the bag in order to unclip it before you can depart again, which is never done until you're ready to go, auto block locked on.

Adjustable Lanyard

If you've used an adjustable lanyard you can just release it until the bag is hanging back on your Y-hang, then unclip.

Monster Loads

A few times I've had to handle loads that would be too heavy to lift alone, and to clip in or out by myself (at one time you'd need to set up a mini haul to get the krab unclipped). In these situations I used the docking cord just like when hauling. At reaching the belay I would clip a locker into the belay, then tie a Munter Mule with a little slack, then continue down until all the weight was on the docking cord, not the Y-hang. When leaving I would get all set to go, then release the docking cord, until the bag was now on the Y-hang again. If I was faced with a difficult transition, say I had to be pulled in by a second, then I would pre-set the Munter Mule, so I could just clip it in as soon as I arrived (no knot tying). This is also a very good way of dealing with people, if you're bringing them down on a Y-hang, most self rescue techniques not envisaging blank walls and hanging belays.

PROBLEM SOLVING

If on the way down you find you need to release yourself from the bags, say you find you're on a rope with a core shot, then you'll need to transfer its weight over onto a prusik tied above your belay device (if you tie it below you will not be able to get your device off the rope. For this you will attach the bag to the prusik via its docking cord, then rap a little further until the bag is now hanging fully from the prusik, and can be unclipped. It's best not to leave the bag hanging from just the prusik, so back it up. Because it's hanging from the docking cord it will be easy to return it to your Y-hang once you're ready to continue.

RAPPEL BELAYS

Once at the new belay anchors, the first climber will either just clip into the bolts and use the bolt's rings to rap off (or leave karabiners for this task), and forego setting up a belay, or set up an equalised belay with a single master point with rap ring or karabiner. The belay can be created as normal, with a master point krab clipped into a sling or cord, equalised to two bolts, the whole set up sacrificed.

But more often, climbers tie their abseil tat (made up from chopped up 7 mm cordelette) directly into the bolt hangers, so they only lose one krab (or just rap through the cord loop).

This approach is fine for standard abseiling, or abseiling with moderate loads, but due to the large loads often involved when rapping a wall, could be dangerous here. Running cord directly through the thin, sharp, or potentially burred edges of bolt hangers (where rap rings aren't available) could dramatically weaken the loop, which could fail if shock loaded (remember you could be running 150 to 200 kg loads through the anchor).

If you don't want to leave karabiners, to avoid this, consider tying into each bolt with a knot with a double bight, such as a double bowline or double figure of eight.

Stepping Down Not Up

On overhanging ground, it is vital that the second person down with the haul bags does not go below the level of the belay, and instead, comes down on to it.

To make this easier to achieve, tie both ropes into the belay with a Munter Hitch (HMS direct to a bolt), and get this as tight as you can while allowing enough slack for the second to rap, creating a quasi Fireman's belay. A Munter Hitch is used here as you might have to make some adjustments to the tension of the rope as they come down, or take in rope as they remove redirects, the aim to have a direct line between anchors.

If this angle is too large, say 45 degrees, it will be hard for a second climber with bags to get to the belay, and so lowering the bag should be considered instead, using one rope as a track line and the other (or ideally a third rope) as your control line, and using a PCP to pull the bags over.

Going Too Far

If you find the second climber has dropped too far below the belay, then you're in a semi rescue situation. Remember that you will have two ropes going from you to them and that the person on the belay should have a PCP. Here is how to sort this mess:

- **A**: If by untying one end of the rope from the belay, this gives you enough rope to throw the second climber that end, then feed this through the PCP and throw it down to them with a karabiner attached. Then simply haul the bag until the weight comes off their Y-hang, and they can release it, at which point you continue to haul the bag all the way to the belay, and the second climber can ascend the rope to the belay.

- **B**: If there is not enough dead rope for **A** to work, then the climber at the belay will need to set up the PCP on one strand of the rap line. Once done the stuck climber will need to transfer the bag to this, then once free, climb up the tied off rope to the belay (tie into the rap rope as a back up).

Last Climber Down

The last climber unties the Stone knot so the ropes can be pulled, then raps with the haul bag(s). Again I must stress that it's vital they do not descend too far below the level of the belay. When redirects are taken out, the climber should consider swinging over for the lower climber to take in some slack on their Munter hitch, creating a direct line between anchors for the descending climber to travel. When they get close to the anchor, the climber should take it very slowly, like they're docking with a space station.

Pulling The Ropes

Leaving the pull strand rope's end clipped into the belay, pull the ropes. It's worth noting that it's easier to pull a static than a dynamic rope, and that a thin rope will slip through the rap anchor easier than a thick rope (leaving karabiners on anchors reduces friction). For this reason pulling a zip line with a haul line is often the ideal combination, but in high wind a falling heavy rope is better than a light one!

LOWERING

Sometimes you won't want to rap with your haul bags, maybe due to them being too heavy, or the fact the next belay is so far away you don't think you can swing over, or maybe you think you can lower them all the way to the ground.

SET UP

The knot of choice for lowering your bags is the Monster Munter as this allows you a greater degree of rope control compared to any other method, even with 300+ kg loads, allowing you to lower bags and people together if need be. Make sure when doing a Monster Munter

that you are using the largest HMS locker you have (DMM Boa or Petzl William etc.) and that the breaking strand is in line with the karabiner's spine, not the gate.

PASSING KNOTS

What the Monster Munter is best for is passing knots, allowing you to lower a load many hundreds of metres without recourse to prusik knots and old school knot passing shenanigans.

All ropes should be tied together with overhand knots (EDK) with 30 cm tails, tied neat and tight (skinny ropes can be tied to thicker ropes), and the ropes stuffed into rope bags, so they feed out well (you don't want tangles mid lower).

Begin lowering and as the overhand knot reaches the Monster Munter it will slip through and around it. Most often the overhand knot catches on the last loop of the Monster Munter knot before popping (don't try and manipulate the knot with your finger, as you can lose it if it gets dragged into the knot, using a krab to flip the loop instead).

Using this setup I've lowered chains of bags many hundreds of metres, and people too, and I think it's one of the best self-rescue techniques there is.

LOWER ON A FIXED LINE

If you need to lower a bag onto a belay that is way over to the side, then you first need to set a zip line between the belays (imagine your bags are going on a death slide), then use the second rope as a lowering line, to lower the bag down the zip line.

01. The leader goes down on one rope (ideally a static), fixed to the belay with

Lowering seven haul bags 400 m on a single seven rope strand

a Butterfly knot. This rope will become the bag's zip line.

02. The bag's zip line will now be fixed between belays, creating a cableway, with the lower end secured with a Munter Mule (so it is releasable).

03. The bag is clipped into the tension zip line with two lockers, and lowered down the zip line from the top belay via a Munter Hitch on the other rope.

04. Once the bag is down, the top climber unties the butterfly knots and raps down as normal (both ropes will be fixed to the belay).

PARACHUTING HAUL BAGS

Getting heavy haul bags down some major big wall can be very tricky, and dangerous, be that when rapping or carried on your back. Being able to throw off the stuff you don't need to survive, can turn a hazardous, potentially danger-ous descent into something manageable. I hope you understand the craziness of throwing haul bags from a wall though. Parachutes can drift anywhere, get hung up, fail, or just go into the twilight zone! Anything thrown off should be viewed as 'disposable' and finding it again a bonus.

THE MORAL AND LEGAL DILEMMA

First off, throwing off a bag is highly dangerous as it could kill someone, and in some places, it is also illegal (US parks), and your skills as a climber should make this unnecessary for all but the most dangerous situations (or lazy climbers).

PACKING FOR THE DROP

When dropping your bag, air is both your friend and your enemy, as hitting the ground hard will see your bag pop like a balloon, but this force can also be used to aid keeping your stuff in one piece.

First off, you need to make some shock absorbing layers in your haul bag, and here you can use your empty water bottles. Place a layer of bottles flat in the bottom with their lid only just screwed on, so the air can just about escape. You can throw in all your trash, but make sure it's compressed hard and tight and double bagged, so it doesn't explode every-where.

Now add any soft stuff, and on top anything more dense, such as pegs, hammers, which should be placed inside plastic bottles, cut and then taped up to stop them cutting into anything. Wires and cams can go on top, webbing and flysheet on top of that.

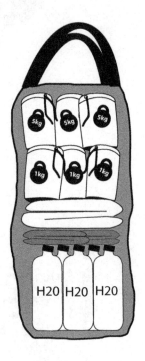

Some people throw off their portaledges but if you're going down a big wall then you should keep that with you, along with bivvy gear, water and food, as sometimes it can take a while to reach the bottom, plus a portaledge is never disposable. With all the main contents, make sure everything is tied and clipped together. Now close the bag very loosely, so that nothing can fall out on the way down, but everything can blow out if it hits the ground hard. Now you're ready to go.

PARACHUTES

There are innumerable types of parachute a big wall team might use or improvise. The old school approach was to make one by using your portaledge flysheet (not expedition style), attaching four long lines from each corner down to the bag. I have sewn in four heavy duty loops onto my flysheet that double up as tie downs and for parachute lines. These lines need to be equal length and should be as long as possible. In action, sometimes this works, sometimes it does not, with factors such as the weight of the fabric, and length of the lines affecting whether or not it deploys or just goes into a death spiral.

An alternative is to use small military surplus drogue chutes or large BASE pilot chutes, as the bag will fall without any drift, and they will take the sting out of a falling bag, making it strike the bottom first. But small chutes don't guarantee to keep your bag in one piece.

Larger army surplus parachutes could be used and will set your kit down as light as a baby, but they're big and bulky and will drift, not good when you're dropping your bags off a wall, not out of a plane. Having lost a few bags, the best option regarding performance, weight and price are the rocket parachutes made for hobby rocket builders, which are very small and cheap, and also simple, with only four lines.

There are many sizes of these chutes, but to have the lowest metres per second drop rate, I'd go for a 3 metre (10 foot) chute (with a 50 kg load, this is around 30 ft per second).

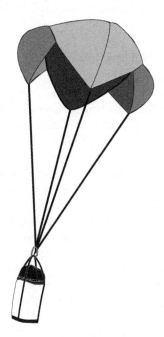

THE DROP

If you're going to throw off your bag, and are just making do with your flysheet, then the standard way to do this is to fold the fly into segments, with the lines folded as well (you can twist the lines a little to keep them together, and this will make the opening less hard). Someone then has the job of throwing the bag as far from the wall as possible, while the other one lets the fly be pulled from their hands (instead of pulling it). It's important that the fly fills with air later rather than sooner, as too soon might see the bag strike the wall and hang up. If you're using a proper chute, then check out and practise how to pack a chute (then you just hold it and throw the bag), and use a stuff sack or have the chute pre packed in a deployment bag clipped to the belay. When throwing the bag, try not to let it tumble as it might just tangle up the chute.

SUICIDE THE BAGS

If the wall below isn't that steep, or you don't have a parachute, then you can just throw the bags, and a haul bag is an amazing piece of kit in that it can tumble and bash for hundreds of metres without blowing apart. When packing to throw, expect the bag to be lost (they have a habit of finding crevasses) or destroyed, so keep everything tied or clipped together. With any of these techniques, make sure you write your name, date, and contact info inside the bag, so someone finding it in fifty years can track you down in the old folk's home (or the police can discover who killed that bird watcher).

WALKING OFF

Most climbers, on reaching the top, will walk down, sometimes with a little abseiling, other times just on their feet. There is always a tendency to want to carry everything down, the loads getting to the point where you can do yourself some real damage (knees, backs, hips).

If the descent includes down climbing, such loads are dangerous, and where a sticky approach shoe would stick with just your bodyweight, might not stick when you add 50 kg. Remember that people have died walking down from walls with haul bags on their backs. Another factor is the muscular damage you do when you carry heavy weights down hill, and after one major carry, I can remember feeling

it in my thighs three weeks on, and in my spine half a year later. If you overload your legs, you might cut into the rest of the time you have, plus overloaded muscles are weak muscles, not good when staggering around on slabs or talus fields.

SPLIT THE LOAD

A better approach is to split your loads and take one down on day 1, then take a rest, then come up and get the other one. This means you can get down faster and safer, then just make getting the other bag a rest day activity, sometimes tying it in with a day route. If you split the load though, make sure you have all the stuff you'll need for the flat land, such as wallet and car keys!

FERRY LOADS

If you stay on top of the wall, you can help your future self by ferrying down a load, taking it as far as you can before walking back up. If you're not camping on top you can ferry two medium weight loads with a lot less pain than one big one - plus you'll be safer and happier doing so. When leaving any bags overnight watch out for animals, hauling your bags up into trees if there are bears or mice lurking.

Don't Rush Down

I'm a big believer in not rushing down from a big wall, especially a wall you've just taken many days to climb. The summit of El Cap, for example, is one the best camping spots on the planet, calm and serene and beautiful. It is a shame to get there with food, time and water to spare only to rush down and get nabbed in the darkness. Stay on top and see the sunrise.

The author degrading his knees on the East Ledges © Charles Sherwood

PARA CLIMBING

Big wall climbing is a perfect - if super tough - adaptive adventure, and I've climbed El Cap with climbers who have been blind and climbers who are wheelchair bound. The vertical world of a wall is somewhere - like the ocean - that can be explored and experienced as long as someone has will and fortitude.

Most climbers with a disability can ascend a rope with slight modifications to the system, with double amputees having an advantage when it comes to rope climbing due to lower weight (I know some ex soldiers who can do endless pull ups without the weight of their legs). Climbers can also lead as long as they're able to step up (the visually impaired climber Steve Bate soloed Zodiac in 2013), while those who cannot lead can usually clean and haul.

The focus of this chapter is dealing with the more profoundly disabled, with some form of paralysis, who are limited to belaying and climbing the rope.

PARA ISSUES

Before embarking on any climb with a para climber, it is vital that both the climber and their team fully understand the physiology of the para climber. This includes:

Osteoporosis

Paralysed limbs will become osteoporotic, leading to a much higher risk of fractures, meaning great care must be taken when moving, keeping the legs and hips protected from impact or twisting. This is compounded by a lack of sensation, meaning absolute care is always required to make sure people are not standing, sitting or pressing on legs while on belays (they will break). This issue needs to be considered when approaching and descending as well, as a para climber cannot be dragged or pushed around.

Skin Damage

Pressure sores, burns, cuts etc can take many months to heal, leaving the climber confined to bed until they do, so must be avoided at all costs. All skin must be covered and protected, and zero tolerance observed at all times in terms of pressure points on the thighs and bottom (check several times a day no stones or karabiners have slipped under the harness). It might also be necessary to check the bottom of the para climber while on the climb to check the harness is not damaging the skin. The use of MTB body armour is recommended for climbing protection, including ankle guards, combined knee and shin protectors and elbow pads.

Suspension Trauma

I've covered this in 'Staying Alive', but it is a factor here, and it's vital again, that the para climber moves from one portaledge to another, and is not left hanging in their harness in between.

Thermoregulation

Paralysis often leads to a loss in thermoregulation, meaning paraplegics can

Karen Darke climbing Zodiac.

rapidly become hypothermic or hyper-thermic. Even in situations where an able bodied person could get away with a t-shirt, a para climber might be shivering. For this reason it's vital to reduce the chance of a severe drop in body temperature by always having the right gear at hand (duvet jackets, duvet trousers, hat, gloves, warm food, a nalgene hot water bottle), or some form of sun protection if needed (umbrella). For bivvying I would recommend the warmest sleeping bag you can find.

Catheters

If you're planning on spending a great deal of time working together, then although embarrassing, it's worth discussing how a paraplegic person goes to the toilet, and the ins and outs of catheters (including superpubic). Harness and clothing must take into account being able to use a catheter (both emptying it and allowing it to flow freely).

Crapping

This is one of the hardest parts of being a para climber, and requires a great deal of work, and so should be factored into the climb strategy. Going every day reduces the length one has to sit on the toilet, but this may be impossible on a portaledge, and can only be done at the base, the summit, and on any large ledges. Reducing food intake (low carb) can be an option, but strength will be reduced. The lightest system for a mobile toilet is a wheelbarrow inner tube (don't forget the pump), or a small camp chair, used in combination with a hole in the ground.

Inclusion

It's vital that the para climber feels they are part of a team, part of the process - not the process itself (i.e., "We're going to drag a disabled guy up El Cap."). Para climbers want to be independent, and want to be as little a burden as possible on those around them, so try to only offer help when it is asked for (never push anyone in a wheelchair unless they ask for help!). When climbing make sure they have a role (coiling ropes, belaying, sorting kit), rather than just letting them 'sit there'. You may feel you're doing them a favour, but it's vital they don't feel that they're just 'luggage'.

EQUIPMENT

Ascending Harness

You can buy adaptive harnesses but these are intended for outdoor centres, not climbing El Cap, and tend to be just modified non-para harnesses. I take the view that a different approach is required, that you need a harness that would work with a mermaid rather than a walking person. The harness itself needs to be light and avoid pressure points, and designed for suspension (climber's harnesses are designed for movement and safety, not hanging in), and cheap for one off use (not $1000). And so I've always used Alpine paragliding harnesses, which tick all my boxes and can be bought new or second hand very cheaply. This style of harness keeps the user in a legs up position, eliminating suspension trauma and pressure points, and works well with the rope system.

Safety Harness

The para climber cannot sleep or go to the toilet in their ascending harness, so needs a very lightweight webbing harness to wear underneath, the modern fabric ski touring harness being ideal (remove any buckles from the back or leg loops).

Pull Up Ascender

This is your main 'pull up' ascender and should be a short chest style ascender (use a model with a twist in the clip hole, such as the Petzl Basic or Climbing Technology Simple), with a pull up bar attached to it (metal bar inserted and bolted into position, with two bike grips glued in place). I would recommend this has its own lanyard to avoid losing it.

Top Ascender & Pulley

This should be a standard handled ascender, and I would recommend adding a 30 cm 'push stick' to the bottom, to allow you to push the ascender higher than arm length. A pulley is attached via an oval screwgate to the top hole of the ascender. Use a camming style lanyard for this which can be released under load (important for switching into rappel mode).

Pro Traxion

This is attached to your ascent harness, is your primary connection, and holds your body in position on the rope. A Micro Traxion can be used, but the Pro can be taken on and off the rope without removing it from its locker, and has less resistance.

Fall Arrest

In some circumstances you might want to use a double rope system, with the climber backed up by the haul line. This is achieved by running a dynamic lanyard from the climber to a fall arrest device on the haul line, such as the Petzl ASAP or DMM Buddy.

Rope

Seeing that a human being is climbing the rope I would go for a 10 mm static line. You can simply use the haul line, but this can slow things up, as the para climber must get to the belay before it's possible to haul.

Portaledges

You will require two portaledges, and these will tend to be hauled up or flagged.

Gloves

Good quality gloves are vital for the para climber in order to keep their hands intact as they will be doing many thousands of pull ups!

SET UP

01. The para climber puts on safety harness, and then ascending harness.

02. Attach Pro Traxion to ascending harness as low as possible (where this is depends on the design of the paragliding harness, and will either be attached through webbing loops or via maillons). I would advise attaching your Traxion via a Petzl OMNI karabiner (this is your suspension point).

03. Attach the rope to the Pro Traxion (this can be done without removing it from the harness), and take in the slack (have the rope coming out of the device so the unloaded rope is facing you).

04. Attach your top ascender to the loaded rope.

05. Thread the slack rope into the pulley and clip this into the top hole on the top ascender, so the rope runs up from the Pro Traxion, to the ascender pulley, then back to you (this will be your pull strand).

06. You have now created a 2:1 system. By pulling on this strand with your pull up ascender you will lift your body about 30 - 60 cm at a time.

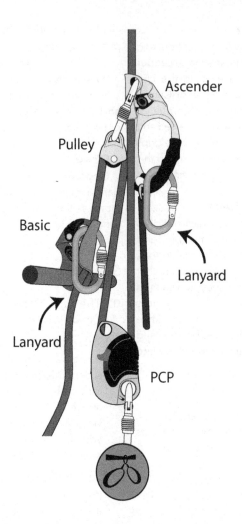

Ascender

Pulley

Basic

Lanyard

Lanyard

PCP

OPERATION

01. Thumb (feather) the cam on your pull up ascender and press the top ascender up as high as you can (thumbing the cam allows the rope to feed through it). The use of a pushing stick allows you to move further before resetting the top ascender.

02. Begin doing pull ups, with each 60 cm stroke on the rope lifting you 30 cm (so halving your bodyweight).

03. When the top ascender gets too close to the Pro Traxion, then reset.

ASCENT TO DESCENT

01. Clip into the rope below you as a back up.

02. When the top ascender is halfway to the Pro Traxion lock it down tight with its lanyard.

03. As you pull down on the pull up ascender release the cam on the Pro Traxion and allow all your weight to go onto the top ascender via it's lanyard.

04. Remove the pulley and karabiner, and pull up ascender.

05. Attach an ABBD to the rope and clip this in to your main suspension point.

06. Remove the Pro Traxion.

07. Take in the slack with the ABBD.

08. Release the lanyard so as to move your weight onto the ABBD.

09. Remove the top ascender and descend.

CLIMBING THE WALL

The system I've always used is designed to be simple to use, and safe, both in terms of the climber's exposure to hazard, as well as reducing fatigue and potential problems with pressure sores and suspension trauma. A three person team is ideal, with the para climber ascending their own rope from one lower portaledge to a higher portaledge, so in between climbs they are sitting on the ledge. The speed of the system does not necessarily have to be any slower than a standard big wall team. Here is how it runs:

01. The leader arrives at the belay with a lead and zip line.

02. They create a belay with two master-points, one for the haul bag, one for the para climber.

03. The haul line, para climbing line, and flagged ledge are hauled up via the zip line.

04. The haul line is attached to the haul masterpoint.

05. The end of the para climbing line is clipped off to the shelf or to a bolt, then attached to the masterpoint with a Munter Mule, making sure you

have several metres of slack between the Munter and the rope end (so you can lower the para climber several metres).

06. The para climber climbs the rope (using the haul line as a backup, or climbing as the haul bag is hauled).

07. When the para climber arrives at the belay, the portaledge is set up below them.

08. The Munter Mule is then released and the para climber is lowered down on the climbing line until they are sitting fully on the ledge.

IDEAL ROUTES

I would recommend routes that are overhanging all the way with easy approaches and descents, as slabs will be a killer to climb. Zodiac on El cap has been climbed several times by para climbers.

GETTING DOWN

The most important issue for me is never getting up, but getting down, and this must be your starting point. On El Cap for example the best option would be to time your climb with the running of the stables, and try and get a horse to bring you down. In some areas you might be able to get a hand bike to the top and cycle down, or have people carry you down in relays, but all have many dangers (I once piggybacked a 65 kg person down the East Ledges, and yes we did get down, but her leg was broken by the end, and my back was screwed for several years after). One option worth considering is descending back down the line of ascent.

KIT LIST

Instead of trying to break down big wall gear into many different categories, I'm going to set down a basic head-to-toe kit list. This is the type of list I'd give to newbie big wall partners, and although this is for summer - California - walls, it can be easily upgraded to winter or alpine walls. I will start with non-technical gear: clothing etc. and then move onto the technical kit.

PERSONAL GEAR - HEAD

Helmet: One of the most vital pieces of kit you have on a wall, a place where things hit your head, and your head hits things frequently.

Bounce testing gear is where a helmet comes in very handy, and you only need to get hit in the head by a few hooks to realise going sans helmet is not cool. Using aiders also creates a flip hazard (the back of your skull, especially around the ears is very vulnerable), as well as head first falls caused by the weight of a rack. Beyond that, there's the usual rock (and ice) falls, people dropping gear, and wild buckling portaledges to deal with.

Lightweight foam helmets are very good at dealing with your head impacting the rock, and ones with venting are better still for hot walls.

I often thread some thin bungee cord across the top of my helmet through which I pass larger two part head torches (light on the front, battery on the back), which stops it being lost if its elastic gets flicked off the helmet's clips.

Sun Hat: A vital piece of gear on both summer and winter walls, a sun hat both creates shade for your eyes as well as gives your face some protection, with dirt

or ripping gear deflected by the visor. I've used these hats on winter walls as well as the visor keeps spindrift off your face and goggles. A peaked hat that fits under a helmet needs to have no stud on the top, and there are many outdoor brands making gear hats. Some climbers fit a Velcro brim to the rim of their helmets, something designed for road crews in hot weather, and although looking funny is very practical for hot weather. Make sure whatever hat you have can be clipped off when not needed (climbing in the night for example).

Neck Guard: If your hat has one of these, ideally it wants to be removable, as then you can let a breeze cool you down. Get one long enough so that when you're looking down it still covers your neck, and choose styles that wrap around your face and neck and are light coloured and baggy, so they don't restrict head movement if caught under your chest harness.

Sunglasses: A wall can be a very hazardous environment for the human eye, with dirt, grit and general wall muck always floating around, as well as the danger from gear smashing you in your face. Whenever you're hammering pitons, bolt drivers or heads, you

Cian O' Leary on a Winter ascent of the Nose.

should be wearing some eye protection, as small shards of steel can often fly off. Getting one of these in your eye on a big multi day wall is an invitation to absolute misery. So sunglasses do double duty, in protecting your eye from both the sun and everything else. I will often carry two pairs of glasses on a big wall, both cheap enough to not worry about them getting trashed, with bendy frames and polycarbonate lenses, one pair with light category one frames and the other category two. All glasses need retainers, and these should be taped on.

Sun Cream: Ideally, most of your body will be covered most of the time, and so I tend not to use sun cream that much, but carry factor 50, taping on a clip loop.

Lip Salve: Like smoking cigarettes, lip salve is a sign of human weakness.

Balaclava: Having something warm to wear in a storm or at night is a good idea, and a balaclava does the job of both a hat and - well - a balaclava, as well as a neck gaiter when not needed. Powerstretch models are great. Make a hole and thread a small loop of 2 mm cord to make a clip loop.

Buff: I bloody hate buffs, but I'm not sure why. Nevertheless they are very handy, both to keep the sun off your neck or the snow out of your collar, and do many other jobs as well, like a towel, emergency knee pad (fold and insert a square of foam) or bandage.

Toothbrush: Keep your toothbrush in your belay jacket along with a small tube of paste and keep your teeth clean. On long multi week walls it's easy to neglect your teeth, but if you're drinking a lot of sugary sports drinks you'll often suffer

from mouth ulcers, so keep 'em clean. On winter walls you can also use this brush to remove ice that's built up on Velcro on your clothing before getting into your sleeping bag. Cut it in half, so it will fit in a pocket without sticking out and add a loop of 2 mm.

Head Torch: There's a school of thought that says that compact LED head torches have become so light that you might as well leave them on your helmet 24/7. On speed ascents where you start and finish in the dark this is often the case anyway. I would recommend that you always have some form of a light source with you at all times, as being able to see is a core survival and safety necessity. The head torch can be stored in your climbing pack, around your neck, in your pocket, or in a pouch on your harness. I will often wear a head torch reversed on my helmet in the day time, and rotate it around when I need it (having it reversed stops it catching on the rock all day long). Small Petzl TIKKA style torches are fine for most climbing, while more powerful beamed torches are better for night climbing, and I always carry two head torches and plenty of batteries. I fit a small lanyard to my head torches with a micro wire gate, clipping this into the helmet strap or a 2 mm loop tied into the helmet itself. This is extra insurance in case you flick your head torch off its clips, easily done when stuck in a chimney or when coiling ropes.

PERSONAL GEAR - UPPER BODY

Long Sleeved Top: This is your primary wall top and protects you from the abrasion of the wall against your skin, as well as the sun and the wind. A baggy top that creates some dead air space between your skin and the outside air is ideal, and a design with a collar protects your neck from gear slings. When you need more air, the sleeves can be rolled up, or the front left open. Some climbers wear regular dress cotton shirts while others wear poly-cotton trekking shirts. A light colour is best and getting a shirt a little bigger than you need is a good idea to make it easier to climb in and cooler. Make sure the top is long enough, so your lower back is never exposed, as your skin around your waist is very quickly burnt.

Bra: If you're wearing a bra, then make sure it's as cool as can be and avoid anything that will rub or press hard when worn under chest harnesses.

T Shirt: It's good to have a mix of clothing, and I would advise not wearing your wall clothes on the approach as you'll stink them out. Instead wear something you can stuff away for the descent, like a t shirt. This is doubly important for winter approaches, when carrying big loads, as you'll be soaked with sweat, so it's vital to have a change of tops once you get there, and women should have a second sports bra for the same reason.

Base Layer: Having a thin base layer to change into at night is nice, as it allows you to take off your smelly clothes, and you'll sleep warmer (salty clothing robs heat and dries slowly). The ideal base layer top should be thin enough to wear in the day even in hot weather, but still be warm when worn under your long sleeved top. I like base layers that have a built in hood and thumb holes and are a little long, so they stay tucked into pants. Wool is the ideal material for multi day/week walls as it doesn't smell as bad.

Mid Weight Insulation: A mid weight fleece is something that is a step up from a base layer, but light enough to be tied

around your waist or stuffed into your hydration pack. This is good when the sun leaves the face, or to layer up for cold nights or storms. This should feature a hood and thumb loops. Add a clip loop to the hem with a loop of 2 mm cord.

Windproof Layer: It's often worth carrying a lightweight nylon windproof or softshell layer, something light and compact enough to stuff in a bladder pack. These are handy for windy afternoons or just to create some dead air warmth when waiting at a belay. Pertex tops are my favourite.

Standard Weight Insulation Layer: Very often just layering up your base and mid-weight layers with a shell or windproof will suffice while moving, putting on a belay jacket once you stop, but on spring or autumn walls you might need more. A standard weight layer should be something that can be climbed in easily and layered up, and ideally provide some protection from wind, showers and snow as well. A thin synthetic insulated top is often ideal for this, again featuring a hood. In the UK the classic top like this would be something like the Montane Prism jacket.

Belay Jacket: This should provide substantial warmth, and I would err on the side of a heavier belay jacket rather than something lighter, as this is often a fundamental piece of survival gear. I would avoid down unless you're assured sub zero temperatures, with the classic belay jacket standard being something like the Patagonia synthetic DAS parka or the Montane Spitfire jacket. This piece of clothing may never be used on a wall, or only while eating on the portaledge or as a pillow but find yourself fighting for survival and this will be a life saver.

Make sure the belay jacket has a super solid clip in loop so you can clip it off to belays or portaledges, and I would not trust little hang tags for this and instead sew my own larger clip loop with bright tape into the hood seam behind the neck.

Shell: A shell is something you hope not to need on a big wall, but it's not something you should ever leave behind. You never really want to be climbing in a shell on a wall, as they tend to get trashed and holed, especially if you're tackling cracks and chimneys. What is important is that the shell is waterproof and that you understand the limits of that waterproofing, that in a storm it'll be pretty useless. Most often when wearing a shell in poor weather you're moving, while on a wall you're often forced to remain static, and if not then water will run down your sleeves and drench you very quickly anyway. And so in any serious storm, your primary protection will be your fly, and if you don't have a portaledge then your bothy bag or bivvy bag. The ideal shell top for a big wall would probably be something like a heavy duty kayaking jacket, with rubber cuffs and neck, carrying a lighter jacket for approach and descent, but climbers tend to make do with what they already have.

PERSONAL GEAR - HANDS

Big Wall Gloves: It is vital that you protect your hands on a big wall, a place that's pretty hostile to the skin. Leather gloves with the fingertips removed are the classic big wall glove, and there are several models you can buy that are climbing specific, with clip in loops and stretch panels fitted. If you make your own, add duct tape where you cut the finger tips off, so the seams don't unravel, and consider just cutting off the last 1 cm of the fingers, rather than half way

down the fingers, as this will protect all your joints much better. Size your gloves a little large as your hands will swell up and tight gloves will no longer fit (they will also shrink when left to dry). Battered cuticles can be very painful on a wall, and so I've often used full-length gloves (with fingertips), but the downside with this is that they need to be removed when free climbing or searching for hook placements.

Crack Jammers: These rubber hand protectors are ideal for mixed walls, where you don't want to be wearing tape for days on end, which although looks cool, is not right for your hands. Crack jammers can be clipped onto your harness and quickly deployed, and I find they make most standard cracks about a grade easier.

Warm Gloves: Having at least one pair of cheap warm fleecy gloves for belaying is nice, and these can be put into service as your main gloves by cutting off the tips if your hands swell up. I tend to keep these in my belay jacket in a small stuff sack, and make sure you add a clip loop to each.

Mitts: For stand alone hand warmth, you cannot beat mittens, plus they are cheaper and lower bulk than shelled mountaineering gloves. On a wall, these will most often be used for belaying when it's cold or windy, or as another piece of storm insurance.

Waterproof Gloves: Having one pair of cheap disposable industrial waterproof gloves, basically like washing up gloves, is another piece of insurance. If you find yourself forced to climb up or down in bad weather, then these can make the difference between life and death, keep-

El Cap Tower, the Nose

ing your fingers moving. There are tons of models in hardware stores, such as Maxi-Flex gloves, and again, these can also do double duty as big wall gloves by cutting off the fingers.

Watch: It's vital everyone has a watch, and not just a phone, so you can tell your progress as you climb, when to speed up, make camp, etc. This is double important when speed climbing. A watch is also vital for getting up on time when time is pressing, or for informing you just how slow time is passing on a miserable bivvy. Instead of some super expensive chunky all-singing-and-dancing watch, I use a dirt cheap Casio F91W (someone told me this is much loved by the SAS). This style of school boy watch is slim enough to be worn on your wrist even when climbing, and is almost disposable. I replace the watch strap with a Velcro NASA strap, making it easier to attach to chest harnesses or sleeping bag pull cords (don't assume a watch worn on your wrist will wake you from a big wall coma).

Hand Repair Balm: Vital on any wall, this small tin of climbing balm is designed to help your hands recover from a hard day's toil. It also seems to reduce the chance of getting infections and can be used on any cuts or skin abrasions, including toes.

Finger Tape: It's worth always carrying a small roll of finger tape to cover cuts on your fingers or cuts in your rope or to tape open karabiners, or tape nuts to your hammer. Keep this on your harness with your knife.

PERSONAL GEAR - LOWER BODY

Shorts: Wearing shorts under your pants rather than cotton tends to make wearing a harness less uncomfortable and sticky when worn for days or weeks on end. Standard polyester shorts with built in stretchy pants or short running tights work best. The trick is to reduce the pressure on the seams of trousers when pressed against the skin by the harness, which can rub you raw. Having shorts is also useful for the approach and descent. You can climb in your shorts, but your legs tend to get a little more battered and sunburnt.

Underwear: For men, one pair of pants will probably suffice, but for women, it's worth carrying more and paying more attention to hygiene on multi week walls. The reason for this is that unfortunately, urinary tract and kidney infections, along with fungal problems such as thrush, seem to be problems that often come up. This might be exacerbated by wearing expensive 'sports' polyester knickers for over a week, instead of changing into cheap cotton knickers every day.

Trousers: Big wall trousers need to be fitted so they can be climbed in, and sized so you can roll them up to the knee so they can be worn like shorts. I would go for light, stretchy, climbing specific trousers designed for moving, rather than heavy duty work trousers, and cotton is worth avoiding as you can get a lot of saturation around your harness and knee pads. Low profile seams are vital to reducing rubbing, and a slightly higher waist stops the hem slipping under the harness. It's good if they are windproof and dry quickly as often you might not be able to throw on a shell quickly. Other features such as a zip pocket is handy to hold a topo, snack bar or pen knife, plus a two-way fly is handy if you're a man.

Base Layer Bottoms: A pair of thin thermal bottoms takes up very little space in the haul bag but can be worn in stormy weather under a shell with or without your big wall pants, or as a stand alone bottoms if you have an 'accident'.

Heavyweight Bottoms: If climbing out of high season, then having a thicker pair of fleece pants is recommended, as these can be worn if pinned down, or can reduce the chance of hypothermia if you have to move in bad weather. Women also tend to feel the cold more, and I've climbed with women who wore this type of pants as their standard pants for the second half of a wall. The best combination of warmth, bulk and 'climbability' would be power stretch tights.

Shell Bottoms: These tend to get worn very little on most walls, but having been caught out without them, I can attest to how quickly wet legs cool you off. Due to the nature of being worn very little on most walls, I would go for cheaper, almost disposable pants most of the time, rather than expensive pants that will just get trashed. If climbing on more hostile walls then good quality salopettes are good as they're often put on in the morning and taken off at night and are a warmer option. Just make sure you have the stuff to repair minor damage.

Puff Pants: Although perhaps better in the 'XS Walls' chapter, these medium weight synthetic pants are suitable for colder walls for belay duty or sleeping in, and are ideal for climbers who feel the cold. In a big wall system, these would usually replace your heavy weight fleece pants, or be used with them as storm insurance, or as emergency bivvy kit if you have no sleeping bag.

PERSONAL GEAR - FEET

Big Wall Boots: What you wear on your feet on a wall depends on the style and length of the route. On some routes

the leader might wear comfortable rock boots with socks on every pitch, switching to light approach shoes for belaying and seconding. Wearing rock boots on lead has a lot of advantages, in that even on full on aid you can exploit foot holds, and when high stepping your feet tend to feel more secure, plus a narrow rock boot can be placed much more easily into aider steps. The downside, which is considerable, is that your feet will get battered, with toes and insteps crushed, to the point where it will almost be impossible to put weight on your feet. For this reason, I'd say that a rock shoe approach should be saved for routes where the climbing is very mixed, or for climbers with the most desensitised feet.

The next step, and the one most widely used is to wear sticky approach shoes, which allow easy free climbing to be done, the approach shoes having some stick and support, and make standing in aiders less painful - up to a point. Go on a steep hard aid route, where you're standing in aider steps for eight hours a day and your feet will become very sore and sensitive. This affects your ability to climb, as painful feet are a constant distraction, meaning often your focus is just getting the weight off your feet, making you rush. The biggest problem comes when high stepping as this puts a lot of force through your feet and so can be excruciating, the effect of this like trying to defuse a bomb while having a migraine.

The final option is one that I use on full on aid routes, and that is to wear solid mountain boots. Having a stiff sole under your instep gives you a great platform for standing around for many hours on end. The drawbacks are that the boots get trashed instead of your feet, and after two weeks on a wall, your brand new boots might be fit for the bin, and I'd not expect to get more than two or three walls from a pair of boots. For this reason, it's often best to use old walking boots or cheap industrial work boots.

Socks: It's vital to look after your feet on a wall, and wearing stinking, sweat soaked socks does not serve that aim well. Have at least three pairs of socks, for the approach, wall, and descent, and maybe more if it's going to be a long route. Always take off your socks at night and give your feet a clean, in particular between the toes. Polyester sports socks or wool are good in that they dry a little faster and don't go as stiff. It's also good to include one pair of warmer wool socks for if things get cold, and these can be left in your sleeping bag for changing into each night, plus they can also do double duty as mitts.

Knee Pads: Although I've climbed walls without knee pads, they save your knees when hauling or leading, where you often brace your body with your knees pressed against the rock. These come in two main types: soft and hard. Soft knee pads are light and cheap and designed for sports such as netball, and when not being used can be slipped down around your ankles. Hard pads are designed for skating or for soldiers, and offer much more protection at the cost of more bulk and weight. I wear different pads depending on the wall I'm climbing, but the soft design is the most flexible.

THE CLIMBING HARNESS

As with most things big wall there are two options, one lightweight, and one heavy.

Rock Harness: The light option is to use the standard harness you use for everything else, an ideal choice if you're climbing mixed free and aid routes. Climbers worry that a standard harness will be uncomfortable on a wall, but all harnesses are uncomfortable after only a short time hanging, whether they're a skinny sports harness or something more akin to a climbing armchair. Ideally when at a belay you will always be sitting on a belay seat, and if not, then standing in your aiders. Real big wall comfort is defined by how well your waist belt and leg loops deal with the loads of hauling, as in most cases you're putting far greater a burden through these components when hauling than you are when only hanging in your harness.

Wall Specific: A heavier option is a harness with more beef to it, thicker waist and legs, designed to take those big wall loads better. This style of harness also tends to have big wall features, including double belay loops, haul loop and beefy but simple racking (remember that most gear will go on your chest harness). Double belay loops are used to free up one belay loop for your belaying, with the other for your lanyards and fifi (some companies recommend one lanyard on each belay loop, but you want your lanyards in the same place. If your harness lacks a second belay loop, but the harness is suitable, you can buy a second belay loop from Yates, or have one sewn on.

Harness Features:

Adjustable Leg Loops: It's not necessary to have adjustable leg loops on a wall, but having this feature makes it easier to put on shell bottoms. Without adjustable leg loops, you can usually contort your legs to get the loops off.

Rear Risers: These are much more important for going to the toilet, but ideally need to be low profile, so they don't dig in when sleeping in the harness. Remember when you take a dump to wrap the risers around your leg loops to avoid them getting 'contaminated'.

Removable Leg Loops: One feature I think is important is a belay loop retainer tab that can be unbuckled, although on most harnesses this is now sewn in to avoid pilot error (where the rope is fed around this tab instead of the leg risers). If the tab can be unbuckled, it means the leg loops can be completely taken off at night.

HARNESS EQUIPMENT

Folding Knife: Like a good sailor, you should always have a knife at hand, both for simple little jobs, like cutting up tomatoes or spreading cheese, and big jobs, like cutting rap tat or your mate's rope if his name's Joe. I like the simple Petzl knives, and a large clip hole is vital. Often the karabiner used to clip this to your harness might end up holding many other things, such as prusiks, finger tape, big wall gloves, so tying a small loop of 4 mm cord through your knife's clip point creates more real-estate for other junk.

Lighter: Carry this with your knife (hang off some cord) so you can melt cord or light the stove.

Prusik Loops: Every climber should have a minimum of one 1.3 metres, soft 5 or 6 mm, prusik loop for abseil back-ups and basic self-rescue. It is best to also carry a second 3 metres long 5 mm foot loop as well, with this doubling up as a mini cordelette, for equalising protection, abseil tat, keeper cords and releasable tie offs.

Belay Device + HMS: Even if you're using an ABBD such as a Petzl Grigri, you still need a belay device, both for descent and for various other jobs. A guide style device such as the DMM Pivot, puts more tools in your tool kit, including hauling and rope climbing, and match this with a good sized HMS locker that takes a Monster Munter knot. I will often also carry a marked or distinctive micro screw-gate clipped into the HMS for when using the device in guide mode (this can be scavenged for other duties as well, but is always returned to its home on the HMS).

Spare Locking Karabiners: In a traditional big wall system, as I describe in this book, you always have two lockers that live permanently on each lanyard. This means you always have lockers for clipping into belays, ascenders, life lines. The primary requirement for extra lockers is for clipping in back up knots or adjusting daisy chains when ascending, increasing the friction on your belay device by running the ropes through two HMS krabs, or securing yourself via the rope.

Nut Tool: Vital for both leading and cleaning. The nut tool is also important for cleaning out cracks. Thread with a loop of 3 mm cord to match the length of the tool, which can be used to clip the tool off to the rope when cleaning stubborn gear. This loop can also be employed to cut through rope and slings. This is done by untying the loop and using it like a wire saw (wrap it once around the material to cut), using the friction to melt the rope or tape.

Appendix

GRADING AND RATINGS

It's not easy to grade a boulder problem of only a single move, the vagaries of height, strength, conditions, gender, mood, psyche or psychosis making the whole affair very subjective. Now scale that up to a pitch of sixty metres, one that may or may not feature fixed gear, some old and some new, as well as edges that could have broken off, or become enhanced through the passage of time. Throw in a mix of aid climbing where advances of gear can turn the expanding horror show of tied off stacked pegs of yesterday into a camming cycle path of tomorrow, or a living end hooking section that can be free climbed with sticky boots and chalk. How about the unknown, that a pitch with a reputation, like the Fly Or Die on Lost In America goes from just a name and a line on a topo marked A4, to become the topic of trip reports and forum beta, where the climber now knows every single placement to come, even who placed the fixed gear. To give a pitch such as that a grading between A1 and A5 can only ever be the roughest guide, a guide that is often more leaning towards the ego than the reality. Now scale that one pitch up to twenty or thirty pitches, with vagaries in weather, from wind and rain to snow and sun, and try and get your head around how a climb of a thousand moves can be distilled into a grade such as VI A3+ 5.8?

The answer is it can't, and grades can only be the most basic of guides, a real understanding based more on who did the first ascent, the popularity of the route, and the word on the street. Nevertheless it's good to understand the basics of grading from A1 to A6. This is the most widely adopted grading system but as is, it often fails to take into account advances in gear, and unlike free grading is capped at the theoretical grade of A6. This means everything is lying between the Nose (A1) and Nightmare On California Street (A5).

Another problem is that the grade gives no indication of the danger involved, as some easy routes can involve very loose rock, where harder routes are just very steep and technical, with the American 'X' or 'R' being worth considering, or the UK E system (E for extermination). A pitch like the A4 Hook Or Book on the 1978 route Sea Of Dreams is basically a whole pitch of hooks with one crappy nest of heads and a hook for pro four fifths up the pitch, meaning it would be easy to kill yourself if you fucked up. At the same time I've climbed modern A4 pitches where you knew the beaks or heads would stop you in a fall, yet they have the same grade. Having the grade A4X or A4R would be a good way around this, and is seen sometimes.

What I'm saying really is that often a pitch has to be evaluated by the leader before committing to it, your eyes and experience often a better judge than some forty year old grade. Another problem with the grade is that pitches can change dramatically when features fall off, making them harder or easier, a bolt or rivet added to a crux pitch taking off the edge.

GRADING BASIC GUIDE

- **A0** (Advanced Dogging, aka "take me there")

Most commonly and unfairly described as 'French Free', a term probably coming from alpinist's focus on speed over style, I class this as Guerrilla aid, an anything goes approach. This style of climbing usually involves improvised gear or minimalist kit (one aider), and is typically a process of grabbing gear and hanging to rest. Much of the Nose can be climbed at A0 when wearing rock boots, but the technique is far from easy, needing far more skill than A1 climbing, requiring the ability to switch from aid to free, swing, tension, and pull, the knack knowing when to do which. When coming across mixed free and aid pitches such as the Lynn Hill Traverse on the Nose, graded A0 5.10d, this means using guerrilla aid you can swing or tension between 5.10d moves (or move), but you cannot simply ape up a line of bolts. A bolt ladder would simply be graded as A0 or A1 with no free grade attached. Even on a bolt ladder, like the one on the East Buttress of Cathedral, you need some skill to yard up bolt to bolt in your rock boots, stepping off bolts to reach the next one, able to bust in to free climbing when they end.

- **A1** (Easy Aid, aka "I'm solid")

This is easier than A0 in my mind, and sometimes such pitches might be better tackled guerrilla style, with a mix of free and A0 aid (or all free). Otherwise the pitch is easy, and safe and straight forward, most often a nut or cam ladder, the classic example being the classic pitches on Zion's Moonlight

Buttress where every single placement is bomber. My own thoughts are that on A1 terrain you should be able to make a big wall belay at any point on the pitch.

- **A2** (Moderate Aid, aka "just watch me here")

This tends to be A1 climbing on steeper terrain, maybe where solid A1 placements are all there, but you need to step a little higher to find them.

- **A2+** (Tricky Aid, aka "actually watch me here")

This is where aiding begins to get a little more interesting as you need to start thinking, and a slap-dash approach could lead to a fall. Such falls could be caused by a short section of flared, dirty, slightly loose rock, or where you have fixed gear that's in a poor state, where failure of one piece should not lead to a zipper fall. It's at this grade that having aid specific gear such as cam hooks and beaks becomes more important, as well as skills in judging placements, testing, and knowing what should be used as pro, and what needs to be used for progression.

- **A3** (Hard Aid, aka "I'm scared")

Don't let the fact this is not A4 fool you, this kind of pitch will feel like A4, as once upon a time it would have been A4. Here you need to have all your skills on hand, especially the ability to bounce test gear. Here you will find multiple body weight only placements, or sections of hooking, meaning you could take long falls or have to deal with dubious rock or fixed gear. This is the grade where you need to apply a bomb disposal level of concentration, paranoia and a big dose of Rabbit foot thinking, namely creating nests of gear to stop any falls you might take on A3 gear (two pieces of A3 pro can make an A1 placement). Good use of beaks, offset cams and cam hooks can tame many old school A3 pitches, giving you more solid pieces on a pitch, but A3 fixed pitches should be treated with a high degree of respect. You don't want to fall off an A3 pitch, but if you do, you are very unlikely to hurt yourself.

- **A3+** (Hard And Dangerous aid, aka "I'm shitting my pants")

This is where things get serious, and that bomb could kill you. Now you're dealing with the same kind of climbing but the outcomes of a fall are more serious, such as corners to fall into, ledges to hit, etc. You don't want to fall, like with A3 climbing, but now you are aware that if you do, you might walk away with more than just a scary story.

- **A4** (Death Aid, aka "I've actually shit my pants")

You have no doubt you're going to die on this pitch if you make one mistake. There is no room to rush or make assumptions about fixed gear. Everything must be tested and second guessed. You might get some solid A1 gear on such a pitch but it won't be handed to you on a plate, might involve nests of gear, and will often come down to your skill and the amount of gear you have at hand. Large racks are vital as you want to maximise every single placement. Such pitches can take several hours, if not all day, and require a great deal of mental and physical stamina, as lowering your guard can get you killed. This grade can feature rivets so it's vital to

get the most out of the protection they offer.

- **A4+** (Double Death, aka "Call the undertaker")

The same as A4 climbing, but on ground where your skills are undermined by the laws of chaos, luck and juju, most often in the form of loose, fragile, uncertain rock. Here you have a random element in your bomb, like a rat running around chewing at the wires. The level of awareness and knowledge gleaned from other pitches like this is your only form of defence, understanding how rock moves, why and where and how, like someone digging into a collapsed building after an earthquake. No matter how skilled you are, you're crazy to climb this style of terrain.

- **A5** (Extreme Aid, aka "Call the Samaritans")

The same as A4+, but features no rivets or bolts, meaning you could theoretically rip an entire pitch. This in itself is not a problem if you fall, as a four hundred foot fall into space is no biggy (in the real world something always stops you). The real danger is a hundred foot fall onto a ledge, which is really the same as A3+, only here, as the grade increases from A3+ to A5, the probability of that death fall increases, and on an A5 pitch I would view all placements as being less than A1, while on A4 this might only be the case for 70% of placements. Having fallen off an A5 pitch, the Natural, on the Reticent wall, where I took a clean 150 foot fall, I feel very lucky, as I know if I'd fallen at the halfway point rather than the end, I'd have bitten Wino tower and might not be here today.

- **A6** (Suicide Aid, aka "Murder suicide")

  This grade is more of a trick or illusion, and means you have A5 climbing above a belay that will not hold a fall, something that's not easy to achieve if you're also hauling off it. Having built non bolted belays on very bad rock that have had ten placements I think this is more theoretical than practical. The trick aspect is you can create an A6 belay by linking pitches when rope soloing without cleaning the previous pitch, but such things are, luckily, so dangerously pointless I doubt anyone would do it.

ALTERNATIVE AID GRADING

In Australia, aid grades go from M1 to M12, which gives a little more nuance to the grading, with M6 being equivalent to the lowest end of A4. I quite like this system as it matches mixed grades, which can be very much like aid climbing in terms of insecurity. Jim Beyer, one of the hardest aid climbers around, subdivides the grade system to match the free system, with A4 broken down to A4a, A4b, A4c etc. Personally, I have no clue how you'd be able to apply this to most climbs, as even A0 to A6 is problematic. Perhaps this is why Jim Bridwell came up with his own system:

NBD = No Big Deal (A1 to A2)
NTB = Not Too Bad (A2+ to A3+)
PDH = Pretty Darn Hard (A4 to A4+)
DFU = Don't Fuck Up (A5 to A6)

AK SYSTEM

I have developed my own grading system, which I call the Fearometer, with grades going from F1 to F4. It is based on a mental measure of how afraid I am.

F1 = I'm not scared
F2 = I'm scared sometimes
F3 = I'm scared all the time
F4 = My belayer is also scared

CLEAN CLIMBING

Clean aid isn't really a thing anymore, it's really just what aid climbing is 95% of the time these days.

The history of clean aid started when climbers began using threaded machine nuts stolen from railway tracks instead of pegs, with the greatest leap being the invention of the rigid Friend by Ray Jardine. Since then the pace of change has been rapid, with new clean gadgets appearing every decade, from RPs and offsets, to Aliens and offset cams, hand placeable beaks and cams the size of your head.

By replacing the A with a C in the decimal system, you indicate that no hammered protection is required, so the Nose for example is graded C1 now, not A1. Personally I think pegs have become so irrelevant to modern climbers, save the birdbeak, that such a distinction is less necessary, as all climbers aim to climb as clean as possible.

The problem with the clean grade is that routes do change, especially sandstone routes, with placements wearing away to dust, meaning on any route harder than C1 I'd always advise bringing a hammer (good to have for cleaning anyway) and some beaks and maybe sawn offs.

The other problem is that although a route like Mescalito might go clean, and get a grade of C3+, it only takes a few heads to rip, or pitons to be cleaned and it becomes impossible to climb clean, meaning you might need a hammer to replace missing gear.

Due to the nature of clean climbing I think it's hard to have clean pitches that go into the A4 range unless you're doing it artificially, by turning A2 climbing into A4 climbing, which for me is not heroic but just false jeopardy designed to raise the grade. It's also good not to judge those who nail and those who do not, as it's rare to have equality in available gear, with one team climbing on Camalots while another has Totems and offsets, making a huge difference.

Why Go Clean?

The most obvious reason for going clean is that it's just faster, but it also means less faff and is less destructive. Once you start hammering pitons you're going to have to hammer them out again. Another advantage of passive pro is that very often you can judge the strength and integrity of a placement more easily compared to a piton, the forces more understandable.

Chasing The 'C' Grades

Call me old fashioned but when I see a pitch graded C4 or A1 I view it as a challenge to climb it clean, but not a prerequisite, especially if a fall will see my legs broken. Clean aid is the best way to go in these situations but don't risk your neck for it. Putting in a piton now and then as protection when your life's on the line is OK. Another thing to remember is that what might have been straightforward in a clean ascent last week might be impossible this week if someone has come along in the meantime and removed a fixed pin or two.

Unclean Climbing

For me the issue is not one of using pitons or not, but rather it's about using such things sensibly, and modern climbers tend to only use gear that is pretty non destructive, the only widely used piton these days being the birdbeak. Knowing how a beak works, how it hooks the rock, is vital in reducing further damage to the rock on existing placements, as well as creating new placements that are sustainable. When you're climbing very thin beak tip cracks there may be a tendency to ignore the beaks 'hook' and focus on the rock's compression of the tip, placing bigger beaks, stacking beaks, or worst of all placing copperheads instead. A beak actually creates a clean hook move for the next beak if cleaned carefully, and only tapped carefully when being reused.

ROUTE LENGTH GRADES

The only length grading that still has any real meaning is the grade VII, the holy grail of big wallers, meaning a wall that takes more than twenty days to climb.

FREE GRADES ON A WALL

These match standard grades, although in reality, many free pitches on a wall don't match the free climbing pitches you'd get on the ground at the same grade. Often a free grade is needed for something that can't be aided, such as chimneys, slabs or offwidths. Free pitches can also be found on sections where there is no protection to aid off, creating free soloing ground – such as the Peregrin Pillar on the Sea Of Dreams – or where the rock is so loose it's safer to trust your sticky boots rather than hooks – like the Coral Sea on Native Sun.

Appendix

BIG WALL KNOTS

This book is not designed to provide information on general knots, but here I'll just briefly cover some knots that you might not be familiar with.

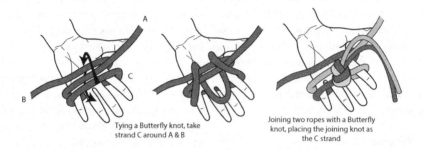

Tying a Butterfly knot, take strand C around A & B

Joining two ropes with a Butterfly knot, placing the joining knot as the C strand

Alpine Butterfly (Butterfly)

This is one of the most important knots in your arsenal, and should be used in any situation where the rope is loaded. No matter how loaded, this knot always comes undone (unlike the figure of eight). To undo it simply rotate strands A and B until the knot loosens up. This is also the best knot for tying out damaged sections of rope, and for joining fixed ropes (for climbing and lowering). Strength: 67% (53% both strands loaded)

Munter Hitch (Italian Hitch)

A vital knot to know, both as an emergency belay/abseil knot, and for lowering out haul bags.

Munter Mule Overhand (MMO)

This is a tied off Munter Hitch, or tied off Monster Munter.

Monster Munter

As discussed in the text, this knot is a real lifesaver, and is easy to tie (just a Munter Hitch inside a Munter Hitch). The main danger of this knot is getting your finger trapped within it when lowering, so take care!

Releasable Hitches

There are many ways to create a releasable connection between an anchor and a load (on a wall the load will invariably be a haul bag). The **Mariner's Hitch** works

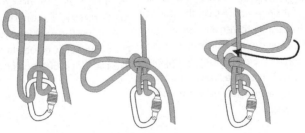

Munter Mule Overhand (MMO)

with both rope or slings, with the **Radium Release Hitch** also having the ability to lower the load. You can also just set up a Munter Mule as used with your haul bags, although I would not recommend this setup unless you can use a double strand of rope (I find a cordelette too

Using the correct knot when you know it will be heavily loaded (I would class heavy loading as greater than body weight) is how to avoid this problem, such as the Butterfly knot, Stone knot and Bowline. If you do come across a knot that is difficult to untie, try the following:

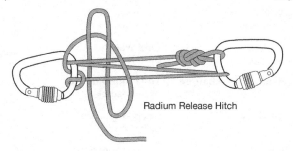

Radium Release Hitch

thin unless doubled). My own favourite is to just keep it simple and tie off the connector with a Monster Munter knot (works like the Radium, but allows the whole length of cord to be employed in lowering).

Tree Tie Off

As simple as it comes, but handy when topping out on walls where trees are your anchors. Just wrap the rope around the tree five times, then either clip the end back into the loaded strand with a locker, two back to back karabiners, or with a knot. This knot is ideal if you're going to be creating very large loads (if doing high friction hauling for example), as there are no loaded knots at the anchor.

UNTYING STUBBORN KNOTS

Getting your knots undone can often be very difficult, and in extreme cases you might have to cut the knot off, with knots that cannot be undone verging on life or death in some situations, which is daft as such problems are easily avoidable.

- **Whip It** If you can strike the knot against the rock as hard as you can this will often soften it up and loosen the knot.

- **Hammer It** You can achieve the same by taking your hammer and bashing the knot.

- **Stamp It**: As above, just stick it on the ground and stamp and roll it under your feet.

- **Marlin spike**: If you have a rigger's knife you can use the marlin spike to force the knot apart.

- **Baby Angle**: You can use a size one baby angle like a marlin spike, forcing and twisting it into the knot to break it apart.

If you are tying a figure of eight knot, or an overhand, and know it will be heavily loaded (such as when setting a cordelette), then clip a karabiner into the heart of the knot, allowing you to tease and worry it open.

RESOURCES

BIBLIOGRAPHY

Climbing Big Walls
by Bridwell & Strassman

Big Walls
by Long and Middendorf

Big Wall Climbing: Elite Technique
by Ogden

How to Big Wall Climb
by McNamara

Big Wall Climbing
by Scott

The Stonemasters
by Long

Training for the New Alpinism
by House & Johnston

Me, Myself & I
by Kirkpatrick

Wilderness Search and Rescue
by Setnika

Life on the Line
by Merchant

Super Alpinism
by Twight

High Angle Rescue
by Vines

Essentials of Sea Survival
by Golden & Tipton

Mixed Emotions
by Child

Postcards from the Edge
by Child

Push
by Caldwell

The Crack Climber's Tech manual
By Peace

Psychovertical
by Kirkpatrick

Cold Wars
by Kirkpatrick

1001 Climbing Tips
by Kirkpatrick

Deep Play
by Pritchard

Gorilla Monsoon
by Long

Climbing Adventures
by Bridwell

Alone on the Wall
by Honnold

Troll Wall
by Howard

To Be Brave
by Robbins

The Art of Freedom
by McDonald

Alpine Warriors
by McDonald

Extreme Eiger
by Gillman

Valley Walls
by Denny

Camp 4
by Roper

The Tower
by Cordes

El Capitan
by Duane

Downward Bound
by Harding

WALL GEAR

Fish Products
fishproducts.com

Rock Exotica
rockexotica.com

D4
bigwallgear.com

Custom Runouts
runoutcustoms.com

Krukonogi
krukonogi.com

Kong
kong.it

Yates
yatesgear.com

Mountain Tools
mtntools.com

Moses Climbing
mosesclimbing.com

Kop De Gas
kopdegas.com

Raumer Climbing
raumerclimbing.com

Grand Wall Equipment
grandwallequipment.ca

Aiguille Alpine
aiguillealpine.co.uk

Climbing Technology
climbingtechnology.com

WEBSITES

**Supertopo.com
andy-kirkpatrick.com
bigwalls.net
yosemitebigwall.com
Riggingforrescue.com
vdiffclimbing.com
terragalleria.com**

CHARTS

CONVERSIONS

Inches	Millimetres
3/63	1.19 mm
1/16	1.58 mm
3/32	2.38 mm
1/8	3.17 mm
5/32	3.96 mm
3/16	4.76 mm
1/4	6.35 mm
5/16	8.46 mm
3/8	9.52 mm
1/2	12.7 mm
9/16	14.28 mm
3/4	19.05 mm
1	25.4 mm

LIQUID

1 Quart	0.94 Litres
1 Gallon	3.78 Litres

ROPE LENGTH

60 Metres	198 feet
70 Metres	230 feet
100 Metres	328 feet

FORCE

KG to KN x 0.00981

KN to KG x 101.972

WIRE STRENGTH (SS)

Cable #	Ø	Ø	Construction	Min Breaking	Min Breaking
#0	1 mm	3/64	7x7	78 kg	0.76 kN
#1	1.5 mm	1/16	7x7	174 kg	1.71 kN
#2	2.5 mm	3/32	7x7	480 kg	4.75 kN
#2	3 mm	3/32	7x19	651 kg	6.39 kN
#3	3.2 mm	1/8	7x19	907 kg	8.89 kN
#4	4 mm	5/32	7x19	1157 kg	11.35 kN

PARACHUTE DESCENT RATE (10ft Chute)

10kg	17.3 ft/sec	5.27 m/sec	18.98 km/hr	11.79 mph
20kg	24.46 ft/sec	7.45 m/sec	26.83 km/hr	16.67 mph
30 kg	29.96 ft/sec	9.13 m/sec	32.87 km/hr	20.42 mph
40 kg	34.6 ft/sec	10.54 m/sec	37.96 km/hr	23.59 mph
50 kg	38.68 ft/sec	11.78 m/sec	42.44 km/hr	26.37 mph

Note: A non lethal descent rate for a human would be between 22 to 24 mph

ACKNOWLEDGEMENTS

There are so many people I need to acknowledge in this book, but seeing as John Middendorf both wrote the forward and injected a huge dose of info into my head via his own book - well I guess I need to thank John first (and not forgetting John Long).

Next come the other writers of books and spreaders of information, whose work has helped me complete this project. These include; Doug Scott, Chongo Chuck, Pitons Pete, Erik Sloan, Chris McNamara, Mike Strassman, Mark Hudon, Mark Synnott, Bryan Law.

Then of course there are all the big wall climbers who have inspire me over the years, and who still do; Alexander Odintsov, Silvo Karo, Greg Child, Eric Kohl, Charlie Porter, Royal and Warren and the gang, Silvia Vidal, The Bird, Zaver Bongard, Jim Beyer and many others.

I'd also like to thank my own wall partners, especially Paul Tattersall and Ian Parnell, for their skill, patience and willingness to keep going up.

Next, without the support of the following people this project would never have been started, and without their constant badgering it would never have been finished! So to all my Kickstarter supporters, thank you, and I hope this book goes some way towards taking you where you want to go (sorry it's been so long in the making!):

1st Sid Vale Scout Group, S Nystrom, T Dimaline, J Luckett, T Greensmith, C H Boesen, S Wilton, M Aw, D Sinclair, S Gitlin, M Krumpholz, L A Tataru, G Burton, N T Forest, M Fraser, T Daniel, J Harris, A Rooney, P Hartman, C Noble, I Durkacz, J Dølvik, D J McCormick, J Larkin, D Yeates, M McCarthy, D Takai, A Motal, C Dey, L Walker, A Hosterman, A Gray, C Giegerich, J Hammond, B Smith, V Vacek, G Mercer, S O'Boyle, M Gyth, E Giske, S Rockarts, G mcfarland, J Kass, A Hwang, E Tombs, D Alie, J V Winkel, S Larson, M Castelli, J Bertucci, G Baxter, H Livingstone, R Duffy, Lars R Frøyland, J Maurin, G Llewellin, B Buehler, R T Woods, K Szuman, W Millar, T Fisher, R Kernan, R Suenram, S Smith, K-E Suurväli, N Nguyen, D Thompson, P Clark, M Kjellsson, D Oughton, K Ondy, G Nathanael, P Dlug, J Webber, E Bassett, B Williams, T Raymond, L Connolly, F Schiffmann, S Cox, F Hansen, S Conway, R Dunne, C Murray-Watters, J Sutherland, O Williams, S Tickle, V Kuklov, N Hazelton, K DeWeese, D Whelan, G Blackman, F Brockners, S Le Feuvre, P R Veit, P Griffiths, R Lee, C Olson, E Gates, M Cristina, K J Wannebo, A McLeod, I Vuorio, N Boet, S Kleeman, J Widmaier, J E Andrews, A Evans, T Maas, M Tilburgs, A Firestone, D Nikas, L Wood, A DiMeglio, JP O'Neil, P Savage, D Rosseau, B Wright, M Ponte, J butler, B McCaul, M Lester, M Sourisseau, B Schneider, K Stewart, N Sandidge, J Andrus, N McLean, J Holterman, N Chun Man To, A Rudden, H Schnait, B Boyer, D Schobben, A Olkkonen, R Hore, A Adkins, A Stewart, L Betsworth, S Reed, K Mokracek,

M Carter, S Hampshire, E Johnstone, Szu-ting Yi, M Potts, J Donigan, J Brunberg, M Frese, Kit Camp, I Kuzin, R Ouellett, B Hanley, T Bateman, R Kelley, L Chapman, S Dilles, K Gregory, B Ranson, R Shade, N as Bose, R Sharpe, M Roddy, J Sawley, D Swan, E Wilson, O Hjort, P Forsberg, C Bell, P Sutherland, B A. S Aubertijn, A Barry, N Chee, P Kirkpatrick, B Lepesant, W Skea, G Young, S Brooke, J Tucker, T Gwilliam, P Johnson, H Crosby, P Boardman, R Lindner, R Miller, T Penrose, K Lai, N Smith, M Pilling, C huon, K O'Dempsey, R Hoppenreijs, T Nunns, A T Jensen, S Fletcher, A Voss, K Matsuyama, P Brindley, J Gans, J Ceballos Villach, C Freeman, K Hornhofer, Z Wasserman, M Williamson, R Dorn, A Tischler, M Rogerson, J Campbell, H Charette, C Gossage, F McLin, R Rönnkvist, B Jackson, M Ruhnau, M Freels, J McKnight, V Kozlov, N Wuelker, F I Björnsson, J Davidson, A F. Webb, N Clarke, J Iggulden, R Callf, C Weeks, W Schneider, J Mansfield, C Dickinson, P Brookes, D Smith, F Bordone Elli, P Simpson, S Lessels, M Samsel, F Iavazzo, M Cooke, D Letts, K Lane, M Munizaga, Michael and Liz, James Lewis, Paolo C Tighe, I Parnell, Va Dumitrica, U Egeberg, A Seger, N Stevenson, D Stone, T Jones, J Carter, K Szilas, A Pierer, Climber Dave, M Sapiecha, T K Yew, O Gibson, J Rastoaca, D Makin, D Bird, R Naylor, B Gill, D Moses, J N Hawkins, K Weaver, T Mc Sweeney, T Holmberg, W Clarkson, D Taylor, T Spooner, N Cooper, C Cookson, S Dennison, D PP, N Ng, MO Chabot, D Lozman, C Bell, W Webb, B Scholz, S Ferry, A Nutley, T Bevins, M Criddle, D Henchliffe, A Arthur, E Ace, R DeLapp, P A Olegovich, M Midgley, P v d Hoogen, J Wright, A Fau, B Gjerdevik, A Darbyshire, J Elsensohn, E Meunier, A McShane, M Tate, M Gylby, D Edwards, B Tsimoyianis, T S Skogedal, A Bielk, S Miles, J Gillmor, B Limbach, V Mangla, A Victor, A Klinterot, R McGregor, M Langby, C Hope-Lang, N Morgan, L Kane, S Sonmor, R Twilley, C Anderson, H Huntington, M Kingsley, M Perrett, R Schenck, N Hingley, C Lorimer, J Johnson, M Foster, T Kühne, M Steible, W Murray, V Hughes, J Bertsch, H Collingridge, R Hironaga, J Fellgård, D Waveman, C Stamler, D Murray, J Madelin, P Browning, M Hand, K Meisel, S Deliflippi, W Zittlau, C D Hicks, B Fingleton, J Theios, D Comer, P Lee, M Vinh, K Ko, G Conlon, J Berry, W Weir, P Gierczak, S Seppälä, O Embréus, K Tanaka, A Lythaby, P Drissen, C Whatley, S Teague, S Mentz, A Mejerblad, D Rozwadowski, J P Hall, B Archibald, C Rightmyer, N Shephard, J J Ramsfjell, S Price, G Wheeler, S Mallory, G Peach, M McCarthy, H Alger, T Sadaoui, J Ruaya, E Hartsink, R Geller, T Khu, G Willis, D Domingue, M Strom, K Copley-Holland, T Mullier, B Chidwick, J Coe, W Nicholson, N Nanuck, G Dunn, G Bonilla, P Hoang, M Adams, F Caberlin, O Batting, J Smith, L Morris, B Brown, B Fredrick, J Jurriens, J Perrine, R Shah, M Sweeney, M Desenberg, V Chan, R Kosowan, J Murphy, J Loeckemann, M Wetmore, J Grenier, F Galbraith, R Fairhurst, M Rawe, B Talley, E Zhang, C Pak, J Lieberman, P Chays, S Warren, A McCartney, J Kuntz, A LaFevers, J Foster, G Bonilla, A Derbis.

Finally, a special thank you goes to my wife Vanessa Kirkpatrick for spending many, many days editing the text of this book and helping with the layout, as well as giving her own views forthrightly, and for beta testing the content on five walls. You are without a doubt my better half!

Thank you all!

INDEX

NOTES

Made in United States
North Haven, CT
15 February 2024

48766777R00261